Modern Real Estate Practice

20th Edition

Fillmore W. Galaty, Wellington J. Allaway, and Robert C. Kyle

Martha R. Williams, JD, Contributing Editor

This publication is designed to provide accurate and authoritative information in regard to the subject matter covered. It is sold with the understanding that the publisher is not engaged in rendering legal, accounting, or other professional advice. If legal advice or other expert assistance is required, the services of a competent professional should be sought.

President: Dr. Andrew Temte
Executive Director, Real Estate Education: Melissa Kleeman-Moy
Development Editor: Jody Manderfeld

MODERN REAL ESTATE PRACTICE 20TH EDITION
©2018 Kaplan, Inc.
Published by DF Institute, Inc., d/b/a Dearborn Real Estate Education
332 Front St. S., Suite 501
La Crosse, WI 54601

Printed in the United States of America
Third revision, August 2020

10   9   8   7   6   5   4   3   2

ISBN: 978-1-4754-6372-9

CONTENTS

PREFACE

Since it first appeared in 1959, *Modern Real Estate Practice* has set the industry standard for real estate education. Whether preparing for a state licensing examination, fulfilling a college or university requirement, looking for specific guidance about buying or renting a home, buying an investment property, or simply expanding your understanding of this fascinating field, you can rely on *Modern Real Estate Practice*, the recognized authority for accurate and comprehensive information presented in a user-friendly format.

Just as today's real estate market is challenging and complex, today's real estate students are increasingly sophisticated and demand a high level of expertise and efficiency. This 20th edition of *Modern Real Estate Practice* meets those expectations. In response to expanding state licensing requirements and the growing body of laws that govern the practice of real estate, this edition contains revisions and new features designed to make it an even more effective tool, no matter what your goal may be.

SPECIAL FEATURES

To access the student question bank—to create customized quizzes and exams from the hundreds of questions in the *Modern Real Estate Practice* text—go to the website and enter your personal Student Access Code: 19671.

www.modernreal estatepractice.com

This 20th edition of *Modern Real Estate Practice* retains the successful features developed for previous editions to reflect the rapid pace of change in the real estate industry.

Website

Modern Real Estate Practice has a website dedicated exclusively to the text and its ancillary products. At www.modernrealestatepractice.com, students and instructors have access to an assortment of study and teaching tools, including a question bank and Instructor Resource materials.

Quick math reference

Inside the front and back covers of the book is a great time-saving reference tool: the most frequently used real estate math equations.

Math concepts

Throughout the book, helpful math hints and answers to commonly asked math questions appear at point of use to help you understand examples in real estate that require math computations.

Math FAQs

This section at the end of the book provides additional math hints and solutions to commonly asked math questions to help you understand basic math concepts and apply them to examples in real estate.

In practice

Throughout the text, there are examples of how the concepts discussed are carried out in everyday real estate practice.

Directory of state licensing agencies

An internet address for every state licensing agency is provided in the appendix. State real estate regulatory agencies typically provide links to state statutes, real estate regulations, required forms, and other useful information. When applicable statutes are provided at a different site, that address is provided as well.

Other internet resources

Throughout the text, *Modern Real Estate Practice* helps connect the student to internet resources by identifying relevant websites whenever appropriate. The student can access the many government and professional association websites that are continually expanded to provide historical, as well as current, information.

Glossary

The glossary features definitions of all key terms, as well as definitions of other important real estate the terms used in the text. It also includes page references that indicate where the terms are defined or explained in the text.

Margin notes

Notes in the margins direct students' attention to important vocabulary terms, concepts, and study tips, as well as internet resources included in the text. The margin notes also help students locate issues for review and serve as memory prompts for more efficient and effective studying.

UNIT FEATURES

Learning objectives

Each unit begins with a list of the unit goals that will help the reader anticipate the unit content.

Key terms

Key terms appear at the beginning of each unit. This feature not only alerts the student on the important vocabulary words that should be noted as the text is read but also helps the student to study and review.

Key point reviews

At the end of each unit is a summary of the most essential content covered in that unit.

Unit quizzes

Demanding fact-pattern problems encourage students to not just memorize but to also understand and apply information. This approach gives students valuable practice in these important test-taking and exam-preparation skills. The questions have been carefully designed to follow the style and content of the most widely used testing services and to demonstrate the types of questions that students will likely encounter on state licensing exams. The answer key includes specific page references to the text.

The fundamental goal of *Modern Real Estate Practice, 20th Edition*, is to help readers understand the dynamics of the real estate industry by providing the critical information needed to pass a licensing examination, buy or sell property, or establish a real estate career.

A FINAL NOTE

With the publication of *Modern Real Estate Practice, 20th Edition*, we think it is fair to consider the book a classic. For more than two generations, this book has provided readers accurate and comprehensive real estate information, but we continue to ask, "What can we do to make a great book even better?"

With this edition, we provide clear, concise content that complements the collective voice of the original authors, while emphasizing contemporary issues such as fair housing, client representation, financing, and the environment. The text provides a balance between key teaching points and the material needed to round out a quality real estate education.

Please let us know what you think of this edition by emailing us at contentinquiries@dearborn .com.

Thank you for your help as you join the ranks of successful *Modern Real Estate Practice* users.

— The Publisher

ACKNOWLEDGMENTS

Like a real estate transaction, this book is the product of teamwork and cooperation among professionals. We would like to express our gratitude and appreciation to the instructors and other real estate professionals whose invaluable suggestions and advice help *Modern Real Estate Practice* remain the industry's leading real estate text. Whether they responded to instructor surveys, provided reviews and suggestions for improving the previous edition, or reviewed the manuscript for this edition, the participation of these professionals—and their willingness to share their expertise—is greatly appreciated.

We would like to specially acknowledge contributing editor Martha R. Williams for her expertise and dedication while working on this edition. Martha received her juris doctor from the University of Texas, is an author and educator, and has practiced law in Texas and California. She is author or coauthor of *Fundamentals of Real Estate Appraisal, The Art of Real Estate Appraisal, How to Use the Uniform Residential Appraisal Report, California Mortgage Loan Brokerage, California Real Estate Principles,* other textbooks, and numerous electronic courses.

REVIEWERS—20TH EDITION

Debbie Martin, CEO, ERA Cape Real Estate, owner Mid Cape Real Estate School

Sal Sedita, Director, Delaware School of Real Estate

Betty Winn, Winn School of Real Estate, LLC

Each new edition of *Modern Real Estate Practice* builds on earlier editions. We gratefully acknowledge the many real estate professionals and others who have contributed to prior editions of this book.

Robert H. Allen, National Real Estate Institute

Penny Alston, Wardley Real Estate School

Jean Anglin, Chattanooga State Community College

Jim Anselmi, Academy Real Estate School

Christopher O. Ashe, Learning Unlimited Doris Barrell, DSB Seminars

Donald R. Bates, Mountain Empire Community College

Thomas E. Battle, Center for Real Estate Education and Research

E. E. Bayliss III, Ford Fairfax Community College

Tom Bowen, Professional School of Real Estate

Paul Boyter, CRS, GRI, McColly School of Real Estate

Dianna Brouthers, Homefinders of America

Thomas Bull, McColly School of Real Estate

Virgil V. Bullis, Sr., Delaware Tech

Leona Busby, Long & Foster Institute of Real Estate

Chuck Byers, Professional Marketing Concepts

Marie Callas, Iowa Association of REALTORS®

Alice W. Cater, Lamar University Institute of Technology

Peter J. Certo, Gabelli School of Business

Charles Civer, Scottsdale Community College

Richard J. Clemmer, D&D School of Real Estate

Ginny Commins, Windermere Education

Kay Knox Crawford, Continual Learning Institute

David Dean, Litchfield County Real Estate School

Gregory Dunn, U.S. Books, Inc.

John Eaton, Ocean School of Real Estate

Dr. Kenneth W. Edwards, GRI, Linn-Benton Community College

Stephen Etzel, Kaplan Professional Schools, Texas

William B. Frost, Weichert Real Estate School

Katherine J. Gandy, Spokane Falls Community College and American Business and Professions Institute

Richard Garnitz, Kelley Academy of Real Estate

Michael Craig Glazer, Ivy Tech State College

Ignacio Gonzales, Mendocino Community College, Ukiah, California

Helen L. Grant, Moseley-Flint Schools of Real Estate, Inc.

Edward A. Guinane, Real Estate School of Siouxland

Randall S. Guttery, PhD, CLU, CLFC, Associate Dean and Professor of Finance and Real Estate, University of North Texas

Terry Hastings, Ridgefield Adult Education

Terry Hayes, Real Estate Brokerage Education

Arthur W. Heinbuch, Allied Institutes of Real Estate

Ray Henry, Arizona Institute of Real Estate

Mary Hibbler-Kee, Bess Technical College/UAB Options

Russell S. Hicks, The Real Estate School

Carl R. Hurst, Hurst Education Center

Diana T. Jacob-Rouhoff, Northwestern State University of Louisiana and Lincoln Graduate Center

F. Jeffrey Keil, J. Sargeant Reynolds Community College

John H. Kilroy, Jefferson County Board of Education

Rick Knowles, Capital Real Estate Training

Dr. Corbet J. Lamkin, Southern Arkansas University

Allen Lamont, Lamont School of Real Estate

Craig Larabee, Larabee School of Real Estate

George W. Lawrence, Master Instructor Faculty, California Association of REALTORS®

Jerome D. Levine, Tunxis Community-Technical College

Richard S. Linkemer, American School of Real Estate, Ltd.

Joyce Magee, Genesee Community College

Denise M. Mancini, J.W. Riker

Charline Mason, Charline Mason Seminars Unlimited

John D. Mathis III, Kaplan Real Estate Education

Peggy Ann McConnochie, Alaska Coastal Homes, Inc.

Paul McLaughlin, Esquire

Thomas L. Meyer, Cape Girardeau School of Real Estate

Coad Miller, Central Nebraska Community College

J. Leo Milotte, CRB, CRS, GRI, Milotte Associates Real Estate School

John R. Morgan, Morgan Testing Services

Monte Needler, Ivy Tech State College

Edward Neeley, Russell & Jeffcoat Real Estate Institute of Training & Education

Robert Neuwoehner, Heartland School of Real Estate

Jessie L. Newman, Grempler Real Estate Institute

Judith A. Nolde, JD, Content Consultant

Mary M. Otis, Northern Virginia Association of REALTORS®

Katherine Pancak, University of Connecticut

Andrew G. Pappas, Capital Community Technical College/Manchester Community Technical College

Joyce D. Remsburg, Trident Technical College

Walter L. Rice, Quality Workshops

John D. Rinehart, CRB, CRS, GRI, The Real Estate Institute of York County, Inc.

Robbie Robison, Allegany College

Kathy Roosa, Kathy Roosa School of Real Estate

Jay Rose, Esq., Tucker School of Real Estate

Phyllis Rudnick, CRS, GRI, Annex Real Estate School

Susann Shadley, Eastern Idaho Technical College

Don Shrum, The Real Estate School, Houston

Sherry Steele, Kaplan Professional Schools, Colorado

Bill Standiford, Ed Smith School of Real Estate

Allan R. Stevenson, GRI, CRB, Frostburg State University

Rita Stuckart, Jack White Real Estate School

Wayne A. Tarter, Greenville Tech

Dennis Tosh, FNC, Inc.

Ruth A. Vella, Omega Real Estate School

Howard E. Walker, Nashville School of Real Estate

Darline C. Waring, Charleston Trident Association of REALTORS®

Cynthia L. Weber, ABC Real Estate School

Donald Dwight Wells, Troy State University

Brenda S. White, Brenda White School of Real Estate

John P. Wiedemer, Houston Community College

Don W. Williams, Alabama Courses in Real Estate—ACRE

Judith B. Wolk, Charleston Trident Association of REALTORS®

Jerry L. Wooten, Tucker School of Real Estate

John Wright, Iowa Real Estate School of Cedar Rapids

UNIT 1

Introduction to the Real Estate Business

LEARNING OBJECTIVES

When you have completed this unit, you will be able to

> **list** the various careers available in the real estate industry;
> **describe** the different classifications and characteristics of real property and the types of housing available for purchase or rental;
> **explain** the factors of supply and demand in the real estate market; and
> **identify** the advantages and disadvantages of investing in real estate.

KEY TERMS

associate licensee	equity buildup	market
appreciation	exchanges	real estate licensee
broker	fair housing	sales associate
capital gain	leverage	salesperson
depreciation	liquidity	supply and demand

OVERVIEW

Real estate transactions are taking place all around us, all the time. When a commercial leasing company rents space in a mall, or the owner of a building rents an apartment, it's a real estate transaction. The most common transaction is the purchase or rental of a home, whether by a first-time buyer, by someone seeking a larger or smaller place to live or a second home, or by an investor interested in the property's income-producing potential. Consumers of real estate services thus include buyers and sellers of homes, tenants and landlords, investors, and developers. Nearly everyone, at some time, is involved in a real estate transaction.

All this adds up to big business—complex transactions that involve trillions of dollars each year in the United States. The services of millions of highly trained individuals are required: attorneys, bankers, trust company representatives, abstract and title insurance company agents, architects, surveyors, accountants, tax experts, and many others, in addition to buyers and sellers. All these people depend on the skills and knowledge of licensed real estate professionals.

REAL ESTATE: A BUSINESS OF MANY SPECIALIZATIONS

Despite the size and complexity of the real estate business, many people think of it as a business of real estate brokers and real estate salespeople only. Actually, the real estate industry is much broader than that. Appraisal, property management, financing, subdivision and development, home inspection, counseling, and education are all separate businesses within the real estate field. To succeed in a complex industry, every real estate professional must have a basic knowledge of these specialized areas and how they impact the real estate industry.

Brokerage

Brokerage is the business of bringing people together in a real estate transaction. A licensed real estate broker acts as a point of contact between two or more people in negotiating the sale, purchase, or rental of property. A **broker** is defined as a person or company licensed to buy, sell, exchange, or lease real property for others and to charge a fee for these services. A licensed real estate **salesperson** is employed by or associated with the broker to perform brokerage activities on behalf of or for the broker, and may also be referred to as a **sales associate** or **associate licensee**.

A **real estate licensee** is a person who has satisfied the requirements of a licensing agency, as authorized by state legislation. The requirements typically include course hours or work experience and passing a state-mandated real estate exam. In some states, every real estate licensee is a broker, but only a managing broker may employ other licensees to act as sales associates, and the managing broker is responsible for the sales associates' conduct. Check the laws in your state to learn the terms used for licensees and the requirements for obtaining a license.

Appraisal

Appraisal is the process of developing an opinion of a property's market value, based on established methods and the *appraiser's* professional judgment. Although brokers should have some understanding of the valuation process and, in some circumstances, may even be asked to estimate the price at which a property is likely to sell, lenders require a professional appraisal for most transactions. Appraisers must have detailed knowledge of the methods of valuation. Appraisers must be not only licensed or certified for many federally related transactions but also licensed or certified in many states to be involved in transactions that are not federally related. The Appraisal Institute, www.appraisalinstitute.org, is the largest trade association of real estate appraisers.

Property management

A *property manager* is a person or company hired to maintain and manage property on behalf of the property owner. By hiring a property manager, the owner is relieved of day-to-day management tasks, such as finding new tenants, collecting rents, finishing or altering space for tenants, ordering repairs, and generally maintaining the property. The scope of the manager's work depends on the terms of the management agreement—the employment contract between the owner and the manager. Whatever tasks are specified, the basic responsibility of

the property manager is to protect the owner's investment and maximize the return on that investment. Depending on the size of the property and/or the scope of the work required, the property manager may need a real estate license or a property management license that is issued by the state in which the property is located. The Building Owners and Managers Association International, www.boma.org, provides useful resources for both owners and managers.

www.boma.org

Financing

Financing is the business of providing the funds that make real estate sales transactions possible. Most sales are financed by a loan that is secured by a mortgage or deed of trust on the property purchased. Individuals involved in financing real estate may work in commercial banks, thrifts (which include savings associations), and credit unions, as well as mortgage banking and mortgage brokerage companies. Federal law requires mortgage loan originators to qualify for the Nationwide Multistate Licensing System and registry (NMLS), found at https://nationwidelicensingsystem.org.

https://nationwide licensingsystem.org

Subdivision and development

Subdivision is the dividing of a single property into smaller parcels. *Development* involves preparation of a site and construction of structures or other improvements. These improvements may be either on-site or off-site. Off-site improvements, such as water lines and storm sewers, are made on public lands to serve the new development. On-site improvements, such as new homes or recreational amenities, are made on individual parcels. While subdivision and development normally are related, they are independent processes that can occur separately.

Home inspection

Home inspection is a profession that combines a practitioner's interest in real estate with skills and training in the construction trades. Many states have recognized the importance of a thorough home inspection by a competent, well-trained inspector by instituting home inspector licensing requirements that include education, training, examinations, and ongoing coursework. The American Society of Home Inspectors, www.homeinspector.org, is a trade group for home inspection professionals.

www.homeinspector .org

A professional home inspector conducts a thorough visual survey of a property's structure, systems, and site conditions and prepares an analytical report that is valuable to both purchasers and homeowners. The inspector examines the property from the chimney to the basement, being alert to deterioration, water intrusion, mechanical, or other observable problems. Often, the home inspection leads to a recommendation for additional examination when warranted by a property condition, such as evidence of mold damage or insect infestation. Cautious consumers, especially those who live in states in which *caveat emptor* (buyer beware) is the law, are relying more and more on the inspector's report to help them make purchase decisions. Frequently, a real estate sales contract will be contingent (conditioned) upon the inspector's report.

Counseling

Counseling involves providing clients with competent independent advice based on sound professional judgment. A real estate counselor helps clients choose among the various alternatives involved in purchasing, leasing, using, or investing in property. A counselor's role is to furnish clients with the information needed to make informed decisions. Professional real estate counselors must have a high degree of industry expertise.

Education

Real estate education is available to both practitioners and consumers. Colleges and universities, private schools, and trade organizations all conduct real estate courses and seminars covering topics from the principles of a prelicensing program to the technical aspects of tax and exchange law. State licensing laws establish the minimum educational requirements for obtaining—and keeping—a real estate license. Continuing education, usually required for license renewal, helps ensure that licensees keep their skills and knowledge current.

Other areas

Many other professionals are involved in real estate, including lawyers who specialize in this area of practice, land-use planners employed by state and local agencies, and tax assessors.

TYPES OF REAL PROPERTY

Just as there are areas of specialization within the real estate industry, there are different types of property in which to specialize. Real estate can be classified as

Six categories of real property
- Residential
- Commercial
- Mixed-use
- Industrial
- Agricultural
- Special purpose

- *residential*—all property used for single-family or multifamily housing, whether in urban, suburban, or rural areas;

- *commercial*—business property, including office space, shopping centers, stores, theaters, hotels, and parking facilities;

- *mixed-use*—property that allows for two or more commercial and residential uses in the same building;

- *industrial*—warehouses, factories, land in industrial districts, and power plants;

- *agricultural*—farms, timberland, ranches, and orchards; or

- *special purpose*—privately owned properties, such as places of worship, schools, and cemeteries, as well as publicly held properties, such as schools, municipal service buildings, and parks.

The market for each type of real property can be divided into three main functions: buying, selling, and leasing. Remember, the most common type of real estate transaction is the purchase of a home or residential property. We will mainly focus on residential transactions, but other types of property transactions are mentioned as well.

IN PRACTICE

Although it is possible for a single real estate firm or an individual real estate professional to perform all the services and handle all classes of property discussed here (unless restricted by a state's license law), this is rarely done. A variety of services may be available within the same real estate firm in small towns, but most firms and professionals specialize to some degree.

Residential property

People buy homes for a variety of reasons. To many people, home ownership is a sign of financial stability. A home is an investment that can appreciate in value, especially over many years of ownership. Even when a loan is necessary to be able to afford the purchase of a home, the interest paid on the loan may be a useful deduction from federal income tax. Home ownership also offers benefits that may be less tangible but no less valuable, such as pride, security, and a sense of belonging to a community.

Financial constraints limit many people to leasing rather than buying a home. Some like the flexibility offered by a lease, or the amenities offered by a housing development or neighborhood where renting is a viable alternative to a home purchase. Renting also means less initial financial commitment, making it possible to use funds for business investment or other purposes.

TYPES OF HOUSING

Some housing types are innovative uses of real estate while also incorporating various ownership concepts. These different forms of housing respond to the demands of a diverse marketplace.

The *single-family detached house* has been one of the most popular housing types, although it has been adapted in urban areas to take the form of the row house that may share a wall with an adjoining property. Often, multistory residences in cities like New York and Chicago have one or more separate living units on each floor, offering the possibility of an owner-occupied building that also provides rental income.

The *apartment building* was the response to housing demand in crowded urban areas. Modern highrise structures can offer residents many amenities. In the suburbs, multifamily housing has taken advantage of greater availability of large tracts of affordable land. An *apartment complex* is made up of a group of apartment buildings with a varying number of units in each building. The buildings may be lowrise or highrise, and the complex may include storage areas, laundry and exercise facilities, parking, security, clubhouse, swimming pool, tennis court, and even a golf course.

The *condominium* is a popular form of residential ownership, offering the security of owning property without the care and maintenance responsibilities a house demands. It is also a popular ownership or rental option in areas where property values make single-family building ownership inaccessible to many people. A condominium owner owns an individual unit and also shares ownership with other unit owners of common facilities (called *common elements*), such as halls, elevators, reception area, laundry room, exercise room, main entrance security system, and surrounding grounds, which may include a swimming pool, clubhouse, tennis court, or other amenities. Management and maintenance of building exteriors and common facilities are provided by the governing association, typically making use of a management company and outside contractors, with expenses paid out of monthly *assessments* charged to owners. While condos are often apartment-style homes, this ownership form includes single-family and even commercial properties.

Condo = conventional ownership; deed

Co-op = proprietary lease

A *cooperative* also has units that share common walls and facilities within a larger building. The owners do not own the units; instead, each owner owns shares in a corporation that holds title to the real estate. Each shareholder receives a *proprietary lease* to a specified unit in the building. Like condominium unit owners, cooperative shareholders pay their proportionate share of the building's expenses.

Planned unit developments (PUDs), sometimes called *master-planned communities*, might consist entirely of residences, but they can also serve to merge such diverse land uses as housing, recreation, and commercial units into one self-contained development. PUDs are planned under special zoning ordinances. These ordinances often permit maximum use of open space by reducing lot sizes and street areas. Owners do not have direct ownership interest in the common areas. A community association is formed to maintain these areas, with fees for expenses collected from the owners. A PUD may be a small development of just a few homes or an entire planned community.

Highrise developments, sometimes called *mixed-use developments* (MUDs), combine office space, stores, theaters, and apartment units into a single vertical community. MUDs are usually self-contained and may offer restaurants, grocery stores, beauty parlors, barbershops, and other attractive and convenient features.

Converted-use properties are factories, warehouses, office buildings, hotels, schools, churches, and other structures that have been converted to residential use. Developers often find renovation of such properties more aesthetically and economically appealing than demolishing a perfectly sound structure to build something new. An abandoned warehouse may be transformed into luxury loft condominium units; an out-of-date hotel may be renovated to create an apartment building; and an unused factory may be recycled into living and work spaces for artists.

Factory-built housing was once the often-derided *mobile home*, the most temporary of residences. Today, what are termed *manufactured homes* are permanent installations built to federal specifications, providing principal residences or vacation homes. The relatively low production cost of assembly-line-type construction in factories unaffected by the elements, coupled with the increased living space available in newer models, makes such homes an attractive option for both manufacturers and buyers. Increased sales have resulted in growing numbers of manufactured home parks that offer complete residential environments with permanent community facilities, as well as semi-permanent foundations and hookups for gas, water, and electricity.

Another type of factory-built housing is the *modular home* with components that are assembled at a building site on a prepared foundation. Workers finish the structure and connect plumbing and wiring. Entire developments can be built at a fraction of the time and cost of conventional stick-built construction.

Fair housing

The decision to purchase or lease housing, and where to do it, should be based on an individual's preferences and finances. Too often, individuals have been denied the housing they prefer based on discriminating factors that should not be considered. Federal law prohibits discrimination in the provision of housing and housing-related services (including lending) based on an individual's race, color, national origin, religion, sex, familial status, or disability.

THE REAL ESTATE MARKET

A **market** exists when goods can be bought and sold. The function of a market is to provide a setting in which supply and demand can establish market value, making it advantageous for buyers and sellers to trade. Other considerations for a homebuyer include the tax benefits of home ownership.

Supply and demand

Prices for goods and services in the market are established by the operation of **supply and demand**. The supply is the quantity of goods or services that can be sold at a given price. In the real estate market, the supply is made up of residential and commercial land and structures. Demand refers to the quantity of goods or services that consumers are willing and able to buy at a given price. In the real estate market, the number of homebuyers and businesses seeking to buy property can vary greatly depending on general economic conditions.

When supply increases and demand remains stable, prices go down. When demand increases and supply remains stable, prices go up.

When supply and demand are roughly balanced, prices are stable and there is neither inflation (prices increasing) or deflation (prices decreasing). When supply increases and demand fails to increase commensurately, prices go down; when demand increases and supply fails to increase sufficiently to satisfy that demand, prices go up. Greater supply means producers need to attract more buyers, so they lower prices. Greater demand means producers can raise their prices because buyers compete for the product.

IN PRACTICE

In 30 years in real estate, broker B has seen supply and demand in action many times. When a computer retailer relocated its distribution center to B's town 10 years ago, more than 100 families were interested in the 60 houses for sale at the time. Those sellers received multiple offers, and most sold their homes for more than the asking prices. On the other hand, 10 years before that, when the nearby naval base closed and 500 civilian jobs were transferred to other parts of the country, it seemed that every other house in town was for sale. There were plenty of sales, but prices were lower than they had been in many years.

Supply and demand in the real estate market

Two characteristics of real estate govern the way the market reacts to the pressures of supply and demand: uniqueness and immobility. *Uniqueness* means that, no matter how identical they may appear, no two parcels of real estate are ever exactly alike; each occupies its own unique geographic location. *Immobility* refers to the fact that property cannot be relocated to satisfy demand where supply is low, nor can buyers always relocate to areas with greater supply. For these reasons, real estate markets are local markets. Each geographic area has different types of real estate and different conditions that drive prices. In these well-defined areas, real estate offices can keep track of the types of property that are in demand, as well as the properties that are available to meet that demand.

IN PRACTICE

Technological advances and market changes have enabled real estate professionals to track trends and conditions that affect their local markets. Computers, the internet, smartphones, digital cameras, e-fax technology, and global positioning systems are just a few of an ever-expanding gallery of tools that help real estate practitioners stay on top of their markets.

Because of real estate's uniqueness and immobility, the market generally adjusts slowly to the forces of supply and demand. Though a home offered for sale can be withdrawn in response to low demand and high supply, it is just as likely that oversupply will result in lower prices. When supply is low, on the other hand, a high demand may not be met immediately because development and construction are lengthy processes. As a result, development tends to occur in uneven spurts of activity.

Even when supply and demand can be forecast with some accuracy, natural disasters such as hurricanes and earthquakes can disrupt market trends. Similarly, a sudden change in the national financial market, a local event such as a business closure, or a regional disruption caused by storm damage can dramatically disrupt a seemingly stable market.

Factors affecting supply

Factors affecting real estate supply are
■ labor force, construction, and material costs;
■ government controls and financial policies; and
■ local government factors.

Factors that tend to affect the supply side of the real estate market's supply and demand balance include labor force availability, construction and material costs, and governmental controls and financial policies.

Labor force, construction, and material costs

A shortage of skilled labor or building materials or an increase in the cost of materials can decrease the amount of new construction. High transfer costs, such as taxes and construction permit fees, can also discourage development. Increased construction costs may be passed along to buyers and tenants in the form of higher sales prices and increased rents that can further slow the market.

Governmental controls and monetary policy

The government's monetary policy can have a substantial impact on the real estate market. The Federal Reserve Board (the Fed) establishes a discount rate of interest for the money it lends to commercial banks. That discount rate has a direct impact on the interest rates the banks charge to borrowers, which in turn plays a significant part in people's ability to buy homes. The Federal Housing Administration (FHA) and the Government National Mortgage Association (Ginnie Mae) can also affect the amount of money available to lenders for mortgage loans.

Even apart from financing concerns, virtually any government action has some effect on the real estate market. For instance, federal environmental regulations may increase or decrease the supply and value of land in a local market. Real estate taxation is one of the primary sources of revenue for local governments. Policies on taxation of real estate can have either positive or negative effects. While high taxes may deter investors, tax incentives may attract new businesses and industries and bring increased employment and expanded residential real estate markets.

Local governments also influence supply. Land-use controls, building codes, and zoning ordinances help shape the character of a community and control the use of land. Careful planning can help stabilize, and even increase, real estate values.

Factors affecting demand

Factors affecting real estate demand are
■ population,
■ demographics, and
■ employment and wage levels.

Factors that tend to affect the demand side of the real estate market include population, demographics, and employment and wage levels.

Population

Because shelter is a basic human need, the demand for housing grows with the population. Although the total population of the country continues to rise, the demand for real estate increases faster in some areas than in others. In some locations, growth has ceased altogether or the population has declined. This may be due to economic changes (such as business closings), social concerns (such as the quality of schools or a desire for more open space), or population changes (such as population shifts from colder to warmer climates). The result can be a drop in demand for real estate in one area, which may be matched by increased demand elsewhere.

Demographics

The study and description of a population is called *demographics*. The population of a community is a major factor in determining the quantity and type of housing in that community. The number of occupants per household and their ages, the ratio of adults to children, the number of retirees, family income, and lifestyle are all demographic factors that contribute to the amount and type of housing needed.

IN PRACTICE

Niche marketing is the phrase used to refer to the targeted marketing of specific demographic populations. For example, as baby boomers age and look for retirement housing, their need or demand is considered a niche market. At the same time, fair housing laws prohibit discriminatory practices against protected classes of individuals.

Employment and wage levels

Decisions about whether to buy or rent and how much to spend on housing are closely related to income. When job opportunities are scarce or wage levels low, demand for real estate usually drops. The market might, in fact, be affected drastically by a single major employer moving in or shutting down. Real estate professionals should stay informed about the business plans of local employers.

As you have seen, the real estate market depends on a variety of economic forces, such as interest rates and employment levels. To be successful, real estate professionals must follow economic trends and anticipate where those trends will lead. How people use their income depends on consumer confidence, which is based not only on perceived job security but also on the availability of credit and the impact of inflation. General trends in the economy, such as the availability of mortgage money and the rate of inflation, will influence people's spending decisions.

Financial considerations for the homeowner

Purchasing a home can offer financial advantages to a buyer, provided the marketplace cooperates. First, if the property's value increases, an eventual sale of the property might bring in more money than the owner's purchase price. Second, as the total mortgage debt is reduced through monthly payments that include part of the principal owed, the owner's actual ownership interest in the property increases. The difference between the market value of the property and the amount still owed on it is the homeowner's **equity** in the property. The equity can be borrowed against in future or realized on a sale of the property. A homeowner's mortgage payments thus help to build personal net worth. The third financial advantage of home ownership may be the tax deductions available to the homeowner for mortgage interest and property tax, if those deductions total more than the amount of the applicable standard deduction. Finally, part of the profit made on the sale of a principal residence is not taxed at all.

Tax deductions

Homeowners may deduct from their gross income some or all of the mortgage interest paid up to a certain point. For mortgages taken out after December 14, 2018, an individual may deduct interest off of debt up to $750,000. Loans in existence prior to that date are not affected, as long as they are not over $1,000,000. If a loan was generated prior to that date and is refinanced, that interest is deductible as well, as long as the amount refinanced is not greater than the original loan amount. Finally, between January 1, 2018, and December 31, 2025, the interest on a second mortgage is no longer tax deductible. State and local real estate taxes can be used as an itemized deduction up to a limit of $10,000. Homeowners may also deduct certain loan origination fees and loan discount points.

Other tax benefits

When a married couple who file a joint tax return sell a principal residence, up to $500,000 in profit (sales price minus purchase price) can be excluded from capital gains tax. A taxpayer who files singly is entitled to a $250,000 exclusion. The exclusion may be used repeatedly, as long as the homeowner has both owned and occupied the property as the principal residence for at least two of the past five years.

A first-time homebuyer may make a penalty-free withdrawal from a tax-deferred individual retirement account (IRA) for the down payment on a home, although the withdrawal is still subject to income tax in that year. The limit on the withdrawal is $10,000 and the amount withdrawn must be spent entirely within 120 days on a down payment to avoid any penalty.

Other tax incentives, such as a tax credit for part of the purchase price, also are offered by the federal government from time to time to encourage homebuying. In addition, many states have their own programs meant to encourage home ownership.

Real estate purchases purely for investment purposes (property that is not to be owner-occupied) offer their own tax and other incentives. Because tax laws are subject to change, real estate professionals should recommend clients consult a competent tax professional for advice.

REAL ESTATE INVESTMENT

Real estate has always been an important part of an investment portfolio. As with any investment, real estate requires careful consideration of both its advantages and disadvantages.

Advantages of real estate investment

Rate of return

Over time—say, 10 to 20 years or more—a real estate investment typically shows an above-average (or even high) *rate of return*. In some parts of the country, an impressive return can be received even after a relatively short period of ownership. In theory, this means that an investor can use borrowed money to finance a real estate purchase and feel relatively sure that the asset, if held long enough, will return a profit, even after accounting for the cost to finance the purchase.

Control

Real estate investments also offer more immediate advantages. Real estate offers investors more control over their investments than other options, such as stocks, bonds, or other securities. The real estate marketplace consists of buyers and sellers who deal directly with each other.

Appreciation

Real estate is an avenue of investment open to those interested in holding property primarily for increasing value, known as **appreciation**. During a period of inflation, of course, the value of all property will rise, but so will the costs of maintaining the property. The *intrinsic value* of real estate is the result of individual choices and preferences for a given geographic area. Residential property in a pleasant neighborhood near employment, shopping, and amenities, will tend to retain and increase in value. Commercial property located close to transportation, suppliers, and a source of employees will also tend to increase in value.

Equity buildup

The amount invested in a property is the owner's *equity*. If the property is financed, the only equity at first is the amount paid as a down payment. As the owner pays down the amount owed by regular payments, however, and if the payments include payment of part of the principal owed on the loan, that principal increases the owner's equity in the property. Appreciation, too, will result in **equity buildup** as the value of the property increases. Accumulated equity is not realized as cash unless a property is sold or refinanced. Equity may be lost if a property's value decreases due to economic conditions or a natural disaster, even if the property is not sold.

Leverage

Leverage is the use of borrowed money to finance an investment. It can be a way to benefit from the potential for increased income from a relatively small initial outlay. As a rule, an investor can receive a maximum return from an initial investment by making a small down payment, paying a low interest rate, and spreading mortgage payments over as long a period as possible.

The risk of an investment is directly proportional to leverage. A high degree of leverage translates into greater risk for the investor, as well as for the lender, because of the high ratio of borrowed money to the value of the property. Lower leverage results in less risk. When property values drop, for whatever reason, the highly leveraged investor may be unable to pay even the financing costs of the property.

Tax benefits

Income tax laws change frequently, and some tax advantages of owning investment real estate are altered periodically by Congress. An investor can make a more educated and profitable real estate purchase with professional tax advice. The Internal Revenue Service (IRS), www .irs.gov, is the best place to start for federal tax information. State and local taxing authorities offer different tax incentives (and disincentives) to investors and information should be sought from those sources, as well. The following are some of the current federal tax benefits available to investors.

Depreciation, or *cost recovery*, allows an investor to recover the cost of an income-producing asset through tax deductions over the asset's useful life. Though investors rarely purchase property without expecting it to appreciate over time, the tax laws recognize that all physical structures deteriorate and lose value over time. Land is not considered a depreciating asset.

Capital gain is the difference between the purchase price of property and its net selling price. A property's cost, or *basis*, determines the amount of gain to be taxed. The investor's initial cost of the property may be increased by physical improvements made to the property, which will add to the property's tax basis. On the other hand, the amount of any depreciation claimed as a tax deduction is subtracted from the basis, resulting in the property's *adjusted basis* for tax purposes. When the investor sells the property, the amount by which the sales price exceeds the property's adjusted basis is the capital gain.

One way to avoid federal taxation on a capital gain is to exchange the investment property for one of the same value. The tax that would have been owed if a sale had occurred is deferred until the property acquired in the exchange is sold. At present, there is no limit to the number of times that a property can be exchanged and taxation deferred. There are strict rules governing property **exchanges**, and failure to fully comply with the rules can mean the loss of the deferral. The law permitting tax-deferred exchanges is also subject to change as Congress considers ways to increase income to the federal treasury.

Disadvantages of real estate investment

Real estate investments are expensive. Large amounts of capital are usually required, even when financing is available. Investing in real estate is difficult without expert advice. Investment decisions must be based on careful study of all facts, reinforced by a thorough knowledge of real estate and how it is affected by the marketplace.l

Liquidity

Liquidity refers to how quickly an asset may be converted into cash. Unlike stocks and bonds, real estate is not highly liquid over the short term. An investor who holds stocks can easily direct a stockbroker to sell stocks when funds are needed. In contrast, a real estate investor may have to sell property at a substantially lower price than desired to bring about a quick sale. If market values are down, the investor who wants to refinance property to free up cash will have to settle for whatever the lender feels the market dictates.

Active management

Real estate requires active management. The investor may choose to personally manage the property or may hire a professional property manager, but management decisions still must be made. If the property has residential or commercial tenants, how much rent should be charged? Is the property and its management in compliance with all federal, state, and local laws? How should repairs and tenant grievances be handled? What is the long-term goal of the property owner? Is the property manager working to achieve that goal?

Risk

Despite its popularity, a real estate investment does not guarantee profit. It involves a high degree of risk. The possibility that an investment property will decrease in value or not generate enough income to make it profitable is a factor that the investor must consider.

KEY POINT REVIEW

Real estate brokerage is the business of bringing people together in a real estate transaction conducted by a **real estate broker** who is a person or company licensed to buy, sell, exchange, or lease real property for others for compensation, or by a **real estate salesperson** (**sales associate**) who conducts brokerage activities on behalf of the broker.

Appraisal is the process of developing an opinion of a property's value (typically, market value) based on established methods and an appraiser's professional judgment. Licensing or certification is required for many federally related transactions, and many states require licensing or certification for other transactions as well.

Property management is conducted by a **property manager**, a person or company hired to maintain and manage property on behalf of the property owner. The property manager's scope of work depends on a **management agreement**, and the basic responsibility of the property manager is to protect the owner's investment while maximizing the owner's financial return.

Financing is the business of providing the funds that make real estate transactions possible through loans secured by a mortgage or deed of trust on the property, with funding provided by commercial banks, thrifts (which include savings associations), credit unions, mortgage bankers, and mortgage brokerage companies.

Subdivision and development involve splitting a single property into smaller parcels (subdividing) and constructing improvements on the land (development).

Home inspection is of interest to both purchasers and homeowners, and an inspection report will show results of a thorough survey of observable property conditions. A state license may be required of a home inspector.

Real estate counseling involves independent advice based on sound professional judgment regarding how to buy, sell, or invest in property.

Types of real property include **residential**, **commercial**, **mixed use**, **industrial**, **agricultural**, and **special purpose**, which can be privately or publically held.

Discrimination in the provision of housing and related services is prohibited by federal law.

The **real estate market** reflects the principle of **supply and demand**, influenced by the **uniqueness** and **immobility** of parcels of real estate. When the supply increases relative to demand, prices go down, and when demand increases relative to supply, prices go up.

The factors affecting the **supply** of real estate include labor force availability, construction and material costs, government controls (environmental restrictions, land use policies, building codes, zoning), and monetary policy that impacts interest rates and the money supply.

The factors affecting the **demand** for real estate include population, demographics, and employment and wage levels.

The buyer of a home can benefit from **tax deductions**, **exclusion of gain** on the sale of the home, and **tax credits**, when available.

Advantages of **investing** in real estate include a typically high **rate of return**, greater **control** over the investment than other options, property **appreciation** over time that leads to **equity buildup**, **leveraging** of funds to provide greater purchasing power, and the **tax benefits** of **depreciation**, **deduction**s, the use of a property **exchange** to avoid taxation, and treatment of income from a property sale as **capital gain**.

Disadvantages of real estate as an investment include its lack of **liquidity**, so that it may take a long time to convert into cash, and the fact that it requires **active management** to make sure it is being managed properly.

UNIT 1 QUIZ

1. A professional opinion of a property's market value, based on established methods and using trained judgment, is performed by
   A. a real estate attorney.
   B. a real estate appraiser.
   C. a real estate counselor.
   D. a home inspector.

2. In general, when the supply of a certain commodity increases,
   A. price tends to rise.
   B. price tends to drop.
   C. demand for it tends to rise.
   D. demand for it tends to drop.

3. Which factor primarily affects supply in the real estate market?
   A. Population
   B. Demographics
   C. Employment
   D. Governmental monetary policy

4. Which factor is *MOST* likely to influence demand for real estate?
   A. Number of real estate professionals in the area
   B. Number of full-time real estate professionals in the area
   C. Wage levels and employment opportunities
   D. Price of new homes being built in the area

5. Property management, appraisal, financing, and development are all examples of
   A. factors affecting demand.
   B. specializations within the real estate industry.
   C. non–real estate professions.
   D. activities requiring broker management and supervision.

6. What type of federal law prohibits discrimination in the provision of housing and housing-related services (including lending) based on an individual's race, color, national origin, religion, sex, familial status, or disability?
   A. Licensing
   B. Lot size
   C. Home ownership
   D. Fair housing

7. A major manufacturer of automobiles announces that it will relocate one of its factories, along with 2,000 employees, to a small town. What effect will this announcement *MOST* likely have on the small town's housing market?
   A. Houses will likely become less expensive.
   B. Houses will likely become more expensive.
   C. Because the announcement involves an issue of demographics, not of supply and demand, housing prices will stay the same.
   D. The announcement involves an industrial property; residential housing will not be affected.

8. A real estate professional who has several years of experience in the industry decided to retire from actively marketing properties. Now this person helps clients choose among the various alternatives involved in purchasing, using, or investing in property. What is this person's profession?
   A. Real estate counselor
   B. Real estate appraiser
   C. Real estate educator
   D. Building inspector

9. Nationwide Multistate Licensing System and Registry was created to register
   A. appraisers.
   B. property managers.
   C. home inspectors.
   D. mortgage loan originators.

10. Schools would be considered part of which real estate classification?
    A. Special purpose
    B. Industrial
    C. Commercial
    D. Residential

11. When demand for a commodity decreases and supply remains the same,
    A. price tends to rise.
    B. price tends to fall.
    C. price is not affected.
    D. the market becomes stagnant.

12. The difference between the cost basis of property and its net selling price is
    A. cost recovery.
    B. capital gain.
    C. leverage.
    D. appreciation.

13. The use of borrowed money to finance an investment is called
    A. appreciation.
    B. leverage.
    C. depreciation.
    D. capital gain.

14. All of the following are categories of the uses of real property EXCEPT
    A. residential.
    B. developmental.
    C. agricultural.
    D. industrial.

15. All of the following would affect demand EXCEPT
    A. population.
    B. demographics.
    C. wage levels.
    D. monetary policy.

16. All of the following affect how quickly the forces of supply and demand work EXCEPT
    A. a property's specific geographic location.
    B. immobility of a property.
    C. degree of standardization of the property's price.
    D. uniqueness of a property.

17. A person who performs a visual survey of a property structure and writes a report for a buyer is
    A. an educator.
    B. a home inspector.
    C. an appraiser.
    D. a property manager.

18. Another name for depreciation is
    A. cost recovery.
    B. leverage.
    C. capital gain.
    D. inflation.

19. A person or company responsible for maintaining a client's property and maximizing the return on the client's investment is serving as
    A. a rental agent.
    B. a building maintenance specialist.
    C. a property manager.
    D. an investment counselor.

20. Detailed information about the age, education, behavior, and other characteristics of members of a population group is called
    A. population analysis.
    B. demographics.
    C. family lifestyles.
    D. household data.

UNIT
2

Real Property and the Law

LEARNING OBJECTIVES

When you have completed this unit, you will be able to

> **discuss** the concepts of land and ownership rights in real property;
> **distinguish** between real and personal property and the basic economic and physical characteristics of real property; and
> **discuss** the limitations of the real estate professional under the law.

KEY TERMS

accession	erosion	real property
accretion	fixture	riparian rights
air rights	improvement	severance
annexation	land	situs
appurtenance	littoral rights	subsurface rights
area preference	manufactured housing	surface rights
avulsion	nonhomogeneity	trade fixture
bundle of legal rights	personal property	water rights
chattel	prior appropriation	
emblements	real estate	

OVERVIEW

Even though real estate can never change its location, it is still a product that has a market in which a variety of transactions take place. The real estate professional is the person who brings together the parties, whether for a sale, lease, exchange, or other type of transaction. As any successful real estate professional will tell you, product knowledge is the key to success. This unit covers the fundamental principles of the product that is at the heart of every real estate transaction.

LAND, REAL ESTATE, AND REAL PROPERTY

The words *land*, *real estate*, and *real property* are often used interchangeably. To most people, they mean the same thing. The terms originated to describe different aspects of ownership interests in land. To fully understand the nature of real estate and the laws that affect it, real estate professionals must be aware of the subtle yet important differences in the meaning of these words.

Land

For the real estate professional, land is more than just a handful of dirt. **Land** is defined as the earth's surface extending downward to the center of the earth and upward to infinity. Land includes naturally attached objects, such as trees, as well as bodies of water found on or under it. (See Figure 2.1.)

FIGURE 2.1:   Land, Real Estate, and Real Property

Land
Earth's surface to the center of the earth and the airspace above the land, including the trees and water

Real Estate
Land plus permanent human-made additions

Real Property
Real estate plus bundle of legal rights

Land thus includes not only the surface of the earth, with the boulders and plants found on it, but also the underlying soil. It includes the *subsurface*, the minerals and substances that lie far below the earth's surface as well as the *airspace*, the air above the earth, all the way into space. Of course, more than 70% of the surface of the earth is not land at all, but water. Federal, state, and local laws govern the ownership and use of those areas within and bordering the United States, including oceans, lakes, and rivers. Private contracts, as well as laws and regulations, can also limit ownership and use rights in the surface, subsurface, and airspace of land.

Three physical characteristics of land

■ Immobility
■ Indestructibility
■ Uniqueness

Physical characteristics of land

Land has three physical characteristics: immobility, indestructibility, and uniqueness.

Immobility

It is true that some of the substances of land are removable and that topography can be changed, but the geographic location of any given parcel of land can never be changed. It is fixed and therefore immobile.

Indestructibility

Land is considered indestructible, even though it is subject to both natural and human forces. Land can be denuded of vegetation by strip mining, paved over for a highway or building, or eroded by a flood or dust storm. The geographic location will still remain, whatever its condition. This permanence of land, coupled with the long-term nature of most improvements, tends to stabilize investments in real property.

The fact that land is indestructible does not, however, change the fact that the improvements on land depreciate and can become obsolete, which may dramatically reduce the land's value. This gradual depreciation should not be confused with the knowledge that the economic desirability of a given location can change.

Uniqueness

Uniqueness, which is also known as **nonhomogeneity**, is the concept that no two parcels of property are exactly the same or in the same location. The characteristics of each property, no matter how small, differ from those of every other, and each property has its own geographic coordinates. An individual parcel has no substitute because each is unique.

Real estate

Real estate is defined as land plus all human-made improvements to the land that are permanently attached (annexed) to it. (See Figure 2.1.)

An **improvement** to land can be any artificial thing attached on or below ground, such as a building, fence, water line or sewer pipe, as well as growing things that are made part of the landscaping.

Real property

Real property is defined as the interests, benefits, and rights that are automatically included in the ownership of real estate. (See Figure 2.1.) In many states, the terms *real estate* and *real property* are synonymous, and are used to refer to both the physical property and the rights of ownership, while other states still make the distinction.

Traditionally, ownership rights of real property are described as a **bundle of legal rights**. These rights include the

- right of possession,
- right to control the property within the framework of the law,
- right of enjoyment (to use the property in any legal manner),
- right of exclusion (to keep others from entering or using the property), and
- right of disposition (to sell, will, transfer, or otherwise dispose of or encumber the property).

The concept of a bundle of rights comes from old English law. In the Middle Ages, a seller transferred property by giving the purchaser a handful of earth or a bundle of bound sticks from a tree on the property. After accepting the bundle, the purchaser became the owner of the tree from which the sticks came and the land to which the tree was attached. Because the rights of ownership (like the sticks) can be separated and individually transferred, the sticks became symbolic of those rights. (See Figure 2.2.)

FIGURE 2.2:   The Bundle of Legal Rights

Possession

Control

Enjoyment

Exclusion

Disposition

Title to real property

The word *title*, as it relates to real property (real estate), has two meanings: (1) the right to or ownership of the property, including the owner's bundle of legal rights; and (2) evidence of that ownership by a deed. Title refers to *ownership* of the property, not to a printed document. The document by which the owner transfers title to the property is the deed.

Real property is often coupled with the word *appurtenance*. An **appurtenance** (something that is transferred with or "runs with" the land) is a right or privilege associated with the property, although not necessarily a physical part of it. Typical appurtenances include parking spaces in multiunit buildings, easements, water rights, and other improvements. An appurtenance is connected to the property, and ownership of the appurtenance normally transfers to the new owner when the property is sold.

IN PRACTICE

When people talk about buying or selling homes, office buildings, and land, they usually call these things real estate. For all practical purposes, the term *real estate* is synonymous with *real property* as defined here. Thus, in everyday usage, *real estate* includes the legal rights of ownership specified in the definition of real property. Sometimes people use the term *realty* instead.

Surface, subsurface, and air rights

Surface rights

Ownership rights in a parcel of real estate that are limited to the surface of the earth are called **surface rights**.

Subsurface rights

The rights to the natural resources below the earth's surface are called **subsurface rights**. An owner may transfer subsurface rights without transferring surface rights, and vice versa. In oil-producing states, real estate is commonly transferred without including the rights to minerals found below ground level. Recently, natural gas found in shale rock beneath the surface that is removed in the process called hydraulic fracturing ("fracking") has become economical and created new interest in subsurface rights in many states. Fracking also has resulted in environmental concerns.

IN PRACTICE

A landowner sells the rights to any oil and gas found beneath the owned farmland to an oil company. Later, the same landowner sells the remaining interests (the surface, air, and limited subsurface rights) to a buyer, reserving the rights to any coal that may be found. This buyer sells the remaining land to yet another buyer but retains the farmhouse, shed, and pasture. After these sales, four parties have ownership interests in the same real estate: (1) the original landowner owns all the coal; (2) the oil company owns all the oil and gas; (3) the first buyer owns the farmhouse, shed, and pasture; and (4) the second buyer owns the rights to the remaining real estate. (See Figure 2.3.)

FIGURE 2.3:   Surface and Subsurface Rights

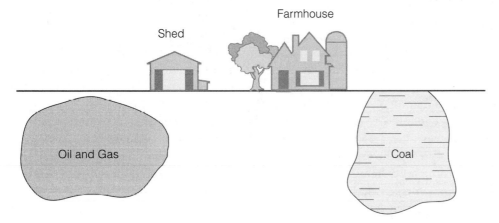

Air rights

The rights to use the space above the earth may be sold or leased independently, provided the rights have not been limited by law. **Air rights** can be an important part of real estate, particularly in large cities, where the air rights over railroad tracks must be purchased or leased to construct office buildings, such as the MetLife Building (formerly the PanAm Building) in New York City and One Prudential Plaza (formerly the Prudential Building) in Chicago. To construct such a building, the developer must purchase not only the air rights but also numerous small portions of the land's surface for the building's foundation supports.

Before air travel was possible, a property's air rights were considered unlimited, extending upward into the farthest reaches of outer space. Now that air travel is common, however, the federal government, through laws, regulations, and court decisions, has put limits on air rights. Today, reasonable interference with these rights is permitted, such as that necessary for aircraft (and presumably spacecraft), as long as the owner's right to use and occupy the land is not unduly lessened. Government and airport authorities often purchase adjacent air rights to provide approach patterns for air traffic.

With the continuing development of solar power, air rights—and, more specifically, light or solar rights—are being closely examined by the courts. A new highrise building that blocks sunlight from a smaller existing building may be found to be interfering with the smaller building's right to sunlight, particularly if systems in the smaller building are solar powered. Air and solar rights are regulated by state and local laws and regulations.

Water rights

Water rights are common-law (historical) or statutory rights held by owners of land adjacent to rivers, lakes, or oceans and are restrictions on the rights of land ownership. Water rights are particularly important in arid western states, where water is a scarce and valuable public commodity, but are also of concern in agricultural areas and population centers.

Whether for agricultural, recreational, or other purposes, waterfront real estate has always been desirable. Each state has strict laws that govern the ownership and use of water as well as the adjacent land. The laws vary among the states, but all are closely linked to climatic and topographical conditions. Where water is plentiful, states may rely on the simple parameters set by the common-law doctrines of riparian and littoral rights. Where water is scarce, a state may control all but limited domestic use of water, according to the doctrine of prior appropriation.

Riparian rights

Common-law rights granted to owners of land along the course of a river, stream, or similar flowing body of water are called **riparian rights**. Although riparian rights are governed by laws that vary from state to state, they generally include the unrestricted right to use the water. As a rule, the only limitation on the owner's use is that such use cannot interrupt or alter the flow of the water or contaminate it in any way. In addition, an owner of land that borders a nonnavigable waterway, (i.e., a body of water unsuitable for commercial boat traffic) owns the land under the water to the exact center of the waterway. Land adjoining commercially navigable rivers, on the other hand, is usually owned to the water's edge, with the state holding title to the submerged land. (See Figure 2.4.) Navigable waters are considered public highways in which the public has an easement or right to travel.

FIGURE 2.4:   Riparian Rights

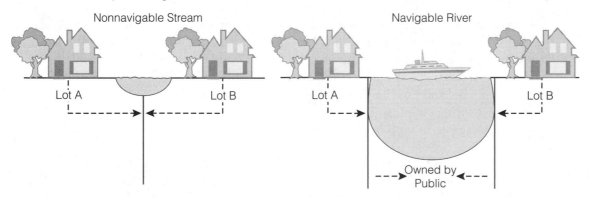

Littoral rights

Closely related to riparian rights are the **littoral rights** of owners whose land borders commercially navigable lakes, seas, and oceans. Owners with littoral rights enjoy unrestricted use of available waters but own the land adjacent to the water only up to the average high-water mark. All land below this point is owned by the government.

In some states, riparian and littoral rights are appurtenant to (run with) the land and cannot be retained when the property is sold. The right to use the water belongs to whoever owns the bordering land and that right cannot be retained by a former owner after the land is sold.

Accretion, erosion, and avulsion

The amount of land an individual owns may be affected by the natural action of water. An owner is entitled to all land created through **accretion**—increases in the land resulting from the deposit of soil by the water's action.

On the other hand, an owner may lose land through the action of the elements. **Erosion** is the gradual and sometimes imperceptible wearing away of the land by natural forces, such as wind, rain, and flowing water. Fortunately, erosion usually takes hundreds or even thousands of years to have any noticeable effect on a person's property. Flash floods or heavy winds, however, can increase the speed of erosion.

If erosion is a slow natural process, avulsion is its opposite. **Avulsion** is the sudden removal of soil by an act of nature. It is an event that causes the loss of land in a much less subtle manner than erosion. An earthquake or a mudslide, for instance, can cause an individual's landholding to become much smaller very quickly.

Doctrine of prior appropriation

In states where water is scarce, ownership and use of water are often determined by the doctrine of **prior appropriation**. Under this doctrine, the right to use any water, with the exception of limited domestic use, is controlled by the state rather than by the landowner adjacent to the water.

To secure water rights in prior appropriation states, a landowner must demonstrate to a state agency that the owner's plans are for *beneficial* use, such as crop irrigation. If the state's requirements are met, the landowner receives a permit to use a specified amount of water for the limited purpose of the beneficial use. Although statutes governing prior appropriation vary from state to state, the priority of water rights is usually determined by the oldest recorded permit date.

Under some state laws, water rights, once granted, attach to the land of the permit holder. The permit holder may sell a water right to another party; however, issuance of a water permit does not grant access to the water source. All access rights-of-way over the land of another (easements) must be obtained from the property owner.

Coastal waters

The United Nations Convention on the Law of the Sea, signed in 1982, is the most recent agreement affecting coastal waters to which the United States is a party. The Law of the Sea identifies territorial waters as those extending up to 12 nautical miles (equivalent to 13.8 land miles) from a base line that is the mean low-water line of a coastal country. The law also recognizes Exclusive Economic Zones that extend 200 nautical miles from the coastal base line. All other ocean waters are considered international waters and are also referred to as the high seas.

The Office of Coastal Survey of the National Oceanic and Atmospheric Administration (NOAA) is a part of the U.S. Department of Commerce. NOAA Electronic Navigational Charts (NOAA EOC) offer detailed information on nautical features and can be viewed at www.nauticalcharts.noaa.gov.

www.nauticalcharts
.noaa.gov

Unit 2

Four economic characteristics of real estate
- Scarcity
- Improvements
- Permanence of investment
- Area preference or situs

Economic characteristics

The four economic characteristics of real property that affect its value as a product in the marketplace are scarcity, improvements, permanence of investment, and area preference.

Scarcity

While a considerable amount of land has not been developed, the supply in a given location that is suitable for a particular use is finite. There is also value in leaving land in its natural condition to preserve species that might otherwise be extinguished, as well as to benefit the earth's environment overall.

Improvements

Building an improvement on one parcel of land can affect the land's value and use, as well as that of neighboring tracts and whole communities. For example, constructing a new business center or selecting a site for toxic waste storage can dramatically change the value of land in a large area.

Permanence of investment

The capital and labor used to build an improvement represent a large fixed investment. Although even a well-built structure can be razed to make way for a newer building, improvements such as drainage, electricity, water, and sewerage remain. The return on such investments tends to be long term and relatively stable.

Area preference

Also known as **situs** ("place"), **area preference** is commonly referred to as "location, location, location." This economic characteristic refers not only to geography but also to the preference for a specific area. Area preference is based on several factors, such as convenience, reputation, and history. It is the unique quality of these preferences that results in the different price points for similar properties. Location is often considered the single most important economic characteristic of land.

IN PRACTICE

A river runs through a town, dividing it more or less in half. Houses on the north side of the river sell for an average of $170,000. On the south side of the river, identical houses sell for more than $200,000. The two areas have equally desirable amenities, but the south side of the river provides a somewhat better view of the downtown area to the east, which may account for the price differential.

REAL PROPERTY VS. PERSONAL PROPERTY

Property may be classified as either real or personal. **Personal property**, sometimes called personalty, is all the property that can be owned and that does not fit the definition of real property. An important distinction between the two is that personal property is movable. Another distinction between real and personal property is their method of transfer. Real property is transferred by deed, while personal property is transferred by a bill of sale. Items of personal property, also called **chattels**, include such tangibles as chairs, tables, clothing, money, bonds, and bank accounts.

Factory-built housing

Factory-built housing is defined as dwellings that are not constructed at the site but are built off-site and trucked to a building lot where they are installed or assembled. Factory-built housing includes modular, panelized, precut, and mobile homes. Use of the term *mobile homes* was phased out with the passage of the National Manufactured Housing Construction and Safety Standards Act of 1976, when manufactured homes became federally regulated. **Manufactured housing** is that which is built specifically to the standards of the Department of Housing and Urban Development (HUD), although the term *mobile home* may still be used. Most states have agencies that administer and enforce the federal regulations for manufactured housing. State and local building codes regulate the construction and installation of other types of factory-built housing. A useful resource is the Manufactured Housing Institute, www.manufacturedhousing.org.

www.manufactured housing.org

The distinction between real and personal property is not always obvious. Factory-built components are found in virtually every building and become part of the real estate once installed. Manufactured housing may be considered personal property, even though its mobility may be limited to a single trip to a park or development to be hooked up to utilities. Any type of factory-built or manufactured housing may, however, be considered real property if it becomes permanently affixed to the land. The distinction is generally one of state law. Real estate professionals should be familiar with local laws before attempting to sell factory-built housing of any type.

Plants

The legal term for plants that do not require annual cultivation (such as trees and shrubbery) is *fructus naturales* (fruits of nature); plant or crops that require annual cultivation are legally known as **emblements** or *fructus industriales* (fruits of labor).

Trees and crops generally fall into one of two classes: (1) Trees, perennial shrubbery, and grasses that do not require annual cultivation are known as *fructus naturales*. These items are considered real estate. (2) Annually cultivated crops such as fruit, vegetables, and grain are known as **emblements**, or *fructus industriales*, and are generally considered personal property. The current owner or tenant is entitled to harvest the crops that result from that individual's labor. For example, when farmland is sold, the seller won't have to dig up growing corn plants and haul them away unless the sales contract says so. The young corn remains on the land. The seller may come back and harvest the corn when it's ready. Perennial crops, such as orchards or vineyards, are not personal property and so transfer with the land.

An item of real property can become personal property by **severance**, which is the act of separating it from the land. For example, a growing tree is part of the land until the owner cuts it down, literally severing it from the property. Similarly, an apple becomes personal property once it is picked from a tree.

It is also possible to change personal property into real property through the process known as **annexation**. For example, if a landowner buys cement, stones, and sand and mixes them into concrete to construct a sidewalk across the land, the landowner has converted personal property (cement, stones, and sand) into real property (a sidewalk).

Real estate professionals need to know whether property is real or personal. An important distinction arises, for instance, when the property is transferred from one owner to another. Real property is conveyed by deed, while personal property is conveyed by a bill of sale or receipt.

Classifications of fixtures

In considering the differences between real and personal property, it is necessary to distinguish between a fixture and personal property.

Fixtures

A **fixture** is personal property that has been so attached to land or a building that, by law, it becomes part of the real property. Examples of fixtures are heating systems, elevator equipment in highrise buildings, radiators, kitchen cabinets, light fixtures, and plumbing. Almost any item that has been added as a permanent part of a building is considered a fixture.

During the course of time, the same materials may change their classification as real or personal property several times, depending on their use and location.

Legal tests of a fixture

In determining whether an item is a fixture, and thus part of the real estate, courts use the following five basic tests, which can be remembered by the acronym *MARIA*:

> **Legal tests of a fixture:**
> - Method of annexation
> - Adaptability of item to land's use
> - Relationship of parties
> - Intention in placing item on the land
> - Agreement of the parties

- *Method of annexation:* How *permanent* is the method of attachment? Can the item be removed without causing damage to the surrounding property, or can any damage caused by the removal be easily repaired?

- *Adaptability of the item for the land's ordinary use:* Is the item being *used* as real property or personal property? For example, a refrigerator is usually considered personal property. However, if a refrigerator has been adapted to match the kitchen cabinetry, it may be considered a fixture.

- *Relationship of the parties:* In general, a court will favor a tenant over a landlord, and a buyer over a seller.

- *Intention of the person in placing the item on the land:* This should be the most important consideration, but the actions of the tenant may not be consistent with the tenant's earlier intention. If an installation is intended to be temporary, it should not be attached in a way that appears to be permanent.

- *Agreement of the parties:* Have the parties agreed on whether the item is real or personal property in the provisions of an offer to purchase or lease?

Although these tests may seem simple, court decisions have been complex and inconsistent. Property that appears to be permanently affixed has sometimes been ruled to be personal property, while property that seems removable has been ruled a fixture. It is important not only for an owner to clarify what is to be sold with the real estate at the very beginning of the sales process but also for a tenant to make certain that items installed for personal use be removable at the conclusion of the lease term.

IN PRACTICE

At the time a property is listed, the seller and the listing agent should discuss which items to include in the sale. Any item that would usually be considered part of the real property (such as a light fixture), and which the seller wishes to remove, should be clearly labeled as remaining with the seller and so noted on any promotional materials, including property listing forms. Most importantly, the written sales contract between the buyer and the seller should specifically list all articles that are being included in the sale, as well as those that are being excluded from it, particularly if any doubt exists as to whether the items are personal property or fixtures (for instance, built-in bookcases, chandeliers, ceiling fans, or exotic shrubbery). This specificity will avoid a misunderstanding between the parties that might result in the collapse of the transaction and an expensive lawsuit. The most commonly disputed items between buyers and sellers are draperies, light fixtures, and appliances.

Trade fixtures

A special category of fixtures includes property used in the course of business. An article owned by a tenant, attached to a rented space or building, and used in conducting a business is a **trade fixture**, or a chattel fixture. Some examples of trade fixtures are hydraulic lifts in an auto repair shop, lanes and pin-setting equipment in a bowling alley, and dining booths in a restaurant. Agricultural fixtures, such as chicken coops and tool sheds, are also included in this category. Trade fixtures must be removed on or before the last day the property is rented. The tenant is responsible for any damage caused by the removal of a trade fixture. Trade fixtures that are not removed become the real property of the landlord. Acquiring the property in this way is known as **accession** (this is related to the legal principle of *constructive annexation*).

IN PRACTICE

A pizza parlor leases space in a small shopping center, and the restaurateur bolts a large iron oven to the floor of the unit. When the pizza parlor goes out of business or relocates, the restaurateur will be able to remove the pizza oven if the bolt holes in the floor can be repaired. The oven is a trade fixture. On the other hand, if the pizza oven was brought into the restaurant in pieces, welded together, and set in concrete, the restaurateur might not be able to remove it without causing structural damage. In that case, the oven might become a fixture and the real property of the building owner.

Trade fixtures differ from other fixtures in the following ways:

- Fixtures belong to the owner of the real estate, but trade fixtures are usually owned and installed by a tenant for the tenant's use.

- Fixtures are considered a permanent part of a building, but trade fixtures are removable. Trade fixtures may be attached to a building so they appear to be fixtures.

In general, fixtures are real property, so they are included in any sale or mortgage. Trade fixtures, however, are considered personal property and are not included in the sale or mortgage of real estate, except by special agreement.

LAWS AFFECTING REAL ESTATE

Laws affecting real estate

- Contract law
- General property law
- Agency law
- Real estate license law
- Federal, state, and local laws and regulations (e.g., consumer protection, environmental, tax, land use, and zoning)

The unique nature of real estate has given rise to an equally unique set of laws and rights. Even the simplest real estate transaction involves a body of complex laws. Real estate professionals must have a clear and accurate understanding of the laws that affect real estate.

The specific areas of law that are important to the real estate professional include contract law, general property law, agency law, and the specific state real estate license law. Federal laws and regulations, such as those involving consumer protection and the environment, as well as federal, state, and local tax laws, also play an important role in real estate transactions. State and local land-use and zoning laws have a significant effect on the practice of real estate, too.

Real estate professionals can't be experts in all areas of real estate law, but they should know and understand some basic principles. Perhaps most important is the ability to recognize problems that should be referred to a competent attorney. Only attorneys are trained and licensed to prepare documents defining or transferring rights in property and to give advice on matters of law. Although real estate professionals may be permitted in their states to provide contract forms and other documents to clients and customers, under no circumstances may real estate professionals act as attorneys unless they are also licensed attorneys representing clients in that capacity.

Because real estate professionals handle transactions that involve the most expensive purchase most consumers will ever make, the need for regulation of licensees' activities has long been recognized. The purpose of real estate license laws is to protect the public from fraud, dishonesty, and incompetence in real estate transactions. All 50 states, the District of Columbia, and all Canadian provinces have passed laws that require real estate brokers and their sales associates to be licensed. Although state license laws are similar in many respects, they differ in some details, such as the amount and type of prelicensing education required.

KEY POINT REVIEW

Land includes the earth's **surface**, its **subsurface** extending downward to the center of the earth, and the **air space** above the surface.

Physical characteristics of land include immobility, indestructibility, and nonhomogeneity (uniqueness).

Subsurface rights include mineral rights and other natural resources that can be leased or sold separately from surface rights. **Air rights** can be sold separately from surface rights and have limitations to enable air travel. **Water rights** can be held by owners of land adjacent to rivers, lakes, or oceans.

Land includes things naturally attached to it, such as trees and crops that do not need cultivation (*fructus naturales*), and perennial crops, orchards, and vineyards (*fructus industriales*).

Real estate includes the land as well as all things permanently attached or annexed to the land, both by nature and by humans.

Real property includes the interests, benefits, and rights that are automatically included in the ownership of unimproved land and real estate.

The **bundle of legal rights** includes the rights of possession, control, enjoyment, exclusion, and disposition.

Title is the right to ownership of real property and the evidence of ownership provided by a written document, called a deed, by which title is transferred.

An **appurtenance** is a right or privilege associated with real property in some way, such as a parking space in a multiunit building, an easement, or water rights, and is normally conveyed to the new owner when the property is sold.

Water rights are determined by common law and statute and include **riparian rights**, which belong to owners of land along a flowing body of water, and **littoral rights**, which belong to owners of land that borders a commercially navigable lake, sea, or ocean. The doctrine of **prior appropriation** is followed in some states and provides that water use, aside from limited domestic use, is controlled by the state rather than the landowner adjacent to the water; to use water, the landowner must demonstrate a beneficial use of the water, such as for irrigation of crops.

Economic characteristics of land include scarcity, improvements, permanence of the investment, and area preference (situs).

Personal property (chattel) includes

- movable items, such as a chair or a sofa;
- **emblements** (*fructus industriales*), annual plantings or crops of grains, vegetables, and fruit;
- items of real property that can become personal property by **severance**;
- items of personal property that can become real property by **annexation** (such as construction materials); and
- factory-built homes, including **manufactured homes**, that can be personal property unless **permanently affixed** to land.

A **fixture** is personal property that has been affixed to the land or to a building so that by law it becomes part of the real property. The legal tests for a fixture include **MARIA**: the **method of annexation**, **adaptability** of the thing for the land's ordinary use, **relationship** of the parties, **intent** in placing the item on the land, and **agreement** of the parties.

Trade fixtures include property attached to the structure but used in the course of business, and can be **personal property**, if removed by the tenant and the premises are returned to original condition before the lease expires; or real property, if left behind by the tenant. The landlord can acquire this type of property by **accession**.

State laws that affect real estate include those on contracts, property, agency, and real estate licensing. There are state and local land-use and zoning laws, as well as federal and state laws concerning consumer protection, the environment, and taxation.

UNIT 2 QUIZ

1. Real estate generally includes all the following *EXCEPT*
   A. trees.
   B. air rights.
   C. annual crops.
   D. mineral rights.

2. A bookstore rents space in a commercial building. The bookstore has large reading tables fastened to the walls and bookshelves bolted to both the ceiling and the floor that create aisles from the front of the store to the back. These were all installed by the bookstore owner. Which of the following *BEST* characterizes the contents of the bookstore?
   A. The shelves and tables are trade fixtures and will transfer when the property owner sells the building.
   B. The shelves and tables are trade fixtures and may properly be removed by the bookstore's owner before the lease expires, with the tenant responsible to the landlord for any damage that the removal causes to the premises.
   C. Because the business is a tenant, the shelves and tables are fixtures and may not be removed except with the building owner's permission.
   D. Because the shelves and tables are attached to the building, they are treated the same as other fixtures.

3. The term *nonhomogeneity* refers to
   A. scarcity.
   B. immobility.
   C. uniqueness.
   D. indestructibility.

4. Another term for *personal property* is
   A. realty.
   B. fixtures.
   C. chattels.
   D. fructus naturales.

5. A property owner wants to use water from a river that runs through the property to irrigate a potato field. To do so, the owner is required by state law to submit an application to the Department of Water Resources describing in detail the plan for beneficial use of the water. If the department approves the owner's application, it will issue a permit allowing a limited amount of river water to be diverted onto the property. Based on these facts, it can be assumed that this property owner's state relies on which rule of law?
   A. Riparian rights
   B. Littoral rights
   C. Doctrine of prior appropriation
   D. Doctrine of highest and best use

6. The owner of a piece of vacant land removed and sold all the topsoil, limestone, and gravel. At the owner's death, which is *TRUE*?
   A. The property no longer exists.
   B. The heir of the deceased inherits the property as is.
   C. The heir of the deceased owns the gravel, limestone, and topsoil, no matter where it is.
   D. The estate of the deceased must restore the property to its original condition.

7. In determining whether an item is real or personal property, a court would *NOT* consider which of the following?
   A. The cost of the item when it was purchased
   B. Whether its removal would cause severe damage to the real estate
   C. Whether the item is clearly adapted to the real estate
   D. Any relevant agreement of the parties in their contract of sale

8. Which of the following is a physical characteristic of land?
   A. Indestructibility
   B. Improvements
   C. Area preference
   D. Scarcity

9. Which of the following describes the act by which real property can be converted into personal property?
   A. Severance
   B. Accession
   C. Conversion
   D. Attachment

10. While moving into a newly purchased home, the buyer discovered that the seller had taken the ceiling fan that hung over the dining room table. The seller had not indicated that the ceiling fan would be removed, and the contract did not address this issue. Which statement is *TRUE*?
    A. Ceiling fans are usually considered real estate.
    B. The ceiling fan belongs to the seller.
    C. Ceiling fans are considered trade fixtures.
    D. Ceiling fans are considered personal property.

11. A buyer purchased a parcel of land and immediately sold the mineral rights to an oil company. The buyer gave up which of the following?
    A. Air rights
    B. Surface rights
    C. Subsurface rights
    D. Vertical rights

12. A truckload of lumber that a homeowner purchased has been left in the driveway for use in building a porch. The lumber is considered
    A. real property.
    B. personal property.
    C. a chattel that is real property.
    D. a trade or chattel fixture.

13. Method of annexation, adaptation to real estate, and agreement between the parties are the legal tests for determining whether an item is
    A. a trade fixture or personal property.
    B. real property or real estate.
    C. a fixture or personal property.
    D. an improvement.

14. Parking spaces in multiunit buildings, water rights, and similar things of value that convey with property are classified as
    A. covenants.
    B. emblements.
    C. chattels.
    D. appurtenances.

15. A resort purchases a large tract of scenic forest land and puts several prefabricated steel buildings there to store landscaping equipment, fuel oil, and propane canisters. Which statement is *TRUE* regarding this situation?
    A. The resort's action constitutes improvement of the property.
    B. The chemicals are considered appurtenances.
    C. The buildings are considered trade fixtures.
    D. Storing fuel oil, which is highly flammable, is not included in the bundle of legal rights.

16. A property owner's land is located along the banks of a river. This owner's water rights are called
    A. littoral rights.
    B. prior appropriation rights.
    C. riparian rights.
    D. hereditaments.

17. A property owner's bundle of legal rights entitles the owner to do all of the following *EXCEPT*
    A. sell the property to a neighbor.
    B. exclude utility meter readers.
    C. erect No Trespassing signs.
    D. enjoy profits from its ownership.

18. According to law, a trade fixture is usually treated as
    A. realty.
    B. an easement.
    C. personalty.
    D. a license.

19. A buyer is interested in a house that is well designed, but is located in a busy area that is problematic for the buyer. The buyer's concern about the property's location is called
    A. physical deterioration.
    B. area preference.
    C. permanence of investment.
    D. immobility.

20. Which of the following is considered personal property?
    A. Wood-burning fireplace
    B. Built-in microwave
    C. Bathtub
    D. Patio furniture

UNIT
3

Interests in Real Estate

LEARNING OBJECTIVES

When you have completed this unit, you will be able to

> **identify** the various types of estates;
> **explain** the difference between liens and other types of encumbrances; and
> **explain** the limitations on private property rights for the welfare of the public.

KEY TERMS

condemnation	escheat	legal life estate
covenants, conditions, and restrictions (CC&Rs)	estate in land	license
	fee simple	lien
deed restrictions	fee simple absolute	life estate
easement	fee simple defeasible	police power
easement appurtenant	fee simple determinable	pur autre vie
easement by necessity	fee simple subject to a condition subsequent	remainder interest
easement by prescription		reversionary interest
easement in gross	freehold estate	taking
eminent domain	future interest	taxation
encroachment	homestead	
encumbrance	inverse condemnation	

OVERVIEW

Ownership of a parcel of real estate includes all or some of the bundle of rights, depending on the type of interest a person holds in the property. Even the most complete ownership the law allows may be limited by public and private restrictions. These restrictions are intended to ensure that one owner's use and enjoyment of the property owned does not interfere with others' use and enjoyment of their property or with the welfare of the general public. For example, a zoning ordinance might not allow a convenience store to be built in a residential neighborhood, a condo association bylaw might prohibit rental of a unit without board approval, and an easement allowing neighbors to use a property owner's private beach might deter a future buyer of the property.

ESTATES IN LAND

An **estate in land** defines the degree, quantity, nature, and extent of an owner's interest in real property. Many types of estates exist, but not all *interests* in real estate are *estates*. To be an estate in land, an interest must allow possession, meaning the holding and enjoyment of the property either now or in the future, and must be measured according to time. Historically, estates in land have been classified primarily by their length of time of possession.

A *freehold estate* is an ownership interest that continues for an indefinite period..

A **freehold estate** lasts for an indeterminable length of time, such as for a lifetime or forever. A freehold estate can be a *fee simple estate* that continues for an indefinite period and may be passed along to the owner's heirs. The forms a fee simple estate may take are shown in Figure 3.1. A freehold estate can also be a *life estate* that is held only for the lifetime of a person (who may not be the holder of the life estate) and ends when that individual dies. The forms of life estates are shown in Figure 3.2. Both types of freehold estates are discussed in the next section.

FIGURE 3.1: Fee Simple Estate

FIGURE 3.2: Life Estate

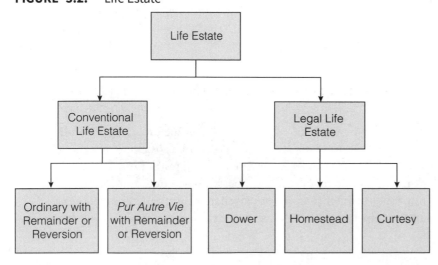

A nonfreehold estate is one for which the length of time of the property's use can be determined. A nonfreehold estate is commonly referred to as a *leasehold estate*.

Fee simple estate

A **fee simple** estate, or **fee simple absolute**, is the highest interest in real estate recognized by law. Fee simple absolute ownership is ownership in which the holder is entitled to all rights to the property by law. This estate is intended to run forever. Upon the death of the owner of a fee simple estate, the property interest passes to

■ the decedent's co-owner, if there is one and the co-ownership was accompanied by a right of survivorship;

■ the person or persons specified in the decedent's will (the devisees); or

■ if the decedent has left no will, to the person or persons designated by the state's law of intestate succession.

The right to use a fee simple estate is limited only by public and private restrictions, such as zoning laws and restrictive covenants.

Fee simple defeasible

A **fee simple defeasible** estate is a qualified fee estate that is subject to the occurrence or nonoccurrence of some specified event. There are two categories of defeasible estate: *fee simple determinable* and *fee simple subject to a condition subsequent*.

A **fee simple determinable** is a fee simple defeasible estate that may be inherited. This estate is qualified by a special limitation (which is an occurrence or event). The language used to distinguish a special limitation—words such as *so long as* or *while* or *during*—is the key to creating this special limitation. The former owner retains a *possibility of reverter*, which is an interest that can be transferred to someone else. If the limitation is violated, the holder of the possibility of reverter (or heir or successor) can reacquire full ownership with no need to bring a legal action in court. The title is automatically transferred to the person who holds the possibility of reverter.

IN PRACTICE

When an owner gives land to a church, *so long as the land is used for only religious purposes*, it is known as a fee simple determinable. The church has the full bundle of rights possessed by a property owner, but one of the "sticks" in the bundle has a special feature. If the church ever decides to use the land for a nonreligious purpose, the holder of the possibility of reverter obtains title without going to court.

Fee simple *determinable*:

■ "So long as"
■ "While"
■ "During"

Fee simple subject to a condition subsequent:

■ "on condition that"

With a **fee simple subject to a condition subsequent**, an owner gives real estate *on condition of* ownership, which means there is a difference in the way the estate will terminate if there is a violation of the condition. With a fee simple subject to a condition subsequent, the estate does not automatically terminate upon violation of the condition of ownership. The owner (or the owner's heir or successor) has the right of reentry but must bring a legal action in court to assert this right.

Unit 3

> **IN PRACTICE**
>
> Land given *on the condition that* there be no consumption of alcohol on the premises is a fee simple subject to a condition subsequent. If alcohol is consumed on the property, the former owner (or the owner's heir or successor) has the right to reacquire full ownership. It will be necessary for that person to go to court to assert that right.

In the defeasible fee estates, the *possibility of reverter* (fee simple determinable) or *right of entry* (fee simple subject to a condition subsequent) will only be possible at some time in the future, and may never take effect. Each of those rights thus is considered a **future interest**.

Life estate

A **life estate** is a freehold estate limited in duration to either the life of the holder of the estate or the life of some other designated person or persons. Figure 3.2 shows the forms a life estate may take.

Unlike other freehold estates, a life estate based on the life of the holder of the estate is not inheritable. It passes to the future owner according to the provisions by which the life estate was created.

The holder of a life estate is called a *life tenant*. A life tenant is not a renter like a tenant associated with a lease. A life tenant is entitled to the rights of ownership and can benefit from both possession and ordinary use, and profits arising from ownership, just as if the individual were a fee simple owner. The life tenant's ownership may be sold, mortgaged, or leased, but it is always subject to the finite limitation of the life estate.

Pur autre vie

A life estate may also be based on the lifetime of a person other than the life tenant. Although a life estate is not considered an estate of inheritance, a life estate **pur autre vie** (for the life of another) provides for inheritance of the property right by the life tenant's heirs, but the right exists only until the death of the identified person or persons. A life estate pur autre vie is often created for people who are physically or mentally incapacitated in the hope of providing incentive for someone to care for them. More than one person could be identified as the measuring life; for instance, a life estate could be granted to a surviving brother by a deceased property owner for the life of the surviving brother's children. As long as one of the children survives, the life estate is in control of the life tenant or the life tenant's successor.

Remainder and reversion

The fee simple owner who creates a life estate must plan for its future ownership. When the life estate ends, it is replaced by a fee simple estate. The future owner of the fee simple estate may be designated in one of two ways:

- **Remainder interest**—The creator of the life estate may name a *remainderman* as the person to whom the property will pass when the life estate ends.
- **Reversionary interest**—The creator of the life estate may choose not to name a remainderman. In that case, ownership returns to the original owner upon the end of the life estate.

IN PRACTICE

To ensure that a surviving spouse would be adequately housed, a married couple with no other heirs drafted wills providing that, on the death of the first spouse, the family house would be held by the surviving spouse in a life estate, with the remainder interest to go to a charitable foundation.

Legal life estate

A **legal life estate** is not created by a property owner, but rather is established by state law. It becomes effective automatically when certain events occur. *Dower, curtesy,* and *homestead* are the legal life estates currently used in some states.

Dower and curtesy provide a nonowning spouse with a means of support after the death of the owning spouse. *Dower* historically was the life estate of a wife in the real estate of her deceased husband. *Curtesy* was a life estate of a husband in the real estate of his deceased wife. (In some states, the terms are used interchangeably.)

States that recognize dower and curtesy typically provide that the nonowning spouse has a lifetime right to a one-half or one-third interest in the real estate, even if the owning spouse wills the estate to others. The surviving spouse benefits because the property cannot be conveyed with clear title until the life estate interest is released; the surviving spouse may release the claim to the property when the value of the interest is paid. Because a nonowning spouse might claim an interest in the future, both spouses should sign the proper documents when real estate is conveyed. The signature of the nonowning spouse would be needed to release any *potential* interest in the property being transferred.

Most states have abolished the common law concepts of dower and curtesy in favor of the Uniform Probate Code (UPC). The UPC gives a surviving spouse the right to an elective share on the death of the other spouse, if the surviving spouse is not satisfied with the decedent's disposition of the property by will. Community property states do not use dower and curtesy.

A **homestead** is a legal life estate in real estate occupied as the family home. In effect, the home (or at least some part of it) is protected from most creditors during the occupant's lifetime. In states that have homestead exemption laws, a portion of the land or value of the property occupied as the family home is exempt from certain judgments for debts, such as charge accounts and personal loans, but not a mortgage for the purchase or improvement of the property. If a debt is secured by the property, including funds advanced under a home equity line of credit, the property cannot be exempt from a judgment on that debt. The homestead also is not protected from real estate taxes billed against the property.

In some states, all that is required to establish a homestead is for the head of a household (who may be a single person) to own or lease the premises occupied by the family as a residence. In other states, the family is required by statute to record a notice of homestead rights. A family can have only one homestead at a time.

How does the homestead exemption actually work? In most states, the homestead exemption merely reserves a certain amount of money for the family in the event of a court sale. In a few states, however, the entire homestead is protected. Once a sale occurs (where permitted), any debts secured by the home (a mortgage, unpaid taxes, or mechanics' liens, for instance) will be paid from the proceeds. Then the family will receive the amount reserved by the homestead exemption. Finally, whatever remains will be applied to the family's unsecured debts.

www.law.cornell
.edu/lii/get_the_law
More information on estates in land can be found at the site of Cornell University Law School's Legal Information Institute, www.law.cornell.edu/lii/get_the_law, by entering "real property" in the search engine at the top of the page.

ENCUMBRANCES

An **encumbrance** is a type of interest in real estate that does not rise to the level of ownership or possession, yet still gives an individual, business, or other entity some degree of use or control of the property. This section covers

- easements and licenses, which permit a limited use of property;

- private restrictions found in property deeds, which cannot impose an illegal requirement;

- liens, which give notice of a claim against the property; and

- encroachments, which can result if a neighboring improvement extends over a property boundary.

Liens

A **lien** is a charge against property that provides security for a debt or an obligation of the property owner. If the obligation is not repaid, the lienholder is entitled to have the debt satisfied from the proceeds of a court-ordered or forced sale of the debtor's property. Real estate taxes, mortgages, judgments, and mechanics' liens all represent possible liens against an owner's real estate.

Private restrictions on the use of real estate

Private restrictions that affect the use of real estate are often found in the deed that conveys title to the property. Once placed in the deed by a previous owner, a **deed restriction** will run with the land, limiting the use of the property by the current owner, as well as future owners to whom the property is subsequently transferred.

A deed restriction cannot violate any law, such as a fair housing law, by attempting to prohibit certain property transfers. A deed restriction that would attempt to do so would be illegal and thus unenforceable.

Covenants, conditions, and restrictions (CC&Rs) are used by a subdivision developer to maintain specific standards in a subdivision, such as by requiring adherence to certain architectural or design specifications for improvements. CC&Rs are detailed in the original development plans for the subdivision that are filed in the public record in the county where the property is located, and they are referred to (incorporated by reference) in the deeds to individual properties in the subdivision. Future purchasers of the property should be given a copy of the CC&Rs and should make review of the CC&Rs a condition of the purchase. The restrictions can be enforced by the developer as long as the developer maintains an interest in any part of the development, and then by any of the subsequent property owners.

Easements

An **easement** is the right to use the land of another for a particular purpose. It may exist in any portion of the real estate, including the airspace above or a right-of-way across the land.

An **easement appurtenant** is attached to the ownership of real estate and allows the owner of that property the use of a neighbor's land. For an easement appurtenant to exist, two adjacent parcels of land must be owned by two different parties. The parcel that benefits from the easement is known as the *dominant tenement*; the parcel over which the easement runs is known as the *servient tenement*. (See Figure 3.3.)

FIGURE 3.3:   Easement Appurtenant

The owner of Lot B has an easement appurtenant across Lot A to gain access to his property from the public road. Lot B is dominant, and Lot A is servient.

An easement appurtenant is part of the dominant tenement. If the dominant tenement is conveyed to another party, the easement transfers with the title. This type of easement will run with the land. It is an encumbrance on the servient property and will transfer with the dominant tenement forever, unless the holder of the dominant tenement legally releases the right or it is terminated in one of the ways that are discussed later in this section. The easement will terminate, for instance, if the owner of the dominant tenement also becomes the owner of the servient tenement (or vice versa). Because the same person then owns both properties, there is no need for the easement to exist.

A *party wall* can be an exterior wall of a building that straddles the boundary line between two lots, or it can be a shared partition wall between two connected properties. The individual lot owners own the half of the wall on their lot, and each has an easement appurtenant in the other half of the wall. The reciprocal interest of each owner in the property of the other is often referred to as a *cross easement*. A written party wall agreement must be used to create the easement rights. Expenses to build and maintain the wall are usually shared. A fence built on the lot line is treated the same as a wall. A party driveway shared by and partly on the land of adjoining owners should be created by written agreement and specify responsibility for maintenance and expenses.

An **easement in gross** is an individual or company interest in or right to use someone else's land. (See Figure 3.4.) A railroad's right-of-way is an easement in gross, as are the rights-of-way of utility easements (such as for a pipeline or power line). Commercial easements in gross may be assigned, conveyed, and inherited. Personal easements in gross are usually not assignable. Generally, a personal easement in gross terminates on the death of the easement owner.

FIGURE 3.4:   Easement in Gross

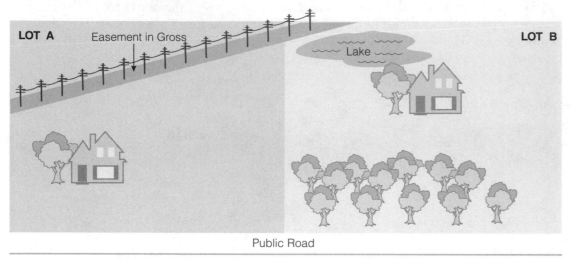

The utility company has an easement in gross across both parcels of land for its power lines.

Creating an easement

An easement is created by a written agreement between the parties that establishes the easement right. The creation of an easement always involves two separate parties; one party owns the land over which the easement runs and the other party benefits from the easement. Two other ways for an easement to be created are by means of an *easement by necessity* and *easement by prescription*.

Easement by necessity

An easement that is created when an owner sells a parcel of land that has no legal access to a street or public way except over the seller's remaining land is an **easement by necessity**. An easement by necessity is created by court order based on the principle that owners must have the right to enter and exit their land—the right of *ingress* (*enter*) and *egress* (*exit*); they cannot be landlocked. Remember, this form of easement is called an easement by *necessity*; it is not merely for convenience.

Easement by prescription

If the claimant has made use of another's land for a certain period of time as defined by state law, an **easement by prescription**, or a *prescriptive easement*, may be acquired. The prescriptive period generally runs from 10 to 21 years. The claimant's use must have been continuous, nonexclusive (the owner isn't excluded from using that part of the property), and without the owner's permission. The use must be visible, open, and notorious, and the owner must have been able to learn of it.

The concept of *tacking* provides that successive periods of continuous occupation by different parties may be combined (tacked) to reach the required total number of years necessary to establish a claim for a prescriptive easement. To tack on one person's possession to that of another, the parties must have been *successors in interest*, such as a deceased individual and the deceased's heir, a landlord and a tenant, or a seller and a buyer.

IN PRACTICE

A property is located in a state with a prescriptive period of 20 years. For the past 22 years, the neighbor to the east has driven across the property's front yard several times a day to reach her garage from a more comfortable angle. The neighbor has an *easement by prescription*.

For 25 years, the neighbor to the west has driven across this same front yard two or three times a year to reach his property when he is in a hurry. This neighbor does not have an easement by prescription because the use was not continuous.

For 15 years, the neighbor to the north parked a car on the same property, next to the garage. Six years ago, the house to the north was sold to a person who continued to park a car next to the garage of the adjoining property. Last year, the buyer acquired an *easement by prescription* through *tacking*.

Terminating an easement

An easement terminates

- when the need no longer exists,
- when the owner of either the dominant or the servient tenement becomes sole owner of both properties,
- by the release of the right of easement to the owner of the servient tenement,
- by the abandonment of the easement (the intention of the parties is the determining factor), or
- by the nonuse of a prescriptive easement.

Note that an easement may not automatically terminate for these reasons. Certain legal steps may be required.

Licenses

A **license** is a personal privilege to enter the land of another for a specific purpose. A license differs from an easement in that it can be terminated or canceled by the owner of the property. If the right to use another's property is given orally or informally, it generally is considered to be a license rather than an easement. A license ends with the death of either party or with the sale of the land.

Encroachments

When a building, fence, or driveway illegally extends beyond the boundaries of the land of its owner or legal building lines, an **encroachment** occurs. An encroachment is usually disclosed by either a physical inspection of the property or a limited survey. If a building encroaches on adjoining land, the neighbor may be able to either recover damages or secure removal of the portion of the building that encroaches. An encroachment that exceeds the state's prescriptive period, however, may give rise to an easement by prescription.

Lis pendens

A *lis pendens* (Latin for *litigation pending*) is a notice filed in the public record of a pending legal action affecting the title to or possession of property. While it does not have a physical effect on property, the lis pendens creates a "cloud on the title" to the property, which may prevent the property from being sold or further encumbered. Recording of a lis pendens should act as an incentive to the property owner to resolve the underlying dispute. When the matter is resolved, the party who filed the lis pendens will record a release to clear the title. If the lis pendens has been recorded without adequate evidence of a bona fide dispute, the property owner can have the lis pendens expunged.

GOVERNMENTAL POWERS

Memory tip
Four governmental powers
- **P**olice power
- **E**minent domain
- **T**axation
- **E**scheat

Individual ownership rights are subject to certain powers, or rights, held by federal, state, and local governments. These limitations on the ownership of real estate are imposed for the general welfare of the community and, therefore, supersede the rights or interests of the individual. Government powers include police power, eminent domain, taxation, and escheat, which can be remembered by the acronym PETE.

Police power

Every state has the power to enact legislation to preserve order, protect the public health and safety, and promote the general welfare of its citizens. That authority is known as a state's **police power**. The state's authority is passed on to municipalities and counties through legislation called *enabling acts*. What is identified as being in the public interest can vary considerably from state to state and region to region. The police power of government is used to enact environmental protection laws, zoning ordinances, and building codes. These include the regulations that govern the use, maximum occupancy, size, location, and construction of real estate.

The government's power to regulate land use is not absolute. A law or regulation must be uniform and nondiscriminatory on its face, even though in practice it may operate to the advantage or disadvantage of a particular owner or owners.

IN PRACTICE

A large area of previously undeveloped land consists of 27 different parcels and is located near the location of a new highway. The land is incorporated into the city limits of Cedar City. The city council conducts the appropriate public hearings on the use of the land and ultimately decides to zone most of the area for residential use and a smaller section for commercial use. Because of its proximity to the highway, the commercially zoned area will keep heavy traffic away from the residential area. Years earlier, all the land was farm land and similarly valued. As a result of the zoning, however, a parcel zoned for commercial use will most likely become far more valuable than a similarly sized parcel zoned for residential use.

Eminent domain

Eminent domain is the government's right to acquire private property for public use; **condemnation** is the actual process of taking property.

Eminent domain is the right of the government to acquire privately owned real estate for public use. Condemnation is the process by which the government exercises this right, by either judicial or administrative proceedings.

Generally, states delegate their power of eminent domain to cities and counties or public entities for public services. For example, a public housing authority might take privately owned land to build low-income housing, or the state's land-clearance commission or redevelopment authority could use the power of eminent domain to allow parcels to be acquired for construction of a new sports arena. If there were no other feasible way to do so, a public railway, utility company, or state highway department might acquire land to extend railroad tracks, bring electricity to a remote new development, or build a highway.

Taking

The concept of the **taking** of property for public use is found in the Fifth Amendment to the U.S. Constitution, which reads, "[N]or shall private property be taken for public use, without just compensation," meaning that when land is taken for public use through the government's power of eminent domain, the owner must be compensated fairly. The rights of the owner of the property also are to be protected by due process of law, as set out in the Fifth and Fourteenth Amendments to the U.S. Constitution. Ideally, the public agency and the owner of the property in question agree on compensation through direct negotiation, and the government purchases the property for a price considered fair by the owner. In some cases, the owner may dedicate the property to the government as a site for a school, park, or another beneficial use. If the owner's consent cannot be obtained, the government agency can initiate condemnation proceedings to acquire the property on payment of just compensation to the owner.

In the past, the proposed use for taking property was to be for the public good. However, in June 2005, the U.S. Supreme Court in *Kelo v. City of New London* significantly changed the definition to a beneficial public use. The court held that local governments can condemn homes and businesses for economic development purposes, even when a private developer is a beneficiary.

In *Kelo*, the city invoked a state statute that authorized the use of eminent domain to promote economic development. The Supreme Court decision leaves it to the states to establish rules that cities must follow when exercising eminent domain powers. *Kelo* caused an uproar when it was decided, and in response, many state legislatures acted to impose a narrower definition of *public use* in eminent domain proceedings to ensure that property would be taken only for public purposes as more commonly understood—roads, bridges, schools, municipal facilities, and so on—and not for commercial endeavors.

Ironically, the City of New London, Connecticut, has failed to benefit from its victory. The city initially sought to avoid losing a $73 million subsidy from the state and attract private development. More than a decade and a recession later, the developer was unable to obtain financing, the Kelo house was moved to another site, and the property is now vacant.

The "taking" concept appeared to further disfavor property owners when the Supreme Court decided, in *Murr v. Wisconsin*, on June 23, 2017, that a property owner could be denied the right to build a second structure on a property that had at one time been two separate parcels, each of which would have been entitled to a building permit, but which ultimately came under the same ownership. In effect, the right to build the second structure was eliminated in what the court considered was "a reasonable land-use regulation."

Inverse condemnation is an action brought by a property owner seeking just compensation for land adjacent to land used for a public purpose when the property's use and value have been diminished. For example, property along a newly constructed highway that could not have been anticipated by nearby property owners may be considered inversely condemned. While the property itself was not used in constructing the highway, the property value may be significantly diminished due to the construction of the highway close to the property. The property owner may bring an inverse condemnation action to be compensated for the loss in value.

It is sometimes very difficult to determine what level of compensation is fair in a particular situation. The compensation may be negotiated between the owner and the government, or the owner may seek a court judgment setting the amount after presentation of evidence of value.

IN PRACTICE

One method used to determine just compensation is the before-and-after method. This method is used primarily where a portion of an owner's property is seized for public use. The value of the owner's remaining property after the taking is subtracted from the value of the whole parcel before the taking. The result is the total amount of compensation due to the owner.

Articles on eminent domain, as well as information on current cases, can be found by going to the website of the National Association of REALTORS®, www.nar.realtor, and entering "eminent domain" in the search engine at the top of the page.

www.nar.realtor

Taxation

Taxation is a charge on real estate to raise funds to finance the operation of government facilities and services. Taxes on real estate include

- annual real property taxes assessed by local and area governmental entities to support school districts, transportation districts, and utility districts;

- taxes on profit realized by individuals and corporations on the sale of real property; and

- special fees that may be levied to finance special projects, such as road or utility installation.

Imposition of real property taxes may be accompanied by an automatic lien on the taxed property. Nonpayment of any of these taxes may allow the taxing body to enforce its lien rights in the property.

Escheat

Escheat is a process by which the state may acquire privately owned real or personal property. State laws provide for ownership to transfer, or **escheat**, to the state when an owner dies and leaves no heirs (as defined by the law) and there is no will or living trust instrument that directs how the real estate is to be distributed. In some states, real property escheats to the county where the land is located; in other states, it becomes the property of the state. Escheat is intended to prevent property from being ownerless or abandoned.

KEY POINT REVIEW

A **freehold estate** lasts for an indeterminable length of time. **Fee simple** is the highest estate recognized by law. **Fee simple defeasible** is an estate that is qualified because it is subject to the occurrence or nonoccurrence of a specified event. A **life estate** is based on the lifetime of the life tenant or someone else **(pur autre vie)**.

An **encumbrance** is a claim, charge, or liability that attaches to real estate. A **lien** is a charge against property that provides security for a debt or obligation of the property owner. **Covenants, conditions, and restrictions (CC&Rs)** are private limitations on the use of land.

An **easement** is a right to use the land of another. An easement is usually created by written agreement between the parties. An **easement appurtenant** is said to run with the land when title is transferred. The **dominant tenement** benefits from the easement, which runs over the **servient tenement**.

An **easement in gross** is an individual or company interest in or right to use another's land. An **easement by necessity** arises when land has no access to a street or public way. An **easement by prescription** is acquired when a claimant has used another's land for the period required by law. The use must be continuous, nonexclusive, visible, open, and notorious.

An easement is **terminated** when the need for it no longer exists, when the owner of either the dominant or servient tenement becomes the owner of both, when the owner of a dominant tenement **releases** the right of easement to the owner of the servient tenement, if the easement is **abandoned**, or by the **nonuse** of a prescriptive easement.

A **license** is a personal privilege to enter the land of another for a specific purpose.

An **encroachment** occurs when all or part of a structure illegally intrudes on the land of another or beyond legal building lines.

A **lis pendens** gives notice of litigation in progress that may affect title to property.

Government powers can be recalled by using the acronym PETE. **Police power** is the state's authority, passed down to counties and municipalities through enabling acts, to legislate to preserve order, protect the public health and safety, and promote the general welfare of citizens. **Eminent domain** is the government's right to acquire privately owned real estate for a public or economically beneficial use through condemnation. **Taxation** can include a charge on real estate to raise funds to meet public needs. **Escheat** occurs when the state takes control of property after the owner dies leaving no will or lawful heirs.

When a **taking** of property occurs, the Fifth Amendment to the U.S. Constitution requires that the owner be given just compensation. A property owner may claim compensation under **inverse condemnation** if an adjacent public land use diminishes the value of the owner's property but the property has not been condemned for public use.

UNIT 3 QUIZ

1. The right of a government body to take owner-
ship of real estate for public use is called
   A. escheat.
   B. eminent domain.
   C. condemnation.
   D. police power.

2. One who has ownership rights of real estate that
could continue forever and which provide that no
other person can claim to be the owner of or have
any ownership control over the property has
   A. fee simple absolute.
   B. life estate.
   C. determinable fee.
   D. condition subsequent.

3. The owner of fee simple title to a vacant lot adjacent to a hospital decided to make a gift of the
lot to the hospital. The deed conveyed ownership
of the lot to the hospital "so long as it is used for
hospital purposes." After completion of the gift,
the hospital will own
   A. a fee simple absolute estate.
   B. a license.
   C. a fee simple determinable.
   D. a leasehold estate.

4. Your neighbors use your driveway to reach the
garage on their property. Your attorney explains
that the neighbors' real estate includes an easement appurtenant giving them the right to do
this. Your property is
   A. the leasehold interest.
   B. the dominant tenement.
   C. the servient tenement.
   D. the license property.

5. A license is an example of
   A. an easement appurtenant.
   B. an encroachment.
   C. a personal privilege.
   D. a restriction.

6. An easement appurtenant
   A. terminates with the sale of the property.
   B. is a right-of-way for a utility company.
   C. is revocable.
   D. runs with the land.

7. A property on Main Street that was formerly a
retail store will become the site of a new city hall,
made possible by the government's power of
   A. escheat.
   B. possibility of reverter.
   C. eminent domain.
   D. taxation.

8. Which of the following is *NOT* an example of
governmental power?
   A. Remainder
   B. Police power
   C. Eminent domain
   D. Taxation

9. A property owner who has the legal right to use a
neighbor's land holds
   A. an estate in land.
   B. an easement.
   C. a police power.
   D. an encroachment.

10. Which of the following is a legal life estate?
   A. Leasehold
   B. Fee simple absolute
   C. Homestead
   D. Determinable fee

11. An owner conveys ownership of a residence to a
church but reserves a life estate in the residence.
The future interest held by the church is
   A. a pur autre vie.
   B. a remainder.
   C. a reversion.
   D. a leasehold.

12. The new owner of a property installs a fence on
the property. By mistake, the fence extends one
foot over the lot line onto a neighbor's property.
The fence is an example of
   A. a license.
   B. an encroachment.
   C. an easement by necessity.
   D. an easement by prescription.

13. A homeowner may be allowed certain protection from judgments of creditors as a result of the state's
    A. littoral rights.
    B. curtesy rights.
    C. homestead rights.
    D. dower rights.

14. A person has permission from a property owner to hike on the owner's property during the autumn months. The hiker has
    A. an easement by necessity.
    B. an easement by condemnation.
    C. riparian rights.
    D. a license.

15. A homestead is a legal life estate in real estate that is
    A. leased by renters.
    B. occupied as the family home.
    C. used as a vacation home.
    D. a secondary residence.

16. Because a homeowner failed to pay the real estate taxes on time, the taxing authority imposed a claim against the homeowner's property. This claim is known as
    A. a deed restriction.
    B. a lien.
    C. an easement.
    D. a reversionary interest.

17. The type of easement that is a right-of-way for a utility company's power lines is
    A. an easement in gross.
    B. an easement by necessity.
    C. an easement by prescription.
    D. a nonassignable easement.

18. The process by which government takes control of a property after the owner dies without a will or lawful heirs is
    A. escheat.
    B. lis pendens.
    C. condemnation.
    D. taxation.

19. A landowner has divided a large parcel of land into smaller parcels and has recently sold a tract near a nature preserve that is landlocked and cannot be entered except through one of the other tracts. The buyer of that property will probably be granted what type of easement by court action?
    A. Easement by necessity
    B. Easement in gross
    C. Easement by prescription
    D. Easement by condemnation

20. All of the following will terminate an easement *EXCEPT*
    A. when the need no longer exists.
    B. nonuse of a prescriptive easement.
    C. abandonment of easement.
    D. release of the right of easement to the dominant tenement.

UNIT 4

Forms of Real Estate Ownership

LEARNING OBJECTIVES

When you have completed this unit, you will be able to

> **distinguish** between ownership in severalty and co-ownership;
> **describe** the various forms of co-ownership in real estate;
> **describe** the key elements of trusts, partnerships, corporations, and LLCs; and
> **identify** the types of property ownership for common-interest properties.

KEY TERMS

common elements	joint tenancy	separate property
community property	limited liability company (LLC)	severalty
condominium	limited partnership	tenancy by the entirety
cooperative	partition	tenancy in common (TIC)
co-ownership	partnership	time-share
corporation	PITT	town house
general partnership	right of survivorship	trust

OVERVIEW

Real estate buyers must determine the type of ownership that best fits their needs. The choice of ownership will affect the ability to transfer the real estate in the future and has tax implications as well. While real estate professionals should be able to identify the basic forms of ownership available in a state, it is up to the prospective buyer to explore the options and make a decision, most likely with the advice of an attorney.

Although the forms of ownership available are controlled by state law, real estate may be held in one of three basic ways. They include ownership in severalty (one owner), co-ownership (more than one owner), and ownership by a trust (property held for the benefit of another).

OWNERSHIP IN SEVERALTY VS. CO-OWNERSHIP

Ownership in **severalty** occurs when property is owned by one individual, corporation, or other entity. The term comes from the fact that a sole owner is *severed* or *cut off* from other owners. The owner in severalty has sole rights to the property and sole discretion to sell, lease, leave as a bequest in a will, or otherwise transfer part or all of the ownership rights to another person.

IN PRACTICE

A grandchild has inherited a condominium from a grandparent. The grandchild owns the property in severalty, making the grandchild the sole owner of the condominium, entitled to all of the rights of ownership.

Co-ownership

When title to a parcel of real estate is held by two or more individuals, those parties are called co-owners or concurrent owners. Most states commonly recognize various forms of **co-ownership**.

FORMS OF CO-OWNERSHIP

Forms of co-ownership

- Tenancy in common (TIC)
- Joint tenancy
- Tenancy by the entirety
- Community property

Individuals may co-own property as tenants in common or joint tenants. Some states also recognize a special form of ownership for co-owners who are married or in a recognized civil union. During the lifetime of the co-owners, there may be no apparent difference between the various types of ownership. Only when the property is conveyed, or when one of the owners dies, will the differences become apparent.

Tenancy in common

A parcel of real estate may be owned by two or more people as tenants in common. In a **tenancy in common (TIC)**, each tenant holds an *undivided interest* in the property. The co-owners have *unity of possession*, meaning that each owner is entitled to possession and use of the entire property, even though each holds only a fractional ownership interest. If there are two co-owners of a property, for instance, and no other division is specified in the deed by which the property was received, each owns a one-half interest. It is the ownership interest, not the property, that is divided.

The deed creating a tenancy in common may or may not state the fractional interest held by each co-owner. If no fractions are stated, the tenants are presumed to hold equal shares; for example, if five people hold title, each owns an undivided one-fifth interest. Each of the shares can also be held by a couple, whether married or in a civil union.

Because the co-owners own separate interests, they can sell, convey, mortgage, or transfer their individual interests in the TIC without the consent of the other co-owners. A share owned by a married couple can be transferred only with the agreement of both parties.

No individual tenant may transfer the ownership of the entire property. When one co-owner dies, the tenant's undivided interest passes according to the decedent's will, to the heirs identified by statute if there is no will, or by the terms of the decedent's living trust, if one was established prior to death. (See Figure 4.1.)

FIGURE 4.1: Tenancy in Common

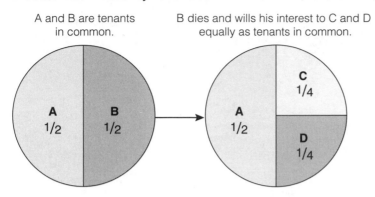

When two or more single individuals or couples acquire title to real estate and the form of ownership is not indicated, the new owners are usually determined to have acquired title as tenants in common. The TIC has become popular in expensive urban areas because it allows a multi-family dwelling to be sold to multiple owners without the need to convert the entire property to the condominium form of ownership, which may entail a lengthy and expensive approval process. The downside of a co-owner's TIC interest is that it may not be as easy to sell as property held in a different form of ownership. Formation of a TIC requires use of an attorney to clarify the terms of ownership.

IN PRACTICE

The problem of owning the right to use an entire property, but having only a fractional ownership interest, usually is resolved by agreement of the co-tenants to specify the part of the property that each will use individually and the part of the property that will be shared. In a residential property with three units, for instance, if there are three TIC interests, each co-tenant may, by agreement of all three, occupy a specified unit, with all three having the right to use all other areas, such as a basement storage space or outdoor space. The agreement should also specify how responsibility for property maintenance, expenses, and taxes is to be shared. Unless all three units are very comparable, this is where any differences may be equalized, with the co-tenant who enjoys the use of the largest or most desirable unit paying a larger portion of the expenses.

Joint tenancy

Most states recognize some form of **joint tenancy** in property owned by two or more people, whether married or unmarried.

The distinguishing feature of a joint tenancy is the **right of survivorship**. Upon the death of a joint tenant, the deceased's interest transfers directly to the surviving joint tenant or tenants. Essentially, there is one less owner. No formal legal action is required, although the death certificate of the deceased owner should be made part of the public record and a copy retained by the surviving owner(s).

If there are only two joint tenants, the death of one of the owners terminates the joint tenancy. If there are three or more joint tenants, at each successive joint tenant's death, the surviving owners acquire the deceased's interest. The last survivor takes title in severalty and has all the rights of sole ownership, including the right to pass the property to any heirs. (See Figure 4.2.)

FIGURE 4.2:   Joint Tenancy With Right of Survivorship

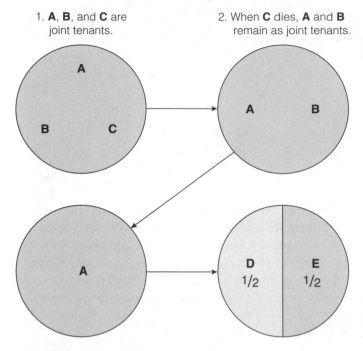

1. **A**, **B**, and **C** are joint tenants.

2. When **C** dies, **A** and **B** remain as joint tenants.

3. When **B** dies, **A** holds title in severalty, which is inheritable.

4. **A** dies and wills his interest to **D** and **E** as tenants in common.

IN PRACTICE

The form under which title to property will be taken should be discussed with an attorney. Remember that real estate professionals may not give legal advice or engage in the practice of law.

Creating a joint tenancy

A joint tenancy can be created only by the intentional act of conveying a deed or giving the property by will or living trust. It cannot be implied or created by operation of law. The instrument must specifically state the parties' intention to create a joint tenancy, and the parties must be explicitly identified as joint tenants.

To create a joint tenancy, four elements or unities are needed, which can be remembered as **PITT**: possession, interest, time, and title.

- Unity of *possession*—all joint tenants hold an undivided right to possession.
- Unity of *interest*—all joint tenants hold an equal ownership interest.
- Unity of *time*—all joint tenants acquire their interests at the same time.
- Unity of *title*—all joint tenants acquire their interests by the same document.

The four requirements or unities are met when the right to possession of a property is acquired by all of the joint owners by means of a single instrument that conveys an equal, undivided interest to all of them, stipulating that they are to be joint owners with the right of survivorship. In some states, identifying the owners as "joint owners" automatically includes the right of survivorship, but use of the wording "with right of survivorship" makes the meaning explicit. Use of a single instrument necessarily means that the right of ownership is conveyed to all of the joint owners at the same time.

Memory tip

The four unities necessary to create a joint tenancy may be remembered as **PITT**:
- **P**ossession
- **I**nterest
- **T**ime
- **T**itle

Terminating a joint tenancy

A joint tenancy is destroyed when any one of the four unities of joint tenancy is terminated. Unless prohibited by state law, joint tenants are free to convey their individual interest in the jointly held property, but doing so destroys the unities of time and title as to that interest. This means that the new owner cannot be a joint tenant, but instead is a tenant in common. If there were only two joint tenants to begin with, the joint tenancy is terminated. If the joint tenancy had more than two owners to begin with, and one of them conveys that interest, there will still be a joint tenancy, but only as to the interests held by the remaining joint tenants; the new owner is a tenant in common.

IN PRACTICE

Sisters A, B, and C hold title to their family home as joint tenants. Sister A conveys her interest to her son, D; D then owns an undivided one-third interest in the property as a tenant in common with B and C, who continue to own their undivided two-thirds interest as joint tenants. (See Figure 4.3.) The difference in the form of ownership means that, unless B and C also convey their separate interests, on the death of either B or C, the surviving sister will be a tenant in common with D, but with a two-thirds interest to D's one-third interest. On the death of the last sister, that sister's share of the TIC will transfer by will or as provided by statute. Unless D is the person to whom the ownership is transferred, D will be a tenant in common with the new owner but D will still have only a one-third interest in the property.

FIGURE 4.3:   Combination of Tenancies

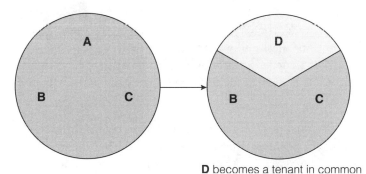

A, **B**, and **C** are joint tenants.   **A** conveys her interest to **D**.

D becomes a tenant in common with **B** and **C** as joint tenants.

Termination of co-ownership by partition suit

Partition is a legal way to dissolve the relationship between co-owners of real estate when the parties do not voluntarily agree to its termination. If the court determines that the property cannot be divided physically into separate parcels without destroying its value, the court will order the real estate sold. The proceeds of the sale will then be divided among the co-owners according to their fractional interests.

IN PRACTICE

Three friends pooled their money to buy a small farm, with the goal of growing produce organically and selling it in the nearby metropolitan area. After learning the requirements to have their produce USDA-certified as organic, one of the owners decides to sell out. After failing to reach an agreement on a suitable buyout price, the friends end up in court, where a judge decides that the property cannot be divided equally and orders it sold and the proceeds divided among the owners.

Ownership by married couples

The property ownership laws of each state identify the forms of property ownership possible within the state. Most states recognize a special form of co-ownership of property that is available only to married couples.

Tenancy by the entirety, recognized in half of the states, is a special form of co-ownership used in some states that allows a spouse to inherit the other spouse's ownership interest upon death. In this form of ownership, each spouse has an equal, undivided interest in the property. (The term *entirety* refers to the fact that the owners are considered one indivisible unit because early common law viewed a married couple as one legal person.) Spouses who are tenants by the entirety have the right of survivorship. During their lives, they can convey title only by a deed signed by both parties. One party cannot convey a one-half interest, and generally they have no right to partition or divide the property.

Community property rights

Community property laws are based on the idea that spouses, rather than merging into one entity, are equal partners in the marriage. Under community property laws, any property acquired during a marriage is considered to be obtained by mutual effort. Today, nine states (Arizona, California, Idaho, Louisiana, Nevada, New Mexico, Texas, Washington, and Wisconsin) uphold this concept. In addition, Alaska allows married residents the option of choosing the community property form of ownership. Although community property law varies among the states that recognize it, all of them recognize two kinds of property: separate property and community property.

Separate property generally is real or personal property that was owned solely by either spouse before the marriage, acquired by gift or inheritance by one spouse during the marriage, or purchased with separate funds during the marriage. Any income earned from a spouse's separate property remains part of that spouse's separate property. Separate property can be mortgaged or conveyed by the owning spouse without the signature of the nonowning spouse.

IN PRACTICE

A spouse who wishes to maintain the character of separate property must be careful not to *commingle* funds that are separate with funds that belong to the community. If the proceeds of the sale of separate property are placed in a community property bank account, for instance, they may thereafter be considered community funds.

Community property consists of real and personal property acquired by either spouse during the marriage. Any conveyance or encumbrance of community property requires the signatures of *both* spouses. Spouses can will their half of the community property to whomever they desire, but upon the death of one spouse, the surviving spouse automatically owns one-half of the remaining property. If a spouse dies without a will, half of the community property already belongs to the surviving spouse and the other half is inherited by the surviving spouse or by the decedent's other heirs, depending on state law. Community property does *not* provide the automatic right of survivorship that joint tenancy does.

Figure 4.4 lists the forms of co-ownership and summarizes how property is held and conveyed under each form.

FIGURE 4.4: Forms of Co-Ownership

Form of Co-Ownership	Property Held	Property Conveyed
Tenancy in common	Each tenant holds a fractional undivided interest with unity of possession only.	The tenants can convey or will their individual interest, but not the entire interest.
Joint tenancy	Unity of ownership. Created by intentional act; unities of possession, interest, time, title.	Right of survivorship; cannot be conveyed to heirs.
Tenants by the entirety	Spouses each have equal undivided interest in property.	Right of survivorship; conveys by deed signed by both parties. One party can't convey one-half interest.
Community property	Spouses are equal partners in marriage. Real or personal property acquired during marriage is community property.	Conveyance requires signature of both spouses. No right of survivorship; when one spouse dies, survivor owns one-half of community property. Other one-half is distributed according to will or, if no will, according to state law.

TRUSTS AND BUSINESS ORGANIZATIONS

A **trust** is a device by which one person transfers ownership of property to someone else to hold or manage for the benefit of a third party. Perhaps a parent wishes to ensure the college education of a child. The parent can transfer an amount sufficient to cover the child's tuition and expenses to a trust account that will be held by the parent's bank, with someone named as trustee of the account. The trustee can be directed to use the funds in the account to pay for the child's college tuition. In this case, the parent is the *trustor*—the person who creates the trust. The child is the *beneficiary*—the person who benefits from the trust. The individual named as *trustee* is the party who holds legal title to the property and is entrusted with carrying out the trustor's instructions regarding the purpose of the trust. The trustee is in the role of a *fiduciary*, a person who acts in confidence or trust and has a special legal relationship with the beneficiary. The trustee's power and authority are limited by the terms of the trust agreement. A trust can be established during the trustor's lifetime, or by will to take effect at the trustor's death.

IN PRACTICE

The legal and tax implications of setting up a trust are complex and vary widely from state to state. Attorneys and tax experts should always be consulted on the subject of trusts.

Most states allow real estate to be held in trust. Depending on the type of trust and its purpose, the trustor, trustee, and beneficiary can all be either people or legal entities, such as corporations. Trust companies are corporations set up for this specific purpose.

Living and testamentary trusts

Property owners may provide for their own financial care or for that of their family by establishing a trust. The trust may be created by agreement during the property owner's lifetime (a *living trust*) or established by will after the owner's death (a *testamentary trust*). (Note that neither of these is related to the document called a living will, which deals with the right to refuse medical treatment.)

The person who creates the trust conveys real or personal property to a trustee (usually a corporate trustee), with the understanding that the trustee will assume certain duties. These duties may include the care and investment of the trust assets to produce an income. After paying the trust's operating expenses and trustee's fees, the income is paid to or used for the benefit of the beneficiary. The trust may continue for the beneficiary's lifetime, or the assets may be distributed when the beneficiary reaches a certain age or when other conditions are met.

In recent years, living trusts have become a major estate planning tool used to minimize the time and costs of probate. In a living trust, the property owner (trustor, grantor, or settler) transfers ownership of real and personal property to a trustee. The trustee is often the trustor. In this way, the owner continues to control the assets of the trust. The trustee may transfer property into and out of the trust, subject to the trust agreement. Upon the death of the trustee, the property passes to the beneficiary or beneficiaries without the need for probate. In the case of community property, the spouses may transfer real and personal property into a trust and name themselves as joint trustees with rights of survivorship. Upon the death of the surviving trustee, the estate is distributed to the beneficiary or beneficiaries.

Land trusts

Real estate is the only asset of a *land trust*. As in all trusts, the property is conveyed to a trustee, and the beneficial interest belongs to the beneficiary. In the case of a land trust, however, the beneficiary is usually also the trustor. While the beneficial interest is personal property, the beneficiary retains management and control of the real property and has the right of possession as well as the right to any income produced by the property or proceeds from its sale. Land trusts are frequently created for the conservation of farmland, forests and other wildlife habitats, coastal land, and scenic vistas.

One of the distinguishing characteristics of a land trust is that the public records usually do not name the beneficiary. A land trust may be used for secrecy when assembling separate parcels. There are other benefits as well. A beneficial interest can be transferred by *assignment*, making the formalities of a deed unnecessary. The beneficial interest in property can be pledged as security for a loan without having a mortgage recorded. Because the beneficiary's interest is personal, it passes at the beneficiary's death under the laws of the state in which the beneficiary resided. If the deceased owned property in several states, additional probate costs and inheritance taxes can be avoided.

A land trust ordinarily continues for a definite term, such as 20 years. If the beneficiary does not extend the trust term when it expires, the trustee is usually obligated to sell the real estate and return the net proceeds to the beneficiary.

Ownership of real estate by business organizations

A business organization is a legal entity that exists independently of its members. Ownership by a business organization makes it possible for many people to hold an interest in the same parcel of real estate. Investors may be organized to finance a real estate project in various ways. Some provide for the real estate to be owned by the entity; others provide for direct ownership by the investors.

Partnership

A **partnership** is an association of two or more persons who carry on a business for profit as co-owners. In a **general partnership**, all the partners participate in the operation and management of the business and share full liability for business losses and obligations. A **limited partnership** consists of one or more general partners, as well as limited partners. The business is run by the general partner or partners. The limited partners are not legally permitted to participate, with the result that each can be held liable for business losses only to the amount invested. The limited partnership is a popular method of organizing investors because it permits investors with small amounts of capital to participate in large real estate projects with minimum personal risk.

If a partner in a general partnership dies, withdraws, or goes bankrupt, the traditional common law result would be to dissolve the partnership, which could be reorganized as a partnership of the surviving partners in order to conduct business. Nearly every state has now adopted the *Uniform Partnership Act*, which provides for the continuation of the existing business even under these circumstances.

In a limited partnership, the partnership agreement may provide for the continuation of the organization after the death or withdrawal of one of the partners.

Corporations

A **corporation** is a legal entity—an artificial person—created under the authority of the laws of the state from which it receives its charter. A corporation is managed and operated by its board of directors, who are selected by the owners of the corporation—its shareholders The members of the board of directors then usually select the officers who are responsible for the day-to-day operation of the corporation. The corporate charter sets forth the powers of the corporation, including its ability to buy and sell real estate (based on a resolution by the board of directors). Because the corporation is a legal entity, it can own real estate in *severalty* or as a *tenant in common* with other natural or artificial persons. Some corporations are permitted by their charters to purchase real estate for any purpose; others are limited to purchasing only the land necessary to fulfill the entities' corporate purposes.

As a legal entity, a corporation continues to exist until it is formally dissolved. The death of one of the officers or directors does not affect title to property owned by the corporation.

Limited liability companies

The **limited liability company (LLC)** is a relatively recent form of business organization in this country, becoming popular only since about 1980, although it has been used in Europe for over a century. An LLC combines the most attractive features of limited partnerships and corporations. The members of an LLC enjoy the limited liability offered by a corporate form of ownership. In addition, the LLC offers the tax advantages of a partnership—income flows directly to the member of the LLC, instead of being subject to the double taxation of a

Unit 4

corporation, with income taxed when received by the corporation, and then taxed again when received as dividends by the shareholders. In addition, the LLC offers a flexible management structure without the complicated requirements of a corporation or the restrictions of a limited partnership. The structure and methods of establishing a new LLC, or of converting an existing entity to the LLC form, vary from state to state.

CONDOMINIUMS, COOPERATIVES, AND TIME-SHARES

A growing urban population, diverse lifestyles, changing family structures, and heightened mobility have created a demand for new forms of property ownership. Condominiums, cooperatives, and time-share arrangements are three types of property ownership that have arisen in residential, commercial, and industrial markets to address changing real estate needs.

See Figure 4.5 for a comparison chart of these types of property ownership.

FIGURE 4.5:   Three Types of Property Ownership

Type	Condominium	Cooperative	Time-Share
Description	Single units are located in lowrise and highrise complexes, as town houses or stand-alone units.	Single units are located in lowrise and highrise complexes.	Multiple purchasers buy interests in real estate—usually resort or hotel property. Each purchaser has right to use unit for set time each year or a number of usage points.
Ownership	Owners have fee title to interior space of units and share title to common areas.	Tenants own shares in a corporation, partnership, or trust that holds title to the building. Tenants have proprietary leases and the right to occupy their respective units.	Time-share estate is a fee simple interest. Time-share use agreement is personal property that expires after a specified time period.
Transfer	Single units are transferred by deed, will, or living trust.	Shares are personal property. Shareholders may sell or transfer shares. Transfer of shares may be restricted by bylaws.	An interest in a time-share estate may be conveyed by deed or will by the owner. An interest in time-share use is personal property that may or may not be transferable according to the contract.
Governance (in addition to state law)	Declaration of condominium and board of directors elected by homeowners	Bylaws of the corporation and board of directors elected by shareholders	Developer

Condominium ownership

The **condominium** form of ownership is used throughout the United States. Condominium laws, often called horizontal property acts, have been enacted in every state. Under these laws, the owner of each unit holds a fee simple title to the unit. The individual unit owners also own a specified share of the undivided interest in the remainder of the building and land, known as **common elements**. Common elements typically include such items as land, courtyards, lobbies, the exterior structure, hallways, elevators, stairways, and the roof, as well as recreational facilities such as swimming pools, tennis courts, and golf courses. (See

Figure 4.6.) Balconies and patios used exclusively by individual units but which must comply with restrictive covenants (such as those regarding use, furnishings, and maintenance) are called limited common elements. Unit owners own the common elements as *tenants in common*, although state law usually provides that condominium unit owners do not have the same right to partition that other tenants in common have.

Condominium ownership is not restricted to highrise buildings. Lowrises, **town houses** that share a wall, and detached structures can all be condominiums.

FIGURE 4.6:   Condominium Ownership

The owner of unit 4 owns the unit, plus an undivided one-fifth share of the elevator, lobby, grounds, and structure.

Owning a condominium

Once a property is established as a condominium, each unit becomes a separate parcel of real estate that is owned in fee simple and may be held by one or more persons in any type of ownership or tenancy recognized by state law. A condominium unit may be mortgaged like any other parcel of real estate, although the condominium project will be required to meet lender requirements. The unit can usually be sold or transferred to whomever the owner chooses, unless the condominium association provides for a *right of first refusal*. In that case, the owner is required to offer the unit at the same price to the other owners in the condominium or the association before accepting an outside purchase offer.

Real estate taxes are assessed and collected on each unit as an individual property. Default in the payment of taxes or a mortgage loan by one unit owner may result in a foreclosure sale of that owner's unit. An owner's default, however, does not affect the other unit owners.

IN PRACTICE

Before buying a condominium, the buyer should do as much background research as possible. Consideration of association fees and rules is critical to understanding all the ramifications of condominium ownership.

Operation and administration

The condominium property is administered by a homeowners association (HOA), which is made up of unit owners. The association may be governed by a board of directors or another elected entity, and it may manage the property on its own or hire a property manager.

Unit 4

The association must enforce any rules it adopts regarding the operation and use of the property. The association is responsible for the maintenance, repair, cleaning, and sanitation of the common elements and structural portions of the property. It must also maintain fire, extended-coverage, and liability insurance.

The expenses of maintaining and operating the condominium building are paid by the unit owners in the form of fees and assessments. Both fees and assessments are imposed and collected by the homeowners association. Recurring fees (called *HOA fees*) are paid by each unit owner. The fees may be due monthly, quarterly, semiannually, or annually, depending on the provisions of the bylaws. If fees are not paid, the association may seek a court-ordered judgment to have the delinquent owner's unit sold to cover the outstanding amount or place a lien on the property. In some states, the association can pursue a foreclosure without first obtaining a court order.

Assessments are special payments required of unit owners to address some specific expense, such as a new roof. Assessments are structured like condo fees: Owners of larger units pay proportionately higher assessments than smaller units. The relative ownership shares are established by the developer prior to the sale of the units.

Cooperative ownership

In a **cooperative**, a corporation holds title to the land and the building. The corporation then offers shares of stock to prospective tenants. The price the corporation sets for each apartment becomes the price of the stock. The purchaser becomes a shareholder in the corporation by virtue of stock ownership and receives a proprietary lease to the apartment for the life of the corporation. Because stock is personal property, the cooperative tenant-owners do not own real estate, as is the case with condominiums. Instead, they own an interest in a corporation that has only one asset: the building.

Operation and management

The operation and management of a cooperative are determined by the corporation's bylaws. Through their control of the corporation, the shareholders of a cooperative control the property and its operation. They elect officers and directors who are responsible for operating the corporation and its real estate assets. Individual shareholders are obligated to abide by the corporation's bylaws.

An important issue in most cooperatives is the method by which shares in the corporation may be transferred to new owners. For instance, the bylaws may require that the board of directors approve any prospective shareholders. In some cooperatives, a tenant-owner must sell the stock back to the corporation at the original purchase price so that the corporation realizes any profits when the shares are resold.

IN PRACTICE

In often publicized events, a well-known celebrity attempts to purchase a unit in a cooperative apartment building and is blocked by the cooperative's board. In refusing to allow a celebrity to purchase shares, the board may cite the unwanted publicity and media attention other tenants might suffer.

Unlike a condominium association, which has the authority to impose a lien on the title owned by someone who defaults on maintenance payments, the burden of any defaulted payment in a cooperative falls on the remaining shareholders. Each shareholder is affected by the financial ability of the others. For this reason, approval of prospective tenants by the board of directors will include financial evaluation. If the corporation is unable to make mortgage and tax payments because of shareholder defaults, the property might be sold by court order in a foreclosure suit. This would destroy the interests of all shareholders, including those who have paid their assessments.

Advantages

Cooperative ownership, despite its risks, has become more desirable in recent years for several reasons. Lending institutions view the shares of stock as acceptable collateral for financing and the availability of financing expands the transferability of shares beyond wealthy cash buyers. As a tenant-owner, rather than a tenant who pays rent to a landlord, the shareholder has some control over the property. Tenants in cooperatives also enjoy certain income tax advantages. The IRS treats ownership of a cooperative as it does a fee simple interest in a single-family home or condominium in regard to deductibility of loan interest and property taxes, and homesellers' tax exclusions. Finally, owners enjoy freedom from maintenance chores.

IN PRACTICE

The laws in some states may prohibit real estate professionals or brokerages from listing or selling cooperative interests because the owners own only personal property. Individuals who participate in these transactions may need a securities license appropriate for the type of cooperative interest involved.

Time-share ownership

Time-share ownership permits multiple purchasers to buy relatively small interests in real estate, typically resort properties. Each purchaser receives the right to occupy the facilities for a certain period. A *time-share estate* includes a real property interest in a specified unit for a particular period of the year, or it can be a designated share of ownership of the property expressed as a fractional interest or number of points. A *time-share use* is a contract right under which the developer owns the real estate. The owner of the time-share use has the right to occupy the facilities for the designated period each year, but only for a certain number of years. At the end of that time, the owner's rights in the property terminate.

The right to transfer the period of occupancy—or even exchange the period of use between properties that are part of the same exchange organization—can make time-share ownership attractive. High development and marketing costs have made time-shares an expensive form of property ownership, however, as evidenced by the discounts offered for resales of time-share interests on various internet sites. Maintenance costs are an ongoing expense, even if the time-share is not used in a given year.

Membership camping may be offered in a form similar to a time-share use. The owner purchases the right to use the developer's facilities, which usually consist of an open area with minimal improvements (such as camper and trailer hookups and restrooms). Normally, the owner is not limited to a specific time for using the property; use is limited only by weather and access.

IN PRACTICE

The laws governing the development and sale of time-share units are complex and vary substantially from state to state. In addition, the sale of time-share properties may be subject to federal securities laws, as well as a state's real estate commission oversight. In many states, time-share properties are now subject to subdivision requirements. Several states have adopted versions of the *Model Real Estate Time-Share Act*, drafted by the National Conference of Commissioners on Uniform State Laws; a summary of the model act is available at www.uniformlaws.org. The model act contains provisions for the management and termination of time-share units and also provides consumer protections for purchasers of time-shares.

www.uniformlaws.org

KEY POINT REVIEW

Ownership in severalty is ownership by one individual, who may be an artificial person, such as a corporation.

Co-ownership by two or more individuals may take one of four forms. In a **tenancy in common (TIC)**, each tenant holds an undivided fractional interest and co-owners have unity of possession. Each interest can be sold, conveyed, mortgaged, or transferred, and will be passed by will or state law when a co-owner dies. A legal action called **partition** can be brought by one or more of the tenants in common to force division or sale of the property.

In a **joint tenancy**, there are four unities (PITT): unity of **possession**, unity of **interest**, unity of **time**, and unity of **title**. Joint tenants enjoy the **right of survivorship**.

A joint tenancy can be terminated by **death** of all but one joint tenant, who then owns the property in severalty; **conveyance** of a joint tenant's interest, but only as to that interest if there were more than two joint tenants originally; or **partition**, the legal action to force division or sale of the property.

Some states recognize a **tenancy by the entirety**, which is available only to spouses and which carries a right of survivorship. Property held by a tenancy by the entirety can be conveyed only by both spouses.

Community property, currently recognized by some states, is property acquired during marriage that is not separate property and requires agreement of both spouses to be conveyed. **Separate property** is property owned by one spouse before marriage, or acquired by one spouse during marriage by gift, inheritance, or with the proceeds of separate property.

A **trust** is a legal arrangement in which property is transferred by the **trustor**, the person creating the trust, to a **trustee**, to be held for the identified **beneficiary**. The trustee acts as a **fiduciary** in carrying out the wishes of the trustor.

In a **land trust**, the beneficiary is also the trustor, but the public record will not identify the beneficiary.

A **partnership** is an association of two or more persons who carry on a business for profit as co-owners in a general or a limited partnership, as provided by state law.

In a **general partnership**, all partners **participate** in operation and management, and partners share **full liability** for business losses and obligations.

A **limited partnership** has both general partners and limited partners. The **general partners** run the business. **Limited partners** do not participate in running the business and are liable for business losses only up to the amount of the individual's investment.

A **limited liability company (LLC)** may be permitted by state law and offers its members the benefits of the limited liability of a corporation, the tax advantages of a partnership, and a flexible management structure.

A **condominium** owner holds fee simple title to the airspace of a unit, as well as an undivided share in the remainder of the building and land, known as the **common elements**, which may be referenced in what are called **horizontal property acts**.

Common elements are owned by condominium unit owners as tenants in common. The condominium is administered by a **homeowners association** of unit owners that may decide to hire an outside property management firm. **Maintenance** of common elements is funded by **fees** charged to each unit owner.

In a **cooperative**, title to the land and the building is held by a corporation, which sells shares of stock to prospective tenants. A purchaser of stock becomes a **shareholder** in the corporation and receives a **proprietary lease** to the apartment for the life of the corporation. The stock is owned as personal property and not real estate.

A **time-share** permits the sale of an **estate** or **use** interest that allows occupancy of a property during a specific period of time, typically weekly. **Time-share** ownership permits multiple purchasers to buy interests in real estate, a form of ownership most commonly found with resort property.

UNIT 4 QUIZ

1. The four unities of possession, interest, time, and title are associated with which of the following?
   A. Community property
   B. Severalty ownership
   C. Tenants in common
   D. Joint tenancy

2. A parcel of property was purchased by two friends. The deed they received from the seller at closing transferred the property without stipulating a form of ownership. The two friends took title as which of the following?
   A. Joint tenants
   B. Tenants in common
   C. Tenants by the entirety
   D. Community property owners

3. Three people are joint tenants with rights of survivorship in a tract of land. One owner conveys his interest to a friend. Which statement is *TRUE*?
   A. The other two owners remain joint tenants.
   B. The new owner has severalty ownership.
   C. They all become tenants in common.
   D. They all become joint tenants.

4. A man owns one of 20 units in fee simple, along with a 5% ownership share in the parking facilities, recreation center, and grounds. What kind of property does he own?
   A. Cooperative
   B. Condominium
   C. Time-share
   D. Land trust

5. A trust is a legal arrangement in which property is held for the benefit of a third party by
   A. a beneficiary.
   B. a trustor.
   C. a trustee.
   D. an attorney-in-fact.

6. According to some states, any real property that either spouse owns at the time of marriage remains separate property. Further, any real property acquired by either spouse during the marriage (except by gift or inheritance or with the proceeds of separate property) belongs to both of them equally. What is this form of ownership called?
   A. Partnership
   B. Joint tenancy
   C. Tenancy by the entirety
   D. Community property

7. Three people were concurrent owners of a parcel of real estate. When one of the owners died, that interest became part of the deceased's estate. The deceased was
   A. a joint tenant.
   B. a tenant in common.
   C. a tenant by the entirety.
   D. a severalty owner.

8. A legal arrangement under which the title to real property is held to protect the interests of a beneficiary is
   A. a trust.
   B. a corporation.
   C. a limited partnership.
   D. a general partnership.

9. A person lives in an apartment building. The land and structures are owned by a corporation, with one mortgage loan securing the entire property. Like the other residents, this person owns stock in the corporation and has a lease to the apartment. This type of ownership is called
   A. condominium.
   B. planned unit development.
   C. time-share.
   D. cooperative.

10. An owner purchased an interest in a house in Beachfront. The owner is entitled to the right of possession only between July 10 and August 4 of each year. Which of the following is *MOST* likely the type of ownership that has been purchased?
    A. Cooperative
    B. Condominium
    C. Time-share
    D. Partnership

11. A corporation is a legal entity, recognized as an artificial person. Property owned solely by the corporation is owned in
    A. trust.
    B. partnership.
    C. severalty.
    D. survivorship tenancy.

12. Which of the following refers to ownership by one person?
    A. Tenancy by the entirety
    B. Community property
    C. Tenancy in common
    D. Severalty

13. A married couple co-owns a farm and has the right of survivorship. This arrangement is *MOST* likely
    A. severalty ownership.
    B. community property.
    C. a tenancy in common.
    D. an estate by the entirety.

14. The real property interest that takes the form of personal property is
    A. ownership in severalty.
    B. cooperative unit ownership.
    C. condominium unit ownership.
    D. tenancy in common.

15. Two people are co-owners of a small office building with the right of survivorship. One of the co-owners dies intestate and leaves nothing to be distributed to heirs. Which of the following would explain why the surviving co-owner acquired the deceased's interest?
    A. Severalty
    B. Joint tenancy
    C. Community property
    D. Condominium

16. Which of the following is *MOST* likely evidence of ownership in a cooperative?
    A. Tax bill for an individual unit
    B. Existence of a reverter clause
    C. Shareholder stock
    D. Right of first refusal

17. An ownership interest that can be an estate interest or a right of use is
    A. a leasehold.
    B. a time-share.
    C. a condominium.
    D. a cooperative.

18. Which statement applies to both joint tenancy and tenancy by the entirety?
    A. There is no right to file a partition suit.
    B. The last survivor becomes a severalty owner.
    C. A deed signed by one owner will convey a fractional interest.
    D. A deed will not convey any interest unless signed by both spouses.

19. Which of the following is *NOT* a form of co-ownership?
    A. Tenancy in common
    B. Ownership in severalty
    C. Tenancy by the entirety
    D. Community property

20. If property is held by two or more owners as joint tenants, the interest of a deceased co-owner will be passed to
    A. the surviving owner or owners.
    B. the heirs of the deceased.
    C. the state, under the law of escheat.
    D. the trust under which the property was owned.

Land Description

LEARNING OBJECTIVES

When you have completed this unit, you will be able to

› **identify** the methods used for describing real estate; and
› **explain** the process involved in identifying and measuring property rights including those above and below the surface.

KEY TERMS

air lots	metes-and-bounds method	rectangular (government)
base lines	monuments	survey system
benchmarks	plat map	sections
datum	point of beginning (POB)	survey
legal description	principal meridians	tiers
lot-and-block (recorded plat)	ranges	township lines
method		townships

OVERVIEW

A street address, while usually enough to find the location of a property or building, is not precise enough to define the perimeter of a parcel of land in a way that excludes all other parcels. A street address will not indicate how large the property is, or where it begins and ends. For real estate to be the subject of a transaction, the description of the property must be *legally sufficient*—that is, the property must be described in a way that will enable a sales contract, lease, deed, or mortgage document to be legally enforceable.

A **legal description** is a detailed way of describing a parcel of land in a document that will be accepted in a court of law. The description is based on information collected through a **survey**—the process by which boundaries are measured by calculating the dimensions and area to determine the exact location of a piece of land. Courts have stated that a description is *legally sufficient* if it allows a surveyor to *locate* the parcel. In this context, *locate* means that the surveyor must be able to define the exact boundaries of the property. Several alternative systems of identification have been developed to express a legal description of real estate.

METHODS OF DESCRIBING REAL ESTATE

There are three basic methods currently used to describe real estate:

- Metes and bounds
- Rectangular (or government) survey
- Lot and block (recorded plat)

Although each method can be used independently, the methods may be combined in some situations. Some states use only one method; others use all three. About 10 states, including Hawaii and Colorado, have properties that are identified by means of a Torrens certificate, which is issued and guaranteed by the state. The Torrens system was created by Robert Torrens in Australia in 1858. Because of the expense involved in verifying a property description before issuing a certificate, the Torrens system was not widely adopted in this country, but it is still popular in Australia, New Zealand, and Canada.

Today, technology allows for greater precision both in land measurement and recordkeeping. The use of a satellite-based geographic information system (GIS) to locate land boundaries and objects with amazing accuracy and the use of computer-assisted design (CAD) programs to create maps have created a new era in land description. The National Geospatial Advisory Committee, www.fgdc.gov/ngac, was created in 1994 to coordinate geographic data acquisition and access. The Federal Bureau of Land Management and the USDA Forest Service were charged in 1998 with the task of developing the National Integrated Land System (NILS) in cooperation with states, counties, and private industry. Recognizing the need for consistent standards of data collection and use, the Cadastral Data Content Standard was created by the Federal Geographic Data Committee, www.fgdc.gov, to integrate information found in publicly available land records. The NILS is being designed to be compatible with land descriptions utilizing both the metes-and-bounds method and the rectangular survey system.

www.fgdc.gov/ngac

www.fgdc.gov

Metes-and-bounds method

The **metes-and-bounds method** of land description is the oldest found in the United States, and it was used in the original 13 colonies, as well as in those states that were being settled while the rectangular survey system was being developed. *Metes* means to measure, and *bounds* means linear directions. The method relies on a property's physical features to determine the boundaries and measurements of the parcel. A metes-and-bounds description starts at a designated place on the parcel, called the **point of beginning (POB)**. The POB is also the point at which the description ends. From there, the surveyor proceeds around the property's boundaries. The boundaries are recorded by referring to linear measurements, natural and artificial landmarks (called *monuments*), and directions. A metes-and-bounds description always ends back at the POB so that the tract being described is completely enclosed.

Monuments

Monuments are fixed objects used to identify the POB, all corners of the parcel or ends of boundary segments, and the location of intersecting boundaries. In colonial times, a monument might have been a natural object such as a stone, a large tree, a lake, or a stream. It also may have been a street, a fence, or other marker. Today, monuments are iron pins or concrete posts placed by the U.S. Army Corps of Engineers, other government departments, or trained private surveyors. Measurements often include the words *more or less* because the location of the monuments is more important than the distances between them. The actual distance between monuments takes precedence over any linear measurements in the description. Because monuments can be moved, surveyors give their final metes-and-bounds reference in terms of cardinal points and distance. They include the statement "to the point of beginning (POB)" to ensure closure and to remove questions if an error in footage prevents closure.

An example of a historical metes-and-bounds description of a parcel of land (pictured in Figure 5.1) follows:

> A tract of land located in Red Skull, Boone County, Virginia, described as follows: Beginning at the intersection of the east line of Jones Road and the south line of Skull Drive; then east along the south line of Skull Drive 200 feet; then south 15° east 216.5 feet, more or less, to the center thread of Red Skull Creek then northwesterly along the center line of said creek to its intersection with the east line of Jones Road; then north 105 feet, more or less, along the east line of Jones Road to the point of beginning.

Figure 5.1:   Metes-and-Bounds Tract

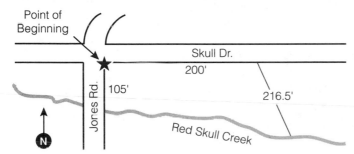

When used to describe property within a town or city, a metes-and-bounds description may begin as follows:

> Beginning at a point on the southerly side of Kent Street, 100 feet easterly from the corner formed by the intersection of the southerly side of Kent Street and the easterly side of Broadway; then . . .

In this description, the POB is given by reference to the corner intersection. Again, the description must close by returning to the POB.

An example of a technically assisted metes-and-bounds description follows:

> Beginning at a point (POB) on the North side of Newberry Street 100.50 feet East from the corner formed by the intersection of the East boundary of Peter Road and the North boundary of Newberry Street; then East 90 degrees, 15 minutes, 200.22 feet; then North 1 degree, 3 minutes, 2 seconds 300 feet; then West 89 degrees, 10 minutes, 3 seconds, 200.05 feet; then direct to the POB.

Metes-and-bounds descriptions are complicated. They can be difficult to understand when they include detailed compass directions or concave and convex lines. Sometimes the lines are curved on an arc or radius that becomes part of the description. Natural deterioration or destruction of the monuments in a description can make boundaries difficult to identify.

Technological advances, such as the use of computers, lasers, satellites, and global positioning systems, have meant a resurgence in property descriptions using points of reference or metes-and-bounds descriptions.

Rectangular (government) survey system

The **rectangular survey system**, sometimes called the *government survey system*, was established by Congress in 1785 to standardize the description of land acquired by the newly formed federal government. By dividing the land into rectangles, the survey provided land descriptions by describing the rectangle(s) in which the land was located. The system is based on two sets of intersecting lines: principal meridians and base lines. The **principal meridians** run north and south, and the **base lines** run east and west. Both are located by reference to degrees of longitude and latitude. Each principal meridian has a name or number and is crossed by a base line. Each principal meridian and its corresponding base line are used to survey a definite area of land, indicated on the map by boundary lines. There are 37 principal meridians in the United States and each is referenced by a name or meridian number.

Each principal meridian describes only specific areas of land by boundaries. No parcel of land is described by reference to more than one principal meridian. The meridian used may not necessarily be the nearest one. Figure 5.2 shows which states use which systems and also shows principal meridians and base lines.

Figure 5.2:   Map of United States Showing Meridians and Base Lines

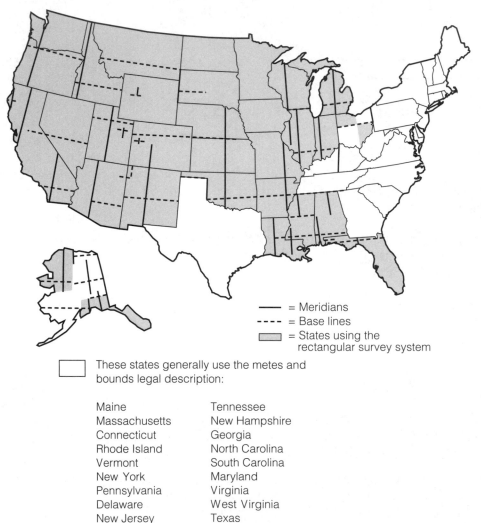

—— = Meridians
---- = Base lines
▨ = States using the rectangular survey system

☐ These states generally use the metes and bounds legal description:

Maine	Tennessee
Massachusetts	New Hampshire
Connecticut	Georgia
Rhode Island	North Carolina
Vermont	South Carolina
New York	Maryland
Pennsylvania	Virginia
Delaware	West Virginia
New Jersey	Texas
Kentucky	Hawaii (not pictured)

Tiers

Lines running east and west, *parallel to the base line* and six miles apart, are called **township lines**. (See Figure 5.3.) They form strips of land called **tiers**. Think of these tiers as being like the tiers of a wedding cake. The tiers are designated by consecutive numbers north or south of the base line. For instance, the strip of land between 6 and 12 miles north of a base line is Township 2 North.

Figure 5.3:   Township Lines

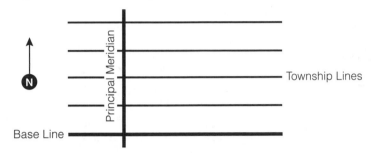

Ranges

The land on either side of a principal meridian is divided into six-mile-wide strips by lines that run north and south, *parallel to the meridian*. These north-south strips of land are called **ranges**. (See Figure 5.4.) They are designated by consecutive numbers east or west of the principal meridian. For example, Range 3 East would be a strip of land between 12 and 18 miles east of its principal meridian.

Figure 5.4:   Range Lines

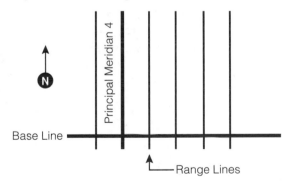

Townships

The directions of township and range lines, and tiers and ranges, may be easily remembered by thinking of the words this way:

T̲ownship lines
R̲ange lines

When the horizontal township lines and the vertical range lines intersect, they form squares, or **townships**, that are the basic units of the rectangular survey system. (See Figure 5.5.) A township is 6 miles square and contains 36 square miles (23,040 *acres*).

Each township is given a legal description. A township's description includes the

- designation of the tier in which the township is located,

- designation of the range, and

- name or number of the principal meridian for that area.

Figure 5.5:   Townships in the Rectangular Survey System

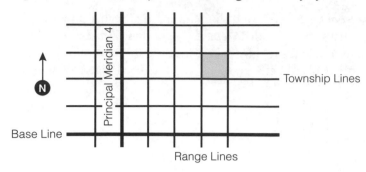

IN PRACTICE

In Figure 5.5, the shaded township is described as Township 3 North, Range 4 East of the Fourth Principal Meridian. This township is in the third tier north of the base line, and in the fourth range east of the principal meridian. Finally, reference is made to the principal meridian because the land being described is within the boundary of land surveyed from that meridian. This description is abbreviated as *T3N, R4E 4th Principal Meridian.*

Sections

> Townships are numbered the same way a field is plowed. Remember: *right to left, left to right, right to left,* and so on.

Townships are subdivided into sections and subsections called halves and quarters, which can be further divided. Each township contains 36 **sections**. Each section is one square mile or 640 acres, with 43,560 square feet in each acre. Sections are numbered 1 through 36, as shown in Figure 5.6. Section 1 is always in the northeast, or upper right-hand, corner. The numbering proceeds right to left to the upper left-hand corner. From there, the numbers drop down to the next tier and continue from left to right, then back from right to left. By law, each Section 16 was set aside for school purposes, and the sale or rental proceeds from this land were originally available for township school use. The schoolhouse was usually located in this section so it would be centrally located for all the students in the township. As a result, Section 16 is commonly called a *school section.*

Figure 5.6:   Sections in a Township

		N			
6	5	4	3	2	1
7	8	9	10	11	12
18	17	16	15	14	13
19	20	21	22	23	24
30	29	28	27	26	25
31	32	33	34	35	36

W (left side)   E (right side)   S (bottom)

Sections are divided into halves (320 acres) and quarters (160 acres). In turn, each of those parts is further divided into halves and quarters. The southeast quarter of a section, which is a 160-acre tract, is abbreviated SE¼. The SE¼ of SE¼ of SE¼ of Section 1 would be a 10-acre square in the lower right-hand corner of Section 1. (See Figure 5.7; the old measurements in chains and rods are defined in Figure 5.9.)

Figure 5.7:   A Section

The rectangular survey system sometimes uses a shorthand method in its descriptions. For instance, a comma may be used in place of the word of: SE¼, SE¼, SE¼, Section 1. It is possible to combine portions of a section, such as NE¼ of SW¼ and N½ of NW¼ of SE¼ of Section 1, which could also be written NE¼, SW¼; N½, NW¼, SE¼ of Section 1. A semicolon means and. Because of the semicolon in this description, the area is 60 acres.

Reading a rectangular survey description

To determine the location and size of a property described in the rectangular or government survey style, *start at the end* and work backward to the beginning, *reading from right to left*. For example, consider the following description (see Figure 5.7):

> The S½ of the NW¼ of the SE¼ of Section 11, Township 8 North, Range 6 West of the Fourth Principal Meridian.

To locate this tract of land from the citation alone, first search for the fourth principal meridian on a map of the United States and note its base line. Then, on a regional map, find the township in which the property is located by counting six range strips west of the fourth principal meridian and eight townships north of its corresponding base line. After locating Section 11, divide the section into quarters. Then divide the SE¼ into quarters, and then the NW¼ of that into halves. The S½ of that NW¼ contains the property in question.

Legal descriptions should always include the name of the county and the state in which the land is located because meridians often relate to more than one state and occasionally relate to two base lines. For example, the description "the southwest quarter of Section 10, Township 4 North, Range 1 West of the Fourth Principal Meridian" could refer to land in either Illinois or Wisconsin.

Math shortcut

To calculate acres in a rectangular survey system description, multiply all the denominators and divide that number into 640 acres. For instance, the SE¼ of SE¼ of SE¼ of Section 1 = 4 × 4 × 4 = 64; 640 ÷ 64 = 10 acres.

Metes-and-bounds descriptions within the rectangular survey system

Land in states that use the rectangular survey system may also require a metes-and-bounds description. This usually occurs in one of three situations: (1) when describing an irregular tract; (2) when a tract is too small to be described by quarter-sections; or (3) when a tract does not follow the lot or block lines of a recorded subdivision or section, quarter-section lines, or other fractional section lines.

Lot-and-block method

The third type of legal description is the **lot-and-block (recorded plat) method**. This system uses lot and block numbers referred to in a **plat map** filed in the public records of the county where the land is located. The plat map is a map of a town, a section, or a subdivision, indicating the location and boundaries of individual properties. The lot-and-block method is used mostly in subdivisions and urban areas.

A lot-and-block survey is performed in two steps. First, a large parcel of land is described either by the metes-and-bounds method or by a rectangular survey. Once this large parcel is surveyed, it is broken into smaller parcels. As a result, a lot-and-block description always refers to a prior metes-and-bounds or rectangular survey description. For each parcel described under the lot-and-block system, the *lot* refers to the numerical designation of any particular parcel. The *block* refers to the name of the subdivision under which the map is recorded. The block reference is drawn from the early 1900s, when a city block was the most common type of subdivided property.

The lot-and-block system starts with the preparation of a *subdivision plat* by a licensed surveyor or engineer. (See Figure 5.8.) On this plat, the land is divided into numbered or lettered lots and blocks, and streets or access roads for public use are indicated. Lot sizes and street details must be described completely and must comply with all local ordinances and requirements. When properly signed and approved, the subdivision plat is recorded in the county in which the land is located. The plat becomes part of the legal description. In describing a lot from a recorded subdivision plat, three identifiers are used:

1. Lot and block number

2. Name or number of the subdivision plat

3. Name of the county and state

The following is an example of a lot-and-block description:

> Lot 71, Happy Valley Estates 2, located in a portion of the southeast quarter of Section 23, Township 7 North, Range 4 East of the Seward Principal Meridian in _____ County, _____ [state].

To locate this parcel, one would start with the map of the Seward principal meridian to identify the township and range reference, then consult the township map of Township 7 North, Range 4 East, and the section map of Section 23. From there, one would look at the quarter-section map of the southeast quarter. The quarter-section map would refer to the plat map for the subdivision known as the second unit (second parcel subdivided) under the name of Happy Valley Estates.

Some lot-and-block descriptions are not dependent on the government survey system and may refer simply to the plat recorded in the land records of the county.

Figure 5.8:   Subdivision Plat Map of Block A

THE SURVEY: MEASURING PROPERTY RIGHTS

Legal descriptions should not be altered or combined without adequate information from a surveyor or title attorney. A licensed surveyor is trained and authorized to locate and determine the legal description of any parcel of land. The surveyor does this by preparing two documents: a survey and a survey sketch. The *survey* states the property's legal description. The *survey sketch* shows the location and dimensions of the parcel. When a survey also shows the location, size, and shape of buildings on the lot, it is referred to as a *spot survey*.

Legal descriptions should be copied with extreme care. An incorrectly worded legal description in a sales contract may result in a conveyance of more or less land than the parties intended. For example, damages suffered from an incorrect description could be extensive if buildings and improvements need to be moved because the land upon which the improvements were made is not owned. Often, even punctuation is extremely critical. Title problems can arise for the buyer who seeks to convey the property at a future date. Even if the contract can be corrected before the sale is closed, the real estate professional risks losing a commission and may be held liable for damages suffered by an injured party because of an improperly worded legal description.

Real estate professionals should be aware of the types of surveys and their uses recognized by state law or local custom. Not all surveys include surveyor liability and warranties of accuracy. An improvement location certificate (ILC), for instance, may be sufficient for some purposes but is not a full survey. It is prepared in a shorter time frame and at less cost, and provides the location of structures and improvements, easements, and any encroachments in relation to property boundaries.

www.nsps.us.com

The National Society of Professional Surveyors provides useful information for real estate professionals and consumers at www.nsps.us.com, including links to state associations and other affiliated organizations.

IN PRACTICE

Because legal descriptions, once recorded, affect ownership of real estate, they should be prepared only by a professional surveyor. Real estate professionals who copy legal descriptions create potential risks for themselves and their clients and customers. The better practice is to refer to a reliable document, such as the deed that transferred the property to the current owner, for a full and accurate legal description.

Measuring elevations

Just as surface rights must be identified, surveyed, and described, so must rights to the property above the earth's surface. Recall that *land* includes the space above the ground. In the same way that land may be measured and divided into parcels, the air may be divided. The owner may subdivide the air space above the land into **air lots**. Air lots are composed of the airspace within specific boundaries located over a parcel of land.

The *condominium laws* passed in all states require that a registered land surveyor prepare a plat map that shows the elevations of floor and ceiling surfaces and the vertical boundaries of each unit with reference to an official *datum* (discussed in the next section). A unit's floor, for instance, might be 60 feet above the datum and its ceiling, 69 feet. Typically, a separate plat is prepared for each floor in the condominium building.

The following is an example of the legal description of a condominium apartment unit that includes a fractional share of the common elements of the building and land:

> UNIT _____, Level ___, as delineated on survey of the following described parcel of real estate (hereinafter referred to as Development Parcel): The north 99 feet of the west ½ of Block 4 (except that part, if any, taken and used for street), in Sutton's Division Number 5 in the east ½ of the southeast ¼ of Section 24, Township 3 South, Range 68 West of the Sixth Principal Meridian, in Denver County, Colorado, which survey is attached as Exhibit A to Declaration made by Colorado National Bank as Trustee under Trust No. 1250, recorded in the Recorder's Office of Denver County, Colorado, as Document No. 475637; together with an undivided _____% interest in said Development Parcel (excepting from said Development Parcel all the property and space comprising all the units thereof as defined and set forth in said Declaration and Survey).

Subsurface rights can be legally described in the same manner as air rights, but they are measured *below* the datum rather than above it. Subsurface rights are used not only for coal mining, petroleum drilling, and utility line location but also for multistory condominiums—both residential and commercial—that have several floors below ground level.

Datum

A **datum** is a point, line, or surface from which elevations are measured or indicated. For the purpose of the United States Geological Survey (USGS), **datum** is defined as the mean sea level at New York Harbor. But virtually all large cities have local official datum that is used instead of the USGS datum. A surveyor would use a datum in determining the height of a

www.usgs.gov

structure or establishing the grade of a street. USGS has information on a variety of climate, land use, and environmental issues, as well as a state site locator, www.usgs.gov.

Monuments

Monuments are traditionally used to mark surface measurements between points. A monument could be a marker set in concrete, a piece of steel-reinforcing bar (rebar), a metal pipe driven into the soil, or simply a wooden stake stuck in the dirt. Because such items are subject to the whims of nature and vandals, their accuracy is sometimes suspect. As a result, surveyors rely most heavily on benchmarks to mark their work accurately and permanently.

Benchmarks are monuments that have been established as permanent reference points throughout the United States. They are usually embossed brass markers set into solid concrete or asphalt bases. While used to some degree for surface measurements, their principal reference use is for marking datums.

IN PRACTICE

All large cities have established a local official datum used in place of the USGS datum. For instance, the official datum for Chicago is known as the *Chicago City Datum*. It is a horizontal plane that corresponds to the low-water level of Lake Michigan in 1847 (the year in which the datum was established) and is considered to be at zero elevation. Although a surveyor's measurement of elevation based on the USGS datum will differ from one computed according to a local datum, it can be translated to an elevation based on the USGS.

Land units and measurements

It is important to understand land units and measurements because they are integral parts of legal descriptions. Some historical measurements are listed in Figure 5.9. Today, the terms *rods* and *chains* are not often used.

Figure 5.9:   Units of Land Measurement

Unit	Measurement
Mile	5,280 feet; 1,760 yards; 320 rods
Furlong	220 yards; 660 feet; 40 rods; 10 chains
Chain	66 feet; 4 rods; 100 links
Rod	16.5 feet; 5.50 yards
Square mile	640 acres (5,280 × 5,280 = 27,878,400 ÷ 43,560)
Acre	43,560 square feet
Cubic yard	27 cubic feet
Square yard	9 square feet
Square foot	144 square inches

MATH CONCEPTS

Land Acquisition Costs

To calculate the cost of purchasing land, use the same unit in which the cost is given. Costs quoted per square foot must be multiplied by the proper number of square feet; costs quoted per acre must be multiplied by the proper number of acres; and so on.

To calculate the cost of a parcel of land of three acres at $1.10 per square foot, convert the acreage to square feet before multiplying:

> 43,560 square feet per acre × 3 acres = 130,680 square feet
>
> 130,680 square feet × $1.10 per square foot = $143,748

To calculate the cost of a parcel of land of 17,500 square feet at $60,000 per acre, convert the cost per acre into the cost per square foot before multiplying by the number of square feet in the parcel:

> $60,000 per acre ÷ 43,560 square feet per acre = $1.38 (rounded) per square foot
>
> 17,500 square feet × $1.38 per square foot = $24,150

KEY POINT REVIEW

Three methods of legal description of land are the metes-and-bounds method, rectangular survey system, and lot-and-block system. The National Integrated Land System is being developed by the federal government to coordinate the land descriptions found in public records, making use of the accuracy in determining and recording property boundaries that is possible with current technology.

The **metes-and-bounds method** measures distances (**metes**), starting from a **point of beginning (POB)**, and following compass directions or angles (**bounds**) to arrive back at the point of beginning. **Monuments** (fixed objects or markers) identify the POB and corners or places where the boundary line changes direction.

The **rectangular survey system (government survey system)** divides land into rectangles called **townships**, measured from the intersection of a **principal meridian** and **base line**, and referenced by degrees of longitude and latitude. **Township lines** within a section run east to west parallel to the base line, six miles apart; **range lines** run north to south parallel to and counted from the principal meridian, six miles apart. Rows of townships are called **tiers** and columns of townships are called **ranges**. A township is divided into 36 **sections** of one square mile (640 acres) each and run from right to left, then left to right, starting at section 1 at the northeast corner of the township and ending at section 36 at the southeast corner of the township.

The **lot-and-block (recorded plat) method** divides a **subdivision** into **block** and **lot** (individual parcel) **numbers** and references all data in a subdivision **plat map**, noting lot sizes, street names, and other required information that is **approved** by the governing body, and filed **in public records** of the county where the land is located.

Survey preparation includes both a **legal description** and a **survey sketch**. A less precise analysis, found in the improvement location certificate (ILC), may be used. The legal description must be included by reference or transcribed **exactly** as written to avoid future problems over incorrect boundaries.

Elevations must be measured if **air lots** above the surface or **subsurface rights below the datum** are to be described and conveyed. Distances are noted as above or below datum, defined by U.S. Geological Survey (USGS) as **mean sea level at New York Harbor**, making use of permanent **benchmarks** that are established throughout the United States and are often based on a **local official datum,** and noting **monuments** marking surface measurements between points.

The most common units of **land measurement** include the

- **mile** of 5,280 feet,
- **acre** of 43,560 square feet (approximately 209 × 209 feet), and
- **square mile** of 640 acres (a section).

UNIT 5 QUIZ

1. What is the proper description of this shaded area of a section using the rectangular survey system?

    A. SW¼ of the NE¼ and the N½ of the SE¼ of the SW¼

    B. N½ of the NE¼ of the SW¼ and the SE¼ of the NW¼

    C. SW¼ of the SE¼ of the NW¼ and the N½ of the NE¼ of the SW¼

    D. S½ of the SW¼ of the NE¼ and the NE¼ of the NW¼ of the SE¼

2. When surveying land, a surveyor refers to the principal meridian that is
    A. furthest from the land being surveyed.
    B. in the same state as the land being surveyed.
    C. not more than 40 townships or 15 ranges distant from the land being surveyed.
    D. within the rectangular survey system area in which the land being surveyed is located.

3. The N½ of the SW¼ of a section contains how many acres?
    A. 20
    B. 40
    C. 60
    D. 80

4. In describing real estate, the method that may use a property's physical features to determine boundaries and measurements is
    A. rectangular survey.
    B. metes and bounds.
    C. government survey.
    D. lot and block.

Questions 5 through 8 refer to the following illustration of one complete township and parts of the adjacent townships.

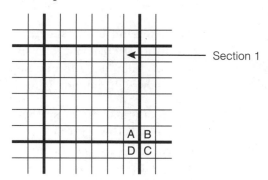

5. The section marked A is which of the following?
    A. School section
    B. Section 31
    C. Section 36
    D. Government lot

6. Which of the following is Section 6?
    A. A
    B. B
    C. C
    D. D

7. The section directly below C is
    A. Section 7.
    B. Section 12.
    C. Section 25.
    D. Section 30.

8. Which of the following is Section D?
    A. Section 1
    B. Section 6
    C. Section 31
    D. Section 36

9. Which of these shaded areas of a section depicts the NE¼ of the SE¼ of the SW¼?

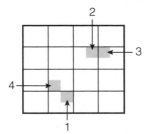

   A. Area 1
   B. Area 2
   C. Area 3
   D. Area 4

10. A buyer purchased a half-acre parcel for $2.15 per square foot. What was the selling price of the parcel?
   A. $774
   B. $1,376
   C. $46,827
   D. $93,654

11. How many acres are contained in the tract described as "beginning at the NW corner of the SW¼, then south along the west line to the SW corner of the section, then east along the south line of the section 2,640 feet, more or less, to the SE corner of the said SW¼, then in a straight line to the POB"?
   A. 80 acres
   B. 90 acres
   C. 100 acres
   D. 160 acres

12. If a farm described as "the NW¼ of the SE¼ of Section 10, Township 2 North, Range 3 West of the 6th. P.M." sold for $4,500 an acre, what was the total sales price?
   A. $45,000
   B. $90,000
   C. $135,000
   D. $180,000

13. As a legal description, "the northwest ¼ of the southwest ¼ of Section 6, Township 4 North, Range 7 West" is defective because it contains no reference to
   A. lot numbers.
   B. boundary lines.
   C. a principal meridian.
   D. a record of survey.

14. A buyer purchases 4.5 acres of land for $78,400. An adjoining owner wants to purchase a strip of this land measuring 150 feet by 100 feet. What should this strip cost the adjoining owner if it is sold for the same price per square foot originally paid?
   A. $3,000
   B. $6,000
   C. $7,800
   D. $9,400

15. Which of the following are *NOT* basic components of a metes-and-bounds description?
   A. Tangible and intangible monuments
   B. Base lines, principal meridians, and townships
   C. Degrees, minutes, and seconds
   D. Points of beginning

16. A property contains 10 acres. How many lots of not less than 50 feet by 100 feet can be subdivided from the property if 26,000 square feet were dedicated for roads?
   A. 80
   B. 81
   C. 82
   D. 83

17. A parcel of land is 400 feet by 640 feet. The parcel is cut in half diagonally by a stream. How many acres are in each half of the parcel?
   A. 2.75
   B. 2.94
   C. 5.51
   D. 5.88

18. What is the shortest distance between Section 1 and Section 36 in the same township?
   A. Three miles
   B. Four miles
   C. Five miles
   D. Six miles

19. In any township, what is the number of the section designated as the school section?
   A. 1
   B. 16
   C. 25
   D. 36

20. The *LEAST* specific method for identifying real property is
   A. rectangular survey.
   B. metes and bounds.
   C. street address.
   D. lot and block.

UNIT 6

Transfer of Title

LEARNING OBJECTIVES

When you have completed this unit, you will be able to

> **describe** the fundamental concepts of title as it relates to the ownership of land, and the processes and instruments used to apply these concepts;
> **describe** the circumstances and conditions which may provide for the involuntary transfer of title; and
> **explain** testate, intestate, wills, and the probate process.

KEY TERMS

acknowledgment	granting clause	special warranty deed
adverse possession	grantor	testate
bargain and sale deed	habendum clause	testator
deed	intestate	title
deed of trust	involuntary alienation	transfer tax
devise	probate	trustee's deed
general warranty deed	quitclaim deed	voluntary alienation
grantee	reconveyance deed	will

OVERVIEW

Transfer of title is an aspect of a real estate sales transaction generally handled by lawyers and title companies. Nonetheless, as with other legal aspects of the transaction, a real estate professional who is aware of the fundamentals of deeds and title issues will better understand the transaction and will know what kind of questions to ask. An informed real estate professional will be able to alert consumers to the need for legal advice to avoid potential title problems.

83

TITLE CONCEPTS

The term *title* has two functions. **Title** to real estate means the *right to or ownership of the land*; it represents the owner's bundle of legal rights. Title also serves as *evidence* of that ownership. A person who holds the title, if challenged in court, would be able to recover or retain ownership or possession of a parcel of real estate. Unlike the title to a motor vehicle, which is a document that transfers ownership, title to real estate is a way of referring to ownership but is not an actual printed document. (There is one exception to that general rule, however. In states that recognize a Torrens certificate, it is the certificate itself that provides evidence of ownership.)

Title to real estate may be transferred voluntarily by sale or gift. Alternatively, title may be transferred involuntarily by operation of law. The property may be transferred while the owner lives or, after the owner dies, either by will or as provided by state law if the owner died without leaving a will.

Voluntary alienation

Voluntary alienation is the legal term for the transfer of title during the property owner's lifetime. An owner may transfer title by making a gift or by selling the property. (As will be discussed later, the actions of a property owner can also determine the disposition of the property on the owner's death.)

A **grantor** conveys property to a grantee.

A **grantee** receives property from a grantor.

A **deed** is the instrument that conveys property from grantor to grantee.

A **deed** is a document by which an owner of real estate conveys the right, title, or interest owned in the parcel of real estate to someone else. The statute of frauds, found in all states, requires that all deeds be in writing. The owner who transfers the property is referred to as the **grantor**, and the person who receives the property is called the **grantee**. A deed is executed (signed) by the grantor. The terms are easier to remember if you keep in mind that the grant<u>or</u> is the property <u>owner</u>. Figure 6.1 lists a number of terms that appear throughout the text that can be remembered in the same way.

FIGURE 6.1:   Remembering Legal Terminology: "OR" vs. "EE"

Product	Property Owner or Person Giving the Right	Recipient
Devise	Devisor	Devisee
Deed	Grantor	Grantee
Legacy	Legator	Legatee
Lease	Lessor	Lessee
Mortgage	Mortgagor	Mortgagee
Offer	Offeror makes the offer	Offeree
Option	Optionor	Optionee
Sublease	Sublessor, who is the original lessee	Sublessee
Trust	Trustor	Trustee

Requirements for a valid deed

Although formal requirements vary, a valid deed generally must contain the following elements:

■   Grantor who has the legal competency to execute the deed

- Grantee named with reasonable certainty to be identified
- Statement of consideration (usually required for recording of the deed)
- Granting clause (words of conveyance)
- *Habendum* clause, which defines the ownership right received by the grantee
- Accurate legal description of the property conveyed
- Any relevant exceptions or reservations to conveyance of full title
- Acknowledgment (notarization) of the signature of the grantor
- Delivery of the deed and acceptance by the grantee to pass title

A deed may include a description of any *limitations* on the conveyance of a full fee simple estate and a statement of any *exceptions and reservations* (also known as *"subject to" clauses*) that affect title to the property.

IN PRACTICE

The deed to each property in a subdivision that is subject to covenants, conditions, and restrictions (CC&Rs) will include a reference to the recorded document that sets out all of the limitations on the property's use.

Grantor

A grantor must be of lawful age, usually at least 18 years old. A deed executed by a minor is generally *voidable*. After reaching legal adult age, the minor can choose to treat the deed as a valid conveyance or can have the conveyance recognized as of no legal effect by a court.

A grantor also must be *legally competent* (of *sound mind*). Generally, any grantor who can understand the action being undertaken is viewed as mentally capable of executing a valid deed. A deed executed by someone who was mentally impaired at the time is voidable, but it is not automatically *void* (of no legal effect). If, however, the grantor has been judged legally incompetent, the deed will be void. Real estate owned by someone who is legally incompetent can be conveyed only with a court's approval.

The grantor's name must be spelled correctly and consistently throughout the deed. If the grantor's name has changed since the title was acquired, as when a person's name is changed following marriage, both names should be shown—for example, "Mary Smith, formerly Mary Jones."

Grantee

To be valid, a deed must name a grantee. The grantee must be specifically named so that the person to whom the property is being conveyed can be readily identified from the deed itself.

IN PRACTICE

Olive Burbank wanted to convey Greenacre to her nephew, Joseph Mara. In the deed, Olive wrote the following words of conveyance: "I, Olive Burbank, hereby convey to Joseph all my interest in Greenacre." The only problem was that Olive also had a son named Joseph, a cousin Joseph, and a neighbor Joseph. The grantee's identity could not be discerned from the deed itself. Olive should have conveyed Greenacre "to my nephew, Joseph Mara."

If more than one grantee is involved, the granting clause should specify their individual rights in the property. For instance, the clause might state that the grantees will take title as joint tenants or tenants in common. This is especially important when specific wording is necessary to create a joint tenancy.

Consideration

A valid deed must contain a clause acknowledging that the grantor has received some form of consideration; that is, something in return for deeding the described property to the grantee. Generally, the amount of consideration is stated in dollars. When a deed conveys real estate as a gift to a relative, love and affection may be sufficient consideration. In most states, it is customary to recite a nominal consideration, such as "$10 and other good and valuable consideration."

Granting clause

A deed must contain a **granting clause**, or words of conveyance, that states the grantor's intention to convey the property. Depending on the type of deed and the obligations agreed to by the grantor, the wording would be similar to one of the following:

- "I, *JKL*, convey and warrant . . ."
- "I, *JKL*, remise, release, alienate, and convey . . ."
- "I, *JKL*, grant, bargain, and sell . . ."
- "I, *JKL*, remise, release, and quitclaim . . ."

A deed that conveys the grantor's entire fee simple interest usually contains wording such as "to *ABC* and to her heirs and assigns forever." If less than the grantor's complete fee simple interest is conveyed, such as a life estate, the wording must indicate that less than a full interest is being conveyed—for example, "to *ABC* for the duration of her natural life."

Habendum clause

When it is necessary to define or explain the ownership to be enjoyed by the grantee, a **habendum clause** may follow the granting clause. The habendum clause begins with the words *to have and to hold*. Its provisions must agree with those stated in the granting clause. For example, if a grantor conveys a time-share interest or an interest less than fee simple absolute, the habendum clause would specify the owner's rights as well as how those rights are limited (a specific time frame or certain prohibited activities, for instance).

Legal description of real estate

To conform to the intent of the grantor, a deed must contain an accurate legal description of the real estate conveyed. Land is considered adequately described if a professional surveyor can locate the property and accurately mark its boundaries using the description.

Exceptions and reservations

A deed may specifically note any encumbrances, reservations, or limitations that affect the title being conveyed. This might include such things as restrictions and easements that run with the land. In addition to citing existing encumbrances, a grantor may reserve some right in the land, such as an easement, for the grantor's use. A grantor may also place certain restrictions on a grantee's use of the property. Developers often restrict the number of houses that may be built on each lot in a subdivision. Such private restrictions must be stated in the deed or contained in a previously recorded document, such as the subdivider's master deed, that is expressly referred to in the deed. Many of these deed restrictions have time limits and often include renewal clauses.

Signature of grantor

To be valid, a deed must be signed by all grantors named in the deed. Some states also require witnesses to or notarization of the grantor's signature, as described below.

Most states permit someone with a *power of attorney* (written specific authority) to sign legal documents for a grantor. The person having power of attorney has written authority to execute and sign one or more legal instruments for another person. The power of attorney will be a special power of attorney if it is created only for a specific act or acts. A general power of attorney provides authority to carry out all of the business dealings of the person giving it. The person with power of attorney does not have to be an attorney-at-law, but could be. Usually, the power of attorney must be recorded in the county where the property is located.

IN PRACTICE

A power of attorney can be a great convenience when all of the co-owners of a property are not available to convey title at the required time. A spouse who is out of the country, for instance, can give a special power of attorney to the other spouse so that property can be conveyed when required.

In some states, a grantor's spouse is required to sign any deed of conveyance to waive any marital or homestead rights. This requirement varies according to state law and depends on the manner in which title to real estate is held.

Many states still require a seal (or simply the word *seal*) to be written or printed after an individual grantor's signature. The corporate seal may be required of a corporate grantor.

Acknowledgment

An **acknowledgment** is a formal declaration under oath that the person who signs a written document does so *voluntarily* and that the signature is genuine. The declaration is made before a registered notary public or an authorized public officer, such as a judge, justice of the peace, or some other person as prescribed by state law. An acknowledgment usually states that the person signing the deed or other document is known to the officer or has produced sufficient identification to prevent a forgery. After verifying the individual's identity, the notary public will also sign and stamp the document, which allows it to be recorded.

An acknowledgment (that is, a formal declaration before a notary public) is not essential to the validity of a deed unless it is required by state statute; however, a deed that is not acknowledged may not be legally sufficient for certain purposes. In most states, for instance, an unacknowledged deed is not eligible for recording—an important act that puts the world on notice as to who owns the property.

Delivery and acceptance

Transfer of title requires both delivery and acceptance of the deed.

A title is not considered transferred until the deed to the property is actually delivered to and accepted by the grantee. The grantor may deliver the deed to the grantee personally or through a third party.

Title is said to *pass* only when a deed is delivered and accepted. The effective date of the transfer of title from the grantor to the grantee is the date of delivery of the deed itself. Delivery and acceptance are usually presumed if the deed has been examined and registered by the county clerk.

Execution of corporate deeds

Although state laws governing a corporation's right to convey real estate vary, two basic rules must be followed:

■ A corporation can convey real estate only by the authority defined in its bylaws or on the basis of a resolution passed by its board of directors. If all or a substantial portion of a corporation's real estate is being conveyed, usually a resolution authorizing the sale must be secured from the shareholders.

■ A deed conveying corporation-owned real estate can be signed only by an authorized officer.

Rules pertaining to not-for-profit corporations vary even more widely. Because the legal requirements must be followed exactly, an attorney should be consulted for all corporate conveyances.

Types of deeds

A deed can take several forms, depending on the extent of the grantor's promises to the grantee. Regardless of any guarantees the deed offers, the grantee will want assurance that the grantor has the right to offer what the deed purports to convey. To obtain this protection, grantees commonly seek evidence of title.

The most common deeds are the following:

■ General warranty deed

■ Special warranty deed

■ Bargain and sale deed

■ Quitclaim deed

■ Deed of trust

■ Reconveyance deed

■ Trustee's deed

■ Deed executed pursuant to a court order

General warranty deed

A **general warranty deed** provides the greatest protection to the buyer because the grantor is legally bound by certain covenants (promises) or warranties. In most states, the warranties are implied by the use of certain words specified by statute. In some states, the grantor's warranties are expressly written into the deed itself. Each state law should be examined, but some of the specific phrases include *convey and warrant* or *warrant generally*. The basic warranties are as follows:

General warranty deed

■ Covenant of seisin
■ Covenant against encumbrances
■ Covenant of further assurance
■ Covenant of quiet enjoyment
■ Covenant of warranty forever

■ *Covenant of seisin*: The grantor warrants that he or she owns the property and has the right to convey title to it. The grantee may recover damages up to the full purchase price if this covenant is broken.

■ *Covenant against encumbrances*: The grantor warrants that the property is free from liens or encumbrances, except for any specifically stated in the deed. Encumbrances generally include mortgages, mechanics' liens, and easements. If this covenant is breached, the grantee may sue for the cost of removing the encumbrances.

■ *Covenant of further assurances*: The grantor promises to obtain and deliver any instrument needed to make the title good. For example, if the grantor's spouse has failed to sign away dower rights, the grantor must deliver a quitclaim deed (discussed below) to clear the title.

■ *Covenant of quiet enjoyment*: The grantor guarantees that the grantee's title will be good against any third party who might bring a court action to establish superior title to the property. If the grantee's title is found to be inferior, the grantor is liable for damages; that is, the grantor will pay the grantee if the title is not good.

■ *Covenant of warranty forever*: The grantor promises to compensate the grantee for the loss sustained if the title fails at any time in the future.

These covenants in a general warranty deed are not limited to matters that occurred during the time the grantor owned the property; they extend back to its origins. The grantor defends the title against defects the grantor created as well as defects created by *all those who previously held title*.

Special warranty deed

Special warranty deed

■ Warranty that grantor received title
■ Warranty that property was unencumbered by grantor

A **special warranty deed** limits the grantor's defense of the title transferred by warranting

■ that the grantor received title; and

■ that the property was not encumbered during the time the grantor held title, except as otherwise noted in the deed.

The grantor promises to defend the title as provided in the covenants of a general warranty deed, but only against the grantor's actions, and not those of earlier owners of the property. The granting clause generally contains these words: "Grantor remises, releases, alienates, and conveys." The grantor may include additional warranties, but they must be specifically stated in the deed. In areas where a special warranty deed is in common use, the purchase of title insurance typically is viewed as providing adequate additional protection to the grantee.

A special warranty deed may be used by fiduciaries such as trustees, executors, and corporations. A special warranty deed is appropriate for fiduciaries because they lack the authority to warrant against acts of predecessors in title (the former owners). A fiduciary may hold title for a limited time without having a personal interest in the proceeds. Sometimes a special warranty deed is used by a grantor who has acquired title at a tax sale.

Bargain and sale deed

Bargain and sale deed

■ Implication that grantor holds title and possession

A **bargain and sale deed** contains no express warranties against encumbrances, but it does *imply* that the grantor holds title and possession of the property. The granting clause usually states a person's or entity's name and the phrase *grants and releases* or *grants, bargains, and sells*. Because the warranty is not specifically stated, the grantee has little legal recourse if title defects appear later. In some areas, this deed is used in foreclosures and tax sales. The buyer should purchase title insurance, if it is not provided by the seller.

A covenant against encumbrances initiated by the grantor may be added to a standard bargain and sale deed to create a *bargain and sale deed with covenant against the grantor's acts*. This deed is equivalent to a special warranty deed. Warranties used in general warranty deeds may be inserted in a bargain and sale deed to give the grantee similar protection.

Quitclaim deed

> **Quitclaim deed**
>
> ■ Used primarily to convey less than fee simple or to cure a title defect

A **quitclaim deed** provides the grantee with the least protection of any deed. It carries *no covenants or warranties* and generally conveys only whatever interest the grantor may have when the deed is delivered. If the grantor has no interest, the grantee will acquire nothing and will have no right of warranty claim against the grantor. A quitclaim deed can convey title as effectively as a warranty deed if the grantor has good title when the deed is delivered, but it provides none of the guarantees of a warranty deed. Through a quitclaim deed, the grantor only *remises, releases, and quitclaims* the grantor's interest in the property, if any.

A quitclaim deed is usually the only type of deed used to convey less than a fee simple estate. This is because a quitclaim deed conveys only the grantor's right, title, or interest without any warranty that the grantor has any right, title, or interest.

A quitclaim deed is frequently used to cure a title defect, called a *cloud on the title*. For example, if the name of the grantee is misspelled on a warranty deed filed in the public record, a quitclaim deed with the correct spelling may be executed to the grantee to perfect the title.

A quitclaim deed is also used when a grantor has apparently *inherited* property but it is not certain that the decedent's title was valid. A warranty deed from the grantor in such an instance would oblige the grantor to warrant good title, while a quitclaim deed would convey only the grantor's interest, whatever it may be.

One of the most common uses of the quitclaim deed is for a simple transfer of property from one family member or co-owner to another.

> **Deed of trust**
>
> *Conveyance from trustor to trustee*

A **deed of trust** (or *deed in trust* in some states) is the means by which a *trustor* conveys real estate to a *trustee* for the benefit of a *beneficiary*. The real estate is held by the trustee to fulfill the purpose of the trust. (See Figure 6.2.)

FIGURE 6.2:   Trust Deeds

IN PRACTICE

A quitclaim deed is frequently used when real property is part of a divorce settlement. Because the parties are familiar with the property and its history, they will agree to a transfer of title without the usual protections afforded by a warranty deed, which would be demanded in a transaction between unrelated parties.

Reconveyance deed

Reconveyance deed

Conveyance from trustee back to trustor

A **reconveyance deed** is used by a trustee to return title to the trustor. For example, when a loan secured by a deed of trust has been fully paid, the beneficiary notifies the trustee. The trustee then conveys the property back to the trustor. As with any document of title, a reconveyance deed should be recorded to prevent title problems in the future. In a "lien theory" state in which a deed of trust is treated as creating a lien on property, rather than transferring title, a document called a *satisfaction of mortgage* fulfills this same purpose.

Trustee's deed

Trustee's deed

Conveyance from trustee to third party

A deed executed by a trustee is a **trustee's deed**. It is used when a trustee conveys real estate held in the trust to anyone other than the trustor. The trustee's deed must state that the trustee is executing the instrument in accordance with the powers and authority granted by the trust instrument.

Deed executed pursuant to a court order

Executors' and administrators' deeds, masters' deeds, sheriffs' deeds, and many others are all deeds executed pursuant to a court order. These deeds are established by state statute and are used to convey title to property that is transferred by will or by court order. The form of the deed must conform to the laws of the state in which the property is located.

One common characteristic of deeds executed pursuant to court order is that the *full consideration* is usually stated in the deed. Instead of "$10 and other valuable consideration," for example, the deed would list the actual sales price.

Transfer tax stamps

Many states have enacted laws providing for a state **transfer tax** (also referred to in some states as a *grantor's tax*) on conveyances of real estate. In these states, the tax is usually payable when the deed is recorded. In some states, the taxpayer purchases *stamps* from the recorder of the county in which the deed is recorded and the stamps must be affixed to the deed before it can be recorded. In other states, the clerk of the court or county recorder simply collects the appropriate transfer tax amount in accordance with state and local law.

The transfer tax may be paid by either the seller or the buyer, or split between them, depending on local custom or agreement in the sales contract. The actual *tax rate* varies and may be imposed at the state, county, and/or city level. For example, the rate might be calculated as $1.10 for every $1,000 of the sales price, as $0.55 for every $500 of the sales price, or as a simple percentage of the sales price.

MATH CONCEPTS

Calculating Transfer Taxes

A state has a transfer tax of $1.50 for each $500 (or fraction of $500) of the sales price of any parcel of real estate. The transfer tax is to be paid by the seller. To calculate the transfer tax due in the sale of a $300,000 house, use the following two steps:

Value ÷ dollar amount per taxable unit = taxable units

Taxable units × rate per unit = tax

In this example:

$300,000 ÷ $500 = 600 taxable units

600 × $1.50 = $900

The seller in this transaction must pay a transfer tax of $900 to the state.

In many states, a *transfer declaration form* (or *transfer statement* or *affidavit of real property value*) must be signed by both the buyer and the seller or their real estate professionals. The transfer declaration states

- the full sales price of the property;
- its legal description;
- the type of improvement;
- the address, date, and type of deed; and
- whether the transfer is between relatives or in accordance with a court order.

Certain deeds may be *exempted* from the tax, such as the following:

- Gifts of real estate
- Deeds not made in connection with a sale (such as a change in the form of co-ownership)
- Conveyances to, from, or between government bodies
- Deeds by charitable, religious, or educational institutions
- Deeds securing debts or releasing property as security for a debt
- Partitions
- Tax deeds
- Deeds pursuant to mergers of corporations
- Deeds from subsidiary to parent corporations for cancellations of stock

INVOLUNTARY ALIENATION

Land may be acquired through the process of accretion or actually lost through erosion. Other acts of nature, such as earthquakes, hurricanes, sinkholes, and mudslides, may also change or destroy a landowner's property. Title to property may be transferred without the owner's consent by **involuntary alienation**. (See Figure 6.3.)

FIGURE 6.3:   Involuntary Alienation

Involuntary transfer by operation of law

Involuntary transfers are usually carried out by operation of law—such as by condemnation, foreclosure of a mortgage loan, or a sale to satisfy delinquent tax or mortgage liens. When a person dies **intestate** (without a valid will), the title to the real estate passes to the heirs identified in the state's law of *intestate succession*. If no heirs can be identified or found, the state will acquire the property by the state's power of *escheat*.

Adverse possession

Adverse possession is another means of involuntary transfer. An individual who makes a claim to certain property, takes exclusive possession of it by excluding the true owner and any other title claimants, and (most important) uses it, may take title away from an owner who fails to use or inspect the property for a period of years. The law recognizes that the use of land is an important function of its ownership.

Usually the possession by the claimant must have the following characteristics, which can be remembered as ONCHA. The property use must be

---

Adverse possession must be ONCHA:
- Open
- Notorious
- Continuous
- Hostile
- Adverse

- *open*—obvious to anyone who looks,

- *notorious*—known by others,

- *continuous*—uninterrupted,

- *hostile*—without the true owner's consent, and

- *adverse*—against the true owner's right of possession.

The necessary period of uninterrupted possession is a matter of state law. The statutory periods range from as few as 5 years in some states to as many as 30 years in others. A shorter time period may be accompanied by the requirement for the adverse possessor to make all property tax payments. A state may allow subsequent adverse owners to *tack* their years of possession together to create the necessary period of adverse use. A subsequent adverse owner usually must take possession under a claim of right, or *color of title*, such as a deed from the prior adverse owner that purports to convey ownership of the property.

To claim legal title, the adverse possessor normally files an action in court to receive undisputed title.

IN PRACTICE

Acquiring title to property by a claim of adverse possession is not a common occurrence. Usually, a claim arises when the titleholder isn't paying attention to the property, which may happen when the owner does not live nearby or if the property is bequeathed to someone who doesn't visit the property. A homeowner who thoughtfully cares for a neighboring vacant property may be tempted to think of applying the concept of adverse possession. Keep in mind, however, that the right of adverse possession is a statutory right. State requirements must be followed carefully to ensure the successful transfer of title. Those who think they might make such a claim should not wait until the end of the statutory period to consult an attorney; doing so early in the process will ensure that all the statutory requirements are met.

CONVEYANCE OF A DECEDENT'S PROPERTY

A person who dies **testate** has prepared a will indicating how that person's real and personal property will be disposed of at the time of death. When a person dies **intestate** (without a valid will), real estate and personal property pass to the decedent's heirs according to the state's *statute of descent and distribution*. In effect, the state makes a will for an intestate decedent.

When a person dies, ownership of real estate passes to

- the co-owner by virtue of a joint tenancy with right of survivorship or a tenancy by the entirety;
- the party or parties named in a valid will; or
- the statutory heirs determined by the state's law of descent and distribution.

Title to property held in joint tenancy with right of survivorship or in tenancy by the entirety needs no court action for title to pass, but the death certificate should be filed so that it becomes part of the record of property ownership.

When title passes by will or descent, the estate must go through a judicial process called **probate** in which the successor to the property title will be recognized; usually, claims against the estate must be satisfied before the designated individual(s) can take possession of the property. The party named in a will could be the trustee of either an existing trust or a *testamentary trust* established by the will.

Transfer of title by will

A **will** is made by a property owner to convey title to real and personal property after the owner's death. This type of property transfer differs from a deed, which *must* be delivered during the lifetime of the grantor and that conveys a present interest in property. While the **testator**, the person who makes a will, is alive, any property included in the will can still be conveyed by the owner. The parties named in a will have no rights or interests as long as the party who made the will is alive; they acquire interest or title only after the owner's death.

Only property owned by the testator at the time of the testator's death may be transferred by will. The gift of real property by will is known as a **devise**, and a person who receives real property by will is known as a *devisee*. The will can also include a bequest of a legacy, which is a gift of personal property.

For title to pass to the devisees, state laws require that, on the death of a testator, the will be filed with the court and probated. *Probate* is the formal judicial process for verifying the validity of a will and accounting for the decedent's assets, and is discussed below. The process can take several months—or considerably longer—to complete before the estate is *settled*.

A will cannot supersede the state laws of dower, curtesy, and homestead, which were enacted to protect the inheritance rights of a surviving spouse in certain real property owned by the decedent. In most states, the surviving spouse is further protected by a statute that provides for certain personal property of the decedent to go to the surviving spouse if the will does not provide the minimum statutory inheritance. In either case, the surviving spouse must decide whether or not to contest the will.

Legal requirements for making a will

A will must be prepared and executed according to the laws of the state in which the testator resides. If the testator owns property in any other state, the will should also comply with the laws of the state in which the real estate is located.

A testator must have legal capacity to make a will. There are no rigid tests to determine legal capacity. Usually, a person must be of *legal age* and of *sound mind*. Legal age varies from state to state. To demonstrate sound mind, the testator must have sufficient mental capacity to understand the nature and extent of the property the testator owns. A testator must also understand that the described property will go to those persons named in the will, who may or may not be the testator's natural heirs—those persons identified by the state law of descent and distribution. The drawing of a will must be a voluntary act, free of any undue influence by other people.

In most states, a written will must be signed by its testator before two or more witnesses, who must also sign the document. The witnesses should not be individuals who are named in the will as recipients of any property. Some states still recognize oral (*nuncupative*) wills or entirely handwritten (*holographic*) wills. Other states do not permit real property to be conveyed by anything other than a formally witnessed, written will.

While living, a testator may alter a will at any time. Any modification or addition to a previously executed will is contained in a separate document called a *codicil*, which must comply with state law to be valid.

Transfer of title by descent

Under a state's statute of descent and distribution, the primary **heirs** of the deceased are the surviving spouse and children by birth or adoption, but the statute will also identify other close blood relatives in the event that the decedent has no surviving spouse or children, including parents, brothers, sisters, aunts, uncles, and, in some cases, first and second cousins.

The right to inherit under laws of descent varies from state to state, and the property of someone who dies intestate is distributed according to the laws of the state in which the property is located. Figure 6.4 illustrates how a state's statute of descent and distribution might provide for an intestate's estate. The specific persons entitled to property, and the various percentages involved, vary from state to state. A real estate professional should never try to determine descent or ownership without consulting legal counsel.

FIGURE 6.4:   Sample Statutory Distributions

Decedent Status	Family Status	How Property Passes
Married, surviving spouse[1]	No children No other relatives	100% to surviving spouse
Married, surviving spouse	Children	50% to surviving spouse 50% shared by children or descendants of deceased child
Married, no surviving spouse	Children	Children share equally, with descendants of a deceased child taking their parent's share
Unmarried, no children	Relatives	100% to father or mother, brothers or sisters, or other relatives (such as grandparents or great-grandparents; uncles or aunts; nieces or nephews; first or second cousins) in order of priority
	No relatives or heirs as defined by state law	100% to state by escheat

[1] Some states allow the decedent's spouse the right to elect a life estate of dower or curtesy in place of the share provided for in the law of descent.

Probate

Probate is a formal judicial process. Probate proceedings take place in the county *in which the decedent last resided*. If the decedent owned real estate in another county, probate would occur in that county as well.

The person who has possession of the will presents it for filing with the court. The court is responsible for determining that the will meets the statutory requirements for its form and execution. If the will was modified or if more than one will exists, the court will decide how these documents should be probated.

The probate court acts on its own volition as well as through the *executor* named in the will or an *administrator* or personal representative appointed by the court if there is no will, or the will fails to name an executor. The court

- publishes required notices of the pending probate;
- proves or confirms the validity of the will, including ruling on any challenges to the will;
- determines the precise assets in the estate of the deceased person; and
- identifies the people to whom the estate's assets are to pass.

The purpose of probate is to properly allocate and distribute the assets of the deceased. All assets must be accounted for, and the decedent's debts must be satisfied before any property is distributed to the heirs. In addition, applicable federal estate taxes and state inheritance taxes must be paid before any distribution. The laws of each state govern probate proceedings as well as the functions of the individuals appointed by will or the court to administer the decedent's affairs. The specific persons entitled to property, and the various percentages involved, vary from state to state.

IN PRACTICE

A real estate broker entering into a listing agreement with the executor or administrator of an estate in probate should be aware that the amount of commission is approved by the court and that the commission is payable only from the proceeds of the sale. The real estate broker will not be able to collect a commission unless the court approves the sale.

In some states, the probate process is not unduly cumbersome, but in other states, it can be lengthy and expensive. One way in which property owners can avoid the delay and expense of probate is by establishing a *living trust* while still living and transferring title to real and personal property to the trust. In a revocable living trust, the person establishing the trust is the trustor as well as the trustee and the terms of the trust can be changed at any time (or terminated) during the life of the trustor. On the trustor's death, the trust need not go through a probate proceeding as title automatically passes to the beneficiary named in the trust.

There are many more details to creation of a living trust, more than be covered adequately here. The advice of an attorney should be sought to create the trust, to successfully transfer property to it, and to file the necessary documentation on the death of the trustor. It is important that all of the trustor's property be transferred to the trust, or part of the estate will still have to go through probate. The living trust also has no effect on the value of the estate for estate tax purposes.

KEY POINT REVIEW

Title is the right to or ownership of land, and can also be evidence of that ownership.

Voluntary alienation is the transfer of title to real estate by **gift** or **sale during one's life**, using some form of **deed**. To create a valid deed, the **grantor** (person who transfers title) must be of legal age and legally competent to execute (sign) the deed. A deed executed by a **minor** is **voidable**. The **grantee** must be identifiable with sufficient certainty.

Consideration (payment) of some form must be stated to record a deed. **The granting clause** (words of conveyance) must be used. The **habendum clause** defines the ownership interest taken by the grantee. An accurate **legal description** of the property conveyed is essential. **Exceptions** or **reservations** to the full transfer of all of the rights of ownership must be noted.

The signature of the grantor(s) must be **acknowledged** by a notary public or other official authorized by the state in which the property is located. Finally, there must be a **delivery** of the deed **and its acceptance** by the grantee.

Types of deeds include the **general warranty deed**, which provides the greatest protection to the grantee and includes the **covenant of seisin**, **covenant against encumbrances**, **covenant of further assurances**, **covenant of quiet enjoyment**, and **covenant of warranty forever**.

The **special warranty deed** includes the warranties that the grantor received title and that the property was not encumbered during the time the grantor held title, except as otherwise noted.

The **bargain and sale deed** implies that the grantor holds title and possession of the property, but there are no express warranties against encumbrances.

The **quitclaim deed** provides the least protection of any deed as it carries no covenants or warranties, and conveys only whatever interest the grantor may have when the deed is delivered.

With a **deed of trust**, a **trustor** conveys real estate to a **trustee** for the benefit of a **beneficiary**. A **reconveyance deed** is used by the trustee to return title to the trustor, but a **trustee's deed** conveys the property to someone other than the trustor. There may also be a **deed executed pursuant to a court order**.

Transfer tax stamps may be required to record a deed.

Involuntary alienation (transfer) of title to property is usually by operation of law. **Using the government's power of eminent domain,** property can be taken for a public purpose, with just compensation paid to the owner. In a **foreclosure**, property is taken by a creditor for nonpayment of a debt secured by real property. **In the process called escheat,** property is taken by the state when no heirs of the deceased can be found.

Property can be acquired by adverse possession when someone who is not the lawful owner takes exclusive possession of the property for the length of time specified by state law in a way that is ONCHA: **<u>o</u>pen**, **<u>n</u>otorious**, **<u>c</u>ontinuous**, **<u>h</u>ostile**, and **<u>a</u>dverse to the interest of the true owner**.

Transfer of title by will occurs when someone dies **testate** (leaving a valid will, prepared as required by state law). A will takes effect only after death and can be changed by **codicil** or revoked while the **testator** is still alive.

A **devise** is a gift of real property by will to the **devisee**. A **bequest** or **legacy** is a gift of personal property.

To pass title to property on death, a will must be **filed with the court** and **probated**.

Wills cannot supersede state laws protecting inheritance rights of a surviving spouse (**dower** or **curtesy**, or benefits granted by homestead laws).

Transfer of title under a state's **statute of descent and distribution** occurs when a person dies **intestate** (without a valid will). The laws of the state where real property is **located** govern property distribution.

UNIT 6 QUIZ

1. The basic requirements for a valid conveyance are governed by
   A. state law.
   B. local custom.
   C. national law.
   D. the law of descent.

2. Every deed must be signed by
   A. the grantor.
   B. the grantee.
   C. the grantor and grantee.
   D. the devisee.

3. A 15-year-old recently inherited a parcel of real estate and has decided to sell it. If the 15-year-old executes a deed conveying the property to a purchaser, such a conveyance would be
   A. valid.
   B. void.
   C. invalid.
   D. voidable.

4. A form authorizing one person to execute documents for another is called
   A. a power of attorney.
   B. a release deed.
   C. a quitclaim deed.
   D. a power to represent.

5. The grantee receives greatest protection with what type of deed?
   A. Quitclaim
   B. General warranty
   C. Bargain and sale with covenant
   D. Executor's

6. Party Y receives a deed from party X. The granting clause of the deed states, "I hereby remise, release, alienate, and convey to Y the following real property." What type of deed has Y received?
   A. Special warranty
   B. Quitclaim
   C. General warranty
   D. Bargain and sale

7. Under the covenant of quiet enjoyment, a grantor
   A. promises to obtain and deliver any instrument needed to make the title good.
   B. warrants that the property is free from liens and encumbrances.
   C. warrants that he or she is the owner and has the right to convey title to the property.
   D. ensures that the title will be good against the title claims of third parties.

8. Which type of deed merely implies but does *NOT* specifically warrant that the grantor holds good title to the property?
   A. Special warranty
   B. Bargain and sale
   C. Quitclaim
   D. Trust deed

9. At which of the following steps did title to the house actually transfer or pass to B?

   Step 1: A decided to convey a house to B.
   Step 2: A signed a deed transferring title to B.
   Step 3: A gave the signed deed to B, who accepted it.
   Step 4: B took the deed to the county recorder's office and had it recorded.

   A. Step 1
   B. Step 2
   C. Step 3
   D. Step 4

10. P signed a deed transferring ownership of P's house to Q. To provide evidence that P's signature was genuine, P executed a declaration before a notary. This declaration is known as
    A. an affidavit.
    B. an acknowledgment.
    C. an affirmation.
    D. an estoppel.

11. Title to real estate may be transferred during a person's lifetime by
    A. devise.
    B. descent.
    C. involuntary alienation.
    D. escheat.

12. A resident of Denver bought acreage in a distant county, never went to see the acreage, and did not use the ground. An artist moved a mobile home onto the land, had a water well drilled, and lived there for 22 years. The artist may become the owner of the land if the artist is in compliance with the state law regarding
    A. requirements for a valid conveyance.
    B. adverse possession.
    C. avulsion.
    D. voluntary alienation.

13. Eminent domain and escheat are two examples of
    A. voluntary alienation.
    B. adverse possession.
    C. transfers of title by descent.
    D. involuntary alienation.

14. A deed contains a promise that the title conveyed is good and a promise to obtain and deliver any documents necessary to ensure good title. This deed contains an example of which covenant?
    A. Further assurances
    B. Seisin
    C. Quiet enjoyment
    D. Warranty forever

15. A deed contains a guarantee that the grantor will compensate the grantee for any loss resulting from the title's failure in the future. This is an example of which covenant?
    A. Warranty forever
    B. Further assurance
    C. Quiet enjoyment
    D. Seisin

16. A person who has died without a will has died
    A. testate.
    B. in valid conveyance.
    C. intestate.
    D. under the acknowledgment clause.

17. Title to real estate can be transferred upon death by what type of document?
    A. Warranty deed
    B. Special warranty deed
    C. Quitclaim deed
    D. Will

18. An owner of real estate was declared legally incompetent and was committed to a state mental institution. While institutionalized, the owner wrote and executed a will. The owner died while still institutionalized and was survived by a spouse and three children. The real estate will pass
    A. to the owner's spouse.
    B. to the heirs mentioned in the owner's will.
    C. according to the state laws of descent.
    D. to the state.

19. Generally, where does a probate proceeding involving real property take place?
    A. Only in the county in which the property is located
    B. Only in the county in which the decedent resided
    C. In both the county where the decedent resided and the county in which the property is located
    D. In the county in which the executor or the beneficiary resides

20. A deed states that the grantors are conveying all their rights and interests to the grantees to have and to hold. This is communicated in
    A. the acknowledgment clause.
    B. the restriction clause.
    C. the covenant of seisin.
    D. the habendum clause.

UNIT 7

Title Records

LEARNING OBJECTIVES

When you have completed this unit, you will be able to

› **explain** the public recordation system and its importance to the title insurer; and
› **explain** the benefits of title insurance and the difference between an owner's policy and a lender's policy.

KEY TERMS

abstract of title	chain of title	subrogation
action to quiet title	constructive notice	title insurance
actual notice	marketable title	title search
attorney's opinion of title	priority	Torrens system
certificate of title	recording	

OVERVIEW

Public records are open to anyone interested in a particular property. A review of the records will reveal the documents, claims, and other details that affect the property's ownership. A prospective buyer, for example, needs to be sure that the seller can convey good title to the property. If the property is subject to any liens or other encumbrances, a prospective buyer or lender needs to know. An attorney or title company typically performs a search of the public records to ensure that good title is being conveyed. A real estate professional should understand what is in the public record and what a search may disclose.

PUBLIC RECORDS

Public records contain detailed information about each parcel of real estate in a city or county. These records are crucial in establishing ownership, giving notice of encumbrances, and establishing priority of liens. They protect the interests of real estate owners, taxing bodies, creditors, and the general public. The real estate recording system includes written documents that affect title, such as deeds and mortgages. Public records regarding taxes, judgments, probate, and marriage also may offer important information about the title to a particular property.

Depending on the jurisdiction in which property is located, the public records are maintained by

- recorders of deeds,
- county clerks,
- county treasurers,
- city clerks,
- collectors, and
- clerks of court.

Notice

Anyone with an interest in a parcel of real estate can take certain steps, called *giving notice*, to ensure that the existence of the interest is made available to the public. The two basic types of notice that can be given are **constructive notice** and **actual notice**.

Constructive notice is the legal presumption that information has been obtained by an individual through due diligence. A document placed in the public record serves as notice to the world of an individual's right or interest in the property. Physical possession of property also serves as constructive notice of the right of the person in possession. Because the information or evidence is readily available to the world, a prospective purchaser or lender is responsible for discovering the interest and is presumed to have done so.

Actual notice means not only that information of an interest in property is available but also that someone is actually aware of it. An individual who has searched the public records or inspected the property has actual notice of what is contained in the records or obvious from the property inspection. If it can be proved that an individual has had actual notice of a property right, that person cannot use a lack of constructive notice (such as an unrecorded deed) to justify a claim.

Recording

In most states, written documents that affect land *must be recorded in the county where the land is located.*

Recording is the act of placing documents in the public record. The specific rules for recording documents are a matter of state law. Although the details may vary, all recording acts essentially provide that any written document that affects any estate, right, title, or interest in land must be recorded in the county (or, in some states, the town) where the land is located to serve as public notice. This way, anyone interested in the title to a parcel of property will know where to look to discover the various interests of all other parties. Recording acts also generally give legal priority to those interests recorded first—the *first in time, first in right* or *first come, first served* principle. There are exceptions to this principle, such as liens for property taxes, special assessments, and delinquent amounts owed to the Internal Revenue Service.

To be *eligible for recording*, a document must be drawn and executed according to state law. For instance, a state may require that the parties' names be typed below their signatures or that the document be acknowledged before a notary public. In some states, the document must be witnessed. Others require that the name of the person who prepared the document appear on it. States may have specific rules about the size of documents and the color and quality of paper they are printed on. Some states require a certificate of real estate value and the payment of current property taxes due for recording. Electronic recording by computer or fax is permitted in a growing number of localities and greatly speeds up the process. A document can be scanned and made available quickly, instead of being required in multiple copies to be manually filed in a process that could take several days.

Priority

Priority refers to the order in which documents or liens were recorded. Many complicated situations can affect the priority of rights in a parcel of real estate—who received a property interest first, who recorded the interest first, who was in possession first, or who had actual or constructive notice. How the courts rule in any situation depends, of course, on the specific facts of the case. These are strictly legal questions that should be referred to the parties' attorneys.

IN PRACTICE

Property owner A listed a house for sale. Buyer B purchased the property from seller A and received a deed. Buyer B did not record the deed but took possession of the property in June. In November, A sold the same property to buyer C who received a deed, which C promptly recorded. C never inspected the property to determine if someone was in possession of it. In this case, by taking possession of the property, B has the superior right to it even though B did not record the deed received from A.

Unrecorded documents

Certain types of liens are not recorded. Real estate taxes and special assessments are liens on specific parcels of real estate and are not usually recorded until after the end of the period for which the taxes or assessments will be due, although some states create a lien right in unpaid taxes from the beginning of the period for which tax is owed. Inheritance taxes and franchise taxes, where applicable, are statutory liens and are placed against all real estate owned by a decedent at the time of death or by a corporation at the time the franchise taxes became a lien. Like real estate taxes, they are not recorded.

Notice of these liens must be gained from sources other than the recorder's office. Evidence of the payment of real estate taxes, special assessments, municipal utilities, and other taxes can be gathered from the tax collector's office, paid tax receipts, and letters from municipalities. Creative measures are often required to get information about *off the record* liens.

Chain of title

The **chain of title** is the record of a property's ownership. Beginning with the earliest owner, a title may pass to many individuals. Because the grantee of the first deed to the property will become the grantor of the next transfer of title, each owner is linked to the next so that a chain is formed. In same way, the title can be worked backward by searching for the record in which the present grantor of the property right received title as the grantee. An unbroken chain of title thus can be traced through conveyances from the present owner back to the earliest recorded owner, and then forward from the earliest recorded owner to the present owner. The chain of title does not include liens and encumbrances or any other document not directly related to ownership.

If ownership cannot be traced through an unbroken chain, a gap in the chain of title or *cloud on the title* is said to exist. In such a case, it is necessary to establish ownership by a court action called an **action to quiet title**. For instance, legal action might be required if a grantor acquired title under one name and conveyed it under another name. Evidence will be presented in court to prove that the grantee in the first transfer is the grantor in the second transfer.

IN PRACTICE

There may be a forged deed in the chain of title, which means that no subsequent grantee, even though innocent of the forgery, acquired legal title. In an action to quiet title brought by an individual currently living on the property and claiming title many years after the forgery, the individual may claim the right of ownership by virtue of adverse possession. Legal title could be acquired by adverse possession even in the case of an invalid document in the chain of title if there were the necessary years of property occupancy (typically, a higher requirement if a forgery has occurred) accompanied by the "color of title" provided by what appeared to each successive owner to be a valid deed.

Title search and abstract of title

A **title search** is an examination of the public records to determine whether any defects exist in the chain of title. The records of the conveyances of ownership are examined, beginning with the present owner. Then the title is traced backward to its origin (or 40 to 60 years or some definite period of time, depending on state statute). The time beyond which the title must be searched can be limited in states that have adopted the Marketable Title Act created by the Uniform Law Commission, www.uniformlaws.org. These states recognize that a review of the same records from, say, the 1800s, over and over again for each conveyance is not a productive use of time or money. This law also extinguishes certain interests and cures certain defects arising before the root of the title is found—the conveyance that establishes the source of the chain of title.

www.uniformlaws.org

Other public records are examined to identify wills, judicial proceedings, and other encumbrances that may affect title. These include a variety of taxes, special assessments, and other recorded liens.

A full **abstract of title** is a summary report of what the title search found in the public records. The person who prepares this report is called an *abstractor*. The abstractor searches all the public records and then summarizes the various events and proceedings that affected the title throughout its history. The report begins with the original grant (or root) and then provides a chronological list of recorded instruments. All recorded liens and encumbrances are included, along with their current status. A list of all of the public records examined is also provided as evidence of the scope of the search.

IN PRACTICE

An abstract of title is a condensed history of those items that can be found in public records. It does not reveal such items as encroachments or forgeries or any interests or conveyances that have not been recorded.

Marketable title

Under the terms of the typical real estate sales contract, the seller is required to deliver to the buyer **marketable title** to the property—that is, title that is acceptable to a reasonably prudent person and which will not subject the buyer to litigation. To be marketable, a title must

- disclose no serious defects and not depend on doubtful questions of law or fact to prove its validity;

- not expose a purchaser to the hazard of litigation or threaten the quiet enjoyment of the property; and

- convince a reasonably well-informed and prudent purchaser, acting on business principles and with knowledge of the facts and their legal significance, that the purchaser could sell or mortgage the property at a later time.

Although a title that does not meet these requirements still can be transferred, it contains certain defects that may limit or restrict its ownership. A buyer cannot be forced to accept a conveyance that is materially different from the one bargained for in the sales contract, but questions of marketable title must be raised by a buyer *before acceptance of the deed.* Once a buyer has accepted a deed with unmarketable title, the only available legal recourse may be to sue the seller under any covenants of warranty contained in the deed.

In some states, a preliminary title search is conducted as soon as an offer to purchase has been accepted. In fact, it may be customary to include a contingency in the sales contract that gives the buyer the right to review and approve the title report before proceeding with the purchase. A preliminary title report also benefits the seller by giving the seller an early opportunity to cure title defects.

PROOF OF OWNERSHIP

Proof of ownership is evidence that title is marketable. A deed by itself is not considered sufficient evidence of ownership. Even though a warranty deed conveys the grantor's interest, it contains no proof of the condition of the grantor's title at the time of the conveyance. The grantee needs assurance that ownership is actually being acquired and that the title is marketable. A certificate of title, title insurance, or a Torrens certificate is commonly used to prove ownership.

Certificate of title

A **certificate of title** is a statement of opinion of the title's status on the date the certificate is issued. *A certificate of title is not a guarantee of ownership.* Rather, it certifies the condition of the title based on an examination of the public records—a title search. The certificate may be prepared by a title company, licensed abstractor, or attorney. An owner, mortgage lender, or buyer may request the certificate.

Although a certificate of title is used as evidence of ownership, it is not perfect. Unrecorded liens or rights of parties in possession cannot be discovered by a search of the public records.

Hidden defects, such as transfers involving forged documents, incorrect marital information, incompetent parties, minors, or fraud, cannot be detected. A certificate offers no defense against these defects because they are unknown. The person who prepares the certificate is liable only for negligence in preparing the certificate.

IN PRACTICE

You earlier learned about the phrase *color of title*. Title may be conveyed in a transaction by a written instrument (such as a deed or will) that is actually inadequate to legally transfer ownership, whether because it was incorrectly executed or because it was executed by someone who did not, in fact, hold title in the first place. State law will specify how title may be perfected (made legally valid) in the event that there is a defect in the title.

Attorney's opinion of title

In some areas of the country, an **attorney's opinion of title** based on a review of the abstract is sufficient evidence of title. Similar to a certificate of title, the attorney's opinion of title does not protect against defects that cannot be discovered from the public records. Many buyers purchase title insurance to defend the title from these defects.

Title insurance

Title insurance is a contract under which the policyholder is protected from losses arising from defects in the title. A title insurance company determines whether the title is insurable, based on a review of the public records. If so, a policy is issued. Unlike other insurance policies that insure against *future losses*, title insurance protects the insured from an event that occurred *before* the policy was issued. Title insurance is considered the best defense of title: the title insurance company will defend any lawsuit based on an insurable defect and pay claims if the title proves to be defective.

After examining the public records, the title company usually issues what may be called a preliminary report of title or a commitment to issue a title policy. This describes the type of policy that will be issued and includes

- the name of the insured party;
- the legal description of the real estate;
- the estate or interest covered;
- conditions and stipulations under which the policy is issued; and
- a schedule of all exceptions, including encumbrances and defects found in the public records and any known unrecorded defects.

The premium for the policy is paid once, at the closing of the transaction. The maximum loss for which the company may be liable cannot exceed the face amount of the policy (unless the amount of coverage has been extended by use of an inflation rider). When a title company makes a payment to settle a claim covered by a policy, the company generally acquires the right to any remedy or damages available to the insured. This right is called **subrogation**.

Coverage

Exactly which defects the title company will defend depends on the type of policy. (See Figure 7.1.) A standard coverage policy normally insures the title as it is known from the public records. In addition, the standard policy insures against such hidden defects as forged documents, conveyances by incompetent grantors, incorrect marital statements, and improperly delivered deeds.

FIGURE 7.1: Owner's Title Insurance Policy

Standard Coverage	Extended Coverage	Not Covered by Either Policy
Defects found in public records	Standard coverage plus defects discoverable through the following:	Defects and liens listed in policy
Forged documents		Defects known to buyer
Incompetent grantors	■ Property inspection, including unrecorded rights of persons in possession	Changes in land use brought about by zoning ordinances
Incorrect marital statements	■ Examination of survey	
Improperly delivered deeds	■ Unrecorded liens not known by policyholder	

Extended coverage as provided by an *American Land Title Association (ALTA) policy* includes the protections of a standard policy plus additional protections. An extended policy protects the homeowner against defects that may be discovered by inspection of the property: rights of parties in possession, examination of a survey, and certain unrecorded liens. Most real estate sales contracts will include a requirement that an ALTA policy be provided.

Title insurance does not offer guaranteed protection against all defects. A title company will not insure a bad title or offer protection against defects that clearly appear in a title search. The policy generally lists certain uninsurable losses, called exclusions. These exclusions typically include zoning ordinances, restrictive covenants, easements, certain water rights, and current taxes and special assessments.

IN PRACTICE

Certain conditions that have been discovered in the title examination, such as encroachments or property improvements that violate zoning requirements (building setback requirements, for example), as well as existing oil and gas leases, will also be excluded from coverage. A defect may be so severe that the title insurance company will refuse to issue a policy, creating an insurmountable obstacle to completing a transaction.

Types of policies

The different types of title insurance policies depend on who is named as the insured. An *owner's policy* is issued for the benefit of the owner (new buyer) and the owner's heirs or devisees and is issued for the property's purchase price. A lender's policy (mortgagee policy) is issued for the benefit of the mortgage lender and the amount of the mortgage loan will determine the amount of the coverage.

The Torrens system

As described previously, the **Torrens system** is a legal registration system used to verify ownership of real estate. Where it is recognized, registration in the Torrens system provides evidence of title without the need for an additional search of the public records. Under the Torrens system, an owner of real property submits a written application to register a title. The application is submitted to the court clerk of the county in which the real estate is located. If the applicant proves ownership, the court enters an order to register the real estate. The registrar of titles is directed to issue a certificate of title. The original Torrens certificate of title in the registrar's office reveals the owner of the land and all mortgages, judgments, and similar liens. It does not, however, reveal federal or state taxes and some other items. The Torrens title system of registration relies on the physical title document itself; a person acquires title only when it is registered.

KEY POINT REVIEW

Constructive notice of a document is assumed when **due diligence** (such as a search of public records and inspection of the property) would reveal its existence. **Actual notice** means that an individual has **direct knowledge** of documents in the public records and facts revealed by an inspection of the property.

To serve as **constructive notice**, and provide **priority** over subsequent documents, a **written document** that affects an **estate**, **right**, **title**, or **interest** in **land** must be **drafted** and **executed** according to state law (**recording acts**) and must be **recorded** in the **public records** that are maintained by the designated **official**, such as the recorder of deeds, county clerk, or city clerk, in the **county** (or city) in which the **property is located**.

Public records are typically **searched** by **title companies** that provide **title insurance** to prospective purchasers based on what the search reveals.

Unrecorded documents that may affect title, such as a tax lien, may not be recorded immediately, yet are still given priority by law and require a search of tax records and other sources.

The **chain of title** is a record of property ownership, but it does not include liens and other encumbrances. A **gap** in the chain or other dispute of ownership creates a **cloud on the title**, which is resolved by a **suit to quiet title**.

An **abstract of title**, prepared by an **abstractor** or an **attorney**, is a **summary** report of what the title search reveals. It includes all **recorded liens and encumbrances** and lists **records searched** but does not indicate forgeries and interests that are unrecorded or could be discovered by property inspection.

A **marketable title** is one that a reasonably well-informed and prudent purchaser would accept because it does **not have serious defects** and does not rely on doubtful questions of law or fact to prove its validity, so that it does not expose the purchaser to litigation or threaten the purchaser's **quiet enjoyment** of the property.

Title insurance is issued as an **owner's policy** or **mortgagee's policy** and protects the insured from losses arising from defects in title and hidden defects, but it also identifies **exclusions** from coverage that typically include readily apparent title defects, zoning, and others.

The **Torrens system** provides a **certificate of title** issued by the county clerk that requires no further search to validate.

UNIT 7 QUIZ

1. A title search in the public records may be conducted by
   A. anyone.
   B. attorneys and abstractors only.
   C. attorneys, abstractors, and real estate professionals only.
   D. anyone who obtains a court order under the Freedom of Information Act.

2. Which statement *BEST* explains why instruments affecting real estate are recorded?
   A. Recording gives constructive notice to the world of the rights and interests claimed in the identified parcel of real estate.
   B. Failing to record will void the transfer.
   C. The instruments must be recorded to comply with the terms of the statute of frauds.
   D. Recording proves the execution of the instrument.

3. A purchaser went to the county building to check the recorder's records, which showed that the seller was the grantee in the last recorded deed and that no mortgage was on record against the property. The purchaser may assume which of the following?
   A. All taxes are paid and no judgments are outstanding.
   B. The seller has good title.
   C. The seller did not mortgage the property.
   D. No one else is occupying the property.

4. The date and time a document was recorded help establish which of the following?
   A. Priority
   B. Abstract of title
   C. Subrogation
   D. Marketable title

5. A buyer bought a house, received a deed, and moved into the residence but neglected to record the document. One week later, the seller died and the heirs in another city, unaware that the property had been sold, conveyed title to a relative, who recorded the deed. Who owns the property?
   A. The buyer
   B. The relative
   C. The seller's heirs
   D. Both the buyer and the relative

6. A property with encumbrances that will outlast the closing
   A. cannot be sold.
   B. can be sold only if title insurance is provided.
   C. cannot have a deed recorded without a survey.
   D. can be sold if a buyer agrees to take it subject to the encumbrances.

7. Which of the following would *NOT* be acceptable evidence of ownership?
   A. Attorney's opinion
   B. Title insurance policy
   C. Abstract
   D. Deed to the current owner signed by the last seller

8. Chain of title is *MOST* accurately defined as
   A. the record of a property's ownership.
   B. a report of the contents of the public record, including all legal proceedings, regarding a particular property.
   C. an instrument or document that protects the insured parties (subject to specific exceptions) against defects in the record of a property's ownership.
   D. the examination of the record and hidden risks such as forgeries, undisclosed heirs, errors in the public records, and so on.

9. A seller delivered title to a buyer at closing. A title search had disclosed no serious defects, and the title did not appear to be based on doubtful questions of law or fact or to expose the buyer to possible litigation. The seller's title did not appear to present a threat to the buyer's quiet enjoyment, and the title insurance policy provided was sufficient to convince a reasonably well-informed person that the property could be resold. The title conveyed would commonly be referred to as
   A. a certificate of title.
   B. an abstract of title.
   C. a marketable title.
   D. an attorney's opinion of title.

10. The person who prepares an abstract of title for a parcel of real estate
    A. searches the public records and then summarizes the events and proceedings that affect title.
    B. insures the condition of the title.
    C. inspects the property.
    D. issues title insurance.

11. Homeowners are frantic because they want to sell their property and the deed is missing. Which of the following is *TRUE*?
    A. They may need to sue for quiet title.
    B. They must buy title insurance.
    C. They do not need the original deed if it has been recorded.
    D. They should execute a replacement deed to themselves.

12. Mortgagee title policies protect which parties against loss?
    A. Buyers
    B. Sellers
    C. Lenders
    D. Buyers and lenders

13. Which of the following are traditionally covered by a standard title insurance policy?
    A. Improperly delivered deeds
    B. Changes in land use because of zoning ordinances
    C. Unrecorded liens not known to the policyholder
    D. Unrecorded rights of persons in possession

14. A written summary of the history of all conveyances and legal proceedings affecting a specific parcel of real estate is called
    A. an adjustment of title.
    B. a certificate of title.
    C. an abstract of title.
    D. a title insurance policy.

15. Which of the following is *NOT* covered by a standard title insurance policy?
    A. Forged documents
    B. Incorrect marital statements
    C. Unrecorded rights of parties in possession
    D. Incompetent grantors

16. Documents referred to as title evidence include
    A. policies of title insurance.
    B. general warranty deeds.
    C. security agreements.
    D. special warranty deeds.

17. All of the following are true regarding public records *EXCEPT*
    A. they give notice of encumbrances.
    B. they establish priority of liens.
    C. they guarantee marketable title.
    D. they provide constructive notice of interests in the identified property.

18. A sells a portion of property to B. B promptly records the deed in the appropriate county office. If A tries to sell the same portion of property to C, which of the following statements is *TRUE*?
    A. C has been given constructive notice of the prior sale because B promptly recorded the deed.
    B. C has been given actual notice of the prior sale because B promptly recorded the deed.
    C. Because C's purchase of the property is the more recent, it will have priority over B's interest, regardless of when B recorded the deed.
    D. Because C purchased the property from its rightful owner, C is presumed by law to be aware of B's prior interest.

19. The *BEST* reason for a buyer to obtain title insurance is
    A. that the mortgage lender requires it.
    B. to ensure that the seller can deliver marketable title.
    C. to ensure that the abstractor has prepared a complete summary of title.
    D. to pay future liens that may be filed.

20. A mortgagee received a title insurance policy on the property a buyer is pledging as security for the mortgage loan. Which of the following is *TRUE*?
    A. The policy is issued for the benefit of the buyer.
    B. The policy guarantees that the buyer's equity will be protected.
    C. The amount of coverage is commensurate with the loan amount.
    D. The amount of coverage increases as the borrower grows older.

UNIT
8

Real Estate Brokerage

LEARNING OBJECTIVES

When you have completed this unit, you will be able to

› **describe** the fundamentals of real estate brokerage and licensing laws;
› **describe** the purpose and basic elements of antitrust laws including price fixing, boycotts, and allocation of markets;
› **discuss** the services provided to real estate practitioners by professional organizations, including the creation and enforcement of ethical codes; and
› **explain** how real estate professionals should use technology in real estate practice to comply with laws and ethical standards.

KEY TERMS

antitrust laws	Electronic Signatures in	minimum level of services
boycott	Global and National	multiple listing service (MLS)
brokerage	Commerce Act (E-Sign)	National Do Not Call Registry
code of ethics	employee	price-fixing
commission	independent contractor	procuring cause
disclaimers	Internet Data Exchange (IDX)	ready, willing, and able buyer
electronic contracting	policy	Uniform Electronic
	managing broker	Transactions Act (UETA)

OVERVIEW

Real estate is an industry driven by small businesses. Most brokerages are not giant national companies, and even those that are members of large franchises are still small businesses at heart, run locally to serve what is essentially a local market. Within a brokerage, no matter how large or small it is, each real estate professional has his own business. To be successful, a real estate professional has to not only know the product—real estate—but also how to run a business. Economics is part of running any operation, as are personnel decisions, such as how many people to hire and in what capacity. What positions are needed? How do you find the right people to fill those jobs? Who's your competition? The answers to these questions are not easy ones, but a successful real estate professional needs to think like a businessperson.

BROKERAGE AND REAL ESTATE LICENSE LAWS

All 50 states, the District of Columbia, and all Canadian provinces license and regulate the activities of real estate professionals. While the laws share a common purpose, the details vary from state to state. Information on state laws and regulations can be found at the websites listed in the appendix. Another good source of information on current laws is the Association of Real Estate License Law Officials (ARELLO), www.arello.org. In addition to individual states, ARELLO's membership includes governing bodies from countries around the globe.

www.arello.org

Purpose of license laws

Real estate license laws protect the public by ensuring a standard of competence and professionalism in the real estate industry. The laws achieve this goal by

- establishing basic requirements for obtaining a real estate license and, in most cases, requiring continuing education to keep a license;

- defining which activities require licensing;

- describing the acceptable standards of conduct and practice for licensees; and

- enforcing those standards through a disciplinary system.

The purpose of these laws is not merely to regulate the real estate industry. Their main objective is to make sure that the rights of purchasers, sellers, tenants, and owners are protected from unscrupulous or negligent practices. The laws are not intended to prevent licensees from conducting their businesses successfully or to interfere in legitimate transactions. Laws cannot guarantee that fair and honest dealing will always prevail in the business of real estate, but by establishing minimum levels of education and standards of behavior, these laws provide a base line for behavior and competency upon which an ethical marketplace can be nurtured and built.

Each state has a licensing authority—a commission, department, division, board, and/or agency—for real estate professionals. This authority has the power to issue licenses, make real estate information available to licensees and the public, and enforce the statutory real estate law.

Each licensing authority has also adopted a set of administrative regulations that administer the statutory law and set operating guidelines for licensees. The regulations have the same force and effect as statutory law, though if they conflict, the statute will prevail. Both regulations and statutory law are usually enforced through fines and the denial, suspension, or revocation of licenses. Civil and criminal court actions also can be brought against violators in some serious cases.

IN PRACTICE

Each state's real estate license laws and the regulations of its real estate commission, board, or other body establish the framework for all of a licensee's activities. It is vital that licensees have a clear and comprehensive understanding of their state's laws and regulations for purposes of the licensing examination, as well as to ensure that the licensee's practice of real estate is both legal and successful. This is especially true for a licensee who holds a license in another state by reciprocity (reciprocal agreement of the states) and who may not have been required to take a special course or examination.

Real estate brokerage

Brokerage is simply the business of bringing parties together. A *real estate broker* is licensed to buy, sell, exchange, or lease real property for others and to charge a fee for those services. A broker may be an *agent* for a client, or broker and client may decide on a different form of representation, if allowed by state law.

A licensed brokerage business may take many forms, as permitted by state law. It may be a sole proprietorship, a corporation, a limited liability company, or a partnership with another real estate broker. The business may be independent of other businesses, or it may be part of a regional or national franchise organization. The business may consist of a single office or multiple branches. A real estate brokerage may specialize in one kind of transaction or service, or it may offer a variety of services. For licensing purposes, the brokerage must have a physical address, but it's most important marketing presence may be its website.

No matter what form it takes, a real estate brokerage has the same demands, expenses, and rewards as any other small business. A real estate broker faces the same challenges as an entrepreneur in any other industry. In addition to mastering the complexities of real estate transactions, the real estate broker must be able to handle the day-to-day details of running a business and set effective policies for every aspect of the brokerage operation:

- Maintaining space and equipment
- Hiring licensed real estate professionals, as well as unlicensed support staff
- Determining compensation
- Directing staff
- Implementing procedures for licensees to follow in carrying out activities permitted by the state's real estate license laws and regulations

IN PRACTICE

A broker should always advise the parties to a real estate transaction to secure legal counsel to protect their interests. Although real estate professionals may bring buyers and sellers together and, in most states, may fill in preprinted blank purchase agreement forms, only an attorney may offer legal advice or prepare legal documents. Real estate professionals who are not attorneys are prohibited from practicing law.

Relationship of broker and sales associate

Although brokerage firms vary widely in size, few brokers today perform their duties without the assistance of other licensed individuals. A *sales associate* might be licensed as a real estate salesperson or be a licensed real estate broker who simply chooses to work for another broker rather than set up an independent brokerage office. This section looks at the relationship of broker and sales associate.

In the traditional definition, a real estate *salesperson* is licensed to perform real estate activities on behalf of a licensed real estate broker. The broker for whom the salesperson works is called the *employing broker*, and both will be subject to the terms of an *employment agreement*, even when the salesperson is an *independent contractor* for tax and other purposes. The distinction is discussed in the next section; regardless of the salesperson's status for tax purposes, the broker is fully responsible for the actions performed in the course of the real estate business by all persons licensed under the broker, which is why the sales associate can never be an independent contractor for purposes of the licensing law.

From now on, we will use the term *sales associate* when we refer to a licensed individual employed by a broker. When we refer to a *broker*, we will mean an employing broker.

A sales associate can carry out *only* those responsibilities delegated by the employing broker and can receive compensation *only* from that broker. As an agent of the broker, the sales associate has no authority to make contracts with or receive compensation from any other party. The agency relationship also makes the broker liable for the acts of a sales associate that fall within the scope of the employment agreement. This *vicarious liability* means that the broker can be held responsible for the conduct while performing brokerage activities of every sales associate employed by the broker.

The complexity of the real estate business and the emphasis on protection of consumer rights has led many states to require that all real estate professionals be licensed as real estate brokers. Even with increased educational requirements, however, the practicalities of running a real estate brokerage require that one broker be identified as the managing or supervising broker. A **managing broker**, who may also be called the supervising broker, is responsible for supervision of the real estate professionals who act on behalf of the brokerage. In a one-office firm, the managing broker may be the broker under whose license the firm has been created. In a larger company, every branch office of the brokerage typically will be required to designate a managing broker for that office location, and the managing broker may be required to live within a certain number of miles of the office. To qualify for the role of managing broker and maintain that status, the real estate professional may have to meet specific education requirements. Note that not all states use the same terminology to refer to managing brokers, brokers, and sales associates. Check your state for the specific language used.

IN PRACTICE

The sales associate must always be supervised by a managing broker. The managing broker cannot delegate office supervision of sales associates to an unlicensed person, although state law should provide for a temporary transfer of the duties of the managing broker to another licensed broker.

Independent contractor vs. employee

The employment agreement between a broker and sales associate should define the nature, obligations, and responsibilities of the relationship. State license laws generally make it clear that a broker is responsible for the acts of the sales associates employed by the brokerage (the traditional employer-employee relationship). This is true regardless of whether a sales associate is considered an employee or an independent contractor for income tax purposes, which will affect the broker's legal obligation to pay and withhold taxes from the sales associate's earnings.

In other businesses, an employer can exercise certain controls over workers who are considered employees and not independent contractors. An employer may require an **employee** to follow rules governing working hours, office routine, attendance at sales meetings, assignment of sales quotas, and adherence to dress codes. An employer is required by the federal government to withhold Social Security taxes and income taxes from wages paid to employees. The employer is also required to pay unemployment compensation taxes on wages paid to one or more employees, as defined by state and federal laws. In addition, employees might receive benefits such as health insurance, profit-sharing plans, and workers' compensation.

In most businesses, the employer's relationship with a person who is an **independent contractor** is very different. As the term implies, an independent contractor operates with more independence than an employee, and the employer may not exercise the same degree of control over an independent contractor's activities. Independent contractors are responsible for paying their own income and Social Security taxes and receive nothing from the employer that could be construed as an employee benefit, such as health insurance or paid vacation time.

Special rules apply when a real estate broker employs other real estate professionals to act on the broker's behalf. Under state license law, the broker is responsible for supervising the business activities of the sales associate and is liable for the actions of the sales associate (the vicarious liability mentioned earlier). The broker's sales associate thus is treated as an employee of the broker, even though the employment agreement between sales associate and broker treats the sales associate as an independent contractor for tax purposes.

Confusion over the nature of the independent contractor status of a real estate sales associate has prompted the Internal Revenue Service (IRS) to issue specific rules to clarify the employer-employee relationship in a real estate office. Under the *qualified real estate agent* category set out in the Internal Revenue Code (26 U.S.C. 3508) found at www.irs.gov, the following three requirements must be met for a sales associate to establish a nonemployee status with the employing broker for tax purposes:

www.irs.gov

- The sales associate must have a current real estate license.

- The sales associate must have a written contract with the broker that specifies that the sales associate will not be treated as an employee for federal tax purposes.

- A substantial portion of the sales associate's income as a real estate professional must be based on sales production or other output and not on the number of hours worked.

IN PRACTICE

Broker K has nine sales associates, all of whom are nonemployees for federal and state tax purposes. To make sure that there is no question of the status of the sales associates, each is compensated based solely on the amount of sales activity generated. None receives an hourly wage or is required to work a certain number of hours per week.

A broker should have a standardized employment agreement drafted and reviewed by an attorney to ensure its compliance with federal law. The broker should also be aware that written agreements carry little weight with an IRS auditor if the actions of the parties contradict the provisions of the contract. Specific legal and tax questions regarding independent contractors should be referred to an attorney or accountant familiar with this issue.

Real estate assistant

A real estate assistant (also known as a personal assistant or professional assistant) can be a combination office manager, marketer, organizer, and facilitator who has a fundamental understanding of the real estate industry. The assistant can be a staff member working for more than one real estate professional but often works for a specific sales associate. The assistant might be required to have a real estate license, depending on the tasks performed. The extent to which the assistant can help the real estate broker or sales associate with transactions will be determined by the state licensing law and regulations. An unlicensed assistant generally may perform duties that include clerical tasks, office management, website development and maintenance, and production of marketing pieces, but with little direct contact with consumers. A licensed assistant, on the other hand, can also set up and host open houses and assist in all aspects of a real estate transaction, including day-to-day contact with consumers.

Most states have very specific rules about what a licensed assistant and an unlicensed assistant may do and how they can be compensated. Usually, an unlicensed personal assistant working for a sales associate can be paid by the sales associate, but a licensed personal assistant working for a sales associate must be paid by the employing broker. For purposes of the real estate licensing laws and regulations, both the sales associate and licensed personal assistant are under the supervision of the employing broker.

IN PRACTICE

A sales associate considering hiring a personal assistant must understand state requirements. The parameters of the relationship should be clear both to the sales associate and the person hired to act as a personal assistant. Even an unlicensed individual could incur liability under the state licensing law, especially if that person conducts activities that require a real estate license.

Broker's compensation

The broker's compensation is specified in the contract with the client. The real estate license law (or statute of frauds) usually will require that there be a written agreement to establish the compensation to be paid. Compensation can be in the form of a **commission** or broker's fee (computed as a percentage of the total sales price), a flat fee, or an hourly rate. The amount of a broker's commission is negotiable in every case. Even subtle attempts to impose uniform commission rates in an area are clearly a violation of state and federal laws. Nevertheless, a broker may set the minimum rate acceptable for that broker's firm; the client is free to work with a different broker if the rate is deemed unacceptable by the client. The important point is for broker and client to agree on a rate before any form of representation is established.

The broker's compensation will also be affected by the participation in the transaction of a broker from another firm, who may be representing one of the parties. Brokers have long realized that the marketing of a property is enhanced when the largest possible number of real estate professionals are aware of the availability of the property and can show it to their clients. Membership in a **multiple listing service (MLS)** provides that marketing opportunity, and the rules of the MLS set out the terms under which brokers agree to *cooperate* in a transaction, including the sharing of the compensation earned.

A commission is considered earned when the work for which the real estate broker was hired has been accomplished. This most likely is different from the time at which the commission is paid; most sales commissions are payable when the sale is consummated by *delivery and acceptance* of the seller's deed. This provision is generally included in the agreement between seller and broker.

To be entitled to receive compensation from a real estate sales transaction, an individual must be

- a licensed real estate broker,

- employed by the buyer or seller under a valid contract, and

- the procuring cause of the sale.

To be considered the **procuring cause** of a sale, the broker must have started or caused an uninterrupted chain of events that resulted in the sale. For example, procuring cause may include activities such as conducting an open house, placing an advertisement in the local real estate advertising magazine, making the property listing available on the internet, and showing the house to the buyer. A broker (or a sales associate of the broker) who causes or completes such a course of action without a contract or without having been promised payment is a volunteer and may not legally claim compensation.

Once a seller accepts an offer from a ready, willing, and able buyer, the real estate broker is entitled to a commission. A **ready, willing, and able buyer** is one who is prepared to buy on the seller's terms and is ready to take positive steps toward consummation of the transaction. A court may prevent the real estate broker from receiving a commission if the real estate broker knew the buyer was unable to perform. If the transaction is not consummated, the real estate broker may still be entitled to a commission if the seller

- has a change of mind and refuses to sell,

- has a spouse who refuses to sign the deed,

- has a title with uncorrected defects,

- committed fraud with respect to the transaction,

- is unable to deliver possession within a reasonable time,

- insists on terms not in the listing (e.g., the right to restrict the use of the property), or

- has a mutual agreement with the buyer to cancel the transaction.

To be a **procuring cause**, the broker or the broker's sales associate must have started an uninterrupted chain of events that resulted in a sale.

A **ready, willing, and able buyer** is one who is prepared to buy on the seller's terms and is ready to complete the transaction.

Sales associate's compensation

The amount of compensation a sales associate receives is set by mutual agreement between the broker and the sales associate. A broker may agree to pay a fixed salary, but usually the compensation is a share of the commissions from transactions originated by the sales associate. In some cases, the sales associate may draw from an account against earned shares of commissions, providing a minimal level of regular income. Some brokers require sales associates to pay all or part of the expenses of advertising listed properties.

Some firms have adopted a 100% commission plan in which each sales associate pays a monthly service charge to the broker to cover the cost of office space, telephone, and supervision in return for keeping 100% of the commissions from the sales the sales associate negotiates. Sales associates on a 100% commission plan pay all of their individual business expenses, such as the salary of a personal assistant or the costs associated with development and maintenance of the sales associate's website.

Other firms have *graduated commission splits* based on a sales associate's achieving specified production goals. For instance, a broker might agree to split commissions 50/50 up to a $25,000 sales associate's share, 60/40 for shares from $25,000 to $30,000, and so on. Commission splits could go up to 80/20 or 90/10, particularly for high producers.

No matter how the sales associate's compensation is structured, as a rule only the employing real estate broker can pay it. In a transaction involving two firms, the entire commission is received by the broker representing the party who pays the commission, and the agreed-upon share of the commission is paid to the cooperating broker. Each broker then pays any employed sales associate who took part in the transaction the amount due to that person.

Unit 8

The method and amount of the compensation received by the sales associate also does not affect the broker's responsibility for the conduct of the sales associate. The real estate license law will always make the broker liable for acts of the sales associate performed in the course of business.

MATH CONCEPTS

Sharing Commissions

A commission might be shared by many people: the broker and sales associate working for the seller, as well as the broker and sales associate working for the buyer. A diagram may help you determine which real estate professional is entitled to receive what amount of the total commission. For example, a sales associate took a listing on a $289,000 house at a 5% commission rate. A sales associate employed by a different firm found the buyer for the property. If the property sold for the listed price, the seller's broker and the buyer's broker shared the commission equally, and the buyer's broker kept 45% of the shared commission, how much did the sales associate employed by the buyer's broker receive?

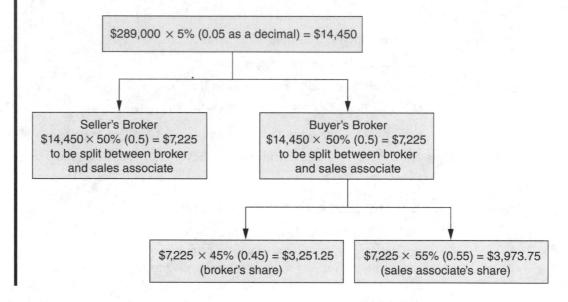

Services offered

One of the more notable impacts of the internet is that it has allowed buyers and sellers to have tremendous access to information about the real estate market, as well as individual properties. The average consumer today is much more knowledgeable about real estate matters, including financing and legal issues, and is accustomed to finding information quickly.

Successful real estate professionals understand and encourage consumers' exploration of the vast resources of the internet but can also identify the services a real estate professional provides and underscore the value of those services. One way in which that can be done is by explaining the tasks that can be performed by a real estate professional as a bundle of services. The next step is to be willing to unbundle those services, customizing the service offered by making a range of options available to the real estate consumer. For example, a real estate professional may want to offer a seller the following services, as permitted by state law:

- Helping the seller prepare the property for sale

- Performing a comparative market analysis (CMA) to assist the seller in pricing the property
- Assisting with marketing the property using the MLS and websites
- Locating and screening a buyer
- Helping fill in the blanks of a sales agreement
- Assisting with negotiations
- Being available to assist with the closing of the transaction

Other services can be directed toward buyers. For example, a real estate professional may offer a buyer the following services, as permitted by state law:

- Working out the economics of renting versus owning
- Helping a buyer with a mortgage preapproval
- Consulting on a buyer's desired location
- Visiting properties with a buyer and checking property information
- Helping fill in the blanks of an offer to purchase
- Assisting with negotiations
- Being available to assist with the closing of the transaction

Limiting services offered

A growing number of brokerages offer limited-service listing agreements. The real estate broker may offer no services other than that of listing a property in the MLS. When sellers enter into this kind of agreement, they are essentially representing themselves, accepting communications from prospective buyers, showing the property, and perhaps hiring an attorney to assist with completing a transaction. If questions emerge during the negotiation or completion of such a transaction, the seller may turn to the real estate professional working for the buyer for answers, which can put the real estate professional in an awkward position or, worse, involve the real estate professional in an unethical or even illegal position if even an implication that the real estate professional has worked on behalf of both parties to the transaction without their informed consent is present.

In response to this potential problem, some states have enacted legislation defining an exclusive brokerage agreement. Other states have proposed regulations that define the **minimum level of services** a consumer should expect from a real estate professional.

For example, one state now requires all exclusive brokerage agreements to specify that the broker—through one or more sponsored sales associates—must, at a minimum,

- accept delivery of and present offers and counteroffers to the client;
- assist the client in developing, negotiating, and presenting offers and counteroffers; and
- answer the client's questions about offers, counteroffers, and contingencies.

Fees

Many real estate professionals use either an hourly rate or a flat fee for particular services. The *fee-for-service* concept can create marketing opportunities for specific services, such as preparing a property for sale, but can also lead to a recognition by the consumer of the value of the real estate professional's knowledge and expertise.

Real estate professionals may also want to develop their own lists of services for sellers and buyers, as well as a specific list of services to help people who decide to sell their own home, known as *for sale by owners* (FSBOs). Again, state law may dictate what the real estate professional can offer. In any event, the property owner should be clear as to the level of representation being offered and how it will affect the services the owner can expect to receive.

Communicating with consumers to identify their real estate needs is key to developing a successful real estate business. It is ultimately the broker who decides whether an unbundling of services is good for the firm.

IN PRACTICE

A buyer wants to buy a house without contracting with a broker but needs help writing an offer. The buyer asks a broker friend to write an offer to purchase, and they agree on the terms of the work. If state law permits, the broker can discuss the terms of the offer with the buyer, help the buyer complete an offer-to-purchase form, and charge the buyer a set fee for the service.

ANTITRUST LAWS

Antitrust violations include

■ price-fixing,
■ the group boycott,
■ allocation of customers,
■ allocation of markets, and
■ tie-in agreements.

The real estate industry is subject to **antitrust laws**. At the federal level, the Sherman Antitrust Act provides specific penalties for a number of illegal business activities. Each state also has its own antitrust laws. These laws prohibit monopolies and any contracts, combinations, and conspiracies among competitors that unreasonably restrain trade—that is, behaviors that interfere with the free flow of goods and services in a competitive marketplace. The most common antitrust violations are price-fixing, the group boycott, allocation of customers or markets, and tie-in agreements.

Price-fixing

Price-fixing is a practice in which competitors agree to set prices or other terms and conditions for products or services rather than letting competition in the open market establish those prices. In real estate, price-fixing occurs when competing brokers agree to set sales commissions, fees, or management rates. Price-fixing is illegal. Real estate brokers must independently determine commission rates or fees for their own firms only. These decisions must be based on a broker's business judgment and revenue requirements. A broker may discuss commissions and fees with real estate professionals who are affiliated with the same brokerage but must not discuss compensation issues with anyone from another real estate firm.

Trade groups, such as associations of REALTORS®, multiple listing services, and other professional organizations, may neither set fees or commission splits, nor deny membership to a real estate broker based on the fees that the broker charges. In fact, no discussion of commissions or fees should ever take place at *any* gathering of two or more real estate professionals from different brokerages.

The challenge for real estate professionals is to avoid even the impression of price-fixing. Hinting to prospective clients that there is a "going rate" of commission or a "normal" fee implies that rates are, in fact, standardized. The broker and sales associates must make it clear to clients that the rate stated is only what that brokerage charges.

Group boycott

A group **boycott** occurs when two or more businesses conspire against another business or agree to withhold their patronage to reduce competition. A group boycott is illegal under antitrust laws.

The most recent example of this type of violation has occurred when traditional full-service brokers have conspired to destroy a competitor's firm by not showing that firm's listings. The competitor may be a so-called discount broker or one who offers unbundled services under the fee-for-service concept discussed earlier. Obviously, if such a scheme succeeds, it diminishes consumer choices by limiting the availability of property.

Allocation of customers or markets

Allocation of customers or markets involves an agreement between real estate brokers to divide their markets and refrain from competing for each other's business. Allocations may be made on a geographic basis, with real estate brokers agreeing to specific territories within which they will operate exclusively. The division may also occur by markets, such as by price range or category of housing. These agreements result in reduced competition.

Tie-in agreements

Finally, *tie-in agreements* (also known as *tying agreements*) are agreements to sell one product only if the buyer purchases another product as well. The sale of the first (desired) product is *tied* to the purchase of a second (less desirable) product. In the real estate business, this can occur if, for instance, a broker will agree to list a seller's home for sale only if the seller agrees to be represented by the broker in the purchase of a new home.

Penalties

The penalties for violating antitrust laws are severe. Under the federal Sherman Antitrust Act, the penalty for fixing prices or allocating markets is a maximum $1 million fine and 10 years in prison. For corporations, the penalty may be as high as $100 million. An individual who has suffered a loss because of an antitrust violation may sue for treble damages—three times the actual damages sustained. In addition, the injured party may recover the cost of the suit, which includes reasonable attorney fees.

PROFESSIONAL ORGANIZATIONS AND ETHICS

www.nar.realtor

Many trade organizations serve the real estate business. Some of them have already been mentioned. The largest is the National Association of REALTORS® (NAR), whose website is www.nar.realtor. NAR is composed of state, regional, and local associations. NAR also sponsors various affiliated organizations that offer professional designations to brokers, salespersons, appraisers, and others who complete required courses in areas of special interest. Members of NAR are entitled to be known as REALTORS® or REALTOR-ASSOCIATES®.

Unit 8

NAR affiliates

NAR has many affiliated institutes, societies, and councils that are available to members who wish to increase their knowledge of a specialized area of real estate practice and earn the accompanying designation. These include the following:

www.cre.org
www.ccim.com
www.irem.org
www.rliland.com
www.rebinstitute.com
www.nar.realtor
/education
/designations-and
-certifications/gri
www.crs.com
www.sior.com
www.wcr.org

- Counselors of Real Estate (CRE)—www.cre.org
- Commercial Investment Real Estate Institute (CIREI)—www.ccim.com
- Institute of Real Estate Management (IREM)—www.irem.org
- REALTORS® Land Institute (RLI)—www.rliland.com
- Certified Real Estate Brokerage Manager (CRB)—www.rebinstitute.com
- Graduate, REALTOR® Institute (GRI)—www.nar.realtor/education/designations-and -certifications/gri
- Council of Residential Specialists (CRS)—www.crs.com
- Society of Industrial and Office REALTORS® (SIOR)—www.sior.com
- Women's Council of REALTORS® (WCR)—www.wcr.org

Other professional associations are mentioned throughout the text.

Professional ethics

Professional conduct involves more than just complying with the law. In real estate, state licensing laws establish the activities that may be performed by a licensee, as well as the activities that are illegal and, therefore, prohibited. Merely complying with the letter of the law may not be enough; however, real estate professionals may perform legally yet not ethically. *Ethics* refers to a system of moral principles, rules, and standards of conduct. These moral principles do two things:

- They establish standards for integrity and competence in dealing with consumers of an industry's services.
- They define a code of conduct for relations within the industry among its professionals.

Code of ethics

One way that an organization can address ethics among its members or in their respective businesses is by adopting a code of professional conduct. A **code of ethics** is a written system of standards for ethical conduct. The code contains statements designed to advise, guide, and regulate behavior. To be effective, a code of ethics must be specific by dictating rules that either prohibit or demand certain behavior. By including sanctions for violators, a code of ethics becomes more effective.

REALTORS® are expected to subscribe to NAR's Code of Ethics. NAR has established procedures for professional standards committees at the local, state, and national levels of the organization to administer compliance to the Code of Ethics. Practical applications of the articles of the code are known as Standards of Practice. The NAR Code of Ethics contains practical applications of business ethics. It can be found at www.nar.realtor/about -nar/governing-documents/code-of-ethics.

www.nar.realtor/about
-nar/governing
-documents/code-of
-ethics

The National Association of Real Estate Brokers (NAREB), whose members are known as *Realtists*, also adheres to a Code of Ethics. NAREB arose out of the early days of the civil rights movement as an association of racial minority real estate brokers in response to the www.nareb.com

conditions and abuses that eventually gave rise to fair housing laws. Today, NAREB remains dedicated to equal housing opportunity and can be found at www.nareb.com.

Many other professional organizations in the real estate industry also have codes of ethics. In addition, many state real estate commissions are required by law to establish codes or canons of ethical behavior for the state's licensees.

TECHNOLOGY IN REAL ESTATE PRACTICE

Most real estate agencies have websites that provide access to extraordinary databases for property and other searches. Trade associations and MLSs form the backbone for much of this information. The National Association of REALTORS® has adopted an **Internet Data Exchange (IDX) policy** that allows all MLS members to have equal rights to display MLS data, while also respecting the rights of the property owner and the real estate broker who represents the property owner to market a property as they wish. A *blanket opt-out* provision provides that those MLS participants interested in keeping their listings from competitors' websites cannot then display other real estate brokers' listings. Real estate brokers who opt out of displaying their listings on competitors' websites can, at the direction of a seller, make an exception and display the seller's property on the MLS website. The NAR IDX policy, which is updated often, can be found at www.nar.realtor/about-nar/policies/internet-data-exchange -idx.

www.nar.realtor/about -nar/policies/internet -data-exchange-idx

While the internet can provide a vast amount of information, much of that information is unverified or comes from questionable sources. Many real estate websites, particularly those that provide links to other sources, have **disclaimers** to indicate that the material on the site is solely for informational purposes and that no warranties or representations have been made. When information is taken from the internet, the source should be one that is known to be reliable.

www.realtor.com
www.zillow.com
www.trulia.com
www.nahb.org

NAR has a property search site available at www.realtor.com, providing consumers access to millions of property listings. Other sites that provide information on current property listings, as well as information on property sales and taxes are www.zillow.com and www.trulia.com. The National Association of Home Builders, www.nahb.org, provides data on new home construction, building materials costs, and building permits issued.

Real estate professionals can purchase website management tools to help with their marketing efforts. These tools help assess the effectiveness of internet marketing by providing statistics on the number of people visiting the site, the most visited pages of the site, the page used to enter and exit the site, and the operating system and browser used by visitors, among other data.

Communication in a digital age

The use of the internet as a means of communication has continued to expand. Just when the latest program or device gains popularity, a new one emerges to eclipse it.

Smartphones

The mobile phone has rapidly evolved from the expensive and clumsy apparatus of the early 1980s to today's sleek smartphone that can provide internet access as well as most of the program capabilities of a computer including document review, modification, and exchange; data storage; photography, and video conferencing.

Email/texting

Email and texting have made communication between real estate professionals and consumers more efficient. Email is an excellent opportunity for the ongoing marketing of a business. Contact information should be kept up to date and appear in every message. State licensing regulations may specify the information that should be provided in every client or customer communication, including electronic communications. Laws against unwanted email messages are discussed later, in the section on prohibited communications.

In communicating with clients or consumers via email, the best practice is to use the subject line in a useful and helpful manner, avoid spelling errors, respond promptly to all email messages, be specific and brief, and pay attention to the size of any file attachments. Never send unsolicited email messages.

The same type of recommendations apply to text messages, which are rapidly overtaking email as the preferred method of client contact. Be clear while being concise, making sure that the subject of the message isn't lost, and avoid too many acronyms. State law may require that all communications by a real estate professional include the licensee's name, address, license number, and (for a sales associate) the name of the employing broker.

Social media

Social media

www.facebook.com

www.twitter.com

www.instagram.com

www.snapchat.com

www.linkedin.com

The latest methods of communicating via the internet include Facebook, Twitter, Instagram, Snapchat, and LinkedIn. Facebook, www.facebook.com, allows users to post a page of information and receive and send messages from identified friends. A real estate professional can establish a presence on Facebook but should always be mindful that information available to the public imposes a level of restraint on comments and photos posted to avoid embarrassment or even potential liability.

Twitter, www.twitter.com, allows users to post short messages called tweets of no more than 140 characters that can be read by others who follow that user. Tweets can be a useful and entertaining way of gathering comments from a number of people on a variety of issues, from politics to entertainment.

Instagram, www.instagram.com, and Snapchat, www.snapchat.com, are other services that allow display of photos and videos, as well as messages.

LinkedIn, www.linkedin.com, emphasizes business networking by allowing users to post resumes and to join groups of those who share similar interests. When users update their information, members of their groups receive those updates. Users can also post announcements or messages to members of their groups, allowing others to post comments or responses in return.

Internet advertising

State laws vary regarding internet advertising. It is important for you to check your own state's laws before engaging in advertising and other marketing activities on the internet. In addition to NAR's Internet Data Exchange policy, internet advertising laws and regulations frequently include the following stipulations:

- All electronic communication by a real estate professional must include the professional's name, office address, and broker affiliation.

- Real estate professionals must disclose their license status on each page of a website that contains an advertisement.

- The listing of only a sales associate's name without the sponsoring broker's name in an advertisement is prohibited.

- An advertisement must be a true, current representation of the information it contains and not be misleading.

Electronic contracting

The legal requirements for a contract will be discussed later, but it is worth noting here that technology and the internet have significantly changed the way in which real estate transactions are performed. **Electronic contracting** is a growing part of real estate practice because it quickly and efficiently integrates information in a real estate transaction between clients, lenders, and title and closing agents. The transactions are conducted through email or fax and can save both time and money.

Two federal acts govern electronic contracting: the **Uniform Electronic Transactions Act (UETA)** and the **Electronic Signatures in Global and National Commerce Act (E-Sign)**.

The Uniform Electronic Transactions Act (UETA) was created by the National Conference of Commissioners on Uniform State Laws, www.uniformlaws.org. At present, UETA has been adopted by all but three states (Illinois, New York, and Washington). The law sets forth basic rules for entering an enforceable contract using electronic means. The primary purpose of UETA is to remove barriers in electronic commerce that would otherwise prevent enforceability of contracts. UETA validates and effectuates electronic records and signatures in a procedural manner and is intended to complement a state's digital signature statute, but it does not in any way require parties to use electronic means. UETA's four key provisions are the following:

- A contract cannot be denied its legal effect just because an electronic record was used.

- A record or signature cannot be denied its legal effect just because it is in an electronic format.

- If a state's law requires a signature on a contract, an electronic signature is sufficient.

- If a state's law requires a written record, an electronic record is sufficient.

www.uniformlaws.org

The Electronic Signatures in Global and National Commerce Act (E-Sign) was passed by Congress in 2000. E-Sign functions as the electronic transactions law in states that have not enacted UETA, and some sections of E-Sign apply to states that have enacted UETA. The purpose of E-Sign is to make contracts (including signatures) and records legally enforceable, regardless of the medium in which they are created. For example, contracts formed using email or transmitted electronically rather than by paper have the same legal significance as those formed on paper.

IN PRACTICE

When entering into a residential sales agreement, it is important for the parties to feel comfortable with and clearly communicate the method chosen for transacting the agreement, whether by paper and ink or by email.

Prohibited communications

Businesses must comply with a variety of prohibitions intended to protect consumers from the intrusions of unwanted communications.

In 2003, federal do-not-call legislation was signed into law, and the Do Not Call Improvement Act of 2007 further strengthened the protections available to consumers. Real estate professionals must comply with the provisions of the **National Do Not Call Registry**, which is managed by the Federal Trade Commission (FTC). The registry is a list of telephone numbers from consumers who have indicated their preference to limit the telemarketing calls they receive. The registry applies to any plan, program, or campaign to sell goods or services through interstate phone calls. The registry does not limit calls by political organizations, charities, collection agencies, or telephone surveyors. The law does apply to a for-profit telemarketer, even if the telemarketer is working for a nonprofit organization. Information for consumers and businesses can be found at www.donotcall.gov.

www.donotcall.gov

Telemarketers and sellers are required to search the registry at least once every 31 days and drop registered consumer phone numbers from their call lists. Normal business relationships are still possible. Real estate professionals may call consumers with whom they have an established business relationship for up to 18 months after the consumer's last purchase, delivery, or payment, even if the consumer is listed on the National Do Not Call Registry. Also, a real estate professional may call a consumer for up to three months after the consumer makes an inquiry or submits an application. Note that if a consumer asks a company not to call, despite the presence of an established business relationship, the company must abide by the consumer's request, which stays in effect permanently.

Even though the federal legislation applies to interstate telephone calls, most states also have do-not-call rules or regulations that apply to in-state calls. It is important to keep up to date with state laws regarding do-not-call policies, as well as the national law.

Similar federal and state laws apply to marketing and business communications by fax and email. The Telephone Consumer Protection Act (TCPA), Junk Fax Prevention Act, and rules of the Federal Communications Commission (FCC) prohibit most unsolicited fax advertisements. There is an exemption for faxes sent as part of an established business relationship. More information can be found at www.fcc.gov/consumers/guides/faqs-about -junk-faxes.

www.fcc.gov
/consumers/guides
/faqs-about-junk-faxes

Junk emails (spam) are prohibited by the federal Controlling the Assault of Non-Solicited Pornography and Marketing Act of 2003, known as the CAN-SPAM Act. An important feature of this law, which applies to commercial electronic mail messages, is that email solicitations must include a means by which the recipient can "unsubscribe" from future messages. A compliance guide for businesses is available at www.ftc.gov/tips-advice/business -center/guidance/can-spam-act-compliance-guide-business.

www.ftc.gov/tips-ad-
vice/business-center/
guidance/can-spam
-act-compliance-guide
-business-act-compli-
ance-guide-business

Additional restrictions on the use of the internet, including mobile apps and ad networks, went into effect on July 1, 2013, as part of the ongoing Children's Online Privacy Protection Act (COPPA). COPPA requires the posting of a privacy policy and limits the personal information that can be collected from children younger than 13, even if a website or app is directed toward a general audience. Details of the law can be obtained at www.ftc.gov/tips -advice/business-center/privacy-and-security/children%27s-privacy.

www.ftc.gov/tips
-advice/business
-center/privacy-and
-security/children%27s
-privacy

KEY POINT REVIEW

All 50 states, Canadian provinces, and the District of Columbia have real estate license laws and rules with the force and effect of law that establish basic requirements for obtaining a real estate license, define which activities require licensing, and enforce standards through a disciplinary system.

A real estate **broker** is licensed to buy, sell, exchange, or lease real property for others for a fee and may operate as a sole proprietorship, partnership, corporation, or limited liability company.

The real estate **brokerage** may be independent or part of a regional or national franchise.

A real estate **sales associate** is a salesperson or broker who is licensed to perform real estate activities **only** on behalf of a licensed real estate broker. The **broker-employer** is liable for the actions of the **sales associate** within the scope of the **employment agreement** or as provided by state law.

An **independent contractor** is an employee who usually receives a commission, with no withholding for Social Security, income tax, and other purposes and has the freedom to set hours and accomplish goals. A real estate broker always has liability and supervisory responsibilities for the real estate related work activities of a sales associate.

An **employee** may receive salary in lieu of or in addition to commission; may receive benefits, such as health insurance, profit-sharing, and workers' compensation; and has an employer who is required to withhold Social Security, income taxes, and other applicable federal and state taxes from earnings. The employer sets hours, duties, and other specifics of the employee's day-to-day work and remains liable for related work activities of the employee.

There are Internal Revenue Service (IRS) requirements for a **qualified real estate agent** to be treated as a **nonemployee** for tax purposes.

A real estate **assistant** may be a licensed employee of the employing broker who is compensated by the broker, or, if unlicensed, is paid by either the sales associate or broker and is limited in the activities that can be undertaken.

A broker's **compensation** can be a **commission** based on a property's sales price, a **flat fee**, or an **hourly rate**.

A broker's **commission** is earned when the seller accepts an offer from a **ready, willing, and able buyer** prepared to buy on the seller's terms and ready to take positive steps toward consummation of the transaction.

A sales associate's compensation is set by mutual agreement of the employing broker and the sales associate.

Fee for services means that a broker's compensation is based on charges for separate activities that the client desires (unbundling of services). Some states now require **minimum services** to be offered by the broker.

Antitrust laws are both state and federal (**Sherman Antitrust Act**) and prohibit **monopolies**, and contracts, combinations, and conspiracies that unreasonably restrain trade, including

- **price-fixing,**
- **group boycott,**

- **allocation of customers or markets**, and

- **tie-in agreements** (tying agreements) that force customers to purchase a product when only another was wanted.

Professional organizations can assist in setting a high level of conduct among real estate professionals by establishing and enforcing a code of ethics.

The **Internet Data Exchange (IDX) policy** of the National Association of REALTORS® allows members to limit the internet distribution of listing information. Overall, the **internet** is invaluable for communication, research, marketing, and advertising of a brokerage and includes the use of email, websites, and social networking, all of which must be conducted in compliance with applicable federal and state laws.

Electronic contracting must take into account the **Uniform Electronic Transactions Act (UETA)**, which has been adopted in most states and the **Electronic Signatures in Global and National Commerce Act (E-Sign)**, which functions as the **electronic transactions** law in states that have not enacted UETA and makes contracts (including signatures) and records legally enforceable, regardless of the medium in which they are created.

Do-not-call legislation is found at federal and state levels. The **National Do Not Call Registry** (regulated by the **Federal Trade Commission**) lists telephone numbers of consumers who have asked to be registered and prohibits interstate calls to those numbers to sell goods or services.

Many states provide their own do-not-call legislation for in-state calls. Other prohibited communications include those defined in the laws regulating junk faxes, as well as the **CAN-SPAM Act**.

Restrictions on collection of information from children younger than 13 by means of the internet, including mobile apps, are specified in **COPPA**, the **Children's Online Privacy Protection Act**.

UNIT 8 QUIZ

1. Which statement *BEST* explains this sentence: "To recover a commission for brokerage services, a broker must *be employed* by a client"?
   A. The broker must work in a real estate office.
   B. The client must make an express or implied agreement to pay a commission to the broker.
   C. The broker must express an interest in representing the client.
   D. The broker must have a sales associate employed in the office.

2. Sales associates who are paid in a lump sum and who are personally responsible for paying their own taxes are probably treated for tax purposes as
   A. employees.
   B. buyer's agents.
   C. independent contractors.
   D. transactional brokers.

3. A sales associate's contract with her broker states that she is not an employee. In the past year, less than half her income was commission, with the rest an hourly wage paid by the broker. The IRS would classify her as
   A. self-employed.
   B. an employee.
   C. an independent contractor.
   D. a part-time real estate salesperson.

4. When acting as an employee rather than an independent contractor, a sales associate may be obligated to
   A. list properties in the sales associate's own name.
   B. work set hours.
   C. accept a commission from another broker.
   D. personally pay all withholding taxes.

5. Terry is the personal assistant of a real estate sales associate. Terry must be paid by the broker who employs the sales associate. This means that
   A. Terry has a real estate license.
   B. the sales associate doesn't make very much money.
   C. Terry is a part-time employee.
   D. ultimate responsibility for Terry's conduct in the performance of work-related activities lies with the sales associate.

6. A broker would have the right to dictate which of the following to an independent contractor?
   A. Number of hours the person would have to work
   B. Work schedule the person would have to follow
   C. Sales meetings the person would need to attend
   D. Conduct in compliance with statutory law and regulations

7. Two real estate professionals were found guilty of conspiring with each other to allocate real estate brokerage markets. A seller suffered an estimated $90,000 loss because of their activities. If the seller brings a civil suit against the two real estate professionals, what can the seller expect to recover?
   A. Nothing, because a civil suit cannot be brought for damages resulting from antitrust activities
   B. Only $90,000—the amount of actual damages the seller suffered
   C. Actual damages plus attorney's fees and costs
   D. $270,000 plus attorney's fees and costs

8. Two sales associates who work for the same firm agree to divide their town into a northern region and a southern region; one sales associate will handle listings in the north, and the other will handle listings in the south. Which statement is *TRUE*?
   A. The agreement does not violate antitrust laws.
   B. The agreement constitutes illegal price-fixing.
   C. The two sales associates have violated the Sherman Antitrust Act and are liable for treble damages.
   D. The two sales associates are guilty of a group boycott with regard to other sales associates in their firm.

9. A state has recently updated its Rules and Regulations for the Real Estate Profession. Which statement is most likely *TRUE* regarding this update?
   A. The rules and regulations are state laws enacted by the legislature.
   B. The rules and regulations do not have the same force and effect as the statutory license law.
   C. The rules and regulations have the same force and effect as the license law itself.
   D. The rules and regulations are not enforceable against real estate professionals.

10. A REALTOR® is *BEST* described as an individual who is
    A. a real estate professional who acts as a point of contact between two or more people in negotiating the sale, purchase, or rental of property.
    B. any real estate professional who assists buyers, sellers, landlords, or tenants in any real estate transaction.
    C. a member of the National Association of Real Estate Brokers who specializes in residential properties.
    D. a real estate licensee and a member of the National Association of REALTORS® (NAR).

11. A broker has established the following office policy: "All listings taken by any sales associate of this real estate brokerage must include compensation based on a 7% commission. No lower commission rate is acceptable." If the broker attempts to impose this uniform commission requirement, which statement is *TRUE*?
    A. A homeowner may sue the broker for violating the antitrust law's prohibition against price-fixing.
    B. The sales associates of the brokerage will not be bound by the requirement and may negotiate any commission rate they choose.
    C. The broker must present the uniform commission policy to the local professional association for approval.
    D. The broker may, as a matter of office policy, legally set the minimum commission rate acceptable for the firm.

12. A real estate company has adopted a 100% commission plan. The monthly desk rent required of sales associates is $1,500, payable on the last day of the month. In August, a sales associate closed a transaction that earned a commission of $11,370 and a second transaction that earned a commission of $6,875. The sales associate's additional expenses for the month were $2,170. How much of the total monthly income did the sales associate keep?
    A. $14,575
    B. $16,075
    C. $16,745
    D. $18,245

13. A sales associate took a listing on a house that sold for $329,985. The commission rate was 5%. A sales associate employed by another broker found the buyer. The seller's broker received 60% of the commission on the sale; the buyer's broker received 40%. If the seller's broker kept 30% and paid the seller's sales associate the remainder, how much did the seller's sales associate earn on this sale?
    A. $4,346.85
    B. $5,774.74
    C. $6,929.68
    D. $8,249.00

14. On the sale of any property, a sales associate's compensation is based on the total commission paid to the broker. The sales associate receives 30% of the first $2,500, 40% of the next amount between $2,500 and $7,500, and 50% of any remaining amount exceeding $7,500. If a property sells for $234,500 and the broker's commission rate is 6.5%, what is the sales associate's total compensation?
    A. $5,847.00
    B. $6,621.25
    C. $6,871.25
    D. $7,621.25

15. The federal law that makes contracts originated, negotiated, and executed over a combination of computer and cell phone enforceable is
    A. CAN-SPAM.
    B. Junk Fax Prevention Act.
    C. COPPA.
    D. UETA.

16. The amount of commission paid to a sales associate is determined by
    A. state law.
    B. the local real estate board.
    C. mutual agreement with the broker.
    D. mutual agreement with the client.

17. A broker was accused of violating antitrust laws. Of the following, the broker was *MOST* likely accused of
    A. not having an equal housing opportunity sign in the office window.
    B. undisclosed dual agency.
    C. price-fixing.
    D. dealing in unlicensed exchange services.

18. A real estate broker was responsible for a chain of events that resulted in the sale of a client's property. This is called
    A. pro forma.
    B. procuring cause.
    C. private offering.
    D. proffered offer.

19. A sales associate wants to be classified by the IRS as a qualified real estate agent—the equivalent of holding independent contractor status for tax purposes. The sales associate must meet all of the following requirements *EXCEPT*
    A. receive substantially all income from the brokerage based on production, not time worked.
    B. perform all work unsupervised by the managing broker.
    C. hold a current real estate license.
    D. have a written agreement with the broker stating that the sales associate will not be treated as an employee for federal tax purposes.

20. A real estate sales associate, classified by the IRS as an independent contractor, receives
    A. a monthly salary or hourly wage.
    B. company-provided health insurance.
    C. a company-provided automobile.
    D. a negotiated share of commissions on transactions.

UNIT
9

Real Estate Agency

LEARNING OBJECTIVES

When you have completed this unit, you will be able to

> **explain** agency concepts and terminology;
> **explain** express and implied agency and an agent's fiduciary duties;
> **define** the types of agency and **identify** which, if any, are involved in real estate practice; and
> **describe** an agent's duties to third-party customers, especially regarding misstatements, misrepresentation, and potential fraud.

KEY TERMS

agency	express agency	listing agreement
agent	express agreement	negligent misrepresentation
buyer representation	fiduciary	nonagent
agreement	fiduciary relationship	principal
buyer's agent	fraud	puffing
client	general agent	single agency
customer	implied agency	special agent
designated agency	implied agreement	transaction broker
designated agent	latent defect	universal agent
dual agency	law of agency	

OVERVIEW

The relationship between a real estate professional and the parties involved in a real estate transaction is not a simple one. A real estate professional can represent a client as an **agent**, but in addition to the parties' assumptions and expectations, the real estate professional acts as a **fiduciary** and is subject to a wide range of legal and ethical requirements designed to protect the seller, the buyer, and the transaction itself. There are other **agency** relationships in the real estate business, including that of sales associate to the employing broker. We will look at the possible agency relationships in a real estate transaction, as well as other types of relationships that can be established.

HISTORY OF AGENCY

Agency relationships in real estate transactions are governed by three kinds of law, which have been mentioned earlier, including

- *common law*, the rules established by tradition and court decisions;

- *statutory law*, the laws enacted by the legislature; and

- *administrative law*, the rules and regulations created by real estate commissions and departments, as authorized by the legislature.

The fundamentals of agency law have remained largely unchanged for hundreds of years, but the nature of real estate brokerage services, particularly those provided in residential sales transactions, has changed significantly in the last half-century.

In the 1950s, the common law doctrine of *caveat emptor* ("let the buyer beware") was the norm; buyers were pretty much on their own. It should have been clear that the real estate broker represented the seller's interests, but buyers often failed to realize that fact.

In the 1960s, the way that buyers and sellers were brought together in real estate transactions began to change. Brokers started to share information about properties they listed, which often resulted in two brokers cooperating to sell a property. The brokers formalized this exchange of information by creating the multiple listing service (MLS). The MLS expedited sales by increasing a single property's exposure to more brokers, and thus more potential buyers. Because it generated more sales, the MLS quickly became a widely used industry service. But one thing remained the same: both brokers still represented the seller's interest. The listing broker had a direct agency relationship with the seller, and the selling broker worked with the listing broker as a subagent of the seller. Because two different brokers would take part in a transaction, it was even less apparent to the buyer that the obligation of both was to work on behalf of the seller.

By the early 1990s, buyers began to demand that they be represented, too. They came to expect not only accurate, factual information but also objective advice, particularly in the face of increasingly complex real estate transactions. As a result, state laws and regulations (and subsequently, MLS rules) were changed to allow a broker to represent a buyer and share in the commission paid to the seller's broker. Buyers have learned to view the real estate professional as the expert on whom they can rely for guidance, and a large percentage of sales contracts are now written by buyer agents.

A real estate broker must comply with the laws and regulations regarding all aspects of a transaction, but an increasing number of brokers are choosing to represent buyers exclusively, just as some brokers prefer to represent sellers. In any case, brokers also must decide how they will cooperate with other brokers, in compliance with the rules of the MLS.

The relationship of a real estate broker and consumer may not be an agency relationship, and other forms of representation that are recognized by state laws will be discussed here. Even as the elements of real estate practice change, however, the underlying assumptions that govern an agency relationship remain intact. Those assumptions are discussed next.

Definitions

The **law of agency,** whether expressed in the common law or statutes, typically includes the following definitions:

An **agent** is a person authorized to act on behalf of the **principal** in dealings with a **third person**.

- **Agent**—the individual who is authorized and consents to represent the interests of another person in dealings with a third person. Many different agency relationships are possible in a real estate transaction. The sales associates of a real estate broker act as agents (representatives) of the broker. In a real estate transaction, a firm's broker will be the agent of a client and may share this responsibility with the sales associates who work for the firm. As agents of the broker, the sales associates historically have had the same relationship to a client of the firm that the broker does. Because of the number of transactions that are "in-house" (the same firm dealing with both seller and buyer), it is now possible for a sales associate to represent a buyer as the buyer's designated agent, even when the sales associate's firm also represents the seller in the transaction.

- **Principal**—the individual who hires the agent and delegates to that agent the responsibility of representing the principal's interests. In a real estate transaction in which an agency relationship is established, the principal is the buyer or the seller or the landlord or the tenant. The broker is the principal in dealings with sales associates.

- **Agency**—the fiduciary relationship between the principal and the agent by which the agent is authorized to represent the principal in one or more transactions.

- **Fiduciary**—the relationship in which the agent is held in a position of special trust and confidence by the principal.

- **Client**—the principal in a real estate transaction for whom a real estate broker acts as agent. The term *client* is also used when a broker represents someone in a relationship other than an agency.

- **Customer**—the third party or nonrepresented consumer who is not a principal but for whom some level of service may be provided and who is entitled to fairness and honesty. The customer may be represented by a separate agent.

- **Nonagent**—(also referred to as a *facilitator, intermediary, transactional broker, transaction coordinator,* or *contract broker*) someone who works with a buyer and a seller (or a landlord and a tenant), assisting one or both parties with the transaction without representing either party's interests. Nonagents are often subject to specific statutory responsibilities. A broker may be considered a nonagent when dealing with a customer (someone other than the person the broker represents).

IN PRACTICE

The general discussion here involves the concepts and principles that govern traditional common law agency relationships. Many states have passed agency legislation that supersedes the common law of agency.

Many agency statutes make the common law duties a matter of statutory law rather than (or in addition to) creating totally new legal relationships. While we are providing an overview of current agency laws, a real estate professional should be familiar with the specific terms of any agency statute adopted by the legislature of the state in which the real estate professional does business. The websites listed in the appendix provide access to statutory law, as well as the rules and regulations of each state's real estate licensing agency.

The client is the principal to whom the agent gives advice and counsel. The agent is entrusted with certain *confidential information* and has *fiduciary responsibilities* (discussed in greater detail later) to the principal. The client can expect full disclosure of all relevant information learned by the agent. In contrast, the *customer* is entitled to factual information and fair and honest dealings as a consumer but does not receive advice and counsel or have an expectation that information disclosed to the agent will remain confidential. The agent works *for* the principal and *with* the customer. This means that the agent supports and defends the principal's interests, not the customer's.

The relationship between the principal and agent must be *consensual*—that is, the principal *delegates* authority, and the agent *consents* to act. The parties must agree to form the relationship.

Just as the agent owes certain duties to the principal, the principal has responsibilities toward the agent. The principal's primary duties are to comply with the agency agreement and cooperate with the reasonable expectations of the agent—that is, the principal must not hinder the agent and must deal with the agent in good faith. The principal also must compensate the agent according to the terms of the agency agreement.

CREATION OF AGENCY

Later, you will learn the legal requirements to create a contractual relationship, along with descriptions of the varieties of contracts that are part of a real estate transaction. Here, some of the elements of an agreement to create an agency relationship are discussed.

An agency relationship may be created by an oral or written agreement between the parties, which is an **express agency**. An agency relationship may also result from the parties' behavior, creating an **implied agency**.

The state may require the real estate licensee to make written disclosure of the possible agency relationships to a prospective client or customer, and stipulate the relationship that will be in effect, in a document that is signed by both the licensee and the client or customer.

Express agency

The principal and the agent may enter into a contract, or an **express agreement**, in which the parties formally express their intention to establish an agency and state its terms and conditions. The agreement may be either oral or written, unless a written agreement is required by law. The employment agreement of broker and sales associate must be in writing.

An agency relationship between a real estate seller and a broker is generally created by a written employment contract, commonly called a **listing agreement** (*seller representation agreement*), which authorizes the broker to find a buyer or a tenant for the owner's property. Although a written listing agreement is usually preferred, some states consider an oral agreement binding in some circumstances, although an exclusive representation agreement must be in writing in order to be enforced in court.

An express agency relationship between a buyer and a broker is created by a **buyer representation agreement**. Similar to a listing agreement, the buyer representation agreement stipulates the activities and responsibilities the buyer expects from the broker in finding the appropriate property for purchase or rent.

Implied agency

An agency may also be created by **implied agreement**. This occurs when the parties act as though they have mutually consented to an agency, even if they have not entered into a formal agency agreement. While neither the real estate professional nor the represented party may have consciously planned to create an agency relationship, they can create one *unintentionally*, *inadvertently*, or *accidentally* by their actions. If the existence of an agency relationship becomes the focus of a legal action, the real estate professional may be in a lose-lose position. If an agency relationship can be shown to have been intended, legal responsibilities may be imposed on the real estate professional even in the absence of a written agency agreement. The real estate professional may also be denied compensation on the grounds that there is no written agreement, as required by law.

IN PRACTICE

Prospective buyers enter a real estate office asking to see a property listed with another brokerage. A real estate sales associate immediately calls the sellers' representative and makes an appointment to show the property. Without having the prospective buyers sign a written representation agreement, the sales associate drives them to the house. The intent of the parties to create an agency relationship can be inferred from the actions of the sales associate.

Even though real estate professionals might be required to disclose their agency status, consumers often find it difficult to understand the complexities of the law of agency. Buyers can easily assume that when they contact a real estate sales associate in order to be shown a property, the real estate sales associate becomes their agent, even though, under the listing contract on the property, the real estate sales associate (through the broker) legally represents the seller. An implied agency with the buyer can result if the words and conduct of the sales associate do not dispel this assumption, which may lead to the creation of an illegal undisclosed dual agency (discussed later). Some states prohibit the creation of agency implied by conduct.

Compensation

In a real estate transaction, *the source of compensation does not determine agency*. An agent does not necessarily represent the person who pays the agent's commission. In fact, agency can exist even if no fee is involved (called a *gratuitous agency*).

The seller's agency agreement may allow the seller's broker to make use of the services of other real estate professionals in the broker's firm, as well as other real estate professionals who are part of the broker's MLS. Under such an arrangement, the compensation for a cooperating broker will be paid by the seller's broker out of the commission paid by the seller. A **buyer's agent** could instead be paid directly by the buyer, which is common in commercial, but not residential, real estate transactions. Any written agency agreement (with seller or buyer) should state how the agent is to be compensated, after all the alternatives are discussed with the client.

Remember, a real estate sales associate can only receive compensation from the sales associate's employing broker.

Unit 9

Memory tip

The six common-law fiduciary duties of an agent are COLD-AC:

Care

Obedience

Loyalty

Disclosure

Accounting

Confidentiality

Fiduciary responsibilities

The agency agreement between a broker and client usually authorizes the broker to act on the principal's behalf. The agent's **fiduciary relationship** of trust and confidence means that the real estate broker owes the principal certain duties. These duties are not simply moral or ethical, they are the law—the common law of agency and/or the statutory law governing real estate transactions. Under the common law of agency, an agent owes the principal the six duties of *care, obedience, loyalty, disclosure, accounting,* and *confidentiality,* which can be remembered as COLD-AC.

Care

Agents must exercise a reasonable degree of care while transacting the business entrusted to them by principals. Principals expect the agent's skill and expertise in real estate matters to be superior to that of the average person. The most fundamental way in which an agent exercises care is to use that skill and knowledge on a principal's behalf. The agent should know all facts pertinent to the principal's affairs, such as the physical characteristics of the property being transferred and the type of financing being used.

If the agent represents the seller, care and skill include helping the seller arrive at an appropriate and realistic listing price, discovering and disclosing facts that affect the seller, and properly presenting, as allowed by law, the contracts and other documents that the seller signs. It also means making reasonable efforts to market the property, such as advertising and holding open houses, and helping the seller evaluate the terms and conditions of offers to purchase.

A real estate broker who represents the buyer is expected to help the buyer locate suitable property and evaluate property values and neighborhood and property conditions, and complete offers and counteroffers, as allowed by law, with the buyer's interest in mind.

A representative who does not make a reasonable effort to properly represent the interests of the principal may be found negligent by a court of law. The representative is liable to the principal for any loss resulting from the representative's negligence or carelessness.

IN PRACTICE

Because real estate firms have, under the law, exposure to liability in what is ordinarily a very expensive and complex transaction, some brokers purchase what is known as *errors and omissions* (E&O) *insurance*. Similar to malpractice insurance in the medical and legal fields, E&O policies cover liability for errors and negligence in the listing and selling activities of a real estate broker and often the broker's sales associates. Some E&O insurance companies also offer policies directly to individual sales associates. Licensing laws in several states now require E&O insurance for brokers and, in some cases, for individual sales associates as well. No insurance policy will protect a real estate professional from a lawsuit or prosecution arising from criminal acts. Insurance companies normally exclude coverage for fraud and violations of civil rights and antitrust laws.

Obedience

The fiduciary relationship obligates an agent to act in good faith at all times, obeying the principal's lawful instructions in accordance with the contract. That obedience is not absolute, however. The agent does not have to obey instructions that are unlawful or unethical. On the other hand, an agent who exceeds the authority assigned in the contract will be liable for any losses that the principal suffers as a result.

Loyalty

The duty of loyalty requires that the agent place the principal's interests above those of all others, including the agent's own self-interest. The agent must be particularly sensitive to any possible conflicts of interest. Because the agent may not act out of self-interest, the negotiation of a sales contract must be conducted without regard to how much the agent will earn in commission. All states forbid agents to buy property listed with them for their own accounts or for accounts in which they have a personal interest without first disclosing that interest and receiving the principal's consent. Neither real estate brokers nor real estate sales associates may sell property in which they have a personal interest without informing the purchaser of that interest.

Disclosure

It is the agent's duty to keep the principal informed of all facts or information that might affect a transaction. The *duty of disclosure* includes relevant information or *material facts* that the agent knows or in some cases should have known.

The real estate agent is obligated to discover facts that a reasonable person would feel are important in choosing a course of action, regardless of whether those facts are favorable or unfavorable to the principal's position. The agent may be held liable for damages for failing to disclose such information. Depending on state law, information that must be disclosed in a sales transaction could include

- the identity of prospective purchasers, which may include any relationships the purchasers might have with the agent (such as when a relative or associate of the agent is a purchaser);
- the purchaser's ability to complete the sale or offer a higher price;
- any interest or prospective interest the agent has in the buyer or the buyer's business (such as the broker's agreement to manage the property after it is purchased); and
- an incorrect market value of the property.

A seller's real estate agent is also expected (and required under many states' laws) to disclose information about known material defects in the property to prospective buyers. This may appear to violate the agent's duty of loyalty to the seller, but this requirement falls under the broader duty to serve the general public and can protect the agent from claims of misrepresentation.

In turn, the buyer's agent must disclose deficiencies of a property and the sales contract provisions and financing that may affect the buyer's decision to purchase. The buyer's agent would suggest the lowest price the buyer should pay based on comparable values, regardless of the listing price. If known, the agent would also disclose how long a property has been listed and why the owner is selling, because such information would affect the buyer's ability to negotiate the lowest purchase price. If the agent represents the seller, of course, disclosure of any of this information without the seller's permission would violate the agent's fiduciary duty to the seller.

Other disclosures are discussed later.

IN PRACTICE

Selling a property "as is" does not negate provisions already in the contract. If the seller truly means "as is," any printed provisions in the contract that relate to the condition of systems and appliances should be amended. The seller must still comply with state laws regarding disclosure of the condition of the property, and selling a property "as is" does not affect the buyer's right to request an inspection of the property. A buyer is free to accept a property in its current condition but has the right to know what that condition is. The buyer is also free to waive the right to a property inspection, if that appears reasonable under the circumstances.

Accounting

The agent must be able to report the status of all funds received from or on behalf of the principal. Most state laws require that a real estate professional give accurate copies of all documents to all affected parties and keep copies on file for a specified period. Most license laws also require monies to be deposited into an escrow account immediately, or within a specified time. Commingling client monies with personal or general business funds is always illegal. *Conversion* is the illegal use of such entrusted money.

Confidentiality

Confidentiality is a key element of fiduciary duties. An agent may not disclose the principal's personal information—for example, the principal's financial condition. If the principal is the seller, the agent may not reveal such things as willingness to accept less than the listing price or urgency to sell, unless the principal has authorized the disclosure, and often the authorization must be in writing. If the principal is the buyer, the agent may not disclose the buyer's willingness to pay a higher price, the buyer's tight moving schedule, or other buyer facts that might affect the principal's bargaining position.

The information that must be kept confidential can change if the business relationship changes, such as when a seller's agent also represents the buyer in what is called *dual agency*.

Depending upon state law, the duty of confidentiality could terminate on conclusion of the agency relationship, or it could extend for a number of years, or forever. Under the NAR Code of Ethics, the duty of confidentiality does not expire. Anything a REALTOR® learns about a client that can be considered confidential must remain confidential forever. Check your state's laws for guidance in dealing with confidentiality issues.

TYPES OF AGENCY RELATIONSHIPS

An agency relationship can be classified based on the extent of the agent's authority. An agent's authority to represent the principal can be broad, or it can include only a certain type of activity or a specific transaction.

A **universal agent** is a person empowered to do anything the principal could do personally. The universal agent's authority to act on behalf of the principal is virtually unlimited. A court-appointed guardian, for instance, will have the authority granted by the court, which can include caring for both the person and the property of the guardian's ward—the individual who is the subject of the guardianship. A real estate professional typically does not have this scope of authority in a real estate transaction.

A **general agent** may represent the principal in a broad range of matters related to a particular business or activity. The general agent may, for example, bind the principal to any contract within the scope of the agent's authority. An entertainer may employ more than one general agent—an agent to find work, as well as a business manager to hire and supervise staff and make other arrangements. A *property manager* hired by the owner of income-producing property is typically a general agent for the owner. A real estate sales associate usually is a general agent of the employing broker, authorized to act as the subagent of the broker in a variety of transactions.

A **special agent**, or *limited agent*, is authorized to represent the principal in one specific act or business transaction only. A real estate broker is usually a special agent. If hired by a seller, the broker is limited to finding a ready, willing, and able buyer for the seller's property. A special agent for a buyer would have the limited responsibility of finding a property that fits the buyer's criteria. A special agent for a tenant will find a property that meets the client's requirements. As a special agent, the real estate broker may not bind the principal to any contract.

> A **general agent** represents the principal in certain business matters *generally*; a **special agent** represents the principal only for *specified transactions*, such as the sale of a house.

Disclosure of agency

Real estate professionals are required to disclose the parties they represent. Understanding the scope of the service a party can expect from the agent allows consumers to make an informed decision about whether to seek their own representation.

Mandatory agency disclosure laws now exist in every state. These laws stipulate when, how, and to whom disclosures must be made. They may, for instance, dictate that a particular type of written form be used. The laws might require that all agency alternatives be explained, including the brokerage firm's policies regarding the firm's services. Frequently, printed brochures outlining agency alternatives are available to a firm's clients and customers.

Whether or not the law requires it, real estate professionals should explain to both buyers and sellers what agency alternatives exist. Good business practice is to make the disclosure of agency before any confidential information is disclosed about an individual's motivation or financial situation. Learn your state's real estate agency disclosure requirements. It may be useful to compare your state's disclosure requirements with those of another state. Here are some examples:

> www.arec.alabama
> .gov/AREC_Bookmark
> /ViewLaw.aspx
> ?LawSectionID=103
>
> www.irec.idaho
> .gov/publcs/agency
> -disclosure-brochure
> .pdf
>
> www.revisor.mn
> .gov/statutes/?id=82.67

Alabama has a Consumer Information Booklet that includes the Real Estate Brokerage Services Disclosure form at www.arec.alabama.gov/AREC_Bookmark/ViewLaw.aspx ?LawSectionID=103.

Idaho's agency disclosure brochure is at www.irec.idaho.gov/publcs/agency-disclosure -brochure.pdf.

Minnesota's agency disclosure requirements can be found at www.revisor.mn.gov/statutes/?id= 82.67.

Single agency

In **single agency**, the agent represents only one party to a transaction. The real estate agent must provide fiduciary common law or statutory duties exclusively to one principal within the transaction (who may be *either* the buyer or the seller—or the landlord or the tenant). The customer is the party not represented by the agent. (See Figure 9.1.)

FIGURE 9.1: Single Agency

While a single agency broker may represent both sellers and buyers (or landlords and tenants) in separate transactions, that broker cannot represent both the buyer and the seller (or the landlord and the tenant) in the same transaction and remain a single agent. Single agency thus avoids conflicts and results in client-based service and loyalty to only one principal in any transaction. On the other hand, it necessarily limits the broker's client base by ruling out the sale of in-house listings to prospective buyers.

Another agency relationship that involves one principal and one agent is the relationship between a real estate broker and a sales associate of that broker. The employing broker is the principal, and the sales associate is authorized to conduct real estate business only as an agent of the employing broker. The sales associate owes the broker the same fiduciary duties that the broker owes to the client—the broker's principal. The sales associate owes those fiduciary duties to the client as well because, as the agent of the broker, the sales associate is the *subagent* of the client.

Seller representation

If a seller enters a listing agreement with a broker to market the seller's real estate, the broker becomes an *agent* of the seller; the seller is the *principal*, the broker's *client*. The broker is obligated to deal honestly with all parties in the transaction and act within the licensing law. The broker is strictly accountable to the principal. The listing contract, the document that usually forms the agency relationship of broker and seller, typically authorizes the broker to use the services of sales associates employed by the broker, as well as the services of other cooperating brokers in marketing the seller's real estate.

Buyer representation

A buyer who contracts with a broker to locate property and represent the buyer's interests in a transaction is the *principal*—the broker's client. The broker, as *agent*, is strictly accountable to the buyer.

Although it has been customary in commercial transactions, *buyer agency* is relatively new to residential practice but is quickly becoming a popular area of expertise. Real estate commissions or boards across the country have developed rules and procedures to regulate the buyer's agent. Local real estate associations have developed agency representation forms and other materials specifically for the buyer's agent. Professional organizations offer assistance, certification, training, and networking opportunities.

A buyer agency relationship is established in the same way as any other agency relationship: by contract or agreement. The buyer's agent may receive a flat fee or a share of the commission or both, depending on the terms of the agency agreement.

Property management

An owner may employ a broker to market, lease, maintain, or manage the owner's property. Such an arrangement is known as *property management*. The broker is made the agent of the property owner through a property management agreement. As in any other agency relationship, the broker has a fiduciary or statutory responsibility to the client-owner. Sometimes, an owner may employ a broker for the sole purpose of marketing the property to prospective tenants. In this case, the broker's responsibility is limited to finding suitable tenants for the owner's property. Some states recognize a special real estate license for those who exclusively handle property rentals.

A broker can also represent the tenant of either residential or commercial property. A knowledgeable real estate broker is an important resource for a transferred employee needing suitable housing, as well as for the owner of a business seeking to find a larger (or smaller) property or expand to an additional location.

Dual agency

In **dual agency**, the agent represents two principals in the same transaction. Dual agency requires equal loyalty to two different principals at the same time—a high burden that means neither principal has the full, undivided loyalty of the agent. Dual agency arises, for example, when a real estate broker is the agent of both the seller and the buyer. The broker's sales associates, as agents of the broker, also have fiduciary or statutory responsibilities to the same principals. The challenge is to fulfill these fiduciary obligations to one principal without compromising the interests of the other. While practical methods of ensuring fairness and equal representation may exist, it should be noted that a dual agent can never fully represent either party's interests because the duty of undivided loyalty cannot be shown to both principals at the same time. Similarly, it is impossible to maintain both confidentiality and full disclosure to parties whose interests are in opposition. (See Figure 9.2.)

FIGURE 9.2:   Dual Agency

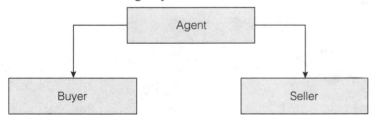

Because of the risks inherent in dual agency—ranging from conflicts of interest to outright abuse of trust—the practice is illegal in some states. In those states where dual agency is permitted, all parties must consent to the arrangement, usually (and always preferably) in writing.

Disclosed dual agency

Although a conflict of interest still exists, disclosure is intended to minimize the risk for the broker. The disclosure alerts the principals that they might have to assume greater responsibility for protecting their interests than they would if they had independent representation. Because the duties of disclosure and confidentiality are sometimes limited by mutual agreement, they must be carefully explained to the parties in order to establish informed consent.

IN PRACTICE

A real estate broker is the agent for the owner of a condominium. A prospective buyer comes into the broker's office and asks her to represent him in a search for a single-family home on a large lot. After several weeks of activity, including two offers unsuccessfully negotiated by the broker, the prospective buyer decides to make an offer on a condominium that he has seen on the broker's website. He tells the broker that he wants to make an offer and asks for the broker's advice on a likely price range. The broker is now in the difficult position of potentially being a dual agent. The broker explains what would be her role as a dual agent—to both the condo seller and the prospective buyer. Both agree that she should represent both of them and both sign the agency disclosure form required by the state. The broker now represents both the seller (who naturally is interested in receiving the highest possible price for his condominium) and the buyer (who is interested in making a successful low offer).

Undisclosed dual agency

A broker may not intend to create a dual agency. It might occur *unintentionally* or *inadvertently*. Sometimes the cause is carelessness. Other times, a sales associate does not fully understand the fiduciary responsibilities of agency. Some sales associates lose sight of other responsibilities when they focus intensely on bringing buyers and sellers together. For instance, a sales associate representing the seller might suggest to a buyer that the seller will accept less than the listing price. Or the same sales associate might promise to persuade the seller to accept an offer that is in the buyer's best interests. Giving a buyer any specific advice on how much to offer can lead the buyer to believe that the sales associate represents the buyer's interests and is acting as the buyer's advocate.

Any of these actions can create an **implied agency** with the buyer and violate the duties of loyalty and confidentiality to the principal-seller. Because neither party has been informed of the situation and given the opportunity to seek separate representation, the interests of both are jeopardized. This undisclosed dual agency violates licensing laws. It can result in the rescission of the sales contract, forfeiture of a commission, a lawsuit for damages, and possible license problems.

IN PRACTICE

In the situation described earlier, if the broker doesn't tell the prospective buyer that she represents the seller of the property, she will be an undisclosed dual agent. The broker has two options. First, knowing the prospective buyer's comfortable financial situation and intense desire for the property, she might choose not to tell the buyer about the dual agency situation. Instead, she could tell him that the condominium's owner will accept nothing less than the full asking price. While this will ensure that the broker receives the maximum possible commission, it will also subject her to severe penalties for violating the state's licensing laws. Alternatively, she can disclose her relationship with the seller, and then she has several options. She could work out a dual agency agreement with both parties in which she legally represents both parties' interests. She could refer the buyer to another broker, enabling her to avoid even the appearance of a conflict of interest. She could also leave the buyer unrepresented.

Designated agency, also called *assigned agency* or *appointed agency*, is available in some states to accommodate an *in-house* sale in which two sales associates of the same broker are involved. The broker designates one sales associate to represent the seller and another sales associate to represent the buyer. Thus, a **designated agent**, or designated representative, is the only sales associate in the company who has a fiduciary responsibility toward the principal. When one sales associate in the company is a designated agent, the other sales associates are free to represent (through the broker) the other party in a transaction. Disclosure of the designated agent status of the sales associates to both parties is required, as is the consent of both parties to the arrangement.

Nonagency

A **nonagent** (also called a **transaction broker**, *facilitator*, *transaction coordinator*, or *contract broker*) is not an agent of either party. A nonagent's job is simply to help both the buyer and the seller with the necessary paperwork and formalities involved in transferring ownership of real property—what may be referred to as *ministerial acts*.

The nonagent is expected to treat all parties honestly and competently, to locate qualified buyers or suitable properties, to help the parties arrive at mutually acceptable terms without acting on behalf of either side, and to assist in the closing of the transaction. The nonagent is equally responsible to both parties and must disclose known defects in a property; however, the nonagent may not negotiate on behalf of either the buyer or the seller and must not disclose confidential information to either party. The buyer and the seller negotiate the sale without the services of the real estate agent(s), though one or both parties may be represented by an attorney during that process.

Termination of agency

An agency may be terminated for any of the following reasons:

- Completion, performance, or fulfillment of the purpose for which the agency was created
- Death or incapacity of either party
- Destruction or condemnation of the property
- Expiration of the terms of the agency
- Mutual agreement by all parties to cancel the contract
- Breach by one of the parties
- By operation of law, as in bankruptcy of the principal (bankruptcy terminates the agency contract and title to the property transfers to a court-appointed receiver)

An agency coupled with an interest cannot be revoked by the principal acting alone, and it is not terminated upon the principal's death. An agency coupled with an interest will occur, for example, when a real estate agent is made a part-owner of a property that is the subject of a transaction.

Even though an agency relationship has terminated, the fiduciary responsibilities of the agent, such as the duty of confidentiality, might continue.

CUSTOMER-LEVEL SERVICES

Even though an agent's primary responsibility is to the principal, the agent also has duties to third parties. When working with a third party, or **customer**, a real estate professional is responsible for adhering to state and federal consumer protection laws, as well as the ethical requirements imposed by professional associations and state regulators. In addition, the real estate professional's duties to the customer typically include

An agent owes a **customer** the duties of *reasonable care and skill, honest and fair dealing*, and *disclosure of known facts* about the property.

- reasonable care and skill in performance,

- honest and fair dealing, and

- disclosure of all facts that the real estate professional knows or should reasonably be expected to know that materially affect the value or desirability of the property.

Opinion vs. fact

Real estate brokers and sales associates must always be careful about the statements they make. They must be sure that the consumer understands whether a statement is an opinion or a fact. Statements of opinion are permissible if not made carelessly and there is no intention to deceive.

Statements of fact, however, must be accurate. Exaggeration of a property's benefits is called **puffing**. While puffing is legal, real estate professionals must ensure that none of their statements can be interpreted as fraudulent. For REALTORS®, puffing is considered unethical even if it is legal. **Fraud** is the intentional misrepresentation of a material fact in such a way as to harm or take advantage of another person. That includes not only making false statements about a property but also intentionally concealing or failing to disclose important facts when there is a duty to disclose.

IN PRACTICE

While showing a potential buyer an average-looking house, the sales associate described even its plainest features as "charming" and "beautiful." Because the statements were obviously the sales associate's personal opinions designed to encourage a positive feeling about the property (or puff it up), the truth of the statements is not an issue.

The misrepresentation or omission does not have to be intentional to result in real estate professional liability. A **negligent misrepresentation** occurs when the real estate professional should have known that a statement about a material fact was false. A real estate professional's lack of awareness of an issue is no excuse. A misrepresentation due to the professional's carelessness will make the professional culpable (subject to liability). If the buyer relies on the real estate professional's statement, the professional will be liable for any damages that result. Similarly, a real estate professional who accidentally fails to perform some act—for instance, forgetting to deliver a counteroffer—may be liable for damages that result from such a negligent omission. Simple negligence can result in an accidental misrepresentation and, while some damages may result, they may be covered by the real estate professional's errors and omissions insurance.

Disclosures

As part of the recent trend for more consumer protection for purchasers, many states have enacted statutes requiring the disclosure of known adverse property conditions to prospective buyers. Generally, these apply to sellers of residential properties, often for those of one to four dwelling units. Prepurchased structural inspections, termite infestation reports, or other protective documentation may also be used. The actual disclosures that sellers are required to make vary according to each state's law.

Environmental hazards

Disclosure of environmental health hazards, which can render properties unusable for the buyer's intended purpose, may be required. For instance, federal law requires the disclosure of lead-based paint hazards. Frequently, the buyer or the buyer's mortgage lender requests inspections or tests to determine the presence or level of risk.

IN PRACTICE

Real estate professionals are encouraged to obtain advice from state and local authorities responsible for environmental regulation whenever the following conditions might be present: toxic-waste dumping; underground storage tanks; contaminated soil or water; nearby chemical or nuclear facilities; and health hazards such as radon, asbestos, and lead paint.

Property conditions

In residential transactions involving property of up to four units, the seller typically has a duty to disclose any known defects that threaten structural soundness or personal safety. A **latent defect** is a hidden structural defect that would not be discovered by ordinary inspection. Buyers may cancel the sales contract or receive damages when a seller fails to reveal known latent defects. The courts also have decided in favor of the buyer when the seller neglected to reveal violations of zoning or building codes. Increasingly, however, there is a growing trend of not only the right but the responsibility of the buyer to discover any material problems with the property. Some states allow the seller to provide a nondisclosure statement to the buyer that places the burden of discovering any adverse property conditions on the buyer.

In addition to the seller's duty in most states to disclose known latent defects, in some states, the agent has an independent duty to conduct a reasonably competent and diligent inspection of the property. It is the real estate professional's duty to discover any material facts that may affect the property's value or desirability, whether or not they are known to or disclosed by the seller. Any such material facts discovered by the real estate professional must be disclosed to prospective buyers. If the real estate professional should have known about a substantial defect that is detected later by the buyer, the real estate professional may be liable to the buyer for any damages resulting from that defect.

IN PRACTICE

A broker knew that a house had been built on a landfill. A few days after the house was listed, one of the broker's salespeople noticed that the living room floor was uneven and sagging in places. In some states, both the broker and the salesperson have a duty to conduct further investigations into the structural soundness of the property. (See *Easton v. Strassburger*, 152 Cal. App. 3d 90, a 1984 California case.) In other states, no such duty exists, but the broker and the salesperson would have the duty of discussing the issue with the seller and advising the buyer to have an inspection performed. They cannot simply ignore the problem or place throw rugs over particularly bad spots and hope buyers won't look underneath. If the seller refuses to disclose the problem, then the broker should refuse the listing.

Stigmatized properties

Stigmatized properties are those that society has found undesirable because of events that occurred there or because of proximity of the property to a known nuisance. A common stigma is a criminal event, such as a homicide, illegal drug manufacturing, gang-related activity, or a suicide. Properties have even been stigmatized by rumors that they are haunted. Because of the potential liability to a real estate professional for inadequately researching and disclosing material facts concerning a property's condition, real estate professionals should be fully aware of any relevant state laws.

IN PRACTICE

A broker was asked by a potential buyer if a particular neighborhood was safe. The broker knew that the area was experiencing a skyrocketing rate of violent crime but assured the buyer that no problem existed. The broker also neglected to inform the buyer that the lot next to the house the buyer was considering had been sold to a waste disposal company for use as a toxic dump. Both might be examples of fraudulent misrepresentation.

Some states have laws regarding the disclosure of information about such properties, designed to protect sellers, real estate professionals, and local property values against a baseless psychological reaction. In other states, the real estate professional's responsibility may be difficult to define because the issue is not a physical defect but merely a perception that a property is undesirable. Many states provide greater statutory direction to real estate professionals by identifying stigmas that are not considered material facts and that therefore do not require disclosure. Federal law may also provide guidance.

IN PRACTICE

A disclosure that a property's previous owner or occupant died of AIDS or was HIV positive constitutes illegal discrimination against a person with a disability under the federal Fair Housing Act and therefore should never be revealed. State law may provide the same prohibition.

Megan's Law

The federal legislation known as Megan's Law promotes the establishment of state registration systems to maintain residential information on every person who kidnaps children, commits sexual crimes against children, or commits sexually violent crimes. Upon release from prison, offenders must register their name with state authorities and indicate where they will be residing, and also inform authorities of a change of residence. The Federal Bureau of Investigation (FBI) maintains an internet site, www.fbi.gov/scams-and-safety/sex-offender-registry, which provides online access to every state's offender registry.

www.fbi.gov/scams
-and-safety/sex
-offender-registry

Megan's Law affects a real estate professional's duty of disclosure. In accordance with state law, a real estate professional may need to request that a customer sign a form that includes information on where the customer may obtain information about the sex offender registry. Depending on the state, a real estate professional may be required to disclose information regarding a released offender if the real estate professional is aware that officials have informed individuals, groups, or the public that a sex offender resides in a particular area. Megan's Law, in effect, creates another category of stigmatized property.

KEY POINT REVIEW

Real estate agency relationships are governed by **common law**, which is established by tradition and court decisions, and **statutory law**, which is passed by state legislatures and other governing bodies.

An **agent** is hired by a principal to act on the principal's behalf. **Agency** is the fiduciary relationship in which the agent is held in a position of special trust and confidence by the principal. In a real estate transaction, the **principal** is the **client**. A **customer** is the nonrepresented party for whom some level of service is provided and who is entitled to fairness and honesty.

A subagent is authorized to work with the agent on behalf of the client. A **nonagent** (also known as a **facilitator**, **intermediary**, **transaction broker**, **transaction coordinator**, or **contract broker**) assists one or both parties with the transaction without representing either party's interests and often is subject to specific statutory responsibilities.

The relationship between principal and agent must be **consensual**. As **express agency** is based on an express agreement between agent and principal, while an **implied agency** will be created when the actions of the parties indicate that they have mutually consented to an agency. The source of the agent's **compensation** does not determine the agency, because the agent may be compensated by someone other than the client, or the agency may exist even if no compensation is involved—a **gratuitous agency**.

An agent has a **fiduciary relationship** of trust and confidence with the principal. The six common-law fiduciary duties can be remembered as **COLD-AC**, which is an acronym for the following:

- **C**are
- **O**bedience
- **L**oyalty
- **D**isclosure
- **A**ccounting
- **C**onfidentiality

A **universal agent** is empowered to do anything the principal could do personally.

A **general agent** represents the principal in a broad range of matters.

A **special agent** represents the principal in one specific act or business transaction only, under detailed instruction.

A **single agency** is one in which an agent represents only one party in a transaction. A real estate broker becomes an agent of the seller by entering into a listing agreement for the seller's property. A **buyer's broker** represents a buyer as an agent to find property that meets the buyer's specifications, as set out in the **buyer representation agreement**.

A **dual agency** is one in which an agent represents two principals in the same transaction. Dual agency, where allowed by state law, requires the **informed consent** of both principals. An **undisclosed dual agency**, which may occur inadvertently, can result in rescission of the sales contract, forfeiture of a commission, a lawsuit for damages, and possibly license suspension or revocation.

A **designated agent** (or **designated representative**) is a sales associate authorized by the broker to represent one party to a transaction, while a different sales associate in the same firm represents the other party to the transaction.

Termination of agency may be accomplished by the

- completion, performance, or fulfillment of purpose of agency;
- destruction or condemnation of the property;
- expiration of the terms of the agency;
- mutual agreement of all parties to the contract;
- breach by one of the parties, who may be liable for damages; or
- operation of law, as in the bankruptcy of the principal.

An **agency coupled with an interest** cannot be revoked by the principal or terminated upon the principal's death.

Statements to clients and customers should be clearly identified as **opinion** or **fact. Puffing** is legal exaggeration of a property's benefits, while **fraud** is the intentional misrepresentation of a material fact to harm or take advantage of another person.

A **negligent misrepresentation** occurs when a real estate professional **should have known** that a statement about a material fact was false and the real estate professional's misrepresentation was due to culpable (careless) negligence rather than simple (accidental) negligence.

The **seller** of residential property may have the duty to disclose any known **latent** (i.e., hidden) **defects** that threaten a building's structural soundness or an occupant's personal safety. In some states, an agent has an independent duty to conduct a **reasonably competent and diligent inspection** of the property and to disclose defects to prospective buyers. Disclosure of environmental hazards may be required.

Stigmatized properties may require an agent to consult an attorney. **Megan's Law** requires states to make available to the public information about how they can determine where persons convicted of sexual offenses live in the community.

UNIT 9 QUIZ

1. In a real estate transaction, the term *fiduciary* typically refers to
   A. the sale of real property.
   B. the people who give someone else the legal power to act on their behalf.
   C. the person who has legal power to act on behalf of another.
   D. the agent's relationship to the principal.

2. The relationship between real estate broker and seller is generally what type of agency?
   A. Special
   B. General
   C. Implied
   D. Universal

3. Which statement is *TRUE* of a real estate broker acting as the agent of the seller?
   A. The broker is obligated to render loyalty to the seller.
   B. The broker can disclose confidential information about the seller to a buyer if it increases the likelihood of a sale.
   C. The broker can agree to a change in price without the seller's approval.
   D. The broker can accept a commission from the buyer without the seller's approval.

4. A real estate broker lists a home for sale for $189,500. Later that same day, a prospective buyer comes into the broker's office and asks for general information about homes for sale in the $130,000 to $140,000 price range but refuses representation by the broker's company at this time. Based on these facts, which statement is *TRUE*?
   A. Both the seller and the potential buyer are the broker's customers.
   B. The seller is the broker's client; the buyer is a customer.
   C. The broker owes fiduciary duties to both seller and buyer.
   D. If the buyer later asks for buyer representation by the broker's firm, it will not be possible because of the firm's earlier agreement with the seller.

5. In a dual agency situation, if it is permitted by state law, a broker may represent both the seller and the buyer in the same transaction provided
   A. the broker informs either the buyer or the seller of this fact.
   B. the buyer and the seller are related by blood or marriage.
   C. both parties consent in writing to the dual agency.
   D. both parties are represented by attorneys.

6. Which event will terminate an agency in a broker-seller relationship?
   A. The broker discovers that the market value of the property is such that an adequate commission will not be earned.
   B. The owner declares personal bankruptcy.
   C. The owner abandons the property.
   D. The broker appoints other brokers to help sell the property.

7. Designated agency is *MOST* likely to occur when
   A. there is a client-buyer and a customer-seller.
   B. the seller and the buyer are represented by different companies.
   C. both the buyer and the seller are customers.
   D. the buyer and the seller are represented by the same company.

8. A real estate broker hired by an owner to sell a parcel of real estate must comply with
   A. the common law of agency in the state in which the property owner lives.
   B. a prospective buyer's instructions.
   C. the concept of caveat emptor.
   D. all lawful instructions of the owner.

9. Which of the following is *NOT* a valid reason to terminate an agency relationship?
   A. The agent found a home for a buyer to purchase, and the sale closed.
   B. The property was condemned.
   C. The buyer wanted to work with a new agent, but the terms of agency had not yet expired and the current agent did not agree to terminate.
   D. The buyer went bankrupt.

10. A seller tells his agent in confidence that he must sell fast and may accept less than the list price. The agent tells a buyer the seller will accept up to $5,000 less than the list price. Which is *TRUE*?
    A. The agent has not violated any agency responsibilities to the seller.
    B. The agent should have disclosed this information, regardless of its accuracy.
    C. Disclosure was improper and possibly illegal, regardless of the agent's motive.
    D. The relationship between the agent and the seller ends automatically if the purchaser submits an offer.

11. A buyer who is a client of the broker wants to purchase a house that the broker has listed. Which statement is *TRUE*?
    A. The broker may proceed to write an offer on the property and submit it.
    B. The broker should refer the buyer to another broker to negotiate the sale.
    C. The seller and the buyer must be informed of the situation and agree in writing to the broker's representing both of them.
    D. The buyer should not have been shown a house listed by the broker.

12. What does the phrase *the law of agency is a common law doctrine* mean?
    A. It is a legal doctrine that is not unusual.
    B. It is one of the rules enacted by legislatures and other governing bodies.
    C. It is part of a body of law established by tradition and court decisions.
    D. It may not be superseded by statutory law.

13. A broker helps a buyer and a seller with paperwork but does not represent either party. This relationship is
    A. dual agency.
    B. prohibited in all states because a broker must always represent one party.
    C. a transactional brokerage.
    D. a designated agency.

14. A real estate sales associate represents a buyer. At their first meeting, the buyer reveals plans to operate a doggrooming business out of the purchased house. The sales associate did not check the local zoning ordinances to determine in which parts of town such a business could be conducted. Which common law duty did the sales associate violate?
    A. Care
    B. Obedience
    C. Loyalty
    D. Disclosure

15. A broker tells a buyer, "This home has the most beautiful river view." In fact, the view includes the river and the back of a shopping center. Which is *TRUE*?
    A. The broker has committed fraud.
    B. The broker is guilty of negligent misrepresentation.
    C. The broker is guilty of intentional misrepresentation.
    D. The broker is merely puffing.

16. A real estate broker's responsibility to keep the principal informed of all the facts that might affect a transaction is the duty of
    A. care.
    B. disclosure.
    C. obedience.
    D. accounting.

17. Which of the following is considered dual agency?
    A. A broker acting for both parties in the same transaction
    B. Two brokerage companies cooperating with each other
    C. A broker representing more than one principal
    D. A broker listing a property and then, after it is relisted with another broker, selling the same property

18. The relationship of broker to client in an agency relationship is that of
    A. a trustee.
    B. a subagent.
    C. a fiduciary.
    D. an attorney-in-fact.

19. A real estate broker acting as the agent of the seller
    A. must promote and safeguard the seller's best interests.
    B. can disclose the seller's minimum price.
    C. should present to the seller only the highest offer for the property.
    D. can accept an offer on behalf of the seller.

20. A broker is permitted to represent both the seller and the buyer in the same transaction when
    A. the principals are not aware of such action.
    B. the broker is a subagent rather than the agent of the seller.
    C. commissions are collected from both parties.
    D. both parties have been informed and agree in writing to the dual representation.

UNIT 10

Client Representation Agreements

LEARNING OBJECTIVES

When you have completed this unit, you will be able to

> **describe** the different types of listing agreements and how they may be terminated;
> **describe** the listing presentation and the information needed for a listing agreement;
> **identify** the listing agreement terms and the responsibilities of both parties; and
> **describe** the types of buyer representation agreements and how they may be terminated.

KEY TERMS

buyer representation agreement	exclusive agency listing	multiple listing service (MLS)
comparative market analysis (CMA)	exclusive buyer representation agreement	net listing
	exclusive right-to-sell listing	open listing

OVERVIEW

A variety of contracts are used throughout the typical real estate sales transaction, including the agreement between a broker and a sales associate; the terms by which the broker makes use of the multiple listing system; the contract that allows the broker to list property for sale; the agreement by which a buyer makes use of the services of a broker; the sales contract that set out the terms of the transaction; and the escrow, title insurance, and other agreements that are required to complete the transaction.

In this unit, we will look at the agreements by which a broker can be employed to act for a seller or a buyer.

REPRESENTING THE SELLER

The employment contract between a broker and a real estate seller is commonly called the *listing agreement*. It is a contract for the professional services of the real estate broker by which the broker is authorized to represent the principal (and the principal's real estate) to consumers. That authorization includes obtaining and submitting offers for the property. As previously discussed, the real estate sales associate's authority to provide brokerage services originates with the broker. Even though the real estate sales associate may perform most, if not all, of the listing services, the listing remains with the broker, who is responsible for the conduct of the sales associate. The sales associate acts as the agent of the broker and the subagent of the seller.

Types of listing agreements

The type of listing agreement used by broker and client determines the rights and obligations of the parties. A listing agreement can be *exclusive* to one broker or made available to multiple brokers. *All states require that an exclusive listing agreement be in writing to be enforceable in court.* (See Figure 10.1.)

FIGURE 10.1: Types of Listing Agreements

Exclusive Right to Sell	Exclusive Agency	Open Listing
Seller employs one broker	Seller employs one broker	Seller employs multiple brokers
Listing broker is paid regardless of who sells the property.	Listing broker is paid only if procuring cause of sale.	Only successful listing broker is paid.
	Seller retains the right to sell without obligation to listing broker.	Seller retains the right to sell without obligation to any listing broker.

Exclusive right-to-sell listing

Exclusive right-to-sell listing
- One authorized listing broker receives a commission.
- Seller pays listing broker regardless of who sells the property.

In an **exclusive right-to-sell listing**, one broker is employed as the seller's sole representative. The listing broker is given the exclusive right, or authorization, to market the seller's property. If the property is sold while the listing agreement is in effect, the seller must pay the broker a commission, *regardless of who sells the property*. In other words, if the seller finds a buyer, with or without the broker's assistance, the seller must pay the broker a commission.

Sellers benefit from this form of agreement because the broker can expend time and money actively marketing the property, making a timely and profitable sale more likely. From the broker's perspective, an exclusive right-to-sell listing offers the greatest opportunity to receive a commission. Because of the protection it offers the broker, many brokers have an office policy that sales associates may only take exclusive right-to-sell listings.

Exclusive agency listing

Exclusive agency listing
- There is one authorized agent.
- Broker receives a commission only if the procuring cause.
- Seller retains the right to sell without obligation.

In an **exclusive agency listing**, one broker is authorized to act as the exclusive agent of the principal, but *the seller retains the right to sell the property without the obligation to pay the broker*. When a request is made by a property owner for this type of agreement, the broker would, understandably, be very reluctant to list the property. The request usually means that the seller is reasonably confident of having the contacts needed to be able to sell the property directly and is only listing the property with a broker to show that the offer to sell is sincere.

For the broker, this type of listing is very risky and somewhat odd because the broker is placed in the position of making the effort to market the property only to be in competition with the client to find a buyer.

Open listing

Open listing

■ There are multiple agents.
■ Only the selling agent is entitled to a commission.
■ Seller retains the right to sell independently without obligation.

In an **open listing** (also known in some areas as a *nonexclusive listing*), the seller retains the right to employ any number of brokers as agents. The listing brokers market the property simultaneously, and the seller is obligated to pay a commission only to the listing broker who successfully produces a ready, willing, and able buyer. If the seller personally sells the property without the aid of any of the listing brokers, the seller is not obligated to pay a commission to any of them.

The terms of an open listing must be negotiated and should be in writing to protect the successful listing broker's ability to collect an agreed-on fee from the seller. An offer to purchase brought to the seller by a buyer's broker should specify the commission or fee to be paid to the buyer's broker out of the sale proceeds, unless the buyer has agreed to compensate the broker by a separate commission or fee.

Net listing

In a **net listing**, the broker is entitled to any amount exceeding the seller's stated net proceeds.

A **net listing** provision specifies that the seller will receive a net amount of money from any sale, with the excess going to the listing broker as commission. The broker is free to offer the property at any price greater than that net amount. Because a net listing can create a conflict of interest between the broker's fiduciary responsibility to the seller and the broker's profit motive, it is illegal in many states and discouraged in others.

Listings involving cooperating brokers

A *multiple listing clause* may be included in an exclusive listing. It is used by brokers who are members of the **multiple listing service (MLS)**. As previously discussed, the MLS is a marketing organization whose broker members make their own exclusive listings available through other brokers who participate in the MLS and gain access to other brokers' listed properties as well. The broker must have the written consent of the seller (which is provided by including the multiple listing clause in the listing agreement) to include the property in an MLS.

The MLS offers advantages to brokers, sellers, and buyers. Brokers develop a sizable inventory of properties and are assured at least a portion of the sales commission if a listing the broker places in the MLS is sold by a participating broker or if the broker sells another broker's listing. Property owners benefit because properties are exposed to a larger market and buyers benefit because they gain access to a wide variety of properties.

The contractual obligations among the member brokers of an MLS vary widely. Most MLSs require that a broker turn over new listings to the service within a specific, fairly short period of time after the broker obtains the listing. The length of time during which the listing broker can offer a property exclusively without notifying the other member brokers varies. Some MLSs permit a broker up to five days before the listing must be submitted to the service.

Under the provisions of most MLSs, a participating broker makes a unilateral offer of cooperation and compensation to other member brokers. The offer is accepted when a *cooperating broker* brings a buyer to the seller and a sale takes place. The cooperating broker typically may choose to work on the seller's behalf as a subagent who bears the same fiduciary responsibilities to the seller as the seller's broker, or the cooperating broker may work as the representative of the buyer. Whether the cooperating broker acts as a subagent of the seller, a *buyer's representative*, or in some other capacity permitted by state law, all initial communication about a buyer's interest in a listed property is broker to broker through the MLS.

IN PRACTICE

Technology has enhanced the benefits of MLS membership. In addition to providing instant access to information about the status of listed properties, MLSs often offer a broad range of other useful information about mortgage loans, real estate taxes and assessments, and municipalities and school districts. Access to the MLS database of active, pending, sold, and expired listings is especially helpful to the real estate professional who needs to suggest an appropriate range of listing prices for a particular property. Computer-assisted searches also help buyers select properties that best meet their needs, narrowing the search parameters before a real estate professional is contacted.

Termination of seller representation

The success of a contract to represent a property seller depends on the broker's professional efforts. Because the broker's services are unique, the agreement to list property for sale cannot be assigned to another broker without the principal's written consent. The property owner cannot force the broker to perform, but the broker's failure to work diligently toward fulfilling the contract's terms constitutes a breach of the listing agreement. If the listing is canceled by the broker, the seller may be entitled to sue the broker for damages.

On the other hand, a property owner could be liable for damages to the broker by refusing to cooperate with the broker's reasonable requests, such as not allowing the broker to show the property to prospective buyers or refusing to proceed with an accepted sales contract.

A broker's agreement to represent a property seller may be terminated for the following reasons:

■ The agreement's purpose is fulfilled by the transfer of title to the buyer.

■ The agreement's term expires.

■ The property is destroyed, or its use is changed by some force outside the owner's control, such as a zoning change or condemnation by eminent domain.

■ Title to the property is transferred by operation of law, as in the case of the owner's bankruptcy or foreclosure.

■ The broker and the seller mutually agree to cancel the agreement.

■ Either the broker or the seller breaches the agreement, such as by the seller's refusal to consider an offer or the broker's refusal to present an offer to the seller.

■ Either the broker or the seller dies or becomes incapacitated. If a sales associate dies or becomes incapacitated, the agreement is still valid.

Expiration of listing period

All exclusive listings should specify a definite period during which the broker is to be employed. In most states, failing to specify a definite termination date in a listing is grounds for the suspension or revocation of a real estate license.

Legislatures and courts also have prohibited or discouraged the use in exclusive listings of *automatic extension clauses*, such as a clause providing for a base period of 90 days that "continues thereafter until terminated by either party hereto by 30 days' notice in writing." Extension clauses are illegal in some states, and many listing contract forms specifically provide (as may be required by law) that there can be no automatic extension of the agreement. Some courts have held that an extension clause actually creates an open listing rather than an exclusive agency agreement.

Some listing contracts contain a *broker protection clause*. This clause provides that the property owner will pay the listing broker a commission if, within a specified number of days after the listing expires, the owner transfers the property to someone the broker originally introduced to the owner. This clause protects a broker from losing a commission in the event that the transaction is not completed (and, perhaps, is intentionally delayed) until after the listing expires.

THE LISTING PRESENTATION

The first opportunity that a property owner has to learn what a real estate brokerage can do to bring about a sale of the owner's property typically is in a *listing presentation* made by a sales associate of the broker. The sales associate will describe the marketing efforts that the brokerage will make to sell the property as quickly as possible.

Before initiating a contract that will go to the broker for review and signature, the sales associate and prospective seller will discuss a variety of issues. The property owner's main concerns typically are the selling price of the property and the net proceeds. The sales associate should already have performed a **comparative market analysis (CMA)**, also known as a competitive market analysis, and should be prepared to discuss the range of value in which the property is likely to fall, as well as the charges that will affect the amount that the seller will receive. The CMA is not a formal appraisal, which must meet separate licensing and other requirements, but instead looks at properties on the market that are similar to the property the seller owns in size, location, and amenities. The sales associate, by examining MLS data, can consider the asking prices of properties currently available, as well as the sales prices of properties that have sold recently and the asking prices on property listings that have expired without a sale being achieved. All of this information should make it easier for the seller to decide on a suitable asking price for the subject property.

Common questions property owners may ask include "How quickly will the property sell?" and "What services will the broker provide during the listing period?" The property owner will also want to know whether the property's condition is suitable for showing to prospective buyers, or if certain improvements should be made. This is the sales associate's opportunity to explain the various types of listing agreements, the ramifications of different agency relationships, the marketing services the broker provides, and the other services, such as "staging" the property to make it as attractive as possible, that could be used to help market the property effectively. At the end of this discussion, the seller should have an idea of what is involved in the sale process and should feel comfortable with the decision to list with the brokerage.

The sales associate will also have questions for the property owner. Before the listing agreement is signed, the seller should provide comprehensive information about the property and indicate any personal concerns about the sale process. Based on this information, the broker can accept the listing with confidence that the seller's goals can be met in a profitable manner for both parties.

Information needed for a listing agreement

Obtaining as many facts as possible about the property ensures that most contingencies can be anticipated. This is particularly important when the listing will be shared with other brokers through the MLS and those real estate professionals must rely on the information taken by the sales associate acting for the listing broker.

The information needed for a listing agreement generally includes the

- names and relationship, if any, of the owners;
- street address and legal description of the property;
- size, type, age, and construction of improvements;
- number of rooms and their sizes;
- dimensions of the lot;
- existing loans, including the name and address of each lender, the type of loan, the loan number, the loan balance, the interest rate, the monthly payment of principal, interest, taxes, and insurance (PITI), whether the loan may be assumed by the buyer and under what circumstances, whether the loan may be prepaid without penalty, and whether or not the lender has approved a *short sale* (one in which the sales price is less than the amount of the outstanding loan balance) and, if so, whether the seller will incur a personal debt for the difference;
- possibility of seller financing or willingness to agree to a lease option in which the property is leased to a prospective buyer who will have the right to purchase the property during or at the end of the lease term at an agreed-upon price;
- amount of any outstanding special assessments and whether they will be paid by the seller or assumed by the buyer;
- zoning classification of the property;
- current (or most recent year's) property taxes;
- neighborhood amenities (e.g., schools, parks and recreation areas, places of worship, and public transportation);
- real property, if any, to be removed from the premises by the seller and any personal property to be included in the sale for the buyer (both the listing contract and the subsequent purchase contract should be explicit on these points);
- any additional information that would make the property more appealing and marketable; and
- required disclosures regarding property condition.

Disclosures

Most states have enacted laws requiring that real estate professionals disclose whose interests they legally represent. It is important that the seller be informed of the company's policies regarding single agency, subagency, buyer agency, dual agency, and any other forms of representation allowed by state law. State law may require a written acknowledgment of required agency disclosures and the seller's agreement to a stated form of representation.

The residential property owner must also disclose the property's condition, as required by law in most states. Property condition disclosures cover a wide range of structural, mechanical, and other conditions that a prospective purchaser should know about in order to make an informed decision. Frequently, state law requires that the property owner complete a standardized form that may require the owner to indicate the condition of specific property features, such as heating and plumbing systems. A real estate professional should always caution a property owner to make truthful disclosures to avoid litigation arising from fraudulent or careless misrepresentations. The real estate professional, while not responsible for investigating the seller's property disclosures, may not conceal property defects that should be readily apparent to the licensee.

THE LISTING CONTRACT

Real estate firms, local and state trade associations, and other groups have worked with their attorneys to draft standardized listing contracts that meet the needs of real estate brokers and their clients, and also comply with the laws and regulations that define acceptable business practices. In some states, independent publishers sell a variety of contract forms that are drafted to meet legal requirements. Even if all the contract wording is not mandated by law, many parts of the agreement may have to use specific wording and appear in a mandated type font and size so that they are clear and conspicuous.

Because contract terms often appear mysterious to the untrained consumer, most states specifically allow a real estate professional to go over the terms of a preprinted contract with a client without risking an accusation of the unlawful practice of law. Figure 10.2 is a sample exclusive right-to-sell listing agreement. It is provided as an example only; many state-specific or regional forms are available online. In addition, many states make available handbooks and other reference materials for real estate professionals, as well as consumers that explain real estate transaction contracts and obligations. Each state real estate agency's website is listed in the appendix.

Listing agreement provisions

Regardless of which type of listing agreement is used, the same considerations arise in most real estate transactions.

Names of all parties to the contract

Anyone who has an ownership interest in the property must be identified and should sign the listing to validate it. If the property has co-owners, that fact should be clearly established. If one or more of the co-owners is married, the spouse's consent and signature on the contract to release any marital rights is required in most states. If the property is in the possession of a tenant, that should be disclosed (along with the terms of the tenancy), and instructions should be included on how the property is to be shown to prospective buyers.

Brokerage firm

The brokerage company name, the employing broker, and if applicable, the sales associate taking the listing must all be identified, even though the sales associate only acts on behalf of the broker and is not a party to the agreement.

Description of the premises

In addition to the street address, the legal description, lot size, and tax parcel number may be required for future purchase offers.

FIGURE 10.2: Sample Listing Agreement

**LISTING CONTRACT:
EXCLUSIVE RIGHT TO SELL**
This form approved by the Minnesota Association of REALTORS®,
which disclaims any liability arising out of use or misuse of this form.
© 2016 Minnesota Association of REALTORS®, Edina, MN

This form is complementary and is provided by the Minnesota Association of REALTORS® for educational purposes only.

1. Date _____

2. Page 1 of _____ pages

3. **DEFINITIONS:** This Contract involves the property located at _____ ,

4. legally described as _____

5. _____ ("Property").

6. Seller is _____ ("Seller").

7. Broker is _____ ("Broker").
    (Real Estate Company Name)

8. This Contract starts on _____ , 20 _____ , and ends at 11:59 p.m. on _____ ,

9. 20 _____ .

10. This Contract may only be canceled by written mutual agreement of the parties.

11. **PRICE:** Seller offers the Property for sale for the price of $ _____ , upon the following

12. terms: _____ .

13. **LISTING:** Seller gives Broker the exclusive right to sell the Property. In exchange, Broker agrees to list and market
14. the Property for sale. Broker may place a "For Sale" sign and a lock box with keys on the Property, unless prohibited by
15. governing authority. Seller understands this Contract DOES NOT give Broker authority to rent or manage the Property.
16. Seller understands Broker may be a member of a Multiple Listing Service ("MLS"), and if Broker is a member of MLS,
17. and where available, Broker may give information to the MLS concerning the Property. Broker may place information
18. on the Internet concerning the Property, including sold information (except as limited in the following MLS Data Feed
19. Options section). If Broker sells the Property, Broker may notify the MLS and member REALTORS® of the price and
20. terms of the sale. Seller acknowledges that neither Broker, the MLS, the Minnesota Association of REALTORS®, nor
21. any other broker is insuring Seller or occupant against theft, loss, or vandalism.

22. **MLS DATA FEED OPTIONS:**

23. EXPLANATIONS AND DEFINITIONS:

24. **"IDX site"** means a web site operated by a broker participating in the MLS on which the broker can advertise the
25. listings of other brokers in MLS, subject to certain MLS rules. The consumer visiting an IDX site is not required to
26. register on the site or to have a brokerage relationship with the broker displaying listings on the site.

27. **"Virtual office web site" ("VOW")** means a web site operated by a broker participating in the MLS that delivers
28. brokerage services to consumers over the world wide web. Visitors to a VOW are required to register on the site (with
29. their name and a real e-mail address) and enter a brokerage relationship with the broker operating the VOW. The
30. broker operating the VOW can then show the visiting customer/client nearly all of the information available to the broker
31. in MLS. The seller(s) of a listing has the right to opt out of certain kinds of data display under the MLS's VOW policy.
32. The MLS imposes various other rules and restrictions on VOWs.

33. For each of the following options, the MLS system automatically defaults to "Yes." Seller's instructions pertaining to the
34. Internet display of the MLS input data for the Property are as follows:

35. **Option 1.** **Listing display on the Internet.** If Seller selects "No," this listing will not be included in MLS data feeds
36.   to Internet web sites that display property listing data, whether intended for advertising the Property or
37.   providing online brokerage services (e.g., VOWs). Brokers participating in MLS can still disclose the listing
38.   to customers/clients via other means, including e-mail, fax, mail, hand delivery, and orally.

39.   Shall the Property listing be displayed on the Internet, including sold information?   ☐ Yes   ☐ No

40.   Seller understands and acknowledges that if Seller has selected "No" for Option 1, consumers who
41.   conduct searches for listings on the Internet will not see information about the Property in response to
42.   their searches.

Figure 10.2:   Sample Listing Agreement

LISTING CONTRACT:
EXCLUSIVE RIGHT TO SELL

43.   Page 2

44.   Property located at _____ .

45.   **If "No" was selected at Option 1, skip Options 2-4. If "Yes" was selected for Option 1, continue to Option 2.**

46.   **Option 2.**   **Listing address (house and unit numbers and street name) display on the Internet.** If Seller selects
47.   "No," the address of the Property will be hidden on web sites receiving data feeds from MLS that result in
48.   Internet listing display, whether intended for advertising the Property or providing online brokerage services
49.   (e.g., VOWs). Brokers participating in MLS can still disclose the address to customers/clients via other
50.   means, including e-mail, fax, mail, hand delivery, and orally.

51.   Shall the listing address (house and unit numbers and street name) be displayed
52.   on the Internet?   ☐ Yes   ☐ No

53.   **Option 3.**   **An automated valuation of the Property listing or a link to an automated valuation of it may be**
54.   **displayed adjacent to the listing.** Some VOWs or IDX sites may provide an automated valuation model
55.   ("AVM") function/service. An AVM uses statistical calculations to estimate the value of a property based
56.   upon data from public records, MLS, and other sources, and incorporating certain assumptions. The
57.   accuracy of AVMs has sometimes been criticized because they do not take into consideration all relevant
58.   factors in valuing a property. Seller, by selecting "no," may prohibit display of an automated valuation of his
59.   or her listing adjacent to the listing.

60.   Shall an automatic valuation of the Property listing or a link to an automated
61.   valuation be displayed adjacent to the listing?   ☐ Yes   ☐ No

62.   **Option 4.**   **Comments or reviews of the Property by persons other than the displaying broker may be displayed**
63.   **with or attached as a link to the listing data of the Property.** Some VOWs or IDX sites may provide
64.   functionality that permits the customers/clients using the VOW or IDX site to enter comments or reviews
65.   with the listing or by hyperlink to such comments or reviews. Note that the broker displaying the listing on
66.   his or her VOW or IDX site may add commentary representing his or her professional judgment regarding
67.   the listing's value, etc.

68.   Shall comments or reviews of the Property by persons other than the displaying
69.   broker be displayed with or attached as a link to the listing data of the Property?   ☐ Yes   ☐ No

70.   **LISTED FOR LEASE:** The Property ☐ **IS** ☐ **IS NOT** currently listed for lease. If **IS**, the listing broker is
---------(Check one.)---------

71.   _____ . If **IS NOT**, Seller ☐ **MAY** ☐ **MAY NOT** list the Property for lease during the
-----------(Check one.)----------

72.   terms of this Contract with another broker.

73.   Nothing in this Contract shall prohibit Broker and Seller from entering into a listing agreement for the lease of this
74.   Property upon terms acceptable to both parties.

75.   **SELLER'S OBLIGATION:** Seller shall notify Broker of relevant information important to the sale of the Property.
76.   Seller shall cooperate with Broker in selling the Property. Seller shall promptly inform Broker about all inquiries Seller
77.   receives about the Property. Seller agrees to provide and pay for any inspections and reports required by any
78.   governmental authority. Seller agrees to provide unit owners' association documents, if required. Seller shall remain
79.   responsible for security, maintenance, utilities, and insurance during the term of this Contract, and for safekeeping,
80.   securing and/or concealing any valuable personal property during Property showings or open houses. Seller shall
81.   surrender any abstract of title and a copy of any owner's title insurance policy for this Property, if in Seller's possession
82.   or control, to buyer or buyer's designated title service provider. Seller shall take all actions necessary to convey
83.   marketable title by the date of closing as agreed to in a purchase agreement. Seller shall sign all documents necessary
84.   to transfer to buyer marketable title to the Property. Seller has the full legal right to sell the Property.

MN:LC:ERS-2 (8/16)

Figure 10.2:   Sample Listing Agreement (continued)

**LISTING CONTRACT:
EXCLUSIVE RIGHT TO SELL**

85.   Page 3

86.   Property located at _____ .

87.   <u>Access to the Property</u>: Seller authorizes access to the Property. Authorizing access means giving permission to another
88.   person to enter the Property, with or without a licensed salesperson present, disclosing to the other person any security
89.   codes necessary to enter the Property, and lending a key to the other person to enter the Property, directly or through
90.   a lockbox. To facilitate the showing and sale of the Property, Seller instructs Broker to:
91.   1.   access the Property;
92.   2.   authorize other brokers and their associates, inspectors, appraisers, contractors, and other industry
93.   professionals to access the Property at reasonable times and upon reasonable notice; and
94.   3.   duplicate keys to facilitate convenient and efficient showings of the Property.
95.   Seller agrees to commit no act which might tend to obstruct Broker's performance here. If the Property is occupied by
96.   someone other than Seller, Seller shall comply with Minnesota law and any applicable lease provisions of an existing
97.   lease and provide tenant with proper notice in advance of any Property showing.

98.   **SELLER CONTENT LICENSE:** In the event Seller provides content, including, but not limited to, any photos or videos
99.   of the Property ("Seller Content") to Broker, Seller grants to Broker a nonexclusive, perpetual, world-wide, transferable,
100.   royalty free license to sub-license (including through multiple tiers), reproduce, distribute, display, perform, and create
101.   derivative works of the Seller Content. Seller represents and warrants that Seller has authority to provide Seller Content
102.   and Seller Content does not violate any restrictions regarding use including any third-party intellectual property rights
103.   or laws. Seller agrees to execute any further documents that are necessary to effect this license.

104.   **NOTICE: THE COMPENSATION FOR THE SALE, LEASE, RENTAL, OR MANAGEMENT OF REAL PROPERTY**
105.   **   SHALL BE DETERMINED BETWEEN EACH INDIVIDUAL BROKER AND THE BROKER'S CLIENT.**

106.   **BROKER'S COMPENSATION:**
107.   Seller agrees to pay Broker a retainer fee of $ _____ at the commencement of this Contract, which
108.   fee should be kept by Broker whether or not Seller sells the Property. The retainer fee will apply toward satisfaction of
109.   any obligation to compensate Broker.

110.   Seller shall pay Broker, as Broker's compensation, _____ percent (%) of the selling price or

111. $ _____ , whichever is greater, if Seller sells or agrees to sell the Property during the term of
112.   this Contract.

113.   Other: _____

114.   In addition, if before this Contract expires Broker presents a buyer who is willing and able to buy the Property at the
115.   price and terms required in this Contract, but Seller refuses to sell, Seller shall still pay Broker the same compensation.
116.   Seller agrees to pay Broker's compensation whether Broker, Seller, or anyone sells the Property. Seller hereby permits
117.   Broker to share part of Broker's compensation with other real estate brokers, including brokers representing only the
118.   buyer. Seller agrees to pay Broker's compensation in full upon the happening of any of the following events:
119.   1.   the closing of the sale;
120.   2.   Seller's refusal to close the sale; or
121.   3.   Seller's refusal to sell at the price and terms specified above.

122.   If, within _____ days *(not to exceed six (6) months)* after the expiration of this Contract, Seller sells or agrees to sell
123.   the Property to anyone who:
124.   1.   during this Contract made inquiry of Seller about the Property and Seller did not tell Broker about the inquiry;
125.   or
126.   2.   during this Contract made an affirmative showing of interest in the Property by responding to an advertisement,
127.   or by contacting Broker or the licensee involved, or was physically shown the Property by Broker and whose
128.   name and address is on a written list Broker gives to Seller within 72 hours after the expiration of this Contract;
129.   then Seller shall still pay Broker the compensation noted here, even if Seller sells the Property without Broker's
130.   assistance. Seller understands that Seller does not have to pay Broker's compensation if Seller signs another valid
131.   listing contract or facilitator services agreement for this Property after the expiration or cancellation of this Contract,
132.   under which Seller is obligated to compensate another licensed real estate broker.

133.   To secure the payment of Broker's compensation, Seller hereby assigns to Broker the gross proceeds from the sale
134.   of the Property in an amount equal to the compensation due to Broker under this Contract.

Figure 10.2:   Sample Listing Agreement (continued)

LISTING CONTRACT:
EXCLUSIVE RIGHT TO SELL

135.   Page 4

136.   Property located at _____ .

137.   **COMPENSATION DISCLOSURE:** Broker's compensation to cooperating brokers shall be as specified in the MLS
138.   unless Broker notifies Seller otherwise in writing.

139.   **CLOSING SERVICES:**

140.   **NOTICE:**   THE REAL ESTATE BROKER, LICENSEE REPRESENTING OR ASSISTING SELLER, OR REAL ESTATE
141.   CLOSING AGENT HAS NOT EXPRESSED AND, UNDER APPLICABLE STATE LAW, MAY NOT EXPRESS
142.   OPINIONS REGARDING THE LEGAL EFFECT OF THE CLOSING DOCUMENTS OR OF THE CLOSING
143.   ITSELF.

144.   After a purchase agreement for the Property is signed, arrangements must be made to close the transaction. Seller
145.   understands that no one can require Seller to use a particular person in connection with a real estate closing and that
146.   Seller may arrange for a qualified closing agent or Seller's attorney to conduct the closing.

147.   Seller's choice for closing services. *(Initial one.)*

148.   _____   _____ Seller wishes to have Broker arrange for the closing.
            (Seller)   (Seller)

149.   _____   _____ Seller shall arrange for a qualified closing agent or Seller's attorney to conduct the closing.
            (Seller)   (Seller)

150.   **ADDITIONAL COSTS:** Seller acknowledges that Seller may be required to pay certain closing costs, which may
151.   effectively reduce the proceeds from the sale.

152.   Seller understands that mortgage financing services are usually paid for by buyer; however, certain insured government
153.   loans may require Seller to pay a portion of the fees for the mortgage loan. Seller understands that Seller shall not be
154.   required to pay the financing fees on any mortgage without giving Seller's written consent.

155.   **FOREIGN INVESTMENT IN REAL PROPERTY TAX ACT ("FIRPTA"):** Section 1445 of the Internal Revenue Code
156.   provides that a transferee ("Buyer") of a United States real property interest must be notified in writing and must withhold
157.   tax from the transferor ("Seller") if the transferor ("Seller") is a foreign person, provided there are no applicable exceptions
158.   from FIRPTA withholding.

159.   Seller represents and warrants that Seller ☐ **IS** ☐ **IS NOT** a foreign person (i.e., a non-resident alien individual,
            -----*(Check one.)*----
160.   foreign corporation, foreign partnership, foreign trust, or foreign estate) for purposes of income taxation.

161.   Due to the complexity and potential risks of failing to comply with FIRPTA, Seller should **seek appropriate legal and**
162.   **tax advice regarding FIRPTA compliance, as Broker will be unable to confirm whether Seller is a foreign person**
163.   **or whether the withholding requirements of FIRPTA apply.**

164.   **WARRANTY:** There are warranty programs available for some properties which warrant the performance of certain
165.   components of a property, which warranty programs Seller may wish to investigate prior to the sale of the Property.

MN:LC:ERS-4 (8/16)

Figure 10.2: Sample Listing Agreement (continued)

LISTING CONTRACT:
EXCLUSIVE RIGHT TO SELL

166.   Page 5

167.   Property located at _____.

---

168.   **AGENCY REPRESENTATION:** If a buyer represented by Broker wishes to buy the Seller's Property, a dual
169.   agency will be created. This means that Broker will represent both the Seller and the buyer, and owe the same
170.   duties to the buyer that Broker owes to the Seller. This conflict of interest will prohibit Broker from advocating exclusively
171.   on the Seller's behalf. Dual agency will limit the level of representation Broker can provide. If a dual agency should arise,
172.   the Seller will need to agree that confidential information about price, terms, and motivation will still be kept
173.   confidential unless the Seller instructs Broker in writing to disclose specific information about the Seller. All other
174.   information will be shared. Broker cannot act as a dual agent unless both the Seller and the buyer agree to it. By
175.   agreeing to a possible dual agency, the Seller will be giving up the right to exclusive representation in an in-house transaction.
176.   However, if the Seller should decide not to agree to a possible dual agency, and the Seller wants Broker to represent
177.   the Seller, the Seller may give up the opportunity to sell the Property to buyers represented by Broker.

178.   <u>Seller's Instructions to Broker:</u>
179.   Having read and understood this information about dual agency, Seller now instructs Broker as follows:
180.   ☐   Seller will agree to a dual agency representation and will consider offers made by buyers represented by
181.   Broker.
182.   ☐   Seller will not agree to a dual agency representation and will not consider offers made by buyers represented
183.   by Broker.

184.   Real Estate Company Name: _____

185.   Seller: _____

186.   By: _____   Seller: _____
                       (Licensee)
187.   Date: _____

---

188.   **OTHER POTENTIAL SELLERS:** Seller understands that Broker may list other properties during the term of this
189.   Contract. Seller consents to Broker representing or assisting such other potential sellers before, during, and after the
190.   expiration of this Contract.

191.   **PREVIOUS AGENCY RELATIONSHIPS:** Broker, or licensee representing or assisting Seller, may have had a previous
192.   agency relationship with a potential buyer of Seller's Property. Seller acknowledges that Seller's Broker, or licensee
193.   representing or assisting Seller, is legally required to keep information regarding the ultimate price and terms the buyer
194.   would accept and the motivation for buying confidential, if known.

195.   **INDEMNIFICATION:** Broker will rely on the accuracy of the information Seller provides to Broker. Seller agrees
196.   to indemnify and hold harmless Broker from and against any and all claims, liability, damage, or loss arising from any
197.   misrepresentation, misstatement, omission of fact, or breach of a promise by Seller. Seller agrees to indemnify and hold
198.   harmless Broker from any and all claims or liability related to damage or loss to the Property or its contents, or any
199.   injury to persons in connection with the marketing of the Property. Indemnification by Seller shall not apply if the damage,
200.   loss, or injury is the result of the gross negligence or willful misconduct of the Broker.

201.   **FAIR HOUSING NOTICE:** Seller understands that Seller shall not refuse to sell or discriminate in the terms, conditions,
202.   or privileges of sale, to any person due to his/her race, color, creed, religion, national origin, sex, marital status, status
203.   with regard to public assistance, handicap (whether physical or mental), sexual orientation, or family status. Seller
204.   understands further that local ordinances may include other protected classes.

205.   **ADDITIONAL NOTICES AND TERMS:** As of this date Seller has not received notices from any municipality, government
206.   agency, or unit owners' association about the Property that Seller has not informed Broker about in writing. Seller agrees
207.   to promptly inform Broker, in writing, of any notices of such type that Seller receives during the term of this Contract.

208.   This shall serve as Seller's written notice granting Broker permission to obtain mortgage information (e.g., mortgage
209.   balance, interest rate, payoff, and/or assumption figures) regarding any existing financing on the Property. A copy of
210.   this document shall be as valid as the original.

MN:LC:ERS-5 (8/16)

Figure 10.2:   Sample Listing Agreement (continued)

LISTING CONTRACT:
EXCLUSIVE RIGHT TO SELL

211.   Page 6

212.   Property located at _____ .

213.   **ELECTRONIC SIGNATURES:** The parties agree the electronic signature of any party on any document related to this
214.   transaction constitute valid, binding signatures.

215.   **CONSENT FOR COMMUNICATION:** Seller authorizes Broker and its representatives to contact Seller by mail, phone,
216.   fax, e-mail, or other means of communication during the term of this Contract and anytime thereafter.

217.   **OTHER:** _____

218.   _____

219.   _____

220.   _____

221.   _____

222.   **BROKER**   **SELLER**

223.   **ACCEPTED BY:** _____   **ACCEPTED BY:** _____
      (Real Estate Company Name)   (Seller)

224.   By: _____   _____
      (Licensee)   (Date)

225.   _____   _____
      (Date)   (Address)

226.   _____   _____
      (Address)   (Phone)

227.   _____   _____
      (Phone)   (E-Mail Address)

228.   _____
      (E-Mail Address)

229.   **SELLER**

230.   **ACCEPTED BY:** _____
                                                                   (Seller)

231.   _____
                                                                   (Date)

232.   _____
                                                                   (Address)

233.   _____
                                                                   (Phone)

234.   _____
                                                                   (E-Mail Address)

235.   **THIS IS A LEGALLY BINDING CONTRACT BETWEEN SELLER AND BROKER.**
236.   **IF YOU DESIRE LEGAL OR TAX ADVICE, CONSULT AN APPROPRIATE PROFESSIONAL.**

MN:LC:ERS-6 (8/16)

Listing price

This is the proposed sales price and is also called the *asking price*. This usually is a starting point for negotiation rather than the amount that will actually be agreed upon in the eventual purchase contract. What the seller will receive is the actual sales price, although the seller's proceeds usually will be reduced by unpaid real estate taxes, special assessments, mortgage debts, seller closing costs, brokerage fee, and any other outstanding obligations. If this is to be a short sale, the approval of the current lienholder(s) of any debts secured by the seller's property must be sought, and that fact should be included in all marketing.

Broker's authority and responsibilities

The contract should specify whether the broker may place a sign on the property and advertise; it should address when the property can be shown, allowing reasonable notice to the seller. It should also address whether or not the broker may accept earnest money on behalf of the seller, and the responsibilities for holding the funds. The broker does not have the authority to sign any legal documents or contracts without first obtaining a power of attorney from the seller or the seller's representative.

Broker's compensation

The circumstances under which the broker will be paid must be specifically stated in the contract. The broker's compensation could be a percentage of the sales price (commission) or a flat rate, and it is usually paid at closing directly by the seller or the party handling the closing. The contract should also indicate whether the compensation may be shared with a cooperating broker.

MATH CONCEPTS

Calculating Sales Price, Commission, and Net to Seller

When a property sells, the sales price equals 100% of the money being transferred. If a broker is to receive a 5% commission, 95% will remain for the seller's other expenses and equity. To calculate a commission using a sales price of $325,000 and a commission rate of 5%, multiply the sales price by the commission rate:

$325,000 × 5% = $325,000 × 0.05 = $16,250 commission

To calculate a sales price using a commission of $16,250 and a commission rate of 6%, divide the commission by the commission rate:

$16,250 ÷ 6% = $16,250 ÷ 0.06 = $270,833 sales price

To calculate a commission rate using a commission of $8,200 and a sales price of $164,000, divide the commission by the sales price:

$8,200 ÷ $164,000 = 0.05, or 5% commission rate

To calculate the net to the seller using a sales price of $125,000 and a commission rate of 4%, multiply the sales price by 100% minus the commission rate:

$125,000 × (100% − 4%) = $125,000 × (96%) = $125,000 × 0.96 = $120,000

The same result can be achieved by calculating the commission ($125,000 × 0.04 = $5,000) and deducting it from the sales price ($125,000 – $5,000 = $120,000); however, this involves unnecessary extra calculations.

$$\frac{\text{commission}}{\text{sales price} \quad \times \quad \text{commission rate}}$$

Real property and personal property

Any personal property that will be included in the sale of the real estate must be explicitly identified. Items of real property that the seller expects to remove at the time of the sale must be specified as well. Some items that may later become points of negotiation might include major appliances, swimming pool and spa equipment, fireplace accessories, window treatments, stacked firewood, and stored heating oil.

Leased equipment

It must be determined if leased equipment—security system, cable television boxes, water softener, special antenna—will be left with the property. If so, the seller is responsible for notifying the equipment's lessor of the change of property ownership.

Proposed dates for closing and buyer's possession

These dates should be based on an anticipated closing date. The listing agreement should allow adequate time for the paperwork involved (including the buyer's qualification for any financing) and the move-in date to be arranged by the seller and the buyer. A short sale means that the lienholder(s) must approve the transaction, possibly at several stages, which will add at least several months to the closing process.

Closing

An attorney, title company, or escrow company should be considered and retained as soon as possible and may be required by state law. A designated party will be needed to complete the paperwork, disburse the funds, and file the proper forms, such as documents to be recorded and documents to be sent to the IRS.

Evidence of ownership

A warranty deed, title insurance policy, abstract of title with an attorney's opinion, or other documentation customary in the area will be used for proof of title.

Encumbrances

All liens will be paid in full by the seller or be assumed by the buyer at the closing.

Home warranty program

To make the property more desirable to potential buyers, the seller or the listing broker may agree at the time of the listing to purchase a home warranty when a sale closes to cover the property's plumbing, electrical, and heating systems, water heaters, duct work, and major appliances.

Termination of the contract

A contract should provide a way for the parties to terminate the agreement and should specify under what circumstances the contract can be terminated. Under certain circumstances, an agreement can be canceled if the seller arbitrarily refuses to sell or cooperate.

Broker protection clause

Brokers may be well advised to protect their interests against possible fraud or a reluctant buyer's change of heart. Usually, the contract will include a period of time during which the broker will be entitled to a fee if a sale is closed with someone who was introduced to the seller by the broker while the contract was in effect.

Warranties by the owner

The owner is responsible for certain assurances and disclosures. Is the property suitable for its intended purpose? Does it comply with the appropriate zoning and building codes? Will it be transferred to the buyer in essentially the same condition as it was originally presented, considering repairs or alterations to be made as provided for in a purchase contract? Are there any known defects that should be revealed to a prospective buyer?

Indemnification (hold harmless) wording

The seller and the broker may agree to hold each other harmless (i.e., not to sue one another) for any incorrect information supplied by one to the other. Indemnification may be offered, regardless of whether the inaccuracies are intentional or unintentional.

Nondiscrimination (equal opportunity) wording

The seller must understand that the property will be shown and offered without regard to the race, color, religion, national origin, familial status, sex, or disability of the prospective buyer. Refer to state and local fair housing laws for a complete listing of protected classes in your area. There are also federal, state, and local laws that prohibit discrimination in lending and other aspects of a real estate transaction.

Antitrust wording

The contract should state that all fees have been negotiated between the seller and the broker; to do otherwise is a violation of antitrust laws.

Signatures of the parties

All parties identified in the contract must sign the contract, including all individuals who have a legal interest in the property. Consent to the use of electronic signatures for required transaction documents reflects the use of email to transfer information about the transaction and greatly speeds the process of securing seller consent to any changes in the contracts terms, such as a change in the list price.

Date the contract is signed

This date may be different from the date the contract actually becomes effective. For example, a sales associate may take the listing and, in some states, then must have the broker sign the contract to accept employment under its terms.

REPRESENTING THE BUYER

Like a listing agreement, a **buyer representation agreement** is an employment contract. In this case, the broker is employed by the buyer and the purpose of the agreement is to find a suitable property. The type of representation will determine the relationship of broker and client. Although the term *buyer agency* may be used to refer to any type of buyer-broker relationship, in some states the buyer and the broker can also establish a relationship that is less than agency. State law will define the nature of the buyer-broker relationship.

An agency agreement will give the buyer a degree of representation possible only in a fiduciary relationship. A broker acting as the agent of the buyer must protect the buyer's interests at all points in the transaction.

Buyer representation provisions

A number of topics must be discussed by broker (typically acting through a sales associate) and buyer before they sign a buyer representation agreement. For instance, a sales associate should make the same disclosures to a prospective buyer that would be made to a prospective seller in a listing presentation. The sales associate should explain the types of representation available and the parties' rights and responsibilities under each. The specific services provided to a buyer-client should be clearly explained.

In an **exclusive buyer representation agreement**, the buyer works with only one broker, although the broker is free to represent other buyer clients. If the representation is not exclusive, the buyer can work with two or more brokers, which may create a problem if more than one broker suggests the same property to the buyer. A *nonexclusive representation* may work if the buyer is considering a purchase in more than one geographic area; each broker's familiarity with a particular area will help find the property or properties that best match the buyer's needs.

www.dlr.sd.gov /realestate/real_estate _transaction_forms .aspx

www.dlr.sd.gov /realestate/consumer _guide.aspx

www.llr.state.sc.us/pol /rec/recpdf/agencylaw brochure05r.pdf

Figure 10.3 is a sample exclusive buyer representation agreement. State, regional, and local contract forms may be available online for your state. For example, the Buyer Agency Agreement required in South Dakota can be found at www.dlr.sd.gov/realestate/real_estate _transaction_forms.aspx. South Dakota has also created a Consumer Guide for home buyers and sellers: www.dlr.sd.gov/realestate/consumer_guide.aspx. South Carolina requires an Agency Disclosure Brochure: www.llr.state.sc.us/pol/rec/recpdf/agencylawbrochure05r.pdf.

Compensation issues should be addressed, whatever the type of representation. The buyer's broker may be compensated in the form of a flat fee for services, an hourly rate, a percentage of the purchase price, or some combination of those methods. The broker may require a *retainer fee* at the time the agreement is signed to cover initial expenses. The retainer may be applied as a credit toward any fees due at the closing. As in any brokerage agreement, the source of compensation does not determine the relationship of the parties. A buyer's broker may be compensated by either the buyer or (through the listing broker) the seller. Issues of compensation are always negotiable.

Unit 10

FIGURE 10.3: Sample Buyer Representation Agreement

This form is complementary and is provided by the Minnesota Association of REALTORS® for educational purposes only.

BUYER REPRESENTATION CONTRACT: EXCLUSIVE

This form approved by the Minnesota Association of REALTORS®, which disclaims any liability arising out of use or misuse of this form.
© 2015 Minnesota Association of REALTORS®, Edina, MN

1. Date _____

2. Page 1 of _____ pages

3. **DEFINITIONS:** Buyer is _____ ("Buyer").

4. Broker is _____ ("Broker").
    (Real Estate Company Name)

5. Buyer gives Broker the exclusive right to locate and/or to assist in negotiations for the purchase, exchange of or option to

6. purchase ("Purchase") property at a price and with terms acceptable to Buyer. This Contract starts on

7. _____ , 20 _____ , and ends at 11:59 p.m. on _____ , 20 _____ .

8. This Contract may only be canceled by written mutual agreement of the parties.

9. **BROKER'S OBLIGATION:** Broker shall make a reasonable effort to locate property acceptable to Buyer. Broker
10. shall use professional knowledge and skills to assist in negotiations for the Purchase of property. Broker shall assist
11. Buyer throughout the transaction. Broker shall act in Buyer's best interest at all times, subject to any limitations imposed
12. by law or dual agency. Broker shall comply with all applicable fair housing and nondiscrimination regulations.

13. **BUYER'S OBLIGATION:** Buyer shall work exclusively with Broker for the Purchase of property. Buyer shall promptly
14. furnish to Broker accurate and relevant personal financial information to ascertain Buyer's ability to Purchase property,
15. if requested. Buyer shall cooperate with Broker in finding a property to Purchase. After a purchase agreement has
16. been accepted by seller, Buyer is legally obligated to Purchase the property. If Buyer refuses to close the Purchase for
17. any reason other than the failure of seller to perform, subject to relevant contingencies, Buyer shall pay Broker all
18. compensation due under this Contract.

19. **NOTICE: THE COMPENSATION FOR THE PURCHASE, LEASE, RENTAL OR MANAGEMENT OF REAL**
20. **PROPERTY SHALL BE DETERMINED BETWEEN EACH INDIVIDUAL BROKER AND THE BROKER'S**
21. **CLIENT.**

22. **BROKER'S COMPENSATION:** *(Fill in all blanks.):*
23. If Buyer, or any other person acting on Buyer's behalf, agrees to Purchase any property during the term of this Contract,
24. the following compensation will apply.
25. 1.   Buyer agrees to pay Broker a retainer fee of $ _____ at the commencement of this Contract,
26.   which fee shall be kept by Broker whether or not Buyer Purchases property. The retainer fee shall apply toward
27.   satisfaction of any obligation to compensate Broker.

28. 2.   Buyer shall pay Broker, as Broker's compensation, _____ percent (%) of the selling price or
29. $ _____ , whichever is greater, when Buyer closes the Purchase, if:

30.   A: Buyer Purchases or agrees to Purchase a property before the expiration of this Contract, even if Buyer does
31.   not use Broker's services; or

32.   B: within _____ days *(not to exceed six (6) months)* after the expiration of this Contract, Buyer Purchases
33.   property which either Broker or licensee representing or assisting Buyer has physically shown Buyer or in which
34.   Buyer has made an affirmative showing of interest to Broker or licensee representing or assisting Buyer before
35.   the expiration of this Contract, as long as Broker has identified this property on a written list Broker gives to
36.   Buyer within 72 hours after the expiration of this Contract.

37. Broker is authorized to negotiate and receive compensation paid by seller, or broker representing or assisting seller, if
38. Broker informs Buyer in writing before Buyer signs an offer to Purchase the property. Any compensation accepted by
39. Broker from seller, or broker representing or assisting seller, ☐ **SHALL** ☐ **SHALL NOT** reduce any obligation of Buyer
    -----------------(Check one.)------------------
40. to pay the compensation by the amount received by seller or broker.

41. Buyer understands that Buyer does not have to pay Broker's compensation if Buyer signs another valid buyer
42. representation contract or facilitator services agreement after the expiration or cancellation of this Contract, under
43. which Buyer is obligated to compensate another licensed real estate broker.

MN:BRC:E-1 (8/15)

FIGURE 10.3: Sample Buyer Representation Agreement (continued)

BUYER REPRESENTATION
CONTRACT: EXCLUSIVE
44.   Page 2

45.   **CAUTION: BUYER'S ACTIONS IN LOCATING A PROPERTY MAY AFFECT PAYMENT OF COMPENSATION BY**
46.   **SELLER(S) AND MAY THEREFORE OBLIGATE BUYER TO PAY ALL OR PART OF THE COMPENSATION**
47.   **IN CASH AT CLOSING. FOR EXAMPLE: THE ACT OF GOING THROUGH AN OPEN HOUSE**
48.   **UNACCOMPANIED BY BUYER'S BROKER OR LICENSEE REPRESENTING OR ASSISTING BUYER;**
49.   **OR SIGNING A PURCHASE AGREEMENT THROUGH ANOTHER BROKER OR WITH OWNER (FOR**
50.   **SALE BY OWNER) MAY REQUIRE BUYER'S PAYMENT OF THE FULL COMPENSATION TO BUYER'S**
51.   **BROKER.**

52.   **GENERAL NATURE OF PROPERTY:** (Including the following property types: existing, new construction or to-be-built.)
53.   *(Check all that apply.)*

54.   ☐ Commercial/Industrial   ☐ Farm   ☐ Recreation
55.   ☐ Residential/Investment   ☐ Residential/Personal   ☐ Vacant Land

56.   **CLOSING SERVICES:**
57.   **NOTICE:**   THE REAL ESTATE BROKER, LICENSEE REPRESENTING OR ASSISTING BUYER OR REAL ESTATE
58.   CLOSING AGENT HAS NOT EXPRESSED AND, UNDER APPLICABLE STATE LAW, MAY NOT EXPRESS
59.   OPINIONS REGARDING THE LEGAL EFFECT OF THE CLOSING DOCUMENTS OR OF THE CLOSING
60.   ITSELF.

61.   After a purchase agreement for the property is signed, arrangements must be made to close the transaction. Buyer
62.   understands that no one can require Buyer to use a particular person in connection with a real estate closing and that
63.   Buyer may arrange for a qualified closing agent or Buyer's attorney to conduct the closing.

64.   Buyer's choice for closing services. *(Initial one.)*

65.   _____ _____   Buyer wishes to have Broker arrange for the closing.
           (Buyer)   (Buyer)

66.   _____ _____   Buyer shall arrange for a qualified closing agent or Buyer's attorney to conduct the closing.
           (Buyer)   (Buyer)

67.   **ADDITIONAL COSTS:** Buyer acknowledges that Buyer may be required to pay certain closing costs, which may
68.   effectively increase the cash outlay at closing.

69.   **FOREIGN INVESTMENT IN REAL PROPERTY TAX ACT ("FIRPTA"):** Section 1445 of the Internal Revenue Code
70.   provides that a transferee ("Buyer") of a United States real property interest must withhold tax from the transferor
71.   ("Seller") if the Seller is a foreign person and no exceptions from FIRPTA withholding apply. A Buyer is personally
72.   liable for the full amount of FIRPTA withholding tax required to be withheld unless the Seller furnishes Buyer with
73.   specific documentation ensuring Buyer is exempt from the withholding requirements as prescribed under 26 USC
74.   §1445. Due to the complexity and potential risks of failing to comply with FIRPTA, including the Buyer's responsibility
75.   for withholding the applicable tax, Buyer should **seek appropriate legal and tax advice regarding FIRPTA compliance,**
76.   **as Broker will be unable to assure Buyer that the transaction is exempt from the withholding requirements.**

77.   **PRIVATE INSPECTION/WARRANTY:** Broker recommends that Buyer obtain a private home inspection to satisfy
78.   himself/herself with the physical condition of the property. Furthermore, there are warranty programs available for some
79.   properties which warrant the performance of certain components of a property, which warranty programs Buyer may
80.   wish to investigate prior to the Purchase of any specific property.

MN:BRC:E-2 (8/15)

FIGURE 10.3: Sample Buyer Representation Agreement (continued)

**BUYER REPRESENTATION
CONTRACT: EXCLUSIVE**
81.   Page 3

82. **AGENCY REPRESENTATION:** If the Buyer chooses to Purchase a property listed by Broker, a dual agency will be
83. created. This means that Broker will represent both the Buyer and the seller, and owe the same duties to the seller that
84. Broker owes to the Buyer. This conflict of interest will prohibit Broker from advocating exclusively on the Buyer's behalf.
85. Dual agency will limit the level of representation Broker can provide. If a dual agency should arise, the Buyer will need
86. to agree that confidential information about price, terms and motivation will still be kept confidential unless the Buyer
87. instructs Broker in writing to disclose specific information about the Buyer. All other information will be shared. Broker
88. cannot act as a dual agent unless both the Buyer and the seller agree to it. By agreeing to a possible dual agency,
89. the Buyer will be giving up the right to exclusive representation in an in-house transaction. However, if the Buyer should
90. decide not to agree to a possible dual agency, and the Buyer wants Broker to represent the Buyer, the Buyer may give
91. up the opportunity to Purchase the properties listed by Broker.

92. Buyer's Instructions to Broker:
93. Having read and understood this information about dual agency, Buyer now instructs Broker as follows:

94. ☐ Buyer will agree to a dual agency representation and will consider properties listed by Broker.

95. ☐ Buyer will not agree to a dual agency representation and will not consider properties listed by Broker.

96. Real Estate Company Name: _____

97.   Buyer: _____

98. By: _____   Buyer: _____
                          (Licensee)

99. Date: _____

100. **OTHER POTENTIAL BUYERS:** Buyer understands that other potential buyers may consider and/or make offers to
101. purchase through Broker the same or similar properties as Buyer is seeking to Purchase. Buyer consents to Broker
102. representing such other potential buyers before, during and after the expiration of this Contract.

103. **PREVIOUS AGENCY RELATIONSHIPS:** Broker or licensee representing or assisting Buyer may have had a previous
104. agency relationship with a seller of a property Buyer is interested in Purchasing. Buyer acknowledges that Buyer's
105. Broker or licensee representing or assisting Buyer is legally required to keep information regarding the ultimate price
106. and terms the seller would accept and the motivation for selling confidential, if known.

107. **NOTICE REGARDING PREDATORY OFFENDER INFORMATION: Information regarding the predatory
108. offender registry and persons registered with the predatory offender registry under MN Statute 243.166 may
109. be obtained by contacting the local law enforcement offices in the community where the property is located
110. or the Minnesota Department of Corrections at (651) 361-7200, or from the Department of Corrections web site at
111. www.corr.state.mn.us.**

112. **ELECTRONIC SIGNATURES:** The parties agree the electronic signature of any party on any document related to this
113. transaction constitute valid, binding signatures.

114. **CONSENT FOR COMMUNICATION:** Buyer authorizes Broker and its representatives to contact Buyer by mail, phone,
115. fax, e-mail or other means of communication during the term of this Contract and any time thereafter.

MN:BRC:E-3 (8/15)

FIGURE 10.3: Sample Buyer Representation Agreement (continued)

**BUYER REPRESENTATION
CONTRACT: EXCLUSIVE**

116.   Page 4

117. **OTHER**: _____

118. _____

119. _____

120. _____

121. _____

122. _____

123. _____

124. _____

125. **BROKER**   **BUYER**

126. **ACCEPTED BY:** _____   **ACCEPTED BY:** _____
     (Real Estate Company Name)   (Buyer)

127. By: _____   _____
     (Licensee)   (Date)

128. _____   _____
     (Date)   (Address)

129. _____   _____
     (Address)   (Phone)

130. _____   _____
     (Phone)   (E-Mail Address)

131. _____
     (E-Mail Address)

132.   **BUYER**

133.   **ACCEPTED BY:** _____
                                                              (Buyer)

134.   _____
                                                              (Date)

135.   _____
                                                              (Address)

136.   _____
                                                              (Phone)

137.   _____
                                                              (E-Mail Address)

138.   **THIS IS A LEGALLY BINDING CONTRACT BETWEEN BUYER AND BROKER.**
139.   **IF YOU DESIRE LEGAL OR TAX ADVICE, CONSULT AN APPROPRIATE PROFESSIONAL.**

MN:BRC:E-4 (8/15)

Termination of buyer representation

Just as with a contract to represent a property seller, the success of a contract to represent a property buyer depends on the chosen broker's professional efforts; the agreement to find a suitable property for the buyer cannot be assigned to another broker without the buyer's written consent. The prospective buyer cannot force the broker to perform, but the broker's failure to work diligently toward fulfilling the contract's terms constitutes a breach of the buyer representation agreement. If the agreement is canceled by the broker, the buyer may be entitled to sue the broker for damages. The buyer could be liable for damages to the broker by refusing to cooperate with the broker's reasonable requests, such as viewing property that the broker has located or refusing to proceed with an accepted sales contract.

A broker's agreement to represent a property buyer may be terminated for the following reasons:

- The agreement's purpose is fulfilled by the transfer of title to the buyer.
- The agreement's term expires.
- The broker and the buyer mutually agree to cancel the agreement.
- Either the broker or the buyer breaches the terms of the agreement, such as by the buyer failing to pay an agreed-upon retainer fee to the broker.
- Either the broker or the buyer dies or becomes incapacitated. If a sales associate dies or becomes incapacitated, the agreement is still valid.

If a transaction fails to be completed through no fault of the buyer or the buyer's broker, the representation will survive, provided the agreement's term has not expired.

Figure 10.4 lists the obligations owed to a buyer by the broker who works for the buyer, as well as the obligations owed to a buyer by the broker who works for the seller. While many of the responsibilities are the same, there are distinct differences that direct the actions of the seller's and buyer's representatives.

FIGURE 10.4   Obligations of Real Estate Broker to Buyer

Broker Works for Seller	Broker Works for Buyer
General Responsibilities	
Be honest with buyer but responsible to seller, including duty of skill and care to promote and safeguard seller's best interests	Be fair with seller but responsible to buyer, including duty of skill and care to promote and safeguard buyer's best interests
Earnest Money Deposit	
Collect amount sufficient to protect seller	Suggest deposit sufficient to indicate sincerity in offer.
Seller Financing	
Encourage financing terms and contract provisions favorable to seller, such as (1 due-on-sale clause, (2) deficiency judgment, (3) secured note.	Suggest terms in best interests of buyer, such as low down payment, long term, no due-on-sale clause, long grace period, security interest limited to the real property (nonrecourse)
Property Condition	
Require seller to fill out all disclosure forms	Require that seller sign property condition statement and confirm representations of condition; require soil and termite inspections, if appropriate; look for negative features and use them to negotiate better price and terms
Documents	
Give buyer a copy of important documents, such as mortgage to be assumed, declaration of restrictions, title report, condominium or homeowners association bylaws	Research and explain significant portions of important documents affecting transaction; refer buyer to expert advisers when appropriate
Negotiation	
Negotiate and bargain in seller's best interests	Negotiate and bargain in buyer's best interests
Showing	
Show buyer properties in which broker's commission is protected, such as in-house or MLS-listed properties; pick best times to show properties; emphasize attributes and amenities	Search for best properties for buyer to inspect, widening marketplace to for-sale-by-owner properties, lender-owned (REO) properties, probate sales, unlisted properties. View properties at different times to find negative features, such as traffic congestion and noise from nearby properties
Property Goals	
Find a buyer whose stated objectives match the seller's property on the seller's price and terms	Counsel buyer as to developing accurate objectives; may find that buyer who wants apartment building might be better off with duplex (two-unit property) or that buyer looking for vacant lot would benefit more from investment in improved property
Offers	
Transmit all offers to seller; consult with seller about possible action steps (e.g., accept offer, counteroffer, reject offer)	Help buyer prepare strongest offer at least risk to buyer
Possession Date	
Consider best date for seller in terms of moving out, notice to existing tenants, impact on insurance, risk of loss provision	Consider best date for buyer in terms of moving in; storage of buyer's possessions, if necessary; favorable risk of loss provision if fire destroys property before closing
Default	
Discuss remedies upon default by either party. Point out to seller any attempt by buyer to limit liability (nonrecourse financing; deposit money as liquidated damages)	Consider having seller pay buyer's sale-related expenses and cancellation charges if seller defaults
Property Value	
No duty to disclose low appraisal or fact broker sold similar unit yesterday for $10,000 less	Review comparable sales from buyer's perspective

KEY POINT REVIEW

A **listing agreement** is an **employment contract** between a real estate broker and a property seller. In all states, an **exclusive listing agreement** must be in writing to be enforceable in court. The broker is a **special agent** of the seller.

As an **agent**, the **broker** is authorized to represent the **principal** and the principal's real estate to consumers. A real estate **sales associate** is a **general agent** of the broker and can carry out listing services only in the name of and under the supervision of the broker.

In an **exclusive right-to-sell listing**, **one broker** is appointed as the seller's **sole** agent, and if the property is sold while the listing is in effect, the broker is entitled to a commission, no matter who sells the property.

An **exclusive agency listing** authorizes **one broker** to act as the **sole** agent of the seller but allows the **seller** to retain the right to sell the property without obligation of payment to the broker.

In an **open listing** (also known as a **nonexclusive listing**), the seller retains the right to employ **any** number of brokers; the seller is obligated to pay a commission **only** to the broker who successfully produces a **ready, willing, and able buyer**; and the seller is not obligated to pay a commission if the seller personally sells the property without the aid of a broker.

A **net listing** in which the excess over the seller's desired net from the sale is paid to the broker as compensation may be prohibited by state law.

A **multiple listing clause** permits cooperation with other brokers in the **multiple listing service (MLS)**.

An **agreement to represent a seller** may be **terminated** when

- the agreement's **purpose** is fulfilled,
- the agreement's **term expires**,
- the property is **destroyed**,
- **title** to the property is transferred by operation of law (e.g., bankruptcy),
- the broker and the seller **mutually agree** to end the agreement,
- either the broker or the seller **breaches** the contract, or
- either party **dies** or becomes **incapacitated**.

All **exclusive listings** should have a **definite termination date** and should not have an automatic extension provision.

The **broker protection clause** preserves a broker's right to compensation if, within a certain number of days after the listing agreement expires, the owner transfers the property to a purchaser who was brought to the seller by the listing broker.

The **listing presentation** is usually made by a sales associate of the broker and is the job interview with a prospective client—the property owner. The sales associate presents information about the firm, the market, and how the firm can provide the best service to the owner. The sales associate also makes a **comparative market analysis (CMA)** to help the seller have a realistic idea of the price range in which the subject property falls.

A **listing agreement** will identify the property owner(s) and the property, describe the property improvements, list any loans held by the owner and their current status, itemize loan and other payments on the property, and provide the details of a short sale, if the lender is willing to accept one.

Disclosures of agency relationships and property condition are important consumer safeguards and may be required by state law.

The listing agreement must specify any **personal property** that will be included in the sale of the real estate, as well as any **fixtures** or other items that will be excluded from the sale. **Leased equipment** also should be identified.

The seller may make a **home warranty** policy available for the buyer.

A **buyer representation agreement** is an employment contract in which a prospective property buyer employs a broker for the purpose of finding a suitable property. State law may specify the type of agreement that is available to the broker when representing a buyer. In an **agency** relationship, the broker will have a **fiduciary** responsibility to the buyer. In an **exclusive buyer representation** agreement, the buyer works with only one broker, but the broker is free to represent other buyer clients.

The buyer's broker will be **compensated** by a retainer, a flat fee for services, an hourly rate, a percentage of the purchase price, or some combination of these methods. The **source of compensation** does not determine the relationship of the parties and compensation is always negotiable.

Buyer representation is **terminated** when

- the agreement's purpose is **fulfilled**,
- the agreement's **term expires**,
- broker and buyer **mutually agree** to cancel the agreement,
- broker or buyer **breaches** the terms of the agreement, or
- broker or buyer **dies** or becomes **incapacitated**.

UNIT 10 QUIZ

1. A property listing taken by a real estate sales associate is technically an employment agreement between the seller and
   A. the broker.
   B. the local multiple listing service.
   C. the sales associate.
   D. the sales associate and broker together.

2. Which of the following is a similarity between an exclusive agency listing and an exclusive right-to-sell listing?
   A. Under each, the seller retains the right to sell the real estate without the broker's help and without paying the broker a commission.
   B. Under each, the seller authorizes only one particular sales associate to show the property.
   C. Both types of listings give the responsibility of representing the seller to one broker only.
   D. Both types of listings are open listings.

3. The listing agreement on a residential property states that it expires on May 2. Which event would terminate the listing before that date?
   A. The agreement is renewed before May 2.
   B. The owner becomes ill on April 29.
   C. On April 15, the owner and agent cancel the agreement.
   D. The house is destroyed by fire on May 3.

4. A seller listed a property with a broker under an exclusive agency listing agreement. If the seller finds a buyer, the seller will owe the broker
   A. no commission.
   B. the full commission.
   C. a partial commission.
   D. only reimbursement for the broker's costs.

5. A broker sold a residence for $485,000 and received $26,675 as commission in accordance with the terms of the listing agreement. What was the broker's commission rate?
   A. 5%
   B. 5.5%
   C. 6%
   D. 6.5%

6. Under a brokerage agreement with a property owner, the broker is entitled to sell the property for any price, as long as the seller receives $85,000. The broker may keep any amount over $85,000 as a commission. This type of listing might be illegal and is called
   A. an exclusive right-to-sell listing.
   B. an exclusive agency listing.
   C. an open listing.
   D. a net listing.

7. Which of the following is a similarity between an open listing and an exclusive agency listing?
   A. Under each, the seller avoids paying the broker a commission if the seller sells the property to someone the broker did not procure.
   B. Each grants a commission to any broker who procures a buyer for the seller's property.
   C. Under each, the broker earns a commission regardless of who sells the property, as long as it is sold within the listing period.
   D. Each grants the exclusive right to sell to whatever broker produces a buyer for the seller's property.

8. The final decision on a property's asking price should be made by
   A. the seller's broker.
   B. the appraised value.
   C. the seller.
   D. the seller's attorney.

9. Which statement is *TRUE* of a listing agreement?
   A. It is an employment contract for the professional services of the broker.
   B. It obligates the seller to transfer the property if the broker procures a ready, willing, and able buyer.
   C. It obligates the broker to work diligently for both the seller and the buyer.
   D. It automatically binds the owner, the broker, and the MLS to its agreed provisions.

10. A broker sold a property that was owned by a bank that had acquired it through foreclosure, and the broker received a 6.5% commission. The broker gave the listing sales associate $3,575, which was 30% of the firm's commission. What was the selling price of the property?
    A. $55,000
    B. $95,775
    C. $152,580
    D. $183,333

11. A seller hired a broker under the terms of an open listing agreement. While that agreement was still in effect, the seller—without informing the first broker—hired another broker from a separate firm under an exclusive right-to-sell listing for the same property. If the first broker produces a buyer for the property whose offer the seller accepts, the seller must pay a full commission to
    A. only the first broker.
    B. only the second broker.
    C. both brokers.
    D. neither broker.

12. A seller listed a residence with a broker. The broker brought an offer at full price and terms of the listing agreement from a buyer who is ready, willing, and able to pay cash for the property, but the seller rejected the buyer's offer. In this situation, the seller
    A. must sell the property.
    B. owes a commission to the broker.
    C. is liable to the buyer for specific performance.
    D. is liable to the buyer for compensatory damages.

13. A buyer signed an agreement with a broker to compensate the broker even if the buyer purchases the property from a relative. This is called
    A. an open buyer representation agreement.
    B. an exclusive agency buyer representation agreement.
    C. an exclusive buyer representation agreement.
    D. an invalid agreement.

14. A prospective buyer signs an agreement with a broker to find a property for the buyer, and the buyer agrees to work only with that broker. While this agreement is in effect,
    A. only one sales associate of the broker can work with the buyer.
    B. the broker can represent other buyers.
    C. the broker cannot show the buyer a property that is listed by the broker.
    D. the sales associate working with the buyer cannot work with other buyers.

15. A seller sold property to a neighbor without the services of a real estate broker; however, the seller still owes a broker a commission because the seller signed
    A. an exclusive agency listing agreement.
    B. an open listing agreement.
    C. an exclusive right-to-sell listing agreement.
    D. a net listing agreement.

16. Most states require that a real estate listing agreement contain
    A. a multiple listing service (MLS) clause.
    B. a definite contract termination date.
    C. an automatic extension clause.
    D. a broker protection clause.

17. Which type of listing is prohibited in some states?
    A. Exclusive right-to-sell
    B. Net listing
    C. Buyer representation
    D. Open listing

18. By executing a listing agreement with a seller, a real estate broker becomes
    A. a procuring cause.
    B. obligated to open a special trust account.
    C. the agent of the seller.
    D. responsible for sharing the commission.

19. The provision in a contract with a property seller that gives additional authority to the broker and obligates the broker to alert other brokers to the availability of the property is
    A. a joint listing clause.
    B. a multiple listing clause.
    C. a net listing clause.
    D. an open listing clause.

20. All of the following are valid reasons for terminating a buyer representation agreement *EXCEPT*
    A. purchase of a property.
    B. death of the sales associate who worked with the buyer.
    C. agreement of the parties.
    D. death of the broker.

UNIT
11

Real Estate Contracts

LEARNING OBJECTIVES

When you have completed this unit, you will be able to

> **describe** the essential elements of a contract;
> **explain** the various means by which a contract may be enforced, terminated, assigned, or replaced; and
> **describe** the primary written agreements and forms used in real estate sales and leasing.

KEY TERMS

amendment	executed contract	rescission
assignment	executory contract	statute of frauds
bilateral contract	express contract	suit for specific performance
breach of contract	implied contract	"time is of the essence"
consideration	land contract	unenforceable contract
contingencies	liquidated damages	unilateral contract
contract	novation	valid contract
counteroffer	offer and acceptance	void contract
disclosure	option	voidable contract
earnest money	owner financing	
enforceable contract	purchase money mortgage	

OVERVIEW

The real estate market is driven by contracts. Both seller and buyer representation agreements are contracts. Options are contracts—and an offer is the first half of a sales contract. Leases and management agreements are contracts. Every aspect of the real estate business involves contracts, and everyone involved in a real estate transaction—even those who are not real estate professionals—should understand what a contract means. A real estate professional must know not only what a contract means but also how one is created, what is required of the parties to the contract, and how the contract is concluded.

CONTRACT LAW

A **contract** is a voluntary promise between two competent parties to perform (or not perform) some legal act in exchange for consideration.

A **contract** is a voluntary agreement or promise between legally competent parties, supported by legal consideration, to perform (or refrain from performing) some legal act. The definition may be easier to understand if its various parts are examined separately.

A contract must be

- *voluntary*—no one may be forced into a contract;

- *an agreement or a promise*—a contract is essentially a promise or set of promises;

- made by *legally competent parties*—the parties must be viewed by the law as capable of making a legally binding promise;

- supported by lawful *consideration*—a contract must be supported by something of value that induces a party to enter into the contract; and

- for a *legal act*—a contract is invalid if it attempts to have an illegal objective.

Real estate professionals use many types of contracts and agreements to carry out their responsibilities to sellers, buyers, landlords, tenants, and the general public. The area of law that governs such agreements is known as *contract law*.

IN PRACTICE

Real estate professionals may be permitted by state law to use contract forms drafted by attorneys and provided by their trade associations or employing brokers. A real estate professional cannot practice law unless also licensed as an attorney. The parties to a transaction, including buyer, seller, landlord, and tenant, always have the option of hiring their own attorney and should never be discouraged from doing so.

Express and implied contracts

A contract is either express or implied. In an **express contract**, the parties state the terms and show their intentions in words, either oral or written. Most real estate contracts are express contracts and are written. In an **implied contract**, the agreement of the parties is demonstrated by their acts and conduct.

Real estate representation agreements should be written in order to comply with the state's real estate law. Exclusive representation agreements must always be written to be enforceable. In addition, the state will probably have a **statute of frauds** requiring certain contracts, such as real estate sales or lease agreements, to be in writing. In any of those cases, only a written agreement can be enforced in a court of law.

Bilateral and unilateral contracts

Contracts are classified as either bilateral or unilateral. In a **bilateral contract**, both parties promise to do something; one promise is given in exchange for another. A real estate sales contract is a bilateral contract because the seller promises to sell a parcel of real estate and transfer title to the property to the buyer, who promises to pay a certain sum of money or other lawful consideration for the property. An exclusive right-to-sell listing contract is a bilateral contract.

Bilateral contract: *Bi* means *two*—must have two promises. **Unilateral** contract: *Uni* means *one*—has only one promise.	A **unilateral contract**, on the other hand, is a one-sided agreement. One party makes a promise in order to entice a second party to do something. The offer made in a unilateral contract is usually accepted by the performance of the party to whom the offer is made. The second party is not legally obligated to act, but if the second party does comply, the first party is obligated to keep the promise.

IN PRACTICE

A brokerage lists a property for sale with the multiple listing service. Any other broker who is part of the multiple listing service may or may not bring a buyer to the listing broker. The offer by the listing broker to share compensation with a cooperating broker is an offer for a unilateral contract. The brokers who receive the offer are not obligated to bring a buyer to the listing broker, but if a cooperating broker does produce a buyer, the listing broker is obligated to share the compensation on the transaction on the terms specified.

Executed and executory contracts

A contract is either executed or executory, depending on whether the agreement has been completed or some obligation under the agreement has yet to be performed. An **executed contract** is one in which all parties have fulfilled their promises; the contract has been performed. The term *executed* is also used to refer to the signing of a contract. An **executory contract** exists when one or both parties still have an act to perform. A sales contract is an executory contract from the time it is signed until closing; ownership has not yet changed hands, and the seller has not received the sales price. At closing, when the contract terms have been met, the sales contract is executed.

Figure 11.1 highlights the issues involved in the formation of a contract.

FIGURE 11.1: Contract Issues

Essential Elements	Classification	Discharge
offer and acceptance	valid, void, voidable	performance
consideration	enforceable, unenforceable	breach
legal purpose	express, implied	remedies (damages, specific performance, rescission)
consent	unilateral, bilateral	
legal capacity	executory, executed	

Creation of a valid contract

Elements of a contract ■ Offer and acceptance ■ Consideration ■ Legally competent parties ■ Consent ■ Legal purpose	A contract must meet certain minimum requirements to be considered legally valid. The following are the essential elements of a contract.

Offer and acceptance

In a real estate sales transaction, the sales contract sets out the offer by the buyer that is accepted by the seller. This is known as **offer and acceptance**. The person who makes the offer is the *offeror*. The person to whom an offer is made is the *offeree*. This requirement is also called *mutual assent*. It means that there must be a meeting of the minds; that is, there must be complete agreement between the parties about the purpose and terms of the contract.

Courts look to the objective intent of the parties to determine whether they intended to enter into a binding agreement. Most states require that the terms and conditions of the sales contract be in writing. The wording of the contract must express all the agreed terms and must be clearly understood by the parties.

An *offer* is a promise made by one party, requesting something in exchange for that promise. The offer is made with the intention that the offeror will be bound to the terms if the offer is accepted. The terms of the offer must be definite and specific and must be communicated to the offeree.

An *acceptance* is a promise by the offeree to be bound by the exact terms proposed by the offeror. The acceptance must be communicated to the offeror. Proposing any deviation from the terms of the offer is considered a rejection of the original offer. The changed offer is known as a *counteroffer* and is explained more fully later. The counteroffer must be accepted for a contract to exist.

Besides being *terminated* by a counteroffer, an offer can be terminated if the offeree fails to accept it before expiration of the time stated in the offer. An offer also may be terminated by the offeree's outright rejection of it.

The offeror may revoke the offer at any time before acceptance. This *revocation* must be communicated to the offeree by the offeror, either directly or through the parties' agents. The offer is revoked if the offeree learns of the revocation and observes the offeror acting in a manner that indicates that the offer no longer exists. For example, if a buyer gives a seller three days to accept an offer and on the third day the buyer's agent calls the seller's agent and revokes the offer, the offer is terminated.

In a complex transaction, usually involving commercial property, the parties may wish to discuss the terms of a potential agreement before initiating a contract. A *letter of intent* can be used to indicate the interest of a prospective buyer or lessee and, if that interest is reciprocated by the property owner, to begin negotiations.

Consideration

The contract must be based on consideration. **Consideration** is something of legal value offered by one party and accepted by another as an inducement to perform or to refrain from performing some act. Consideration is some interest or benefit accruing to one party, or some loss or responsibility by the other party. There should be a statement of the promised consideration in a contract to show that something of value will be given in exchange for the promise of the transfer of the described property, even if the amount of the consideration is yet to be determined. For example, a contract to purchase 300 acres of land could state that the consideration is the promise to pay the appraised value of the land as of a certain date.

Consideration must be *good and valuable* between the parties. The courts usually do not inquire into the adequacy of consideration. Adequate consideration could be a promise of love and affection or it could be a substantial sum of money. Anything that has been bargained for and exchanged is legally sufficient to satisfy the requirement for consideration. The only requirements are that the parties agree and that no undue influence or fraud has occurred.

Consent

A contract must be entered into by consent as a free and voluntary act of each party. Each party must be able to make a prudent and knowledgeable decision without undue influence. A mistake, misrepresentation, fraud, undue influence, or duress would deprive a person of that ability. If any of these circumstances is present, there is no valid offer and acceptance and the contract is voidable by the injured party. If the other party were to sue for breach, the injured party could use lack of voluntary assent as a defense.

Legal purpose

A contract must be for a legal purpose—that is, even with all the other elements (consent, competent parties, consideration, and offer and acceptance), the contract must have a legal reason for existence. A contract for an illegal purpose or for the performance of an act against public policy is not a valid contract.

Legally competent parties

All parties to the contract must have legal capacity, meaning they must be of legal age and have enough mental capacity to understand the nature or consequences of their actions in the contract. In most states, 18 is the age of contractual capacity. If it is discovered that a party is not legally competent, the contract is voidable at the option of the person who lacks competency.

Validity of a contract

A contract may be
- valid—has all legal elements;
- void—lacks one or more elements and has no legal force or effect;
- voidable—has all legal elements on its face, but it may be rescinded or disaffirmed; or
- unenforceable—appears to have all legal elements but cannot be enforced in court.

A contract can be described as valid, void, voidable, or unenforceable, depending on the circumstances.

A **valid contract** meets all the essential elements that make it legally sufficient, or enforceable, and is binding in a court of law.

A **void contract** has no legal force or effect because it lacks some or all the essential elements of a contract. A contract that is void was never a legal contract. For example, the use of a forged name in a listing contract would make the contract void.

IN PRACTICE

High demand for rental housing has led to a number of scams in which a property is listed fraudulently on an internet rental site. The party listing the property may claim to be the owner or even a representative of a property management firm. The intent, of course, is to procure a deposit and rental payment from an unsuspecting victim. Any purported rental agreement that is executed without the consent of the true owner of the property is void.

A **voidable contract** appears on the surface to be valid, but it may be rescinded or disaffirmed by one or both parties based on some legal principle. A voidable contract is considered by the courts to be valid if the party who has the option to disaffirm the agreement does not do so within a period of time. A contract with a minor, for instance, is voidable. A contract entered into by a mentally ill person is usually voidable during the mental illness and for a reasonable period after the person is cured. If a contract was made under duress, with misrepresentation, under the influence, and with intent to defraud, it is also voidable.

An **enforceable contract** meets all the elements of a valid contract, including compliance with any applicable statute of frauds or other law that requires it to be in writing and signed by the parties. An **unenforceable contract** may also appear on the surface to be valid; however, neither party can sue the other to force performance. For example, an oral agreement for the sale of a parcel of real estate would be unenforceable; the defaulting party could not be taken to court and forced to perform. There is, however, a distinction between a suit to force performance and a suit for damages, which may be possible even with an oral agreement. An unenforceable contract is still said to be *valid as between the parties*. This means that once the agreement is fully executed by the transfer of the deed and purchase price, satisfying both parties, neither has reason to initiate a lawsuit to force performance.

DISCHARGE OF CONTRACTS

A contract is *discharged* when the agreement is terminated. A contract terminates when it has been completely performed, with all its terms fulfilled, but a contract may be terminated for another reason, such as a party's breach or default.

Performance of a contract

Each party to a contract has certain rights and duties to fulfill. The question of when a contract must be performed is an important factor. Many contracts call for a specific time by which the agreed acts must be completely performed. Some contracts provide that "**time is of the essence**," which means that each of the elements of the contract must be performed within the specified time. A party who fails to perform an obligation under the contract on time is liable for breach of contract.

When a contract does not specify a deadline for performance, the acts it requires should be performed within a reasonable time. The interpretation of what constitutes a reasonable time depends on the situation. Courts can declare a contract invalid because the contract did not contain a time or date for performance.

Assignment

Assignment refers to a transfer of rights or duties under a contract. Generally rights and obligations may be assigned to a third party as long as they do not involve a contract for personal services. Obligations may be delegated, but the original party remains liable unless specifically released. Many contracts have a clause that will either allow or forbid assignment.

IN PRACTICE

A homeowner signs an exclusive right-to-sell agreement with a broker. Because the contract is for the services that the particular broker will provide, the broker cannot assign the agreement to a different broker.

Novation

Assignment =
substitution of parties

Novation =
substitution of a new
contract

Substitution of a new contract for an existing contract is called **novation**. The new agreement may be between the same parties, or a new party may be substituted for either in a *novation* of the parties. The parties' intent must be to discharge the old obligation. When there are many changes to a real estate contract and it is faxed, scanned, or otherwise re-transmitted several times, it may become difficult to decipher. Novation occurs when a new, clear contract with all the accepted changes is signed by all the parties.

Breach of contract

A contract may be terminated if it is breached by one of the parties. A **breach of contract** is a violation of any of the terms or conditions of a contract. A seller who fails to deliver title to the buyer breaches a sales contract. The breaching or defaulting party assumes certain burdens, and the nondefaulting party has certain legal and/or equitable remedies.

If the seller breaches a real estate sales contract, the buyer may sue for *specific performance* unless the contract specifically states otherwise. In a **suit for specific performance**, the buyer asks the court to force the seller to go through with the sale and transfer the property as previously agreed. The buyer may choose to sue for damages, in which case the seller is asked to pay for any costs and hardships suffered by the buyer as a result of the seller's breach.

If the buyer defaults, the seller can sue for damages or sue for the purchase price. A suit for the purchase price is an action for damages, but it has the same result as a suit for specific performance: The seller tenders the deed and the buyer is required to pay the agreed price.

The contract may limit the remedies available to the parties. A *liquidated damages* clause in a real estate purchase contract specifies the amount of money to which the seller is entitled if the buyer breaches the contract. The liquidated damages in the event that the buyer defaults may be specified as the buyer's earnest money deposit (down payment), although in some states, the amount of liquidated damages in a residential purchase contract is limited to a specific percentage of the purchase price—say, 3%—even if the buyer has made a down payment for a larger amount.

Statute of limitations

Every state limits the time during which parties to a contract may bring a legal action, or lawsuit, to enforce their rights. The statute of limitations varies for different legal actions, and any rights not enforced within the applicable time period are lost.

Other reasons for termination

A contract may also be discharged or terminated when any of the following occurs:

■ *Partial performance of the terms, along with a written acceptance* by the party for whom acts have not been done or to whom money is owed. If the parties agree that the work performed is close enough to completion, for example, they can agree that the contract is discharged even if some minor elements remain unperformed.

■ *Substantial performance*, in which one party has substantially performed on the contract but does not complete all the details exactly as the contract requires. Such performance may be enough to force payment, with certain adjustments for any damages suffered by the other party. For example, if a newly constructed addition to a home is finished except for polishing the brass doorknobs, the contractor is entitled to the final payment.

■ *Impossibility of performance*, in which an unforeseen circumstance has made an act required by the contract impossible or impracticable. Sometimes, a contract will cover a contingency, such as the destruction of property to be transferred. At other times, an event will occur that makes fulfillment of the contract terms a practical impossibility, such as when a buyer is laid off and can no longer afford to complete the purchase.

■ *Mutual agreement* of the parties to cancel the contract. Cancellation by one party will terminate a contract but does not automatically return the parties to their original position, unless provided by law (such as the right of cancellation that accompanies some consumer contracts) or by the terms of the agreement.

■ *Operation of law*, such as in the voiding of a contract by a minor, or as a result of fraud, or because a contract was altered without the written consent of all parties involved. **Rescission** returns the parties to their original positions before the contract, so any monies or property exchanged must be returned. Rescission is normally a contractual remedy for a breach, but a contract may also be rescinded by the mutual agreement of the parties.

IN PRACTICE

If a contract contains any ambiguity, the court will generally interpret the agreement against the party who prepared it. In a contract between a business and a consumer, the court will tend to favor the consumer unless it can be shown that the consumer signed the contract with full knowledge of and consent to its terms.

CONTRACTS USED IN THE REAL ESTATE BUSINESS

The written agreements most commonly used by real estate professionals are

■ client representation agreements,

■ real estate sales contracts,

■ options,

■ escrow agreements,

■ property management agreements,

■ leases, and

■ owner financing contracts, such as land contracts or contracts for deed.

We will now discuss real estate sales contracts, options to purchase real estate, and owner financing contracts.

Use of contract forms

The practice of law includes preparing legal documents, such as deeds and mortgages, and offering advice on legal matters. A real estate professional who is not a licensed attorney cannot practice law. Nevertheless, many states have specific guidelines for when and how real estate professionals may assist consumers with contract preparation. These guidelines, which specify the activities that are not considered the practice of law or which can be performed by non-attorneys, are created by state real estate officials, court decisions, or statutes. Often, brokerage representation agreements, agency and property disclosure forms, and parts of residential property sales agreements must comply word for word with statutory language.

A real estate professional also may be permitted to fill in the blanks on other preprinted documents, such as those created by bar associations, real estate trade associations, and attorneys for real estate firms, as directed by the client. No separate fee may be charged for completing the forms.

The parties to a real estate transaction always should be advised to have sales contracts and other legal documents examined by their lawyers before they sign them to ensure that the agreements accurately reflect their intentions. When preprinted forms do not sufficiently cover special provisions in a transaction, the parties should have an attorney draft an appropriate contract.

IN PRACTICE

Real estate professionals should always be aware of the source of any preprinted document, particularly those that have not come from the state, a trade association, or their employer's attorney and have not been approved by the firm. The forms made available by a national publishing company, for instance, may or may not be state-specific, and should always be shown to and approved by the firm, acting on the advice of counsel, before being used. Just because a preprinted form is available doesn't mean that the real estate professional should offer it to a client.

Sales contracts

A real estate sales contract contains the complete agreement between a buyer of a parcel of real estate and its seller. It establishes the legal rights and obligations of buyer and seller. Depending upon the area, the contract may be referred to as an offer to purchase, a contract of purchase and sale, a purchase agreement, an earnest money agreement, or a deposit receipt.

In addition to the essential elements of a contract, a real estate sales contract will include

- the sales price and terms;
- an adequate description of the property and improvements;
- a statement of the kind and condition of the title and the form of deed to be delivered by the seller;
- the kind of title evidence required, who will provide it, and how many defects in the title will be eliminated; and
- a statement of all the terms of the agreement between the parties, including any contingencies—conditions that must be met to successfully complete the transaction.

Offer

The real estate sales agreement is an offer to purchase real estate when it has been prepared, signed by the prospective buyer, and communicated to the seller. Typically, the buyer's offer is presented by the buyer or the buyer's representative to the seller or the seller's representative.

If either party is represented by a real estate professional, the real estate professional must be the one who sends or receives communications on behalf of the client. If the buyer's offer is accepted by the seller and the seller signs the document, it becomes a sales contract.

Counteroffer

A **counteroffer** is a *new* offer; it rejects the original offer.

Any change by the seller to the terms proposed by the buyer creates a **counteroffer**. The original offer ceases to exist because the seller has rejected it. The buyer may accept or reject the seller's counteroffer. If the buyer desires, the process may continue by making another counteroffer. Any change in the last offer results in a new counteroffer until either the parties reach agreement or one party walks away.

An offer or counteroffer *may be withdrawn at any time before it has been accepted*, even if the person making the offer or counteroffer agreed to keep the offer open for a set period.

Acceptance

If the seller agrees to the original offer or a later counteroffer *exactly* as it is made and signs the document, the offer has been accepted and a contract is formed. The seller's representative advises the buyer (through the buyer's representative, if there is one) of the seller's acceptance and a copy of the contract is provided to each party. The next step is the approval of the parties' attorneys, if the contract calls for it.

An offer is not considered accepted until the person making the offer has been notified of the other party's acceptance. When the parties communicate through a representative or at a distance, questions may arise regarding whether an acceptance, rejection, or counteroffer has occurred. All offers, acceptances, or other responses should be transmitted as soon as possible and acknowledged by the recipient to avoid later questions of proper communication.

Binder

In some states, and particularly in a complex transaction involving commercial or industrial property, a buyer's offer may be presented in a shorter document known as a *binder*, or *letter of intent*, instead of a complete sales contract. The binder states the essential terms of the offer and acknowledges that the buyer's representative has received the buyer's deposit. A more formal and complete contract of sale is drawn up by an attorney once the seller accepts and signs the binder.

Earnest money deposits

It is customary, although not essential, for a purchaser to provide a deposit when making an offer to purchase real estate. This deposit, usually in the form of a check, is called **earnest money**. The earnest money deposit is evidence of the buyer's intention to carry out the terms of the contract in good faith. The amount of the deposit is a matter to be agreed on by the parties but typically is an amount sufficient to

- discourage the buyer from defaulting,
- compensate the seller for taking the property off the market, and
- cover any expenses the seller might incur if the buyer defaults.

In many states, the earnest money check is given to the seller's agent on acceptance of the offer to purchase by the seller. When the disposition of the funds has been determined, they will be placed in an escrow account according to the terms of the escrow agreement, the contract between the buyer, the seller, and the escrow holder that sets forth the rights and responsibilities of each. The escrow holder will collect and then disburse the funds and documents that are necessary to close the transaction.

If there is a delay in presentation of an offer or negotiations are lengthy, most states require that earnest money be deposited in a broker's escrow or trust account, where it is held until the offer to purchase is accepted or rejected. The escrow account must be separate from the broker's business or personal account. A separate escrow account does not have to be opened for each earnest money deposit received; all deposits may be kept in one account. A broker must maintain full, complete, and accurate records of all earnest money deposits. The broker's (and any involved sales associate's) real estate license may be revoked or suspended if deposits are not managed properly. In some areas, it is customary for deposits to be held in escrow by the seller's attorney. If the offer is not accepted, the earnest money deposit is immediately returned to the would-be buyer. If the offer is accepted, the funds are delivered to the escrow holder according to the terms of the escrow agreement.

Equitable title

When a buyer signs a contract to purchase real estate that is accepted by the seller, the buyer does not immediately receive title to the land. Title transfers only upon delivery and acceptance of a deed. After both buyer and seller have executed a sales contract, however, the buyer acquires an interest in the land known as *equitable title*. A person who holds equitable title has rights that vary from state to state. Equitable title may give the buyer an insurable interest in the property.

Destruction of premises

In some states, once the sales contract is signed by both parties, the buyer assumes the risk of any damage to the property that may occur before closing the contract. In other states, laws and court decisions have placed the risk of loss on the seller. More than a dozen states, including California, Illinois, New York, and Texas, have adopted the Uniform Vendor and Purchaser Risk Act, which can be viewed at www.uniformlaws.org. The act specifically provides that the seller bear any loss that occurs before the title passes or the buyer takes possession.

www.uniformlaws.org

Liquidated damages

To simplify matters in the event that one party breaches a contract, the parties may agree on a certain amount of money that will compensate the nonbreaching party. Such money is called **liquidated damages**. If a sales contract specifies that the earnest money deposit is to serve as liquidated damages in the event that the buyer defaults, the seller will be entitled to keep the deposit if the buyer refuses to perform without good reason. The seller who keeps a deposit as liquidated damages may not sue for any further damages if the contract provides that the deposit is the seller's sole remedy (usually, the purpose of liquidated damages). State law may limit the amount of the deposit that can be retained as liquidated damages.

Provisions of a sales contract

All real estate sales contracts contain a number of provisions, or clauses. Most sales contracts include the following information:

- Purchaser's name and a statement of the purchaser's obligation to purchase the property, sometimes including how the purchaser intends to take title

- Adequate description of the property, such as the street address; while a street address is adequate to describe most residential properties in a sales contract, it is not adequate for the legal description that will be included in the deed

- Seller's name and a statement of the type of deed the seller agrees to provide, including any covenants, conditions, and restrictions

- Purchase price and how the purchaser intends to pay for the property, including earnest money deposits, additional cash from the purchaser, and the conditions of any anticipated mortgage financing

- Identification of the closing or settlement agent and closing or settlement instructions

- Date for the closing of the transaction and the transfer of possession of the property to the purchaser

- Title evidence that will be satisfactory to the buyer

- Method by which real estate taxes, rents, fuel costs, and other expenses are to be prorated

- Outcome of the contract should the property be damaged or destroyed between the time of signing and the closing date

- Liquidated damages, specific performance, or other statement of remedies available in the event of default

- Contingencies or conditions of the sale

- Personal property to be left with the premises for the purchaser (such as major appliances or lawn and garden equipment)

- Fixtures or other items that could be considered part of the real property that are to be removed by the seller before the closing (such as a chandelier or fireplace screen)

- Transfer of any applicable warranties on items such as heating and cooling systems or built-in appliances

- Identification of any leased equipment that must be transferred to the purchaser or returned to the lessor (such as cable television boxes or a water softener)

- Transfer or payment of any outstanding special assessments

- Purchaser's right to inspect the property shortly before the closing or settlement (often called the final walk-through)

- Documents to be provided by each party and when and where they will be delivered

- Dated signatures of all parties. In some states, the seller's nonowning spouse may be required to release potential marital or homestead rights. In most states, there must be an agency disclosure statement that indicates the form of representation provided by the real estate professional(s). Documents can be transmitted and signed electronically using one of a variety of software programs, in compliance with the Uniform Electronic Transactions Act (www.uniformlaws.org), which has been adopted by all states except Illinois, New York, and Washington. Those states have their own laws governing electronic transactions.

Contingencies

Conditions that must be satisfied before a sales contract is fully enforceable are **contingencies**. The contract clause that provides a contingency will include the following three elements:

- The action necessary to satisfy the contingency
- The time frame within which the action must be performed
- The party who is responsible for paying any costs involved

The most common contingencies are as follows:

- A *mortgage contingency* protects the buyer's earnest money in the event that the buyer is unable to secure a mortgage on the property.

- An *inspection contingency* provides that the buyer may obtain certain inspections of the property and may cancel the contract if the inspections indicate an unsatisfactory or unsafe property condition. Inspections may include those for wood-boring insects, lead-based paint, structural and mechanical systems, sewage facilities, and radon or other toxic materials. Buyer and seller can usually come to an agreement on any work indicated by a property inspection, and the party responsible for paying for the work.

- A *property sale contingency* protects a buyer who has to sell a home in order to buy the seller's property. This provision protects the buyer from owning two homes at the same time and also helps ensure the availability of cash for the purchase.

- A *lienholder approval*, if the contract is a short sale.

The seller may insist on an *escape clause*, which permits the seller to continue to market the property until all the buyer's contingencies have been satisfied or removed. The buyer may retain the right to eliminate the contingencies if the seller receives a more favorable offer. (Note that contingencies create a *voidable contract*; if the contingencies are rejected or not satisfied, the contract is void.)

IN PRACTICE

The real estate professional should avoid recommending sources for any inspection or testing services. If a buyer suffers any injury as a result of a provider's negligence, the real estate professional might also be named in any lawsuit. The better practice is to give the client the names of several professionals who offer high-quality services.

Amendments and addendums

A change or modification to the existing content of a contract is an **amendment**. An amendment can also be a change to the existing words or provisions in a preprinted contract form. Amendments to the contract form must be separately initialed or signed by all parties prior to or at the time that the contract is signed.

Even after there is agreement on the contract terms and the contract has been signed by both parties, there may be a need to change one of the contract provisions. If that happens, a separate agreement stipulating the changed provision can be executed by the parties.

IN PRACTICE

Seller and buyer have agreed to a sales contract that provides for a closing of the transaction in 60 days. In the next few weeks, it becomes obvious that, because of a backlog in the lender's underwriting department, a closing in 60 days will not be possible. The parties agree to amend the contract by allowing for 30 more days within which to complete the contract terms, executing a document that changes the provision requiring closing "within 60 days of contract acceptance" to "within 90 days of contract acceptance."

An **addendum** is any provision added to an existing contract that may change or be an addition to the content of the original. An addendum includes the original contract's provisions *by reference*, meaning the addendum mentions the original contract and must be signed by all parties. For example, an addendum might be an agreement to split the cost of repairing certain items discovered in a home inspection.

Disclosures

Many states have enacted mandatory property condition disclosure laws, which help consumers make informed decisions. **Disclosure** of property conditions may be included as part of a sales contract or may be required in a separate document that is presented to the buyer before an offer to purchase is made. Many states require separate forms for disclosing environmental problems.

Options

An **option** is a contract by which an optionor (generally an owner) gives an optionee (a prospective purchaser or tenant) the right to buy or lease the owner's property at a fixed price within a certain period of time. The optionee pays a fee as consideration for the option right. The optionee must then decide whether to exercise the option right or allow the option to expire. An option is enforceable by the optionee only (a unilateral contract). Options must contain all the elements of a valid contract.

A lease may include an option for the tenant to purchase the property. A residential lease option may also provide for a portion of the lease payment to be applied to the purchase price if the tenant decided to exercise the option. Options on commercial real estate frequently depend on some specific conditions being fulfilled, such as obtaining a zoning change or a building permit. The optionee may be obligated to exercise the option if the optionor has expended resources and money to see that conditions specified in the option are met. Similar terms could also be included in a sales contract.

Owner financing contracts

A traditional lender does not always have to be involved in the financing of a real estate purchase. With **owner financing**, the seller provides credit for all or part of the funds that will allow the buyer to move forward with the transaction.

A real estate sale can be made under a **land contract**, also called a *contract for deed*, a *contract of sale*, a *bond for title*, an *installment contract*, a *land sales contract*, or *articles of agreement for warranty deed*. Under a typical land contract, the owner/seller (also known as the *vendor*) retains legal title. The buyer, or the vendee, takes possession and gets equitable title to the property. The buyer agrees to give the seller a down payment and pay regular monthly installments of principal and interest over a number of years. The buyer also agrees to pay real estate taxes, insurance premiums, repairs, and upkeep on the property. Although the buyer obtains possession under the land contract, in its oldest form the seller is not obligated to execute and deliver a deed to the buyer until the terms of the contract have been satisfied—that is, all payments due to the seller have been made. Any early pay-off must occur if the buyer obtains a mortgage loan to pay off the contract balance. Although a land contract is usually assumable by subsequent purchasers, it generally must be approved by the seller.

IN PRACTICE

State legislatures and courts have recognized the harsh result that may occur if a buyer under a land contract breaches the terms of the contract by missing a single payment, even after many years of fulfilling the terms of the agreement. Depending on the state, the buyer under a land contract may have an equitable interest in the property after as little as one year of successfully making contract payments. This means that the statutory requirements for a foreclosure must be followed if the vendor wants to take back the property, and also that the defaulting vendee is entitled to a share of the proceeds of a forced sale.

The seller who finances a sale can also make use of a **purchase money mortgage** in which the buyer receives title to the property but places a security interest on it—the mortgage—in favor of the seller. The terms of the mortgage will dictate how it can be foreclosed in the event that the buyer defaults on the purchase. There is another way in which a property owner can help a buyer complete a transaction. If the buyer cannot obtain all the money needed for the purchase from a traditional lender, the seller may be willing to "take back a second" by holding part of the debt as a second mortgage. The lender will still have the priority interest in the property in the event that the buyer defaults, but the seller will have a secondary interest. This can be a very useful tool if the buyer has an insufficient down payment, provided the lender is made aware of and approves the arrangement.

KEY POINT REVIEW

A **valid contract** is a voluntary agreement based on the consent of the parties to the agreement. An offer by one party (**offeror**) is accepted by the other (**offeree**). A contract can be **revoked** by the offeror up to the time of acceptance. The parties must be of **legal age** and able to understand the **nature or consequences** of their actions. The contract must be supported by **consideration**—something of value, which could be love and affection—and must have a **legal act** as its objective.

A contract may be **express** (in words) or **implied** by the conduct of parties and may be required to be **in writing** to be **enforceable** in a court of law. A contract may be **bilateral** (having obligations on both sides) or **unilateral** (a promise by one side that can be accepted by performance of the other side). A contract may be **executed** (all parties have fulfilled their promises) or **executory** (one or both parties still have an act to perform).

A contract is **voidable** if it may be **rescinded** or **disaffirmed** by one or both parties. A contract with a minor is *voidable*. A contract is **void** if one of the essential elements is missing. If a mistake, misrepresentation, fraud, undue influence, or duress occurs, there is no mutual consent or meeting of the minds, which means that an essential element of the contract is missing and the contract is *void*.

A contract may be **discharged** (completed) by

- **performance**, which completes the contract terms;
- **partial performance**, if agreeable to both parties;
- **substantial performance**, depending on circumstances;
- **impossibility of performance** (required acts cannot be legally accomplished); **assignment** (transfer of rights to **assignee** or **delegation** of duties, if allowed by the contract);
- **novation** (substitutes a new contract or party for the original);
- **breach** by one of the parties without legal cause, in which case a **liquidated damages clause** may specify the amount the seller will receive if the buyer defaults;
- failure to enforce contract within **statute of limitations;**
- **mutual agreement** of the parties;
- **operation of law**, as when a contract is void from inception;
- **rescission**, which returns the parties to their original pre-contract positions, so any property or funds that have been transferred must be returned; or
- **cancellation,** which also is a termination of the contract.

The written agreements most often used in residential real estate transactions by real estate professionals are **client representation agreements**, **sales contracts**, **options**, **escrow agreements**, **property management agreements**, **leases**, and **owner financing agreements**, such as land contracts or contracts for deed.

A real estate sales contract is usually accompanied by an **earnest money deposit**, which may be held in a broker's escrow or trust account until an escrow is arranged to complete a property purchase or the funds are returned to the would-be buyer if there is no sales agreement.

The sales contract usually will identify the **parties** and the **property** that is the subject of the transaction, indicate the amount that the buyer is including with the offer to serve as **earnest money**, how the buyer intends to **finance** the purchase, who will serve as the **closing agent** for the transaction, when the transaction is to **close** and **possession** of the property delivered to the buyer, **fixtures** or other items on the property that are not part of the sale, **personal property** of the seller that will be included in the sale, **inspections** that will be made by the buyer, **seller disclosures** that are required by law, and other provisions.

The **contingencies** included in a sales contract allow the buyer to have an attorney review the contract, secure financing, conduct necessary inspections, and perform other activities.

Amendments and **addendums** can be used to alter the terms of a preprinted contract during the negotiation of the sale or to include additional terms after the contract has been signed by the parties.

An **option** allows the **optionor** (owner) to give the **optionee** the right to purchase the property at a later date at the price fixed in the **option agreement**.

Owner financing can assist a buyer by providing a credit for some or all of the purchase price. A **land contract**, also known as a **contract for deed**, **bond for title**, **installment contract**, **land sales contract**, or **articles of agreement for warranty deed**, must comply with state law. With a **purchase money mortgage**, the buyer receives title to the property immediately but places a security interest on the property in favor of the seller.

UNIT 11 QUIZ

1. A legally enforceable agreement under which both parties promise to do something for each other is called
   A. an escrow agreement.
   B. a legal pledge.
   C. a bilateral contract.
   D. an option agreement.

2. A person approaches an owner and says, "I'd like to buy your house." The owner says, "Sure," and they agree on a price. What kind of contract is this?
   A. Implied
   B. Unenforceable
   C. Void
   D. No contract

3. A contract is said to be bilateral if
   A. one of the parties is a minor.
   B. the contract has yet to be fully performed.
   C. only one party to the agreement is bound to act.
   D. both parties to the contract exchange binding promises.

4. During the period after a real estate sales contract is signed, but before title actually passes, the status of the contract is
   A. voidable.
   B. executory.
   C. unilateral.
   D. implied.

5. A contract for the sale of real estate that does not state the consideration and provides no basis on which the consideration could be determined is considered
   A. voidable.
   B. executory.
   C. void.
   D. enforceable.

6. A buyer and a seller sign a contract to purchase. The seller backs out, and the buyer sues for specific performance. What is the buyer seeking in this lawsuit?
   A. Money damages
   B. New contract
   C. Deficiency judgment
   D. Transfer of the property

7. In a preprinted sales contract, several words were crossed out or inserted by the parties. To eliminate future controversy as to whether the changes were made before or after the contract was signed, the usual procedure is to
   A. have both parties initial or sign in the margin near each change.
   B. write a letter to each party listing the changes.
   C. have each party write a letter to the other approving the changes.
   D. redraw the entire contract.

8. A buyer makes an offer on a seller's house and the seller accepts. Both parties sign the sales contract. At this point, the buyer has what type of title to the property?
   A. Equitable
   B. Voidable
   C. Escrow
   D. Contract

9. The sales contract says the buyer will purchase only if an attorney approves the sale by the following Saturday. The attorney's approval is
   A. a contingency.
   B. a reservation.
   C. a warranty.
   D. a consideration.

10. A real estate broker uses earnest money placed in the company trust account to pay for the rent owed on the brokerage's office. Using escrow funds for this purpose is
    A. illegal, unless the client has approved the expenditure.
    B. legal if the trust account is reimbursed by the end of the calendar month.
    C. legal if the seller gives consent in writing.
    D. illegal.

11. An option to purchase binds which of the following parties?
    A. Buyer only
    B. Seller only
    C. Neither buyer nor seller
    D. Both buyer and seller

12. A buyer and a seller enter into a real estate sales contract. Under the contract's terms, the buyer will pay the seller $500 a month for 10 years. The seller will continue to hold legal title, while the buyer will live in the home and pay all real estate taxes, insurance premiums, and regular upkeep costs. What kind of contract do the buyer and seller have?
    A. Option contract
    B. Contract for mortgage
    C. Unilateral contract
    D. Land sales contract

13. The purchaser of real estate under an installment contract
    A. generally pays no interest charge.
    B. receives title immediately.
    C. is not required to pay property taxes for the duration of the contract.
    D. has only an equitable interest in the property's title.

14. Under the statute of frauds, all contracts for the sale of real estate must be
    A. originated by a real estate professional.
    B. on preprinted forms.
    C. in writing to be enforceable.
    D. accompanied by earnest money deposits.

15. If, upon the receipt of an offer to purchase a property, the seller makes a counteroffer, the prospective buyer is
    A. bound by the original offer.
    B. not able to counter the counteroffer.
    C. bound by whichever offer is lower.
    D. relieved of the original offer.

16. A buyer makes an offer to purchase certain property listed with a real estate professional and leaves an escrow deposit with the real estate professional to show good faith. The real estate professional should
    A. immediately apply the deposit to the listing expenses.
    B. put the deposit in an account, as provided by state law.
    C. give the deposit to the seller when the offer is presented.
    D. put the deposit in the real estate professional's personal checking account.

17. While suffering from a mental illness that caused delusions, hallucinations, and loss of memory, a person signed a contract to purchase real estate. Which statement regarding the contract to purchase is *TRUE*?
    A. The contract is voidable.
    B. The contract is void.
    C. The contract lacks consent.
    D. The contract is fully valid and enforceable.

18. A real estate professional has found a buyer for a seller's home. The buyer has indicated in writing a willingness to buy the property for $1,000 less than the asking price and has provided an earnest money check for $5,000. The seller is out of town for the weekend, and the real estate professional has been unable to inform the seller of the signed document. At this point, there is
    A. a voidable contract.
    B. an offer.
    C. an executory agreement.
    D. an implied contract.

19. A buyer and a seller agree on a purchase price of $300,000 for a house. The contract contains a clause stating that "time is of the essence." Which statement is *TRUE*?
    A. The closing must take place within a reasonable period before the stated date.
    B. A "time is of the essence" clause is not binding on either party.
    C. The closing date must be stated as a particular calendar date, and not simply as a formula, such as "two weeks after loan approval."
    D. If the closing date passes and no closing takes place, the contract may be rescinded by the party who was ready to settle on the scheduled date.

20. A buyer signs a contract under which he is given the right to purchase a property for $130,000 anytime in the next six months. The buyer pays the current owner $500 at the time that contract is signed. Which of the following *BEST* describes this agreement?
    A. Contingency
    B. Option
    C. Installment
    D. Sales

Real Estate Financing

LEARNING OBJECTIVES

When you have completed this unit, you will be able to

> **describe** the factors that contribute to housing affordability, including mortgage terms and ability to pay;
> **describe** the terms, conditions, and use of the promissory note;
> **explain** the elements and use of security instruments, the mortgage and deed of trust, and the roles, rights, and obligations of the parties involved in each;
> **describe** the various types of real estate financing;
> **explain** the distinction between a judicial foreclosure and a non-judicial foreclosure, and the process involved in each; and
> **describe** the various consumer protections related to homeownership.

KEY TERMS

acceleration clause	deficiency judgment	negative amortization
adjustable-rate mortgage (ARM)	discount points	negotiable instrument
	equity	note
alienation clause	foreclosure	novation
amortized loan	growing-equity mortgage	PITI (principal, interest, taxes,
assumption of mortgage	homeowners insurance	and insurance)
balloon payment	hypothecation	prepayment penalty
beneficiary	index	promissory note
Comprehensive Loss	interest	release deed
Underwriting Exchange	interest-only loan	reverse mortgage
(CLUE)	loan origination fee	satisfaction of mortgage
debt to income (DTI)	loan-to-value ratio (LTV)	short sale
deed in lieu of foreclosure	margin	straight loan
deed of reconveyance	mortgage	"subject to"
deed of trust	mortgagee	trustor
defeasance clause	mortgagor	usury

OVERVIEW

In the United States, relatively few homes that are to be owner-occupied are purchased for cash. Most such homes are bought with borrowed money, and a lending industry has been created to service the financial requirements of homebuyers. Here, we will examine housing affordability—what it takes to purchase a home, and whether the investment is manageable. We then look at the ways in which real estate is financed. We conclude with a discussion of homeowners property insurance, an essential element to loan approval.

IN PRACTICE

A real estate professional should refer a prospective buyer to a lender to be preapproved for a loan prior to showing properties to the buyer. It is important for the real estate professional to be knowledgeable about real estate financing programs and products in order to provide quality service, especially when representing a buyer, but it is also important for the buyer to be realistic about the type and amount of financing that the buyer can acquire.

HOUSING AFFORDABILITY

Congress, state legislatures, and local governments work diligently to increase the affordability of housing. At the start of this century, creative financing, low-interest loans, interest-only loans, and flexible lending standards helped initiate housing loans to an ever-broader pool of borrowers, including many who would not have qualified for a housing loan otherwise. As a result, according to the U.S. Bureau of the Census, by June of 2004, 69.2% of households were homeowners. That proved to be a high point, however, and the homeownership rate has been falling ever since. By 2012, many borrowers had defaulted and a record number of foreclosures meant that real estate prices fell precipitously. In addition, a recessionary period and high unemployment made matters even worse, both for homeowners in distress and those who would otherwise have entered the housing market. By 2015, most areas of the country saw an increase in sales and property values; however, for many, those increases were modest, and the overall rate of homeownership continued to decline. According to the Census Bureau, www.census.gov, the annual average homeownership rate for 2016 was 63.4%, the lowest rate in the last half-century.

Certainly, not everyone wants to or should own a home. Home ownership involves substantial commitment and responsibility. People whose work requires frequent moves or whose financial position is uncertain particularly benefit from renting. Renting also provides more leisure time by freeing tenants from management and maintenance.

Those who choose home ownership over renting must evaluate many factors before they decide to purchase property. And the purchasing decision must be weighed carefully in light of each individual's financial circumstances.

The decision to buy or to rent property involves considering

- how long a person wants to live in a particular area,
- a person's financial situation,
- housing affordability,
- current mortgage interest rates,
- tax consequences of owning versus renting property, and
- what might happen to home prices and tax laws in the future.

Unfortunately, recent history has shown that there are those who will commit *mortgage fraud* in applying for a home loan by exaggerating income or assets, minimizing or concealing debt obligations, or providing a false employment history. Loan applicants have also been victims of *predatory lending* practices that result in too-high loan fees and abusive interest rates. To help curb such practices, HUD now certifies housing counselors to assist borrowers in knowing their responsibilities and rights. Information on the Housing Counseling Certification program is at www.hudexchange.info/programs/housing-counseling/.

Mortgage terms

Mortgage terms and payment plans are two of the biggest factors when deciding whether to own or rent a home. Although many loan programs of the past are no longer offered or are offered only to highly qualified borrowers, mortgages on less stringent terms are still available to those who qualify. The Federal Housing Administration (FHA) and the U.S. Department of Veterans Affairs (VA), for example, have programs with low down payments and lower credit score requirements. They, too, have tightened lending standards in recent years.

Ownership expenses and ability to pay

The basic costs of owning a home are **PITI**—
■ **P**rincipal,
■ **I**nterest,
■ **T**axes, and
■ **I**nsurance

Home ownership involves many expenses, including utility costs, such as electricity, natural gas, heating oil, water, trash removal, and sewer charges, in addition to routine maintenance and repairs. Owners also must pay real estate taxes, buy property insurance, and repay (with interest) the mortgage loan used to purchase the property—what lenders refer to as **PITI** (principal, interest, taxes, and insurance).

www.equifax.com
www.experian.com
www.transunion.com

To determine what a prospective buyer can afford, most home mortgage lenders use a computerized underwriting system that considers various factors, including the loan applicant's credit report and credit score. There are three major credit reporting companies in the United States: Equifax (www.equifax.com), Experian (www.experian.com), and TransUnion (www.transunion.com).

CHECKING YOUR CREDIT REPORT

www.annualcredit report.com/index .action

The *credit report* is important in acquiring a loan for a home or other major purchase, obtaining a credit card, being approved for a lease, and even in acquiring a new job. Because of its significance to the consumer in so many ways, the federal government requires each of the major credit reporting companies to make a free copy of the report available annually to every consumer for whom a report is available. The free reports can be obtained at www .annualcreditreport.com. (Don't be confused by similarly named sites that charge for this service.) Because each of the credit reporting agencies is required to comply with the law, the consumer can request a free report every four months from a different company each time, making it possible to monitor one's credit status on a regular basis.

www.myfico.com /credit-education /credit-report-credit -score-articles/

A *credit score* is prepared by a credit reporting company and is based on a consumer's past history of credit use, including income, outstanding loans, number of credit accounts open, outstanding credit lines, number of accounts opened and closed, payment history, and credit inquiries. The credit score, often called the FICO score because it can be created from software developed by Fair Isaac and Company, can range from a low of 300 to a high of 850, the best score. Lenders will require a minimum credit score for a loan, often dependent on whether or not the lender will sell the mortgage after initiating it or the borrower is making use of a government-sponsored program, such as those of FHA and VA. More information on the FICO score is at www.myfico.com/credit-education/credit-report-credit-score-articles/.

Lenders generally look at a loan applicant's percentage of **debt to income (DTI)**. A homebuyer who is able to provide at least 10% of the purchase price as a down payment, for instance, could be expected to incur a monthly PITI payment of no more than 28% of the borrower's gross (pretax) monthly income. Monthly payments on all debts—normally including long-term debt such as car payments, student loans, or other mortgages—would be expected to not exceed 36% of gross monthly income. Expenses such as insurance premiums, utilities, and routine medical care would not be included in the 36% figure but would be expected to be covered by the remaining 64% of the buyer's monthly income. The formula can vary, depending on the type of loan program and the borrower's earnings, credit history, number of dependents, and other factors. The borrower's credit score now plays a key role in the lending decision, though the debt-to-income ratio is still important.

IN PRACTICE

A prospective homebuyer wants to know how much to budget for a purchase. The buyer has a gross monthly income of $5,000. If the required down payment can be made, the buyer's allowable housing expense may be calculated as follows:

$5,000 gross monthly income × 28% = $1,400 total housing expense allowed

$5,000 gross monthly income × 36% = $1,800 total housing and other debt expense allowed

If actual monthly non-housing debts exceed 8% of gross income (36%–28%), and the borrower is unable to reduce that amount, the monthly payment must be lowered proportionately because the debts and housing payment combined cannot exceed 36% of gross monthly income. Lower debts would not result in a higher allowable housing payment, but would be considered a factor for approval.

The lender will also consider the **loan-to-value ratio (LTV)**, which is the amount of the loan as a percentage of the purchase price of the property. If a borrower makes a down payment of 10% of the purchase price and borrows the rest, the LTV is 90%. The lower the LTV (the greater the down payment), the less risk is assumed by the lender.

PROMISSORY NOTE

The purchase of a home usually requires borrowing a substantial amount—or all—of the purchase price. In exchange for a lender providing the needed funds, the borrower promises to repay the debt with interest.

The **promissory note**, called the *note* or *financing instrument*, is a borrower's personal promise to repay a debt according to the agreed terms. A promissory note executed by a borrower (the *maker* or *payor*) is a contract with the lender (the *payee*). The note generally states the amount of the debt, the time and method of payment, and the rate of interest. When signed by the borrower and other necessary parties, the note becomes a legally enforceable and fully negotiable instrument of debt. When the terms of the note are satisfied, the debt is discharged. If the terms of the note are not met, the lender may foreclose on any property that was used as security for the debt. When a note is unsecured (there is no collateral provided for the debt), the lender can sue to collect on the note.

A **note** is a **negotiable instrument**, similar to a check or bank draft. The payee who holds the note may transfer the right to receive payment to a third party in one of two ways:

■ By signing the instrument over (that is, by *assigning* it) to the third party

■ By delivering the instrument to the third party

IN PRACTICE

Most home loans are sold by the lenders who have made them, which is useful because it means that more funds are made available for future borrowers. Home loans are bought and sold in the *secondary mortgage market*.

Interest

Interest is a charge for the use of money, expressed as a percentage of the remaining balance of the loan. A lender charges interest on the principal (amount borrowed that has not yet been repaid) over the term of the loan, usually monthly. Interest may be due at either the end or the beginning of each payment period. Payments made at the end of a period are known as payments *in arrears*. This payment method is the general practice, and home loans often call for end-of-period payments due on the first of the following month. Payments may also be made at the beginning of each period and are known as payments *in advance*. Whether interest is charged in arrears or in advance is specified in the note. This distinction is important if the property is sold before the debt is repaid in full.

Usury

Charging interest in excess of the maximum rate allowed by law is called **usury**. To protect consumers from unscrupulous lenders, many states have enacted laws limiting the interest rate that may be charged on loans. In some states, a lender that makes a usurious loan is permitted to collect the borrowed money, but only at the legal rate of interest. In others, a usurious lender may lose the right to collect any interest or may lose the entire amount of the loan in addition to the interest.

As of March 31, 1980, federal law *exempts* federally related residential first mortgage loans made after that date from state usury laws. A federally related transaction is one that involves a federally chartered or insured lending institution or an agency of the federal government. Because federal law always preempts state law on the same subject, the federal law means that most home loans are not subject to state usury protections. Private lenders are still subject to state usury laws, however.

Loan origination fee

The processing of a mortgage application is known as *loan origination*. When a home loan is originated, a **loan origination fee**, or transfer fee, is charged by most lenders to cover the expenses involved in generating the loan. These expenses include the loan officer's salary and the lender's other costs of doing business. A loan origination fee is not prepaid interest; rather, it is a charge that must be paid to the lender. The loan origination fee will vary, depending on how competitive a lender chooses to be, but typically is about 1% of the loan amount.

IN PRACTICE

Because many real estate loans are made by private loan companies that may not be covered by federal regulations, it is important that a borrower insist on receiving a statement in advance from the lender that clearly states the total amount of the loan closing costs and the effective interest rate, in order to avoid unpleasant surprises at closing.

Discount points

Discount points are used to increase the lender's *yield* (rate of return) on its investment. For example, the interest rate that a lender charges for a loan might be less than the yield an investor demands. To make up the difference, the lender charges the borrower discount points. The number of points charged depends on two factors:

- The difference between the loan's stated interest rate and the yield required by the lender
- How long the lender expects it will take the borrower to pay off the loan

A **point** is 1% of the amount being borrowed; it is not 1% of the purchase price.

For borrowers, one discount point equals 1% of the loan amount (not purchase price) and is charged as prepaid interest at the closing. For instance, three discount points charged on a $100,000 loan would be $3,000, which is $100,000 × 3%, or $100,000 × 0.03. If a house sells for $100,000 and the borrower seeks an $80,000 loan, each point would be $800, not $1,000. The points in a new acquisition may be paid in cash at closing by the buyer (or, of course, by the seller on the buyer's behalf, as negotiated by the parties) rather than being financed as part of the total loan amount.

To determine how many points are charged on a loan, divide the total dollar amount of the points by the amount of the loan. For example, if the loan amount is $350,000 and the charge for points is $9,275, how many points are being charged?

$9,275 ÷ $350,000 = 0.0265 or 2.65% or 2.65 points

Prepayment penalty

Most mortgage loans are paid in installments over a long period of time. As a result, the total interest paid by the borrower may add up to more than the principal amount of the loan. That does not come as a surprise to the lender; the total amount of accrued interest is carefully calculated during the origination phase to determine the profitability of each loan. If the borrower repays the loan before the end of the term, the lender collects less than the anticipated interest. For this reason, some mortgage notes contain a *prepayment clause*. This clause requires that the borrower pay a **prepayment penalty** against the unearned portion of the interest for any payments made ahead of schedule, typically during the first years of the loan. This gives the lender the assurance of a certain level of income earned on the loan.

Lenders may not charge prepayment penalties on mortgage loans insured or guaranteed by the federal government or on those loans that have been sold on the secondary mortgage market to one of the government-sponsored enterprises, such as Fannie Mae.

SECURITY INSTRUMENT

Mortgage loans are secured loans. Mortgage loans have two parts: the debt itself and the security for the debt. When a property is mortgaged, the owner must *execute* (sign) two separate instruments—the financing instrument that creates the debt and the security instrument that specifies the property that the debtor will use as collateral for the debt. The financing instrument is the promissory note (discussed earlier), which states the amount owed. Depending on the state, the security instrument will take the form of either a mortgage or a deed of trust, though both are commonly referred to as a mortgage, and will specify the property used to secure the loan. A mortgage creates a lien on the property; the deed of trust actually transfers legal title from the borrower to a third party to hold on behalf of the lender while the borrower's debt is still outstanding. This section looks at the differences in how each form of security interest is created and how each is enforced.

A basic principle of property law is that no one can convey more than he actually owns. This principle also applies to a mortgage. The owner of a fee simple estate can mortgage the fee. The owner of a leasehold or subleasehold can mortgage that leasehold interest. The owner of a condominium unit can mortgage the fee interest in the condominium. Even the owner of a cooperative unit may be able to offer that property interest (the owner's stock in the underlying corporation) as security for a loan.

Hypothecation

In mortgage lending practice, a borrower is required to make specific real property security (collateral) for the loan. In the process called **hypothecation**, the debtor retains the right of possession and control of the secured property, while the creditor receives an equitable right in the property. The right to foreclose on the property in the event a borrower defaults is contained in the security agreement, which takes the form of either a mortgage or a deed of trust, as discussed next.

Mortgage

A **mortgage** is a lien on the real property of a debtor. The borrower, or **mortgagor**, receives a loan and in return gives a promissory note and mortgage to the lender, called the **mortgagee**. The mortgage is a voluntary, specific lien. If the debtor defaults, the lender can sue on the note and foreclose on the mortgage. When the loan is paid in full, the mortgagee issues a document called a **satisfaction of mortgage**, which can be filed in the public record as evidence of the removal of the security interest, which would otherwise continue to be an encumbrance on the ownership interest of the borrower. The judicial process for foreclosure of a mortgage depends on state law and on whether the state treats the mortgage as a lien or as a conveyance of some part of the title to the property.

In a mortgage or **lien theory** state, the mortgagor retains both legal and equitable title to property that serves as security for a debt. The mortgagee has a lien on the property but the mortgage is nothing more than collateral for the loan. If the mortgagor defaults, the mortgagee must go through a formal foreclosure proceeding in court to obtain legal title. If the foreclosure is approved by the court, the property is offered for sale at public auction, and the funds from the sale are used to pay the balance of the remaining debt. In some states, a defaulting mortgagor may *redeem* (buy back) the property during a certain period after the sale, the *statutory right of redemption*. A borrower who fails to redeem the property during that time loses the property irrevocably. See Figure 12.1 for a diagram of how a mortgage works.

FIGURE 12.1: Mortgages

Mortgage — Two Parties

When the Money Is Borrowed

- Mortgagor (Borrower)
  - Note and Mortgage
  - Loan $
- Mortgagee (Lender)

When the Money Is Repaid

- Mortgagor (Borrower)
  - Pays the Loan $
  - Satisfaction of Mortgage
- Mortgagee (Lender)

Deed of trust

In some states, lenders prefer to use a three-party security instrument known as a **deed of trust**. A trust deed conveys bare legal title (naked title)—that is, title without the right of possession—from the borrower to a third party, called the *trustee*. The trustee holds legal title on behalf of the lender, the holder of the promissory note, who is known as the **beneficiary.** On full payment of the underlying debt, the lender/beneficiary notifies the trustee, who returns legal title to the trustor.

In a deed of trust or *title theory* state, such as Arizona, the borrower is the trustor who conveys *legal title* to the trustee but retains *equitable title* and the right of possession. Legal title is returned to the borrower/trustor only when the debt is paid in full (or some other obligation is performed).

The deed of trust establishes the actions that the trustee may take if the borrower, the **trustor**, defaults under any of the deed of trust terms. In states where deeds of trust are generally preferred, foreclosure procedures for default, which must comply with state law, are usually simpler and faster than for mortgage loans. On notification of the borrower's default, the trustee is authorized to sell the secured property, providing the proceeds to the beneficiary, the lender. If the sale proceeds are greater than the amount owed on the debt, the borrower receives the difference, less penalty fees and court costs.

Usually, the lender chooses the trustee and reserves the right to substitute trustees in the event of the trustee's death or dismissal. State law usually dictates who may serve as trustee. Although the deed of trust is particularly popular in certain states, it is used all over the country. See Figure 12.2 for a diagram of how a deed of trust works.

FIGURE 12.2: Deed of Trust

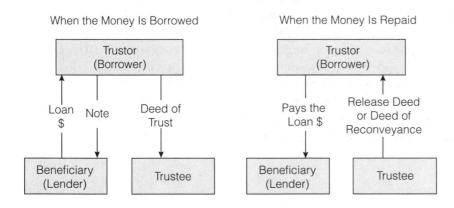

Deed of Trust — Three Parties

When the Money Is Borrowed

When the Money Is Repaid

Trustor (Borrower)

Loan $ | Note | Deed of Trust

Beneficiary (Lender) | Trustee

Trustor (Borrower)

Pays the Loan $ | Release Deed or Deed of Reconveyance

Beneficiary (Lender) | Trustee

IN PRACTICE

In the financing of a commercial or industrial real estate venture that involves a large loan and several lenders, the borrower generally executes a single deed of trust to secure as many notes as necessary. Sometimes a large note will be secured by multiple parcels of real property, as in a subdivision, and there will be a separate security instrument for each parcel.

A mortgage or deed of trust must clearly establish that the property is security for a debt, identify the lender and the borrower, and include an accurate legal description of the property. Both instruments incorporate the terms of the promissory note by reference, which coordinates the note and security instrument, and both should be signed by all parties who have an interest in the real estate.

IN PRACTICE

In reality, the differences between the parties' rights in a lien theory state and those in a title theory state are more technical than actual. Regardless of the practice in any particular state, all borrowers and lenders observe the same general requirements to protect themselves in a loan transaction. As with any contract, the parties must be legally competent, their signatures valid and attested, and adequate consideration exchanged.

Duties of the borrower

The borrower—whether a mortgagor or a trustor—is required to fulfill certain obligations created by the mortgage or deed of trust. These usually include the following:

- Payment of the debt in accordance with the terms of the promissory note
- Payment of all real estate taxes on the property used as security
- Maintenance of adequate insurance to protect the lender in the event that the property is destroyed or damaged by fire, windstorm, or other hazard
- Maintenance of the property in good repair at all times
- Receipt of lender authorization before making any major alterations on the property

Failure to meet any of these obligations can result in a borrower's default. The loan documents may, however, provide for a grace period (such as 30 days) during which the borrower can meet the obligation and cure the default. If the borrower does not do so, the lender has the right to take the steps described next.

Provisions for default

The mortgage or deed of trust typically includes an **acceleration clause** to assist the lender in foreclosure. If a borrower defaults, the lender has the right to accelerate the maturity of the debt. This means the lender may declare the *entire* principal balance due and payable *immediately*. Without an acceleration clause, the lender would have to sue the borrower every time a payment was overdue.

Other provisions in a mortgage or deed of trust enable the lender to take care of the property in the event of the borrower's negligence or default. If the borrower does not pay taxes or insurance premiums, or fails to make necessary repairs on the property, the lender may step in and do so. The lender has the power to protect the security (the real estate).

IN PRACTICE

In financing a real estate sale, a lender will seldom accept an unsecured promissory note because there would be no backup for the loan. If a borrower defaulted, the lender would be forced to sue for a money judgment. In the meantime, the debtor might dispose of the property and hide assets. In some states, a money judgment cannot be used to foreclose on a debtor's personal residence. Because of these, and other reasons, lenders prefer a security interest in real property.

Assignment of the mortgage

As noted earlier, a promissory note usually is a negotiable instrument. This means that, without changing the provisions of the contract, the note may be sold to a third party, such as an investor or another mortgage company. The original mortgagee (the *assignor*) endorses the note to the third party (the *assignee*) and executes an *assignment* of mortgage. The assignee becomes the new owner of the debt and security instrument. When the debt is paid in full (or satisfied), the assignee is required to execute the document that releases the security interest.

Release of the mortgage lien or deed of trust

When all loan payments have been made and the promissory note has been paid in full, the borrower will want the public record to show that the debt has been satisfied and that the lender is divested of all rights conveyed under the mortgage or deed of trust. By the provisions of the **defeasance clause** in the financing instrument, the lender is required to execute a **satisfaction of mortgage** (also known as a *release* or *discharge*) when the note has been fully paid. This document returns to the borrower all interest in the real estate originally conveyed to the lender. Entering this release in the public record shows that the debt has been removed from the property.

When a real estate loan secured by a deed of trust has been completely repaid, the beneficiary must make a written request that the trustee convey the title to the property back to the grantor. The trustee executes and delivers a *deed of reconveyance* (sometimes called a **release deed**) to the trustor. The deed to the trustor conveys the same rights and powers that the trustee was given under the deed of trust. It should include a notarized acknowledgment and be recorded in the public records of the county in which the property is located.

If the mortgage or deed of trust has been assigned, the satisfaction of mortgage or reconveyance deed must be executed and recorded by the assignee or mortgagee.

Tax and insurance reserves

As discussed previously, many lenders require that borrowers provide a reserve fund to meet future real estate taxes and property insurance premiums. This fund is called an *impound* or *escrow account*. When the mortgage or deed of trust loan is made, the borrower starts the reserve by depositing funds to cover the amount of unpaid real estate taxes. If a new insurance policy has just been purchased, the insurance premium reserve will be started with the deposit of one-twelfth of the insurance premium liability. The borrower's monthly loan payments will include PITI: principal, interest, taxes, and insurance. Other costs also may be included, such as flood insurance. Federal regulations limit the total amount of reserves that a lender may require.

IN PRACTICE

The borrower should make sure that property taxes and insurance payments have been made by the holder of an impound account by their respective due dates. The borrower should also keep track of any increases in taxes or insurance payments, in order to deposit a sufficient amount into the impound account.

Flood insurance reserves

The National Flood Insurance Reform Act of 1994 imposes certain mandatory obligations on lenders and loan servicers to set aside (*escrow*) funds for flood insurance on new loans for property in flood-prone areas. This means that if a lender or servicer discovers that a secured property is in a flood hazard area, it must notify the borrower. The borrower then has 45 days to purchase flood insurance. If the borrower fails to procure flood insurance, the lender must purchase the insurance on the borrower's behalf. The cost of the insurance may be charged back to the borrower. More information on flood insurance, which can be a critical part of home ownership, is provided later.

Buying "subject to" or assuming a seller's mortgage or deed of trust

When a person purchases real estate that has an outstanding mortgage or deed of trust, the buyer may take the property in one of two ways. The property may be purchased **"subject to"** the mortgage or deed of trust, or by **assumption of mortgage**, in which the buyer assumes the mortgage or deed of trust and agrees to pay the debt. This technical distinction becomes important if the buyer defaults and the mortgage or deed of trust is foreclosed.

When the property is sold *subject to* the mortgage, the buyer is not personally obligated to pay the debt in full. The buyer takes title to the real estate knowing that she must make payments on the existing loan. Upon default, the lender forecloses and the property is sold by court order to pay the debt. If the sale does not pay off the entire debt, the purchaser is not liable for the difference. In some circumstances, however, the original seller might continue to be liable.

In contrast, a buyer who purchases a property and assumes the seller's debt becomes personally obligated for the payment of the entire debt. If a seller wants to be completely free of the original mortgage loan, the seller(s), buyer(s), and lender must execute a **novation** agreement in writing. The novation makes the buyer solely responsible for any default on the loan. The original borrower (seller) is freed of any liability for the loan.

The existence of a lien does not prevent the transfer of property; however, when a secured loan is assumed, the mortgagee or beneficiary must approve the assumption and any release of liability of the original mortgagor or trustor. Because a loan may not be assumed without lender approval, the lending institution would require the assumer to qualify financially, and many lending institutions charge a transfer fee to cover the costs of changing the records. This charge can be paid by either the buyer or the seller.

Alienation clause

The lender may want to prevent a future purchaser of the property from being able to assume the loan, particularly if the original interest rate is low. For this reason, most lenders include an **alienation clause** (also known as a *resale clause*, *due-on-sale clause*, or *call clause*) in the note. An alienation clause provides that when the property is sold, the lender may either declare the entire debt due immediately or permit the buyer to assume the loan at an interest rate acceptable to the lender. Land contracts that involve a due-on-sale clause also limit the assumption of the contract.

Recording a mortgage or deed of trust

The mortgage document or deed of trust must be recorded in the recorder's office of the county in which the real estate is located. Recording gives constructive notice to the world of the borrower's obligations. Recording also establishes the lien's priority. If the property is registered in the Torrens system, notice of the lien must be entered on the original Torrens certificate.

Priority of a mortgage or deed of trust

Priority of mortgages and other liens normally is determined by the order in which they were recorded. A mortgage or deed of trust on land that has no prior mortgage lien is a *first mortgage* or *first deed of trust*. If the owner later executes another loan for additional funds, the new loan becomes a *second mortgage* or *second deed of trust* (or a *junior lien*) when it is recorded. Second loans represent greater risk to the lender, and they usually have a higher interest rate.

In the event that a second lien has a higher amount than the first, the lender may require a *subordination agreement*, in which the first lender subordinates or lowers its lien position to that of the second lender. To be valid, both lenders must sign the agreement.

TYPES OF LOANS

Real estate can be financed in a variety of ways. The most popular forms of financing are discussed next. Most provide for some form of *amortization*, with each payment including part of the loan principal, so that the entire principal is paid off by the end of the loan term.

Straight loan

With a **straight loan** (also known as a *term loan* or **interest-only loan**) the borrower makes periodic payments of interest only, followed by the payment of the principal *in full at the end of the term*. Straight loans were once the only form of home loan available, but are now generally used for home improvements and second mortgages rather than for residential first mortgage loans. A loan may provide for interest-only payments in the beginning years, to make payments affordable.

Amortized loan

Each payment in an **amortized loan** partially pays interest as well as a portion of the principal owed. Most mortgage and deed of trust loans are amortized loans. The word *amortize* literally means to kill off. The amount borrowed is gradually paid back over the loan term. The payment period usually ranges from 10 to 30 years. At the end of the loan term, the full amount of the principal and all interest due is reduced to zero. Such loans are known as *direct reduction loans*.

With a *fully amortized loan*, or *level-payment loan*, the lender credits each payment first to the interest due, then to the principal amount of the loan. While each payment remains the same, the portion applied to repayment of the principal grows and the interest due declines as the unpaid balance of the loan is reduced. If the borrower pays additional amounts that are applied directly to the principal, the loan will amortize more quickly. The required payment stays the same, but more of each payment goes toward paying down the principal, thereby shortening the loan term.

IN PRACTICE

Financial calculators can accurately perform the standard mortgage lending calculations, and most commercial lenders provide mortgage calculators on their websites. Nonetheless, it is valuable to understand how the calculations are performed.

Adjustable-rate mortgage (ARM)

The **adjustable-rate mortgage (ARM)** begins at one rate of interest, then fluctuates up or down during the loan term, based on a specified economic indicator. Because the interest rate may change, the mortgagor's loan payment may change. Details of how and when the interest rate will change are included in the note. When there is not much difference in interest rate between a fixed and an adjustable-rate loan, the ARM is less appealing. Common components of an ARM include the following:

■ The **index** is an economic indicator that is used to adjust the interest rate in the loan. Most indexes are tied to U.S. Treasury securities. The adjustment period establishes how often the rate may be changed, which could be monthly, quarterly, or annually. If interest rates are going up, the longest adjustment period benefits the borrower. If interest rates are going down, the borrower benefits from a shorter adjustment period.

■ Usually, the interest rate is the index rate plus a premium, called the **margin**. The margin represents the lender's cost of doing business.

■ *Rate caps* limit the amount the interest rate may change. Most ARMs have two types of rate caps—periodic and life-of-the-loan (or aggregate). A periodic rate cap limits the amount the rate may increase over a stated term, usually a year. A life-of-the-loan rate cap limits the amount the rate may increase over the entire life of the loan.

The mortgagor can be protected from unaffordable individual payments by a *payment cap*. The payment cap sets a maximum amount for payments, but the difference between the payment made and the full payment amount will be added to the remaining mortgage balance. The amount of the loan actually increases (instead of decreasing) in the process called **negative amortization**. If property values do not increase as anticipated, or the borrower can no longer afford to make mortgage payments, negative amortization can result in the borrower owing more than the property is worth—the unhappy situation of being *under water*. The *option ARM* that allowed negative amortization as one of the borrower's choices was a contributing factor to many of the foreclosures that suppressed the housing market in many parts of the country.

The lender may offer a conversion option that permits the mortgagor to convert from an adjustable-rate to a fixed-rate loan at certain intervals during the life of the mortgage.

Growing-equity mortgage

A **growing-equity mortgage** is also called a *rapid-payoff mortgage*. The growing-equity mortgage uses a fixed interest rate, but payments of principal are increased according to an index or schedule. The total payment thus increases, and the loan is paid off more quickly. A growing-equity mortgage is most frequently used when the borrower's income is expected to keep pace with the increasing loan payments.

MATH CONCEPTS

The Mortgage Amortization Triangle

If you know the monthly payment and interest rate on a loan, you can easily track how much of each month's payment is being applied toward principal and how much is applied toward interest.

Always begin with the top box and follow the direction of the arrows to perform the calculations described in each box for each month's calculation. Your result will show how much of a given month's mortgage payment goes to pay principal and what portion pays interest on the loan to the lender. For instance, if you wanted to see how much the loan principal would be reduced after three months, you would "go around the triangle" three times.

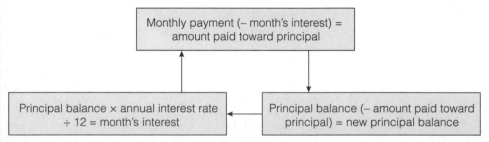

For example, using the Mortgage Factor Chart in Figure 12.3, assume a 15-year mortgage loan for $150,000 at a 3.75% annual interest rate and a monthly payment of $1,090.50 (150,000 ÷ 1,000 × 7.27 = $1,090.50). You can see how the triangle can help you determine the amount of principal and interest in each payment for the first two months of the loan (shown in each box as "1" and "2").

The principal balance on the loan at the end of the second month (the beginning of the third month) 148,754.56.

What is the principal balance on this loan at the end of the third month?

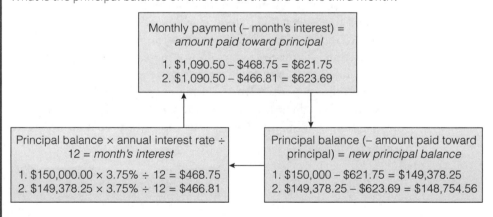

Solution

Step 1: $148,754.56 × 3.75% ÷ 12 = $464.86

Step 2: $1,090.50 − $464.86 = $625.64

Step 3: $148,754.56 − $625.64 = $148,128.92

Principal balance at the end of the third month is $148,128.92

FIGURE 12.3: Mortgage Factor Chart

How to use this chart	Rate	Term 15 Years	Term 30 Years		Rate	Term 15 Years	Term 30 Years
To use this chart, start by finding the appropriate interest rate. Then follow that row over to the column for the appropriate loan term. This number is the *interest rate factor* required each month to amortize a $1,000 loan. To calculate the principal and interest (PI) payment, multiply the interest rate factor by the number of 1,000s in the total loan.	3	6.91	4.22		6	8.44	6.00
	3⅛	6.97	4.28		6⅛	8.51	6.08
	3¼	7.03	4.35		6¼	8.57	6.16
	3⅜	7.09	4.42		6⅜	8.64	6.24
	3½	7.15	4.49		6½	8.71	6.32
	3⅝	7.21	4.56		6⅝	8.78	6.40
	3¾	7.27	4.63		6¾	8.85	6.49
	3⅞	7.33	4.70		6⅞	8.92	6.57
For example, if the interest rate is 6% for a term of 30 years, the interest rate factor is 6.00. If the total loan is $200,000, the loan contains 200 1,000s. Therefore, 200 × 6.00 = $1,200 PI.	4	7.40	4.77		7	8.98	6.65
	4⅛	7.46	4.85		7⅛	9.06	6.74
	4¼	7.52	4.92		7¼	9.12	6.82
	4⅜	7.59	4.99		7⅜	9.20	6.91
	4½	7.65	5.07		7½	9.27	6.99
	4⅝	7.71	5.14		7⅝	9.34	7.08
	4¾	7.78	5.22		7¾	9.41	7.16
	4⅞	7.84	5.29		7⅞	9.48	7.25
	5	7.91	5.37		8	9.56	7.34
	5⅛	7.97	5.44		8⅛	9.63	7.43
	5¼	8.04	5.52		8¼	9.71	7.52
	5⅜	8.10	5.60		8⅜	9.78	7.61
	5½	8.17	5.68		8½	9.85	7.69
	5⅝	8.24	5.76		8⅝	9.93	7.78
	5¾	8.30	5.84		8¾	10.00	7.87
	5⅞	8.37	5.92		8⅞	10.07	7.96
					9	10.15	8.05

Balloon payment loan

When the periodic payments on a loan are not enough to fully pay off the principal of the loan by the time the final payment is due, the final payment will be larger than the others. State law will provide the definition, but typically a **balloon payment** is a final payment that is at least twice the amount of any other payment. The loan will be considered a *partially amortized loan* because some of the principal has been paid, with some still owed at the end of the term.

It is frequently assumed that if payments are made promptly, the lender will extend the balloon payment for another limited term. The lender, however, is not legally obligated to grant this extension and can require payment in full when the note is due.

Reverse mortgage

A **reverse mortgage** allows a homeowner aged 62 or older to borrow money against the equity built up in the home. The borrowed money may be used for any purpose and the borrower decides if the funds will be paid out in a lump sum, fixed monthly payments, an open line of credit, or another option. The borrower is charged a fixed rate of interest on amounts paid out by the lender, but the lender does not need to be repaid until the property is sold or the borrow defaults (perhaps by failing to maintain the property), moves, or dies. With the recent recession and volatility of the stock market, the reverse mortgage has become a popular method of providing more income for other expenses while allowing the homeowner to remain in the home. It is important to remember, however, that the usual property tax, insurance, maintenance, and utility costs must still be paid by the homeowner, and these may be more substantial than the income produced by the reverse mortgage. Also, with the equity in the home reduced, the homeowner will have fewer resources on which to draw in the event that a move to a smaller property, an assisted-living facility, or a nursing home becomes necessary.

_____
www.hud.gov
_____

The most popular reverse mortgages are those insured by FHA through its Home Equity Conversion Mortgage (HECM) program. For more information, go to www.hud.gov and enter "reverse mortgage" in the search feature.

FORECLOSURE

Foreclosure is a legal procedure in which property pledged as security for a debt is sold to satisfy the debt when a borrower defaults on any required payment or fails to fulfill any of the other obligations set forth in the mortgage or deed of trust. Any unpaid lienholder, regardless of priority position, can initiate foreclosure proceedings; however, foreclosure of a junior lien means that the liens with higher priority remain in place and the buyer takes title subject to those liens. The foreclosure of a lien with highest priority brings the rights of the parties and all junior lienholders to a conclusion. It passes title to the person holding the mortgage document, the beneficiary of a deed of trust, or a third party who purchases the property at a *foreclosure sale*. The property is sold *free of the foreclosing mortgage and all junior liens*.

The purchaser on foreclosure of a debt secured by real property could be the mortgagee—the lender—and the property then becomes part of the lender's *REO (real estate owned)* portfolio. The lender then becomes responsible for maintaining the property and paying the expenses of ownership, including property taxes.

IN PRACTICE

Institutional lenders are not in the business of managing property, so they try to minimize their REO portfolios, but dealing with an institutional seller can be a frustrating experience for a prospective buyer. In some areas, a buyer should be prepared for a much longer than usual time for acceptance of an offer to purchase as well as a lengthy period before the sale is closed, during which there may be repeated requests from the seller that must be addressed. In other areas, the volume of REO sales has prompted lenders to expedite the sale process. In any event, an attractive sales price may make the purchase of an REO property worth any aggravation.

Methods of foreclosure

There are three general types of foreclosure proceedings—judicial, nonjudicial, and strict foreclosure. The specific provisions and procedures depend on state law.

Judicial foreclosure

Judicial foreclosure allows the property to be sold by court order after the mortgagee has given sufficient public notice. When a borrower defaults, the lender may *accelerate* the due date of the remaining principal balance, along with all overdue monthly payments and interest, penalties, and administrative costs. The lender's attorney can then file a suit to foreclose the lien. After presentation of the facts in court, if the court grants the request, the property is ordered sold. A public sale is advertised and held, and the real estate is sold to the highest bidder.

Nonjudicial foreclosure

Some states allow nonjudicial foreclosure procedures to be used when the security instrument contains a *power-of-sale clause*. In nonjudicial foreclosure, no court action is required. In those states that recognize deed of trust loans, the beneficiary is generally given the power of sale, which is conducted by the trustee. Some states allow a similar power of sale to be used with a mortgage loan, if specified in the terms of the mortgage.

To institute a nonjudicial foreclosure, the trustee or mortgagee will send a notice of default to the borrower indicating the amount that must be paid to make the debt current, as well as the action that will be taken if the required payment is not made. If the borrower fails to *cure* the default within the specified time, a notice of foreclosure will be sent to the borrower, indicating when and where the property will be sold at public auction. The notice of foreclosure will be recorded within a designated period to give notice to the public of the intended auction. The notice is generally provided by newspaper advertisements that state the total amount due and the date of the public sale. After selling the property, the trustee or mortgagee may be required to file a notice of sale or affidavit of foreclosure.

Strict foreclosure

In some states, a lender may acquire mortgaged property through a *strict foreclosure* process. First, appropriate notice must be given to the delinquent borrower. Once the proper documents have been prepared and recorded, the court establishes a deadline for the balance of the defaulted debt to be paid in full. If the borrower does not pay off the loan by that date, the court simply awards full legal title to the lender. No sale takes place. Strict foreclosure is more common when personal property is used to secure a debt.

Deed in lieu of foreclosure

As an alternative to foreclosure, a lender may be willing to accept a **deed in lieu of foreclosure** from the borrower. This is sometimes known as a *friendly foreclosure* because it is carried out by mutual agreement rather than by lawsuit. The deed in lieu of foreclosure eliminates any equity that the homeowner may have had in the property. The disadvantage of the deed in lieu of foreclosure to the lender is that it does not eliminate junior liens. In a foreclosure action, all junior liens are eliminated. Also, by accepting a deed in lieu of foreclosure, the lender usually loses any rights pertaining to FHA or private mortgage insurance or VA guarantees. Finally, a deed in lieu of foreclosure is still considered an adverse element in the borrower's credit history.

Unit 12

Redemption

Most states give defaulting borrowers a chance to redeem their property through the *equitable right of redemption*. If, after default but before the foreclosure sale, the borrower (or any other person who has an interest in the real estate, such as another creditor) pays the lender the amount in default, plus costs, the debt will be reinstated. In some cases, the person who redeems may be required to repay the accelerated loan in full. If some person other than the mortgagor or trustor redeems the real estate, the borrower becomes responsible to that person for the amount of the redemption.

Certain states also allow defaulted borrowers a period in which to redeem their real estate after the sale. During this period (which may be as long as one year), the borrower has a *statutory right of redemption*. The mortgagor who can raise the necessary funds to redeem the property within the statutory period pays the redemption money to the court. Because the debt was paid from the proceeds of the sale, the borrower can take possession free and clear of the former defaulted loan. The court may appoint a receiver to take charge of the property, collect rents, and pay operating expenses during the redemption period. (See Figure 12.4.)

FIGURE 12.4: Redemption

| Equitable Redemption (*before the sale*) | Statutory Redemption (*after the sale*) |

Date of Default — Date of Sale — End of Redemption Rights

Deed to purchaser at sale

If redemption is not made, or if state law does not provide for a redemption period, the successful bidder at the foreclosure sale receives a deed to the real estate. Officials such as a sheriff, an officer of the court, or a trustee executes this deed to the purchaser to *convey whatever title the borrower had*.

Deficiency judgment

The foreclosure sale may not produce enough cash to pay the loan balance in full after deducting expenses and accrued unpaid interest. In that case, the mortgagee may be entitled to a *personal judgment* against the borrower for the unpaid balance. Such a judgment is a **deficiency judgment**. It may also be obtained against any endorsers or guarantors of the note and against any owners of the mortgaged property who assumed the debt by written agreement. If any money remains from the foreclosure sale after paying the debt and any other liens (such as a second mortgage or a mechanic's lien), expenses, and interest, those proceeds are paid to the borrower.

Some states prohibit a deficiency judgment on a purchase money loan for the borrower's principal residence. A lender could decide not to pursue a deficiency judgment, even though entitled to one, but the defaulting borrower could then be faced with short sale situation.

Short sale

Since 2008, many parts of the country have experienced a severe drop in market values of all kinds of real estate. While the market has improved somewhat in many places, a prospective property seller may still be faced with a proposed sales price that is less than the amount outstanding on the seller's mortgage debt. In such a situation, the lender may permit a **short sale** in which the sales price is less than the remaining indebtedness. Contact the lender before marketing the property to determine whether or not the short sale would be accepted and, if so, how low a sales price the lender would be willing to approve.

The listing of a property for which a short sale has been approved should always disclose that fact. The lender will expect to approve the sales contract negotiated by buyer and seller and will also be informed of the progress of the transaction, giving final approval before the closing. Lender approvals will add several months or longer to the closing of the transaction, and the buyer should be aware of the lengthy period before the transaction can be completed. This might be acceptable to a buyer who is satisfied that the sales price is worth the wait; another buyer might not be able to wait that long.

A lender's willingness to approve a short sale may result in forgiveness of part of the borrower's debt. In addition to the seller's loss of any equity in the property, the forgiveness of part of the seller's mortgage debt has been considered by the IRS to be income to the seller/borrower and thus subject to income tax. The widespread dismay at this outcome resulted in the passage by Congress of the Mortgage Forgiveness Debt Relief Act of 2007. The law allows a taxpayer to exclude from income the forgiveness of part of the mortgage debt on the taxpayer's principal residence on a sale of the property, restructuring of an existing mortgage loan, or foreclosure of a mortgage loan. Subsequent legislation extended this provision through January 1, 2017.

CONSUMER PROTECTIONS

As directed by the Wall Street Reform and Consumer Protection Act of 2010 (Dodd-Frank), the Consumer Financial Protection Bureau (CFPB) issued new mortgage disclosure rules that took effect January 10, 2014. A consumer information pamphlet, which was released in January 2013, can be found at www.consumerfinance.gov. The pamphlet explains information that the mortgage lender must provide to the borrower and also provides contact information for the borrower to initiate a complaint if the lender is not following the rules. The lender must

www.consumerfinance
.gov

- provide billing information in writing;

- give the borrower two months' warning if an adjustable-rate mortgage will have a rate change;

- promptly credit the borrower's payments;

- respond quickly when the borrower asks about paying off the loan;

- not charge for insurance the borrower doesn't need, or over-charge for insurance the lender provides if the borrower fails to do so ("force-placed insurance");

- quickly resolve complaints, generally within 30 to 45 business days, and share information;

- have and follow good customer service policies and procedures;

- contact the borrower to help when the borrower is having trouble making payments;

- work with the borrower, if the borrower is having trouble paying the mortgage, before starting or continuing foreclosure; and

- allow the borrower to seek review of the decision about a loan workout request.

The CFPB also created two new forms to be provided to the borrower after the loan application and before the close of the transaction. These forms are discussed later.

Homeowners insurance

A home is usually the biggest purchase many people ever make. Most homebuyers recognize the importance of protecting their investment by insuring it. A lender will require that a homeowner obtain insurance when the loan is secured by the property. While owners can purchase individual policies that insure against destruction of property by fire or windstorm, injury to others, and theft of personal property, most buy a **homeowners insurance** policy to cover all these risks.

Coverage and claims

The most common homeowners policy is called a *basic form*. The basic form provides property coverage against

- fire and lightning,
- glass breakage,
- windstorm and hail,
- explosion,
- riot and civil commotion,
- damage by aircraft,
- damage from vehicles,
- damage from smoke,
- vandalism and malicious mischief,
- theft, and
- loss of property removed from the premises when it is endangered by fire or other perils.

Broad-form homeowners insurance covers

- falling objects;
- damage due to the weight of ice, snow, or sleet;
- collapse of all or part of the building;
- bursting, cracking, burning, or bulging of a steam or water heating system or of appliances used to heat water;
- accidental discharge, leakage, or overflow of water or steam from within a plumbing, heating, or air-conditioning system;
- freezing of plumbing, heating, and air-conditioning systems and domestic appliances; and
- damage to electrical appliances, devices, fixtures, and wiring from short circuits or other accidentally generated currents.

Additional insurance is available to cover almost all possible perils. Special apartment and condominium policies generally provide fire and windstorm, theft, and public *liability coverage* for injuries or losses sustained within the unit, but they usually do not cover losses or damages to the structure. The basic structure is insured by either the landlord or the condominium owners association.

Most homeowners insurance policies contain a *coinsurance clause*. This provision usually requires that the owner maintain insurance equal to a specified percentage (usually 80%) of the *replacement cost* of the dwelling (not including the price of the land). An owner who has this type of policy may make a claim for the full cost of the repair or replacement of the damaged property without deduction for depreciation or annual wear and tear.

IN PRACTICE

A homeowner's insurance policy is for 80% of the replacement cost of the home, or $80,000. The home is valued at $100,000, and the land is valued at $40,000. The homeowner sustains $30,000 in fire damage to the house. The homeowner can make a claim for the full cost of the repair or replacement of the damaged property without a deduction for depreciation. If the owner has insurance of only $70,000, the claim will be handled in one of two ways. The owner will receive either actual cash value (replacement cost of $30,000 less depreciation cost of say $3,000, or $27,000), or the claim will be prorated by dividing the percentage of replacement cost actually covered (0.70) by the policy's minimum coverage requirement (0.80). So, 0.70 divided by 0.80 equals 0.875, and $30,000 multiplied by 0.875 equals $26,250.

Comprehensive Loss Underwriting Exchange

The **Comprehensive Loss Underwriting Exchange (CLUE)** is a database of consumer claims history that enables insurance companies to access prior claims information in the underwriting and rating process. The database contains up to five years of personal property claims history. The reports include policy information such as name, date of birth, policy number, and claim information date (date and type of loss, amounts paid, and description of property covered). More information about the CLUE report, and how one can be obtained, is at http://oci.wi.gov/pub_list/pi-207.htm.http://oci.wi.gov/pub_list/pi-207.htm.

http://oci.wi.gov/
pub_list/pi-207.htm

National Flood Insurance Program

The National Flood Insurance Act of 1968 was enacted by Congress to help owners of property in flood-prone areas by subsidizing flood insurance and by taking land-use and land-control measures to improve future management for floodplain areas. The Federal Emergency Management Agency (FEMA) administers the National Flood Insurance Program (NFIP). The Army Corps of Engineers has prepared maps that identify specific flood-prone areas throughout the country. To finance property with federally related mortgage loans, owners in flood-prone areas must obtain flood insurance.

In flood-prone areas identified as *special flood hazard areas* (*SFHAs*), flood insurance is required on all types of buildings—residential, commercial, industrial, and agricultural—used as security for a federally related mortgage loan. The insurance must cover either the value of the property or the amount of the mortgage loan, subject to the maximum limits available. Policies are written annually and can be purchased from any licensed property insurance broker, the NFIP, or the designated servicing companies in each state. A borrower who can produce a survey showing that the lowest part of the building is located above the 100-year flood mark may be exempted from the flood insurance requirement, even if the property is in a flood-prone area. A flood insurance premium reduction is available for communities that participate in NFIP's voluntary Community Rating System (CRS) by taking floodplain management steps to reduce flood losses, facilitating accurate insurance ratings, and promoting awareness of flood insurance issues.

Even when it is not required, flood insurance should be considered for all properties in coastal states subject to hurricanes and in any state through which major rivers run. The cost of flood insurance will increase the property owner's expenses, which will be taken into consideration by the lender when making a financing decision. Higher expenses mean that a borrower will qualify for a lower loan amount, or may be charged a higher interest rate, but a lower interest rate will be no comfort if the property suffers unexpected flood damage.

IN PRACTICE

A flood insurance policy is separate from a homeowners insurance policy, which many property owners fail to realize until it is too late. Flood insurance is not retroactive; it must be purchased before a disaster occurs. Flood insurance is not effective until 30 days after it is purchased, unless the lender requires it.

Flood insurance: what's covered and what's not

FEMA defines a flood as "a general and temporary condition of partial or complete inundation of two or more acres of normally dry land or two or more properties from

- an overflow of inland or tidal waves,

- an unusual and rapid accumulation or runoff of surface waters,

- mudflows or mudslides on the surface of normally dry land, or

- the collapse of land along the shore of a body of water (under certain conditions)."

The physical damage to a building or personal property "directly" caused by a flood is covered by flood insurance policies. For example, damage from sewer backups is covered if it results directly from flooding. Flood policies exclude coverage for losses such as swimming pools, cars, money, animals, groundcover, or underground systems.

www.fema.gov
/national-flood
-insurance-program

Policies are of two types: replacement cost value (RCV) or actual cost value (ACV). Deductibles and premiums vary accordingly. More information is at www.fema.gov/national-flood-insurance-program.

IN PRACTICE

NFIP has been called on to aid in many disasters, such as the flooding along the Mississippi River and its tributaries in 1993 and the extensive damage caused by Hurricane Sandy along the Eastern Seaboard in 2013. The $60 billion required to satisfy claims from Hurricane Sandy resulted in NFIP increasing its debt to $27 million. Congressional action is likely to help place NFIP on firmer financial footing. An appraisal should indicate whether or not a property is located in a floodplain.

KEY POINT REVIEW

The true cost of home ownership—from down payment to **PITI (principal, interest, taxes, and insurance)** and utility and maintenance costs—must be considered to determine whether it is a desirable alternative to renting a home. A prospective borrower's **credit report**, **credit score**, and **percentage of debt to income (DTI)** will be considered by a lender. The difference between the amount owed on a property and its current market value is the property owner's **equity**.

A **mortgage loan** will require two instruments: the **financing instrument** and the **security instrument**. A **promissory note**, as a financing instrument, is a contract with a lender that sets out the terms under which a borrower promises to repay a debt. A promissory note is a **negotiable instrument** that can be transferred to a third party.

Interest is a charge for the use of money; charging an excessive rate of interest is called **usury, but most home loans are exempt from state usury laws**. **Discount points** are a percentage of a loan amount and are charged by a lender to increase the lender's yield on its investment. A mortgage loan may include a **prepayment penalty**.

A home mortgage loan is **secured** by the borrower's real property in the process called **hypothecation**. The borrower retains the right of possession and control of the property. The security agreement can be either a mortgage or deed of trust.

In a **mortgage**, the **mortgagor** (owner) borrows money from the **mortgagee** (lender), and the real estate purchased with the borrowed money is used as **security** for the debt.

A **deed of trust** transfers **title** from the **trustor** (property owner) to a **trustee,** who holds it on behalf of a **beneficiary** (lender).

When a mortgage loan is paid in full, a **defeasance clause** requires the lender to execute a **satisfaction** (**release** or **discharge**) that is **recorded** to clear title. If the borrower **defaults**, the lender can **accelerate** the due date of the remaining principal balance and all other payments and costs.

A **deed of trust** executed by the borrower is **recorded** in the county in which property is located. The **trustor** transfers **legal title** to the **trustee** but retains equitable title and has the right to possession and use of the mortgaged property.

When the loan is paid in full, a **defeasance clause** requires the beneficiary to request the trustee to execute and deliver to the trustor a **deed of reconveyance** (release deed) to return legal title to the trustor.

If the borrower **defaults**, the lender can **accelerate** the due date of the remaining principal balance and all overdue costs. If the borrower continues in default, a **deed of trust with power of sale** allows the beneficiary (lender) to ask the trustee to conduct the **trustee's sale** without court action. A **mortgage with power of sale** also enables a sale without court action.

An **impound (escrow) account** may be required to create a reserve fund to ensure that future tax, property insurance, and other payments are made.

The **National Flood Insurance Reform Act of 1994** imposes obligations on lenders and loan servicers to set aside escrow funds for flood insurance on new loans for property in flood-prone areas.

When property with an outstanding mortgage or deed of trust is conveyed, the new owner may **take title** in one of two ways, if allowed by the loan document:

1. **"Subject to"**—the **new owner** makes payments on existing loans but is **not personally liable** if the property is sold on default and proceeds of the sale do not satisfy debt. "Subject to" is no longer in use.

2. **Assuming** the existing mortgage or deed of trust and agreeing to pay the debt—the **new owner** takes personal responsibility for existing loans and is subject to a **deficiency judgment** if the property is sold on default and proceeds of the sale do not satisfy the debt.

An **alienation clause (due-on-sale clause)** in a loan document requires full payment on the sale of the property and can prevent future purchasers of the property from assuming the loan.

Priority of mortgages and other liens is determined by the order in which they were recorded. **Priority** may be changed by **subordination agreement**.

Most forms of real estate financing provide for **amortization** of the loan payments so that the principal of the loan is paid off by the end of the loan term. A **straight loan** is an interest-only loan. With an **adjustable-rate mortgage (ARM)**, the interest rate changes over the term of the loan according to an identified economic indicator—the **index**. A **margin** is added to the index to determine the rate the borrower will pay and a **rate cap** sets the highest interest rate that can be charged at any point over the life of the loan. Rate **adjustments** are made monthly, quarterly, or annually, as agreed between borrower and lender. The loan might have a **conversion** option that allows it to be converted to a fixed-rate loan.

With a **growing-equity mortgage**, payments of principal are increased each month to pay off the loan more quickly. A **balloon payment** typically is a final loan payment that is at least twice as much as any other payment.

A **reverse mortgage** can be used by someone age 62 or older to receive one or more payments that result in a claim by the lender on the equity in the mortgaged property when the homeowner moves from the property, dies, defaults on one of the loan terms, or sells the property.

If a **judicial foreclosure** is granted, the **judge** orders the property sold. A **public sale** is advertised and the real estate is sold to the **highest bidder**. The borrower has **equitable right of redemption** within a time period (before and/or after sale) allowed by state law. No court action is necessary to begin the sale process if the mortgage or deed of trust has a **power-of-sale** clause.

The mortgagee may have the right to a **deficiency judgment** against the borrower for an unpaid balance, **when allowed by state law**, if the sale proceeds are less than the amount owed. The court can **award title** to the **lender** and no sale occurs in a **strict foreclosure**. The lender may accept a **deed in lieu of foreclosure** from a defaulting borrower, but title is **subject to junior liens** that are eliminated in a foreclosure.

In a **short sale**, the lender agrees to accept less than the amount of the remaining indebtedness in order to allow the property to be sold.

Homeowners insurance, which will be required by a mortgage lender, will protect against loss due to natural disasters, accidents, theft, and fire. The **Comprehensive Loss Underwriting Exchange (CLUE)** database allows insurers to share information on a consumer's claims history. The **Federal Emergency Management Agency (FEMA)** administers the National Flood Insurance Program.

UNIT 12 QUIZ

1. A charge of three discount points on a $120,000 loan equals
   A. $450.
   B. $3,600.
   C. $4,500.
   D. $116,400.

2. A prospective buyer needs to borrow money to buy a house. The buyer applies for and obtains a real estate loan from a mortgage company. Then the buyer signs a note and a mortgage. In this example, the buyer is called
   A. the mortgagor.
   B. the beneficiary.
   C. the mortgagee.
   D. the vendor.

3. A prospective buyer needs to borrow money to buy a house. The buyer applies for and obtains a real estate loan from a mortgage company. Then the buyer signs a note and a mortgage. In this example, the mortgage company is
   A. the mortgagor.
   B. the beneficiary.
   C. the mortgagee.
   D. the vendor.

4. The borrower under a deed of trust is known as
   A. the trustor.
   B. the trustee.
   C. the beneficiary.
   D. the vendee.

5. A loan in which the borrower makes only interest payments is called
   A. a fixed-rate loan.
   B. an adjustable-rate mortgage.
   C. a straight loan.
   D. a reverse mortgage.

6. What type of law limits the interest rate that is allowed to be charged?
   A. Trustee law
   B. A usury law
   C. The statute of frauds
   D. Contract law

7. After a foreclosure sale, the borrower who has defaulted on the loan may seek to pay off the mortgage debt plus any accrued interest and costs under what right?
   A. Equitable redemption
   B. Defeasance
   C. Usury
   D. Statutory redemption

8. Which clause would give a lender the right to have all future installments become due upon default?
   A. Escalation
   B. Defeasance
   C. Alienation
   D. Acceleration

9. What document is available to the mortgagor when the mortgage debt is completely repaid?
   A. Satisfaction of mortgage
   B. Defeasance certificate
   C. Deed of trust
   D. Mortgage estoppel

10. Who is entitled to a reverse mortgage?
    A. A homeowner age 62 or older
    B. The owner of an unencumbered home
    C. A homebuyer who cannot qualify for a regular loan
    D. An investor who rents a home only to senior citizens

11. A loan that provides for the full payment of the principal over the life of the loan is
    A. a reverse mortgage.
    B. an indexed loan.
    C. an amortized loan.
    D. a balloon payment.

12. All the following clauses in a loan agreement enable the lender to demand that the entire remaining debt be paid immediately EXCEPT
    A. a due-on-sale clause.
    B. a defeasance clause.
    C. an acceleration clause.
    D. an alienation clause.

13. Which of the following allows a mortgagee to proceed to a foreclosure sale without going to court first?
    A. Waiver of redemption right
    B. Power of sale
    C. Alienation clause
    D. Possession rights

14. The mortgagee foreclosed on a property after the borrower defaulted on the loan payments. The unpaid balance of the loan at the time of the foreclosure sale was $140,000, but at the foreclosure sale, the house sold for only $129,000. If permitted by state law, what must the lender do to recover the $11,000 the borrower still owes?
    A. Sue for damages
    B. Sue for specific performance
    C. Seek a judgment by default
    D. Seek a deficiency judgment

15. Discount points on a mortgage are computed as a percentage of
    A. the selling price.
    B. the loan amount.
    C. the closing costs.
    D. the down payment.

16. In one state, a lender holds a lien on real property offered as collateral for a loan. The borrower retains both legal and equitable title to real property. If the borrower defaults on the loan, the lender must go through formal foreclosure proceedings to recover the debt. This state can be *BEST* characterized as what kind of state?
    A. Lien theory
    B. Mortgage theory
    C. Intermediate theory
    D. Title theory

17. In one state, a mortgagee holds legal title to real property offered as collateral for a loan, and the mortgagor retains the rights of possession and use. If the borrower defaults, the lender is entitled to immediate possession and rents. This state can be *BEST* characterized as what kind of state?
    A. Lien theory
    B. Mortgage theory
    C. Intermediate theory
    D. Title theory

18. A homebuyer has a mortgage that provides for increasing payments over the life of the loan so that it can be paid off earlier than would be the case with a regular amortized loan. The homebuyer has
    A. a mortgage with power of sale.
    B. a growing-equity mortgage.
    C. a balloon payment loan.
    D. a reverse mortgage.

19. A junior lien may become first in priority if the original lender agrees to execute
    A. a deed of trust.
    B. a subordination agreement.
    C. a second mortgage agreement.
    D. a call clause.

20. A buyer purchased a home under an agreement that made the buyer personally obligated to continue making payments under the seller's existing mortgage. If the buyer defaults and the court sale of the property does not satisfy the debt, the buyer will be liable for making up the difference. The buyer has
    A. purchased the home subject to the seller's mortgage.
    B. assumed the seller's mortgage.
    C. benefited from the alienation clause in the seller's mortgage.
    D. benefited from the defeasance clause in the seller's mortgage.

UNIT
13

Government Involvement in Real Estate Financing

LEARNING OBJECTIVES

When you have completed this unit, you will be able to

> **explain** the primary and secondary mortgage marketplaces, the roles of the parties in each, and the impact on the parties through government influence;
> **describe** the difference between conventional, government, and private loan programs available for real estate financing;
> **describe** the various alternative and special-purpose loan programs which can meet a borrower's special needs; and
> **explain** the primary government regulations which govern real estate lending and provide consumer protection against unfair lending practices.

KEY TERMS

blanket loan	Federal Deposit Insurance	open-end loan
buydown	Corporation (FDIC)	package loan
certificate of reasonable value	Federal Reserve System (Fed)	primary mortgage market
(CRV)	FHA-insured loan	private mortgage insurance
Community Reinvestment Act	Freddie Mac	(PMI)
of 1977 (CRA)	Ginnie Mae	Real Estate Settlement
construction loan	government-sponsored	Procedures Act (RESPA)
conventional loan	enterprises (GSEs)	Regulation Z
Equal Credit Opportunity Act	home equity loan	sale-and-leaseback
(ECOA)	mortgage insurance premium	secondary mortgage market
Fannie Mae	(MIP)	triggering terms
Farmer Mac	Office of the Comptroller of	Truth in Lending Act (TILA)
	the Currency (OCC)	VA-guaranteed loan

OVERVIEW

In this unit, we will consider the overall financial marketplace, and refer to any loan secured by either a mortgage or a deed of trust as a mortgage loan.

We will look at the ways in which the federal government is involved in real estate financing. A mortgage that has no direct federal involvement (even though it may be made by a federally chartered lender) is called a *conventional* loan. Loans that have direct federal involvement include those insured by the Federal Housing Administration (FHA) or guaranteed by the U.S. Department of Veterans Affairs (VA).

INTRODUCTION TO THE REAL ESTATE FINANCING MARKET

The real estate financing market has the following three basic components:

- Government influences, primarily the Federal Reserve System
- The primary mortgage market
- The secondary mortgage market

Under the umbrella of the monetary policy set by the Federal Reserve System, lenders that are part of the primary mortgage market originate loans that are bought, sold, and traded in the secondary mortgage market. Qualified state chartered banks may also join the Fed.

The Federal Reserve System

The role of the **Federal Reserve System** (the Fed), acting through its Board of Governors, is to maintain sound credit conditions, help counteract inflationary and deflationary trends, and create a favorable economic climate. The Federal Reserve System divides the country into 12 federal reserve districts, each served by a federal reserve bank. All nationally chartered banks must join the Fed and purchase stock in its district reserve banks. Detailed information about the Fed is found at www.federalreserve.gov.

www.federalreserve
.gov

The Fed regulates the flow of money and interest rates in the marketplace through its member banks by controlling the rate charged for loans it makes to them, called the *discount* rate, as well their *reserve requirements*—the minimum level of funds that an institution must maintain. The discount rate charged by the Fed influences the *prime rate* (also called the *base rate*) that member institutions charge for credit card loans, small business loans, and other forms of financing.

When the discount rate rises, interest rates on all sorts of loans will rise, making funding harder to obtain. When the discount rate is lowered, interest rates will go down, making borrowed funds easier to obtain, an incentive to businesses as well as homebuyers. The Fed's reserve requirements place funds out of circulation; when reserve requirements are increased, lender solvency is improved but funding is harder to obtain.

The Fed acts on the open market to stimulate the economy at a time of recession by increasing the amount of money in circulation by buying Treasury securities. The Fed can also act to control inflation by decreasing the amount of money in circulation by selling Treasury securities.

The primary mortgage market

The **primary mortgage market** is made up of the lenders that originate mortgage loans. These lenders make money available directly to borrowers. From a borrower's point of view, a loan is a means of financing an expenditure; from a lender's point of view, a loan is an investment. All investors look for profitable returns on their investments. Income on a loan is realized from the following two sources:

- Finance charges collected at closing, such as loan origination fees and discount points
- Recurring income, the interest collected during the term of the loan

Lenders can sell mortgage loans, which produces income to make more loans, and some lenders derive income from servicing loans for investors who have purchased the loans, or servicing loans made by other mortgage lenders. Servicing a loan involves

- collecting payments (including taxes and insurance, if the borrower must maintain an impound account as part of the loan agreement),
- accounting,
- bookkeeping,
- preparing insurance and tax records,
- processing payments of taxes and insurance, and
- following up on loan payment and delinquency.

Major lenders of home mortgage and commercial property loans include the following:

- *Savings associations* (also called *thrifts*) and *commercial banks.* These institutions are known as *fiduciary lenders* because of their fiduciary obligations to protect and preserve their depositors' funds. Mortgage loans are perceived as secure investments for generating income and enable these institutions to pay interest to their depositors. Fiduciary lenders are subject to the standards and regulations established by the **Office of the Comptroller of the Currency (OCC)**, www.occ.gov. Deposits in insured institutions are covered up to the specified limit, currently $250,000 per depositor, per account, by the **Federal Deposit Insurance Corporation (FDIC)**, www.fdic.gov.

www.occ.gov
www.fdic.gov

- *Insurance companies.* Insurance companies accumulate large sums of money from the premiums paid by their policyholders. While part of this money is held in reserve to satisfy claims and cover operating expenses, much of it is free to be invested in profit-earning enterprises, such as large commercial real estate loans.

- *Credit unions.* Credit unions are cooperative organizations whose members place money in savings accounts. In the past, credit unions made only short-term consumer and home improvement loans. Now, they routinely originate longer-term first and second mortgage and deed of trust loans. Federally chartered credit unions are regulated by the National Credit Union Association (NCUA), www.ncua.gov. NCUA insures deposits of up to $250,000 in all federal credit unions as well as the majority of state-chartered credit unions.

www.ncua.gov

- *Pension funds.* Pension funds usually have large amounts of money available for investment. Because of the comparatively high yields and low risks offered by mortgages, pension funds have begun to participate actively in financing real estate projects. Most real estate activity for pension funds is handled through mortgage bankers and mortgage brokers. The Pension Real Estate Association, www.prea.org, is a nonprofit organization of public and corporate pension funds, endowment funds, and other institutional real estate investors.

www.prea.org

■ *Endowment funds.* Many commercial banks and mortgage bankers handle investments for endowment funds. The endowments of hospitals, universities, colleges, charitable foundations, and other institutions provide a good source of financing for low-risk commercial and industrial properties.

■ *Investment group financing.* Large real estate projects, such as highrise apartment buildings, office complexes, and shopping centers, are often financed as joint ventures through group financing arrangements like syndicates, limited partnerships, and real estate investment trusts.

■ *Mortgage banking companies.* Mortgage banking companies originate mortgage loans with money belonging to insurance companies, pension funds, and individuals, as well as funds of their own. They make real estate loans with the intention of selling them to investors and receiving a fee for servicing the loans. Mortgage banking companies are generally organized as stock companies. As a source of real estate financing, they are subject to fewer lending restrictions than are commercial banks or savings associations. They are not mortgage brokers.

■ *Mortgage brokers.* Mortgage brokers are not lenders, but they are mentioned here because they are intermediaries who bring borrowers and lenders together. Mortgage brokers locate potential borrowers, process preliminary loan applications, and submit the applications to lenders for final approval. They do not service loans once the loans are made. Mortgage brokers also may be real estate brokers who offer these financing services in addition to their regular real estate brokerage activities.

The Secure and Fair Enforcement for Mortgage Licensing Act of 2008 (SAFE Act) requires states to license mortgage loan originators according to national standards and also requires all state agencies to participate in the Nationwide Mortgage Licensing System and Registry (NMLS), www.nmlsconsumeraccess.org, as of January 1, 2011. The NMLS Resource Center is at https://nationwidelicensingsystem.org/Pages/default.aspx.

https://nationwide licensingsystem.org/ Pages/default.aspx

All mortgage loan originators (MLOs) must register annually and meet other requirements. NMLS is the sole system of licensure for mortgage companies for 57 state agencies and the sole system of licensure for MLOs for 59 state and territorial agencies.

☑ IN PRACTICE

A growing number of consumers apply for mortgage loans via the internet, particularly for a loan refinancing. Many major lenders have websites that offer information to potential borrowers regarding their current loan programs and requirements. In addition, online brokerages link lenders with potential borrowers. The best sites allow comparison of loan terms across a variety of loan programs. New borrowers are cautioned to make sure that there is the opportunity for a phone or in-person consultation before making any mortgage decision.

The secondary mortgage market

In addition to the primary mortgage market, where loans are originated, there is a **secondary mortgage market** in which loans are bought and sold only after they have been funded (closed). The secondary mortgage market thus helps lenders raise capital to make additional mortgage loans and is especially useful when money is in short supply. By freeing capital for additional loans, the secondary market stimulates both the housing construction market and the mortgage market. The lender benefits, not only by raising additional capital, but also by avoiding interest rate risks on adjustable rate loans when interest rates fall, as well as on fixed rate loans if interest rates rise, and by making a profit on the sale. In addition, the lender may continue to service the loan and collect a fee for that service.

In the secondary market, a number of mortgage loans are assembled into blocks called *pools*. The mortgages can be pooled by the lender who sells them or, more frequently, by the organization that purchases them. Securities that represent shares in these pooled mortgages are then sold to investors or other organizations. The key players in the secondary mortgage market were created by the federal government in the decades following the Great Depression and World war II to help increase loan opportunities for homebuyers. They are referred to collectively as **government-sponsored enterprises (GSEs)**. (See Figure 13.1.)

FIGURE 13.1: Government-Sponsored Enterprises (GSEs)

Institution	Secondary Market Function
Fannie Mae	Conventional, FHA-insured, VA-guaranteed loans
Freddie Mac	Mostly conventional loans
Ginnie Mae	Special assistance loans

Fannie Mae

Originally the Federal National Mortgage Association, **Fannie Mae** was created as a government agency in 1938. It became a completely private shareholder-owned corporation in 1968, although it is still under congressional supervision. Fannie Mae buys from a lender a block or pool of mortgages that may then be used as collateral for *mortgage-backed securities* that are sold on the global market.

The housing collapse that was felt around the country starting in 2006 brought into question the value a great many of the mortgages that Fannie Mae had purchased and resold to investors. In September 2008, Fannie Mae was placed into the conservatorship of the Federal Housing Finance Agency (FHFA), www.fhfa.gov. Fannie Mae continues to operate and provide a secondary market for mortgage loans, although with massive federal investment to protect its investors. Fannie Mae deals in conventional as well as FHA-insured and VA-guaranteed loans.

www.fhfa.gov

One of the most important features of the GSEs has been their development of standardized loan application, credit report, appraisal and other forms that are required for loans they purchase, as well as detailed guidelines for the lending process. Fannie Mae has a consumer-oriented site at www.fanniemae.com, and a site for lenders that provides access to its forms and guides at www.fanniemae.com/singlefamily.

www.fanniemae.com
www.fanniemae.com
/singlefamily

Freddie Mac

Originally called the Federal Home Loan Mortgage Corporation, **Freddie Mac** was created in 1970 as a privately owned corporation but is also now under government conservatorship. Freddie Mac continues to provide a secondary market for mortgage loans, primarily conventional loans.

www.freddiemac.com

Many lenders use the standardized forms and follow the guidelines issued by Fannie Mae and Freddie Mac. More information on Freddie Mac is available at www.freddiemac.com.

Farmer Mac

The Federal Agricultural Mortgage Corporation (**Farmer Mac**) is privately owned and publicly traded, and was established by Congress in 1988 to create a secondary market for agricultural mortgage and rural utilities loans and the portions of agricultural and rural development loans guaranteed by the U.S. Department of Agriculture (USDA). Farmer Mac is part of the Farm Credit System and is regulated by the Farm Credit Administration. Farmer Mac guarantees payment of principal and interest on the loans it purchases and pools those loans for sale. Farmer Mac has not had the financial difficulties that have plagued Fannie Mae and Freddie Mac in recent years, primarily because market values in rural areas have not gone through the wide swings that most urban areas have experienced. Information on Farmer Mac is at www.farmermac.com; Farmer Mac has a subsidiary, Farmer Mac II, LLC, found at www .farmermac2.com.

www.farmermac.com
www.farmermac2.com

Ginnie Mae

www.ginniemae.gov

The Government National Mortgage Association, **Ginnie Mae**, was created in 1968 and has always been a governmental agency. Information on this agency can be found at www .ginniemae.gov. Ginnie Mae is a division of the Department of Housing and Urban Development (HUD), organized as a corporation without capital stock. Ginnie Mae does not buy or sell loans or issue mortgage-backed securities. Instead, Ginnie Mae administers special-assistance programs and guarantees investment securities issued by private offerors (such as banks, mortgage companies, and savings and loan associations) and backed by pools of FHA-insured and VA-guaranteed mortgage loans. The *Ginnie Mae pass-through certificate* is a security interest in a pool of mortgages that provides for a monthly pass-through of principal and interest payments directly to the certificate holder. Such certificates are guaranteed by Ginnie Mae.

LOAN PROGRAMS

Mortgage loans can be classified based on their loan-to-value ratio (LTV). The LTV is the ratio of debt to the value of the property, where the value is the sales price or appraised value, whichever is less. The *lower* the ratio of debt to value, the *higher* the down payment by the borrower. For the lender, the higher down payment means a more secure loan, which minimizes the lender's risk.

IN PRACTICE

If the appraised value of a property is less than the sales price, the buyer/borrower will renegotiate the contract with the seller so that the sales price is reduced to the appraised value, or the buyer will make an additional down payment (the difference between the sales price and the appraised value). If appraised value is higher than the sales price, the sales price is considered the property value. The buyer does not get a financial "bonus" from the lender for negotiating a price that is lower than the property's appraised value.

MATH CONCEPTS

Determining LTV

If a property has an appraised value of $200,000, secured by an $180,000 loan, the LTV is 90%:

$180,000 ÷ $200,000 = 90%

Conventional loans

Conventional loans are viewed as the most secure loans because their loan-to-value ratios are often lowest. The ratio may be 80% of the value of the property or less because the borrower may make a down payment of at least 20%. Because the payment of the debt rests on the ability of the borrower to pay, the lender carefully evaluates both the property and the prospective borrower. In determining the amount of the loan, the lender relies primarily on its appraisal of the property. To decide the buyer's willingness and ability to pay, information from credit reports, the buyer's credit score, and other factors, such as qualifying ratios and work history, are very important. Usually with a 20% down payment and a conventional loan, no additional insurance or guarantee on the loan is necessary to protect the lender's interest. A loan with less than a 20% down payment usually will require *private mortgage insurance*. A conventional loan is not government insured or guaranteed, unlike FHA-insured and VA-guaranteed loans.

IN PRACTICE

A foreclosure can be a long, messy proposition that has a negative effect on the borrower, the borrower's family, and the neighborhood in which the property is located. Even after a foreclosure, the lender can sue a defaulting borrower on the promissory note when it is a "recourse" loan that allows the lender to obtain a deficiency judgment against the borrower's assets. Lenders usually do not want to take this route unless it is absolutely necessary. Making sure that both property and borrower are qualified for the requested financing is the best protection against an unsuccessful loan.

Today, the secondary mortgage market has a significant impact on borrower qualifications, standards for the collateral, and documentation procedures followed by lenders. Loans must meet strict criteria to be sold to Fannie Mae and Freddie Mac. Lenders still can be flexible in their lending decisions, but they may not be able to sell unusual loans in the secondary market. Fannie Mae's Eligibility Matrix showing its eligibility requirements is at www .fanniemae.com/content/eligibility_information/eligibility-matrix.pdf.

www.fanniemae.com /content/eligibility _information/eligibility -matrix.pdf

The Federal Housing Finance Agency (FHFA) publishes the maximum loan limits for loans sold to Fannie Mae and Freddie Mac. Beginning January 1, 2018, the maximum loan limit for a single-family home was set from $453,100 to $679,650, in high-cost areas. Specific loan limits are established for each county (or equivalent), and the loan limit may be lower for each specific high-cost area. Updates on loan limits are at www.fanniemae.com/singlefamily/loan -limits.

www.fanniemae .com/singlefamily /loan-limits

Loans that exceed the stated limits are called *nonconforming loans* or *jumbo loans* and are not marketable, but they may be held in the lender's investment portfolio, along with other loans the lender may have made that don't meet the underwriting guidelines of FHA, VA, or Fannie Mae/Freddie Mac. A real estate professional who is aware that such portfolio loans are possible may find this knowledge valuable when working with a borrower in unusual circumstances and a lender who is flexible.

Private mortgage insurance

One way a borrower can obtain a conventional mortgage loan with a down payment that is less than 20% of the purchase price is by obtaining **private mortgage insurance (PMI)**. The borrower purchases an insurance policy that provides the lender with funds in the event of borrower default on the loan. This allows the lender to assume more risk so that the loan-to-value ratio can be higher than for other conventional loans. PMI protects the top portion of a loan, usually 20% to 30%, against borrower default. This means that, if the property is sold at a foreclosure sale for less than the outstanding balance of the loan, the PMI usually is enough to make up the difference.

The borrower pays a monthly premium or fee while PMI is in force, which may be made part of the loan payment. The Homeowner's Protection Act of 1998 (HPA) requires that the lender automatically terminate the PMI payment if the borrower has accrued at least 22% equity in the home and is current on mortgage payments.

IN PRACTICE

The 22% of equity that HPA has set as the point at which PMI can be canceled is based on the purchase price of the home. If market appreciation or improvements made by the borrower have increased the value of the home, the lender is not required by HPA to consider those factors but may be willing to do so. The borrower must contact the lender to find out how to proceed. The lender may require an appraisal, at the borrower's expense, to document the increase in value.

FHA-insured loans

The Federal Housing Administration (FHA), which operates under HUD, neither builds homes nor lends money. The term **FHA loan** actually refers to a loan that is *insured* by the agency. An FHA-insured loan must be made by an FHA-approved lending institution. The FHA insurance provides additional security to the lender. As with private mortgage insurance, the FHA insures lenders against loss from borrower default. For information on FHA programs, go to www.hud.gov and enter "FHA Resource Center" in the search box at the top of the page.

www.hud.gov

The most popular FHA program covers fixed-rate loans for 10 to 30 years on one- to four-family residences. FHA does not set interest rates, but it does limit lender fees and specifies how closing costs and down payment may be paid and by whom, and regulates rate increases and caps on adjustable-rate loans. FHA-insured loans are competitive with other types of loans, often because an FHA-insured loan can be made even when the borrower makes a relatively low down payment, resulting in a high LTV. The maximum loan amounts that FHA will insure, by state and county, are available by going to www.hud.gov and entering "FHA mortgage limits" in the search box. By law, FHA loans cannot charge prepayment penalties.

Other types of FHA-insured loans include adjustable-rate mortgages, home improvement and rehabilitation loans, and loans for the purchase of condominiums. Specific standards for condominium complexes and the ratio of owner-occupants to renters must be met for a loan on a condominium unit to be insured by FHA.

Currently, a borrower can obtain an FHA-insured loan with a down payment as low as 3.5% of the purchase price on a one- to four-unit structure, and certain closing costs can be included in the loan amount. A lower down payment may be possible with one of the special programs discussed later in this section. The borrower is charged a mortgage insurance premium (MIP) for all FHA loans. The borrower is also responsible for paying an annual premium that is usually charged monthly. The up-front premium is charged on all FHA loans, except those for the purchase of a condominium, which require only a monthly MIP.

The mortgaged real estate must be appraised by an approved FHA appraiser, and the borrower must meet standard FHA credit qualifications. Financing for manufactured homes and factory-built housing is also available, both for those who own the land that the home is on and also for manufactured homes that are, or will be, located on another plot of land.

If the purchase price exceeds the FHA-appraised property value, the buyer may pay the difference in cash as part of the down payment, although some exceptions are made for special programs.

Discount points

The lender of an FHA-insured loan may charge discount points in addition to a loan origination fee. The payment of points is a matter of negotiation between the seller and the buyer. As of November 2009, if the seller pays more than 6% of the costs normally paid by the buyer (such as discount points, the loan origination fee, the mortgage insurance premium, buydown fees (prepaid interest), other prepaid items, and impound or escrow amounts), the lender will treat the payments as a reduction in sales price and recalculate the mortgage amount accordingly.

Assumption rules

A qualified buyer may assume an existing FHA-insured loan. The application consists of a credit check to demonstrate whether the person assuming the loan is financially qualified. The process is quicker and less expensive than applying for a new loan. Sometimes, the older loan has a lower interest rate and no appraisal is required.

The assumption rules for FHA-insured loans vary, depending on the date the loan was originated. As of December 15, 1989, an assumption is not permitted without complete buyer qualification.

HUD home sales

Foreclosures of FHA-insured homes by HUD provide opportunities for both homebuyers and investors. HUD accepts bids on foreclosed properties only from real estate professionals who are registered with HUD and does not deal with the general public directly. Properties are sold in "as-is" condition, which means that HUD will not make repairs prior to the sale. Some homes can need extensive work, which also means that minimum bids can be set quite low, making a purchase of such a property a good investment for a buyer willing to make the required renovations.

HUD allows an early bidding period for those who intend to be owner-occupants; properties are made available to investors only after that period has elapsed, if the property remains unsold. HUD has special programs that may offer a reduced down payment on property that is purchased with an FHA-insured loan. HUD's Good Neighbor Next Door program is intended to help revitalize certain areas by allowing law enforcement officers, firefighters, emergency medical technicians, and pre-kindergarten through grade 12 teachers to purchase eligible property in those areas at a 50% discount off the list price. The buyer must occupy the property as the buyer's sole residence for a minimum of 36 months. Property listings, which are available in about 10 states, and more information on HUD property sales and programs can be found at www.hudhomestore.com.

www.hudhomestore
.com

Unit 13

VA-guaranteed loans

The U.S. Department of Veterans Affairs (VA) is authorized to guarantee loans used to purchase or construct homes for eligible veterans and their spouses (including unremarried spouses of veterans whose deaths were service-related). The VA also guarantees loans to purchase manufactured homes and the lots on which to place them. Information on the VA can be found at www.va.gov, and the VA-guaranteed loan program is explained at www .benefits.va.gov/homeloans.

www.va.gov

www.benefits.va.gov
/homeloans

A veteran who meets any of the following time-in-service criteria is eligible for a VA-guaranteed loan:

- 90 days of active service for service people currently on active duty and veterans of at least 90 days of active service during World War II, the Korean War, the Vietnam conflict, and the Gulf War (which extends to the present time)

- A minimum of 181 days of active service during interconflict periods between July 26, 1947, and September 6, 1980

- Two full years of service during any peacetime period since 1980 (since 1981 for officers) or the full period (at least 181 days) for which the veteran was called or ordered to active duty

- Six or more years of continuous duty as a reservist in the Army, Navy, Air Force, Marine Corps, or Coast Guard, or as a member of the Army or Air National Guard

The VA assists veterans in financing the purchase of homes with little or no down payment at market interest rates. The VA issues rules and regulations that set forth the qualifications, limitations, and conditions under which a loan may be guaranteed. The owner must live on the property. The veteran must apply for a certificate of eligibility. This certificate sets forth the maximum guarantee to which the veteran is entitled, but the veteran must still qualify for the loan with the lender. For individuals with full eligibility, no down payment is required for a loan up to the maximum guarantee limit.

There is no VA dollar limit on the amount of the loan a veteran can obtain; this limit is determined by the lender and the qualification of the buyer. The VA limits the amount of the loan it will guarantee, however. For 2018, the guarantee limit was 25% of a loan of up to $453,100 on a one-unit property for most of the country, with a higher loan limit for some areas of Alaska, California, Colorado, District of Columbia, Florida, Guam, Hawaii, Idaho, Maryland, Massachusetts, New Hampshire, New Jersey, New York, Pennsylvania, Rhode Island, Tennessee, Utah, Virginia, Virgin Islands, Washington, West Virginia, and Wyoming.

IN PRACTICE

The VA loan guarantee is tied to the current conforming loan limit for Fannie Mae and Freddie Mac. On a conforming loan of $453,100, the VA guarantee is $453,100 × 25%, or $113,275.

The VA also issues a **certificate of reasonable value (CRV)** for the property being purchased. The CRV states the property's current market value based on a VA-approved appraisal. The CRV places a ceiling on the amount of a VA-guaranteed loan allowed for the property. If the purchase price is greater than the amount cited in the CRV, the veteran may pay the difference in cash.

The VA borrower pays a loan origination fee to the lender, as well as a funding fee to the U.S. Department of Veterans Affairs. The funding fee is a percentage of the loan amount; the percentage varies based on the type of loan ad military category of the veteran. There is *no* funding fee for

- a veteran who is receiving VA compensation for a service-connected disability,

- a veteran who would be entitled to receive compensation for a service-connected disability if the veteran did not receive retirement or active duty pay, or

- the surviving spouse of a veteran who died in service or from a service-connected disability.

Other loan costs

The lender sets the loan interest rate, discount points, and closing costs. Closing costs such as the VA's property appraisal, the credit report, state and local taxes, and recording fees may be paid by the veteran purchaser, the seller, or shared by both. The veteran is not allowed to pay for the termite report, unless the loan is a refinance. No commissions, brokerage fees, or buyer broker fees may be charged to the veteran buyer.

The seller is allowed to pay for some closing costs, up to 4% of the loan amount, including prepaid closing costs, the VA funding fee, payoff of credit balances or judgments for the veteran, and temporary interest buydowns. Reasonable discount points may be charged on a VA-guaranteed loan, and either the veteran or the seller may pay them. Discount points are not included in the 4% limit.

Prepayment privileges

As with an FHA-insured loan, the borrower under a VA-guaranteed loan can prepay the debt at any time without penalty.

Assumption rules

VA-guaranteed loans made on or after March 1, 1988, are no longer assumable without prior consent from the lender.

Agricultural loan programs

The Farm Service Agency (FSA) is a federal agency of the Department of Agriculture. The FSA offers programs to help families purchase or operate family farms and has taken over the functions of the former Farmers Home Administration (FmHA). Through the Rural Housing and Community Development Service (RHCDS), FSA also provides loans to help families purchase or improve single-family homes in rural areas (generally areas with populations of fewer than 10,000 people). FSA loan programs fall into two categories: guaranteed loans that are made and serviced by private lenders and guaranteed for a specific percentage by the FSA, and loans made directly by the FSA. More information on FSA programs can be found at www.fsa.usda.gov.

www.fsa.usda.gov

The Farm Credit System (Farm Credit) provides loans to farmers, ranchers, rural homeowners, agricultural cooperatives, rural utility systems, and agribusinesses. Unlike commercial banks, Farm Credit banks and associations do not take deposits. Instead, loanable funds are raised through the system-wide sale of bonds and notes in capital markets. More information is at www.farmcreditnetwork.com.

www.farmcredit
network.com

OTHER FINANCING TECHNIQUES

Because borrowers often have different needs, a variety of financing techniques have been created that apply to various types of property. We have already discussed the owner-financed transaction that can be secured by means of a purchase money mortgage. There are also ways of structuring financing in a variety of situations.

Package loan

A **package loan** includes real and personal property. In recent years, these kinds of loans have been very popular with developers and purchasers of unfurnished condominiums. Package loans usually include furniture, drapes, the kitchen range, microwave oven, refrigerator, dishwasher, washer, dryer, and other appliances as part of the sales price of the home.

Blanket loan

A **blanket loan** covers more than one parcel or lot. It is usually used by a developer to finance a subdivision, but it can also be used to finance the purchase of improved properties or to consolidate multiple loans on a single property. A blanket loan usually includes a provision known as a *partial release clause*. This clause permits the borrower to obtain the release of any one lot or parcel from the blanket lien by repaying a certain amount of the loan. The development lender issues a partial release from the mortgage lien on the entire property for each parcel sold. The release form from the lender will include a provision that the lien will continue to cover all other unreleased lots. In this way, the lender retains a security interest in the unsold property for the remaining development loan balance, yet each purchaser of an improved or unimproved lot can obtain secured financing on that parcel.

IN PRACTICE

Developer M has obtained financing for Shady Acres, a residential development, under the terms of a blanket loan issued by First State Bank. M grades the property, brings in utility lines, builds roads, and then markets the buildable lots to construction companies. As each lot or group of lots is sold, First State Bank is paid a proportionate share of its development loan by the developer and releases its lien rights as to that parcel. This allows each of the purchasers to obtain financing that will cover building construction costs. The purchaser of more than one lot may obtain a blanket loan that will release that lender's lien as to individual properties when construction is completed and properties are sold to home buyers. Each homebuyer can then obtain a mortgage loan secured by the property.

Open-end loan

An **open-end loan** provides a security interest when a *note* is executed by the borrower to the lender, but also secures any future *advances* of funds made by the lender to the borrower. The interest rate on the initial amount borrowed is fixed, but interest on future advances may be charged at the market rate in effect at that time. An open-end loan is often a less costly alternative to a home improvement loan. It allows the borrower to increase the debt to its original amount, or the maximum amount stated in the note, after the debt has been reduced by payments over a period of time. The note will include the terms and conditions under which the loan can be opened, and the provisions for repayment.

Construction loan

A **construction loan** is made to finance the construction of improvements on real estate such as homes, apartments, and office buildings. The lender commits to the full amount of the loan but disburses the funds in payments during construction. These payments are also known as *draws*. Draws are made to the general contractor or the owner for that part of the construction work that has been completed since the previous payment. Before each payment, the lender inspects the work. The general contractor must provide the lender with adequate waivers that release all mechanics' lien rights for the work covered by the payment.

Construction loans are generally *short-term* or *interim* financing. The borrower pays interest only on the monies that have actually been disbursed. The borrower is expected to arrange for a permanent loan, also known as an *end loan* or *take-out loan*, which will pay off (take out) the construction financing lender when the work is completed by paying the principal owed on the construction loan.

Sale-and-leaseback

Sale-and-leaseback arrangements, while not loans, are used to finance large commercial or industrial properties. The land and the building, usually used by the seller for business purposes, are sold to an investor. The real estate then is leased back by the investor to the seller, who continues to conduct business on the property as a tenant. The buyer becomes the landlord, and the original owner becomes the tenant. This enables a business to free money tied up in real estate to be used as working capital.

Buydown

A **buydown** is a way to temporarily (or permanently) lower the interest rate on a mortgage or deed of trust loan. Perhaps a homebuilder wishes to stimulate sales by offering a lower-than-market rate. Or a first-time residential buyer may have trouble qualifying for a loan at the prevailing rates. The buyer's relatives or the sellers might want to help the buyer qualify. In any case, a lump sum is paid in cash to the lender at the closing. The payment offsets (and so reduces) the interest rate and monthly payments during the mortgage's first few years. Typical buydown arrangements reduce the interest rate by 1% to 2% over the first one to two years of the loan term. After that, the rate rises. The hope is that the borrower's income will also increase, making it more likely that the borrower will be able to pay the increased monthly payments. In a permanent buydown, a larger up-front payment reduces the effective interest rate for the life of the loan.

IN PRACTICE

As recent history has shown, a borrower should not overestimate the ability to meet future payment obligations. Holding onto employment—with or without an increase in income—may be the best that can be managed. The risk of incurring a property foreclosure should be carefully considered.

Home equity loan

A **home equity loan** is a source of funds that takes advantage of the equity built up in a home. The original mortgage loan remains in place; the home equity loan is junior to the original lien. Although the home equity loan will carry a higher interest rate than a purchase loan, it is an alternative to refinancing because only the amount borrowed will be subject to the higher rate. As an added benefit, the interest paid on a home equity loan of up to

$100,000 is deductible from federal income tax. A home equity loan can be used for a variety of financial needs, such as to

- finance the purchase of an expensive item, such as a boat;

- consolidate existing installment loans or credit card debt; and

- pay medical, education, home improvement, or other expenses.

A home equity loan can be taken out as a fixed loan amount or as a line of credit. With the *home equity line of credit*, called a *HELOC*, the lender extends a line of credit that the borrower can use at will. One downside to a HELOC is that the full amount of the line of credit will appear on the borrower's credit report, even though it is not being used. On the upside, the home equity loan could eventually lead to a new first mortgage loan. The homeowner could refinance all outstanding mortgage loans at some point with a single new loan at an attractive interest rate, in which case the original mortgage loan and the home equity loan would be paid off.

IN PRACTICE

The decision to borrow against the equity in a home should not be made lightly. Using the funds to make home improvements should at least result in a higher property value, building up additional equity to replace some or all of that encumbered. The prospect of paying off other kinds of debts (particularly, credit card and auto loans) may be enticing, but those debts probably won't result in the possible loss of one's home.

FINANCING LEGISLATION

The federal government regulates the lending practices of mortgage lenders through the Truth in Lending Act (TILA), Equal Credit Opportunity Act (ECOA), Community Reinvestment Act of 1977 (CRA), and Real Estate Settlement Procedures Act (RESPA). Recent legislation to assist property owners during the economic downturn is also discussed.

Truth in Lending Act and Regulation Z

Regulation Z, enacted by the Federal Reserve Board to enforce the **Truth in Lending Act (TILA)**, requires that credit institutions inform borrowers of the true cost of obtaining credit. With proper disclosures, borrowers can compare the costs of various lenders to avoid the uninformed use of credit. Regardless of the amount, *Regulation Z generally applies when a credit transaction is secured by a residence*. The regulation does *not* apply to business or commercial loans or to agricultural loans of any amount. Information on the law can be found at the site of the Office of the Comptroller of the Currency, www.occ.treas.gov, by entering "truth in lending" in the search box.

www.occ.treas.gov

Under TILA, a consumer must be fully informed of all finance charges and the true cost of the financing before a transaction is completed. The finance charge disclosure must include any loan fees, finder's fees, service charges, and points, as well as interest. In the case of a mortgage loan made to finance the purchase of a dwelling, the lender must compute and disclose the *annual percentage rate (APR)* that takes into account the fees, points, and other charges incurred in loan origination, in addition to the nominal interest rate on the loan.

In 2009, the Helping Families Save Their Homes Act amended TILA by requiring that consumers be notified of the sale or transfer of their mortgage loans. The party acquiring the loan, whether a purchaser or assignee, must provide the required disclosures no later than 30

www.federalreserve
.gov/boarddocs/sup
manual/cch/til.pdf

www.consumerfinance
.gov

www.consumerfinance
.gov/learnmore/

days after the date on which the loan was acquired. The Consumer Compliance Handbook for Regulation Z can be found at www.federalreserve.gov/boarddocs/supmanual/cch/til.pdf.

The Dodd-Frank Wall Street Reform and Consumer Protection Act of 2010 (Dodd-Frank) transferred most of the Federal Reserve's responsibilities for enforcing TILA in July, 2011, to the new Consumer Financial Protection Bureau (CFPB). Information on the reasons why CFPB was created, including mortgage loan abuses by lenders, can be found at www.consumerfinance.gov. CFPB's booklet on TILA is at www.consumerfinance.gov/learnmore/.

Creditor

A *creditor*, for purposes of Regulation Z, is any person who extends consumer credit more than 25 times each year or more than 5 times each year if the transactions involve dwellings as security. The credit must be subject to a finance charge or payable in more than four installments by written agreement.

Three-business-day right of rescission

In the case of most consumer credit transactions covered by Regulation Z, the borrower has three business days in which to rescind (cancel) the transaction by notifying the lender. *This right of rescission does not apply to owner-occupied residential purchase-money or first mortgage or deed of trust loans.* It does, however, apply to refinancing a home mortgage or taking out a home equity loan.

Advertising

Regulation Z provides strict rules for real estate advertisements (in all media, including newspapers, flyers, signs, billboards, websites, radio or television ads, and direct mailings) that refer to mortgage financing terms. General phrases like "flexible terms available" may be used, but if details are given, they must comply with the act. The APR must be stated.

Advertisements for buydowns or reduced-rate mortgages must include both the term to which the interest rate applies and the APR. If a variable-rate mortgage is advertised, the advertisement must include

- the number and timing of payments,
- the amount of the largest and smallest payments, and
- a statement of the fact that the actual payments will vary between these two extremes.

Specific credit terms, such as down payment, monthly payment, dollar amount of the finance charge, or term of the loan, are called **triggering terms**. These terms may not be advertised unless the advertisement includes the following information:

- Cash price
- Required down payment
- Number, amounts, and due dates of all payments
- APR
- Total of all payments to be made over the term of the mortgage (unless the advertised credit refers to a first mortgage or deed of trust to finance the acquisition of a dwelling)

Penalties

A creditor who fails to comply with any requirement of TILA, other than certain advertising provisions, may be held liable to the consumer for actual damages and the cost of any legal action together with reasonable attorney's fees. In other actions, a creditor may be liable to a consumer for twice the amount of the finance charge, at a minimum of $400 and a maximum of $4,000, plus court costs, attorney's fees, and any actual damages. Alternatively, a successful class action alleging that a creditor understated the APR and/or finance charge could make the creditor liable for punitive damages of the lesser of $500,000 or 1% of the creditor's net worth, plus attorney's fees and court costs. In addition, a willful violation is a misdemeanor punishable by a fine of up to $5,000, one year's imprisonment, or both.

Equal Credit Opportunity Act

The federal **Equal Credit Opportunity Act (ECOA)** prohibits discrimination in the lending process based on the credit applicant's race, color, religion, national origin, sex, marital status, age (provided the applicant is of legal age), or receipt of public assistance. The ECOA requires that credit applications be considered only on the basis of income, the stability of the source of that income, net worth (total assets and liabilities), and credit rating. Information for consumers is available at www.consumer.ftc.gov/articles/0347-your-equal-credit-opportunity -rights.

www.consumer.ftc .gov/articles/0347 -your-equal-credit -opportunity-rights

The Equal Credit Opportunity Act (ECOA) prohibits discrimination in granting credit based on
■ race,
■ color,
■ religion,
■ national origin,
■ sex,
■ marital status,
■ age, and
■ receipt of public assistance.

The protections offered by ECOA are both similar (race, color, religion, and national origin) and different from those of the Fair Housing Act; ECOA includes age, marital status, and receipt of public assistance. Real estate professionals should be aware of the protections offered by this law because their clients should not face discrimination when applying for a loan to buy a property or when applying to rent one.

A creditor may not consider age unless the applicant is too young to legally sign a contract, which is usually 18, although the creditor may consider age if determining if income will drop due to retirement. Lenders are prohibited from discriminating against recipients of public assistance programs such as food stamps and rent subsidies. Lenders may not ask questions about a spouse, unless the spouse is also applying for credit; they may not discount a woman's income or assume that she will leave the workforce to raise children.

www.consumer.ftc .gov/articles/pdf-0096 -fair-credit-reporting -act.pdf

If a loan application is rejected, ECOA and the federal Fair Credit Reporting Act (FCRA) require that the lender detail the reasons for the rejection in a statement that must be provided to the loan applicant within 30 days. The loan applicant also has the right under FCRA to a free copy of any credit report that was considered in the loan application process. Additional state protections may also apply. Information for consumers is at www.consumer .ftc.gov/articles/pdf-0096-fair-credit-reporting-act.pdf.

The agency that enforces ECOA depends on the type of financial institution involved. The ECOA is enforced by the Federal Trade Commission (FTC) and the Department of Justice as well as other agencies.

Community Reinvestment Act of 1977 (CRA)

Community reinvestment refers to the responsibility of financial institutions to help meet their communities' needs for low-income and moderate-income housing. Under the **Community Reinvestment Act of 1977 (CRA)**, updated in 1995 and 2005, financial institutions are expected to meet the deposit and credit needs of their communities; participate and invest in local community development and rehabilitation projects; and participate in loan programs for housing, small businesses, and small farms. Information on the Community Reinvestment Act and other programs is at www.federalreserve.gov/communitydev/cra_about.htm and www.ffiec.gov/cra/.

The law requires any federally regulated financial institution to prepare a statement containing

■ a definition of the geographic boundaries of its community;

■ an identification of the types of community reinvestment credit offered, such as residential housing loans, housing rehabilitation loans, small-business loans, commercial loans, and consumer loans; and

■ comments from the public about the institution's performance in meeting its community's needs.

The institutions must post a public notice that their community reinvestment activities are subject to federal review, and they must make the results of those reviews public.

Real Estate Settlement Procedures Act

The federal **Real Estate Settlement Procedures Act (RESPA)** applies to any residential real estate transaction involving a new first mortgage loan. RESPA is designed to ensure that the buyer and the seller are both fully informed of all costs related to closing the transaction. Under the TILA-RESPA Integrated Disclosure rule (TRID), the disclosures required by TILA and RESPA have been combined into two new disclosure forms created by the Consumer Financial Protection Bureau.

Automated underwriting and scoring

For lenders, *automated underwriting* procedures can shorten loan approvals from weeks to minutes. Automated underwriting also tends to lower the cost of loan application and approval by reducing a lender's time spent on the approval process by as much as 60%. Freddie Mac uses a system called *Loan Prospector*. As of June 1, 2015, Freddie Mac no longer charges lenders a fee (previously $20 per transaction) to use its automated underwriting service, to encourage its use. Fannie Mae has a system called *Desktop Underwriter*, which reduces approval time to minutes, based on the borrower's credit report, a paycheck stub, and a drive-by appraisal of the property. Complex or difficult mortgages can be processed in less than 72 hours. Through automated underwriting, one of a borrower's biggest headaches in buying a home—waiting for loan approval—is eliminated. In addition, prospective buyers can strengthen their purchase offer by including proof of loan approval.

When used in automated underwriting systems, the application of credit scores has become somewhat controversial. Critics of scoring are concerned that the scores may not be accurate or fair, and in the absence of human discretion, they could result in making it more difficult for low-income and minority borrowers to obtain mortgages.

Freddie Mac has the following to say about automated underwriting:

> Whether using traditional or automated methods, underwriters must consider all three areas of underwriting—collateral, credit reputation, and capacity. When reviewing collateral, underwriters look at house value, down payment, and property type. Income, debt, cash reserves, and product type are considered when underwriters are looking at capacity. Credit scores are simply one consideration when underwriters are reviewing credit reputation. Even lenders who use an automated underwriting system such as Loan Prospector, still rely on human judgment when the scoring system indicates that the loan application is a higher risk.

KEY POINT REVIEW

The **Federal Reserve System (Fed)** consists of 12 federal reserve district banks. The Fed regulates the flow of money and interest rates.

The **primary mortgage market** consists of lenders that originate mortgage loans.

In the **secondary mortgage market**, loans are bought and sold after being funded.

Fannie Mae has shareholders but is under the conservatorship of the Federal Housing Finance Agency (FHFA). It creates **mortgage-backed securities** using pool of mortgages as collateral; and deals in conventional, FHA, and VA loans.

Freddie Mac also has shareholders and is under the conservatorship of FHFA. It has authority to purchase mortgages, pool them, and use them as security for **bonds** sold on the open market.

Ginnie Mae (**Government National Mortgage Association**) is entirely a government agency, a division of the **Department of Housing and Urban Development (HUD)**, organized as a corporation but without corporate stock, that administers **special-assistance programs**, and guarantees **mortgage-backed securities** using FHA and VA loans as collateral.

Conventional loans are the most secure loans. The **loan-to-value ratio (LTV)** is often lowest for these loans—traditionally 80%—but the LTV may be as high as 100%. Conventional loans are **not** government-insured or guaranteed. Conventional loans meet all the requirements of the secondary market, set by Fannie Mae and Freddie Mac, for **conforming loans**. **Nonconforming loans** (jumbo loans) must be retained in the lender's investment portfolio.

Private mortgage insurance (PMI) may be required for LTVs higher than 80%, that is, down payments of less than 20%. Federal law requires PMI to **automatically** terminate if the borrower has accumulated 22% equity in the home (based on purchase price or original appraised value, whichever is less) *and* is current on mortgage payments. **Fannie Mae** and **Freddie Mac** have extended the automatic termination option to all loans that are in good standing and have had no additional financing added to the original loan.

FHA-insured loans are backed by the **Federal Housing Administration (FHA)**, which is part of HUD. FHA does not make loans but insures loans made by an FHA-approved lending institution. The FHA **mortgage insurance premium (MIP)** has an up-front fee along with monthly installments. **VA-guaranteed loans** are backed by the **U.S. Department of Veterans Affairs** and are available to eligible veterans and spouses.

The **Farm Service Agency (FSA)**, formerly **Farmers Home Administration (FmHA)**, is part of the Department of Agriculture and has programs to help families purchase or operate family farms, including the Rural Housing and Community Development Service (RHCDS) and the **Farm Credit System (Farm Credit)**.

The **package loan** includes all personal property and appliances as well as real estate.

A **blanket loan** covers more than one parcel or lot, and a **partial release clause** allows a borrower to pay off part of a loan to remove the liens from one parcel or lot at a time.

An **open-end loan** secures the current loan to the borrower and future advances made by the lender to the borrower.

Construction loans are used to finance construction of property improvements.

A sale-and-leaseback arrangement can be used to finance large commercial or industrial properties. A **buydown** is a payment made at closing to reduce the interest rate on the loan.

A **home equity loan** (**home equity line of credit** or **HELOC**) is junior to the original lien.

The **Truth in Lending Act (TILA)** is implemented by **Regulation Z**, now enforced by the Consumer Financial Protection Bureau, and requires that, when a loan is secured by a residence, the lender must inform the borrower of the true cost of obtaining credit. The borrower has a **three-business-day right of rescission**. **Advertising** is strictly regulated, using **triggering terms** to mandate what must be disclosed, and there are civil and criminal penalties for violations.

The **Equal Credit Opportunity Act (ECOA)** prohibits **discrimination** in granting or arranging credit on the basis of race, color, religion, national origin, sex, marital status, age (as long as the applicant is not a minor), or receipt of public assistance.

The **Fair Credit Reporting Act (FCRA)** requires that reasons for a loan application rejection be provided to the applicant within 30 days and that the applicant be given the right to a free copy of any credit report that was considered in the loan application process.

The **Community Reinvestment Act (CRA)** requires financial institutions to help meet the need for affordable housing in their communities.

The **Real Estate Settlement Procedures Act (RESPA)** covers costs related to the closing of a residential transaction.

Automated underwriting (loan processing) programs provide loan approvals quickly and include Fannie Mae's *Desktop Underwriter* and Freddie Mac's *Loan Prospector*. A credit score may be used as part of a loan application evaluation process.

Unit 13

UNIT 13 QUIZ

1. The buyers purchased a residence for $395,000, making a down payment of $79,000 and obtaining a loan for the balance. The loan is
   A. a nonconforming loan.
   B. a package mortgage.
   C. a balloon note.
   D. a purchase money mortgage.

2. A buyer purchased a new residence from a builder for $350,000. The buyer made a down payment of $30,000 and obtained a $320,000 mortgage loan. The builder of the house paid the lender 3% of the loan balance for the first year and 2% for the second year. This represented a total savings for the buyer of $16,000. What type of mortgage arrangement is this?
   A. Open-end
   B. Package
   C. Blanket
   D. Buydown

3. Which of the following is *NOT* a participant in the secondary mortgage market?
   A. Fannie Mae
   B. Ginnie Mae
   C. Credit union
   D. Freddie Mac

4. One of the federal laws requiring disclosure to a loan applicant who is rejected for a loan on the basis of a credit report is
   A. the Real Estate Settlement Procedures Act.
   B. the Community Reinvestment Act.
   C. the Fair Credit Reporting Act.
   D. the Truth in Lending Act.

5. If buyers seek a mortgage on a single-family house, they would be *LEAST* likely to obtain the mortgage from
   A. a mutual savings bank.
   B. a life insurance company.
   C. a credit union.
   D. a commercial bank.

6. The conservatorship of Fannie Mae and Freddie Mac is the responsibility of
   A. the Federal Housing Finance Agency.
   B. the Federal Housing Authority.
   C. the Office of the Comptroller of the Currency.
   D. the Federal Reserve System.

7. What is the source of the rules that govern the use of real estate advertisements in all media, if they include mortgage financing terms?
   A. Equal Credit Opportunity Act
   B. Fair Lending Act
   C. Community Reinvestment Act
   D. Regulation Z of the Truth in Lending Act

8. A developer received a loan that covers five parcels of real estate and provides for the release of the mortgage lien on each parcel when certain payments are made on the loan. This type of loan arrangement is called
   A. the purchase money loan.
   B. the blanket loan.
   C. the package loan.
   D. the wraparound loan.

9. Funds for FHA-insured loans are usually provided by
   A. the FHA.
   B. the Federal Reserve.
   C. approved lenders.
   D. the seller.

10. The provisions of Regulation Z require all of the following to be disclosed to a residential buyer *EXCEPT*
    A. discount points.
    B. brokerage commissions.
    C. a loan origination fee.
    D. the loan interest rate.

11. What is the position of home equity line of credit (HELOC) in relation to the original lien?
    A. Equal
    B. Junior
    C. First in priority
    D. No relationship

12. The buyers purchased a model home and all its furnishings and appliances by using
    A. a package loan.
    B. a blanket loan.
    C. a FHA-insured loan.
    D. a buydown.

13. The primary activity of Freddie Mac is to
    A. guarantee mortgages with the full faith and credit of the federal government.
    B. buy and pool blocks of conventional mortgages.
    C. act in tandem with Ginnie Mae to provide special assistance in times of tight money.
    D. buy and sell VA and FHA mortgages.

14. The federal Equal Credit Opportunity Act allows lenders to discriminate against potential borrowers on the basis of
    A. preferred neighborhood.
    B. marital status.
    C. country of national origin.
    D. amount of income.

15. The buyers of a residence in Happy Hollow have a mortgage that allows them to borrow additional funds that will be secured by the home at any time. They have
    A. a closed-end loan.
    B. an open-end loan.
    C. a provisional loan.
    D. a fully adjustable loan.

16. Programs to help families purchase or operate family farms are provided by
    A. Ginnie Mae
    B. the Farm Service Agency.
    C. Fannie Mae
    D. the Federal Housing Finance Agency.

17. If a lender agrees to make a loan based on an 80% LTV, what is the amount of the loan if the property appraises for $114,500 and the sales price is $116,900?
    A. $83,200
    B. $91,300
    C. $91,600
    D. $92,900

18. The document that sets forth the maximum loan guarantee to which a veteran is entitled is
    A. the funding statement.
    B. the certificate of eligibility.
    C. the certificate of reasonable value.
    D. the certificate of discharge.

19. The law that requires lenders to find ways to help meet the housing needs of those of low and moderate incomes is
    A. the Dodd-Frank Act.
    B. the Equal Credit Opportunity Act.
    C. the Community Reinvestment Act.
    D. the Real Estate Settlement Procedures Act.

20. Which of the following requires that all advertising that references mortgage financing terms contain certain disclosures?
    A. Equal Credit Opportunity Act
    B. Fair Housing Act
    C. Community Reinvestment Act
    D. Truth in Lending Act (Regulation Z)

UNIT

14

Closing the Real Estate Transaction

LEARNING OBJECTIVES

When you have completed this unit, you will be able to

› **describe** the steps involved to achieve conveyance of clear and marketable title, including compliance with all applicable laws;
› **describe** closing procedures and the respective roles of all parties;
› **explain** the Real Estate Settlement Procedures Act (RESPA) and the Mortgage Disclosure Improvement Act (MDIA);
› **identify** all buyer and seller charges and credits contained in a closing statement; and
› **explain** the financial entries and mathematical calculations contained in a closing statement.

KEY TERMS

accrued items	escrow account	prorations
affiliated business arrangement (ABA)	escrow closing	Real Estate Settlement Procedures Act (RESPA)
closing	impound account	survey
Closing Disclosure	Loan Estimate	TILA-RESPA Integrated
closing statement	Mortgage Disclosure Improvement Act (MDIA)	Disclosure Rule (TRID)
credit	mortgage servicing transfer	
debit	statement prepaid items	

OVERVIEW

The conclusion of the real estate sales transaction is the **closing**, when title to the real estate is transferred in exchange for payment of the purchase price. Until closing preparations begin, a real estate professional's relationship is primarily with the buyer or the seller. During the closing period, new players come on the scene: appraisers, inspectors, loan officers, insurance agents, and lawyers. Negotiations may continue, usually based on issues revealed by property inspections, sometimes right up until the property is finally transferred. A thorough knowledge of the closing process is the best defense against the risk of a transaction failing.

PRECLOSING PROCEDURES

Closing is the point at which ownership of a property is transferred in exchange for the payment of the purchase price.

Closing involves two major events. First, the promises made in the sales contract are fulfilled; second, the mortgage funds are distributed to the buyer. Before the property changes hands, however, each party—buyer and seller—usually will have specific concerns that must be addressed. As emphasized previously, the closing process is based on the provisions of the sales contract, making it important that the parties treat the negotiation for the purchase of the property—the process of offer and acceptance—very seriously.

Many real estate professionals maintain a list of events that must take place prior to the actual closing in order to avoid surprises that might lead to delays.

Buyer's concerns

Both the buyer and the buyer's lender must be sure that the seller can deliver the title that was promised in the purchase agreement and that the property is now in essentially the same condition it was in when the buyer and the seller agreed to the sale. A home inspection will alert the buyer to any issues that were not immediately apparent when the buyer viewed the property, as well as problems with mechanical systems that an inspection may reveal.

The buyer's concerns thus involve examination of examination of

- the results of any inspections, such as termite, radon, water and septic systems, structural inspections, or required repairs;
- the survey;
- the title evidence, including the seller's deed and any documents demonstrating the removal of undesired liens and encumbrances; and
- any lease, if a tenant resides on the premises.

A thorough inspection of the property by a professional home inspector, who may have to be licensed by the state, may allay many of the buyer's concerns, or identify problems to be resolved. (See Figure 14.1.)

Final property inspection

In the real estate contract, the buyer usually reserves the right to make a *final inspection*, often called a *walk-through*, shortly before the closing takes place. The buyer, accompanied by the real estate professional, verifies that necessary repairs have been made, that the property has been well maintained, that all fixtures are in place, and that no unauthorized removal or alteration of any part of the improvements has taken place. It is not a time to reopen negotiations, but to verify that the condition of the property is in compliance with the terms of the contract.

Survey

A **survey** provides information about the exact location and size of the property. Typically, the survey indicates the location of all buildings, driveways, fences, and other improvements located on the premises. The survey should also indicate any existing easements and encroachments. The cost of the survey is negotiated in the sales contract. The survey is important in verifying the legal description of the property.

FIGURE 14.1: For Your Protection, Get a Home Inspection

CAUTION

U.S. Department of Housing
and Urban Development
Federal Housing Administration (FHA)

OMB Approval No: 2502-0538
(exp. 07/31/2009)

For Your Protection:
Get a Home Inspection

Why a Buyer Needs a Home Inspection

A home inspection gives the buyer more detailed information about the overall condition of the home prior to purchase. In a home inspection, a qualified inspector takes an in-depth, unbiased look at your potential new home to:

- ✔ Evaluate the physical condition: structure, construction, and mechanical systems;
- ✔ Identify items that need to be repaired or replaced; and
- ✔ Estimate the remaining useful life of the major systems, equipment, structure, and finishes.

Appraisals are Different from Home Inspections

An appraisal is different from a home inspection. Appraisals are for lenders; home inspections are for buyers. An appraisal is required to:

- ✔ Estimate the market value of a house;
- ✔ Make sure that the house meets FHA minimum property standards/requirements; and
- ✔ Make sure that the property is marketable.

FHA Does Not Guarantee the Value or Condition of your Potential New Home

If you find problems with your new home after closing, FHA can not give or lend you money for repairs, and FHA can not buy the home back from you. That is why it is so important for you, the buyer, to get an independent home inspection. Ask a qualified home inspector to inspect your potential new home and give you the information you need to make a wise decision.

Radon Gas Testing

The United States Environmental Protection Agency and the Surgeon General of the United States have recommended that all houses should be tested for radon. For more information on radon testing, call the toll-free National Radon Information Line at 1-800-SOS-Radon or 1-800-767-7236. As with a home inspection, if you decide to test for radon, you may do so before signing your contract, or you may do so after signing the contract as long as your contract states the sale of the home depends on your satisfaction with the results of the radon test.

Be an Informed Buyer

It is your responsibility to be an informed buyer. Be sure that what you buy is satisfactory in every respect. You have the right to carefully examine your potential new home with a qualified home inspector. You may arrange to do so before signing your contract, or may do so after signing the contract as long as your contract states that the sale of the home depends on the inspection.

EQUAL HOUSING
OPPORTUNITY

HUD-92564-CN (6/06)

CAUTION

IN PRACTICE

Relying on an old survey is not a good idea; the property should be resurveyed prior to closing, even in the rare instance that it is not required by the title company or lender. A current survey confirms that the property purchased is exactly what the buyer wants and that no encroachments have arisen since the last transfer of title.

Title evidence

The buyer and the buyer's lender will require that the seller's title comply with the terms of the real estate contract. Although practices vary from state to state, most require that the seller produce a current abstract of title or title commitment from a title insurance company. When an abstract of title is used, the purchaser's attorney examines it and issues an opinion of title. The attorney's opinion of title is a statement of the quality of the seller's title, and it lists all liens, encumbrances, easements, conditions, and restrictions that appear in the record and to which the seller's title is subject. The attorney's opinion is not a guarantee of title. You previously learned about how ownership is proven and the importance of examining the chain of title for various defects.

> The *title* or *opinion of title* discloses all liens, encumbrances, easements, conditions, and restrictions on the property.

When the purchaser pays cash or obtains a new loan to purchase the property, the seller's existing loan is paid in full and satisfied on the record. The exact amount required to pay the existing loan is provided in a current *payoff statement* from the lender, effective the date of closing. The payoff statement notes the unpaid amount of principal, the interest due through the date of the proposed payment, the fee for issuing the certificate of satisfaction or *release deed*, credits to the seller (if any) for tax and insurance reserves, and the amount of any prepayment penalty. The same procedure is followed for any other liens, such as a second mortgage or home equity loan, that must be released before the buyer takes title.

If the buyer assumes the seller's existing mortgage loan, the buyer needs to know the exact balance of the loan as of the closing date. Usually, the lender is required to provide the buyer with a mortgage reduction certificate, which certifies the amount owed on the mortgage loan, the interest rate, and the date and amount of the last interest payment.

The closing agent examines the title commitment or the abstract that was issued several days or weeks before the closing. Because liens may have been filed during the interval, two searches of the public record are often made. The first search shows the status of the seller's title on that date. The second search, known as a *bring down*, is made after the closing and before any new documents are filed.

As part of the later search, the seller may be required to execute an *affidavit of title*, a sworn statement in which the seller assures the title insurance company (and the buyer) that no other defects in the title have occurred since the date of the title examination (e.g., judgments, bankruptcies, divorce, unrecorded deeds or contracts, unpaid repairs or improvements that might lead to mechanics' liens). The affidavit gives the title insurance company a basis on which to sue the seller should the statements in the affidavit be incorrect.

In areas in which real estate sales transactions are customarily closed through an escrow, the escrow instructions usually provide for an extended coverage policy to be issued to the buyer effective the date of closing. The seller then has no need to execute an affidavit of title.

IN PRACTICE

Real estate professionals often assist in preclosing arrangements as part of their service to customers. In some states, real estate professionals are required to advise the parties of the approximate expenses involved in closing when a real estate sales contract is signed. In other states, real estate professionals have a statutory duty to coordinate and supervise closing activities. Aside from state laws on this issue, a real estate professional without a specific role in the closing may still be the person with the greatest knowledge of the details of the transaction. Because of this, many real estate professionals feel it is part of their fiduciary duty to be present at a face-to-face closing.

Seller's concerns

The seller's main interest is to receive payment for the property, so the seller will want assurance that the buyer has obtained the necessary financing and will have sufficient funds to complete the sale. In turn, the seller may have a list of tasks required by the purchase agreement to complete. Unless the seller owns the property free and clear of any mortgage debt, there must also be a payoff statement from the seller's lender(s), noting the amount owed that will be paid out of the sale proceeds. Both parties, along with their attorneys or real estate professionals, will want to inspect the disclosure statement made prior to closing to make sure that all monies involved in the transaction have been accounted for properly.

Real estate professional's role at closing

Depending on local practice, the real estate professional's role at closing can vary from simply collecting the commission to conducting the proceedings. In the states that require an attorney's participation, a real estate professional's responsibility is essentially finished as soon as the real estate contract is signed. Even so, most real estate professionals continue to be involved all the way through closing on behalf of their clients because it is also in a real estate professional's best interest that the transaction moves successfully and smoothly to a conclusion. This may mean actively arranging for title evidence, surveys, appraisals, and inspections or repairs related to structural conditions, water supplies, sewage facilities, or toxic substances.

Although real estate professionals do not always conduct closing proceedings, they usually attend. Often, the parties look to their real estate professionals for guidance, assistance, and information during what can be a stressful experience. Real estate professionals must be thoroughly familiar with the procedures involved in preparing the disclosure statement provided prior to closing, including the proration of costs involved in closing the transaction, which will be discussed later.

IN PRACTICE

Even in a state that does not require an attorney at closing, the real estate professional should never discourage the seller's or the buyer's use of an attorney, before and/or at closing. The real estate professional can, however, provide guidance on the importance of selecting a competent, experienced real estate attorney. The attorney must be knowledgeable about real estate documents and closing practices in order for the transaction to close smoothly.

Unit 14

Lender's interest in closing

Whether a buyer obtains new financing or assumes the seller's existing loan, the lender wants to protect its security interest in the property and ensure that its mortgage lien has priority over other liens. The lender may require a survey, a pest control or another inspection report, or a certificate of occupancy (for a newly constructed building). In order to ensure that the buyer takes good and marketable title at closing, lenders generally require that the buyer obtain a mortgagee's title insurance policy.

The buyer must also provide a fire and hazard insurance policy (along with a receipt for the premium). Usually, the homeowners insurance policy the buyer purchases combines the required hazard insurance on the structure, as well as insurance on the buyer's personal property.

The lender typically will request that a reserve account be established for tax and insurance payments so that the buyer sets aside funds for these large expenses of homeownership. The lender may even require representation by its own attorney at closing.

Internal Revenue Service reporting requirements

Certain real estate closings must be reported to the Internal Revenue Service (IRS) on Form 1099-S. The affected properties include a sale or exchange of

- land (improved or unimproved), including air space;

- an inherently permanent structure, including any residential, commercial, or industrial building;

- a condominium unit and its appurtenant fixtures and common elements (including land); or

- shares in a cooperative housing corporation.

Information to be reported includes the sales price, the amount of property tax reimbursement credited to the seller, and the seller's Social Security number. If the closing agent does not notify the IRS, the responsibility for filing the form falls on the mortgage lender, although the real estate professionals or the parties to the transaction ultimately could be held liable.

CONDUCTING THE CLOSING

Closing is known by different names in different areas. In some areas, for instance, closing is called *settlement and transfer*. The closing process also takes different forms, depending on state law, local custom, or the convenience of the parties. In some parts of the country, the parties to a transaction sit around a table and exchange copies of documents as they are executed, a process known as *passing papers*. ("We passed papers on the new house Wednesday morning.") In other regions, the buyer and the seller never meet; the paperwork is handled by an escrow agent in a process known as *closing escrow*. ("We'll close escrow on our house next week.") The main concerns are always that the buyer receive marketable title and the seller receive the purchase price.

Face-to-face closing

In a *face-to-face closing*, the parties may meet for the first time.

A face-to-face closing may be held at the office of the title company, the lending institution, an attorney for one of the parties, the real estate professional, the county recorder, or the escrow company. In many cases, this is the first and only time the buyer and the seller will meet. Those attending a closing may include

- the buyer;
- the seller;
- the real estate professionals (both the buyer's and the seller's representatives);
- the seller's and the buyer's attorneys;
- a representative of the lending institution involved with the buyer's new mortgage loan, the buyer's assumption of the seller's existing loan, or the seller's payoff of an existing loan; and
- a representative of the title insurance company.

Closing agent or closing officer

The closing agent may be a representative of the title company or lender, the real estate professional representing one of the parties, or the buyer's or the seller's attorney. Some title companies and law firms employ paralegal assistants who conduct closings for their firms.

The closing agent orders and reviews the title insurance policy or title certificate, survey, property insurance policy, and other items. After the sales contract is reviewed, the disclosure statement that indicates the division of income and expenses between the parties is prepared. Finally, the time and place of closing is arranged.

The exchange

The exchange is made when the parties are satisfied that everything is in order. After the buyer and the seller have signed all the necessary paperwork, the seller delivers the signed deed to the buyer, who accepts it. All pertinent documents are then recorded in the correct order to ensure continuity of title. For instance, if the seller pays off an existing loan and the buyer obtains a new loan, the seller's satisfaction of mortgage must be recorded before the seller's deed to the buyer. Because the buyer cannot pledge the property as security for the new loan until ownership has been transferred, the buyer's new mortgage or deed of trust is recorded only after the seller's deed to the buyer is recorded.

IN PRACTICE

A face-to-face or roundtable closing can be challenging and may not be the best approach to use if there has been friction between buyer and seller leading up to the closing. In addition, there may be a confidentiality or privacy concern in having all parties present to hear all discussions, questions asked, or concerns raised. Having the closing agent ferry documents between separate rooms in which each of the parties and their representatives are sequestered may be the best way to avoid any risk of conflict at such a stressful moment.

Closing in escrow

In an *escrow closing*, a
third party coordinates
the closing activities
on behalf of the buyer
and the seller.

In an **escrow closing**, a disinterested third party is authorized to act as *escrow agent*, or *escrow holder*, and coordinate the closing activities. The selection of the escrow agent is determined by negotiation, custom, or state law. The escrow agent may be an attorney, a title company, a trust company, an escrow company, or the escrow department of a lending institution. Although a few states do not permit certain transactions to be closed in escrow, escrow closings are used to some extent in most states.

Escrow procedure

After the sales contract is signed, the buyer and seller execute escrow instructions to the escrow agent. Once the escrow instructions are received by the escrow agent, they can be changed only at the written direction of both buyer and seller. The real estate professional who is holding the earnest money turns it over to the escrow agent, who deposits it in a special trust, or escrow, account.

The buyer and the seller deposit all pertinent documents and other items with the escrow agent before the specified date of closing.

The seller deposits

- the deed conveying the property to the buyer;
- title evidence (abstract and attorney's opinion of title, certificate of title, title insurance, or Torrens certificate);
- existing hazard insurance policies;
- a letter or mortgage reduction certificate from the lender stating the exact principal remaining (if the buyer is assuming the seller's loan);
- affidavits of title (if required);
- a payoff statement (if the seller's loan is to be paid off); and
- other instruments or documents necessary to clear the title or to complete the transaction.

The buyer deposits

- the balance of the cash needed to complete the purchase, usually in the form of a certified check;
- loan documents (if the buyer secures a new loan);
- proof of hazard insurance, including (where required) flood insurance; and
- other necessary documents, such as inspection reports required by the lender.

The escrow agent has the authority to examine the title evidence. When marketable title is shown in the name of the buyer, all other conditions of the escrow agreement have been met, and the parties have received the disclosure statement, the agent is authorized to disburse the purchase price to the seller, minus all charges and expenses. The agent then records the deed and, if a new loan has been obtained by the buyer, the mortgage or deed of trust.

If the escrow agent's examination of the title discloses liens, a portion of the purchase price can be withheld from the seller. The withheld portion is used to pay the liens to clear the title.

If the seller cannot clear the title, or if for any reason the sale cannot be consummated, the escrow instructions usually provide that the parties be returned to their former status, as if no sale occurred. The escrow agent returns the documents of title to the seller and returns the purchase money to the buyer.

LEGISLATION RELATED TO CLOSING

The **Real Estate Settlement Procedures Act (RESPA)** is a federal law that requires certain disclosures about the mortgage and settlement process and prohibits certain practices that increase the cost of settlement services, such as kickbacks and referral fees. The **Mortgage Disclosure Improvement Act (MDIA)** has changed how buyers, sellers, lenders, mortgage brokers, title agents, and real estate professionals prepare for a closing. The Consumer Financial Protection Bureau (CFPB) issued the **TILA-RESPA Integrated Disclosure rule (TRID)** to implement provisions of the Dodd-Frank Act intended to combine and clarify financing disclosures to consumers. This rule applies to transactions originating on or after October 3, 2015.

Real Estate Settlement Procedures Act (RESPA)

RESPA regulations apply to a first-lien residential mortgage loan made to finance the purchase of a one- to four-family home, cooperative, or condominium, for either investment or occupancy, as well as second or subordinate liens for home equity loans when a purchase is financed by a federally related mortgage loan. A federally related loan is one made by a bank, savings association, or other lender whose deposits are insured by a federal agency; a loan insured by the FHA or guaranteed by the VA; a loan administered by HUD; and a loan intended to be sold by the lender to Fannie Mae, Ginnie Mae, or Freddie Mac. RESPA is administered by HUD.

RESPA does not apply to the following:

- Loans on large properties (i.e., more than 25 acres)
- Loans for business or agricultural purposes
- Construction loans or other temporary financing
- Vacant land (unless a dwelling will be placed on the property within two years)
- A transaction financed solely by a purchase-money mortgage taken back by the seller
- An installment contract (contract for deed)
- A buyer's assumption of a seller's existing loan—but if the terms of the assumed loan are modified, or if the lender charges more than $50 for the assumption, the transaction is subject to RESPA regulations

RESPA prohibits certain practices that increase the cost of settlement services:

- Section 8 prohibits kickbacks and fee-splitting for referrals of settlement services, and unearned fees for services not actually performed. Violators are subject to criminal and civil penalties, including a fine up to $10,000 and/or imprisonment up to one year. The consumer may privately pursue a violator in court; the violator may be liable for an amount up to three times the amount of the charge paid for the service.
- Section 9 prohibits the home seller from requiring that the buyer purchase title insurance from a particular company. The buyer may sue the seller for such a violation; the violator is liable for up to three times the amount paid for the title insurance.
- Section 10 prohibits the lender from requiring excessive escrow account deposits for such items as taxes and hazard insurance.

Affiliated business arrangement (ABA)

To streamline the settlement process, a real estate firm, title insurance company, mortgage broker, home inspection company, or even a moving company may agree to offer a package of services to consumers, a system known as an **affiliated business arrangement (ABA)**. RESPA permits an ABA between a real estate brokerage and a mortgage company or other settlement service provider when

- there is a 1% or more common ownership between the companies, as long as the consumer is clearly informed of the relationship among the service providers,

- participation is not required,

- other providers are available, and

- the only thing of value received from the arrangement, in addition to permitted payments for services provided, is a return on the ownership interest.

Fees must be reasonably related to the value of the services provided and must not be fees exchanged among the affiliated companies simply for referring business to one another.

Other RESPA requirements

RESPA prohibits the lender from requiring the borrower to deposit funds in an escrow account for taxes and insurance that exceed certain limits, thus preventing the lender from taking advantage of the borrower. While RESPA does not require that an escrow account be set up, certain government loan programs and some lenders require that an escrow account be established as a condition of a loan. RESPA places limits on the amount that a lender may require: on a monthly basis, the lender may require only one-twelfth of the total of the disbursements for the year, plus an amount necessary to cover a shortage in the account. No more than one-sixth of the year's total disbursements may be held as a cushion (a cushion is not required). Once a year, the lender must perform an escrow account analysis and return any amount over $50 to the borrower.

A **mortgage servicing transfer statement** is required if the lender intends to sell or assign the right to service the loan to another loan servicer. The loan servicer must notify the borrower 15 days before the effective date of the loan transfer, including in the notice the name and address of the new servicer, toll-free telephone numbers, and the date the new servicer will begin accepting payments. If the borrower makes a timely payment to the old servicer within 60 days of the loan transfer, the borrower cannot be penalized.

TILA-RESPA Integrated Disclosure Rule

The TILA-RESPA Integrated Disclosure Rule (TRID), (also called the "Know Before You Owe" mortgage disclosure rule or TRID) replaces the four previous disclosure forms with two new forms: the Loan Estimate and the Closing Disclosure. The Consumer Financial Protection Bureau (CFPB) prepared these forms to make it easier for consumers to understand the costs involved in closing. The new forms were required for transactions originating on or after October 3, 2015. The forms apply to most consumer mortgage transactions, but not to home equity lines of credit, reverse mortgages, or mortgages secured by a mobile home or a dwelling that is not attached to land. The forms also do not apply to a creditor who makes five or fewer mortgages in a year. Although the burden of implementing these reforms is the responsibility of the lender, real estate professionals should be aware of current requirements because failure to meet the standards can and will delay closings.

Loan Estimate form

The **Loan Estimate** form replaces the initial Truth in Lending Statement (TIL) and the Good Faith Estimate (GFE). This form highlights the information that historically has been the most important to consumers. Interest rate, monthly payment, and total closing costs are clearly presented on the first page. The Loan Estimate form must be provided to the consumer three business days after a loan application is submitted to the lender. The Loan Estimate must contain the exact language specified by the CFPB, making it easier for borrowers to compare loan conditions from one lender to another.

The only fee that the lender may collect before the loan applicant receives the Loan Estimate is the fee for a credit report. Once the Loan Estimate is issued, the lender is committed to making the loan on the indicated terms and may only modify the Loan Estimate in certain specific instances. If certain information or circumstances change after the original Loan Estimate is issued, a new Loan Estimate must be issued.

Some closing costs or fees may or may not change prior to settlement.

The fees are divided into three categories:

- No tolerance—fees that may not increase before closing: lender charges for taking, underwriting, and processing the loan application, including points, origination fee, and yield spread premium

- 10% tolerance—fees that cannot increase by more than 10% in any given category: settlement services for which the lender selects the provider or for which the borrower selects the provider from the lender's list, title services and title insurance if the lender selects the provider, and recording fees

- Unlimited tolerance—fees for services that are out of the lender's control: services for which the borrower chooses the provider (such as escrow and title insurance), impounds for taxes, mortgage interest, and the cost of homeowners insurance

The last page of the Loan Estimate is a summary of the loan terms that the consumer can use to compare different loans and terms to aid in price shopping. The lender is responsible for the accuracy of the Loan Estimate as well as the actual costs that the lender charges, which are shown on the Closing Disclosure form.

http://www.consumer
finance.gov/regulatory
-implementation/tila
-respa/

The new form is shown in Figure 14.2. Additional sample forms can be found at http://www.consumerfinance.gov/regulatory-implementation/tila-respa/.

Closing Disclosure form

The **Closing Disclosure** form itemizes all charges that are normally paid by a borrower and a seller in connection with settlement, whether required by the lender or another party, or paid by the lender or any other person. The Closing Disclosure form replaces the HUD-1 Settlement Statement and the final TIL. The form provides more information about the costs of taxes and insurance and how the interest rate and payments may change in the future. It also warns consumers about things they may want to avoid such as prepayment penalties. The borrower must receive a completed Closing Disclosure at least three business days before the closing. If a new Closing Disclosure is required because a creditor has made a significant change to the loan terms (such as an increase in the APR greater than 0.125%, a different loan product, or the addition of a prepayment penalty), a new three-day waiting period begins.

A completed sample form is shown in Figure 14.3. For more information and updates from the Consumer Financial Protection Bureau (CFPB) regarding this rule, visit the CFPB website.

FIGURE 14.2: Loan Estimate

Save this Loan Estimate to compare with your Closing Disclosure.

Loan Estimate

DATE ISSUED
APPLICANTS

PROPERTY
SALE PRICE

LOAN TERM
PURPOSE
PRODUCT
LOAN TYPE ☐ Conventional ☐ FHA ☐ VA ☐ _____
LOAN ID #
RATE LOCK ☐ NO ☐ YES, until

Before closing, your interest rate, points, and lender credits can change unless you lock the interest rate. All other estimated closing costs expire on

Loan Terms	Can this amount increase after closing?
Loan Amount	
Interest Rate	
Monthly Principal & Interest *See Projected Payments below for your Estimated Total Monthly Payment*	
	Does the loan have these features?
Prepayment Penalty	
Balloon Payment	

Projected Payments	
Payment Calculation	
Principal & Interest	
Mortgage Insurance	
Estimated Escrow *Amount can increase over time*	
Estimated Total Monthly Payment	
Estimated Taxes, Insurance & Assessments *Amount can increase over time*	**This estimate includes** **In escrow?** ☐ Property Taxes ☐ Homeowner's Insurance ☐ Other: *See Section G on page 2 for escrowed property costs. You must pay for other property costs separately.*

Costs at Closing	
Estimated Closing Costs	Includes in Loan Costs + in Other Costs – in Lender Credits. *See page 2 for details.*
Estimated Cash to Close	Includes Closing Costs. *See Calculating Cash to Close on page 2 for details.*

Visit **www.consumerfinance.gov/mortgage-estimate** for general information and tools.

Figure 14.2:   Loan Estimate (continued)

Closing Cost Details

Loan Costs

A. Origination Charges

   % of Loan Amount (Points)

B. Services You Cannot Shop For

C. Services You Can Shop For

D. TOTAL LOAN COSTS (A + B + C)

Other Costs

E. Taxes and Other Government Fees

Recording Fees and Other Taxes
Transfer Taxes

F. Prepaids

Homeowner's Insurance Premium (months)
Mortgage Insurance Premium (months)
Prepaid Interest (per day for   days @   )
Property Taxes (months)

G. Initial Escrow Payment at Closing

Homeowner's Insurance	per month for	mo.
Mortgage Insurance	per month for	mo.
Property Taxes	per month for	mo.

H. Other

I. TOTAL OTHER COSTS (E + F + G + H)

J. TOTAL CLOSING COSTS

D + I
Lender Credits

Calculating Cash to Close

Total Closing Costs (J)

Closing Costs Financed (Paid from your Loan Amount)

Down Payment/Funds from Borrower

Deposit

Funds for Borrower

Seller Credits

Adjustments and Other Credits

Estimated Cash to Close

Adjustable Payment (AP) Table

Interest Only Payments?	
Optional Payments?	
Step Payments?	
Seasonal Payments?	
Monthly Principal and Interest Payments	
First Change/Amount	
Subsequent Changes	
Maximum Payment	

Adjustable Interest Rate (AIR) Table

Index + Margin
Initial Interest Rate
Minimum/Maximum Interest Rate
Change Frequency
First Change
Subsequent Changes
Limits on Interest Rate Changes
First Change
Subsequent Changes

Figure 14.2: Loan Estimate (continued)

Additional Information About This Loan

LENDER	**MORTGAGE BROKER**
NMLS/___ LICENSE ID	**NMLS/___ LICENSE ID**
LOAN OFFICER	**LOAN OFFICER**
NMLS/___ LICENSE ID	**NMLS/___ LICENSE ID**
EMAIL	**EMAIL**
PHONE	**PHONE**

Comparisons	Use these measures to compare this loan with other loans.
In 5 Years	Total you will have paid in principal, interest, mortgage insurance, and loan costs.
	Principal you will have paid off.
Annual Percentage Rate (APR)	Your costs over the loan term expressed as a rate. This is not your interest rate.
Total Interest Percentage (TIP)	The total amount of interest that you will pay over the loan term as a percentage of your loan amount.

Other Considerations

Appraisal	We may order an appraisal to determine the property's value and charge you for this appraisal. We will promptly give you a copy of any appraisal, even if your loan does not close. You can pay for an additional appraisal for your own use at your own cost.
Assumption	If you sell or transfer this property to another person, we ☐ will allow, under certain conditions, this person to assume this loan on the original terms. ☐ will not allow assumption of this loan on the original terms.
Homeowner's Insurance	This loan requires homeowner's insurance on the property, which you may obtain from a company of your choice that we find acceptable.
Late Payment	If your payment is more than ___ days late, we will charge a late fee of _____
Refinance	Refinancing this loan will depend on your future financial situation, the property value, and market conditions. You may not be able to refinance this loan.
Servicing	We intend ☐ to service your loan. If so, you will make your payments to us. ☐ to transfer servicing of your loan.

Confirm Receipt

By signing, you are only confirming that you have received this form. You do not have to accept this loan because you have signed or received this form.

_____	_____	_____	_____
Applicant Signature	Date	Co-Applicant Signature	Date

Figure 14.3:   Closing Disclosure

Closing Disclosure

This form is a statement of final loan terms and closing costs. Compare this document with your Loan Estimate.

Closing Information

Date Issued	4/15/2013
Closing Date	4/15/2013
Disbursement Date	4/15/2013
Settlement Agent	Epsilon Title Co.
File #	12-3456
Property	456 Somewhere Ave Anytown, ST 12345
Sale Price	$180,000

Transaction Information

Borrower	Michael Jones and Mary Stone 123 Anywhere Street Anytown, ST 12345
Seller	Steve Cole and Amy Doe 321 Somewhere Drive Anytown, ST 12345
Lender	Ficus Bank

Loan Information

Loan Term	30 years
Purpose	Purchase
Product	Fixed Rate
Loan Type	☒ Conventional ☐ FHA ☐ VA ☐ _____
Loan ID #	123456789
MIC #	000654321

Loan Terms

Loan Terms		Can this amount increase after closing?
Loan Amount	$162,000	**NO**
Interest Rate	3.875%	**NO**
Monthly Principal & Interest *See Projected Payments below for your Estimated Total Monthly Payment*	$761.78	**NO**
		Does the loan have these features?
Prepayment Penalty		**YES** • **As high as $3,240** if you pay off the loan during the first 2 years
Balloon Payment		**NO**

Projected Payments

Payment Calculation		Years 1-7		Years 8-30
Principal & Interest		$761.78		$761.78
Mortgage Insurance	+	82.35	+	—
Estimated Escrow *Amount can increase over time*	+	206.13	+	206.13
Estimated Total Monthly Payment		**$1,050.26**		**$967.91**

Estimated Taxes, Insurance & Assessments *Amount can increase over time* *See page 4 for details*	$356.13 a month	**This estimate includes** ☒ Property Taxes ☒ Homeowner's Insurance ☒ Other: Homeowner's Association Dues *See Escrow Account on page 4 for details. You must pay for other property costs separately.*	**In escrow?** YES YES NO

Costs at Closing

Closing Costs	$9,712.10	Includes $4,694.05 in Loan Costs + $5,018.05 in Other Costs – $0 in Lender Credits. *See page 2 for details.*
Cash to Close	$14,147.26	Includes Closing Costs. *See Calculating Cash to Close on page 3 for details.*

Unit 14

Figure 14.3: Closing Disclosure (continued)

Closing Cost Details

Loan Costs		Borrower-Paid		Seller-Paid		Paid by Others
		At Closing	Before Closing	At Closing	Before Closing	
A. Origination Charges		**$1,802.00**				
01 0.25 % of Loan Amount (Points)		$405.00				
02 Application Fee		$300.00				
03 Underwriting Fee		$1,097.00				
04						
05						
06						
07						
08						
B. Services Borrower Did Not Shop For		**$236.55**				
01 Appraisal Fee	to John Smith Appraisers Inc.					$405.00
02 Credit Report Fee	to Information Inc.		$29.80			
03 Flood Determination Fee	to Info Co.	$20.00				
04 Flood Monitoring Fee	to Info Co.	$31.75				
05 Tax Monitoring Fee	to Info Co.	$75.00				
06 Tax Status Research Fee	to Info Co.	$80.00				
07						
08						
09						
10						
C. Services Borrower Did Shop For		**$2,655.50**				
01 Pest Inspection Fee	to Pests Co.	$120.50				
02 Survey Fee	to Surveys Co.	$85.00				
03 Title – Insurance Binder	to Epsilon Title Co.	$650.00				
04 Title – Lender's Title Insurance	to Epsilon Title Co.	$500.00				
05 Title – Settlement Agent Fee	to Epsilon Title Co.	$500.00				
06 Title – Title Search	to Epsilon Title Co.	$800.00				
07						
08						
D. TOTAL LOAN COSTS (Borrower-Paid)		**$4,694.05**				
Loan Costs Subtotals (A + B + C)		$4,664.25	$29.80			

Other Costs		Borrower-Paid		Seller-Paid		Paid by Others
E. Taxes and Other Government Fees		**$85.00**				
01 Recording Fees	Deed: $40.00 Mortgage: $45.00	$85.00				
02 Transfer Tax	to Any State			$950.00		
F. Prepaids		**$2,120.80**				
01 Homeowner's Insurance Premium (12 mo.) to Insurance Co.		$1,209.96				
02 Mortgage Insurance Premium (mo.)						
03 Prepaid Interest ($17.44 per day from 4/15/13 to 5/1/13)		$279.04				
04 Property Taxes (6 mo.) to Any County USA		$631.80				
05						
G. Initial Escrow Payment at Closing		**$412.25**				
01 Homeowner's Insurance $100.83 per month for 2 mo.		$201.66				
02 Mortgage Insurance per month for mo.						
03 Property Taxes $105.30 per month for 2 mo.		$210.60				
04						
05						
06						
07						
08 Aggregate Adjustment		– 0.01				
H. Other		**$2,400.00**				
01 HOA Capital Contribution	to HOA Acre Inc.	$500.00				
02 HOA Processing Fee	to HOA Acre Inc.	$150.00				
03 Home Inspection Fee	to Engineers Inc.	$750.00			$750.00	
04 Home Warranty Fee	to XYZ Warranty Inc.			$450.00		
05 Real Estate Commission	to Alpha Real Estate Broker			$5,700.00		
06 Real Estate Commission	to Omega Real Estate Broker			$5,700.00		
07 Title – Owner's Title Insurance (optional) to Epsilon Title Co.		$1,000.00				
08						
I. TOTAL OTHER COSTS (Borrower-Paid)		**$5,018.05**				
Other Costs Subtotals (E + F + G + H)		$5,018.05				
J. TOTAL CLOSING COSTS (Borrower-Paid)		**$9,712.10**				
Closing Costs Subtotals (D + I)		$9,682.30	$29.80	$12,800.00	$750.00	$405.00
Lender Credits						

Figure 14.3:   Closing Disclosure (continued)

Calculating Cash to Close

Use this table to see what has changed from your Loan Estimate.

	Loan Estimate	Final	Did this change?
Total Closing Costs (J)	$8,054.00	$9,712.10	**YES** • See **Total Loan Costs (D)** and **Total Other Costs (I)**
Closing Costs Paid Before Closing	$0	– $29.80	**YES** • You paid these Closing Costs **before closing**
Closing Costs Financed (Paid from your Loan Amount)	$0	$0	**NO**
Down Payment/Funds from Borrower	$18,000.00	$18,000.00	**NO**
Deposit	– $10,000.00	– $10,000.00	**NO**
Funds for Borrower	$0	$0	**NO**
Seller Credits	$0	– $2,500.00	**YES** • See Seller Credits in **Section L**
Adjustments and Other Credits	$0	– $1,035.04	**YES** • See details in **Sections K and L**
Cash to Close	$16,054.00	$14,147.26	

Summaries of Transactions

Use this table to see a summary of your transaction.

BORROWER'S TRANSACTION

K. Due from Borrower at Closing	$189,762.30
01 Sale Price of Property	$180,000.00
02 Sale Price of Any Personal Property Included in Sale	
03 Closing Costs Paid at Closing (J)	$9,682.30
04	
Adjustments	
05	
06	
07	
Adjustments for Items Paid by Seller in Advance	
08 City/Town Taxes to	
09 County Taxes to	
10 Assessments to	
11 HOA Dues 4/15/13 to 4/30/13	$80.00
12	
13	
14	
15	

L. Paid Already by or on Behalf of Borrower at Closing	$175,615.04
01 Deposit	$10,000.00
02 Loan Amount	$162,000.00
03 Existing Loan(s) Assumed or Taken Subject to	
04	
05 Seller Credit	$2,500.00
Other Credits	
06 Rebate from Epsilon Title Co.	$750.00
07	
Adjustments	
08	
09	
10	
11	
Adjustments for Items Unpaid by Seller	
12 City/Town Taxes 1/1/13 to 4/14/13	$365.04
13 County Taxes to	
14 Assessments to	
15	
16	
17	

CALCULATION	
Total Due from Borrower at Closing (K)	$189,762.30
Total Paid Already by or on Behalf of Borrower at Closing (L)	– $175,615.04
Cash to Close ☒ From ☐ To Borrower	**$14,147.26**

SELLER'S TRANSACTION

M. Due to Seller at Closing	$180,080.00
01 Sale Price of Property	$180,000.00
02 Sale Price of Any Personal Property Included in Sale	
03	
04	
05	
06	
07	
08	
Adjustments for Items Paid by Seller in Advance	
09 City/Town Taxes to	
10 County Taxes to	
11 Assessments to	
12 HOA Dues 4/15/13 to 4/30/13	$80.00
13	
14	
15	
16	

N. Due from Seller at Closing	$115,665.04
01 Excess Deposit	
02 Closing Costs Paid at Closing (J)	$12,800.00
03 Existing Loan(s) Assumed or Taken Subject to	
04 Payoff of First Mortgage Loan	$100,000.00
05 Payoff of Second Mortgage Loan	
06	
07	
08 Seller Credit	$2,500.00
09	
10	
11	
12	
13	
Adjustments for Items Unpaid by Seller	
14 City/Town Taxes 1/1/13 to 4/14/13	$365.04
15 County Taxes to	
16 Assessments to	
17	
18	
19	

CALCULATION	
Total Due to Seller at Closing (M)	$180,080.00
Total Due from Seller at Closing (N)	– $115,665.04
Cash ☐ From ☒ To Seller	**$64,414.96**

Figure 14.3: Closing Disclosure (continued)

Additional Information About This Loan

Loan Disclosures

Assumption

If you sell or transfer this property to another person, your lender

☐ will allow, under certain conditions, this person to assume this loan on the original terms.

☒ will not allow assumption of this loan on the original terms.

Demand Feature

Your loan

☐ has a demand feature, which permits your lender to require early repayment of the loan. You should review your note for details.

☒ does not have a demand feature.

Late Payment

If your payment is more than *15* days late, your lender will charge a late fee of *5% of the monthly principal and interest payment.*

Negative Amortization (Increase in Loan Amount)

Under your loan terms, you

☐ are scheduled to make monthly payments that do not pay all of the interest due that month. As a result, your loan amount will increase (negatively amortize), and your loan amount will likely become larger than your original loan amount. Increases in your loan amount lower the equity you have in this property.

☐ may have monthly payments that do not pay all of the interest due that month. If you do, your loan amount will increase (negatively amortize), and, as a result, your loan amount may become larger than your original loan amount. Increases in your loan amount lower the equity you have in this property.

☒ do not have a negative amortization feature.

Partial Payments

Your lender

☒ may accept payments that are less than the full amount due (partial payments) and apply them to your loan.

☐ may hold them in a separate account until you pay the rest of the payment, and then apply the full payment to your loan.

☐ does not accept any partial payments.

If this loan is sold, your new lender may have a different policy.

Security Interest

You are granting a security interest in
456 Somewhere Ave., Anytown, ST 12345

You may lose this property if you do not make your payments or satisfy other obligations for this loan.

Escrow Account

For now, your loan

☒ will have an escrow account (also called an "impound" or "trust" account) to pay the property costs listed below. Without an escrow account, you would pay them directly, possibly in one or two large payments a year. Your lender may be liable for penalties and interest for failing to make a payment.

Escrow		
Escrowed Property Costs over Year 1	$2,473.56	Estimated total amount over year 1 for your escrowed property costs: *Homeowner's Insurance Property Taxes*
Non-Escrowed Property Costs over Year 1	$1,800.00	Estimated total amount over year 1 for your non-escrowed property costs: *Homeowner's Association Dues* You may have other property costs.
Initial Escrow Payment	$412.25	A cushion for the escrow account you pay at closing. See Section G on page 2.
Monthly Escrow Payment	$206.13	The amount included in your total monthly payment.

☐ will not have an escrow account because ☐ you declined it ☐ your lender does not offer one. You must directly pay your property costs, such as taxes and homeowner's insurance. Contact your lender to ask if your loan can have an escrow account.

No Escrow		
Estimated Property Costs over Year 1		Estimated total amount over year 1. You must pay these costs directly, possibly in one or two large payments a year.
Escrow Waiver Fee		

In the future,

Your property costs may change and, as a result, your escrow payment may change. You may be able to cancel your escrow account, but if you do, you must pay your property costs directly. If you fail to pay your property taxes, your state or local government may (1) impose fines and penalties or (2) place a tax lien on this property. If you fail to pay any of your property costs, your lender may (1) add the amounts to your loan balance, (2) add an escrow account to your loan, or (3) require you to pay for property insurance that the lender buys on your behalf, which likely would cost more and provide fewer benefits than what you could buy on your own.

Figure 14.3:   Closing Disclosure (continued)

Loan Calculations

Total of Payments. Total you will have paid after you make all payments of principal, interest, mortgage insurance, and loan costs, as scheduled.	$285,803.36
Finance Charge. The dollar amount the loan will cost you.	$118,830.27
Amount Financed. The loan amount available after paying your upfront finance charge.	$162,000.00
Annual Percentage Rate (APR). Your costs over the loan term expressed as a rate. This is not your interest rate.	4.174%
Total Interest Percentage (TIP). The total amount of interest that you will pay over the loan term as a percentage of your loan amount.	69.46%

Questions? If you have questions about the loan terms or costs on this form, use the contact Information below. To get more information or make a complaint, contact the Consumer Financial Protection Bureau at **www.consumerfinance.gov/mortgage-closing**

Other Disclosures

Appraisal
If the property was appraised for your loan, your lender is required to give you a copy at no additional cost at least 3 days before closing. If you have not yet received it, please contact your lender at the information listed below.

Contract Details
See your note and security instrument for information about
• what happens if you fail to make your payments,
• what is a default on the loan,
• situations in which your lender can require early repayment of the loan, and
• the rules for making payments before they are due.

Liability after Foreclosure
If your lender forecloses on this property and the foreclosure does not cover the amount of unpaid balance on this loan,

☒ state law may protect you from liability for the unpaid balance. If you refinance or take on any additional debt on this property, you may lose this protection and have to pay any debt remaining even after foreclosure. You may want to consult a lawyer for more information.

☐ state law does not protect you from liability for the unpaid balance.

Refinance
Refinancing this loan will depend on your future financial situation, the property value, and market conditions. You may not be able to refinance this loan.

Tax Deductions
If you borrow more than this property is worth, the interest on the loan amount above this property's fair market value is not deductible from your federal income taxes. You should consult a tax advisor for more information.

Contact Information

	Lender	Mortgage Broker	Real Estate Broker (B)	Real Estate Broker (S)	Settlement Agent
Name	Ficus Bank		Omega Real Estate Broker Inc.	Alpha Real Estate Broker Co.	Epsilon Title Co.
Address	4321 Random Blvd. Somecity, ST 12340		789 Local Lane Sometown, ST 12345	987 Suburb Ct. Someplace, ST 12340	123 Commerce Pl. Somecity, ST 12344
NMLS ID					
ST License ID			Z765416	Z61456	Z61616
Contact	Joe Smith		Samuel Green	Joseph Cain	Sarah Arnold
Contact NMLS ID	12345				
Contact ST License ID			P16415	P51461	PT1234
Email	joesmith@ ficusbank.com		sam@omegare.biz	joe@alphare.biz	sarah@ epsilontitle.com
Phone	123-456-7890		123-555-1717	321-555-7171	987-555-4321

Confirm Receipt

By signing, you are only confirming that you have received this form. You do not have to accept this loan because you have signed or received this form.

_____   _____
Applicant Signature   Date

_____   _____
Co-Applicant Signature   Date

Unit 14

Your Home Loan Toolkit

The CFPB developed an information booklet called *Your Home Loan Toolkit*, which must be provided by a creditor to a mortgage applicant as part of the loan application process, although other real estate professionals, such as brokers, are encouraged to make the booklet available to prospective borrowers. The booklet provides the borrower with general information about settlement (closing) and how to find the best mortgage. It provides numerous resources for further information, as well as a line-by-line description of the Loan Disclosure form. More information on *Your Home Loan Toolkit* is available from the CFPB by going to www.consumerfinance.gov. As of October 3, 2015, *Your Home Loan Toolkit* replaced the previously mandated *Settlement Cost Booklet*.

www.consumerfinance
.gov

Kickbacks and referral fees

RESPA prohibits the payment of kickbacks, or unearned fees, in any real estate settlement service.

It prohibits a referral fee when no services are actually rendered. The payment or receipt of a fee, a kickback, or anything of value for a referral for settlement services includes activities such as mortgage loans, title searches, title insurance, attorney services, surveys, credit reports, and appraisals.

IN PRACTICE

Although RESPA's requirements are aimed primarily at lenders, real estate professionals fall under RESPA when they refer buyers to particular lenders, title companies, attorneys, or other providers of settlement services. Real estate professionals who offer computerized loan origination are also subject to regulation. Remember: Buyers have the right to select their own providers of settlement services.

Mortgage Disclosure Improvement Act

The Mortgage Disclosure Improvement Act (MDIA), which took effect July 31, 2009, changed how buyers and sellers, lenders, mortgage brokers, title agents, and real estate professionals prepare for a closing. The intent of this law is to prevent the consumer from receiving an encitingly low interest rate at the initial loan application and then learning at settlement that the lender is charging more in fees.

The requirements of the MDIA are now incorporated into the CFPB disclosure requirements. Until the applicant/borrower receives the Loan Estimate, the lender may collect only a reasonable fee for accessing the applicant's credit history. In addition, the lender must provide a statement to the loan applicant indicating that the applicant is not obligated to complete the transaction simply because disclosures were provided or because the individual applied for a loan. Generally, if the APR increases more than 0.125% from that stated in the Closing Disclosure, the creditor must provide a new disclosure with a revised APR and wait an additional three business days before closing the loan. The consumer is permitted to accelerate the process if a personal emergency, such as a foreclosure, exists.

Before closing, everyone involved in the real estate transaction should check and double-check that the Loan Estimate and Closing Disclosure forms are consistent with the original application.

PREPARATION OF CLOSING STATEMENTS

A typical real estate transaction requires accounting for the expenses incurred by either party, generally on the Closing Disclosure, which is required for any federally related closing. All expenses must be itemized to arrive at the exact amount of cash required from the buyer and the net proceeds that will be paid to the seller. These include prorated items—those prepaid by the seller for which the seller must be reimbursed (such as taxes) and expenses the seller has incurred but for which the buyer will be billed (such as mortgage interest paid in arrears when a loan is assumed).

How the closing statement works

A **debit** is an amount to be paid by the buyer or the seller.

A **credit** is an amount payable to the buyer or the seller.

The **closing statement** is an accounting of the parties' debits and credits. A **debit** is a charge—an amount that a party owes and must pay at closing. A **credit** is an amount entered in a person's favor—an amount that has already been paid, an amount being reimbursed, or an amount the buyer promises to pay in the form of a loan.

To determine the amount a buyer must bring to closing, any buyer expenses and prorated amounts for items prepaid by the seller are added to the purchase price. Then the buyer's credits are totaled. Credits to the buyer include the earnest money (already paid), the balance of the loan the buyer obtains or assumes, and the seller's share of any prorated items the buyer will pay in the future.

Finally, the total of the buyer's credits is subtracted from the total of the buyer's debits to arrive at the actual amount of cash the buyer must bring to closing. The buyer usually brings a cashier's or certified check.

A similar procedure is followed to determine the net proceeds to the seller. The seller's debits are subtracted from the seller's credits. Seller credits include the purchase price plus the buyer's share of any prorated items that the seller has prepaid. The seller's debits include expenses to be paid by the seller, the seller's share of prorated items to be paid by the buyer, and the balance of any mortgage loan or other lien that the seller must satisfy. (See Figure 14.4.)

Broker's commission

The responsibility for paying a real estate broker's commission will have been determined by previous agreement. If the broker represents the seller, the seller is normally responsible for paying the commission. If a representation agreement exists between a broker and the buyer or if two representatives are involved, one for the seller and one for the buyer, the commission *may* be distributed as an expense between both parties or according to some other arrangement.

Attorney's fees

If either of the parties' attorneys will be paid from the closing proceeds, that party will be charged with the expense in the closing statement. This expense may include fees for the preparation or review of documents or for representing the parties at settlement.

FIGURE 14.4: Credits and Debits

Item	Credit to Buyer	Debit to Buyer	Credit to Seller	Debit to Seller	Prorated
Principal amount of new mortgage	√				
Payoff of existing mortgage				√	
Unpaid principal balance if assumed mortgage	√			√	
Accrued interest on existing assumed mortgage	√			√	√
Tenant's security deposit	√			√	
Purchase money mortgage	√			√	
Unpaid water and other utility bills	√			√	√
Buyer's earnest money	√				
Selling price of property		√	√		
Fuel oil on hand (valued at current market price)		√	√		√
Prepaid insurance and tax reserve for mortgage assumed by buyer		√	√		√
Refund to seller of prepaid water charges and similar utility expenses		√	√		√
Prepaid general real estate taxes		√	√		√

Note: This chart is based on generally applicable practices. Closing practices may be different in your state or county.

Recording expenses

The seller usually pays for any recording charges (filing fees) necessary to clear all defects and furnish the purchaser with a marketable title. Items customarily charged to the seller include the recording of any release deed or satisfaction of mortgage, quitclaim deed, affidavit, or satisfaction of a mechanic's lien. The buyer pays for recording charges that arise from the actual transfer of title. Usually, such items include the recording of the deed that conveys title to the purchaser and a mortgage or deed of trust executed by the buyer for the benefit of the lender.

Transfer tax

Most states, counties, and local municipalities require some form of transfer tax, conveyance fee, or tax stamps on real estate conveyances. Responsibility for this charge varies according to local practice and the terms of the sales contract.

Title expenses

Responsibility for title expenses varies according to local custom. In most areas, the seller is required to furnish evidence of good title and pay for the title search. If the buyer's attorney inspects the evidence or if the buyer purchases title insurance policies, the buyer is charged for the expense.

Loan fees

For a new loan, the lender generally charges an origination fee and could possibly charge discount points, particularly if the borrower wants a below-market interest rate.

Tax reserves and insurance reserves (escrow or impound accounts)

Most mortgage lenders require that borrowers provide funds to pay future real estate taxes and insurance premiums. These funds are held in an **escrow account** or **impound account**. A borrower starts the account at closing by depositing funds to cover at least the amount of unpaid real estate taxes from the date of the lien to the end of the current month. (The buyer receives a credit from the seller at closing for any unpaid taxes.) Afterward, an amount equal to one month's portion of the estimated taxes is included in the borrower's monthly mortgage payment.

The borrower is responsible for maintaining adequate property insurance as a condition of the mortgage loan. The first year's premium is paid in full at closing if it has not been paid earlier by the buyer, effective on the date of closing. The borrower's monthly loan payment typically will include principal and interest on the loan (unless the payment is interest-only), plus one-twelfth of the estimated taxes and insurance (PITI) that will be owed at the end of the coming year. The taxes and insurance are held by the lender in an escrow account until the bills are due.

IN PRACTICE

RESPA permits lenders to maintain a cushion equal to one-sixth of the total estimated amount of annual taxes and insurance. However, if state law or mortgage documents allow for a smaller cushion, the lesser amount prevails.

Appraisal fee

Either the seller or the purchaser pays the appraisal fee, depending on who orders the appraisal. When the buyer obtains a mortgage, it is customary for the lender to require an appraisal, in which case, the buyer usually bears the cost, although this is always a negotiable item. If the fee is paid at the time of the loan application, it is reflected on the closing statement as having been paid before closing.

Survey fee

The purchaser who obtains new mortgage financing customarily pays a survey fee. The sales contract may require that the seller furnish a survey.

Additional fees

If the borrower's loan is insured by FHA, the borrower owes a lump sum for payment of the mortgage insurance premium (MIP) if it is not financed as part of the loan. The borrower of a VA-guaranteed loan pays a funding fee directly to the Department of Veterans Affairs at closing. If a conventional loan carries private mortgage insurance (PMI), the buyer prepays one year's mortgage insurance premium at closing.

Accounting for expenses

Expenses paid out of the closing proceeds are debited only to the party making the payment. Occasionally, an expense item (e.g., an escrow fee, a settlement fee, or a transfer tax) may be shared by the buyer and the seller. In that case, each party is debited for that individual's share of the expense.

PRORATIONS

Most closings involve the division of financial responsibility between the buyer and the seller for such items as loan interest, taxes, rents, fuel, and utility bills. These allowances are allocated between the parties in the required proportions, or **prorations**. Prorations are necessary to ensure that expenses and credits are divided fairly between the seller and the buyer.

General rules for prorating

The rules or customs governing the computation of prorations for the closing of a real estate sale vary widely from state to state. The following are some general guidelines for preparing the closing statement:

- In most states, the seller owns the property on the day of closing, and prorations or apportionments are usually made up to and including the day of closing. A few states specify that the buyer owns the property on the closing date. In that case, adjustments are made as of the day preceding the day on which title is closed.

- Mortgage interest, general real estate taxes, water taxes, insurance premiums, and similar expenses are usually computed by using 360 days in a year and 30 days in a month. In some areas, however, prorations are computed on the basis of the actual number of days in the calendar month of closing. The agreement of sale should specify which method will be used.

- On almost every mortgage loan, the interest is paid in arrears. A mortgage payment due on June 1, for example, includes interest due for May. The buyer who places a new mortgage loan on May 31 may be pleasantly surprised to learn that the first mortgage payment is not due for another month.

- Accrued or prepaid general real estate taxes are usually prorated at the closing. In some states, real estate taxes are paid in advance; that is, if the tax year runs from January 1 to December 31, taxes for the coming year are due on January 1. In this case, the seller, who has prepaid a year's taxes, should be reimbursed for the portion of the year remaining after the buyer takes ownership of the property. In other areas, taxes are paid in arrears, on December 31 for the year just ended. In that case, the buyer should be credited by the seller for the time the seller occupied the property. When the amount of the current real estate tax cannot be determined definitely, the proration is usually based on the last obtainable tax bill, often with a percentage increase—say, 10%—to account for a likely reassessment.

- Special assessments for municipal improvements such as sewers, water mains, or streets are usually paid in annual installments over several years, with annual interest charged on the outstanding balance of future payments. The seller normally makes the current payments, and the buyer assumes all future payments. The special assessment installment generally is not prorated at the closing. A buyer may insist that the seller allow the buyer a credit for the seller's share of the interest to the closing date. The agreement of sale may address the manner in which special assessments will be handled at closing.

- Rent is usually adjusted on the basis of the actual number of days in the month of closing. The seller customarily receives the rents for the day of closing and pays all expenses for that day. If any rents for the current month are uncollected when the sale is closed, the buyer often agrees by a separate letter to collect the rents, if possible, and remit the prorated share to the seller.

- A security deposit made by a tenant to cover the cost of repairing damage caused by the tenant, or the last month's rent which has been collected in advance, are generally transferred by the seller to the buyer without prorating. The only exception would be if the property were being transferred in the last month of the lease; thus, the last month's rent would be prorated.

Accrued items = buyer credits

Prepaid items = seller credits

Accrued items are expenses to be prorated (such as water bills and interest on an assumed mortgage) that are owed by the seller but will be paid after the sale by the buyer. The seller pays for these items by giving the buyer credits for them at closing.

Prepaid items are expenses to be prorated (such as fuel oil in a tank) that have been prepaid by the seller but not fully used up, so they become credits to the seller.

The arithmetic of prorating

The computation of a proration involves identifying a yearly charge for the item to be prorated, then dividing by 12 to determine a monthly charge for the item. Also, it is usually necessary to identify a daily charge for the item by dividing the monthly charge by the number of days in the month. These smaller portions are then multiplied by the number of months or days in the prorated period to determine the accrued or unearned amount that will be figured in the settlement.

Using this general principle, there are two methods of calculating a proration:

- The yearly charge is divided by a 360-day year (called a banking or statutory year), or 12 months of 30 days each.
- The yearly charge is divided by 365 (a calendar year) to determine the daily charge, and the actual number of days in the proration period is determined, with this number multiplied by the daily charge.

The final proration figure will vary slightly, depending on which computation method is used. The final figure also will vary according to the number of decimal places to which the division is carried. All the proration calculations here are computed by carrying the division to three decimal places and then rounding to the nearest cent only after the final proration figure is determined.

Accrued items

When the real estate tax is levied for the calendar year and is payable during that year or in the following year, the accrued portion is for the period from January 1 to the date of closing (or to the day before the closing in states where the sale date is excluded). If the current tax bill has not yet been issued, the parties must agree on an estimated amount based on the previous year's bill and any known changes in assessment or tax levy for the current year. If the assessment for the current year is not known, the parties may agree to add an estimated amount, say 10%, to the amount of the last assessment.

Sample proration calculation

Assume that a sale is to be closed on September 17. Using a 360-day year, prorate the current real estate taxes of $3,600 for the accrued period of 8 months, 17 days. First determine the prorated cost of the real estate tax per month and day:

$3,600 ÷ 12 months = $300 per month

$300 ÷ 30 days = $10 per day

Next, multiply these figures by the accrued period and add the totals to determine the prorated real estate tax:

$300 × 8 months = $2,400

$10 × 17 days = $170

$2,400 + 170 = $2,570

Thus, the accrued real estate tax for 8 months and 17 days is $2,570. This amount represents the seller's accrued earned tax. It will be a credit to the buyer and a debit to the seller on the closing statement.

To compute this proration using the actual number of days in the accrued period, the following method is used:

The accrued period from January 1 to September 17 runs 260 days (January's 31 days plus February's 28 days and so on, plus the 17 days of September).

$3,600 ÷ 365 days = $9.863 per day

$9.863 × 260 days = $2,564.38

Although these examples show proration as of the date of settlement, the agreement of sale may indicate otherwise. For instance, if the buyer's possession date does not coincide with the settlement date, the parties could prorate according to the date of possession.

IN PRACTICE

On state licensing examinations, tax prorations are usually based on a 30-day month (360-day year) unless specified otherwise. This may differ from local custom regarding tax prorations. Many title insurance companies provide proration charts that detail tax factors for each day in the year. To determine a tax proration using one of these charts, multiply the factor given for the closing date by the annual real estate tax.

MATH CONCEPTS

Computing Interim Interest

Interim interest is charged by a lender when a borrower obtains a new loan. This interest is called *interim* because it is for the interim period of time from the day of closing through the end of the closing month. Most real estate loan interest is paid in arrears, but interim interest is an example of interest paid in advance.

If closing on a loan on June 12, the borrower will owe interim interest for 19 days. The first full payment (PI) will be due August 1; this payment will include interest for July. If the closing is September 21, interim interest for 10 days will be paid at closing, and the first full payment will be due November 1 (paying interest for October).

For Example

A borrower is closing on a $114,300 loan with an interest rate of 4.75% on November 18. How much interim interest will be due at closing? The first full payment is due January 1.

30 days in November – 18 (days until closing) = 12 days + 1 (day of closing) = 13 days

$114,300 × 4.75% = 5,429.25 annual interest

$5,429.25 ÷ 360 = $15.081 interest per day

$15.081 × 13 days = $196.053 interim interest due at closing

$196.05 interim interest due at closing is the answer (rounded to the nearest cent).

Prepaid items

A tax proration might be a prepaid item. Because real estate taxes may be paid in the early part of the year, a tax proration calculated for a closing that will take place later in the year must reflect the fact that the seller has already paid the tax. For example, in the preceding problem, suppose that all taxes had been paid. The buyer would then have to reimburse the seller; the proration would be credited to the seller and debited to the buyer.

In figuring the tax proration, the number of future days, months, and years for which taxes have been paid must be ascertained. The formula commonly used for this purpose is as follows:

	Years	Months	Days
Taxes paid to (Dec. 31, end of tax year)	20XX	12	30
Date of closing (Sept. 17, 20XX)	20XX	− 9	− 17
Period for which tax must be paid		3	13

This formula will calculate the amount the buyer will reimburse the seller for the unearned portion of the real estate taxes. The prepaid period determined by the formula for prepaid items is three months and 13 days. Three months at $300 per month equals $900, and 13 days at $10 per day equals $130. Add these two figures to determine that the proration is $1,030 credited to the seller and debited to the buyer.

Sample prepaid item calculation

One example of a prepaid item is a water bill. Assume that the unmetered water is billed in advance by the city. The six months' billing is $480 for the period ending October 31 ($480 ÷ 6 = $80 per month). The sale is to close on August 3. Because the water bill is paid through October 31, the prepaid time must be computed. Using a 30-day basis, the prepaid period is the 27 days left in August plus two full months. To compute one day's cost, divide $80 by 30, which equals $2.667 per day. The computation is as follows:

27 × $2.667 per day = $72.000

2 months × $80 = $160.000

$232.009 or $232.01

This is a prepaid item; it is credited to the seller and debited to the buyer on the closing statement.

To figure this proration based on the actual days in the month of closing, the following process would be used:

$80 per month ÷ 31 days in August	= $2.581 per day
August 4 through August 31	= 28 days
28 days × $2.581	= $78.268
2 months × $80	= $160.000
$72.268 + $160	= $232.268 or $232.27

KEY POINT REVIEW

Closing (settlement and transfer) is the point at which ownership of a property is transferred in exchange for the selling price.

To complete a transaction, the buyer requires the survey; title evidence; results of necessary inspections; an affidavit of title from the seller and, where applicable, documents showing the removal of prior encumbrances; the deed from the seller; and the lease, if a tenant resides on the premises. The buyer will expect to make a successful final property inspection (walk-through) and to receive a closing statement showing the amount and distribution of funds.

To complete the transaction, the seller will need the payoff statement from the seller's lender noting the amount owed; evidence that the buyer has the necessary funds; and a closing statement showing the distribution of funds.

The lender will want assurance that its lien rights will have priority and will want the buyer to obtain a mortgagee's title insurance policy.

The **Internal Revenue Service (IRS)** may require completion and submission of the Form 1099-S statement of income to the seller showing the seller's Social Security number. Form 1099-S is filed by a closing agent or the mortgage lender, with the real estate professionals or the parties being ultimately liable for the filing.

Depending on state law and local custom, closing may take place at a face-to-face meeting of the parties at the escrow company, title company, lender's office, or attorney's office, or the parties may execute documents separately and never meet.

An **escrow holder** (**escrow agent**) is a disinterested third party authorized to coordinate the closing activities.

The **Real Estate Settlement Procedures Act (RESPA)** is a federal law enacted to protect consumers in the settlement process by requiring accurate and timely information about the actual costs of a transaction, eliminating **kickbacks** and other referral fees, prohibiting the seller from requiring the buyer to buy title insurance from a particular company, and prohibiting lenders from requiring excessive escrow account deposits.

RESPA does not apply to a transaction financed solely by a purchase-money mortgage taken back by a seller, installment contracts (contract for deed), or a buyer's assumption of a seller's existing loan.

The CFPB has produced *Your Home Loan Toolkit*, a booklet that must be provided by a lender to every person from whom they receive or for whom they prepare a loan application (except for refinancing).

The **Loan Estimate form** must be provided to the borrower no later than three business days after receiving a loan application. The **Closing Disclosure** given to the borrower and the seller itemizes all charges to be paid in connection with closing.

The Loan Estimate and Closing Disclosure forms developed by the CFPB are required for transactions originating on or after October 3, 2015.

Affiliated business arrangements (ABA) that make use of companies with a shared ownership require notice to clients.

A **mortgage servicing transfer statement** must be given by the lender to the borrower if the lender intends to sell or assign the servicing rights to the borrower's loan.

A **closing statement** involves an accounting of the amounts paid by or received by the parties.

A **debit (give)** is a charge that must be paid by the buyer or the seller at closing. A **credit (receive)** is the amount entered in favor of the buyer or the seller. In most instances, a debit to one party is a credit to the other party.

Certain charges are **prorated**, divided between the buyer and the seller, in one of two ways. A yearly charge can be divided by a **360-day year** (banking year), or 12 months of 30 days each. A yearly charge could be divided by a **365-day year** (366 days in leap year) to determine the daily charge, the actual number of days in the proration period is determined, and the number of days is multiplied by the daily charge. In most states, the charges are prorated as of the date of closing, with the seller being responsible for the date of closing.

UNIT 14 QUIZ

1. Which statement is *TRUE* of real estate closings in most states?
   A. Closings are generally conducted by real estate professionals.
   B. The buyer usually receives the rent for the day of closing.
   C. The buyer must reimburse the seller for any title evidence provided by the seller.
   D. The seller usually pays the expenses for the day of closing.

2. All encumbrances and liens shown on the report of title, other than those waived or agreed to by the purchaser and listed in the contract, must be removed so that the title can be delivered free and clear. The removal of such encumbrances is typically the duty of
   A. the buyer.
   B. the seller.
   C. the real estate professional.
   D. the title company.

3. Legal title *ALWAYS* passes from the seller to the buyer
   A. on the date of execution of the deed.
   B. when the closing statement has been signed.
   C. when the deed is placed in escrow.
   D. when the deed is delivered and accepted.

4. Which item would a lender generally require at the closing?
   A. Title insurance commitment
   B. Market value appraisal
   C. Application
   D. Credit report

5. A buyer purchases a home in an area where closings are traditionally conducted in escrow. Which item would a buyer deposit with the escrow agent before the closing date?
   A. Deed to the property
   B. Title evidence
   C. Estoppel certificate
   D. Cash needed to complete the purchase

6. The Closing Disclosure must be used to illustrate all settlement charges for
   A. every real estate transaction.
   B. transactions financed by VA and FHA loans only.
   C. residential transactions financed by federally related mortgage loans.
   D. all transactions involving commercial property.

7. A mortgage reduction certificate is executed by
   A. an abstract company.
   B. an attorney.
   C. a lending institution.
   D. a grantor.

8. At closing, the principal amount of a purchaser's new mortgage loan is
   A. a credit to the seller.
   B. a credit to the buyer.
   C. a debit to the seller.
   D. a debit to the buyer.

9. At closing, the earnest money left on deposit with a real estate broker is
   A. a credit to the seller.
   B. a credit to the buyer.
   C. a balancing factor.
   D. a debit to the buyer.

10. The annual real estate taxes on a property amount to $18,000. The seller has paid the taxes in advance for the calendar year. If the closing is set for June 15, which statement is *TRUE*?
    A. Credit the seller $8,250; debit the buyer $9,750.
    B. Credit the seller $18,000; debit the buyer $8,250.
    C. Credit the buyer $9,750; debit the seller $9,750.
    D. Credit the seller $9,750; debit the buyer $9,750.

11. If a seller collected rent of $900 from the buyer, payable in advance, on August 1, which statement is *TRUE* at the closing on August 15, if the closing date is an expense to the seller? (Use a 30-day month)
    A. The seller owes the buyer $900.
    B. The buyer owes the seller $900.
    C. The seller owes the buyer $450.
    D. The buyer owes the seller $450.

12. Security deposits should be listed on a closing statement as a credit to
    A. the buyer.
    B. the seller.
    C. the lender.
    D. the real estate professional.

13. A building was purchased for $850,000, with 10% down and a loan for the balance. If the lender charged the buyer two discount points, how much cash did the buyer need at closing if the buyer incurred no other costs?
    A. $17,000
    B. $85,000
    C. $100,300
    D. $102,000

14. Which charge noted on the Closing Disclosure must be the same or less than the charge noted on the Loan Estimate form?
    A. Cost of settlement services when the lender selects the provider
    B. Lender charges for taking and underwriting the loan
    C. Cost of settlement services when the borrower selects the provider from the list provided by the lender
    D. Cost of homeowners insurance

15. At closing, the listing agent's commission is usually shown as
    A. a credit to the seller.
    B. a credit to the buyer.
    C. a debit to the seller.
    D. a debit to the buyer.

16. At the closing of a real estate transaction, the person performing the settlement gave the buyer a credit for certain accrued items. These items were
    A. bills relating to the property that had already been paid by the seller.
    B. bills relating to the property that the buyer must pay.
    C. all of the seller's real estate bills.
    D. all of the buyer's real estate bills.

17. At closing, an item prepaid by the seller is
    A. debited to the seller.
    B. evenly divided between the buyer and the seller.
    C. credited to the buyer.
    D. credited to the seller.

18. The purpose of the Real Estate Settlement Procedures Act (RESPA) is to
    A. make sure buyers do not borrow more than they can repay.
    B. make real estate professionals more responsive to buyers' needs.
    C. help buyers know how much money is required.
    D. ensure that buyers know all settlement costs that will be charged to them.

19. The document that provides the borrower with general information about settlement costs, RESPA provisions, and what happens at settlement is
    A. *What You Should Know About RESPA.*
    B. *Your Home Loan Toolkit.*
    C. the Closing Disclosure form.
    D. the Loan Estimate form.

20. Under the TILA-RESPA Integrated Disclosure Rule (TRID), a lender must extend the closing how many days if the annual percentage rate (APR) has changed more than 0.125% before closing?
    A. Two business days
    B. Three business days
    C. Four business days
    D. Five business days

UNIT 15

Real Estate Taxes and Other Liens

LEARNING OBJECTIVES

When you have completed this unit, you will be able to

› **describe** the characteristics of statutory and equitable liens;
› **describe** general taxes and special assessment taxes; and
› **explain** real property liens, including judgments and taxes, as well as the protection and limitations they offer the respective parties.

KEY TERMS

ad valorem tax	involuntary lien	statutory lien
assessment equalization factor	judgment	statutory right of redemption
	junior lien	subordination agreement
equitable lien	lien	tax lien
equitable right of redemption	mechanic's lien	tax sale
estate tax	mill	vendor's lien
general lien	mortgage lien	voluntary lien
general real estate tax	special assessment	writ of attachment
inheritance tax	specific lien	

OVERVIEW

The ownership of real estate is subject to certain obligations imposed by state and local governments, usually in the form of taxes that become a *lien* against the property. A creditor or a court can also place a claim against property to secure payment for a debt or other obligation. The ability to place a lien on property helps provide assurance to governments, lenders, homeowners associations, and those who provide work or services to improve property that the property owner will meet financial obligations incurred by virtue of owning the property.

LIENS

A **lien** is a charge or claim against a person's property made to enforce the payment of money. Whenever someone borrows money, the lender generally requires some form of *security*. Security (also called *collateral*) is something of value that the borrower promises to give the lender if the borrower fails to repay the debt. When the lender's security is in the form of real estate, the security interest is called a mortgage lien. Property can thus be used to ensure payment for work performed, material provided, or debts incurred.

Liens are not limited to security for borrowed money. Liens can be enforced against property by a government agency for payment of property tax owed by the owner. A lien also can be used to force the payment of an assessment or other special charge.

> All liens are encumbrances, but not all encumbrances are liens.

A lien represents an interest in ownership, but it does not constitute actual ownership of the property. It is an encumbrance on the owner's title. An *encumbrance* is any charge or claim that attaches to real property and lessens its value or impairs its use. An encumbrance does not necessarily prevent the transfer or conveyance of the property, but because an encumbrance is attached to the property, it transfers along with it. Liens differ from other encumbrances because they are financial or monetary in nature and attach to the property because of a debt. Other encumbrances may be physical in nature and may affect the owner's use of the property, such as easements or encroachments.

If a lien is not paid in the allotted time, the lienholder may foreclose on the lien, potentially forcing the sale of the property as set out by state law. Depending on how the lien was created, a lienholder may be required to initiate a legal action to force the sale of the property or acquire title. In other cases, the sale of the property can take place without a court hearing. The debt is paid out of the proceeds of the sale; any remaining amount goes to the debtor.

Types of liens

> **Memory tip**
> Four ways to create a lien (VISE):
> ■ **V**oluntary
> ■ **I**nvoluntary
> ■ **S**tatutory
> ■ **E**quitable

There are many different types of liens. One way that liens are classified is by how they are created. A **voluntary lien** is created intentionally by the property owner's action, such as when someone takes out a mortgage loan. An **involuntary lien** is not a matter of choice; it is created by law and may be either statutory or equitable. A **statutory lien** is created by statute. A real estate **tax lien**, for example, is an involuntary, statutory lien. It exists without any action by the property owner. An **equitable lien** arises out of common law. A court-ordered judgment that requires a debtor to pay the balance on a delinquent charge account, and which can be filed in the county where the debtor owns property, would create an involuntary, equitable lien on the debtor's real estate.

Liens may be classified according to the type of property involved. **General liens** affect all the property, both real and personal, of a debtor. This includes judgments, estate and inheritance taxes, decedent's debts, corporate franchise taxes, and Internal Revenue Service taxes. A lien on real estate differs from a lien on personal property. A lien attaches to real property *at the moment it is filed and recorded*. In contrast, a lien does not attach to personal property *until the personal property is seized*.

Specific liens are secured by specific property and affect only that particular property. Specific liens on real estate include vendors' liens, mechanics' liens, mortgage liens, real estate tax liens, and liens for special assessments and utilities. A **vendor's lien** is a lien belonging to the vendor (seller) for the unpaid purchase price of the property, when the vendor has not taken any other lien or security, such as a mortgage, beyond the personal obligation of the purchaser. Vendors' liens in real estate are uncommon and arise out of the use of owner financing to sell property.

Effect of lien on title

The existence of a lien does not necessarily prevent a property owner from transferring title to someone else. The lien might reduce the value of the real estate because few buyers will take on the risk of a property that has a lien on it. Because the lien attaches to the property, not the property owner, a new owner might lose the property if the creditors take court action to enforce payment. Once in place, a lien *runs with the land* and will bind all successive owners until the lien is paid or settled and title is cleared by the filing of a *release of lien* by the lienholder.

IN PRACTICE

A buyer should insist on a title search before closing a real estate transaction so that any recorded liens are revealed. If liens are present, the buyer may decide to purchase at a lower price or at better terms, require that the liens be removed, or refuse to complete the purchase.

Priority of liens

Priority of liens refers to the order in which claims against the property will be *satisfied* if the property is sold by the debtor. In general, the rule for priority of liens is *first to record, first in right (priority).* In accordance with state law, the priority of payment typically is established by the date the liens are placed in the public record of the county in which the property is located. If the holder of the first lien to be recorded forecloses on that lien, the proceeds of the property sale are used to pay that lien; if there are any funds remaining, the holder of any other lien is paid, with the former property owner receiving anything that remains after all lien holders are paid off. The holder of a **junior lien** (one that comes after an earlier lien) can foreclose on that lien, but the property will still be subject to the lien or liens with higher priority.

There are some notable exceptions to this rule. For instance, real estate taxes and special assessments generally take priority over all other liens, regardless of the order in which the liens are recorded. This means that outstanding real estate taxes and special assessments are paid first from the proceeds of a court-ordered sale.

IN PRACTICE

It is important for a creditor to have the highest lien priority because it will mean that the creditor will be paid first if it becomes necessary to bring about a forced sale of the debtor's property. A creditor in the second or later position may receive little or nothing from the sale.

Subordination agreements are written agreements between lienholders to change the priority of mortgage, judgment, and other liens. Under a subordination agreement, the holder of a superior or prior lien agrees to permit a later lienholder's interest to take precedence.

IN PRACTICE

The seller of a vacant parcel of land often finances the purchase for a builder, claiming the first lien priority, but will then agree to subordinate that interest to the interest of the lender who provides financing for the construction of a home on the lot. The construction lender will insist on having first lien priority but, because the overall property value will be increased by the improvements made to it, the seller of the land is willing to bear the risk that, in the event of a forced sale of the property, the proceeds of the sale will be sufficient to cover both liens.

REAL ESTATE TAX LIENS

There are two types of real estate taxes: general real estate taxes and special assessments or improvement taxes. Both are levied against specific parcels of property and automatically become liens on those properties.

The ownership of real estate is subject to certain governmental powers. One of these is the right of state and local governments to impose (levy) taxes to pay for their functions. Because the location of real estate is permanently fixed, the government can levy taxes with a high degree of certainty that the taxes will be collected. The annual taxes levied on real estate in most states usually have priority over previously recorded liens and may be enforced by a court-ordered sale.

Ad valorem tax

The **general real estate tax** is an **ad valorem tax**. *Ad valorem* is Latin for "according to value." Ad valorem taxes are based on the value of the property being taxed and are specific, involuntary, statutory liens. Real estate property taxes are a favored source of revenue for local governments because real estate cannot be hidden and is relatively easy to value. Property taxes pay for a wide range of government services and programs, including those of

- states;
- counties;
- cities, towns, boroughs, and villages;
- school districts (local elementary and high schools, publicly funded junior colleges, and community colleges);
- drainage districts;
- hospital districts;
- water districts;
- sanitary districts;
- transportation districts; and
- parks, forest preserves, and recreation districts.

Exemptions from general taxes

Most state laws exempt certain real estate from taxation. Such property must be used for tax-exempt purposes, as defined in the statutes. The most common exempt properties are owned by

- cities,
- various municipal organizations (such as schools, parks, and playgrounds),

- state and federal governments,
- religious and charitable organizations,
- hospitals, and
- educational institutions.

Many state laws also allow special exemptions to reduce real estate tax bills for certain property owners or land uses. For instance, senior citizens, veterans, and persons with a disability are frequently granted reductions in the *assessed values* of their homes. In some states, low-income seniors may request a property tax freeze on the principal residence, which means that the tax assessed will not increase during the remaining years of the senior's ownership and use of the property. In an effort to stem the recent record number of home foreclosures, some states have subsidized low-income homeowners' tax bills, without regard to the owners' ages.

Some state and local governments offer real estate tax reductions to attract industries and sports franchises. Many states also offer tax reductions for agricultural land.

Assessment

Real estate is valued for tax purposes by county or township assessors or appraisers. This official valuation process is called *assessment*. A property's assessed value is generally based on the sales prices of comparable properties, although practices may vary. Land values may be assessed separately from buildings or other improvements, and different valuation methods may be used for different types of property. State law may provide for property to be periodically reassessed.

Sometimes, a property owner believes that an error was made in determining the assessed property value—usually that the assessment is too high in comparison with the assessments of neighboring properties. Such owners may present their objections to a local board of appeal or board of review. A protest or appeal regarding a tax assessment may ultimately be taken to court.

Equalization

In some jurisdictions, when it is necessary to correct inequalities in statewide tax assessments, an **assessment equalization factor** is used to achieve uniformity. An equalization factor may be applied to raise or lower assessments in a particular district or county. The assessed value of each property in the area is multiplied by the equalization factor and the tax rate is then applied to the equalized assessment.

Tax rates

The process of arriving at a real estate tax rate begins with the adoption of a budget by each taxing district. Each budget covers the financial requirements of the taxing body for the coming fiscal year. The fiscal year may be the January through December calendar year or some other 12-month period designated by statute. The budget must include an estimate of all expenditures for the year.

The next step is appropriation, which means that a taxing body authorizes the expenditure of funds and provides for the sources of the funding. Appropriation generally involves the adoption of an ordinance or the passage of a law that states the specific terms of the proposed taxation. Some states require voter approval of any real property tax increase.

After appropriation or approval by voters, the amount to be raised from the general real estate tax is imposed on property owners through a *tax levy*. A tax levy is the formal action taken to impose the tax, usually by a vote of the taxing district's governing body.

The tax rate for each taxing body is determined by state law or computed separately. Unless the tax rate has already been determined by state law, the total monies needed for the coming fiscal year are divided by the total assessments of all real estate located within the taxing body's jurisdiction.

The tax rate may be stated in a number of ways. In many areas, it is expressed in mills. A **mill** is $\frac{1}{1000}$ of a dollar, or $0.001. The tax rate may be expressed as a mills-per-dollar ratio—for instance, in dollars per hundred or in dollars per thousand. A tax rate of 0.032, or 3.2%, could be expressed as 32 mills, or $3.20 per $100 of assessed value or $32 per $1,000 of assessed value.

IN PRACTICE

An easy way to recall the value of a mill is to remember that there are 10 mills in a penny.

Tax bills

A property owner's tax bill is computed by applying the tax rate to the assessed valuation of the property.

IN PRACTICE

A property is assessed for tax purposes at $160,000. At a tax rate of 3%, or 30 mills, the tax owed on the property is $4,800 ($160,000 × 0.03). If an equalization factor of 120% is used, the computation is in two steps: $160,000 × 1.20 = $192,000, and $192,000 × 0.03 = $5,760. The tax owed on the property is $5,760.

The due dates for tax payments (also called the penalty dates) are set by statute. Taxes may be payable in 2 installments (semiannually), 4 installments (quarterly), or 12 installments (monthly). In some areas, taxes become due at the beginning of the current tax year and must be paid in advance (e.g., the year 2015 taxes must be paid at the beginning of 2014). In other areas, taxes are payable during the year after the taxes are levied (e.g., 2015 taxes are paid throughout 2015). In some states, taxes are paid one year in arrears, and you cannot pay any portion of the ad valorem taxes during the current year (e.g., 2014 taxes could not be paid until the tax books open in 2015). In still other areas, a partial payment is due in the year the tax is imposed, with the balance due in the following year (e.g., 2015 taxes are payable partly during 2015 and partly during 2016).

Some states offer discounts and monthly payment plans to encourage prompt payment of real property taxes. Penalties, typically in the form of monthly interest charges on overdue taxes, are added to all taxes that are not paid when due.

Enforcement of tax liens

Real estate taxes must be valid to be enforceable. That means they must be charged properly, must be used for a legal purpose, and must be applied equitably to all property. As previously mentioned, tax liens usually are given priority over all other liens against a property. Real estate taxes that have remained delinquent for the statutory period can be collected through a **tax sale** of the property. While the methods and details of the various states' tax sale procedures differ substantially, the results are the same.

A tax sale is usually held according to a published notice after a court has rendered a judgment for overdue taxes, penalties, and administrative costs and has ordered that the property be sold. The sale is advertised in local newspapers, and a notice of sale is posted on the affected property. The county sheriff or other public official then holds a public sale of the property. Because a specific amount of delinquent tax and penalty must be collected, the purchaser at a tax sale must pay at least that amount. A *certificate of sale* is usually given to the highest bidder when that bidder pays the delinquent tax amount in cash. The certificate of sale gives the holder the right to take possession of the property.

The holder of the certificate of sale may not immediately receive the deed to the property. Some states grant a period of redemption after the tax sale. In this case, the defaulted owner (or the defaulted owner's creditors) may redeem the property by paying the amount collected at the tax sale plus interest and charges (including any taxes levied since the sale). This is known as a **statutory right of redemption**. If the property is not redeemed within the statutory period, the certificate holder can apply for a *tax deed (sheriff's deed)*. The quality of the title conveyed by a tax deed varies from state to state.

In some states, the delinquent taxpayer may redeem the property any time before the tax sale. The taxpayer exercises this **equitable right of redemption** by paying the delinquent taxes plus interest and charges (any court costs or attorney's fees). An owner who does not exercise this right may force a sale.

Special assessments and local improvement district taxes

A **special assessment** is a tax charged on real estate to fund public improvements to the property, and it creates a lien for the amount of the assessment on the property. Property owners in the improvement area are required to pay for the improvements because their properties benefit directly from them. For example, the construction of paved streets, curbs, gutters, sidewalks, storm sewers, or street lighting increases the value of properties that benefit from them. The additional tax paid by the homeowner of those properties covers the cost of the improvements.

A special assessment is generally paid in equal annual installments over a period of years. The first installment is usually due during the year following the public authority's approval of the assessment. The first bill includes one year's interest on the property owner's share of the entire assessment. Subsequent bills include one year's interest on the unpaid balance. Property owners have the right to prepay any or all installments to avoid future interest charges.

For large-scale improvement projects such as streets, sidewalks, and water or sewer construction, a local improvement district (LID) may be created. An LID is a specific geographical area formed by a group of property owners working together to fund needed capital improvements. LID taxation is simply a financing method available for the design and construction of public improvements.

In some parts of the country, strict subdivision regulations and LIDs have just about eliminated special assessments. Most items for which assessments have traditionally been levied are now required to be installed at the time of construction as a condition of a subdivision's approval.

OTHER LIENS ON REAL PROPERTY

In addition to real estate tax and special assessment liens, a variety of other liens may be charged against real property.

Mortgage lien

A **mortgage lien** is a specific, voluntary lien on real estate given to a lender by a borrower as security for a real estate loan. It becomes a lien on real property when the lender records the documents in the county where the property is located. Lenders generally require a preferred lien, called a first mortgage lien. This means that no other liens against the property (aside from real estate taxes) can take priority over the mortgage lien. As mentioned earlier, subsequent liens are referred to as junior liens.

Mechanic's lien

A **mechanic's lien** is a specific, involuntary lien that gives security to persons or companies that perform labor or furnish material to improve real property. A mechanic's lien is available to contractors, subcontractors, architects, equipment lessors, surveyors, laborers, and other providers. This type of lien is filed when the owner has not fully paid for the work or when the general contractor has been compensated but has not paid the subcontractors or suppliers of materials. Statutes in some states prohibit subcontractors from placing liens directly on certain types of property, such as owner-occupied residences. While laws regarding mechanics' liens vary from state to state, there are many similarities.

To be entitled to a mechanic's lien, the person who did the work must have had a contract with the owner or the owner's authorized representative, such as a general contractor. A person claiming a mechanic's lien must file a notice of lien in the public record of the county where the property is located within a certain time after the work has been completed. A lien waiver is required for a contractor to receive a payment from the owner's construction loan. Once the work is completed and accounts paid, the owner will ask for a release or satisfaction of lien to be filed to clear the property title.

According to state law, priority of a mechanic's lien may be established as of the date the construction began or materials were first furnished; the date the work was completed; the date the individual subcontractor's work was either commenced or completed; the date the contract was signed or work was ordered; or the date a notice of the lien was recorded, filed, posted, or served. In some states, mechanics' liens may be given priority over previously recorded liens, such as mortgages.

If improvements that were not ordered by the property owner have commenced, the property owner should execute a document called a *notice of nonresponsibility* to be relieved from possible mechanics' liens. By posting this notice in some conspicuous place on the property and recording a verified copy of it in the public record within the time specified by statute, the owner gives notice that he or she is not responsible for the work done. This may prevent the filing of mechanics' liens on the property.

IN PRACTICE

In most states, a mechanic's lien takes priority from the time it attaches, even though a claimant's notice of lien will not be filed in the public record until sometime later. A prospective purchaser of property that has been recently constructed, altered, or repaired should be cautious about possible unrecorded mechanics' liens against the property.

Judgment

A **judgment** is a decree issued by a court. When the decree establishes the amount a debtor owes and provides for money to be awarded, it is called a *money judgment.* These often result from damages caused to one person by another person through a wrongful act, breach of contract, or nonpayment of a debt.

A judgment is a general, involuntary, equitable lien on both real and personal property owned by the debtor. A judgment is not the same as a mortgage because no specific parcel of real estate was given as security at the time the debt was created. A lien automatically covers only property located within the county in which the judgment is issued, so a notice of the lien must be filed in any county to which a creditor wishes to extend the lien coverage. Judgments expire after a number of years but, in some states, can be renewed indefinitely by the judgment creditor.

To enforce a judgment, the creditor must obtain a *writ of execution* from the court. A writ of execution directs the sheriff to seize and sell as much of the debtor's property as is necessary to pay both the debt and the expenses of the sale. A judgment does not become a lien against the personal property of a debtor until the creditor orders the sheriff to assess the property and the charge is actually made.

A judgment lien's priority is established by one or a combination of the following (as provided by state law):

- Date the judgment was entered by the court
- Date the judgment was filed in the recorder's office
- Date a writ of execution was issued

When real property is sold to satisfy a debt, the debtor should demand a legal document known as a *satisfaction of judgment* (or *satisfaction piece*). Filing the satisfaction of judgment clears the record of the lien. In those states using a deed of trust, a deed of reconveyance must be filed with either the clerk of the court or, in some states, the recorder of deeds.

Lis pendens

There is often a considerable delay between the time a lawsuit is filed and the time final judgment is rendered. When any suit that affects title to or possession of real estate is filed, a special notice, known as a lis pendens is recorded. A lis pendens is not itself a lien, but rather notice of a possible future lien. Recording a lis pendens notifies prospective purchasers and lenders that there is a potential claim against the property. It also establishes a priority for the later lien. The lien is backdated to the recording date of the lis pendens.

Attachment

To prevent a debtor from conveying title to previously unsecured real estate while a court suit is being decided, a creditor may seek a **writ of attachment**. A writ of attachment is a court order against the property of another person that directs the sheriff or other officer of the court to seize or take control of a property. By this writ, the court retains custody of the property until the suit concludes. Most *attachments* arise from an action for payment of an unsecured debt. For example, a plaintiff in a lawsuit may attach a defendant's property to gain a security interest in order to foreclose the property or to prevent the defendant from disposing of property that may be needed to pay a judgment.

Estate and inheritance tax liens

Federal **estate taxes** and state **inheritance taxes** (as well as the debts of decedents) are general, statutory, involuntary liens that encumber a deceased person's real and personal property. These taxes and debts are normally paid or cleared in probate court proceedings.

Lien for municipal utilities

Municipalities often have the right to impose a specific, equitable, involuntary lien on the property of an owner who refuses to pay bills for municipal utility services.

Bail bond lien

A real estate owner who is charged with a crime that will result in a trial may post bail in the form of real estate rather than cash. The execution and recording of such a bail bond creates a specific, statutory, voluntary lien against the owner's real estate. If the accused fails to appear in court, the lien may be enforced by the sheriff or another court officer.

Corporation franchise tax lien

State governments generally levy a corporation franchise tax on corporations as a condition of allowing them to do business in the state. Such a tax is a general, statutory, involuntary lien on all real and personal property owned by the corporation.

IRS tax lien

www.irs.gov

A federal tax lien, or **Internal Revenue Service (IRS) tax lien**, results from a person's failure to pay any portion of federal taxes, such as income and withholding taxes. A federal tax lien is a general, statutory, involuntary lien on all real and personal property held by the delinquent taxpayer. Its priority, however, is based on the date of filing or recording; it does not supersede previously recorded liens. The same rules apply to most state income tax liens. Information on federal tax liens can be found at www.irs.gov.

KEY POINT REVIEW

A **lien** is a claim of a creditor or taxing authority against the **real property** of a debtor that is used as **security** to ensure repayment of the debt.

A lien is not an ownership interest in real estate; it is an **encumbrance** that transfers with it (**runs with the land**) and lessens its value or impairs its use because it binds all successive owners until paid and cleared. If a debtor **defaults** in payment of a debt secured by property, the **lienholder** can force the **sale** of the property, or **acquire title**.

Creation of a lien may be **voluntary**, if it is created by action of the property owner, such as a mortgage or **involuntary**, if it is created without the property owner's express permission. It may also be **statutory**, if it is permitted by statute, or **equitable**, if it is granted by a court.

A **general lien** affects all of a debtor's property, both real and personal; a **specific lien** affects only identified property.

Priority of liens determines the order in which claims will be **satisfied** (paid off). Generally, the first lien to be recorded will take priority, but real estate taxes and special assessments usually take priority over all other liens. If a junior lien is foreclosed, the property is still subject to prior liens. A **subordination agreement** between lienholders can be used to change the order of priority.

Real estate taxes are *ad valorem* taxes based on the value of the property taxed.

Property **assessments** (valuations) are conducted by county or township tax **assessors** or appraisers. **Assessed value** is generally based on sales prices of comparable properties. **An equalization factor** may be applied to correct inequalities in statewide tax assessments.

The **tax rate** for each taxing body is computed separately and may be expressed in **mills**. A mill is $\frac{1}{1000}$ of a dollar, or $0.001. Mills may be shown as dollars per hundred or thousand dollars of assessed value.

Delinquent taxes can be collected through a **tax sale** following statutory notice requirements. The **taxpayer** usually has **equitable right of redemption** any time before a tax sale. The state may allow a **statutory right of redemption** following a tax sale. If there are **no bidders** at the tax sale, the property may be forfeited to the state.

Special assessments are levied and create a lien on property that benefits from public improvements, such as properties located in a **local improvement district (LID)**, and are always specific and statutory, but may be voluntary or involuntary, and are usually paid in annual installments over a period of years.

A **mortgage lien** is a voluntary lien given to a lender by a borrower as security for a real estate loan. The lien takes effect when the lender **records** the documents in the county where the property is located. A **first mortgage lien** on a property, when recorded, has **priority** over other liens (except for tax liens); subsequent liens are **junior liens**.

A **mechanic's lien** is a specific, involuntary lien that gives a security interest in real property to persons or companies that perform labor or furnish material to improve the property. A mechanic's lien is **filed** when an **owner** has not fully paid for work or the **general contractor** has been compensated but has not paid subcontractors or suppliers of materials.

A property owner who did not order improvements that are being made should execute, post, and record a **notice of nonresponsibility** to be relieved from possible lien claims.

A **judgment**, a decree issued by a court, is a general, involuntary, equitable lien on both real and personal property owned by a debtor and must be filed in **every county** in which the judgment debtor owns property.

While a lawsuit is pending, a **lis pendens** can be filed to give notice of an action pending relating to the title or possession of real property and establish priority of the claimant, and a **writ of attachment** can be sought from the court to authorize the sheriff to seize the property that the debtor may attempt to transfer. A **writ of execution** can be obtained from the court to enforce a judgment.

Estate and inheritance tax liens are general, statutory, involuntary liens that encumber a deceased person's real and personal property and are normally paid or cleared in a probate proceeding.

A **lien for municipal utilities** is a specific, equitable, involuntary lien on the property of the owner who refuses to pay bills for municipal utility services.

A **corporation franchise tax lien** is a general, statutory, involuntary lien on real and personal property owned by the corporation.

An **IRS tax lien** is a general, statutory, involuntary lien on all real and personal property held by a delinquent taxpayer; it does not supersede previously recorded liens (which is also true of most state income tax liens).

UNIT 15 QUIZ

1. Which lien affects all real and personal property of a debtor?
    A. Specific
    B. Voluntary
    C. Involuntary
    D. General

2. Priority of liens refers to which of the following?
    A. Order in which a debtor assumes responsibility for payment of obligations
    B. Order in which liens will be paid if property is sold to satisfy a debt
    C. Dates liens are filed for record
    D. Fact that specific liens have greater priority than general liens

3. A lien on real estate made to secure payment for a specific municipal improvement project is which of the following?
    A. Mechanic's lien
    B. Special assessment lien
    C. Ad valorem
    D. Utility lien

4. Which of the following is classified as a general lien?
    A. Mechanic's lien
    B. Bail bond lien
    C. Judgment
    D. Real estate taxes

5. Which lien usually would be given highest priority in disbursing funds from a foreclosure sale?
    A. Mortgage dated last year
    B. Real estate taxes due
    C. Mechanic's lien for work started before the mortgage was made
    D. Judgment rendered the day before foreclosure

6. A specific parcel of real estate has a market value of $160,000 and is assessed for tax purposes at 75% of market value. The tax rate for the county in which the property is located is 40 mills. The tax bill will be
    A. $6,400.
    B. $5,000.
    C. $5,200.
    D. $4,800.

7. Which tax targets homeowners in particular?
    A. Personal property tax
    B. Franchise tax
    C. Real property tax
    D. Luxury tax

8. A mechanic's lien claim arises when a contractor has performed work or provided material to improve a parcel of real estate on the owner's order and the work has not been paid for. Such a contractor has a right to
    A. tear out the work.
    B. record a notice of the lien.
    C. record a notice of the lien and file a court suit within the time required by state law.
    D. have personal property of the owner sold to satisfy the lien.

9. What is the annual real estate tax on a property valued at $135,000 and assessed for tax purposes at $47,250, with an equalization factor of 125%, when the tax rate is 25 mills?
    A. $945
    B. $1,181
    C. $1,418
    D. $1,477

10. Which of the following is a voluntary, specific lien?
    A. IRS tax lien
    B. Mechanic's lien
    C. Mortgage lien
    D. Seller's lien

11. A buyer purchased a parcel of real estate. Title has passed, but to date the buyer has not paid the purchase price in full, as originally agreed. If the seller wants to force payment, which remedy is the seller entitled to seek?
    A. Attachment
    B. Mechanic's lien
    C. Lis pendens
    D. Judgment

12. A general contractor recently filed suit against a homeowner for nonpayment. The contractor now learns that the homeowner has listed the property for sale with a real estate professional. In this situation, which of the following will the contractor's attorney use to protect the contractor's interest?
    A. Seller's lien
    B. Buyer's lien
    C. Assessment
    D. Lis pendens

13. Which statement *MOST* accurately describes special assessment liens?
    A. They are general liens.
    B. They are paid on a monthly basis.
    C. They take priority over mechanics' liens.
    D. They cannot be prepaid in full without penalty.

14. Which of the following creates a lien on real estate?
    A. Easement running with the land
    B. Unpaid mortgage loan
    C. License
    D. Encroachment

15. Which statement is *TRUE* of both a mortgage lien and a judgment lien?
    A. It must be entered by the court.
    B. It involves a debtor-creditor relationship.
    C. It is a general lien.
    D. It is an involuntary lien.

16. A mechanic's lien would be available to all of the following *EXCEPT*
    A. subcontractors.
    B. contractors.
    C. surveyors.
    D. real estate professionals.

17. The right of a defaulted taxpayer to recover property before its sale for unpaid taxes is
    A. the statutory right of reinstatement.
    B. the equitable right of appeal.
    C. the statutory right of assessment.
    D. the equitable right of redemption.

18. Which of the following is a specific, involuntary, statutory lien?
    A. Real estate tax lien
    B. Income tax lien
    C. Estate tax lien
    D. Judgment lien

19. General real estate taxes levied for the operation of the government are
    A. assessment taxes.
    B. ad valorem taxes.
    C. special taxes.
    D. improvement taxes.

20. All of the following probably would be exempt from real estate taxes *EXCEPT*
    A. public hospitals.
    B. golf courses operated by the park district.
    C. synagogues and churches.
    D. apartment buildings.

UNIT
16

Real Estate Appraisal

LEARNING OBJECTIVES

When you have completed this unit, you will be able to

> **explain** appraisal concepts and the process employed by the appraiser;
> **differentiate** between value and price; and
> **describe** the three approaches to value.

KEY TERMS

accrued depreciation	economic life	progression
anticipation	external obsolescence	property inspection waiver
appraisal	functional obsolescence	(PIW)
Appraiser Independence	gross income multiplier (GIM)	reconciliation
Requirements (AIR)	gross rent multiplier (GRM)	regression
assemblage	highest and best use	sales comparison approach
broker's price opinion (BPO)	income approach	sales price
capitalization rate	law of diminishing returns	substitution
change	law of increasing returns	supply and demand
competition	market data approach	*Uniform Standards of*
conformity	market value	*Professional Appraisal*
contribution	net operating income (NOI)	*Practice (USPAP)*
cost approach	physical deterioration	value
depreciation	plottage	

OVERVIEW

Appraisal is a distinct area of specialization within the world of real estate professionals. Most real estate transactions require an appraisal by a licensed or certified real estate appraiser to provide a clearer understanding of the market's response to a subject property. Real estate professionals also must be aware of the fundamental principles of valuation in order to complete an accurate and effective comparative market analysis (CMA) that assists seller clients in arriving at a reasonable asking price and buyer clients to make appropriate offers based on current market conditions. A broker's price opinion (BPO), less expensive than an appraisal, might be requested by a lender when property is refinanced. In addition, knowledge of the appraisal process allows the real estate professional to recognize a questionable appraisal.

APPRAISING

An **appraisal** is an opinion of value based on supportable evidence and approved methods. An *appraisal report* is an opinion of market value on a property given to a lender or client with detailed market information. An *appraiser* is an independent professional trained to provide an *unbiased* opinion of value in an impartial and objective manner, following an identified appraisal process. Appraising is a professional service performed for a fee; it is a breach of accepted practice and ethics to collect a commission for an appraisal based on the value of the property appraised.

An accurate, objective appraisal is an important part of a real estate transaction, as well as a safeguard against a fraudulent transaction. The Dodd-Frank Act required changes to the Truth in Lending Act and other legislation to prohibit the coercion and other activities that influenced appraisals in many cases of fraud that occurred during the housing crisis of the past decade. Fannie Mae initiated **Appraiser Independence Requirements (AIR)** that took effect October 15, 2010. A copy of the AIR can be found at www.fanniemae.com/content/fact_sheet/appraiser-independence-requirements.pdf.

www.fanniemae
.com/content/fact
_sheet/appraiser
-independence
-requirements.pdf

Regulation of appraisal activities

Title XI of the Financial Institutions Reform, Recovery, and Enforcement Act of 1989 (FIRREA) requires that any appraisal used in connection with a federally related transaction be performed by a competent individual who is licensed or certified by the state in which the appraiser practices. Every state now has an appraiser licensing agency, which is required by FIRREA to be separate from the agency that licenses real estate professionals.

A federally related transaction is any real estate-related financial transaction in which a federal financial institution or regulatory agency is engaged. These transactions involve the sale, lease, purchase, investment, or exchange of real property. They also include the use of real property as security for a loan or an investment, including mortgage-backed securities. Appraisals of residential property valued at $250,000 or less are exempt and need not be performed by licensed or certified appraisers. Nonresidential properties valued at more than $250,000 (raised to $500,000 in 2018) require a certified appraiser.

There are limited exceptions to the appraisal requirements. Fannie Mae will not require a new appraisal for a limited cash-out refinancing when borrower and lender are the same, the original appraisal was performed no more than 12 months earlier (if performed more than four months earlier, an appraisal update is required), and the property should be in substantially the same condition (no significant updates or deterioration) that would affect market value.

Given the many properties that have had appraisals entered in Fannie Mae's Collateral Underwriter (CU) database, some loans purchased by Fannie Mae are eligible for a **property inspection waiver (PIW)**. Fannie Mae's Desktop Underwriter (DU) system will search the property address for an appraisal; if the first and last names of the borrowers on the earlier and present loan match, Fannie Mae will consider a PIW. If the earlier appraisal was flagged for any reason (perhaps an over valuation), the PIW will not be issued.

Appraiser qualifications

State licensing and certification criteria for appraisers must conform to the requirements of the Appraisal Subcommittee of the Federal Financial Institutions Examination Council, as recommended by the Appraiser Qualifications Board (AQB) of the Appraisal Foundation. The Appraisal Foundation is a not-for-profit organization composed of representatives of the major appraisal and related groups. In conducting an appraisal, an appraiser must follow the *Uniform Standards of Professional Appraisal Practice (USPAP)* established by the Appraisal Standards Board (ASB) of the Appraisal Foundation. Members of the AQB meet regularly to review and make recommendations for changes to the level of education and experience required of appraisers. Members of the ASB also meet often to discuss revisions and updates to *USPAP*. Both of these boards are composed of practicing appraisers, state officials, and educators. The Appraisal Foundation has also created the Appraisal Practices Board (APB), which "offers voluntary guidance to appraisers, regulators and users of appraisal services on recognized valuation methods and techniques for all valuation disciplines."

www.appraisal
foundation.org
www.uspap.org

More information about the Appraisal Foundation and links to all of the Appraisal Foundation boards can be found at www.appraisalfoundation.org. USPAP undergoes review and revision in a two-year cycle starting with an even-numbered year; the current update can be found at www.uspap.org.

Organizations for appraisers

Most appraisers work as independent contractors, even when they are employed by a large appraisal management company, but appraisers are also employed by public agencies. Numerous trade associations are available for appraisers and are valuable sources of education, legal updates, and networking opportunities. Some of the largest are the following:

www.appraisers.org
www.asfmra.org
www.appraisalinstitute
.org
www.iaao.org
www.irwaonline.org
www.naifa.com

- American Society of Appraisers—www.appraisers.org
- American Society of Farm Managers and Rural Appraisers, Inc.—www.asfmra.org
- Appraisal Institute—www.appraisalinstitute.org
- International Association of Assessing Officers—www.iaao.org
- International Right of Way Association—www.irwaonline.org
- National Association of Independent Fee Appraisers—www.naifa.com

Comparative market analysis

Not all estimates of value are made by professional appraisers. As you have already learned, real estate professionals often prepare a comparative market analysis (CMA) for a seller or buyer. A CMA is distinctly different from an appraisal report offered by a licensed or certified appraiser. An appraisal is based on a detailed analysis of market conditions, the features of the subject property and comparable properties in the neighborhood, recent sales and listings, land value and current construction cost—all the elements that a lender wants to consider in determining whether or not to make a loan and accept the property as security for the debt. The CMA focuses on properties similar to the subject property in size, location, and amenities for the purpose of deriving a likely listing price or offering price. The CMA analysis is based on

- recently closed properties (solds),
- properties currently on the market (competition for the subject property), and
- properties that did not sell (expired listings in the area).

Broker's price opinion (BPO)

A **broker's price opinion (BPO)** is a less-expensive alternative for evaluating property that is often used by lenders working with home equity lines, refinancing, portfolio management, loss mitigation, and collections. Although some BPOs are more extensive, including information about the neighborhood and an interior analysis, many are simply "drive bys" that verify the existence of the property, along with a listing of comparable sales. A BPO should not be confused with an appraisal, which consists of more in-depth analysis of gathered information and which may be performed only by a licensed or certified appraiser. A BPO cannot be used if the matter involves a federally related transaction that requires an appraisal and/or the transaction occurs in a state that requires one. Information on how a BPO is used in certain Fannie Mae programs, perhaps a short sale or deed in lieu of foreclosure, can be obtained by entering "BPO" in the search box at www.fanniemae.com /singlefamily.

www.fanniemae.com /singlefamily

The appraisal process

The key to an accurate appraisal lies in the methodical collection and analysis of data. The appraisal process is an orderly set of procedures used to collect and analyze data to arrive at a justifiable opinion of value. The value sought most often is market value, though an appraisal also can be made to determine a different value, such as a property's insurance value, salvage value, or assessment value. The data needed by the appraiser can be divided into two basic classes:

1. General data, which covers the nation, region, city, and neighborhood. The appraiser researches the physical, economic, social, and political influences that affect the value and potential of the subject property.

2. Specific data, which covers the type and features of improvements to the subject property as well as comparable properties that are similar to and competitive with the subject property.

Figure 16.1 outlines the steps an appraiser takes in carrying out an appraisal assignment.

Once the approaches have been reconciled and an opinion of value has been reached, the appraiser prepares a report for the client. The report should

■ identify the real estate and real property interest being appraised;

■ state the purpose and intended use of the appraisal;

■ define the value sought;

■ state the effective date of the value and the date of the report;

■ state the extent of the process of collecting, confirming, and reporting the data;

■ list all assumptions and limiting conditions that affect the analysis, opinion, and conclusions of value;

■ describe the information considered, the appraisal approaches used, and the reasoning that supports the report's conclusions (if an approach was excluded, the report should explain why);

■ describe the appraiser's opinion of the highest and best use of the real estate;

■ describe any additional information that may be appropriate to show compliance with the specific guidelines established in *USPAP* or to clearly identify and explain any departures from those guidelines; and

■ include a signed certification, as required by *USPAP*.

FIGURE 16.1: The Appraisal Process

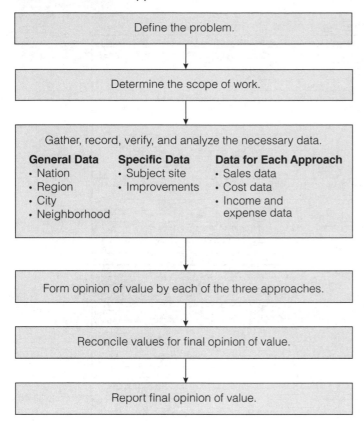

Define the problem.

Determine the scope of work.

Gather, record, verify, and analyze the necessary data.

General Data
- Nation
- Region
- City
- Neighborhood

Specific Data
- Subject site
- Improvements

Data for Each Approach
- Sales data
- Cost data
- Income and expense data

Form opinion of value by each of the three approaches.

Reconcile values for final opinion of value.

Report final opinion of value.

Uniform Residential Appraisal Report

Figure 16.2 shows the *Uniform Residential Appraisal Report (URAR)*, which is the form required by many government agencies. It illustrates the types of detailed information required of an appraisal of residential property. It also highlights the extensive list of certifications required of the appraiser and is accompanied by a page of instructions. A copy of the form can also be found at www.fanniemae.com/content/guide_form/1004.pdf.

www.fanniemae.com /content/guide_form /1004.pdf

IN PRACTICE

Technology has come to the appraisal office, just as it has to the real estate office. Software can be used to make completing the URAR more efficient; the completed electronic form can be attached to a transmittal letter and sent electronically to the client along with digital copies of any exhibits, such as maps and photos.

While the appraiser does not determine value, neither is value determined by what the seller wants to receive, what the buyer wants to pay, or what the real estate professional suggests. The appraiser, relying on experience and expertise in valuation theories, develops an objective report that supports the value indicated by the market. Sellers and real estate professionals may not agree with the appraiser's value, and may argue that it is lower than they think that it should be. Since the appraisal is most often ordered by a lender, who will make a loan decision based on the property's appraised value, the appraiser must be able to back up the appraisal report with quantifiable data. It is the lender who will want to know, "If there is a loan default, at what price can the property probably be sold to recover the remaining loan balance?" The lender is relying on the skill of the appraiser to answer this question.

FIGURE 16.2: Uniform Residential Appraisal Report (URAR)

Uniform Residential Appraisal Report   File

The purpose of this summary appraisal report is to provide the lender/client with an accurate, and adequately supported, opinion of the market value of the subject property.

SUBJECT

Property Address	City	State	Zip Code
Borrower	Owner of Public Record	County	
Legal Description			
Assessor's Parcel #	Tax Year	R.E. Taxes $	
Neighborhood Name	Map Reference	Census Tract	

Occupant ☐ Owner ☐ Tenant ☐ Vacant   Special Assessments $ ☐ PUD   HOA $ ☐ per year ☐ per month
Property Rights Appraised ☐ Fee Simple ☐ Leasehold ☐ Other (describe)
Assignment Type ☐ Purchase Transaction ☐ Refinance Transaction ☐ Other (describe)
Lender/Client   Address
Is the subject property currently offered for sale or has it been offered for sale in the twelve months prior to the effective date of this appraisal? ☐ Yes ☐ No
Report data source(s) used, offering price(s), and date(s).

CONTRACT

I ☐ did ☐ did not analyze the contract for sale for the subject purchase transaction. Explain the results of the analysis of the contract for sale or why the analysis was not performed.

Contract Price $ Date of Contract   Is the property seller the owner of public record? ☐ Yes ☐ No Data Source(s)
Is there any financial assistance (loan charges, sale concessions, gift or downpayment assistance, etc.) to be paid by any party on behalf of the borrower? ☐ Yes ☐ No
If Yes, report the total dollar amount and describe the items to be paid.

NEIGHBORHOOD

Note: Race and the racial composition of the neighborhood are not appraisal factors.

Neighborhood Characteristics			One-Unit Housing Trends			One-Unit Housing		Present Land Use %	
Location ☐ Urban	☐ Suburban	☐ Rural	Property Values ☐ Increasing	☐ Stable	☐ Declining	PRICE	AGE	One-Unit	%
Built-Up ☐ Over 75%	☐ 25–75%	☐ Under 25%	Demand/Supply ☐ Shortage	☐ In Balance	☐ Over Supply	$ (000)	(yrs)	2-4 Unit	%
Growth ☐ Rapid	☐ Stable	☐ Slow	Marketing Time ☐ Under 3 mths	☐ 3–6 mths	☐ Over 6 mths	Low		Multi-Family	%
Neighborhood Boundaries						High		Commercial	%
						Pred.		Other	%

Neighborhood Description

Market Conditions (including support for the above conclusions)

SITE

Dimensions	Area	Shape	View

Specific Zoning Classification   Zoning Description
Zoning Compliance ☐ Legal ☐ Legal Nonconforming (Grandfathered Use) ☐ No Zoning ☐ Illegal (describe)
Is the highest and best use of the subject property as improved (or as proposed per plans and specifications) the present use? ☐ Yes ☐ No If No, describe

Utilities	Public	Other (describe)		Public	Other (describe)	Off-site Improvements—Type	Public	Private
Electricity	☐	☐	Water	☐	☐	Street	☐	☐
Gas	☐	☐	Sanitary Sewer	☐	☐	Alley	☐	☐

FEMA Special Flood Hazard Area ☐ Yes ☐ No FEMA Flood Zone   FEMA Map #   FEMA Map Date
Are the utilities and off-site improvements typical for the market area? ☐ Yes ☐ No If No, describe
Are there any adverse site conditions or external factors (easements, encroachments, environmental conditions, land uses, etc.)? ☐ Yes ☐ No If Yes, describe

IMPROVEMENTS

General Description		Foundation		Exterior Description	materials/condition	Interior	materials/condition
Units ☐ One ☐ One with Accessory Unit		☐ Concrete Slab ☐ Crawl Space		Foundation Walls		Floors	
# of Stories		☐ Full Basement ☐ Partial Basement		Exterior Walls		Walls	
Type ☐ Det. ☐ Att. ☐ S-Det./End Unit		Basement Area	sq. ft.	Roof Surface		Trim/Finish	
☐ Existing ☐ Proposed ☐ Under Const.		Basement Finish	%	Gutters & Downspouts		Bath Floor	
Design (Style)		☐ Outside Entry/Exit ☐ Sump Pump		Window Type		Bath Wainscot	
Year Built		Evidence of ☐ Infestation		Storm Sash/Insulated		Car Storage ☐ None	
Effective Age (Yrs)		☐ Dampness ☐ Settlement		Screens		☐ Driveway # of Cars	
Attic ☐ None		Heating ☐ FWA ☐ HWBB ☐ Radiant		Amenities ☐ Woodstove(s) #		Driveway Surface	
☐ Drop Stair ☐ Stairs		☐ Other Fuel		☐ Fireplace(s) # ☐ Fence		☐ Garage # of Cars	
☐ Floor ☐ Scuttle		Cooling ☐ Central Air Conditioning		☐ Patio/Deck ☐ Porch		☐ Carport # of Cars	
☐ Finished ☐ Heated		☐ Individual ☐ Other		☐ Pool ☐ Other		☐ Att. ☐ Det. ☐ Built-in	

Appliances ☐ Refrigerator ☐ Range/Oven ☐ Dishwasher ☐ Disposal ☐ Microwave ☐ Washer/Dryer ☐ Other (describe)
Finished area **above** grade contains: Rooms   Bedrooms   Bath(s)   Square Feet of Gross Living Area Above Grade
Additional features (special energy efficient items, etc.)

Describe the condition of the property (including needed repairs, deterioration, renovations, remodeling, etc.).

Are there any physical deficiencies or adverse conditions that affect the livability, soundness, or structural integrity of the property? ☐ Yes ☐ No If Yes, describe

Does the property generally conform to the neighborhood (functional utility, style, condition, use, construction, etc.)? ☐ Yes ☐ No If No, describe

FIGURE 16.2: Uniform Residential Appraisal Report (URAR) (continued)

Uniform Residential Appraisal Report   File

There are	comparable properties currently offered for sale in the subject neighborhood ranging in price from $				to $		.
There are	comparable sales in the subject neighborhood within the past twelve months ranging in sale price from $				to $		.

FEATURE	SUBJECT	COMPARABLE SALE # 1		COMPARABLE SALE # 2		COMPARABLE SALE # 3	
Address							
Proximity to Subject							
Sale Price	$		$		$		$
Sale Price/Gross Liv. Area	$ sq. ft.	$ sq. ft.		$ sq. ft.		$ sq. ft.	
Data Source(s)							
Verification Source(s)							
VALUE ADJUSTMENTS	DESCRIPTION	DESCRIPTION	+(-) $ Adjustment	DESCRIPTION	+(-) $ Adjustment	DESCRIPTION	+(-) $ Adjustment
Sale or Financing Concessions							
Date of Sale/Time							
Location							
Leasehold/Fee Simple							
Site							
View							
Design (Style)							
Quality of Construction							
Actual Age							
Condition							
Above Grade	Total Bdrms. Baths	Total Bdrms. Baths		Total Bdrms. Baths		Total Bdrms. Baths	
Room Count							
Gross Living Area	sq. ft.	sq. ft.		sq. ft.		sq. ft.	
Basement & Finished Rooms Below Grade							
Functional Utility							
Heating/Cooling							
Energy Efficient Items							
Garage/Carport							
Porch/Patio/Deck							
Net Adjustment (Total)		☐ + ☐ -	$	☐ + ☐ -	$	☐ + ☐ -	$
Adjusted Sale Price of Comparables		Net Adj. % Gross Adj. %	$	Net Adj. % Gross Adj. %	$	Net Adj. % Gross Adj. %	$

I ☐ did ☐ did not research the sale or transfer history of the subject property and comparable sales. If not, explain

My research ☐ did ☐ did not reveal any prior sales or transfers of the subject property for the three years prior to the effective date of this appraisal.

Data source(s)

My research ☐ did ☐ did not reveal any prior sales or transfers of the comparable sales for the year prior to the date of sale of the comparable sale.

Data source(s)

Report the results of the research and analysis of the prior sale or transfer history of the subject property and comparable sales (report additional prior sales on page 3).

ITEM	SUBJECT	COMPARABLE SALE # 1	COMPARABLE SALE # 2	COMPARABLE SALE # 3
Date of Prior Sale/Transfer				
Price of Prior Sale/Transfer				
Data Source(s)				
Effective Date of Data Source(s)				

Analysis of prior sale or transfer history of the subject property and comparable sales

Summary of Sales Comparison Approach

Indicated Value by Sales Comparison Approach $

Indicated Value by: **Sales Comparison Approach** $ **Cost Approach** (if developed) $ **Income Approach** (if developed) $

This appraisal is made ☐ "as is", ☐ subject to completion per plans and specifications on the basis of a hypothetical condition that the improvements have been completed, ☐ subject to the following repairs or alterations on the basis of a hypothetical condition that the repairs or alterations have been completed, or ☐ subject to the following required inspection based on the extraordinary assumption that the condition or deficiency does not require alteration or repair:

Based on a complete visual inspection of the interior and exterior areas of the subject property, defined scope of work, statement of assumptions and limiting conditions, and appraiser's certification, my (our) opinion of the market value, as defined, of the real property that is the subject of this report is
$, as of   , which is the date of inspection and the effective date of this appraisal.

FIGURE 16.2: Uniform Residential Appraisal Report (URAR) (continued)

Uniform Residential Appraisal Report   File

ADDITIONAL COMMENTS

COST APPROACH TO VALUE (not required by Fannie Mae)

Provide adequate information for the lender/client to replicate the below cost figures and calculations.

Support for the opinion of site value (summary of comparable land sales or other methods for estimating site value)

ESTIMATED ☐ REPRODUCTION OR ☐ REPLACEMENT COST NEW	OPINION OF SITE VALUE .... = $
Source of cost data	Dwelling Sq. Ft. @ $ .... =$
Quality rating from cost service Effective date of cost data	Sq. Ft. @ $ .... =$
Comments on Cost Approach (gross living area calculations, depreciation, etc.)	
	Garage/Carport Sq. Ft. @ $ .... =$
	Total Estimate of Cost-New .... = $
	Less Physical Functional External
	Depreciation =$( )
	Depreciated Cost of Improvements.. =$
	"As-is" Value of Site Improvements.. =$
Estimated Remaining Economic Life (HUD and VA only) Years	Indicated Value By Cost Approach .... =$

INCOME APPROACH TO VALUE (not required by Fannie Mae)

Estimated Monthly Market Rent $ X Gross Rent Multiplier   = $ Indicated Value by Income Approach

Summary of Income Approach (including support for market rent and GRM)

PROJECT INFORMATION FOR PUDs (if applicable)

Is the developer/builder in control of the Homeowners' Association (HOA)? ☐ Yes ☐ No   Unit type(s) ☐ Detached ☐ Attached

Provide the following information for PUDs ONLY if the developer/builder is in control of the HOA and the subject property is an attached dwelling unit.

Legal name of project

Total number of phases   Total number of units   Total number of units sold

Total number of units rented   Total number of units for sale   Data source(s)

Was the project created by the conversion of an existing building(s) into a PUD? ☐ Yes ☐ No   If Yes, date of conversion

Does the project contain any multi-dwelling units? ☐ Yes ☐ No   Data source(s)

Are the units, common elements, and recreation facilities complete? ☐ Yes ☐ No   If No, describe the status of completion.

Are the common elements leased to or by the Homeowners' Association? ☐ Yes ☐ No   If Yes, describe the rental terms and options.

Describe common elements and recreational facilities

FIGURE 16.2:   Uniform Residential Appraisal Report (URAR) (continued)

Uniform Residential Appraisal Report   File

This report form is designed to report an appraisal of a one-unit property or a one-unit property with an accessory unit; including a unit in a planned unit development (PUD). This report form is not designed to report an appraisal of a manufactured home or a unit in a condominium or cooperative project.

This appraisal report is subject to the following scope of work, intended use, intended user, definition of market value, statement of assumptions and limiting conditions, and certifications. Modifications, additions, or deletions to the intended use, intended user, definition of market value, or assumptions and limiting conditions are not permitted. The appraiser may expand the scope of work to include any additional research or analysis necessary based on the complexity of this appraisal assignment. Modifications or deletions to the certifications are also not permitted. However, additional certifications that do not constitute material alterations to this appraisal report, such as those required by law or those related to the appraiser's continuing education or membership in an appraisal organization, are permitted.

SCOPE OF WORK: The scope of work for this appraisal is defined by the complexity of this appraisal assignment and the reporting requirements of this appraisal report form, including the following definition of market value, statement of assumptions and limiting conditions, and certifications. The appraiser must, at a minimum: (1) perform a complete visual inspection of the interior and exterior areas of the subject property, (2) inspect the neighborhood, (3) inspect each of the comparable sales from at least the street, (4) research, verify, and analyze data from reliable public and/or private sources, and (5) report his or her analysis, opinions, and conclusions in this appraisal report.

INTENDED USE: The intended use of this appraisal report is for the lender/client to evaluate the property that is the subject of this appraisal for a mortgage finance transaction.

INTENDED USER: The intended user of this appraisal report is the lender/client.

DEFINITION OF MARKET VALUE: The most probable price which a property should bring in a competitive and open market under all conditions requisite to a fair sale, the buyer and seller, each acting prudently, knowledgeably and assuming the price is not affected by undue stimulus. Implicit in this definition is the consummation of a sale as of a specified date and the passing of title from seller to buyer under conditions whereby: (1) buyer and seller are typically motivated; (2) both parties are well informed or well advised, and each acting in what he or she considers his or her own best interest; (3) a reasonable time is allowed for exposure in the open market; (4) payment is made in terms of cash in U. S. dollars or in terms of financial arrangements comparable thereto; and (5) the price represents the normal consideration for the property sold unaffected by special or creative financing or sales concessions* granted by anyone associated with the sale.

*Adjustments to the comparables must be made for special or creative financing or sales concessions. No adjustments are necessary for those costs which are normally paid by sellers as a result of tradition or law in a market area; these costs are readily identifiable since the seller pays these costs in virtually all sales transactions. Special or creative financing adjustments can be made to the comparable property by comparisons to financing terms offered by a third party institutional lender that is not already involved in the property or transaction. Any adjustment should not be calculated on a mechanical dollar for dollar cost of the financing or concession but the dollar amount of any adjustment should approximate the market's reaction to the financing or concessions based on the appraiser's judgment.

STATEMENT OF ASSUMPTIONS AND LIMITING CONDITIONS: The appraiser's certification in this report is subject to the following assumptions and limiting conditions:

1. The appraiser will not be responsible for matters of a legal nature that affect either the property being appraised or the title to it, except for information that he or she became aware of during the research involved in performing this appraisal. The appraiser assumes that the title is good and marketable and will not render any opinions about the title.

2. The appraiser has provided a sketch in this appraisal report to show the approximate dimensions of the improvements. The sketch is included only to assist the reader in visualizing the property and understanding the appraiser's determination of its size.

3. The appraiser has examined the available flood maps that are provided by the Federal Emergency Management Agency (or other data sources) and has noted in this appraisal report whether any portion of the subject site is located in an identified Special Flood Hazard Area. Because the appraiser is not a surveyor, he or she makes no guarantees, express or implied, regarding this determination.

4. The appraiser will not give testimony or appear in court because he or she made an appraisal of the property in question, unless specific arrangements to do so have been made beforehand, or as otherwise required by law.

5. The appraiser has noted in this appraisal report any adverse conditions (such as needed repairs, deterioration, the presence of hazardous wastes, toxic substances, etc.) observed during the inspection of the subject property or that he or she became aware of during the research involved in performing this appraisal. Unless otherwise stated in this appraisal report, the appraiser has no knowledge of any hidden or unapparent physical deficiencies or adverse conditions of the property (such as, but not limited to, needed repairs, deterioration, the presence of hazardous wastes, toxic substances, adverse environmental conditions, etc.) that would make the property less valuable, and has assumed that there are no such conditions and makes no guarantees or warranties, express or implied. The appraiser will not be responsible for any such conditions that do exist or for any engineering or testing that might be required to discover whether such conditions exist. Because the appraiser is not an expert in the field of environmental hazards, this appraisal report must not be considered as an environmental assessment of the property.

6. The appraiser has based his or her appraisal report and valuation conclusion for an appraisal that is subject to satisfactory completion, repairs, or alterations on the assumption that the completion, repairs, or alterations of the subject property will be performed in a professional manner.

FIGURE 16.2: Uniform Residential Appraisal Report (URAR) (continued)

Uniform Residential Appraisal Report   File

APPRAISER'S CERTIFICATION: The Appraiser certifies and agrees that:

1. I have, at a minimum, developed and reported this appraisal in accordance with the scope of work requirements stated in this appraisal report.

2. I performed a complete visual inspection of the interior and exterior areas of the subject property. I reported the condition of the improvements in factual, specific terms. I identified and reported the physical deficiencies that could affect the livability, soundness, or structural integrity of the property.

3. I performed this appraisal in accordance with the requirements of the Uniform Standards of Professional Appraisal Practice that were adopted and promulgated by the Appraisal Standards Board of The Appraisal Foundation and that were in place at the time this appraisal report was prepared.

4. I developed my opinion of the market value of the real property that is the subject of this report based on the sales comparison approach to value. I have adequate comparable market data to develop a reliable sales comparison approach for this appraisal assignment. I further certify that I considered the cost and income approaches to value but did not develop them, unless otherwise indicated in this report.

5. I researched, verified, analyzed, and reported on any current agreement for sale for the subject property, any offering for sale of the subject property in the twelve months prior to the effective date of this appraisal, and the prior sales of the subject property for a minimum of three years prior to the effective date of this appraisal, unless otherwise indicated in this report.

6. I researched, verified, analyzed, and reported on the prior sales of the comparable sales for a minimum of one year prior to the date of sale of the comparable sale, unless otherwise indicated in this report.

7. I selected and used comparable sales that are locationally, physically, and functionally the most similar to the subject property.

8. I have not used comparable sales that were the result of combining a land sale with the contract purchase price of a home that has been built or will be built on the land.

9. I have reported adjustments to the comparable sales that reflect the market's reaction to the differences between the subject property and the comparable sales.

10. I verified, from a disinterested source, all information in this report that was provided by parties who have a financial interest in the sale or financing of the subject property.

11. I have knowledge and experience in appraising this type of property in this market area.

12. I am aware of, and have access to, the necessary and appropriate public and private data sources, such as multiple listing services, tax assessment records, public land records and other such data sources for the area in which the property is located.

13. I obtained the information, estimates, and opinions furnished by other parties and expressed in this appraisal report from reliable sources that I believe to be true and correct.

14. I have taken into consideration the factors that have an impact on value with respect to the subject neighborhood, subject property, and the proximity of the subject property to adverse influences in the development of my opinion of market value. I have noted in this appraisal report any adverse conditions (such as, but not limited to, needed repairs, deterioration, the presence of hazardous wastes, toxic substances, adverse environmental conditions, etc.) observed during the inspection of the subject property or that I became aware of during the research involved in performing this appraisal. I have considered these adverse conditions in my analysis of the property value, and have reported on the effect of the conditions on the value and marketability of the subject property.

15. I have not knowingly withheld any significant information from this appraisal report and, to the best of my knowledge, all statements and information in this appraisal report are true and correct.

16. I stated in this appraisal report my own personal, unbiased, and professional analysis, opinions, and conclusions, which are subject only to the assumptions and limiting conditions in this appraisal report.

17. I have no present or prospective interest in the property that is the subject of this report, and I have no present or prospective personal interest or bias with respect to the participants in the transaction. I did not base, either partially or completely, my analysis and/or opinion of market value in this appraisal report on the race, color, religion, sex, age, marital status, handicap, familial status, or national origin of either the prospective owners or occupants of the subject property or of the present owners or occupants of the properties in the vicinity of the subject property or on any other basis prohibited by law.

18. My employment and/or compensation for performing this appraisal or any future or anticipated appraisals was not conditioned on any agreement or understanding, written or otherwise, that I would report (or present analysis supporting) a predetermined specific value, a predetermined minimum value, a range or direction in value, a value that favors the cause of any party, or the attainment of a specific result or occurrence of a specific subsequent event (such as approval of a pending mortgage loan application).

19. I personally prepared all conclusions and opinions about the real estate that were set forth in this appraisal report. If I relied on significant real property appraisal assistance from any individual or individuals in the performance of this appraisal or the preparation of this appraisal report, I have named such individual(s) and disclosed the specific tasks performed in this appraisal report. I certify that any individual so named is qualified to perform the tasks. I have not authorized anyone to make a change to any item in this appraisal report; therefore, any change made to this appraisal is unauthorized and I will take no responsibility for it.

20. I identified the lender/client in this appraisal report who is the individual, organization, or agent for the organization that ordered and will receive this appraisal report.

Freddie Mac Form 70   March 2005   Page 5 of 6   Fannie Mae Form 1004   March 2005

FIGURE 16.2:   Uniform Residential Appraisal Report (URAR) (continued)

Uniform Residential Appraisal Report   File

21. The lender/client may disclose or distribute this appraisal report to: the borrower; another lender at the request of the borrower; the mortgagee or its successors and assigns; mortgage insurers; government sponsored enterprises; other secondary market participants; data collection or reporting services; professional appraisal organizations; any department, agency, or instrumentality of the United States; and any state, the District of Columbia, or other jurisdictions; without having to obtain the appraiser's or supervisory appraiser's (if applicable) consent. Such consent must be obtained before this appraisal report may be disclosed or distributed to any other party (including, but not limited to, the public through advertising, public relations, news, sales, or other media).

22. I am aware that any disclosure or distribution of this appraisal report by me or the lender/client may be subject to certain laws and regulations. Further, I am also subject to the provisions of the Uniform Standards of Professional Appraisal Practice that pertain to disclosure or distribution by me.

23. The borrower, another lender at the request of the borrower, the mortgagee or its successors and assigns, mortgage insurers, government sponsored enterprises, and other secondary market participants may rely on this appraisal report as part of any mortgage finance transaction that involves any one or more of these parties.

24. If this appraisal report was transmitted as an "electronic record" containing my "electronic signature," as those terms are defined in applicable federal and/or state laws (excluding audio and video recordings), or a facsimile transmission of this appraisal report containing a copy or representation of my signature, the appraisal report shall be as effective, enforceable and valid as if a paper version of this appraisal report were delivered containing my original hand written signature.

25. Any intentional or negligent misrepresentation(s) contained in this appraisal report may result in civil liability and/or criminal penalties including, but not limited to, fine or imprisonment or both under the provisions of Title 18, United States Code, Section 1001, et seq., or similar state laws.

SUPERVISORY APPRAISER'S CERTIFICATION: The Supervisory Appraiser certifies and agrees that:

1. I directly supervised the appraiser for this appraisal assignment, have read the appraisal report, and agree with the appraiser's analysis, opinions, statements, conclusions, and the appraiser's certification.

2. I accept full responsibility for the contents of this appraisal report including, but not limited to, the appraiser's analysis, opinions, statements, conclusions, and the appraiser's certification.

3. The appraiser identified in this appraisal report is either a sub-contractor or an employee of the supervisory appraiser (or the appraisal firm), is qualified to perform this appraisal, and is acceptable to perform this appraisal under the applicable state law.

4. This appraisal report complies with the Uniform Standards of Professional Appraisal Practice that were adopted and promulgated by the Appraisal Standards Board of The Appraisal Foundation and that were in place at the time this appraisal report was prepared.

5. If this appraisal report was transmitted as an "electronic record" containing my "electronic signature," as those terms are defined in applicable federal and/or state laws (excluding audio and video recordings), or a facsimile transmission of this appraisal report containing a copy or representation of my signature, the appraisal report shall be as effective, enforceable and valid as if a paper version of this appraisal report were delivered containing my original hand written signature.

APPRAISER	**SUPERVISORY APPRAISER (ONLY IF REQUIRED)**
Signature_____	Signature_____
Name _____	Name _____
Company Name _____	Company Name _____
Company Address_____	Company Address _____
_____	_____
Telephone Number _____	Telephone Number _____
Email Address _____	Email Address _____
Date of Signature and Report_____	Date of Signature _____
Effective Date of Appraisal _____	State Certification #_____
State Certification #_____	or State License #_____
or State License #_____	State _____
or Other (describe) _____ State # _____	Expiration Date of Certification or License _____
State _____	
Expiration Date of Certification or License _____	**SUBJECT PROPERTY**
	☐ Did not inspect subject property
ADDRESS OF PROPERTY APPRAISED	☐ Did inspect exterior of subject property from street
_____	Date of Inspection _____
_____	☐ Did inspect interior and exterior of subject property
APPRAISED VALUE OF SUBJECT PROPERTY $ _____	Date of Inspection _____
LENDER/CLIENT	
Name _____	**COMPARABLE SALES**
Company Name _____	
Company Address_____	☐ Did not inspect exterior of comparable sales from street
_____	☐ Did inspect exterior of comparable sales from street
Email Address _____	Date of Inspection _____

VALUE

To have **value** in the real estate market—that is, monetary worth based on desirability—a property must have the following characteristics, which can be remembered as DUST:

The characteristics of value
■ **D**emand
■ **U**tility
■ **S**carcity
■ **T**ransferability

■ *Demand*—the need or desire for possession or ownership backed by the financial means to satisfy that need

■ *Utility*—the property's usefulness for its intended purposes

■ *Scarcity*—a finite supply

■ *Transferability*—the relative ease with which ownership rights are transferred from one person to another

Market value

The goal of an appraiser most often is to estimate or express an opinion of a property's market value. **Market value** generally is considered the most probable price that a property should bring in a competitive and open market under all conditions requisite to a fair sale. The buyer and the seller are both assumed to be acting prudently and knowledgeably and the price is not affected by undue stimulus. The property's most probable price is not the average price for such properties, or the highest price possible.

A determination of market value thus requires that

■ the buyer and the seller are unrelated and acting without undue pressure;

■ both the buyer and the seller are well informed of the property's use and potential, including both its defects and its advantages;

■ a reasonable time is allowed for exposure of the property in the open market;

■ payment is made in cash or its equivalent; and

■ the price paid for the property is a normal market price, unaffected by special financing amounts or terms, services, fees, costs, or credits incurred in the market transaction.

Market price

Market value—an opinion of a property's worth

Market price—the asking, offer, or sales price of a property

Market value is an opinion of value based on an analysis of data. The data may include not only an analysis of comparable sales but also an analysis of potential income, expenses, and replacement costs. *Market price*, on the other hand, is a property's asking, offer, or sales price.

Cost

One of the most common misconceptions about valuing property is that its cost represents its market value. Cost and market value may be the same. In fact, when the improvements on a property are new, cost and value are likely to be equal. But more often, cost does not equal market value. For example, a homeowner may install a swimming pool for $30,000; however, the cost of the improvement may not add $30,000 to the value of the property.

Basic principles of value

A number of economic principles can affect the value of real estate. The most important are defined in the following.

Anticipation

According to the principle of **anticipation**, value is created by the expectation that certain events will occur. For instance, the value of a house may be affected if rumors circulate that a major employer in the area will be going out of business. In the same way, a neighborhood may see an increase in property values if a major employer announces that it is moving to the area. The income approach to value is based on the principle of anticipation.

Change

No physical or economic condition remains constant; this is the principle of **change**. Real estate is subject to natural phenomena such as tornadoes, fires, and routine wear and tear. The real estate business is subject to market demands, like any other business. An appraiser must be knowledgeable about both the past and the predictable future effects of natural phenomena and the behavior of the marketplace.

Competition

The interaction of supply and demand creates **competition**. Profitable businesses tend to attract competition. For example, the success of a retail store may cause investors to open similar stores in the area. This tends to mean less profit for all stores concerned unless the purchasing power in the area substantially increases.

Conformity

The principle of **conformity** means that maximum value is created when a property is in harmony with its surroundings. Maximum value is realized if the use of land conforms to existing neighborhood standards. In a single-family residential neighborhood, for instance, buildings should be similar in design, construction, size, and age. Many parts of the country have experienced the "tear-down" phenomenon in which a large, expensive new home replaces a smaller, mid-century home that is more typical of others in the neighborhood. The new home will not realize its maximum value because it has violated the principle of conformity—at least, until a significant number of such conversions has taken place.

Contribution

Under the principle of **contribution**, the value of any part of a property is measured by its effect on the value of the whole parcel. Installing a swimming pool, greenhouse, or private bowling alley may not add value to the property equal to its cost, but remodeling an outdated kitchen or bathroom might.

Highest and best use

The most profitable single use of a property is its **highest and best use**. The use must be

- physically possible,
- legally permitted,
- economically or financially feasible, and
- the most profitable or maximally productive.

The highest and best use of a site can change with social, political, and economic forces. A parking lot in a busy downtown area, for example, may not maximize the land's profitability to the same extent that an office building would. On the other hand, if the downtown area has an oversupply of office space but is short of parking areas, the parking lot may be the most profitable current use of the land.

Increasing and diminishing returns

The addition of improvements to land and structures tends to increase a property's market value, but only up to a certain point. Beyond that point, additional improvements no longer affect a property's value because buyers or renters in the market cannot be expected to pay more for the property. As long as money spent on improvements produces an increase in income or value, the **law of increasing returns** applies. At the point where additional improvements do not increase income or value, the **law of diminishing returns** applies. No matter how much money is spent on the property, the property's value does not keep pace with the expenditures. A remodeled kitchen or bathroom might increase the value of a house; adding restaurant-quality appliances and hand-crafted wood floors, however, could be costs that the owner would not be able to recover.

IN PRACTICE

The law of diminishing returns sometimes creates an awkward situation during a listing appointment. The owner is proud of all the improvements that have been made to the property and may produce a box filled with receipts for all the additions that have been made to the property over the years. When the real estate professional presents the carefully prepared CMA, however, it becomes clear that the probable market value of the property will not cover the cost of the improvements. The real estate professional must be prepared to explain why it would be foolhardy for the owner to set a listing price high enough to cover all of those costs. The real estate professional must also know how to react if the owner chooses to ignore the evidence presented by the CMA. A property listing that languishes on the market because the listing price is too high is bad for everyone.

Plottage

Plottage: the individual value of two adjacent properties may be greater if they are combined in an assemblage than if each is sold separately.

The principle of **plottage** is in evidence when the consolidation of adjacent lots into a single larger one produces a greater total land value than the sum of the two sites valued separately. For example, two adjacent lots valued at $35,000 each might have a combined value of $90,000 if consolidated. The process of merging two separately owned lots under one owner is known as **assemblage**. *Plottage* is the amount that the value of the combined properties is increased by successful assemblage.

Regression and progression

In general, the worth of a better-quality property is adversely affected by the presence of a lesser-quality property. This is known as the principle of **regression**. Thus, in a neighborhood of modest homes, a structure that is larger, better maintained, or more luxurious would tend to be valued in the same range as the less lavish homes. Conversely, under the principle of **progression**, the value of a modest home would be higher if it were located among larger, fancier properties.

Substitution

According to the principle of **substitution**, the maximum value of a property tends to be set by how much it would cost to purchase an equally desirable and valuable substitute property. Substitution is the foundation of the sales comparison approach to appraising that is discussed later.

Supply and demand

The principle of **supply and demand** operates in the real estate market just as it does in the market for any product. The value of a product depends on the supply—the number of such products available in the marketplace. When the supply of similar properties increases, their value decreases and when demand for such properties increases, their value increases.

IN PRACTICE

The factors of supply and demand tend to operate in a cycle and point out how the immovability of real estate is a critical part of that cycle. When there is a high demand for homes and relatively few properties available for sale, prices will go up. This could be caused by a number of factors, from business expansion in the area to a natural disaster that destroys part of the housing supply. At the same time, another area may be experiencing a glut of properties on the market, usually because of dismal economic conditions that force companies to close or downsize. Some residents will choose to move to where the work is, putting even more properties on the market and also placing additional pressure on businesses that struggle to survive as a declining, and less prosperous, population reduces the demand for their products and services.

THE THREE APPROACHES TO VALUE

To arrive at an accurate opinion of value, an appraiser traditionally uses one or more of three basic valuation techniques: the sales comparison approach, the cost approach, and the income approach. The three methods serve as checks against each other and using more than one approach helps the appraiser narrow the range of the final conclusion of value. Each approach is most useful with a specific type of property.

The sales comparison approach

In the **sales comparison approach** (also known as the **market data approach**), value is obtained by comparing the property being appraised—the subject property—with recently sold comparable properties—properties similar to the subject in location and features. Because no two parcels of real estate are exactly alike, each comparable property must be analyzed for differences and similarities between it and the subject property. This approach is a good example of the principle of substitution, discussed above. The **sales price** of a comparable is adjusted to reflect the impact on value of any differences between the subject and comparable. The elements of comparison for which adjustments must be made include the following:

- *Property rights.* An adjustment must be made when less than fee simple—the full legal bundle of rights—is involved. An adjustment could be made because of the presence of a land lease, ground lease, life estate, easement, deed restriction, and/or encroachment.

- *Financing concessions.* The financing terms under which a property was sold must be considered, including mortgage loan terms and owner financing or an interest rate buydown by a builder-developer.

- *Market conditions.* Interest rates, supply and demand, and other economic indicators must be analyzed.

- *Conditions of sale.* Adjustments must be made for motivational factors that would affect the sale, such as foreclosure, a sale between family members, or some nonmonetary incentive.

- *Market conditions since the date of sale.* An adjustment must be made if economic changes occur between the date of sale of the comparable property and the date of the appraisal.

- *Location or area preference.* Similar properties might differ in price from neighborhood to neighborhood or even between locations within the same neighborhood.

- *Physical features and amenities.* Physical features, such as the structure's age, size, and condition when compared to the subject property, may require adjustments.

The sales comparison approach is usually considered the most reliable of the three approaches in appraising single-family homes, where the intangible benefits of home ownership may be difficult to measure otherwise. Figure 16.3 is an abbreviated version of the information that an appraiser will provide a client, but it illustrates the kind of comparisons and value adjustments that are made.

FIGURE 16.3: Sales Comparison Approach to Value

| | Subject Property | Comparable Properties | | |
		A	B	C
Sales price		$262,000	$252,000	$265,000
Financing concessions	none	none	none	none
Date of sale		current	current	current
Location	good	same	poorer +4,500	same
Age	6 years	same	same	same
Size of lot	60' × 135'	same	same	larger –5,000
Landscaping	good	same	same	same
Construction	brick	same	same	same
Style	ranch	same	same	same
No. of rooms	8	same	same	same
No. of bedrooms	4	same	poorer +4,500	same
No. of baths	2½	same	same	better –500
Sq. ft. of living space	2,500	same	same	better –2,000
Other space (basement)	full basement	same	same	same
Condition—exterior	average	better –2,500	poorer +2,000	better –2,500
Condition—interior	good	same	same	better –1,500
Garage	3-car attached	same	same	same
Other improvements	none	none	none	none
Net adjustments		–2,500	+11,000	–11,500
Adjusted value		$259,500	$263,000	$253,500

Note: The value of a feature that is present in the subject but not in the comparable property is added to the sales price of the comparable. The value of a feature that is present in the comparable but not in the subject property is subtracted from the sales price of the comparable. A good way to remember this is as follows: CBS stands for "comp better, subtract"; and CPA stands for "comp poorer, add." The adjusted sales prices of the comparables represent the probable range of value of the subject property. From this range, a single market value estimate can be selected.

The cost approach

The **cost approach** to value also is based on the principle of substitution. The cost approach consists of five steps:

1. Estimate the value of the land as though it were vacant and available to be put to its highest and best use.

2. Estimate the current cost of constructing buildings and improvements.

3. Estimate the amount of **accrued depreciation** (loss in value) resulting from the property's physical deterioration, external depreciation, and functional obsolescence.

4. Deduct the accrued depreciation estimated in Step 3 from the construction cost estimated in Step 2.

5. Add the estimated land value from Step 1 to the depreciated cost of the building and site improvements derived in Step 4 to arrive at the total property value.

For example:

Value of the land	=	$50,000
Current cost of construction	=	$180,000
Accrued depreciation	=	$20,000
$180,000 – $20,000	=	$160,000
$50,000 ı $160,000	–	$210,000

In this case, the total property value is $210,000.

An example of the cost approach to value, applied to the same property as in Figure 16.3, is shown in Figure 16.4.

FIGURE 16.4:   Cost Approach to Value

Subject Property	
Land valuation: Size 60' × 135' @ $450 per front foot	$ 27,000
Plus site improvements: driveway, walks, landscaping, etc.	10,000
Total	$ 37,000
Building valuation: replacement cost	
2,500 sq. ft. @ $75 per sq. ft.	$187,500
Less depreciation:	
Physical depreciation	
Curable (items of deferred maintenance)	
exterior painting	$4,000
Incurable (structural deterioration)	9,750
Functional obsolescence	0
External obsolescence	0
Total depreciation	$13,750
Depreciated value of building	$173,750
Indicated value by cost approach	$210,750

Depreciation

In a real estate appraisal, **depreciation** is a loss in value for any reason. It refers to a condition that adversely affects the value of an improvement to real property. Land is not considered a depreciating asset; it retains its value indefinitely, except in such rare cases as an urban parcel that is rezoned, improperly developed land, or misused farmland. Depreciation is the result of a negative condition that affects real property.

IN PRACTICE

Depreciation for appraisal purposes is not the same as depreciation for tax reporting purposes. Depreciation for appraisal purposes represents the actual loss in value caused by property deterioration, damage, or obsolescence. Depreciation for tax purposes is an annual deduction from taxable income for a term of years, as permitted by IRS regulations, which may even allow the term of years to be shortened so that accelerated depreciation can be taken.

Depreciation is considered curable or incurable, depending on whether it can be corrected economically. For appraisal purposes, depreciation is divided into three classes, according to cause:

- **Physical deterioration.** A curable item is one in need of repair, such as painting (deferred maintenance), that would result in an increase in value equal to or exceeding its cost. An item is incurable if it is a defect caused by physical wear and tear and its correction would not be economically feasible or contribute a comparable value to the building, such as an extensive crack in the foundation. The cost of a major repair may not warrant the financial investment.

- **Functional obsolescence.** Obsolescence means a loss in value from the market's response to the item. Outmoded or unacceptable physical or design features that are no longer considered desirable by purchasers are considered curable if they can be replaced or redesigned at a cost that would be offset by the anticipated increase in ultimate value. Outmoded plumbing, for instance, is usually easily replaced. Room function may be redefined at no cost if the basic room layout allows for it. A bedroom adjacent to a kitchen, for example, may be converted to a family room. Currently undesirable physical or design features that cannot be easily remedied because the cost of the cure would be greater than its resulting increase in value are considered incurable. A four-bedroom home with only one bathroom is likely to suffer from incurable functional obsolescence.

- **External obsolescence.** If depreciation is caused by negative factors not on the subject property, such as environmental, social, or economic forces, it is always incurable. The loss in value cannot be reversed by spending money on the property. For example, close proximity to a polluting factory is a factor that cannot be cured by the owner of the subject property.

The easiest but least precise way to determine depreciation is the straight-line method, also called the economic age-life method. Depreciation is assumed to occur at an even rate over a structure's **economic life**, the period during which it is expected to remain useful for its original intended purpose. The property's cost is divided by the number of years of its expected economic life to derive the amount of annual depreciation.

For instance, a $420,000 property may have a land value of $90,000 and an improvement value of $330,000. If the improvement is expected to last 60 years, the annual straight-line depreciation would be $5,500 ($330,000 divided by 60 years). Such depreciation can be calculated as an annual dollar amount or as a percentage of a property's improvements.

The cost approach is most useful in the appraisal of newer or special-purpose buildings such as schools, churches, and public buildings. Such properties are difficult to appraise using other methods because there are seldom enough local sales to use as comparables and because the properties do not ordinarily generate income.

Much of the functional obsolescence and all the external obsolescence can be evaluated only by considering the actions of buyers in the marketplace.

The income approach

The **income approach** to value is based on the present value of the right to future income. It assumes that the income generated by a property will determine the property's value. The income approach is used for valuation of income-producing properties such as apartment buildings, office buildings, retail stores, and shopping centers and is based on anticipation. A simplified version of the computations used in applying to income approach is shown in Figure 16.5. In estimating value using the income approach, an appraiser must take the following five steps:

Income approach
Gross
Income
Vacancy
Expenses
Net operating income

1. Estimate the property's annual potential gross income. An estimate of economic rental income must be made based on market studies. Current rental income may not reflect the current market rental rates, especially in the case of short-term leases or leases about to terminate. Potential income also includes income to the property from such sources as vending machines, parking fees, and laundry machines.

2. Deduct an appropriate allowance for vacancy and rent loss, based on the appraiser's experience, and arrive at the effective gross income.

3. Deduct the annual operating expenses from the effective gross income to arrive at the annual **net operating income (NOI)**. Management costs are always included, even if the current owner manages the property. Mortgage payments (principal and interest) are debt service and are not considered operating expenses. Capital expenditures are not considered expenses; however, an allowance can be calculated representing the annual usage of each major capital item.

4. Estimate the price a typical investor would pay for the income produced by this particular type and class of property. This is done by estimating the rate of return (or yield) that an investor will demand for the investment of capital in this type of building. This rate of return is called the **capitalization rate** (or "cap" rate) and is determined by comparing the relationship of net operating income with the sales prices of similar properties that have sold in the current market. For example, a comparable property that is producing an annual net income of $15,000 is sold for $187,500. The capitalization rate is $15,000 divided by $187,500, or 8%. If other comparable properties sold at prices that yielded substantially the same rate, it may be concluded that 8% is the rate that the appraiser should apply to the subject property.

5. Apply the capitalization rate to the property's annual net operating income to arrive at the estimate of the property's value.

FIGURE 16.5: Income Capitalization Approach to Value

Potential gross annual income		$60,000
Market rent (100% capacity)		
Income from other sources (vending machines and pay phones)	+600	
	$60,600	
Less vacancy and collection losses (estimated) @ 4%		−2,424
Effective gross income		$58,176
Expenses:		
Real estate taxes	$9,000	
Insurance	1,000	
Heat	2,500	
Maintenance	6,400	
Utilities, electricity, water, gas	800	
Repairs	1,200	
Decorating	1,400	
Replacement of equipment	800	
Legal and accounting	600	
Advertising	300	
Management	3,000	
Total		$27,000
Annual net operating income		$31,176

Capitalization rate = 10% (overall rate)

Capitalization of annual net income: $31,176 ÷ 0.10 = $311,760

Market value by income approach = $311,760

With the appropriate capitalization rate and accurate projected annual net operating income, the appraiser can obtain an estimate of value by applying the income approach.

This formula and its variations are important in dealing with income property:

> Income ÷ rate = value
>
> Income ÷ value = rate
>
> Value × rate = income

For example:

> Net operating income ÷ capitalization rate = value
>
> $18,000 income ÷ 9% cap rate = $200,000 value or
>
> $18,000 income ÷ 8% cap rate = $225,000 value

Note the relationship between the rate and the value. As the rate goes down, the value increases.

Gross rent or gross income multipliers

If a buyer is interested in purchasing a one- to four-unit residential rental property, the **gross rent multiplier (GRM)** based on monthly rental income could be used for a rough approximation of value. If the buyer is interested in purchasing five or more units, a **gross income multiplier (GIM)** based on annual income could be used.

The formulas are as follows:

■ For a property with one to four residential units that has no income from other sources:

Sales price ÷ monthly gross rent = gross rent multiplier (GRM)

■ For a property with five or more units and commercial properties with income from a variety of sources:

Sales price ÷ annual gross income = gross income multiplier (GIM)

For example, if a home recently sold for $155,000 and its monthly rental income was $1,250, the GRM for the property would be

$155,000 ÷ $1,250 = 124 GRM

If a commercial property recently sold for $155,000 and its annual rental income was $15,000, the GIM for the property would be

$155,000 ÷ $15000 = 10.33 GIM

To establish an accurate GRM, an appraiser must have recent sales and rental data from at least four properties that are similar to the subject property. The resulting GRM can then be applied to the estimated fair market rental of the subject property to arrive at its market value. The formula would be as follows:

Rental income × GRM = Estimated market value

Figure 16.6 shows some examples of GRM comparisons.

Reconciliation

When the three approaches to value are applied to the same property, they normally produce three separate indications of value. (Compare Figure 16.3 with Figure 16.4.) **Reconciliation** is the act of analyzing and effectively weighing the findings from the three approaches. In reconciliation, an appraiser explains not only the appropriateness of each approach but also the relative reliability of the data within each approach in line with the type of value sought. The appraiser should also explain how the data reflect the current market.

FIGURE 16.6: Gross Rent Multiplier

Comparable No.	Sales Price	Monthly Rent	GRM
1	$280,000	$1,800	155.56
2	243,000	1,350	180.00
3	287,000	2,000	143.50
4	262,500	1,675	156.72
Subject	?	1,750	?

Note: Based on an analysis of these comparisons, comparables 2 and 3 show extremes. Based on monthly rent between comparables 1 and 4, a GRM of 156.72 seems reasonable for homes in this area. In the opinion of an appraiser, the estimated value of the subject property would be $1,750 × 156.72, or $274,260.

The process of reconciliation is not simply taking the average of the three estimates of value. An average implies that the data and logic applied in each of the approaches are equally valid and reliable and should, therefore, be given equal weight. In fact, however, certain approaches are more valid and reliable with some kinds of properties than with others.

For example, in appraising a home, the income approach is rarely valid, and the cost approach is of limited value unless the home is relatively new. Therefore, the sales comparison approach is usually given greatest weight in valuing single-family residences. In the appraisal of income or investment property, the income approach normally is given the greatest weight. In the appraisal of churches, libraries, museums, schools, and other special-use properties, where little or no income or sales revenue is generated, the cost approach usually is assigned the greatest weight. From this analysis, or reconciliation, a single opinion of market value is produced.

KEY POINT REVIEW

An **appraisal** provides the appraiser's opinion of **value** based on supportable evidence and appraisal methods, as defined by the *Uniform Standards of Professional Appraisal Practice (USPAP)* established by the Appraisal Foundation's **Appraisal Standards Board**.

An **appraiser** must be state-licensed or certified for an appraisal performed as part of a **federally related transaction**. The **Appraiser Qualifications Board** sets minimum education and experience requirements for licensing or certification and the **Appraisal Practices Board** recommends acceptable business practices.

The **Uniform Residential Appraisal Report (URAR)** is required by Fannie Mae and Freddie Mac.

A **comparative market analysis (CMA)** is a report by a real estate professional of market statistics, but it is not an appraisal.

A **broker's price opinion (BPO)** may be used in transactions involving home equity lines, refinancing, portfolio management, loss mitigation, and collections.

Value is created by **d**emand, **u**tility, **s**carcity, and **t**ransferability of property (**DUST**). **Market value** is the most probable price that property should bring in a fair sale, but not necessarily the same as the **price** asked or paid or the **cost** to construct.

The basic principles of value include **anticipation** of certain events, **change** that can be physical or economic, **competition** for clients and customers, **conformity** of properties in a neighborhood, and **contribution** to a property's value of any individual improvement. A property's **highest and best use** is the use that is physically possible, legally permitted, economically or financially feasible, and the most profitable or maximally productive. The **law of increasing and diminishing returns** is in evidence when additional property improvements no longer bring a comparable increase in property value.

Plottage is the increase in value that can result when two or more parcels of land are combined in the process called **assemblage**. The principle of **progression** is in evidence when a property's value is enhanced because of more valuable properties in the vicinity; the opposite is true and the principle of **regression** is in effect when a property's value is lower because of less valuable properties in the vicinity.

The principle of **substitution** is the foundation of the sales comparison approach. A buyer will not want to pay more for a property than it would cost to purchase an equally desirable and suitable property. The principle of **supply and demand** dictates that prices will rise when demand is high relative to supply, and prices will fall when supply is high relative to demand.

The **sales comparison approach** (**market data approach**) makes use of sales of properties comparable to the property that is the subject of the appraisal by adding or subtracting from the sales price of each comp the value of a feature present or absent in the subject property versus the comparable.

The **cost approach** uses the current **cost** of constructing building and other property improvements and an estimate of **accrued depreciation** using the **straight-line method** (**economic age-life method**), or an estimate of individual items of **physical deterioration**, **functional obsolescence**, or **external obsolescence**.

The **income approach** is based on the present value of the right to future income arrived at by these steps:

1. Estimating annual potential **gross income**

2. Deducting an allowance for **vacancy and rent loss** to find **effective gross income**

3. Deducting **annual operating expenses** to find **net operating income (NOI)**

4. Estimating the **rate of return** (**capitalization rate** or **cap rate**) for the subject by analyzing cap rates of similar properties

5. Deriving an estimate of the subject's market value by applying the cap rate to the property's annual NOI using this formula: **net operating income ÷ capitalization rate = value**

Reconciliation is the process by which the validity and reliability of the results of the approaches to value are weighed objectively to determine the appraiser's final opinion of value.

UNIT 16 QUIZ

1. Which appraisal method uses a rate of investment return?
   A. Sales comparison approach
   B. Cost approach
   C. Income approach
   D. Gross income multiplier method

2. The characteristics of value include which of the following?
   A. Competition
   B. Scarcity
   C. Anticipation
   D. Balance

3. There are two vacant adjacent lots in an area zoned for commercial use, each worth approximately $50,000. If their owner sells them as a single lot, however, the combined parcel will be worth $120,000. What principle does this illustrate?
   A. Substitution
   B. Plottage
   C. Regression
   D. Progression

4. The amount of money a property is likely to command in the marketplace is its
   A. intrinsic value.
   B. market value.
   C. subjective value.
   D. book value.

5. A homeowner constructs a five-bedroom brick house with an indoor pool in a neighborhood of modest two-bedroom and three-bedroom frame houses on narrow lots. The value of this house is *MOST* likely to be affected by what principle?
   A. Progression
   B. Assemblage
   C. Change
   D. Regression

6. The owners of a modest ranch house in a neighborhood of larger, more expensive homes may find that the value of their home is affected by what principle?
   A. Progression
   B. Increasing returns
   C. Competition
   D. Regression

7. For appraisal purposes, accrued depreciation is *NOT* caused by
   A. functional obsolescence.
   B. physical deterioration.
   C. external obsolescence.
   D. accelerated depreciation.

8. The term *reconciliation* refers to which of the following?
   A. Loss of value due to any cause
   B. Separating the value of the land from the total value of the property to compute depreciation
   C. Analyzing the results obtained by the different approaches to value to form an opinion of value
   D. The process by which an appraiser determines the highest and best use for a parcel of land

9. If a property's annual net income is $24,000 and it is valued at $300,000, what is its capitalization rate?
   A. 8%
   B. 10.5%
   C. 12%
   D. 15%

10. Which of the following is *NOT* used by an appraiser applying the income approach to value?
    A. Annual net operating income
    B. Capitalization rate
    C. Accrued depreciation
    D. Annual gross income

11. An appraiser asked for an opinion of the value of an existing shopping center would probably give the *MOST* weight to which approach to value?
    A. Cost approach
    B. Sales comparison approach
    C. Income approach
    D. Index method

12. The market value of a parcel of real estate is
    A. an estimate of its future benefits.
    B. the amount of money paid for the property.
    C. an estimate of the most probable price it should bring.
    D. its value without improvements.

13. Capitalization is the process by which annual net operating income is used to
    A. determine cost.
    B. estimate value.
    C. establish depreciation.
    D. determine potential tax value.

14. From the reproduction or replacement cost of a building, the appraiser deducts depreciation, which represents
    A. the remaining economic life of the building.
    B. remodeling costs to increase rentals.
    C. loss of value due to any reason.
    D. costs to modernize the building.

15. All of the following factors would be important in comparing properties under the sales comparison approach to value *EXCEPT*
    A. differences in dates of sale.
    B. differences in financing terms.
    C. differences in appearance and condition.
    D. differences in original cost.

16. Which of the following is *TRUE* about a comparative market analysis?
    A. It is made by a professional appraiser.
    B. It is the same as an appraisal.
    C. It is based on a detailed market analysis of market conditions, property features, recent sales and listings, land value, and construction costs.
    D. None of these.

17. What is the key to an accurate appraisal?
    A. Methodical collection and analysis of data
    B. Years of experience the appraiser has
    C. Appraising in a market with high supply
    D. Appraising in a market with high demand

18. The appraised value of a residence with four bedrooms and one bathroom would probably be reduced because of
    A. external obsolescence.
    B. functional obsolescence.
    C. curable physical deterioration.
    D. incurable physical deterioration.

19. Which principle of value indicates that a developer's very profitable real estate project will attract others to engage in similar activity in the same area and thus drive down profits?
    A. Anticipation
    B. Competition
    C. Value
    D. Progression

20. Change, contribution, plottage, and substitution are some of the basic principles that affect what aspect of real estate?
    A. Demand
    B. Depreciation
    C. Value
    D. Supply

UNIT 17

Leases

LEARNING OBJECTIVES

When you have completed this unit, you will be able to

› **explain** the essential elements of leasehold interests;
› **describe** the essential terms of a lease agreement;
› **distinguish** the various types of leases; and
› **explain** the means by which the lease may be terminated and discharged and the remedies available to the parties for its breach.

KEY TERMS

actual eviction	holdover tenancy	purchase option
assignment	lease	renewal option
constructive eviction	lease purchase	rent
estate (tenancy) at sufferance	leasehold estate	reversionary right
estate (tenancy) at will	lessee	right of first refusal
estate (tenancy) for years	lessor	sale-and-leaseback
estate (tenancy) from period to period	month-to-month tenancy	security deposit
gross lease	net lease	sublease
ground lease	nondisturbance clause	
	percentage lease	

OVERVIEW

Real estate professionals should be knowledgeable about the local rental market to better assist prospective buyers who may need temporary housing, those who prefer to rent a home or cannot afford to purchase one, or investor-buyers, or to manage their own portfolios. In any case, anyone with an interest in rental property should be aware of the basic provisions of leases and other landlord-tenant issues.

LEASING REAL ESTATE

The record number of property foreclosures in recent years has been accompanied by an increase in the number of residential rental properties, both because foreclosed owners have become renters and because investors have taken advantage of the decline in market values to increase their portfolios. There has been a drop in the rate of home ownership from a record high of 69% in 2004 to 63.7% in 2015, and a corresponding increase in the number of households residing in rental units. Additional statistics on the housing market are available from the U.S. Census Bureau, www.census.gov.

_____
www.census.gov
_____

The foundation of the relationship between a property owner and tenant is the lease. A **lease** is a contract between a **lessor** (the owner of real estate, or landlord) and a **lessee** (the tenant). A lease transfers the lessor's rights to exclusive possession and use of the property to the tenant for a specified period of time and establishes the consideration the lessee is to pay **rent** for use of the property. Rent is a fixed, periodic payment made by a tenant of a property to the owner for possession and use, usually by prior agreement of the parties. Other rights and obligations of the parties are also set forth. The landlord retains a **reversionary right** to possession after the lease term expires.

The statute of frauds in most states requires lease agreements for more than one year to be in writing to be enforceable. In general, oral leases for one year or less that can be performed within a year of their making are enforceable. A written lease should be executed (signed) by both the lessor and the lessee.

IN PRACTICE

Even though an oral lease, such as a lease for one year commencing from the day of agreement, may be enforceable, it is always better practice to put a lease agreement in writing. A written lease signed by both landlord and tenant provides concrete evidence of the terms and conditions to which the parties have agreed.

Leasehold estates

A tenant's right to possess real estate for the term of the lease is called a **leasehold estate** (less-than-freehold). A leasehold is generally considered personal property. When the tenant assumes many of the landowner's obligations under a lease for life or for more than 49 years, certain states give the tenant some of the benefits and privileges of ownership, such as the right to use the leasehold interest as security for a loan.

Just as there are several types of freehold (ownership) estates, there are different kinds of leasehold estates. (See Figure 17.1.)

FIGURE 17.1: Leasehold Estates

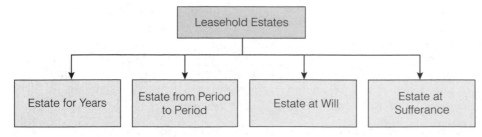

Estate for years

An **estate (tenancy) for years** is a leasehold estate that continues for a definite period. That period may be years, months, weeks, or even days. An estate for years (sometimes called an *estate for term*) always has specific starting and ending dates. When the estate expires, the lessee is required to vacate the premises and surrender possession to the lessor. No notice is required to terminate the estate for years because the lease agreement states a specific expiration date. When the date comes, the lease expires, and the tenant's rights are extinguished.

If both parties agree, the lease for years may be terminated before the expiration date. Otherwise, neither party may terminate without showing that the lease agreement has been breached. Any extension of the tenancy requires that a new contract be negotiated.

As is characteristic of all leases, a tenancy for years gives the lessee the right to occupy and use the leased property according to the terms and covenants contained in the lease agreement. A lessee has the right to use the premises for the entire lease term and that right is unaffected by the original lessor's death or the sale of the property, unless the lease states otherwise. If the original lease provides for an option to renew, no further negotiation is required; the tenant merely exercises the option.

Estate from period to period

An **estate (tenancy) from period to period**, or *periodic tenancy*, is created when the landlord and tenant enter into an agreement for an indefinite time—that is, the lease does not contain a specific expiration date. Such a tenancy is created initially to run for a definite amount of time—for instance, month to month, week to week, or year to year—but the tenancy continues indefinitely until proper notice of termination is given. Rent is payable at definite intervals. A periodic tenancy is characterized by *continuity* because it is automatically renewable under the original terms of the agreement until one of the parties gives notice to terminate. In effect, the payment and acceptance of rent extend the lease for another period. A **month-to-month tenancy**, for example, is created when a tenant takes possession with no definite termination date and pays monthly rent. Periodic tenancy is often used in residential leases.

IN PRACTICE

A landlord and a tenant who is unsure how long the apartment will be needed have agreed that an apartment can be rented by the month without specifying the number of months the lease will run. The lease simply continues until either the landlord or the tenant gives proper notice to terminate.

If the original agreement provides for the conversion from an estate for years to a periodic tenancy, no negotiations are necessary; the tenant simply exercises the option.

An estate from period to period also might be created when a tenant with an estate for years remains in possession, or holds over, after the lease term expires. If no new lease agreement has been made, a **holdover tenancy** is created. The landlord may evict the tenant or treat the holdover tenant as one who holds a periodic tenancy. The landlord's acceptance of rent usually is considered conclusive proof of acceptance of the periodic tenancy. The courts customarily rule that a tenant who holds over can do so for a term equal to the term of the original lease, provided the period is for one year or less. For example, a tenant with a lease for six months would be entitled to a new six-month tenancy, but if the original lease were for five years, the holdover tenancy could not exceed one year. Some leases stipulate that in the absence of a renewal agreement, a tenant who holds over does so as a month-to-month tenant.

To terminate a periodic estate, either the landlord or the tenant must give proper notice. The form and timing of the notice may be established by state statute. Normally, the notice must be given at least one period in advance. For example, to terminate an estate from week to week, one week's notice is required; to terminate an estate from month to month, one month's notice is required. For an estate from year to year, however, the notice requirements vary from two months to six months. Many states have statutory notice requirements.

Estate at will

Estate (tenancy) at will:

- *Indefinite term*
- *Possession with landlord's consent*

An **estate (tenancy) at will** gives the tenant the right to possess property with the landlord's consent for an unspecified or uncertain term. An estate at will is a tenancy of indefinite duration; it continues until it is terminated by either party giving proper notice. No initial period of occupancy is specified, as is the case in a periodic tenancy. An estate at will is automatically terminated by the death of either the landlord or the tenant. It may be created by express agreement or by operation of law. During the existence of a tenancy at will, the tenant has all the rights and obligations of a lessor-lessee relationship, including the duty to pay rent at regular intervals. As a practical matter, tenancy at will is rarely used in a written agreement and is viewed skeptically by the courts.

IN PRACTICE

A landlord tells a tenant that two months after the end of the tenant's lease someone else will be moving into the apartment. The landlord gives the current tenant the option to continue to rent the unit until the new tenant is ready to move in. If the tenant agrees, an estate (tenancy) at will is created.

Estate at sufferance

Estate (tenancy) at sufferance:

- *Tenant's previously lawful possession continues without landlord's consent*

An **estate (tenancy) at sufferance** arises when a tenant who lawfully took possession of real property continues in possession of the premises without the landlord's consent after the right of possession has expired. This estate can arise when a tenant for years fails to surrender possession at the lease's expiration.

When a tenant fails to surrender possession, or *holds over*, the tenant is responsible for the payment of rent at the existing terms and rate. A lease may contain a holdover clause, in which case that provision will govern the rights of both the landlord and the tenant. If a lease does not contain such a clause, then state law will govern and will typically offer three options:

- The landlord can accept rent offered by the tenant, thereby creating a new tenancy under conditions of the original lease, a *holdover tenancy*. If the original lease term was greater than one year, generally the new tenancy is limited to one year.

- The landlord can treat the tenant as a *tenant at sufferance* by either objecting to the tenant holding over or informing the tenant of such treatment, thus creating a month-to-month or periodic tenancy. The landlord receives rent, and both parties have to provide notice within a certain period of terminating the arrangement.

- The landlord can treat the tenant as a trespasser and proceed with an eviction and damages action. Under this situation, the landlord must comply with the *notice to quit* requirements in the lease as well as state law regarding the landlord-tenant relationship.

LEASE AGREEMENTS

Most states require no special wording to establish the landlord-tenant relationship. The lease may be written, oral, or implied, depending on the circumstances and the requirements of the statute of frauds. The law of the state where the real estate is located must be followed to ensure the validity of the lease.

Requirements of a valid lease

A lease is a contract between the lessor (landlord) and the lessee (tenant). To be valid, a lease must meet the following requirements, which are essentially the same as in any other contract:

- *Capacity to contract.* The parties must have the legal capacity to contract; that is, be of legal age and sound mind.

- *Legal objective.* The objective of the lease must not be prohibited by any law.

- *Offer and acceptance.* Acceptance The parties must reach a mutual agreement (meeting of the minds) on all the terms of the contract.

- *Consideration.* The lease must be supported by valid consideration—an exchange of promises. The landlord promises to provide occupancy and the tenant promises to pay rent. Rent is typically monetary, although the tenant could provide agreed-upon labor in maintaining or fixing up the property. Because a lease is a contract, the rent and other terms may not be changed unless both parties agree to the changes in a writing that is executed in the same manner as the original lease.

The leased premises should be clearly described. For most residential leases, the street address or the street address and the apartment number is usually sufficient. If supplemental space is part of the rental, it should be clearly identified. If the lease covers land, such as a ground lease, then a legal description should be used. There should be no ambiguity.

Preprinted lease agreements are usually better suited to residential leases. Commercial leases are generally more complex, have different legal requirements, and may include complicated calculations of rent and maintenance costs. Drafting a commercial lease—or even a complex residential lease, for that matter—may constitute the practice of law. Unless the real estate professional is also an attorney, legal counsel should be sought.

IN PRACTICE

For a complex lease, the professional can use a two- or three-page form to facilitate a preliminary agreement on the basic terms of the lease, subject to approval of a final draft prepared by an attorney (usually, the attorney for the landlord). The final document would then require execution by both parties.

Possession of premises

The lessor, as the owner of the real estate, is usually bound by the *covenant of quiet enjoyment* that the lessee can occupy the premises without interference from the owner or anyone else. Quiet enjoyment does not have anything to do with barking dogs or late-night motorcycles. The lease usually stipulates the conditions under which the landlord may enter the property to perform maintenance, to make repairs, or for other stated purposes. Except in emergencies, adequate notice to the tenant is usually required, which may be stipulated in the lease or by state law.

Use of premises

A lessor may restrict a lessee's use of the premises through provisions included in the lease. For example, the property is leased only to the lessee "and shall be used strictly as a residence and for no other purpose." Use restrictions are particularly common in leases for stores or other commercial space. For example, a lease may provide that the leased premises are to be used only as a real estate office and for no other purpose. In the absence of such clear limitations, a lessee may use the premises for any lawful purpose.

Term of lease

The term of a lease—the period for which the lease will run—should be stated precisely, including the beginning and ending dates together with a statement of the total period of the lease. For instance, a lease might run "for a term of 30 years beginning June 1, 2018, and ending May 31, 2048." A perpetual lease for an inordinate amount of time or an indefinite term usually will be ruled invalid, but if the language of the lease and the surrounding circumstances clearly indicate that the parties intended such a term, the lease will be binding on the parties. Some states prohibit leases that run for 100 years or more.

Security deposit

Tenants are often required to provide a **security deposit**, which is held by the landlord during the lease term. The security deposit usually is available to the landlord if the tenant defaults on payment of rent or destroys the premises. Real estate professionals should be aware of state laws that govern security deposits: how they may be held, maximum amounts, whether interest must be paid, and how and when they are returned. To safeguard against nonpayment of rent, landlords may require an advance rental payment or a contract for a lien on the tenant's property or may require the tenant to have a third person guarantee payment.

IN PRACTICE

A lease should specify whether a payment is a security deposit or an advance on rent. If it is a security deposit, the tenant is usually not entitled to apply it to the final month's rent. If it is an advance on rent, the landlord must treat it as income for tax purposes.

Improvements

Neither the landlord nor the tenant is required to make any improvements to the leased property. The tenant may, however, make improvements with the landlord's permission or as required to make the rented premises accessible, as discussed in the next paragraph. In most residential properties, any alterations become the property of the landlord. In many commercial leases, however, the tenant is permitted to install and remove trade fixtures— those articles attached to a rental space that are required to conduct the tenant's business. Trade fixtures may be removed before the lease expires, provided the tenant restores the premises to the previous condition, with allowance for the wear and tear of normal use.

Accessibility

The federal Fair Housing Act makes it illegal to discriminate against a prospective tenant on the basis of the tenant's real or perceived disability. A tenant with a disability must be permitted to make reasonable modifications to a property at the tenant's own expense. If the modifications would interfere with a future tenant's use, the landlord may require that the premises be restored to their original condition at the end of the lease term. The Americans with Disabilities Act (ADA) will also affect a landlord's obligations when a commercial property or place of public accommodation is being leased. Updates of access issues and accessibility guidelines are provided by the United States Access Board, www.access-board.gov.

www.access-board.gov

Maintenance of premises

Most states require a lessor of residential property to maintain dwelling units in a habitable condition. The landlord must make any necessary repairs to common areas, such as hallways, stairs, and elevators, and maintain safety features, such as fire sprinklers, smoke alarms, and adequate lighting. Residential tenants do not have to make any repairs, but they must return the premises in the same condition they were received, with allowances for ordinary wear and tear. Lessees of commercial and industrial properties usually maintain the premises and are often responsible for making their own repairs.

Destruction of premises

The obligation to pay rent for damaged or destroyed premises differs depending on the type of property and the lease. Usually, residential tenants are permitted to reduce their rent payments in proportion to the amount of space they are unable to use. Likewise, tenants who lease only part of a building, such as office or commercial space, generally are not required to continue to pay rent after the leased premises are destroyed. In some states, if the property was destroyed as a result of the landlord's negligence, the tenant can recover damages.

On the other hand, tenants who have constructed buildings on leased land, often agricultural or industrial land, are still obligated for the payment of rent even if the improvements are damaged or destroyed. If the buildings are destroyed, tenants must turn to their property insurer for a covered loss.

Assignment and subleasing

In an **assignment** of a lease, a tenant transfers the entire leasehold interest to another person. The new tenant is legally obligated to comply with all of the promises the original tenant made in the lease.

Under a **sublease**, a tenant transfers less than the entire leasehold interest by *subletting* the premises to a new tenant. The original tenant remains responsible for rent being paid by the new tenant and for any damage done to the rental during the lease term. The new tenant is responsible only to the original tenant to pay the rent due. The sublessor's (original lessee's) interest in the real estate is known as a *sandwich lease*.

Assignment and subleasing are allowed only when a lease specifically permits them. In both an assignment and a sublease, details of the arrangement should be in writing. In most cases, the sublease or assignment of a lease does not relieve the original lessee of the obligation to pay rent. The landlord may, however, agree to waive the former tenant's liability. Most leases prohibit a lessee from assigning or subletting without the lessor's consent. This permits the lessor to retain control over the occupancy of the leased premises. As a rule, the lessor must not unreasonably withhold consent.

Online rental services have become very popular and have been used by both property owners and renters to make accommodations available on a short-term basis. More jurisdictions are placing restrictions on such rentals, which may be seen as a way to avoid the legal protections typically available to tenants, landlords, property owners, and neighbors who live in the same building or complex. Local governments may be concerned that the protections available to hotel guests are ignored. Some jurisdictions limit the term of such rentals, and some impose a minimum number of days (such as 31 days) that a property can be rented out.

Recording a lease

Anyone who inspects a leased property receives actual notice of the tenant's occupancy. For this reason, it is usually considered unnecessary to record a lease, although most states allow a lease to be recorded in the county in which the property is located. Furthermore, leases of three years or longer often are recorded as a matter of course. Some states require that a long-term lease be recorded, especially when the lessee intends to mortgage the leasehold interest.

A lease will typically run with the land; a change in the ownership of the leased fee estate doesn't affect the leasehold unless there is a provision in the lease providing for termination of an existing tenancy under specified circumstances or as provided by state law. Existing tenants usually have the right to remain in possession until the lease expires. A prospective buyer of property, especially an occupied single-family home, should inquire about the status of the occupants. The title records are searched for any recorded leases as part of the purchase transaction.

Nondisturbance clause

A **nondisturbance clause** is included in the financing instrument used to mortgage leased premises. By accepting this provision, the mortgagee agrees not to terminate the tenancy of the lessee(s), so long as the lessee is current in payment of the required rent, should the mortgagee foreclose on the mortgagor's building.

Options

A lease may contain a clause that grants the lessee the privilege of renewing the lease (called a **renewal option**). The lessee must, however, give notice of intent to exercise the option. Some leases grant the lessee the option to purchase the leased premises (called a **purchase option**). This option normally gives the tenant the right to purchase the property at a predetermined price within a certain period, possibly the lease term. The lease might also contain a **right of first refusal** that allows the tenant the opportunity to buy the property before the owner accepts an offer from another party. The lease option may stipulate that the tenant is to be given credit toward the purchase price for some percentage of the rent paid, as the parties negotiate.

IN PRACTICE

All the general statements concerning provisions of a lease are controlled largely by the terms of the agreement and state law. Landlord-tenant laws vary from state to state. Great care must be exercised in reading the entire lease document before signing it because every clause in the lease has an economic and legal impact on either the landlord or the tenant. Although preprinted lease forms are available, there is no such thing as a standard lease. When complicated lease situations arise, legal counsel should be sought.

TYPES OF LEASES

A lease can be characterized by the manner in which rent payments are determined as well as the type of property being leased. There are three basic forms of lease payments: the gross lease, the net lease, and the percentage lease. (See Figure 17.2.) A variable lease will combine one of these forms of payment with adjustments in the amount of rent to be paid.

Gross lease

In a **gross lease**, the tenant pays a fixed rent and some or all of the utility expenses, while the landlord pays all taxes, insurance, repairs, any other utility expenses, and maintenance connected with the property (usually called *property charges* or *operating expenses*). Residential and commercial office leases are most often gross leases.

IN PRACTICE

The landlord may pay for water, trash collection, and sewerage fees, while the tenant pays for items such as electricity, gas, and cable or other access to phone, television, and internet services.

Net lease

In a **net lease**, the tenant pays all or most of the property expenses, such as hazard insurance, property taxes, and/or common area maintenance (CAM) charges, in addition to the rent. The monthly rental is net income for the landlord after operating costs have been paid. Leases for entire commercial and industrial buildings and the land on which they are located, ground leases, and long-term leases are usually net leases.

Percentage lease

Either a gross lease or a net lease may be a **percentage lease**. This type of lease is generally used for retail business leases. The rent is based on a minimum fixed rental fee plus a percentage of the gross income received by the tenant doing business on the leased property. The percentage charged is negotiable and varies depending on the nature of the business, location of the property, and general economic conditions.

FIGURE 17.2: Types of Leases

Type of Lease	Lessor	Lessee
Gross lease	Pays property charges (taxes, repairs, insurance, maintenance, some or all utilities)	Pays basic rent plus some utility costs
Net lease	May pay some property charges	Pays basic rent plus all or most property charges
Percentage lease (commercial and industrial)	Often pays property charges (taxes, repairs, insurance, maintenance, some utilities)	Pays basic rent plus percentage of gross sales (may pay property costs, such as utilities)

Variable lease

A lease may allow for increases in the rental charges during the lease term. A *graduated lease* provides for specified rent increases at set future dates. An *index lease* allows rent to be increased or decreased periodically based on changes in the consumer price index or some other indicator.

Other types of leases

Ground lease

When a landowner leases unimproved land to a tenant who agrees to erect a building on the land, the lease is usually called a **ground lease**. It is most often used in commercial and industrial property development. Ground leases typically involve separate ownership of the land and the buildings. These leases must be long enough to make the transaction desirable to the tenant investing in the building. They often run for terms of 50 to 99 years.

Ground leases are generally *net leases*: the lessee must pay rent on the ground, as well as real estate taxes, insurance, upkeep, utilities, and repairs. At the end of the lease term, any tenant-built structures on the property usually become the property of the landlord.

Oil and gas lease

When an oil company leases land to explore for oil and gas, a special lease agreement must be negotiated. Except for enough surface space to conduct extraction operations, the lease covers subsurface rights. Usually, the landowner receives a cash payment for executing the lease. If no well is drilled within the period stated in the lease, the lease expires, although most oil and gas leases permit the oil company to continue its rights for another year by paying another flat rental fee. Such rentals may be paid annually until a well is produced. If oil or gas is found, the landowner usually receives a percentage of its value as a royalty. As long as oil or gas is obtained in significant quantities, the lease continues indefinitely. Oil and gas leases, even after they have expired, are often listed as exclusions in title insurance policies.

Lease purchase

A **lease purchase** is used when a tenant wants to purchase the property but is not yet able to do so. Perhaps the tenant cannot obtain favorable financing or clear title, or the tax consequences of a purchase are currently unfavorable. The terms of the sale are negotiated and agreed to at the time that the lease is signed. A down payment is paid, which may or may not be refundable, and part of the periodic rent may be applied toward the purchase price of the property. Both parties hope that, by the time the lease expires, the tenant's issues have been resolved and financing can be obtained or the tenant can purchase the property outright.

Sale-and-leaseback

In a **sale-and-leaseback**, the property owners sell the property and then lease it back for an agreed period and rental. The original owners pull out their equity to use on other projects and are also able to reduce their taxable income when they pay rent to the new owner. The new owner has a reliable source of rental income for an extended time.

IN PRACTICE

The sale-and-leaseback is often used by a company that owns its own office building but is in need of capital, perhaps for business expansion. The building can be sold to obtain funds, but the company will be allowed to remain in the building as a tenant and pay rent to the new owners.

DISCHARGE OF A LEASE

As with any contract, a lease is discharged when the contract terminates. Termination can occur either when all parties have fully performed their obligations under the agreement, or when the parties agree to cancel the lease. If the tenant, for instance, offers to surrender the leasehold interest, and if the landlord accepts the tenant's offer, the lease is terminated. A tenant who simply abandons leased property, however, remains liable for the terms of the lease—including the rent. The terms of the lease will usually indicate whether the landlord is obligated to try to re-rent the space. If the landlord intends to sue for unpaid rent, however, most states require an attempt to mitigate damages by re-renting the premises to limit the amount owed.

The lease does not terminate if the parties die or if the property is sold. There are two exceptions to this general rule. First, a lease from the owner of a life estate ends with the death of the person on whose life the estate is measured. Second, the death of either party terminates a tenancy at will. In all other cases, the heirs of a deceased landlord are bound by the terms of existing valid leases.

If leased real estate is sold or otherwise conveyed, the new landlord takes the property subject to the rights of the tenants. A lease agreement may contain language that permits a new landlord to terminate existing leases, although this is much more common in commercial properties than in residential properties. The clause, known as a *sale clause*, requires that the tenant be given some period of notice before the termination. Because the new owner takes title subject to the rights of the tenant, the sale clause enables the new landlord to claim possession and negotiate a new lease under new terms and conditions.

A tenancy may also be terminated by operation of law, as in a bankruptcy, foreclosure, or condemnation proceeding in an eminent domain action.

Breach of lease

When a tenant breaches (violates) any lease provision, the landlord may sue the tenant to obtain a judgment to cover past-due rent, damages to the premises, or other defaults. Likewise, when a landlord breaches any lease provision, the tenant is entitled to certain remedies. The rights and responsibilities of the landlord-tenant relationship are governed by state law.

Suit for possession—actual eviction

When a tenant breaches a lease or improperly retains leased premises, the landlord may regain possession through a legal process known as **actual eviction**. The landlord must serve notice on the tenant before commencing the lawsuit. Most lease terms require at least a 10-day notice in the case of default. In many states, however, only a five-day or three-day notice is necessary when the tenant defaults in the payment of rent. When a court issues a judgment for possession to a landlord, the tenant must vacate the property. If the tenant fails to leave, the landlord can have the judgment enforced by a court officer, who forcibly removes the tenant and the tenant's possessions. The landlord then has the right to re-enter and regain possession of the property. In some states, in cases of nonpayment of rent, a landlord also has the right to *distrain*, that is, to seize the tenant's property for rent in arrears, generally by changing the locks and giving notice. Most states require a court order to pursue the remedy of *distraint*.

Tenants' remedies—constructive eviction

If a landlord breaches any clause of a lease agreement, the tenant has the right to sue and recover damages against the landlord. If the leased premises become unusable for the purpose stated in the lease, the tenant may have the right to abandon them. This action, called **constructive eviction**, terminates the lease agreement. The tenant must prove that the premises have become unusable because of the conscious neglect of the landlord. To claim constructive eviction, the tenant must leave the premises while the conditions that made the premises uninhabitable exist.

FOR EXAMPLE

A tenant's lease requires that the landlord furnish heat. The landlord fails to repair a defective furnace, and no heat is provided to the tenant's apartment during the winter months. The tenant is forced to abandon the apartment. Because the lack of heat was due to the landlord's negligence, the tenant has been constructively evicted.

Protenant legislation

For the most part, leases are drawn up primarily for the benefit of the landlord. Due to tenants' rights movements and increased consumer awareness, however, most states have adopted all or part of the Uniform Residential Landlord and Tenant Act that was created in 1972, amended slightly in 1974, and updated in 2015, by what is now the National Conference of Commissioners on Uniform State Laws, www.uniformlaws.org. The model law addresses the need for both parties to a lease to fulfill certain basic obligations. The act addresses such issues as

www.uniformlaws.org

- the landlord's right of entry,
- maintenance of the premises,
- the tenant's protection against retaliation by the landlord for complaints,
- the disclosure of the property owner's name and address to the tenant, and
- specific remedies available to both the landlord and the tenant if a breach of the lease agreement occurs.

The law's revisions cover security deposits, disposition of tenant property, and lease termination in a situation involving domestic violence or sexual assault.

Fair housing and civil rights laws

The federal fair housing and civil right laws that were previously covered affect landlords and tenants just as they do sellers and purchasers. All persons must have access to housing of their choice without any differentiation in terms and conditions based on race, color, religion, national origin, sex, disability, or familial status. State and local municipalities have their own fair housing laws that add protected classes such as age and sexual orientation. Withholding an apartment that is available for rent, segregating certain people in separate sections of an apartment complex or parts of a building, and charging people in the protected classes different amounts for rent or security deposits all constitute violations of the law.

IN PRACTICE

The fair housing laws require that the same tenant criteria be applied to families with children that are applied to adults. A landlord cannot charge a different amount of rent or security deposit because one of the tenants is a child. While landlords have historically argued that children are noisy and destructive, the fact is that many adults are also noisy and destructive.

It is important to remember that a violation of federal or state fair housing laws can occur even without deliberate intent to discriminate—and even if a prospective tenant asks for the kind of assistance that would make a real estate professional guilty of discrimination.

IN PRACTICE

The Manero family from Thailand moved to Oakton and contacted a real estate professional for assistance in finding a rental property. The real estate professional asked a number of questions to determine what kind of housing the family sought, their budget, and what part of town they preferred. Mrs. Manero insisted that she wanted to live in a part of town that they had heard about where a number of Thai families lived. She asked the real estate professional to find them a house in that part of town. The real estate professional complied but was subsequently disciplined by the state's real estate licensing agency and also fined by the fair housing division of the state's attorney general's office. The real estate professional learned, the hard way, that he should have informed the Maneros that he could show them properties in any part of town they requested that were within their budget but could not direct them to a neighborhood based on the nationality of the residents.

KEY POINT REVIEW

A **lease** is a contract between the **lessor** (the owner of real estate, also called the **landlord**) and the **lessee** (the **tenant**) that transfers possession and use of the property, lasts for a specified period, and is made in return for consideration (possession and payment).

The **statute of frauds** in most states requires that leases for more than one year be **in writing to be enforceable**. The lessor has a **reversionary right** to possession of property when a lease expires.

The **leasehold estate** of the lessee can be one of the following:

■ An **estate for years (tenancy for years)** continues for a definite period. A **holdover tenancy** may be created when a tenant with an estate for years stays on after the lease term expires and the landlord accepts rent payment.

■ An **estate from period to period (periodic tenancy)** has no specific expiration date, but rent is payable at definite intervals and the lease term has continuity because it automatically renews. A **month-to-month tenancy** is a common form of residential lease.

■ An **estate at will (tenancy at will)** has no specified initial term, is created by **express agreement** or **operation of law**, and can be **terminated** by the landlord or the tenant at any time on proper notice.

■ An **estate at sufferance (tenancy at sufferance)** is created when the tenant stays on without the landlord's consent after termination. The landlord's acceptance of rent creates a holdover tenancy, or the landlord can treat the tenant as a trespasser and begin eviction proceedings and an action for damages under state law.

A **valid lease** requires parties with **CLOAC** (**C**apacity to contract, **L**egal objective, **O**ffer and **A**cceptance, and valid **C**onsideration). A lease typically includes a **description** of leased premises, implied **covenant of quiet enjoyment** and a **nondisturbance clause**, limitations on tenant's **use** of the property and the **term** (length) of the lease, **security deposit** that must comply with state law, and a statement as to whether **improvements** may be made by the tenant.

Fixtures installed by a tenant generally become the landlord's property unless they are removable **trade fixtures**. Federal fair housing law requires the landlord to allow a tenant with a disability to make **reasonable modifications** to the premises. The **Americans with Disabilities Act (ADA)** requires that commercial nonresidential property be free of barriers or that reasonable accommodations be provided.

A typical lease will also include a provision that **maintenance** of premises will be performed by the landlord in compliance with state law; whether or not an **assignment** of the lease will be permitted, and if so, whether the assignment will relieve the tenant of further obligation to the landlord; and whether or not a **sublease** will be permitted and under what terms. **Recording** of the lease may be required by state law. An **option** may give the tenant the right to renew the lease, the right to purchase the leased property, or the right of first refusal if the landlord decides to sell the property.

A **gross lease** requires the tenant to pay rent and the landlord to pay the expenses of ownership, such as taxes, insurance, and maintenance. A **net lease** requires the tenant to pay rent plus all or most property expenses, with the landlord also paying some property expenses. In a **percentage lease**, the tenant pays rent plus a percentage of gross sales and may pay property expenses.

A **variable lease** allows an increase in rent during the lease period. A **graduated lease** states specific rent increases. An **index lease** allows rent changes (up or down) based on the consumer price index or other indicator.

A **ground lease** involves separate ownership of land and buildings. An **oil and gas lease** allows exploration for and removal of oil and gas. In a **lease purchase**, part of the rent may be applied to the purchase price. A **sale-and-leaseback** allows the original owner to use the property as a tenant while freeing up capital for other business purposes.

The remedies for **breach** of a lease are governed by state law. The landlord may bring **suit for possession** (actual eviction), or the tenant may claim a **constructive eviction** if the premises are uninhabitable.

The **Uniform Residential Landlord and Tenant Act** has been adopted by many states in whole or in part and was updated in 2015.

Federal fair housing and **civil right laws** affect landlords and tenants just as they do sellers and purchasers.

UNIT 17 QUIZ

1. Which transaction is *BEST* described as involving a ground lease?
   A. A landowner agrees to let a tenant drill for oil on a property for 75 years.
   B. The tenant agrees to pay a proportionate, increased rental based on annual appraisals of the rented property.
   C. A landlord charges a commercial tenant separate amounts for the land and the leased building.
   D. The tenant pays a base amount for the property plus a percentage of business-generated income.

2. A tenant enters into a commercial lease that requires a monthly rent of a minimum fixed amount, plus an additional amount determined by the tenant's gross receipts exceeding $5,000. This type of lease is called
   A. a standard lease.
   B. a gross lease.
   C. a percentage lease.
   D. a net lease.

3. If a tenant moved out of a rented store building because access to the building was blocked as a result of the landlord's negligence,
   A. the tenant would have no legal recourse against the landlord.
   B. the landlord may be liable for the rent until the expiration date of the lease.
   C. the landlord may have to provide substitute space.
   D. the tenant may be entitled to recover damages from the landlord.

4. A tenant moves a pet into an apartment community that has a no-pets policy. The landlord wishes to remove the tenant due to the breach. The legal process to remove a tenant is known as
   A. constructive eviction.
   B. eminent domain.
   C. actual eviction.
   D. partial eviction.

5. A tenant still has five months remaining on a one-year apartment lease. When the tenant moves to another city, the tenant transfers possession of the apartment to a friend for the entire remaining term of the lease. The friend pays rent directly to the tenant. In this situation, the tenant has become
   A. an assignor.
   B. a sublessor.
   C. a sublessee.
   D. a lessor.

6. A tenancy is which the tenant continues in possession after the lease has expired, without the landlord's permission is
   A. a tenancy for years.
   B. a periodic tenancy.
   C. a tenancy at will.
   D. an estate at sufferance.

7. A tenant's tenancy for years will expire in two weeks. The tenant plans to move to a larger apartment across town when the current tenancy expires. In order to terminate this agreement, the tenant must
   A. give the landlord immediate notice or the lease will automatically renew.
   B. give the landlord one week's prior notice or the lease will automatically renew.
   C. do nothing because the agreement will terminate automatically at the end of the current term.
   D. sign a lease for the new apartment, which will automatically terminate the existing lease.

8. When a tenant holds possession of a landlord's property without a current lease agreement and without the landlord's approval,
   A. the tenant is maintaining a gross lease.
   B. the landlord can file suit for possession.
   C. the tenant has no obligation to pay rent.
   D. the landlord may be subject to a constructive eviction.

9. Under the negotiated terms of a commercial lease, the landlord is required to maintain the water heater used in a health club. If the tenant is unable to get hot water because of a faulty water heater that the landlord has failed to repair after repeated notification, the tenant could do all of the following *EXCEPT*
   A. sue the landlord for damages.
   B. order a new water heater and deduct the payment from the rent.
   C. abandon the premises claiming constructive eviction.
   D. terminate the lease agreement.

10. A lessee has a one-year leasehold interest in a house. The lease automatically renews itself at the end of each year. The lessee's interest is referred to as a tenancy
    A. for years.
    B. from period to period.
    C. at will.
    D. at sufferance.

11. Rent would *BEST* be described as
    A. contractual consideration to a third party.
    B. consideration for the use of real property.
    C. all monies paid by the lessor to the lessee.
    D. the total balance owed under the terms of a lease.

12. Under the terms of a net lease, a commercial tenant would usually be responsible for paying all of the following property expenses *EXCEPT*
    A. mortgage debt service.
    B. maintenance expenses.
    C. fire and extended coverage insurance.
    D. real estate taxes.

13. Which of the following describes a net lease?
    A. An agreement in which the tenant pays a fixed rent and the landlord pays all taxes, insurance, and expenses related to the property
    B. A lease in which the tenant pays rent, plus some—or most—of the operating expenses related to the property
    C. A lease in which the tenant pays the landlord a percentage of the monthly income derived from the property
    D. An agreement granting an individual a leasehold interest in fishing rights for a shoreline property

14. A tenancy in which the tenant continues in possession after the lease has expired, without the landlord's permission, is
    A. a tenancy for years.
    B. a periodic tenancy.
    C. a tenancy at will.
    D. a tenancy at sufferance.

15. A tenant's right to possess real estate for a definite period with a specific starting and ending date is
    A. an estate for years.
    B. an estate at will.
    C. an estate at sufferance.
    D. an estate from period to period.

16. Which of the following describes a gross lease?
    A. An agreement in which the tenant pays a fixed rent and some or all of the utilities and the landlord pays all taxes, insurance, and expenses related to the property
    B. A lease in which the tenant pays rent plus some of the operating expenses related to the property
    C. A lease in which the tenant pays the landlord a percentage of the monthly income derived from the property
    D. An agreement allowing the tenant to terminate the lease if certain conditions near the premises become unbearable

17. A tenant signs a lease that includes a schedule of rent increases on specific dates over the course of the lease term. What kind of lease has this tenant signed?
    A. Percentage
    B. Net
    C. Graduated
    D. Index

18. A tenant signs a lease that includes the following clause: "The stated rent under this agreement will be increased or decreased every three months based on the percentage change in the consumer price index (CPI) for that period." What kind of lease has this tenant signed?
    A. Percentage
    B. Net
    C. Graduated
    D. Index

19. The death of either the landlord or the tenant will terminate the lease and the parties' heirs will *NOT* be bound by its terms under which of the following tenancies?
    A. Tenancy for years
    B. Periodic tenancy
    C. Tenancy at will
    D. Tenancy at sufferance

20. The tenant leases a heated apartment during a bitterly cold winter, but soon after the tenant moves in, the landlord fails to provide heat because of a defective central heating unit. The tenant vacates the premises and refuses to pay any rent. This is an example of
    A. abandonment.
    B. actual eviction.
    C. constructive eviction.
    D. lessor negligence.

UNIT
18

Fair Housing

LEARNING OBJECTIVES

When you have completed this unit, you will be able to

> **explain** the significance of the Civil Rights Act of 1866 to equal opportunity in housing;
> **describe** the various federal laws which protect Americans from unfair housing practices;
> **describe** blockbusting, steering, redlining, and other abusive housing practices;
> **list** the various recourses available to the aggrieved person who believes illegal discrimination has occurred including acts of real estate professionals; and
> **describe** the importance to real estate professionals and the public of understanding and complying with fair housing laws.

KEY TERMS

administrative law judge (ALJ)
Americans with Disabilities Act (ADA)
blockbusting
Civil Rights Act of 1866
conciliation

Department of Housing and Urban Development (HUD)
Fair Housing Act
Fair Housing Amendments Act
Housing for Older Persons Act (HOPA)

redlining
steering
Title VIII of the Civil Rights Act of 1968

OVERVIEW

Real estate professionals and their clients and customers reflect the wide diversity of America's population. The ability to buy or rent adequate housing allows an individual or family to achieve and maintain a satisfying lifestyle. Housing discrimination takes its toll on its immediate victims, and it also reflects poorly on the society that allows it to exist. In short, when legal action is required to correct abuses, the end result benefits all. Understanding and working within the context of fair housing laws is critical to creating and maintaining a vibrant and ultimately profitable real estate market for everyone. We will examine the history of federal fair housing executive, legislative, and judicial actions, but states and local jurisdictions may provide even greater recognition of opportunities to work against the many forms of discrimination. Later, we will also consider the fair lending practices that help make financing available for home purchasers on an equitable basis.

EQUAL OPPORTUNITY IN HOUSING

The civil rights laws that affect the real estate industry recognize the importance of having the opportunity to live where one chooses. Federal, state, and local fair housing or equal opportunity laws affect every phase of a real estate transaction, from listing to closing. Together, they help ensure that housing is not denied on the basis of an individual's race, nationality, religion, or other characteristic specified in federal, state, or local law.

While the passage of laws may establish a code for public conduct, centuries of discriminatory practices and attitudes, reinforced by public and private conduct, are not so easily changed. Just as real estate professionals must not allow their own prejudices to interfere with the ethical and legal conduct of their profession, they must not allow discriminatory attitudes of property owners or property seekers to affect compliance with fair housing laws. Complying with fair housing laws is not always easy because it requires thoughtful consideration of both one's own actions and those of others. In addition to obeying the law and "doing the right thing," it is important to remember that failure to comply with fair housing laws not only subjects a real estate professional to both civil and criminal penalties but also constitutes grounds for disciplinary action by the licensing authority.

IN PRACTICE

Real estate professionals must have a thorough knowledge of federal, state, and local fair housing laws. State and local laws may be broader than the federal requirements by providing protections for more classes of persons and may be applicable to all real property transactions, not just the residential transactions that are the focus of federal law. State and local licensing rules may provide for fines, and state penalties may include suspension or revocation of an offender's license for violation of any fair housing law.

The Civil Rights Act of 1866

The federal government's effort to end discrimination in the provision of housing began with the passage of the **Civil Rights Act of 1866**. The law prohibits discrimination based on race in every property transaction but was largely ignored.

Housing was not the only area subject to discrimination. The U.S. Supreme Court's 1896 decision in *Plessy v. Ferguson*, which involved segregated railway cars, upheld racial segregation in public facilities—the "separate but equal" doctrine. It would be a long time before that injustice was corrected. President Franklin Delano Roosevelt signed Executive Order 8802 on June 25, 1941, prohibiting racial discrimination in the national defense industry. President Harry S. Truman signed Executive Order 9981 on June 26, 1948, ending racial discrimination in the U.S. armed forces.

In 1954, *Plessy* was overturned by the U.S. Supreme Court's decision in *Brown v. Board of Education*, which held that separate schools for black and white students were inherently unconstitutional. On September 9, 1957, President Dwight D. Eisenhower signed into law the Civil Rights Act of 1957, which authorized the Attorney General to seek federal injunctions to protect the voting rights of African Americans. Finally, in 1968, the Supreme Court, in *Jones v. Mayer*, held that there was a constitutional basis for the Civil Rights Act of 1866 in the 13th Amendment to the U.S. Constitution, which prohibits slavery. It is now recognized that the 1866 law prohibits all racial discrimination in the sale or rental of publicly or privately held property, without exception, whether facilitated by a real estate professional or sold or rented by the owner. Where race is involved, no exceptions apply.

In subsequent cases, the U.S. Supreme Court has expanded the definition of the term *race* to include ancestral and ethnic characteristics, including certain physical, cultural, or linguistic traits that are shared by a group with a common national origin. These rulings are significant because discrimination on the basis of race, as it is now defined, allows a complaint to be brought under the provisions of the Civil Rights Act of 1866.

IN PRACTICE

A real estate professional is not obligated to provide ethnic-diversity information to homebuyers. At issue in a 2001 case from Ohio, *Hannah v. Sibcy Cline Realtors*, was whether a real estate professional had the fiduciary duty to (1) inform a client whether a neighborhood was ethnically diverse or (2) direct the client to resources that provided such information. The court concluded that while real estate professionals might choose to provide such information to clients or direct clients to resources about the ethnic diversity of a particular area, the real estate professionals do so at their own risk and there is no fiduciary duty to do so. The risk, of course, is that the real estate professional might be accused of illegally steering a client to a particular neighborhood based on the racial, ethnic, or other protected characteristics of its residents. Steering is discussed in more detail later.

The 1866 Civil Rights Act applies only to racial discrimination, but 1968 also saw passage of a federal law that prohibits specific discriminatory practices throughout the real estate industry.

FAIR HOUSING ACT

Title VIII of the Civil Rights Act of 1968, signed into law by President Lyndon B. Johnson on April 11 of that year, was amended by the Housing and Community Development Act of 1974 and the **Fair Housing Amendments Act** of 1988, and is known as the **Fair Housing Act**. It prohibits discrimination in housing based on

The Fair Housing Act prohibits discrimination based on
■ race, color,
■ national origin,
■ religion,
■ sex,
■ familial status, or
■ disability.

- ■ race,
- ■ color,
- ■ national origin,
- ■ religion,
- ■ sex,
- ■ familial status, or
- ■ disability.

The Fair Housing Act also prohibits discrimination against individuals because of their association with persons in the protected classes.

The Fair Housing Act originally prohibited discrimination based on race, color, religion, or national origin. The Housing and Community Development Act added sex to the list of protected classes, and the Fair Housing Amendments Act added disability and familial status (i.e., households with children), although an exception was made for certain housing intended for persons age 55 or older. The amended act also changed the penalties for violations of the law, making them more severe, and added the right to seek damages, such as those for noneconomic injuries (humiliation, embarrassment, inconvenience, and mental anguish).

Unit 18

In 1995, Congress passed the **Housing for Older Persons Act (HOPA)**, which repealed the requirement that housing intended for those age 55 or older have "significant facilities and services" designed for seniors. HOPA still requires that at least 80% of occupied units have one person age 55 or older living in them. The act prohibits the awarding of monetary damages against those who, in good faith, reasonably believed that property designated as housing for older persons was exempt from familial status provisions of the Fair Housing Act.

The Fair Housing Act is administered by the **Department of Housing and Urban Development (HUD)**, and information on fair housing can be found by going to www.hud .gov and entering "fair housing" in the search box at the top of the page. HUD has established rules and regulations that further interpret the practices affected by the law. In addition, HUD distributes an equal housing opportunity poster, available at www.hud.gov. (See Figure 18.1.) The poster declares that the office in which it is displayed promises to adhere to the Fair Housing Act and pledges support for affirmative marketing and advertising programs.

www.hud.gov

IN PRACTICE

When HUD investigates a real estate broker for discriminatory practices, it may consider failure to prominently display the equal housing opportunity poster in the broker's place of business as evidence of discrimination. If a real estate brokerage is accused of a fair housing violation and has not displayed the poster, the burden of proof may shift from the complainant (the party alleging discrimination) to the broker. This means that the broker would have to prove that there had been no act of discrimination rather than the complainant proving that there had been an act of discrimination.

Definitions

HUD's regulations provide specific definitions that clarify the scope of the Fair Housing Act.

Dwelling

The regulations define a *dwelling* as any building or part of a building designed for occupancy as a residence by one or more families. This includes a single-family house, a condominium, a cooperative, and manufactured or other factory-built housing, as well as vacant land on which any of these structures will be built.

Family/familial status

A family can be as small as a single individual. *Familial status* is defined as one or more individuals under age 18 living with a parent or guardian. It also includes a woman who is pregnant and anyone who is in the process of assuming custody of a child under age 18. Housing that qualifies for older people is exempt. Otherwise, single or multifamily housing must be made available to families with children under the same terms and conditions applied to anyone else. It is illegal to advertise properties as being for adults only or to indicate a preference for a certain number of children. Landlords and condominiums/cooperatives cannot restrict the number of occupants with the intent of eliminating families with children. Any occupancy standards must be based on objective factors, such as sanitation or safety.

FIGURE 18.1: Equal Opportunity Housing Poster

U. S. Department of Housing and Urban Development

**EQUAL HOUSING
OPPORTUNITY**

**We Do Business in Accordance With the Federal Fair
Housing Law**

(The Fair Housing Amendments Act of 1988)

It is Illegal to Discriminate Against Any Person Because of Race, Color, Religion, Sex, Handicap, Familial Status, or National Origin

---

In the sale or rental of housing or residential lots

In advertising the sale or rental of housing

In the financing of housing

In the provision of real estate brokerage services

In the appraisal of housing

Blockbusting is also illegal

**Anyone who feels he or she has been
discriminated against may file a complaint of
housing discrimination:**
     1-800-669-9777 (Toll Free)
     1-800-927-9275 (TTY)
     www.hud.gov/fairhousing

**U.S. Department of Housing and
Urban Development
Assistant Secretary for Fair Housing and
Equal Opportunity
Washington, D.C. 20410**

Previous editions are obsolete

form HUD-928.1 (8/2011)

Unit 18

IN PRACTICE

An elderly tenant was terminally ill and requested that no children be allowed in the vacant apartment next door because the children's noise would make the situation more difficult. The owner of the apartment building agreed and refused to rent that unit to families with children. Although the intent was to make things easier for a dying tenant, the owner was nonetheless found to have violated the Fair Housing Act by discriminating on the basis of familial status.

Disability

A *disability* is included in the Fair Housing Act as a *handicap*, although the word *disability* is now the preferred term. A disability is a physical or mental impairment that substantially limits one or more of a person's major life activities and includes having a record of having such an impairment, or being regarded as having such an impairment, even if one does not exist. It is unlawful to discriminate against prospective buyers or tenants on the basis of disability. Persons who have AIDS are protected by fair housing laws under this classification. The classification does not include current, illegal use of, or addiction to, a controlled substance, as defined in the Controlled Substances Act.

IN PRACTICE

Just as the federal Fair Housing Act's protection of persons with a disability does not include those who are current users of illegal or controlled substances, it also does not extend to individuals who have been convicted of the illegal manufacture or distribution of a controlled substance. The law does prohibit discrimination against those who are participating in addiction recovery programs; for instance, a landlord could lawfully discriminate against a cocaine addict but not against someone who is in a drug recovery program.

Landlords must make reasonable accommodations to existing policies, practices, or services to permit persons with disabilities to have equal enjoyment of the premises. It would be reasonable to expect a landlord to permit a support animal (such as a guide dog) in a normally no-pets building or to provide a designated parking space in a generally unreserved lot for a person with a disability.

People with disabilities must be permitted to make necessary, reasonable modifications to the premises at their own expense. Such modifications might include lowering door handles or installing bath rails to accommodate a person in a wheelchair. Failure to permit reasonable modification constitutes illegal discrimination.

The law recognizes that some reasonable modifications might make a rental property undesirable to the general population. In such a case, the landlord is allowed to require that the property be restored to its previous condition when the lease period ends, aside from reasonable wear and tear. Where it is necessary to ensure with reasonable certainty that funds will be available to pay for the restorations at the end of the tenancy, the landlord may negotiate, as part of a restoration agreement, a provision requiring that the tenant pay into an interest-bearing escrow account, over a reasonable period, a reasonable amount of money not to exceed the cost of the restorations. The interest in the account accrues to the benefit of the tenant. A landlord may not increase the required security deposit for a person with a disability, however.

The law does not prohibit restricting occupancy exclusively to persons with a disability in dwellings that are designed specifically for their accommodation.

In newly constructed multifamily buildings with an elevator and four or more units, the public and common areas must be accessible to persons with a disability, and doors and hallways must be wide enough for wheelchairs. The entrance to each unit must be accessible, as well as the light switches, electrical outlets, thermostats, and other environmental controls. A person using a wheelchair should be able to use the kitchen and bathroom; bathroom walls should be reinforced to accommodate later installation of grab bars. Ground-floor units must meet these requirements in buildings that do not have an elevator. Real estate professionals should be aware that state and local laws may have stricter standards.

Exemptions to the Fair Housing Act

The federal Fair Housing Act covers most housing but does exempt

- owner-occupied buildings with no more than four units,
- single-family housing sold or rented without the use of a real estate professional, and
- housing operated by organizations and private clubs that limit occupancy to members.

The rental of rooms or units in an owner-occupied building of no more than four units is exempt from the Fair Housing Act.

The sale or rental of a single-family home is exempt from the Fair Housing Act when the transaction meets all of the following conditions:

- The home is owned by an individual who does not own more than three such homes at one time (and who does not sell more than one every two years).
- A real estate professional is <u>not</u> involved in the transaction.
- Discriminatory advertising is not used.

Housing owned by a religious organization may be restricted to people of the same religion if membership in the organization is not restricted on the basis of race, color, or national origin. A private club that is not open to the public may restrict the rental or occupancy of lodgings that it owns to its members, as long as the lodgings are not operated commercially. Membership in a private club must be open to people of all races, colors, and national origins.

IN PRACTICE

The Metropolitan Club accepts members who have graduated from Grandiose University, a private institution. At its building in downtown Metropolis, the club has some sleeping rooms that it makes available to members at a nominal cost for no more than a one-week stay every year. Because the rooms are provided as a member convenience and not operated as a commercial venture, their use can be limited to members of the Metropolitan Club.

The Fair Housing Act does not require that housing be made available to an individual whose tenancy would constitute a direct threat to the health or safety of other individuals or would result in substantial physical damage to the property of others.

Housing for older persons

As mentioned earlier, while the Fair Housing Act protects families with children, the Housing for Older Persons Act (HOPA) provides that certain properties can be restricted to occupancy by older persons. Housing intended for persons age 62 or older or housing occupied by at least one person 55 years of age or older per unit (where 80% of the units are occupied by individuals 55 or older) is exempt from the familial status protection. Such "senior housing" typically will allow temporary occupancy by younger visitors, such as permitting overnight visits for up to two weeks per year.

Americans with Disabilities Act

Although the **Americans with Disabilities Act (ADA)** is not a housing law, it still has a significant effect on the real estate industry. ADA requires reasonable accommodations in employment and access to goods, services, and public buildings. The law is important because real estate professionals are often employers, and their offices are public spaces. ADA's goal is to enable individuals with disabilities to become part of the economic and social mainstream of society. Information can be found online at www.ada.gov.

www.ada.gov

Title I of ADA requires that employers, including real estate professionals, make reasonable accommodations that enable an individual with a disability to perform essential job functions. Reasonable accommodations include making the work site accessible, restructuring a job, providing part-time or flexible work schedules, and modifying equipment that is used on the job. The provisions of the ADA apply to any employer with 15 or more employees.

Title III of ADA requires that individuals with disabilities have full accessibility to businesses, goods, and public services. As a result, building owners and managers of commercial spaces must be constantly alert to ensure that obstacles are removed. The Americans with Disabilities Act Accessibility Guidelines (ADAAG) contain detailed specifications for designing parking spaces, curb ramps, elevators, drinking fountains, toilet facilities, and directional signs to ensure maximum accessibility. Unless a real estate professional is a qualified ADA expert, it is best to advise commercial clients to seek the services of an attorney, an architect, or a consultant who specializes in ADA issues.

IN PRACTICE

In 1999, the U.S. Supreme Court strictly limited the definition of *persons with disabilities* protected by the ADA. As a result, ADA excludes individuals whose disability, such as nearsightedness, can be corrected. In 2002, the U.S. Supreme Court narrowed the definition even further by stating that in determining whether a person has a disability, you may ask whether the impairment prevents or restricts the person from performing tasks that are ordinarily of central importance to daily life.

ADA and the Fair Housing Act

ADA exempts from its requirements:

■ property that is covered by the Fair Housing Act, which already prohibits discrimination on the basis of disability, and

■ property that is exempt from coverage by the Fair Housing Act, such as housing for those age 55 or older.

Some properties are subject to both laws. For example, in an apartment complex, the rental office is a place of public accommodation. As such, it is covered by ADA and must be accessible to persons with a disability at the owner's expense. Individual rental units would be covered by the Fair Housing Act. A tenant who wished to modify the unit to make it accessible would be responsible for the cost.

Issues of housing and disability discrimination are often litigated in the courts. For example, in *Wells v. State Manufactured Homes,* a 2005 case before the U.S. District Court, District of Maine, the landlord ordered the owner of a manufactured housing unit to move from the community because he claimed she violated the no-pets provision of her rental agreement. The landlord refused to make a reasonable accommodation for the owner's emotional disability by permitting her to keep a dog. She filed suit under the ADA and Fair Housing Act. The court held that there was no violation of the Fair Housing Act or the ADA. The court said she failed to establish that her mental impairment substantially limited a major life activity and so did not meet the definition of a disability under ADA.

IN PRACTICE

Real estate professionals need a general knowledge of ADA's provisions in dealing with clients and customers. It is necessary for a real estate broker's workplace and employment policies to comply with the law. Amendments to ADA are periodically introduced in the U.S. Congress, and it is important to be aware of changes in the law. Real estate professionals who are building managers must ensure that the properties managed are legally accessible. ADA compliance questions also may arise with regard to a client's property listed for sale or lease. Unless the real estate professional is a qualified ADA expert, it is best to advise commercial clients to seek the services of an attorney, architect, or consultant who specializes in ADA issues.

FAIR HOUSING ISSUES

For fair housing and other civil rights laws to accomplish their goal of prohibiting discrimination, real estate professionals must apply them routinely. Compliance also means that real estate professionals avoid violating not only the law but also the ethical standards of the profession. The following discussion examines legal and ethical issues that continue to confront real estate professionals.

Blockbusting

Blockbusting is the act of encouraging people to sell or rent their homes by claiming that the entry of a protected class of people into the neighborhood will have some sort of negative impact on property values. Blockbusting was a common practice during the 1950s and 1960s when unscrupulous real estate professionals profited by fueling "white flight" from cities to suburbs. Any message from a real estate professional, however subtle, that property should be sold or rented because the neighborhood is "undergoing changes" is considered blockbusting. It is illegal to assert that the presence of certain persons will cause property values to decline, crime or antisocial behavior to increase, or the quality of schools to suffer.

A critical element in blockbusting, according to HUD, is the profit motive. A property owner may be intimidated into selling a property at a depressed price to the blockbuster, who in turn sells the property to another person at a higher price. Another term for this activity is *panic selling.* To avoid accusations of blockbusting, real estate professionals should use good judgment when choosing locations and methods for marketing their services and soliciting listings.

Steering

Steering is the channeling of homeseekers to particular neighborhoods or discouraging potential buyers from considering some areas. In the rental process, steering occurs when the landlord puts members of a protected class on a certain floor or building. Another form of steering occurs when the landlord tells a prospective tenant that no vacancy exists when, in fact, there is a vacancy. When the misstatement is made on the basis of a protected class, the prospect is steered away from that building. In any case, it is an illegal limitation of a purchaser's or renter's options.

Advertising

Advertisements of property for sale or rent may not include language indicating a preference or limitation. No exception to this rule exists, regardless of how subtle the choice of words. HUD's regulations include the types of language that are considered discriminatory. One such regulation can be found at www.hud.gov/sites/documents/DOC_7781.PDF. Figure 18.2 shows some examples of language that is permitted and language that is considered discriminatory and not permitted. An advertisement that is gender specific, such as "female roommate sought," is allowed as long as the advertiser seeks to share living quarters with someone of the same gender. The media used for promoting property or real estate services cannot target one population to the exclusion of others. The selective use of media, whether by language or geography, may have discriminatory impact. For instance, advertising property only in a Korean-language newspaper tends to discriminate against non-Koreans. Similarly, limiting advertising to a cable television channel available only to white suburbanites may be construed as a discriminatory act. If an advertisement appears in general-circulation media as well, however, it may be legal.

www.hud.gov/sites /documents/DOC _7781.PDF

FIGURE 18.2: HUD's Advertising Guidelines

Category	Rule	Permitted	Not Permitted
Race Color National origin	No discriminatory limitation/ preference may be expressed	"master bedroom" "good neighborhood"	"exclusive neighborhood" "English-speaking only"
Religion	No religious preference/ limitation	"chapel on premises" "kosher meals available" "Merry Christmas"	"no Muslims" "nice Christian family" "near great Catholic school"
Sex	No explicit preference based on sex	"mother-in-law suite" "master bedroom" "female roommate sought"	"great bachelor pad" "wife's dream kitchen"
Disability	No exclusions or limitations based on disability	"wheelchair ramp" "walk to shopping"	"no wheelchairs" "able-bodied tenants only"
Familial status	No preference or limitation based on family size or nature	"two-bedroom" "family room" "quiet neighborhood"	"married couple only" "no more than two children" "empty nester's dream house"
Photographs or illustrations of people	People should be clearly representative and nonexclusive	Illustrations showing multiple ethnicities, family groups, singles, etc.	Illustrations showing only individuals in ethnic dress, African American families, only white adults, etc.

IN PRACTICE

The Fair Housing Council of Oregon filed a complaint against a local multiple listing service (MLS), charging that the phrase "adults only over 40" was included in the "Remarks" section of a condominium listing. While the condominium association's bylaws actually did contain the (illegal) age restriction, the Fair Housing Council argued that including the phrase in the listing constituted discrimination against families with children in violation of the Fair Housing Act. The MLS paid $30,000 to settle with HUD, $20,000 of which went to support the antidiscrimination efforts of the Fair Housing Council of Oregon. The MLS also agreed to conduct regular computerized searches of its database for 67 different discriminatory words and phrases.

Appraising

Those who prepare appraisals or any statements of valuation—whether formal or informal, oral or written (including a comparative market analysis prepared by a real estate professional)—may consider any factors that affect value. Race, color, religion, national origin, sex, disability, and familial status are factors that may not be considered, however.

Redlining

The practice of refusing to make mortgage loans or issue insurance policies in specific areas for reasons other than the economic qualifications of the applicants is known as **redlining**. Redlining refers to literally drawing a line around particular areas. This practice is often a major contributor to the deterioration of older neighborhoods. Redlining is frequently based on racial grounds rather than on any real objection to an applicant's creditworthiness. The federal Fair Housing Act prohibits discrimination in mortgage lending and covers not only the actions of primary lenders but also activities in the secondary mortgage market. A lending institution, however, can refuse a loan solely on sound economic grounds.

Intent and effect

If an owner or real estate professional purposely sets out to engage in blockbusting, steering, or other unfair activities, the intent to discriminate is obvious. However, owners and real estate professionals must examine their activities and policies carefully to determine whether they have unintentional discriminatory effects. Whenever policies or practices result in unequal treatment of people in the protected classes, they are considered discriminatory, regardless of any innocent intent. This "effects" test is applied by regulatory agencies to determine whether an individual has been discriminated against.

Response to concerns of terrorism

Landlords and property managers have been developing new security procedures in response to concerns of terrorist attacks. These procedures have focused on protecting buildings and residents. Landlords and property managers are also educating residents on signs of possible terrorist activity and how and where to report it. At the same time, landlords and property managers need to ensure that their procedures and education do not infringe on the fair housing rights of others.

For screening and rental procedures, it is unlawful to screen housing applicants on the basis of race, color, religion, sex, national origin, disability, or familial status. According to

HUD, landlords and property managers have been inquiring about whether they can screen applicants on the basis of citizenship status. The Fair Housing Act does not specifically prohibit discrimination based solely on a person's citizenship status. Therefore, asking applicants for citizenship documentation or immigration status papers during the screening process does not violate the Fair Housing Act. For many years, the federal government has been asking for these documents in screening applicants for federally assisted housing. HUD provides a specific procedure for collecting and verifying citizenship papers.

IN PRACTICE

During an interview with a landlord, a woman mentions that she left her native country to study at the local university. The landlord is concerned about the woman's visa and whether it will expire during the lease term. The landlord asks the woman for documentation to determine how long she can legally live in the United States. The landlord asks for this information, regardless of her race or national origin. The landlord has not violated the Fair Housing Act.

ENFORCEMENT OF THE FAIR HOUSING ACT

The federal Fair Housing Act is administered by the Office of Fair Housing and Equal Opportunity under the direction of the secretary of HUD. Any aggrieved person who believes illegal discrimination has occurred may file a complaint with HUD within one year of the alleged act. HUD also may initiate its own complaint. Complaints may be reported to the Office of Fair Housing and Equal Opportunity, Department of Housing and Urban Development, Washington, DC 20410, or to the Office of Fair Housing and Equal Opportunity in care of the nearest HUD regional office. Complaints may also be submitted directly to HUD using an online form available on the HUD website.

Upon receiving a complaint, HUD initiates an investigation. Within 100 days of the filing of the complaint, HUD either determines that reasonable cause exists to bring a charge of illegal discrimination or dismisses the complaint. During this investigation period, HUD can attempt to resolve the dispute informally through conciliation. **Conciliation** is the resolution of a complaint by obtaining assurance that the person against whom the complaint was filed (the respondent) will remedy any violation that may have occurred. The respondent further agrees to take steps to eliminate or prevent discriminatory practices in the future. If necessary, these agreements can be enforced through civil action.

The aggrieved person has the right to seek relief through administrative proceedings. An administrative proceeding is a hearing held before an **administrative law judge (ALJ)**. An ALJ has the authority to award actual damages to an aggrieved party and, if it is believed the public interest will be served, to impose a monetary penalty. HUD increased the maximum civil penalty for violation of the Fair Housing Act, effective August 16, 2016. Adjusting the previous penalty amounts for inflation, the fine is now $19,987 for the first violation that occurs on or after that date, $49,467 if there was a violation in the preceding five years, and $98,935 for the third or more violation within seven years. The penalty previously ranged from up to $16,000 for a first offense to $70,000 for a third violation within seven years.

In addition to civil penalty amounts, actual damages and attorney's fees and costs may be awarded to the victim of housing discrimination. The ALJ also has the authority to issue an injunction to order the offender to either do something (such as rent an apartment to the complaining party), or refrain from doing something (such as acting in a discriminatory manner).

The parties may elect civil action in federal court at any time within two years of the discriminatory act. For cases heard in federal court, unlimited punitive damages can be awarded in addition to actual damages. The court can also issue injunctions.

The attorney general, upon finding reasonable cause to believe that any person or group is engaged in a pattern or practice of resistance to the full enjoyment of any of the rights granted by the federal fair housing laws, may file a civil action in any federal district court. Civil penalties may result in an amount not to exceed $50,000 for a first violation and an amount not to exceed $100,000 for second and subsequent violations, in addition to the victim's actual damages, attorney's fees, and costs, as well as compensation for humiliations, mental distress, and loss of housing rights. The U.S. Department of Justice is at www.justice.gov. Recent cases can be found at www.justice.gov/crt/recent-accomplishments-housing-and-civil -enforcement-section.

www.justice.gov

www.justice
.gov/crt/recent
-accomplishments
-housing-and-civil
-enforcement-section

Complaints brought under the Civil Rights Act of 1866 are taken directly to federal courts. The only time limit for action is a state's statute of limitations for torts (injuries one individual inflicts on another).

IN PRACTICE

On April 10, 2017, the United States filed a complaint alleging that the owners and operators of a 16-unit rental apartment complex in Wichita, Kansas violated the Fair Housing Act on the basis of familial status by terminating the lease of a tenant who asked to add her baby granddaughter to her lease and making statements indicating that they had a policy of not renting to households with children. (*United States v. Pritchard* (D. Kan.))

State and local enforcement agencies

Many states and municipalities have their own fair housing laws. If a state or local law is substantially equivalent to the federal law, all complaints filed with HUD are referred to the local enforcement agency. To be considered substantially equivalent, the local law and its related regulations must contain prohibitions comparable to those in the federal law. In addition, the state or locality must show that its local enforcement agency takes sufficient affirmative action in processing and investigating complaints and in finding remedies for discriminatory practices. All real estate professionals should be aware of their states' fair housing laws, as well as applicable local ordinances.

Threats or acts of violence

Working in real estate is not generally considered dangerous, but some real estate professionals may find themselves the targets of threats or violence merely for complying with fair housing laws. The Fair Housing Act protects the rights of those who seek the benefits of the fair housing laws. It also protects owners and real estate professionals who aid or encourage the enjoyment of fair housing rights. Threats, coercion, and intimidation are punishable by criminal action. In such a case, the victim should report the incident immediately to law enforcement officials.

IMPLICATIONS FOR REAL ESTATE PROFESSIONALS

The real estate industry is largely responsible for creating and maintaining an open housing market. Real estate professionals are a community's real estate experts. With the privilege of profiting from real estate transactions comes the social and legal responsibilities to ensure that everyone's civil rights are protected. Establishing relationships with community and fair housing groups to discuss common concerns and find solutions to problems is a worthwhile activity. Real estate professionals who actively work to improve their community will earn a reputation for being concerned citizens, which may well translate into a larger consumer base.

Consequences

Fair housing is the law. The consequences for anyone who violates the law are serious. In addition to the financial penalties, the livelihood of a real estate professional may be in jeopardy if the real estate license is suspended or revoked. That the offense was unintentional is no defense. Real estate professionals must scrutinize their practices and be particularly careful not to fall victim to clients or customers who expect them to discriminate.

KEY POINT REVIEW

Equal opportunity in housing is intended to create a marketplace in which persons of similar financial means have a similar range of housing choices. Equal opportunity laws apply to owners, real estate professionals, apartment management companies, real estate organizations, lending agencies, builders, and developers.

The **Civil Rights Act of 1866** prohibits all racial discrimination in real estate transactions, with no exceptions, and was upheld in *Jones v. Mayer* in 1968.

Race has been defined by the U.S. Supreme Court to include ancestral and ethnic characteristics, including certain physical, cultural, or linguistic traits that are shared by a group with a common national origin.

The **federal Fair Housing Act** is Title VIII of the **Civil Rights Act of 1968**, as amended, and prohibits discrimination in housing based on **race**, **color**, **national origin**, **religion**, **sex**, **familial status**, or **disability**. The Fair Housing Act does not prohibit discrimination based solely on a person's citizenship status. Illegal activities include steering, blockbusting, and redlining.

The **Housing and Community Development Act of 1974** added **sex** to the list of protected classes. The **Fair Housing Amendments Act of 1988** added **disability** and **familial status** to the protected classes. The Fair Housing Act is administered by HUD, which established rules and regulations to further clarify the law, and created the Equal Housing Opportunity poster.

Exemptions from the Fair Housing Act (but not the Civil Rights Act of 1866) include

- rentals in **owner-occupied buildings** with no more than four units;
- housing operated by organizations and private clubs that limit occupancy to members; and
- the sale or rental of a **single-family home** when fewer than three homes are owned by an **individual**, discriminatory advertising is not used, and a real estate professional is not involved in the transaction.

The **Housing for Older Persons Act of 1995 (HOPA)** repealed facilities and services requirements for housing intended for persons age 55 or older. Housing is **exempt** from familial status protection if it is restricted to persons **age 62** or older, or if 80% of the units are occupied by persons **age 55** or older.

Familial status extends fair housing protections to families with children, meaning a family including a woman who is pregnant or in which one or more individuals under the age of 18 live with either a parent or a guardian.

A **disability** is a physical or mental impairment that substantially limits one or more of an individual's major life activities. Reasonable modifications to property to make it usable by an individual with a disability must be allowed, but the individual must return the property to its former condition on vacating it.

The **Americans with Disabilities Act (ADA)** prohibits discrimination in employment and public accommodations. Access to facilities and services in commercial properties must be provided when **reasonably achievable** in existing buildings, with higher standards for new construction/remodeling. Exempt properties include those covered by federal fair housing laws.

HUD enforces the Fair Housing Act. A complaint must be brought within one year of the alleged act of discrimination. Within 100 days of filing a complaint that is not referred by HUD to a local enforcement agency, HUD dismisses or goes forward with a charge of illegal discrimination. Conciliation is the resolution of a complaint within 100 days of filing when a respondent promises to remedy any violation.

A complaint brought to HUD may be heard by an **administrative law judge (ALJ)**, with remedies that may include a fine or injunction. A civil action may be brought in federal court by the complainant within two years of the alleged discriminatory act. The attorney general may bring a civil action in federal court.

Complaints under the Civil Rights Act of 1866 go directly to federal court.

Real estate professionals must act legally, doing their part to avoid discriminatory practices.

UNIT 18 QUIZ

1. Under the Fair Housing Act, which action is legally permitted?
   A. Advertising property for sale only to a special group
   B. Altering the terms of a loan for a member of a protected class
   C. Refusing to make a mortgage loan to a member of a protected class because of a poor credit history
   D. Telling a member of a protected class that an apartment has been rented when in fact it has not

2. Complaints relating to the Civil Rights Act of 1866
   A. must be taken directly to federal courts.
   B. are no longer reviewed in the courts.
   C. are handled by HUD.
   D. are handled by state enforcement agencies.

3. Why is the Civil Rights Act of 1866 unique?
   A. It has been broadened to protect the aged.
   B. It adds welfare recipients as a protected class.
   C. It contains "choose your neighbor" provisions.
   D. It provides no exceptions that would permit racial discrimination.

4. A real estate professional said to a homeowner, "I hear *they're* moving in. There goes the neighborhood! Better put your house on the market before values drop!" This is an example of what illegal practice?
   A. Steering
   B. Blockbusting
   C. Redlining
   D. Fraudulent advertising

5. The act of directing homeseekers toward or away from particular areas, either to maintain or to change the character of the neighborhood, is
   A. blockbusting.
   B. redlining.
   C. steering.
   D. permitted under the Fair Housing Act of 1968.

6. A lender's refusal to lend money to potential homeowners attempting to purchase properties located in particular ethnic neighborhoods is known as
   A. redlining.
   B. blockbusting.
   C. steering.
   D. prequalifying.

7. All of the following would be permitted under the federal Fair Housing Act *EXCEPT*
   A. an expensive club in New York renting rooms only to members who are graduates of a particular university.
   B. the owner of a 20-unit residential apartment building renting to men only.
   C. a Catholic convent refusing to furnish housing for a Jewish man.
   D. an owner refusing to rent the other side of the duplex in which she lives to a family with children.

8. It is illegal for a lending institution to refuse to make a residential real estate loan in a particular area based on
   A. the ethnicity of the residents of the area.
   B. the applicant's questionable economic situation.
   C. the applicant not being of legal age.
   D. the deteriorated condition of the premises.

9. Which agency, upon receiving a complaint regarding a Fair Housing Act violation, investigates?
   A. HUD
   B. HOPA
   C. DOJ
   D. ADA

10. Housing that qualifies for exemption from familial status provisions
    A. includes housing intended for persons 50 or older.
    B. includes a restriction that 80% of the units be occupied by persons 55 or older.
    C. is not permitted under the federal Fair Housing Act.
    D. is permitted for owner-occupied buildings with four or more units.

11. Which statement describes the Supreme Court's decision in the case of *Jones v. Alfred H. Mayer Company*?
    A. Racial discrimination is prohibited by any party in the sale or rental of real estate.
    B. Sales by individual residential homeowners are exempted, provided the owners do not use real estate professionals.
    C. Laws against discrimination apply only to federally related transactions.
    D. Persons with disabilities are a protected class.

12. After a real estate professional takes a sale listing of a residence, the owners specify that they will not sell the home to any Chinese family. The real estate professional should do which of the following?
    A. Advertise the property exclusively in newspapers marketed to persons of Chinese heritage.
    B. Explain to the owners that the instruction violates federal law and that the real estate professional cannot comply with it.
    C. Abide by the owners' directions despite the fact that they conflict with the fair housing laws.
    D. Require that the owners sign a separate legal document stating the additional instruction as an add-on to the listing agreement.

13. The fine for a first violation of the federal Fair Housing Act could be as much as
    A. $19,987.
    B. $37,525.
    C. $65,654.
    D. $100,000.

14. A single man with two small children has been told by a real estate professional that homes for sale in a condominium complex are available only to married couples with no children. Which statement is *TRUE*?
    A. Because a single-parent family can be disruptive if the parent provides little supervision of the children, the condominium is permitted to discriminate against the family under the principle of rational basis.
    B. Condominium complexes are exempt from the fair housing laws and can therefore restrict children.
    C. The man may file a complaint alleging discrimination on the basis of familial status.
    D. Restrictive covenants in a condominium take precedence over the fair housing laws.

15. The following ad appeared in the newspaper: "For sale: 4 BR brick home; Redwood School District; excellent Elm Street location; short walk to St. John's Church; and right on the bus line. Move-in condition; priced to sell." Which statement is *TRUE*?
    A. The ad describes the property for sale and is very appropriate.
    B. The fair housing laws do not apply to newspaper advertising.
    C. The ad should state that the property is available to families with children.
    D. The ad should not mention St. John's Church.

16. A suit may be filed in federal court by a person aggrieved by an alleged act of discrimination under the Fair Housing Act
    A. within two years of the discriminatory act.
    B. no later than one year after the discriminatory act.
    C. with the approval of the state or county nondiscrimination officer.
    D. if the Federal Housing Administration refuses to pursue the case.

17. The federal Fair Housing Act does *NOT* prohibit
    A. blockbusting.
    B. discriminatory advertising.
    C. redlining.
    D. discriminating on the basis of marital status.

18. Which of the following is legal?
    A. Charging a family with children a higher security deposit than those with no children
    B. Requiring a person with a disability to establish an escrow account for the costs to restore a property after it has been modified
    C. Picturing only white people in a brochure as the "happy residents" in a housing development
    D. Refusing to sell a house to a person who has a history of mental illness

19. The landlord's lease prohibits tenants from altering the property in any way. A young woman who uses a wheelchair cannot maneuver over the doorstep into her apartment by herself. In addition, she cannot access the bathroom facilities in her wheelchair. Which of the following is *TRUE*?
    A. The landlord is responsible for making all apartments accessible to people with disabilities.
    B. The tenant cannot remedy these conditions because of the terms of the lease.
    C. The landlord should not have rented this apartment to the tenant.
    D. The tenant is entitled to make the necessary alterations.

20. The provisions of the federal Fair Housing Act apply
    A. in all states.
    B. in those states that have ratified the act, but not in other states.
    C. only in those states that do not have substantially equivalent laws.
    D. only in those states that do not have specific state fair housing laws.

UNIT 19

Property Management

LEARNING OBJECTIVES

When you have completed this unit, you will be able to

> **describe** the various property management assignments available in the property management field and the role of the property manager in each;
> **explain** the essential elements of the property management agreement;
> **list** the primary responsibilities of the property manager;
> **describe** the various federal laws, which the property manager must know and follow in the performance of management; and
> **describe** the implementation of risk management procedures to insure the safety and security of a managed property's tenants as well as to protect the landlord from liability and loss.

KEY TERMS

budget comparison statement	multiperil policies	risk management
cash flow report	operating budget	routine maintenance
corrective maintenance	preventive maintenance	surety bonds
management agreement	profit and loss statement	tenant improvements
management plan	property manager	workers' compensation acts

OVERVIEW

Property management involves the leasing, managing, marketing, and overall maintenance of real estate owned by others, usually rental property. Although some owners of rental units manage their own properties (a real estate license is not required to do so), most rental properties are professionally managed. Many mortgage lenders require that investors hire a professional property manager to manage their properties.

In many states, property managers are required to hold a real estate broker's or property manager's license. As with all real estate services, a real estate sales associate can only manage property with the consent of the employing broker and in the broker's name.

THE PROPERTY MANAGER

The role of the **property manager** is complex, requiring the manager to wear many hats. It is not unusual for a property manager to be a market analyst, salesperson, accountant, advertising specialist, and maintenance person—all in the same day. In addition, the property manager frequently interacts with people in various professions, including lawyers, environmental engineers, and accountants. The three principal responsibilities of the property manager are to

> A property manager must
> - achieve the goals of the owners,
> - generate income, and
> - preserve and/or increase the value of the property.

- achieve the objectives of the property owners,

- generate income for the owners, and

- preserve and/or increase the value of the investment property.

The property manager carries out the goals of the property owners. In the process, the property manager is responsible for maintaining the owner's investment and making sure the property earns income. These goals can be accomplished in several ways. The physical property must be maintained in good condition. Suitable tenants must be found, rent must be collected, and employees must be hired and supervised. The property manager is responsible for budgeting and controlling expenses, keeping proper accounts, and making periodic reports to the owner. In all of these activities, the manager's primary goal is to operate and maintain the physical property in such a way as to preserve and enhance the owner's capital investment.

Some property managers work for property management companies. These firms manage properties for a number of owners under management agreements. A property manager in a general agency relationship with the property owner could be an independent contractor with great authority and discretion in management decisions. A property manager or an owner may employ building managers to supervise the daily operations of a building. In some cases, these individuals might be residents of the building.

IN PRACTICE

In most states, licensed real estate professionals are permitted to manage properties for others. Some states have separate property management licenses. When directly employed by the owner, nonlicensed individuals are permitted by some states to manage properties. While some states require licensing in order to manage condominium or cooperative homeowners associations, others do not. Some states require an on-site manager for residential income-producing properties having more than a certain number of units; for example, California requires a manager on-site for residential properties of 16 or more units.

Securing management business

Possible clients of a property management business include

- corporate owners,

- apartment buildings,

- owners of small rental residential properties,

- homeowners associations,

- investment syndicates,

- trusts, and

- owners of office buildings.

A good reputation is often the manager's best advertising. A manager who consistently demonstrates the ability to increase property income over previous levels, while meeting legal requirements and enhancing the property's attractiveness to tenants, should have little difficulty finding new business.

Before contracting to manage any property, the professional property manager should be certain that the building owner has realistic income expectations. Necessary maintenance, unexpected repairs, and effective marketing all take time and money. In addition, most states have landlord-tenant laws that require the landlord-owner to keep the property repaired and make sure it complies with building codes. Through the agency relationship with the owner, the property manager becomes responsible for repairs and the building's condition.

New opportunities

Specialization has opened a range of new opportunities

Well-trained specialists are needed to manage shopping centers, commercial buildings, and industrial parks, in addition to the more visible management of residential properties. The following are just a few of the specialties that have an ongoing need for competent managers.

Community association management

The prevalence of homeowners and condominium associations combined with complex planning and development codes have placed new demands on property managers. Working as part of a team, property managers assist in providing a comprehensive array of services to volunteer boards. Many states now require at least a real estate license or an association management license for those who specialize in managing associations.

Housing for seniors

Opportunities abound in managing housing for those age 55 and older, including federally assisted housing programs. In addition to marketing, managers of senior housing are often responsible for the operation of the facility, as well as housekeeping, meal service, social event planning, and medical emergency planning. When subsidized housing is involved, the property manager needs to be familiar with state and federal rules pertaining to eligibility requirements and income verification.

Manufactured homes

Homes built in factories meeting HUD specifications are called manufactured homes or HUD-code homes. These homes may be placed on individually owned land, but more than a third are sited in communities. A tenant may rent only the "pad," the land on which the home is sited, or the home itself. Many communities, especially those in the sun belt states, are geared toward seniors; managers at these communities must be effective at building community spirit.

Resort housing

Managing second-home and resort rentals presents specific challenges. A resort manager must be able to care for and maintain often-vacant properties and be able to attract and manage short-term tenants. Many such properties are located in high-risk areas for natural disasters such as hurricanes, so the manager must be able to prepare for an emergency as well as to work with insurance adjusters.

Concierge services

A new area for property managers to specialize in is the training and managing of concierge staff for office buildings and other settings. Concierge staff are responsible for anything from arranging for taxi rides to assisting with internet-enabled equipment for a conference.

Asset management

An asset manager monitors a portfolio of properties similar to a securities portfolio by analyzing the performance of the properties and making recommendations to the owners of the properties. Real property asset management helps clients decide what type of real estate to invest in—commercial, residential, industrial, or agricultural—and which property is best to purchase, the best financial sources for a real estate purchase, and when to dispose of property.

Corporate property manager

Hiring a corporate property manager allows a corporation to invest in real estate and increase its capital, even if the corporation is not necessarily knowledgeable about property management. Typically, the corporate property manager is an employee of the corporation and not an independent contractor.

Leasing agent

A leasing agent is usually an independent contractor working on a commission basis. Leasing agents are usually in high demand because of their skill in securing lessees.

Professional associations

Most metropolitan areas have local associations of building and property owners and managers that are affiliates of regional and national associations. Many of these professional organizations provide information and contacts for all aspects of property management. Many also provide well-respected designations that help open doors for the property manager who is willing to fulfill the educational and/or experience requirements that a designation requires. The better-known associations include the following:

www.boma.org
www.bomi.org
www.caionline.org
www.irem.org
www.icsc.org
www.naahq.org
www.nahb.org
www.narpm.org

- Building Owners and Managers Association International (BOMA)—commercial real estate, www.boma.org

- Building Owners and Managers Institute International (BOMI)—education programs for commercial property and facility management industries, www.bomi.org

- Community Associations Institute (CAI)—homeowners associations, condominiums, and other planned communities, www.caionline.org

- Institute of Real Estate Management (IREM)—multifamily and commercial real estate designation, www.irem.org

- International Council of Shopping Centers (ICSC)—shopping centers worldwide, www .icsc.org

- National Apartment Association (NAA)—multifamily housing industry, www.naahq.org

- National Association of Home Builders (NAHB)—all aspects of home building, www .nahb.org

- National Association of Residential Property Managers (NARPM)—single-family and small residential properties, www.narpm.org

THE MANAGEMENT AGREEMENT

The first step in taking over the management of any property is to enter into a **management agreement**, a contract creating a general agency relationship between the owner and the property manager. The management agreement defines the duties and responsibilities of each party; it is a guide used in operating the property, as well as a reference in case of any future disputes.

The property manager's role

The property manager is typically considered a *general agent*. As an agent, the property manager is charged with the fiduciary responsibilities of care, obedience, accounting, loyalty, confidentiality, and disclosure. Property managers are usually empowered to make many more decisions on behalf of the owner than a real estate professional can make in the real estate professional's representation of a seller or a buyer. After entering into an agreement with a property owner, a manager handles the property the same way the owner would. In all activities, the manager's first responsibility is to realize the highest return on the property in a manner consistent with the owner's instructions and applicable law. As in any other contract in which the duties and responsibilities of the parties are specified, the management agreement should be in writing, and it should include the following points:

- *Description* of the property.

- *Time period* the agreement covers and specific provisions for *termination*.

- *Definition of the manager's responsibilities.* All the manager's duties should be specifically stated in the contract. Any limitations or restrictions on what the manager may do should be clearly stated.

- *Statement of the owner's purpose and responsibilities.* The owner should clearly state what the manager is to accomplish. One owner may want to maximize net income, while another may want to increase the capital value of the investment. What the manager does depends on the owner's long-term goals for the property. The agreement also should list the owner's responsibilities for management expenses, such as payroll, advertising, insurance, and management fees.

- *Extent of the manager's authority.* This provision should state what authority the manager is to have in matters such as hiring, firing, and supervising employees; fixing rental rates for space; and making expenditures and authorizing repairs. Repairs that exceed a certain expense limit may require the owner's written approval.

- *Reporting.* The frequency and detail of the manager's periodic reports on operations and financial position should be agreed on. These reports serve as a means for the owner to monitor the manager's work. They also form a basis for both the owner and the manager to spot trends that are important in shaping management policy. The state real estate commission usually will have regulations concerning reporting.

■ *Compensation.* The management fee or other form of compensation may be based on a percentage of gross or net income, a fixed fee, or some combination of these and other factors. The compensation provision of the agreement should state the base fee, as well as any leasing fees, supervision fees, or other commissions or compensations.

■ *Allocation of costs.* The agreement should state which of the property manager's expenses—such as office rent, office help, telephone, advertising, and association fees—will be paid by the manager. Other costs will be paid by the owner.

■ *Liability.* The agreement should require that the manager be included as an additional insured on the property liability policy.

■ *Antitrust provisions.* Management fees are subject to the same antitrust considerations as sales commissions. They cannot be standardized in the marketplace, because standardization would be considered price-fixing. The fee must be negotiated between the agent and the principal. In addition, the property manager may be entitled to a commission on new rentals and renewed leases.

■ *Equal opportunity statement.* Residential property management agreements should include a statement that the property will be shown, rented, and otherwise made available to all persons, regardless of race, color, religion, sex, disability, national origin, or family status, and to any class of person protected by local, state or federal law.

MATH CONCEPTS

Rental Commissions

Residential property managers often earn commissions when they find tenants for a property. Rental commissions are usually based on the annual rent from a property. The commission on a year's lease may be one month's rent, or may be a percentage of the projected lease payments. For example, if an apartment unit rents for $3,200 per month, the lease is for one year, and the commission payable is 8%, the commission is calculated as follows:

$3,200 per month × 12 months = $38,400

$38,400 × 0.08 = $3,072

THE PROPERTY MANAGER'S RESPONSIBILITIES

Property management begins with a **management plan** prepared by the property manager. A management plan outlines the details of the owner's objectives with the property, as well as what the property manager expects to accomplish and how, including all financial objectives.

The management plan

In preparing a management plan, a property manager analyzes three factors: the owner's objectives, the regional and neighborhood market, and the specific property. Occupancy, absorption rates, and new starts are critical indicators. The plan also includes a budgetary section on sources of revenue and anticipated expenses. While the management plan is a document for the present, it is forward-looking in determining the feasibility of a property owner's long-term goals for a specific property.

Financial reports

One of the primary responsibilities of a property manager is maintaining financial reports, including an operating budget, cash flow report, profit and loss statement, and budget comparison statement. While there are no standard formats for these reports, they have some similarity, and it is important for the property manager to adapt a report to meet an owner's needs. The reports are sent to the property owner at the agreed-upon intervals, by mail or email, but the property manager should meet the client at least once a year to go over the property's financial status in detail. Not only is this helpful to the owner's understanding of the property's performance, it is an excellent way for the property manager to demonstrate the levels of service and expertise that are being provided to the client.

Operating budget

The projection of income and expense for the operation of a property over a one-year period is called an **operating budget**. This budget, developed before attempting to rent property, is based on anticipated revenues and expenses and provides the owner the amount of expected profit. The property uses the operating budget as a guide for the property's financial performance in the present and future.

Once a property manager has managed a property for a length of time, an operating budget may be developed based on the results of the profit and loss statement in comparison to the original budget (actual versus projected). After making the comparison, a new operating budget is prepared for a new time period in the future.

Cash flow report

A **cash flow report** is a monthly statement that details the financial status of the property. Sources of income and expenses are noted, as well as net operating income and net cash flow. The cash flow report is the most important financial report because it provides a picture of the current financial status of a property.

Income

Income includes gross rentals collected, delinquent rental payments, utilities, vending machine proceeds, contracts, late fees, and storage charges. In some properties, there is space that is not income producing, such as the property manager's office. The rental value of the property that is not producing income is subtracted from the gross rental income to equal the gross collectible, or billable, rental income.

Any losses from uncollected rental payments or evictions are deducted from total gross income to arrive at net operating income.

Expenses

A property will incur both fixed and variable expenses. Fixed expenses are those that remain fairly predictable, even though they may increase or decrease somewhat, such as employee wages and other administrative expenses, utilities, and other basic operating costs. Variable expenses may be recurring or nonrecurring and can include capital improvements, building repairs, and landscaping.

Cash flow

Cash flow is derived as shown below. The entry for "debt service" in the third equation includes any mortgage payments on the property.

gross rental income + other income – losses incurred = total income

total income – operating expenses = net operating income

net operating income – debt service – reserves = cash flow

Profit and loss statement

A **profit and loss statement** is a financial picture of revenues and expenses used to determine whether a business has made money or suffered a loss. It may be prepared monthly, quarterly, semiannually, or annually. The statement is created from the monthly cash flow reports and does not include itemized information. A formula for a profit and loss statement is as follows:

gross receipts – operating expenses – total mortgage payment + mortgage loan principal = net profit

Budget comparison statement

The **budget comparison statement** compares actual results with the original budget, often giving either percentages or a numerical variance of actual versus projected income and expenses. Budget comparisons are especially helpful in identifying trends in order to help with future budget planning.

Renting the property

Effective rental of the property being managed is essential to ensure its long-term financial health. A property manager may use the services of a leasing agent. The real estate professional acting as leasing agent will be concerned solely with renting space and will not be responsible for maintaining and managing the property.

Setting rental rates

While some municipalities control rent increases for residential tenants, most communities allow the market to determine the amount of rent that a tenant should pay. Because rental rates are influenced primarily by supply and demand, property managers should conduct a detailed survey of the competitive space available in the neighborhood, emphasizing similar properties. In establishing rental rates, property managers must consider the following:

■ The rental income must be sufficient to cover the property's fixed charges and operating expenses.

■ The rental income must provide a return on the owner's investment.

■ The rental rate should be comparable with prevailing rates in comparable buildings in the area; it may be slightly higher or slightly lower, depending on the desirability of the property.

■ The current vacancy rate in the property is a good indicator of how much of a rent increase might be possible. A building with a low vacancy rate is a better candidate for an increase than one with a high vacancy rate.

A rental rate for residential space is usually stated as the monthly rate *per unit*. Commercial leases—including office, retail, and industrial space rentals—are usually stated according to either annual or monthly rates *per square foot*.

An elevated level of vacancy may indicate poor management, a defective or undesirable property, or rental rates that are too high for the market or the property. A high occupancy rate may mean that rental rates are too low. Before adjusting the rental rates, the manager should investigate the rental market to determine whether a rent increase is warranted.

Marketing

To ensure that a property generates income, the property manager must attract the most reliable tenants. The marketing strategy must take into consideration the property itself, the supply and demand in the area where the property is located, and the amount of money available for advertising.

Advertising

All advertising and promotional activities must comply with federal, state, and local nondiscrimination laws. The content cannot market to members of a protected class, but also must not discriminate on the basis of a prospective tenant's race, color, religion, sex, national origin, familial status, or disability. To ensure that a property generates income, the property manager must attract the best tenants.

Advertising methods are numerous and include internet sites and social media, newspapers, brochures, radio, television, and direct mail.

Management activities

Because property management firms are often known by reputation, it is important for a firm to maintain good public relations. One way to cultivate public relations is through community involvement and charitable giving.

Firms can also write and issue public service announcements (PSAs) or press releases regarding special projects. These announcements can attract the attention of the media and, ultimately, prospective tenants.

Marketing and advertising costs

A cost-benefit analysis helps a property manager assess whether a particular advertising method worked to attract new tenants. Property marketing expenses are usually figured on a cost-per-prospect-per-lease basis. For example, if a three-bedroom apartment rents for $4,500, is typically viewed by 10 prospects before it is leased, and a single newspaper advertisement is the only marketing, an $1,200 newspaper ad would cost $120 per prospect.

www.apartmentfinder
.com
www.apartmentguide
.com
www.craigslist.org
www.forrent.com
www.realtor.com
www.trulia.com
www.zillow.com

The internet has significantly expanded a property manager's ability to reach consumers. Online apartment vacancy listing sites include www.apartmentfinder.com, www.apartmentguide.com, www.craigslist.org, www.forrent.com, www.realtor.com, www.trulia.com, and www.zillow.com.

Selecting tenants

The residential property manager must be sure to comply with all federal, state, and local fair housing laws in selecting tenants. Although fair housing laws do not apply to commercial properties, commercial property managers need to be aware of federal, state, and local antidiscrimination and equal opportunity laws that may govern industrial or retail properties, including the Americans with Disabilities Act.

The commercial property manager should be sure that the premises are suitable for the tenant in terms of size, location, and amenities, and that the tenant can afford the space. A commercial tenant's business should be compatible not only with the building but also with the businesses of the other tenants. Managers should always ask commercial tenants about the potential for expansion. Because the property may not have enough room for expansion, the manager could soon lose the tenant to a larger space.

IN PRACTICE

Some commercial leases prohibit the introduction of similar businesses. In any event, introduction of competitors into the same property should be undertaken with care because competitors in the same location will often decrease the activity of both businesses and soon one or the other will seek to move.

Most states have strict requirements as to how security deposits should be handled by the property manager: how soon they must be deposited, into what kind of account, and when they must be refunded. In general, funds belonging to others, such as security deposits and collected rents, should be placed into a trust or escrow account. Property managers should not use any of these funds personally (conversion) or mix the funds into a personal account (commingling).

Collecting rents

A property manager should accept only those tenants who can be expected to meet their financial obligations. The manager should investigate financial references, check with local credit bureaus, and when possible, interview a prospective tenant's former landlord to ensure the tenant is able to meet financial obligations. Financial qualification standards must be applied in a similar fashion to all applicants to avoid even the appearance of a discriminatory practice.

MATH CONCEPTS

Calculating Monthly Rent per Square Foot (Commercial)

Determine the total square footage of the rental premises (generally floor space only).

50 feet

30 feet   30 feet

50 feet

50 feet × 30 feet = 1,500 square feet

Find the total annual rent.

> $2,500 per month × 12 months = $30,000 per year

Divide the total annual rent by the total square feet to determine the annual rate per square foot.

> $30,000 ÷ 1,500 square feet = $20 per square foot

Convert the annual rate to a monthly rate.

> $20 ÷ 12 months = $1.67 per square foot (rounded to nearest cent)

The terms of rental payment should be spelled out in the lease agreement, including

- time and place of payment,
- provisions and penalties for late payment and returned checks, and
- provisions for cancellation and damages in case of nonpayment.

The property manager should establish a firm and consistent collection plan. The plan should include a system of notices and records that complies with state and local law.

Every attempt must be made to collect rent without resorting to legal action. Legal action is costly and time consuming, and does not contribute to good tenant relations. In some cases, however, legal action is unavoidable. In these instances, a property manager must be prepared to initiate and follow through, in cooperation with the property owner's or management firm's attorney, on the necessary legal steps.

Maintaining good relations with tenants

The ultimate success of a property manager depends on the ability to maintain good relations with tenants. Dissatisfied tenants are more likely to vacate the property early. A high tenant turnover rate results in greater expenses for advertising and redecorating and less profit for the owner due to uncollected rents. Empty units and storefronts can also damage a property's reputation—and its perceived desirability.

An effective property manager establishes a good communication system with tenants—and prospective tenants. An internet site that highlights property features and solicits new tenants can also have a section limited to residents that posts activities, maintenance updates, and other news to keep tenants informed and involved. Email notices, printed and electronic newsletters, and posted memoranda, especially when updated on a regular basis, are also useful.

Above all, maintenance and service requests must be attended to promptly, and all lease terms and building rules must be enforced consistently and fairly. A manager who fails to treat all tenants the same in terms of rent collection and enforcement of lease terms or rules and regulations will create ill will among tenants and might even be violating fair housing laws. A good manager is tactful and decisive, and acts to benefit both owner and occupants.

The property manager must be able to address residents who do not pay rent on time or who violate building regulations. When one tenant fails to follow the rules, the other tenants often become frustrated and dissatisfied. Careful recordkeeping shows whether rent is remitted promptly and in the proper amount. Records of all lease renewal dates should be kept so that the manager can anticipate a lease expiration and retain a good tenant who might otherwise move when the lease term ends.

Maintaining the property

One of the most important functions of a property manager is the supervision of property maintenance. A manager must learn to balance the services provided with their cost—that is, to satisfy tenants' needs while keeping operating expenses within budget.

To maintain property efficiently, the manager must be able to assess the building's needs and how best to meet those needs. Because staffing and scheduling requirements vary with the type, size, and geographic location of the property, the owner and the manager usually agree in advance on maintenance objectives. In some cases, the best plan may be to operate a low-rent property with minimal expenditures for services and maintenance. Another property may be more lucrative if kept in top condition and operated with all possible tenant services. A well-maintained, high-service property can command premium rental rates.

A primary maintenance objective is to protect the physical integrity of the property over the long term. For example, preserving the property by repainting the exterior or replacing the heating system helps decrease long-term maintenance costs. Keeping the property in good condition involves the following three types of maintenance:

Types of maintenance
- Preventive
- Repair or corrective
- Routine

■ Preventive

■ Repair or corrective

■ Routine

Preventive maintenance includes regularly scheduled activities such as painting and seasonal servicing of appliances and systems. Preventive maintenance preserves the long-range value and physical integrity of the building. This is both the most critical and the most neglected maintenance responsibility. Failure to perform preventive maintenance invariably leads to greater expense in other areas of maintenance.

Repair or **corrective maintenance** involves the actual repairs that keep the building's equipment, utilities, and amenities functioning. Repairing a toilet, fixing a leaky faucet, and replacing a broken air-conditioning unit are acts of corrective maintenance.

A property manager also must supervise the **routine maintenance** of the building. Routine maintenance includes such day-to-day duties as performing minor carpentry and plumbing repairs, and providing regularly scheduled upkeep of heating, air-conditioning, and landscaping.

IN PRACTICE

One of the major decisions a property manager faces is whether to contract for maintenance services from an outside firm or to hire on-site employees. The property manager will make the decision on what is most cost-effective for the owner. This decision should be based on a number of factors, including the

- size of the building,
- complexity of the tenants' requirements,
- time and expense involved, and
- availability of suitable labor.

A commercial or industrial property manager often is called on to make **tenant improvements** (*or build-outs*). These are construction alterations to the interior of the building to meet a tenant's particular space needs. Such alterations range from simply repainting or recarpeting to completely gutting the interior and redesigning the space by

Construction involves making a property meet a tenant's needs.

erecting new walls, partitions, and electrical systems. Tenant improvements are especially important when renting new buildings. In new construction, the interiors are usually left incomplete so that they can be adapted to the needs of individual tenants. One matter that must be clarified is which improvements will be considered trade fixtures (personal property belonging to the tenant) and which will belong to the owner of the real estate.

Modernization or renovation of buildings that have become functionally obsolete and thus unsuited to today's building needs is also important. The renovation of a building often enhances its marketability and increases its potential income. At the same time, federal and state regulations regarding lead-based paint, asbestos, and other hazardous substances that may be found in or around a structure can entail expensive remediation efforts.

Environmental concerns

The environment is an increasingly important property management issue. A variety of environmental issues, from waste disposal to air quality, must be addressed by the property manager. Tenant concerns, as well as federal, state, and local regulations, determine the extent of the manager's environmental responsibilities. Property managers are not expected to be experts in all of the disciplines necessary to operate a property; they are expected to be knowledgeable in many diverse subjects, most of which are technical in nature. Environmental concerns are one such subject.

Recycling facilities may be required by law, but even if they are not, the manager may want to provide them for tenants, which can benefit the environment, as well as make the property more marketable. Hazardous wastes produced by employees or tenants must be properly disposed of. Even the normally nonhazardous waste of an office building must be controlled to avoid violation of laws requiring segregation and recycling of types of waste. Residential property managers of buildings constructed before 1978 must provide lead-based paint disclosure forms to all new tenants. Environmental audits also identify issues relating to asbestos, radon, and mold.

Air quality issues are a key concern for those involved in property management and design. *Building-related illness (BRI)* and *sick building syndrome (SBS)* are illnesses that are more prevalent today because of energy efficiency standards used in construction that make buildings more airtight with less ventilation. BRI is a clinically diagnosed condition that can be attributed directly to airborne building contaminants. Symptoms include asthma, hypersensitivity, and some allergies. SBS is more typical in an office building, and symptoms include fatigue, nausea, dizziness, headache, and sensitivity to odors. Often, increasing ventilation or replacing interior features, such as carpeting, can solve air quality problems.

FEDERAL LAWS PROHIBITING DISCRIMINATION

Federal laws prohibiting discrimination in the provision of housing, accommodations, services, and access to credit affect the property management profession. The Americans with Disabilities Act, the Equal Credit Opportunity Act, and the Fair Housing Act all help to ensure that consumer rights are not violated.

The Americans with Disabilities Act

www.ada.gov

The Americans with Disabilities Act (ADA), www.ada.gov, has had a significant impact on the responsibilities of the property manager, in both building amenities and employment issues.

ADA Title I provides that any employer of 15 or more employees must adopt nondiscriminatory employment procedures. In addition, an employer must make reasonable accommodations to enable an individual with a disability to perform essential job functions.

Property managers also must be familiar with ADA Title III, which prohibits discrimination in commercial properties and public accommodations. ADA requires that companies ensure that people with disabilities have full and equal access to facilities and services. (See Figure 19.1).

FIGURE 19.1: Reasonable Modifications to Public Facilities or Services

 Provide doors with automatic opening mechanisms

 Provide menus (and real estate listings) in a large-print or braille format

 Install an intercom so customers can contact a second-floor business in a building without an elevator

 Lower public telephones

 Add grab bars to public restroom stalls

 Permit guide dogs to accompany customers

 Provide a shopper's assistant to help disabled customers

 Provide ramps in addition to entry stairs

IN PRACTICE

A prospective tenant is visually impaired. The property manager should be prepared to provide a lease agreement that is in large, easy-to-read type or that is printed in Braille, as required.

To protect owners of existing structures from the massive expense of extensive remodeling, the ADA recommends reasonably achievable accommodations to provide access to the facilities and services. Existing barriers must be removed when this can be accomplished in a readily achievable manner with little difficulty and at reasonable cost. The following are typical examples of readily achievable modifications:

- Ramping or removing an obstacle from an otherwise accessible entrance
- Lowering wall-mounted public telephones
- Adding raised letters and Braille markings on elevator buttons
- Installing auditory signals in elevators
- Reversing the direction in which doors open

Alternative methods can be used to provide reasonable accommodations if extensive restructuring is impractical or if retrofitting is unduly expensive. For example, installing a cup dispenser at a water fountain that is too high for a person in a wheelchair may be more practical than installing a lower water fountain.

IN PRACTICE

Federal, state, and local laws may provide additional requirements for accommodating people with disabilities. Real estate professionals should be aware of the full range of laws to ensure that their practices are in compliance.

New construction and remodeling must meet higher standards of accessibility and usability because it costs less to incorporate accessible features in the design than to retrofit. Though the law intends to provide for people with disabilities, many accessible design features and accommodations benefit everyone. Such *universal design* can enhance a property's desirability and be a successful marketing concept.

The property manager typically is responsible for determining whether a building meets ADA accessibility requirements. The property manager also must prepare a plan for retrofitting a building that is not in compliance when removal of existing barriers is readily achievable and can be performed without much difficulty or expense. Some tax advantages may be available to help offset the expense of ADA compliance. ADA experts may be consulted, as well as architectural designers who specialize in accessibility issues.

IN PRACTICE

The U.S. Department of Justice has ADA specialists available to answer general information questions about compliance issues. The ADA Information Line is 800-514-0301 (TTY: 800-514-0383).

Equal Credit Opportunity Act

The Equal Credit Opportunity Act (ECOA) prohibits a lender from denying a loan based on a person's race, color, religion, national origin, sex, marital status, age, or receipt of public assistance. The ECOA affects the property manager in several ways. A manager should use the same lease application for every applicant. If a manager requires a credit report from one applicant, the manager should require credit reports from all applicants. The manager should be consistent in evaluating the income and debt of applicants and in determining whether to rent to an applicant. A complete copy of the law can be found at www.fdic.gov/regulations /laws/rules/6500-1200.html.

Guiding principle: what you do for one, do for all.

www.fdic.gov /regulations/laws /rules/6500-1200.html

Fair Housing Act

The federal Fair Housing Act and its amendments prohibit discrimination in the sale, rental, or financing of housing based on race, color, religion, national origin, sex, familial status, or disability. Property managers need to ensure that their marketing practices do not violate fair housing laws. For example, blockbusting and steering are prohibited. *Blockbusting* is encouraging people to rent or to sell a property by claiming that the entry of a protected class of people into the neighborhood will have a negative impact on property values. *Steering* is the channeling of protected class members to certain buildings or neighborhoods. The Department of Justice has information on fair housing issues at www.justice.gov/crt/fair -housing-act-1.

www.justice.gov /crt/fair-housing-act-1

Unit 19

IN PRACTICE

Many fair housing complaints are related to property management issues that could have been avoided by treating all rental applicants with the same courtesy and respect. A fair housing training program can be useful at any stage of a real estate professional's career and is often a requirement for license renewal.

RISK MANAGEMENT

Enormous monetary losses can result from unexpected or catastrophic events. As a result, one of the most critical areas of responsibility for a property manager is **risk management**.

Risk management techniques

Risk management involves answering the question, What happens if something goes wrong? The perils of any risk must be evaluated in terms of options. In considering the possibility of a loss, the property manager must decide whether it is better to

Memory tip

The four alternative risk management techniques:

Avoid

Control

Transfer

Or

Retain

- *avoid it* by removing the source of risk (e.g., a swimming pool may pose an unacceptable risk);

- *control it* by preparing for an emergency before it happens (by installing sprinklers, fire doors, and security systems);

- *transfer it* by shifting the risk onto another party (by taking out an insurance policy); or

- *retain it* by deciding that the chances of the event occurring are too small to justify the expense of any other response (an alternative might be to take out an insurance policy with a large deductible, making the policy less expensive).

Security of tenants

Recent court decisions in several states have held owners and their agents responsible for physical harm that was inflicted on tenants by intruders. These decisions have prompted property managers and owners to think about how to protect tenants and secure apartments from intruders. After the terror attacks of September 11, 2001, and subsequent incidents, managers of all types of properties have increased awareness of security issues. A professional security analysis can help identify areas of concern and suggest possible remedies.

There is also concern caused by wrongdoing or criminal behavior inflicted by tenants on other tenants in a building. Many leases now have a crime-free provision that makes criminal activity, such as drug use or assault, grounds for eviction.

Types of insurance

Just as it is for homeowners, insurance is a first line of defense in risk management for other real property owners and managers. Numerous forms of insurance policies are available, covering a wide range of possible events that might result in devastating loss. A single policy may cover risks in one or more categories.

Tenant's insurance

The property manager should notify tenants that they must obtain renter's insurance, known as HO-4, in order to protect their personal belongings. The real estate owner can only insure what is owned (i.e., the building); the owner of the building cannot insure the personal property of tenants. Residential tenants need an HO-4 or renter's policy to insure their personal property. Business tenants can obtain their own business or commercial policy.

Commercial insurance

An insurance audit should be performed by a competent, reliable insurance agent who is familiar with insurance issues for the type of property involved. The audit will indicate areas in which greater or lesser coverage is recommended and will highlight particular risks. The final decision, however, is made by the property owner.

Common types of coverage available to income property owners and managers include the following:

- *Fire and hazard.* Fire insurance policies provide coverage against direct loss or damage to property from a fire on the premises. Standard fire coverage can be extended to include other hazards, such as windstorm, hail, smoke damage, or civil insurrection.

- *Flood.* Flood insurance is always a separate policy from home, rental, or building insurance policies. A flood insurance policy is available to any property located in a community participating in the National Flood Insurance Program (NFIP). It covers flooding caused by heavy rains, melting snow, inadequate drainage systems, or failed levees or dams. Consult www.fema.gov/national-flood-insurance-program.

- *Consequential loss, use, and occupancy.* Also known as *loss of rent* or *business interruption insurance*, consequential loss insurance covers the results of a disaster. Consequential loss can include the loss of rent or revenue to a business that occurs if the business's property cannot be used.

- *Contents and personal property.* This type of insurance covers building contents and personal property during periods when they are not actually located on the premises.

- *General liability.* General liability insurance covers the risks an owner assumes whenever the public enters the building. A claim paid under this coverage is used for medical expenses incurred by a person who is injured in the building or on the property as a result of the owner's negligence. Claims for medical or hospital payments for injuries sustained by building employees hurt in the course of their employment are covered by state laws known as **workers' compensation acts**.

- *Casualty.* Casualty insurance policies include coverage against theft, burglary, vandalism, and machinery damage, as well as health and accident insurance.

- *Surety bonds.* **Surety bonds** cover an owner against financial losses resulting from an employee's criminal acts or negligence while performing assigned duties.

Many insurance companies offer **multiperil policies** for apartment buildings. Such a policy offers an insurance package that includes standard types of commercial coverage, such as fire, hazard, public liability, and casualty. Special coverage for terrorism, earthquakes, and floods is also available. Remember that flood insurance is always a separate policy.

Condominium associations carry insurance on all the *common elements*, and cooperatives carry insurance on the building. Condominium owners and proprietary lease owners must carry their own casualty and liability insurance, as well as insurance to cover the destruction of their

www.fema.gov/national-flood-insurance-program

Unit 19

unit's contents by fire or other hazard. If condominium owners rent out space to tenants, the tenants must carry their own personal property insurance.

The property manager may also want to carry insurance to cover the management office and its contents, as well as professional malpractice claims. For example, a property manager may want to consider purchasing errors and omissions (E&O) insurance to protect against any financial management mistakes.

Insurance claims

Two methods are used to determine the amount of a claim under an insurance policy. One method considers the *depreciated* or *actual cash value* of the damaged property; the property is not insured for what it would cost to replace it but rather for what it was originally worth, less the depreciation in value that results from use and the passage of time. The other method considers *current replacement cost*—the building or property is insured for what it would cost to rebuild or replace today. When purchasing insurance, the property manager must act on the owner's decision as to whether the property should be insured at full replacement cost or at depreciated cost. Full replacement cost coverage is generally more expensive than depreciated cost coverage.

As with homeowners insurance policies, commercial policies include *coinsurance clauses* that require the insured to carry fire coverage, usually in an amount equal to 80% of a building's replacement value.

Property managers can encounter legal issues with insurance claims. For example, if the property owner is not available to file an insurance claim, the property manager must have proper authorization, such as a power of attorney.

KEY POINT REVIEW

A **property manager**, whether an individual or a company, acts as the **general agent** of the investment property owner in administering the property to achieve the **objectives** of the owner, generate **income**, and preserve and/or increase the property's **value**.

Property management functions may require a real estate or property management **license**, as provided by state law.

Property managers may undertake **asset management** by helping the owner to decide the **type** of real estate in which to invest (residential or commercial), the **best** property to purchase, the **financial resources** necessary to fund the purchase, and the best time to **dispose** of the property.

A **leasing agent** is usually a state-licensed real estate professional working as an **independent contractor** or property manager on a commission basis.

A **corporate property manager** is usually an **employee** of the corporation.

A **management plan** and **management agreement** should define the expectations and responsibilities of the parties.

A **cash flow report** will summarize income and expenses.

Periodic **profit and loss statements** provide general financial information. **Net profit** is determined by computing **gross receipts**, then subtracting operating expenses and interest paid on a mortgage loan. A **budget comparison statement** compares actual results with the original budget.

Rents typically are determined at a **monthly rate per unit** for residential property and at a **monthly rate per square foot** for commercial property.

A building manager **selects tenants** while complying with all applicable federal, state, and local fair housing, antidiscrimination, and equal opportunity laws.

Commercial tenant considerations typically include **the suitability** of the building in terms of size, location, and amenities; **compatibility** of the prospective tenant with the building and other tenants; and the **availability** of space for expansion, if necessary.

Adequate property maintenance includes **preventive** maintenance, timely **repairs** or corrective actions, and the **routine** activities that help preserve the property and enhance its desirability to tenants.

The **environmental concerns** that require the attention of the property manager include the **disposal of hazardous wastes**, the **lead-based paint disclosure** for residential property constructed before 1978, **building-related illness (BRI)**, and **sick building syndrome (SBS)**.

Federal laws affecting property management include the following:

- **Americans with Disabilities Act (ADA)**, which includes
    - **Title I**, which applies to **employers** with 15 or more employees and provides for employment of qualified job applicants, regardless of disability, with reasonable accommodations
    - **Title III**, which prohibits discrimination in **commercial properties and public accommodations** and requires that access to facilities and services be provided

when reasonably achievable in existing buildings, with a higher standard for new construction or remodeling

- **Equal Credit Opportunity Act (ECOA)**, which prohibits lenders from denying a loan based on a person's race, color, religion, national origin, sex, marital status, age, or receipt of public assistance; additional protections may be added by state or local laws

- Federal **Fair Housing Act**, which prohibits discrimination in the sale, rental, or financing of housing based on race, color, religion, national origin, sex, familial status, or disability; additional protected individuals may be added by state or local laws

Risk management includes treatment of risk by deciding whether to <u>a</u>**void** it, <u>c</u>**ontrol** it, **transfer** it, <u>or</u> <u>r</u>**etain** it (**ACTOR**) and focuses on tenant security and types of insurance available. The renter's insurance policy that covers the renter's personal property is the HO-4 policy.

UNIT 19 QUIZ

1. Which type of insurance coverage insures an employer against *MOST* claims for job-related injuries?
   A. Consequential loss
   B. Workers' compensation
   C. Casualty
   D. Surety bond

2. Avoid, control, transfer, or retain are the four alternative techniques of
   A. tenant relations.
   B. acquiring insurance.
   C. risk management.
   D. property management.

3. Adaptations of property specifications to suit tenant requirements are
   A. tax-exempt improvements.
   B. tenant improvements.
   C. prohibited by most nonresidential leases.
   D. generally not a good idea.

4. A guest slips on an icy apartment building stair and is hospitalized. A claim against the building owner for medical expenses may be paid under which of the following policies held by the owner?
   A. Workers' compensation
   B. Casualty
   C. Liability
   D. Fire and hazard

5. All of the following should be included in a management agreement *EXCEPT*
   A. a description of the property.
   B. compensation.
   C. restrictions regarding ages of children.
   D. the extent of the manager's authority.

6. A property manager is offered a choice of three insurance policies with different deductibles. If the property manager selects the policy with the highest deductible, which risk management technique is being used?
   A. Avoiding risk
   B. Retaining risk
   C. Controlling risk
   D. Transferring risk

7. Asbestos, sick building syndrome (SBS), and lead-based paint are all examples of
   A. issues beyond the scope of a property manager's job description.
   B. problems found only in newly constructed properties.
   C. issues that arise under the Americans with Disabilities Act (ADA).
   D. environmental concerns that a property manager may have to address.

8. The manager of a commercial building has many responsibilities in connection with the operation and maintenance of the structure. The manager would normally be considered the agent of
   A. the building's owner.
   B. the building's tenants.
   C. both the owner and the tenants.
   D. neither the owner nor the tenants.

9. Which of the following would be considered a variable expense when a manager develops an operating budget?
   A. Employee wages
   B. Utilities
   C. Building repairs
   D. Basic operating costs

10. In *MOST* market areas, rents are determined by
    A. supply and demand factors.
    B. the local apartment owners' association.
    C. HUD.
    D. a tenants' union.

11. An apartment complex is severely damaged by a tornado, making it uninhabitable. What type of insurance covers the landlord against the resulting loss of rent?
    A. Fire and hazard
    B. Liability
    C. Consequential loss, use, and occupancy
    D. Casualty

12. A property manager hires a full-time maintenance person. While repairing a faucet in one of the apartments, the maintenance person steals some jewelry and the tenant sues the owner. The property manager could protect the owner against this type of loss by purchasing
    A. liability insurance.
    B. workers' compensation insurance.
    C. a surety bond.
    D. casualty insurance.

13. Residential leases are usually expressed as
    A. an annual or monthly rate per square foot.
    B. a percentage of total space available.
    C. a monthly rate per unit.
    D. an annual rate per room.

14. A property manager repairs a leaking sink. This is classified as which type of maintenance?
    A. Preventive
    B. Corrective
    C. Routine
    D. Construction

15. A property manager who enters into a management agreement with an owner is usually
    A. a special agent.
    B. a general agent.
    C. a universal agent.
    D. a designated agent.

16. A statement sent to an owner that does not reflect the entire debt service as an expense is called
    A. a cash flow report.
    B. a profit and loss statement.
    C. a budget comparison statement.
    D. an operating budget statement.

17. An insurance policy package that includes standard commercial property coverage such as fire, hazard, public liability, and casualty is called what kind of policy?
    A. Coinsurance
    B. Multiperil
    C. Universal
    D. Surety

18. Removing existing barriers when readily achievable in public buildings, such as adding Braille markings to elevator buttons, is a requirement of which law?
    A. Fair Housing Act
    B. Equal Credit Opportunity Act
    C. Americans with Disabilities Act
    D. Regulation Z

19. Title III of the Americans with Disabilities Act (ADA) impacts which type of property?
    A. Residential
    B. Industrial
    C. Commercial and public accommodations
    D. Privately owned

20. In evaluating rental applications, it is important for the property manager to establish consistent criteria for acceptable debt and income ratios in order to be in compliance with
    A. federal antitrust laws.
    B. the Americans with Disabilities Act.
    C. Regulation Z.
    D. the Equal Credit Opportunity Act.

UNIT 20

Land-Use Controls and Property Development

LEARNING OBJECTIVES

When you have completed this unit, you will be able to

> **explain** the concept of police power and the provisions under which it protects the public's health, safety, and welfare;
> **explain** zoning ordinances, permits, and property use;
> **define** building codes as they relate to the requirements and restrictions placed on construction standards;
> **explain** the issues and regulations involved in subdivisions;
> **explain** non-governmental (private) land-use restrictions: covenants, conditions, and restrictions (CC&Rs); and
> **describe** the various laws and agencies which regulate land sales.

KEY TERMS

buffer zone	density zoning	plat map
building code	developer	restrictive covenants
certificate of occupancy	enabling acts	subdivider
comprehensive plan	Interstate Land Sales Full	subdivision
conditional-use permit	Disclosure Act (ILSA)	variance
covenants, conditions, and	nonconforming use	zoning ordinances
restrictions (CC&Rs)	planned unit development	
deed restrictions	(PUD)	

OVERVIEW

In most areas of the United States, local governments have developed comprehensive planning that restricts how land may be used, with the goal of orderly and planned growth. Real estate professionals must be knowledgeable about local land-use restrictions in order to avoid showing a buyer a property that is not suitable for the buyer's intended commercial or residential use.

The buyer of a home within a subdivision or planned unit development that is subject to a residential community association will also be subject to limitations that appear in the property deed or specific rules that are created and enforced by the association. An individual parcel of real estate may be subject to restrictions that a prior owner has included in the deed or a document that has been made part of the property's chain of title.

While no one expects real estate professionals to become experts in land use, they should be aware of these issues and be able to direct their clients to appropriate sources of additional information.

LAND-USE CONTROLS

Land use is controlled through public and private limitations as well as through the direct ownership of land by federal, state, and local governments. According to the U.S. Department of Agriculture (USDA), more than 60% (1.35 billion acres) of the total 2.3 billion acres of land area in the United States is privately owned. The federal government owns more than 29% of the land, over a third of which is in Alaska, while state and local governments own about 9%, and about 3% is Indian trust land. These percentages change very little over time. In 2007, about 1% of U.S. land (22 million acres) was in foreign ownership. Urban land acreage increased fourfold from 1945 to 2007, to 61 million acres, about twice the rate of population growth in that time. The latest report by the USDA on major uses of land in the United States (compiled in 2007 and published in 2011) can be found at www.ers.usda .gov/data-products/major-land-uses.aspx, or enter "major land uses" in the search box at www .usda.gov.

www.ers.usda.gov
/data-products/major
-land-uses.aspx

Here, you will learn about how property development and use is regulated at every level.

Government ownership

Government-owned land is used for national parks and forests, military bases, federal office buildings, schools, museums, state parks, government buildings, and municipal parks and buildings, as well as streets, highways, and bridges. Beyond direct ownership of land, government controls on property use range from regulation of the use and disposal of hazardous materials by the federal government to the design, construction, and type of buildings that are permitted at the local level.

The *police power* of government is the source of its authority to create regulations needed to protect the public's health, safety, and welfare. Through **enabling acts**, states delegate to counties and local municipalities the authority to enact ordinances in keeping with general laws. The degree to which governmental bodies seek to regulate land uses varies and is often a reflection of the priorities of local residents. While there may be little objection anywhere to regulations that control noise, air, and water pollution, the topic of population density (lot and building sizes) can elicit strong reactions.

The comprehensive plan

Local governments, municipalities, and counties establish development goals by creating a **comprehensive plan**. The comprehensive plan, also known as a *master plan*, is not a regulatory document, but a guide that tries to anticipate changing needs. The comprehensive plan usually is long term, perhaps 20 years or longer, and often includes (a) a general plan that can be revised and updated more frequently, (b) plans for specific areas, and (c) strategic plans. Systematic planning for orderly growth usually considers the following elements:

- Land use—determining how much land may be proposed for residences, industries, businesses, agriculture, traffic and transit uses, utilities, community facilities, parks and recreational facilities, floodplains, and areas of special hazards

- Housing needs of present and anticipated residents, including rehabilitation of declining neighborhoods, as well as new residential developments

- Movement of people and goods, including highways and public transit, parking facilities, and pedestrian and bikeway systems

- Community facilities and utilities such as schools, libraries, hospitals, recreational facilities, fire and police stations, water resources, sewerage, waste treatment and disposal, storm drainage, and flood management

- Energy conservation to reduce energy consumption and promote the use of renewable energy sources

The preparation of a comprehensive plan involves surveys, studies, and analyses of housing, demographic, and economic characteristics and trends. The plan typically is drafted by a *planning commission* and approved by the city council or other governing body following a period for public comment at hearings held for that purpose. A municipality's planning activities may be coordinated with other government bodies and private interests to achieve orderly growth and development.

IN PRACTICE

After the Great Chicago Fire of 1871 reduced most of the city's downtown to rubble and ash, the city engaged planner Daniel Burnham to lay out a design for Chicago's future. The resulting Burnham Plan of orderly boulevards linking a park along Lake Michigan with other large parks and public spaces throughout the city established an attractive and workable urban space. The plan is still being implemented today.

ZONING

Zoning ordinances implement the comprehensive plan and regulate and control the use of land and structures within designated land-use districts, in part by separating conflicting land uses. If the comprehensive plan is the big picture, zoning provides the details that carry out the comprehensive plan.

Although no nationwide or statewide zoning ordinances exist, the federal government and the states regulate land use through coastal management, environmental laws, and scenic easements.

Zoning affects such things as

- permitted uses of each parcel of land,

- lot sizes,

- types of structures,

- building heights,

- setbacks (the minimum distance from property boundaries that structures may be built),

- style and appearance of structures,

- density (the ratio of land area to structure area), and

- protection of natural resources.

www1.nyc.gov

www.pittsburghpa
.gov/dcp/zoning

www.portlandoregon
.gov/bps/31612

Zoning ordinances should conform to the comprehensive plan, but both must remain flexible to meet the changing needs of society. Extensive information on how the zoning process works can be found at the websites for New York City, www1.nyc.gov; Pittsburgh, www .pittsburghpa.gov/dcp/zoning; and Portland, www.portlandoregon.gov/bps/31612.

IN PRACTICE

The changing nature of the U.S. economy has resulted in areas of vacant factories and warehouses in many cities. Some cities have revised zoning ordinances to permit new residential or commercial developments in areas once zoned strictly for industrial use. Coupled with tax incentives, the changes have lured developers back into the cities. The resulting housing is often stylishly contemporary, conveniently located, and affordable. In some cities, rundown waterfront areas have become attractive recreational spaces that revitalize surrounding commercial and residential areas.

Zoning classifications

Zoning ordinances have traditionally designated land for residential, commercial, industrial, and agricultural uses. These land-use areas are further divided into subclasses. For example, a residential area may be subdivided to provide for detached single-family dwellings, semidetached structures containing not more than four dwelling units, lowrise apartment buildings without elevators (walkups), and highrise apartment buildings.

A **planned unit development (PUD)** is a development where land is set aside for mixed-use purposes, such as residential, commercial, and public areas. Zoning regulations may be modified for PUDs. PUDs tend to also be heavily regulated by private restrictions, including limitations on building design, materials, landscaping, and use.

Zoning ordinances

To meet both the growing demand for a variety of housing types and the need for innovative residential and nonresidential development, municipalities have adopted ordinances for subdivisions and planned residential developments. Some municipalities also use **buffer zones** to ease the transition from one use to another. A buffer zone is typically a strip of land separating land dedicated to one use from land dedicated to another use. For example, landscaped parks, playgrounds, and hiking trails may be used to screen residential areas from nonresidential zones. Certain types of zoning that focus on special land-use objectives are used in some areas. These include

- *bulk zoning* to control density and avoid overcrowding by imposing restrictions such as setbacks, building heights, and percentage of open area or by restricting new construction projects;

- *aesthetic zoning* to specify certain types of architecture for new buildings; and

- *incentive zoning* to ensure that certain uses are incorporated into developments, such as requiring the street floor of an office building to house retail establishments.

Constitutional issues

Zoning can be a highly controversial issue and often raises questions of constitutional law. The Fourteenth Amendment to the U.S. Constitution prevents the states from depriving "any person of life, liberty, or property, without due process of law." The ongoing question is, How can a local government enact zoning ordinances that protect the public safety and welfare without violating the constitutional rights of property owners? Due process of law means that citizens can discuss zoning ordinances before they are enacted in public hearings. Those affected by the proposed change are provided notice of such hearings and have the opportunity to attend and be heard.

Any land-use legislation that is destructive, unreasonable, arbitrary, or confiscatory usually is considered void. Furthermore, zoning ordinances must not violate the various provisions of the state's constitution. Commonly applied tests in determining the validity of ordinances require that

- power be exercised in a reasonable manner;

- provisions be clear and specific;

- ordinances be nondiscriminatory;

- ordinances promote the public health, safety, and general welfare under the government's police power; and

- ordinances apply to all property in a similar manner.

Is a zoning restriction ever an unconstitutional *taking* that entitles a property owner to compensation for a resulting loss in property value? Unlike the loss of ownership that occurs when title to property is taken, zoning leaves title in the landowner, but limits the owner's use of the property. On June 23, 2017, the U.S. Supreme Court decided the case of *Murr v. Wisconsin* by refusing to grant any relief to the property owner in the form of compensation for a diminution in the property's value created by a state law. The inheritors of two adjoining but separately titled and separately taxed parcels were prohibited from building a structure on one of the parcels because there was already a structure on the other parcel and the two parcels were under the same ownership.

Zoning permits

Compliance with zoning can be monitored by requiring that a property owner obtain a permit before beginning any development. A permit will not be issued unless the proposed development conforms to the permitted zoning, among other requirements. A *zoning permit* is usually required before a *building permit* will be issued.

Nonconforming use

Frequently, a lot or an improvement does not conform to the zoning use because it existed before the enactment or amendment of the zoning ordinance. Such a **nonconforming use** may be allowed to continue legally as long as it complies with the regulations governing nonconformities in the local ordinance, until the improvement is destroyed or torn down, or until the current use is abandoned. If the nonconforming use is allowed to continue indefinitely, it is considered to be grandfathered into the new zoning.

Real estate professionals should never assume, nor allow their clients to assume, that an existing nonconforming use will be allowed to continue. A prospective buyer should verify with the local zoning authorities the conditions under which the use is allowed to remain or whether changes are permitted.

Unit 20

IN PRACTICE

Under a city's original zoning ordinances, a small grocery store was well within a commercial zone. When the zoning map was changed to accommodate an increased need for residential housing, the grocery store was grandfathered into the new zoning.

Zoning hearing board

Most communities have a zoning hearing board (or zoning board of appeal) to hear testimony about the effects a zoning ordinance may have on specific parcels of property. A petition for an exception to the zoning law may be presented to the appeals board, as described next.

Variances and conditional-use permits

Once a plan or zoning ordinance is enacted, property owners and developers know what they can and cannot do on their property. Nevertheless, a property owner may want to use the property in a way that differs to some degree from what the zoning would allow. Generally, the property owner in such a situation may request either a *conditional-use permit* or a *variance* to allow a use that does not meet current zoning requirements.

> A **conditional-use permit** allows a non-conforming but related land use.
>
> A **variance** permits a prohibited land use to avoid undue hardship.

A **conditional-use permit** (also known as a special-use permit) may be granted to a property owner to allow a special use of property that is defined as an allowable conditional use within that zone, such as a house of worship or daycare center in a residential district. For a conditional-use permit to be appropriate, the intended use must meet certain standards set by the municipality.

A **variance** will provide relief if a zoning regulation deprives an owner of the reasonable use of the property. To qualify for a variance, the owner must demonstrate the unique circumstances that make the variance necessary. In addition, the owner must prove that the regulation has caused harm or created a burden. A variance might also be sought to provide relief if an existing zoning regulation creates a physical hardship for the development of a specific property. For example, if an owner's lot is level next to a road but slopes steeply 30 feet away from the road, the zoning board may allow a variance so the owner can build closer to the road than the setback allows.

Both variances and conditional-use permits are issued by zoning boards only after public hearings. Owners of nearby properties must be given an opportunity to voice their opinions.

A property owner also can seek a change in the zoning classification of a parcel of real estate by obtaining an amendment to the district map or zoning ordinance for that area; that is, the owner can attempt to have the zoning changed to accommodate an intended use of the property.

BUILDING CODES AND CERTIFICATES OF OCCUPANCY

Most municipalities have enacted ordinances to specify construction standards that must be met when repairing or erecting buildings. These are called **building codes**, and they set many requirements for such things as materials and standards of workmanship, sanitary equipment, electrical wiring, and fire prevention. Not all building codes are local. Florida has adopted a statewide building code as a way to help protect properties against the massive destruction caused by hurricanes. California requires specific building standards to help protect structures and fixtures from damage that can be caused by earthquakes. Many jurisdictions have adopted the International Building Code that was developed by the International Code Council, www .iccsafe.org, and is regularly reviewed and updated.

www.iccsafe.org

Permits

A property owner who wants to build a structure or alter or repair an existing building usually must obtain a building permit. Through the permit requirement, municipal officials are made aware of new construction or alterations and can verify compliance with building codes and zoning ordinances. An inspector will closely examine the plans and conduct periodic inspections of the work to ensure that the construction complies with relevant ordinances and codes. Once the completed structure has been inspected and found satisfactory, the building official will issue a **certificate of occupancy** or occupancy permit.

The certificate of occupancy indicating that the property is suitable for habitation must be issued before anyone moves in and usually before a lender will allow closing. Most municipalities allow for transfer of property ownership without the need to comply with the most current building codes. The exceptions are usually for safety reasons, such as the California requirement that a water heater be strapped in place for protection in an earthquake. Federal regulations may also be applicable, such as the design and construction requirements of the Americans with Disabilities Act (ADA).

If the construction of a building or an alteration violates a deed restriction, the issuance of a building permit will not cure this violation. A building permit is merely evidence of the applicant's compliance with municipal regulations.

Similarly, communities with historic districts, or those that are interested in maintaining a particular look or character, may have aesthetic ordinances. These laws require that all new construction or restorations be approved by a special board. The board ensures that the new structures will blend in with existing building styles. Owners of existing properties will need to obtain approval to have their homes painted or remodeled.

IN PRACTICE

The subject of planning, zoning, and restricting the use of real estate is extremely technical, and the interpretation of the law is not always clear. Questions concerning any of these subjects in relation to real estate transactions should be referred to legal counsel. The prospective property owner should also be aware of the costs for various permits.

SUBDIVISION

Most communities have adopted **subdivision** and land development ordinances as part of their comprehensive plans. Just as no national zoning ordinance exists, no uniform planning and land development legislation affects the entire country. Laws governing subdividing and land planning are controlled by the state and local governing bodies where the land is located. Rules and regulations developed by state agencies may provide certain minimum standards. Many local governments have established standards that are higher than the minimum standards.

Subdivider and developer

A **subdivider** is a person who buys undeveloped acreage and divides it into smaller lots for sale to individuals or developers or for the subdivider's own use. A subdivision ordinance will include provisions for submitting and processing a proposed subdivision. A **developer**, who may also be a subdivider, improves the land, constructs homes or other buildings on the lots, and sells them. Developing is generally a more extensive activity than subdividing.

Land development plan

Before the actual subdividing can begin, the subdivider must go through the process of land planning. The resulting land development plan must comply with the municipality's comprehensive or master plan. Although comprehensive plans and zoning ordinances are not necessarily inflexible, a plan that requires a change to either must undergo a long, expensive, and frequently complicated process that will include public hearings and action by multiple governing bodies.

Subdivision plan

In plotting out a subdivision according to local planning and zoning controls, a subdivider determines the size as well as the location of the individual lots. The maximum or minimum size of a lot is generally regulated by local ordinances and must be considered carefully. Most subdivisions are laid out by use of lots and blocks. An area of land is designated as a block, with the area making up the block then divided into individual building lots.

The land itself must be studied, usually in cooperation with a surveyor, so that the subdivision takes advantage of natural drainage and land contours. A subdivider should provide for utility easements, as well as easements for water and sewer mains. A developer is often required to submit an environmental impact report with the application for subdivision approval. This report explains what effect the proposed development will have on the surrounding area.

One negative aspect of subdivision development is the potential for increased tax burdens on all residents, both inside and outside the subdivision. To protect local taxpayers against the costs of a heightened demand for public services, many local governments strictly regulate nearly all aspects of subdivision development and may impose impact fees. *Impact fees* are charges made in advance to cover anticipated expenses involving off-site capital improvements, such as additional water and sewer facilities, new roads, and school expansions.

Plat map

From the land development and subdivision plans, the subdivider draws the plat map. A **plat map** is a detailed map illustrating the geographic boundaries of individual lots. The plat map shows the lots, blocks, sections, streets, public easements, and monuments in the prospective subdivision. (See Figure 5.8 for an example of a subdivision plat map.) The plat map may also include engineering data and restrictive covenants. The plat map must be approved by the municipality before it can be recorded. Once a plat map is properly recorded, it may be used to describe the individual parcels of real property. A metes-and-bounds or government survey system description will pinpoint the location of the subdivision plat map on the surface of the earth, which will become part of its description.

Subdivision density

Zoning ordinances typically dictate minimum lot sizes, as well as population density requirements for subdivisions and land developments. For example, a zoning restriction may set the minimum lot area on which a subdivider can build a single-family housing unit at 10,000 square feet. This means that the subdivider can build four houses per acre. Many zoning authorities establish special **density zoning** standards for certain subdivisions. Density zoning ordinances restrict the average maximum number of houses per acre that may be built within a particular subdivision. If the area is density zoned at an average maximum of four houses per acre, for instance, the subdivider may choose to cluster building lots to achieve an open effect. Regardless of lot size or number of units, the subdivider will be in compliance with the ordinance as long as the average number of units in the development, called its *gross density*, remains at or below the maximum density allowed.

PRIVATE LAND-USE CONTROLS

Not all restrictions on the use of land are imposed by government bodies. As already mentioned, certain restrictions to control and maintain the desirable quality and character of a property or subdivision may be created by private parties, including the property owners themselves. These restrictions are separate from and in addition to the land-use controls exercised by the government, but a private restriction cannot violate a federal, state, or local law. Any restriction that would attempt to do so would be void.

Deed restrictions are limitations to the use of property imposed by a past owner or the current owner by inclusion in the deed to the property and are binding on future grantees.

Restrictive covenants

Like deed restrictions, **restrictive covenants** or **covenants, conditions, and restrictions (CC&Rs)**, are private rules set up by the developer that establish standards for all the parcels within the defined subdivision or PUD. The developer's restrictions may be imposed through a covenant in the deed or by a separate recorded declaration that is referenced in the deed. CC&Rs typically govern the type, height, and size of buildings that individual owners can erect, as well as land use, architectural style, construction methods, setbacks, and square footage. CC&Rs are enforced by the homeowners association (HOA) that is set up by the developer and turned over to the homeowners when a specified number of properties has been sold.

Unlike most deed restrictions, many CC&Rs have time limitations; for example, a restriction might state that it is "effective for a period of 25 years from this date." After the specified time, the restriction becomes inoperative or it may be extended if approved by the required number of owners. The rules of the HOA may also allow a specified number of homeowners to change a CC&R.

Restrictive covenants are usually considered valid if they are reasonable restraints that benefit all property owners in the subdivision; that is, they protect property values or safety. If a restriction is too broad, it may be construed as preventing the free transfer of property. If a restrictive covenant or condition is judged unenforceable by a court, the estate will stand free from the invalid covenant or condition. A restrictive covenant, just as with a deed restriction, cannot be used for an illegal purpose, such as the exclusion from a subdivision of members of certain races, nationalities, or religions.

Unit 20

Private land-use controls may be more restrictive of an owner's use than the local zoning ordinances. The rule is that the more restrictive of the two takes precedence. For example, local zoning ordinances may not address the use of a shed on a residential lot, but the CC&Rs in a particular subdivision may prohibit sheds, which means that a property owner in that subdivision may not place a shed on the property.

Private restrictions can be enforced in court when one lot owner or the HOA applies to the court for an injunction to prevent another lot owner from violating the recorded restrictions. The court injunction will direct the violator to stop or remove the violation. The court retains the power to punish the violator for failing to obey. If another lot owner or the HOA fails to take prompt action while a violation is occurring, the right to an injunction can be lost. The court might state that the right was lost through *laches*—that is, the legal principle that a right may be lost through undue delay or failure to assert it.

IN PRACTICE

A real estate professional should consider inserting a contingency in a purchase contract whenever there is doubt about any public or private restrictions which may exist, especially when knowing this information is important to the buyer. Real estate professionals must also be careful to stay informed about publicized changes in zoning so that a misrepresentation charge cannot later be made against the real estate professional who "knew or should have known" this information.

REGULATION OF LAND SALES

Just as the sale and use of property within a state are controlled by state and local governments, the sale of property in one state to buyers in another state is subject to strict federal and state regulations.

Interstate Land Sales Full Disclosure Act

The U.S. Congress created the **Interstate Land Sales Full Disclosure Act (ILSA)** to prevent fraudulent marketing schemes that may arise when land is sold without being seen by the purchasers. The Act was amended by the Dodd-Frank Act in 2011 and its administration is now under the authority of the Consumer Financial Protection Bureau. A full copy of the revised law is at www.hud.gov. Under ILSA, the property seller is required to file a statement of record with CFPB before offering unimproved lots in interstate commerce by telephone or through the mail. The statement of record must contain numerous disclosures about the property.

www.hud.gov

A developer is also required to provide each purchaser or lessee of property with a printed report before the purchaser or lessee signs a purchase contract or lease. The report must disclose specific information about the property, including the

- type of title being transferred to the buyer,
- number of homes currently occupied on the site,
- availability of recreation facilities,
- distance to nearby communities,
- utility services and charges, and
- soil conditions and foundation or construction problems.

If the purchaser or lessee does not receive a copy of the report before signing the purchase contract or lease, the consumer may have grounds to void the contract.

The act provides a number of exemptions. For instance, it does not apply to subdivisions consisting of fewer than 25 lots or to those in which each lot is 20 acres or more. Lots offered for sale solely to developers also are exempt from the act's requirements, as are lots on which buildings exist or where a seller is obligated to construct a building within two years.

State subdivided land sales laws

Many states have enacted their own subdivided land sales laws. Some affect only the sale to state residents of land located outside the state. Other states' laws regulate sales of land located both inside and outside the state. These state land sales laws tend to be stricter and more detailed than the federal law. Real estate professionals should be aware of the law in their state, if any, and how it compares with federal law.

KEY POINT REVIEW

Land use is controlled and regulated through **public restrictions, such as** planning, zoning, building codes, and subdivision plans; **private restrictions** imposed by deed; and direct ownership of land by federal, state, and local governments.

The **police power** of the state is its authority to create regulations to protect the public health, safety, and welfare. State enabling acts allow the state's police power to be passed down to municipalities and other local governing authorities. A **comprehensive plan (master plan)** created by a local government usually covers land use, housing needs, movement of people and goods, community facilities and utilities, and energy conservation.

Zoning ordinances are local laws implementing the land uses designated in the comprehensive plan and typically cover items such as **permitted uses**, lot sizes, types of structures, building heights, setbacks, style and appearance of structures, density, and protection of natural resources.

Zoning classifies property by uses and types, such as **commercial**, **industrial**, **residential**, agricultural, and **planned unit developments (PUDs)**.

Other ways in which zoning is used include **buffer zones** separating residential from nonresidential areas, **bulk zoning** to control density, **aesthetic zoning** to specify certain types of architecture for new buildings, and **incentive zoning** to require certain uses in developments.

Zoning is enforced through the use of **permits**. An individual case may be considered by a **zoning hearing board (or zoning board of appeals)**, which may decide to allow a **nonconforming use** to continue, grant a **variance** from a zoning ordinance to permit a prohibited land use to avoid undue hardship, or grant a **conditional-use permit (special-use permit)**.

Building codes require permits for new construction and remodeling of or additions to existing construction. State and federal regulations may add additional requirements.

A **certificate of occupancy** is issued upon satisfactory completion of work for which a **building permit** was issued.

Subdivision and land development ordinances may be created by the state or may be made part of a local government's comprehensive plan. **A subdivider** buys undeveloped acreage and divides it into smaller lots for sale to individuals or developers. A **developer** improves land and constructs homes or other buildings that are then sold.

A **plat map (subdivision map)** shows geographic boundaries of separate land parcels, usually by showing **blocks** of land divided into individual **lots**. A **subdivision plan** describes subdivision features, including utility easements, in compliance with zoning and other laws.

Private land-use controls include **deed restrictions** that are placed in a deed and the **covenants, conditions, and restrictions (CC&Rs)** placed or referenced in deeds to all property owners in a subdivision.

The **federal Interstate Land Sales Full Disclosure Act (ILSA)** regulates the interstate sale of unimproved lots in subdivisions of 25 or more lots of less than 20 acres each. The law does not apply to subdivisions sold solely to developers. **State subdivision laws** may also apply to sales within the state of subdivisions located either inside or outside the state.

UNIT 20 QUIZ

1. A subdivision declaration reads, "No property within this subdivision may be further subdivided for sale or otherwise, and no property may be used for other than single-family housing." This is an example of
   A. a restrictive covenant.
   B. an illegal reverter clause.
   C. R-1 zoning.
   D. a conditional-use clause.

2. A landowner who wants to use property in a manner that is prohibited by a local zoning ordinance but which would benefit the community can apply for which of the following?
   A. Conditional-use permit
   B. Prescriptive easement
   C. Occupancy permit
   D. Property allowance

3. What is *NOT* included in public land-use controls?
   A. Subdivision regulations
   B. Covenants, conditions, and restrictions
   C. Environmental protection laws
   D. Comprehensive plan specifications

4. Under its police powers, a municipality may regulate all of the following about housing in a development *EXCEPT*
   A. lot sizes.
   B. building uses.
   C. ethnicity of owners.
   D. type of structure.

5. The purpose of a building permit is to
   A. indicate the property is suitable for habitation.
   B. maintain municipal control over the amount of building.
   C. provide evidence of compliance with municipal regulations.
   D. show compliance with restrictive covenants.

6. Zoning powers are conferred on municipal governments in which of the following ways?
   A. By state enabling acts
   B. Through the master plan
   C. By popular local vote
   D. Through city charters

7. A town located near a small recreational lake enacts a new zoning code. Under the new code, commercial buildings are not permitted within 1,000 feet of the lake. A commercial building that is permitted to continue in its former use even though it is built on the lakeshore is an example of
   A. nonconforming use.
   B. variance.
   C. special use.
   D. adverse possession.

8. To determine whether a location can be put to future use as a retail store, one would examine
   A. the building code.
   B. the list of permitted nonconforming uses.
   C. the housing code.
   D. the zoning ordinance.

9. All of the following are legal deed restrictions *EXCEPT*
   A. types of buildings that may be constructed.
   B. allowable race of purchasers.
   C. activities that are not to be conducted at the site.
   D. minimum size of buildings to be constructed.

10. A restriction in a seller's deed may be enforced by which of the following?
    A. Court injunction
    B. Zoning board of appeal
    C. City building commission
    D. State legislature

11. A property owner owns a large tract of land. After an adequate study of all the relevant facts, the owner legally divides the land into 30 lots suitable for the construction of residences. In this situation, the property owner is acting as
    A. a subdivider.
    B. a developer.
    C. a land planner.
    D. an urban planner.

12. A map illustrating the sizes and locations of streets and lots in a subdivision is called
    A. a gridiron plan.
    B. a survey.
    C. a subdivision plat map.
    D. a property report.

13. In one city, developers are limited by the zoning law to constructing no more than an average of three houses per acre in any subdivision. What does this restriction regulate?
    A. Clustering
    B. Gross density
    C. Out-lots
    D. Covenants

14. Which of the following is a variance?
    A. An exception to a zoning ordinance
    B. A court order prohibiting certain activities
    C. A reversion of ownership
    D. A nullification of an easement

15. Permitted land uses and set-asides, housing projections, transportation issues, and objectives for implementing future controlled development would all be found in a community's
    A. zoning ordinance.
    B. comprehensive plan.
    C. enabling act.
    D. land-control law.

16. Which of the following items would usually *NOT* be shown on the plat map for a new subdivision?
    A. Easements for sewer and water mains
    B. Land to be used for streets
    C. Numbered lots and blocks
    D. Prices of residential and commercial lots

17. A plat for a proposed subdivision is submitted to
    A. the municipality.
    B. the property owners.
    C. the developer.
    D. the state.

18. Restrictive covenants
    A. are no longer effective when the title is transferred.
    B. apply only until the developer has conveyed the title.
    C. can be removed by a court of competent jurisdiction.
    D. apply to and bind successive owners of the property.

19. To protect the public from fraudulent interstate land sales, a developer involved in interstate land sales of 25 or more lots must
    A. provide each purchaser with a printed report disclosing details of the property.
    B. pay the prospective buyer's expenses to see the property involved.
    C. provide preferential financing.
    D. allow a 30-day cancellation period.

20. When is a certificate of occupancy issued?
    A. When the owner of a multifamily residential property wishes to limit the number of individuals who may live in a single unit
    B. At the time a property owner applies for a building permit
    C. After building construction work has been inspected and found satisfactory by the municipal inspector
    D. When an application for a variance or conditional-use permit has been granted by the zoning board

UNIT
21

Environmental Issues and the Real Estate Transaction

LEARNING OBJECTIVES

When you have completed this unit, you will be able to

> **identify** the basic environmental hazards the real estate professional should be aware of for the protection of client interests as well as the personal risk of liability for nondisclosure;
> **describe** groundwater, water table, and the provisions of the Safe Drinking Water Act;
> **describe** the issues involved with underground storage tanks, and the associated legal requirements facing the property owner;
> **explain** the regulation involved in the creation and operation of waste disposal sites and in the control of brownfields;
> **list** the various federal laws which protect the public from uncontrolled hazardous waste, and the liability issues facing those who violate any of these laws; and
> **explain** the responsibilities and duties of real estate professionals regarding environmental issues.

KEY TERMS

asbestos
brownfields
carbon monoxide (CO)
chlorofluorocarbons (CFCs)
Comprehensive
  Environmental Response,
  Compensation, and Liability
  Act (CERCLA)
encapsulation
environmental impact
  statement (EIS)

environmental site
  assessment (ESA)
formaldehyde
groundwater
hydraulic fracturing (fracking)
lead
Lead-Based Paint Hazard
  Reduction Act (LBPHRA)
mold
polychlorinated biphenyls
  (PCBs)
radon

Small Business Liability
  Relief and Brownfields
  Revitalization Act
Superfund Amendments and
  Reauthorization Act (SARA)
underground storage tanks
  (USTs)
urea-formaldehyde foam
  insulation (UFFI)
water table
wetlands

OVERVIEW

Environmental issues are health issues, and health issues based on environmental hazards have become real estate issues. Although real estate professionals are not expected to have the technical expertise necessary to determine whether a hazardous substance is present on or near a property, they should be familiar with state and federal environmental laws and the regulatory agencies that enforce them. In that way, the real estate professional can alert a prospective purchaser to the need for authoritative information about hazardous substances in order to make an informed purchase decision.

HAZARDOUS SUBSTANCES

Pollution and hazardous substances in the environment are of interest to real estate professionals because they affect the attractiveness, safety, desirability, and market value of cities, neighborhoods, and backyards. No one wants to live in a toxic environment. (See Figure 21.1.) You will see various references to the Environmental Protection Agency (EPA), www.epa.gov, which was created by Congress in 1970 to oversee many of the laws passed since then to protect and restore the environment.

www.epa.gov
www.hud.gov

Rules of the Department of Housing and Urban Development (HUD), www.hud.gov, also come into play.

FIGURE 21.1: Environmental Hazards

State laws are also of concern when discussing environmental hazards. A state-mandated disclosure about the condition of the property and any known environmental issues is usually required by a seller of property with one to four dwelling units. In the past, real estate professionals tended to accept seller-supplied disclosure forms without question, trusting that all was accurate and complete. Today that trust is risky business. In fact, some states impose a burden on the real estate professional to discover problems and ask questions. Similarly, real estate professionals should inform buyers of the need to ask and discover and not rely on disclosure forms as a warranty or guarantee. As a rule, sellers are to disclose what they are aware of, but buyers are put on notice of the responsibility to discover hazards they are concerned about.

IN PRACTICE

It is important that real estate professionals and sellers provide property disclosures to prospective buyers when required by law. For example, in the 2003 South Dakota case of *Saiz v. Horn*, homebuyers found substantial defects in the home they purchased. The buyers learned that the seller had in the past given prospective buyers a disclosure statement revealing the property's defects but had not provided it to the buyers. The court found that the real estate professional should have told the homebuyers that the sellers had a legal duty to provide them with a disclosure statement.

Asbestos

Asbestos is a fire-resistant mineral that was once used extensively as insulation and to strengthen other materials. A component of more than 3,000 types of building materials, asbestos was first used in the early 1900s and is found in most construction, including residential, built from the early 1940s until 1978, when its use was banned. The EPA estimates that about 107,000 primary and secondary schools and 733,000 public and commercial buildings have asbestos-containing materials (ACMs).

Asbestos was used to cover pipes, ducts, and heating and hot water units. Its fire-resistant properties made it a popular material for use in floor tile, exterior siding, roofing products, linoleum flooring materials, joint compounds, wallboard material, backing, and mastics. Though some ACMs are easy to identify (e.g., older insulation around heating and water pipes), identifying asbestos may be more difficult when it is behind walls or under floors.

Asbestos-based products can create airborne contaminants that may result in respiratory diseases.

Asbestos is highly *friable*, meaning that as it ages, asbestos fibers easily break down into tiny, very light filaments that stay in the air a long time when it is disturbed or exposed, as often occurs during renovation or remodeling. Those who have inhaled asbestos fibers often develop serious and deadly respiratory diseases decades later. While federal regulations establish guidelines for owners of public and commercial buildings to test for asbestos-containing materials, there are no guidelines regarding the presence of asbestos in residential properties.

Because improper removal procedures may further contaminate the air within the structure, the removal process requires state-licensed technicians and specially sealed environments. The waste generated must be disposed of at a licensed facility, which further adds to the cost of removal. **Encapsulation**, or the sealing off of disintegrating asbestos, is an alternate method of asbestos control that may be preferable to removal in certain circumstances, provided the condition of the encapsulated asbestos is monitored periodically to make sure it is not disintegrating.

Only a certified asbestos inspector should perform an asbestos inspection of a structure to identify which building materials may contain asbestos. The inspector can also provide recommendations and costs associated with remediation. Buyers should be aware of where ACMs are located so that they are not disturbed during any repair, remodeling, demolition, or even routine use. Appraisers also should be aware of the possible presence of asbestos.

www.epa.gov/asbestos

More information on asbestos-related issues can be found at www.epa.gov/asbestos. Numerous publications that provide guidance, information, and assistance with asbestos issues are available.

Lead-based paint and other lead hazards

Although prohibited for use in housing as of 1978, **lead** has been used as a pigment and drying agent in alkyd oil-based paints, stains, and varnishes. Lead-based paint may be on any interior or exterior surface, but it is particularly common on doors, windows, and other woodwork, but can even be found in wallpaper. The federal government estimates that lead is present in about 75% of all private housing built before 1978; that's approximately 57 million homes, ranging from apartments to mansions. Information on lead hazards and abatement can be found at www.epa.gov/lead.

www.epa.gov/lead

Lead from paint or other sources can result in damage to the brain, nervous system, kidneys, and blood. Children younger than six are particularly vulnerable.

Children younger than six are the most vulnerable to damage from excessive lead levels, which can cause learning disabilities, developmental delays, reduced height, and poor hearing. Excessive exposure in adults can induce anemia and hypertension, trigger gallbladder problems, and cause reproductive problems in both men and women.

Lead dust can be ingested from the hands of a crawling infant, inhaled by any occupant of a structure, or ingested from the water supply because of lead pipes or lead solder. Soil and groundwater may be contaminated by everything from lead plumbing in leaking landfills to discarded skeets and bullets from an old shooting range. High levels of lead have been found in the soil near waste-to-energy incinerators.

In 1996, the EPA and HUD issued final regulations under the **Lead-Based Paint Hazard Reduction Act (LBPHRA)** of 1992, requiring disclosure of the presence of any known lead-based paint hazards to potential buyers or renters. The federal law does not require that anyone test for the presence of lead-based paint, however. Under later regulations, EPA imposed training and certification requirements, which took effect June 23, 2008, for renovators of certain property containing lead-based paint.

The EPA now requires the following from sellers, landlords, and renovators of residential dwellings built before 1978:

www.epa.gov/sites /production/files/ documents/selr_eng .pdf

www.epa.gov/sites/ production/files/2017 -06/documents/pyf_ color_booklet_format _2017_508.pdf

www.gpo.gov/home -page

www.epa.gov/lead

www.epa.gov/ getleadsafe

- Landlords must disclose known information on lead-based paint and hazards before leases take effect. Leases must include a disclosure form regarding lead-based paint.

- Sellers have to disclose known information on lead-based paint and hazards prior to execution of a contract for sale. Sales contracts must include a completed disclosure form about lead-based paint. (See Figure 21.2.) This is the form for sellers and is slightly different from the form for landlords. Real estate professionals should use EPA-written disclosure forms rather than creating their own forms. The form shown can be found at www.epa.gov/sites/production/files/documents/selr_eng.pdf.

- Buyers must have up to 10 days to conduct a risk assessment or inspection for the presence of lead-based paint hazards. Buyer and seller can mutually agree in writing to lengthen or shorten that time period, or the buyer may waive the inspection.

- Real estate professionals must provide buyers and lessees with "Protect Your Family from Lead in Your Home," the pamphlet created by the EPA, HUD, and the U.S. Consumer Product Safety Commission. The pamphlet can be downloaded from www.epa .gov/sites/production/files/2017-06/documents/pyf_color_booklet_format_2017_508 .pdf or ordered from the Government Publishing Office, 202-512-1800 or www.gpo .gov/home-page.

- Anyone who is paid to perform work that disturbs paint in housing, schools, and child care facilities built before 1978 must be trained and certified in EPA lead-based work practices. This includes residential rental property owners/managers, general contractors, and special trade contractors (e.g., painters, plumbers, carpenters, electricians). The Renovation, Repair, and Painting (RR&P) program involves prerenovation education, including distribution of the pamphlet *Renovate Right* to the property owner before work commences. It can be found at www.epa.gov/lead. General information about the program is at www.epa.gov/lead/renovation-repair-and-painting-program.

- Real estate professionals must ensure that all parties comply with the law.

- Sellers, lessors, and renovators are required to disclose any prior test results or any knowledge of lead-based paint hazards. With only a very narrow exception, all real estate professionals (subagent, buyer's representative, transaction facilitator) are required to advise sellers to make the required disclosures. Only buyer's representatives who are paid entirely by the buyer are exempt.

IN PRACTICE

The EPA and HUD are serious about enforcement of lead-based paint notification rules.

No company is too big or too small to escape scrutiny. On September 28, 2016, the EPA and the Department of Justice announced a settlement with Sears Home Improvement Products Inc. that resolved alleged violations of the Lead Renovation, Repair and Painting Rule for work performed by Sears' contractors during home renovation projects across the country. In addition to paying a $100,000 civil penalty, Sears must implement a comprehensive, corporate-wide program to ensure that the contractors it hires to perform work minimize lead dust from home renovation activities. On October 17, 2016, the EPA announced a fine of $69,398 against a Portland, Oregon based remodeling firm, Hammer and Hand Inc., for failing to follow lead-safe work practices while renovating two older homes in Portland in 2015.

A home can be inspected for lead hazards in the following ways:

- *Paint inspection.* A paint inspection will provide the lead content of every different type of painted surface in a home. This inspection will not indicate whether the paint is a hazard or how the homeowner should deal with it.

- *Risk assessment.* A risk assessment indicates whether there are any sources of serious lead exposure, such as peeling paint or lead dust. It also describes what actions can be taken to address the hazards.

www.epa.gov/lead /forms/lead-hotline -national-lead -information-center

EPA guidance pamphlets, a list of professionals qualified to inspect or assess for lead-based paint, and other information about lead-based hazards are available from the National Lead Information Center at 800-424-5323 and www.epa.gov/lead/forms/lead-hotline-national-lead -information-center.

FIGURE 21.2: Disclosure of Lead-Based Paint and Lead-Based Paint Hazards

---

Disclosure of Information on Lead-Based Paint and/or Lead-Based Paint Hazards

Lead Warning Statement

Every purchaser of any interest in residential real property on which a residential dwelling was built prior to 1978 is notified that such property may present exposure to lead from lead-based paint that may place young children at risk of developing lead poisoning. Lead poisoning in young children may produce permanent neurological damage, including learning disabilities, reduced intelligence quotient, behavioral problems, and impaired memory. Lead poisoning also poses a particular risk to pregnant women. The seller of any interest in residential real property is required to provide the buyer with any information on lead-based paint hazards from risk assessments or inspections in the seller's possession and notify the buyer of any known lead-based paint hazards. A risk assessment or inspection for possible lead-based paint hazards is recommended prior to purchase.

Seller's Disclosure

(a) Presence of lead-based paint and/or lead-based paint hazards (check (i) or (ii) below):

    (i) _____ Known lead-based paint and/or lead-based paint hazards are present in the housing (explain).

    _____

    (ii) _____ Seller has no knowledge of lead-based paint and/or lead-based paint hazards in the housing.

(b) Records and reports available to the seller (check (i) or (ii) below):

    (i) _____ Seller has provided the purchaser with all available records and reports pertaining to lead-based paint and/or lead-based paint hazards in the housing (list documents below).

    _____

    (ii) _____ Seller has no reports or records pertaining to lead-based paint and/or lead-based paint hazards in the housing.

Purchaser's Acknowledgment (initial)

(c) _____ Purchaser has received copies of all information listed above.

(d) _____ Purchaser has received the pamphlet *Protect Your Family from Lead in Your Home.*

(e) Purchaser has (check (i) or (ii) below):

    (i) _____ received a 10-day opportunity (or mutually agreed upon period) to conduct a risk assessment or inspection for the presence of lead-based paint and/or lead-based paint hazards; or

    (ii) _____ waived the opportunity to conduct a risk assessment or inspection for the presence of lead-based paint and/or lead-based paint hazards.

Agent's Acknowledgment (initial)

(f) _____ Agent has informed the seller of the seller's obligations under 42 U.S.C. 4852(d) and is aware of his/her responsibility to ensure compliance.

Certification of Accuracy

The following parties have reviewed the information above and certify, to the best of their knowledge, that the information they have provided is true and accurate.

Seller	Date	Seller	Date
Purchaser	Date	Purchaser	Date
Agent	Date	Agent	Date

Radon

Radon is a naturally occurring, colorless, odorless, tasteless, radioactive gas produced by the decay of other radioactive substances. Radon is measured in picocuries (a unit of radiation) contained in a liter of air (pCi/L). Radon is found in every state and territory with radon levels in the outdoor air averaging 0.4 pCi/L. Fans and thermal "stack effects" (i.e., rising hot air draws cooler air in from the ground through cracks in the basement and foundation walls) pull radon into buildings.

The potential for developing lung cancer from exposure to radon is a function of the extent and the length of a person's exposure to radon. Radon has been classified as a Class A known human carcinogen. Furthermore, smokers have a radon risk factor 15 times greater than nonsmokers.

Because neither the EPA nor current scientific consensus has been able to establish a "threshold" safe level of radon exposure, the EPA suggests an "action" level of 4 pCi/L. The action level of 4 was chosen because 95% of the time, current technology can bring the level below 4, and 75% of the time, levels can be reduced to 2 pCi/L. A radon mitigation system is less expensive when installed during construction. Mitigation consists of removing the radon before it seeps into the house by means of a fan installed in a pipe running from the basement to the attic to draw the radon up and out.

Home testing may be done with passive devices, such as alpha track detectors and a charcoal canister. Continuous monitors require electrical power and usually a trained technician. Test results are normally received within 10 days or so when using a passive device (immediately when using an electric continuous monitor). Although a 90-day testing period is most accurate, the EPA developed a 48-hour procedure that can be used in a real estate transaction. The 48-hour test can satisfactorily predict whether a home's annual average is at or above 4 pCi/L in 94% of cases.

www.epa.gov/radon

Because one out of every 15 homes probably needs mitigation, before looking at properties, real estate professionals should discuss radon concerns with their buyers. Real estate professionals can direct buyers to www.epa.gov/radon for the *Consumer's Guide to Radon* and additional information about testing and mitigation methods.

Formaldehyde

Formaldehyde, a colorless chemical with a strong, pronounced odor, is used widely in the manufacture of building materials and many household products because of its preservative characteristics. Often emitted as a gas, formaldehyde is one of the most common and problematic volatile organic compounds (VOCs) and is one of the few indoor air pollutants that can be measured. Formaldehyde was listed as a hazardous air pollutant in the Clean Air Act Amendments of 1990. Its use and effects are described at www.epa.gov/formaldehyde.

www.epa.gov
/formaldehyde

Formaldehyde is classified as a "probable human carcinogen" (i.e., causing cancer in animals and probably in humans). For the 10 to 20% of the population that is "sensitive" to formaldehyde, formaldehyde may trigger respiratory problems (shortness of breath, wheezing, chest tightness, asthma), as well as eye and skin irritations (burning sensations in the eyes and throat). It is a major contributor to sick building syndrome (SBS) in commercial properties.

The largest source of formaldehyde in any building is likely to be the off-gassing from pressed-wood products made using adhesives that contain urea-formaldehyde (UF) resins. Pressed-wood products include particleboard, hardwood plywood paneling, and medium-density fiberboard. It is also used in carpeting and ceiling tiles. Since 1985, HUD has regulated the use of plywood and particleboard so that they conform to specified formaldehyde-emission levels in the construction of prefabricated homes and manufactured housing. The latest regulations that will be enforced by the EPA under the Formaldehyde Standards for Composite Wood Products Act enacted in 2010, went into effect on May 22, 2017. More information can be found at www.epa.gov/formaldehyde.

Urea-Formaldehyde Foam Insulation (UFFI), once popular, then banned, and now legal again, is rarely used. When incorrectly mixed, UFFI never properly cures, resulting in strong emissions shortly after installation. Studies have shown that formaldehyde emissions generally decrease over time, so homes where UFFI was installed many years ago are unlikely to still have high levels of formaldehyde unless the insulation is exposed to extreme heat or moisture. Real estate professionals should check their state's property disclosure form to see whether UFFI must be disclosed. Appraisers should also be aware of the presence of formaldehyde.

Carbon monoxide

Carbon monoxide (CO) is a colorless, odorless, and tasteless gas that occurs as a by-product of burning fuels such as wood, oil, and natural gas, owing to incomplete combustion. Carbon monoxide is quickly absorbed by the body, where it inhibits the blood's ability to transport oxygen, resulting in dizziness and nausea. As CO concentrations increase, the symptoms become more severe, and death may occur within a short time. According to the Consumer Product Safety Commission, www.cpsc.gov, more than 150 deaths from accidental non-fire-related carbon monoxide poisoning associated with consumer products occur in the United States each year. Thousands of other individuals require hospital emergency room care annually. Many cases arise from the use of portable generators in areas that have undergone a natural disaster. More information can be found at www.cpsc.gov/Safety-Education/Safety -Guides.

www.cpsc.gov/Safety -Education/Safety -Guides

In addition to portable generators, furnaces, water heaters, space heaters, fireplaces, and wood stoves all produce CO as a natural result of their combustion of fuel. When these units are functioning properly and are properly ventilated, their CO emissions are not a problem; however, improper ventilation or equipment malfunctions can allow large quantities of CO to be released into a residence or commercial structure in a very short amount of time. CO is a problem often encountered by property managers if tenants use kerosene heaters. More information is available at www.epa.gov.

www.epa.gov/indoor -air-quality-iaq/carbon -monoxides-impact -indoor-air-quality

IN PRACTICE

Carbon monoxide detectors are available, sometimes in combination with smoke detectors, and their use is required in residential buildings in more than half of the states. Even if they are not, a property manager should discuss with the landlord the importance of installing a detector in any rental property that is equipped with an appliance or heater that might create a CO problem. Annual maintenance of heating systems also helps avoid CO exposure.

Polychlorinated biphenyls

Polychlorinated biphenyls (PCBs) consist of more than 200 chemical compounds that are not found naturally in nature. Flame resistant, they were often used in electrical equipment, such as transformers, electrical motors in refrigerators, caulking compounds, and hydraulic oil in older equipment. The EPA has classified PCBs as reasonably carcinogenic, and these chemicals have been implicated in lower fertility and shortened life spans. Although the commercial distribution of PCBs was banned in 1979, PCBs remain in the environment because burning them at more than 2,400 degrees in a closed environment is the only known way to destroy them.

PCBs are most likely a concern for commercial and industrial property managers. These managers should ask the local utility company to identify and remove any type of transformer that might be a source of PCBs. If the PCBs leak into the environment, penalties and removal methods are expensive.

Chlorofluorocarbons

Chlorofluorocarbons (CFCs) are nontoxic, nonflammable chemicals used as refrigerants in air conditioners, refrigerators, and freezers. CFCs are also used in aerosol sprays, paints, solvents, and foam-blowing applications. Although CFCs are safe in most applications and are inert in the lower atmosphere, once CFC vapors rise to the upper atmosphere, where they may survive from 2 to 150 years, they are broken down by ultraviolet light into chemicals that deplete the ozone layer.

Global treaties have sought to reduce the production levels of CFCs. The manufacture of these chemicals ended for the most part in 1996, with exceptions for production in developing countries, medical products (e.g., asthma inhalers), and research.

Although newer air conditioners use a different product, older appliances may leak CFCs and should be properly disposed of to prevent further leakage. A buyer's representative may wish to advise the client to consider upgrading to newer, more energy-efficient and environmentally safe appliances.

Only EPA-certified technicians should do any work on a refrigeration system, especially the larger systems found in commercial and industrial buildings. Approved equipment should carry a label reading, "This equipment has been certified by ARI/UL to meet EPA's minimum requirements for recycling and recovery equipment."

Mold

Mold can be found almost anywhere and can grow on almost any organic substance, as long as moisture, oxygen, and an organic food source are present. Moisture feeds mold growth. If a moisture problem is not discovered or addressed, mold growth can gradually destroy what it is growing on. In addition, some molds can cause serious health problems, including allergic reactions and asthma attacks. Some molds are known to produce potent toxins and/or irritants.

Some moisture problems in homes and buildings have been directly linked to recent changes in construction practices. Some of these practices have resulted in buildings that are too tightly sealed, preventing adequate ventilation. Building materials, such as drywall, may not allow moisture to escape easily. The material used in drywall wicks moisture to the nutrition source of glue and paper. Vinyl wallpaper and exterior insulation finish systems (EIFS), also known as synthetic stucco, also do not allow moisture to escape. Other moisture problems include roof leaks, unvented combustion appliances, and landscaping or gutters that direct water to the building.

General mold information, as well as guidelines for the remediation and/or cleanup of mold and moisture problems in schools and commercial buildings can be found at www.epa.gov /mold.

_____
www.epa.gov/mold

Mold is an important issue for real estate professionals, particularly because homeowners insurance policies now generally exclude mold from coverage. Plaintiffs may name property sellers, landlords, property management companies, and real estate professionals as defendants in a case, in addition to construction and insurance companies.

IN PRACTICE

In a 2005 Wisconsin case, *Eddy v. B.S.T.V., Inc.*, a couple sued a real estate company for failing to disclose mold contamination in the home they purchased. The real estate company's insurer refused to provide coverage, stating that the insurance policy had specific exclusion clauses that would not cover property damage arising out of a real estate professional's failure to render professional services. The couple bringing the lawsuit alleged that the real estate professionals breached the real estate company's professional-service responsibilities and that, therefore, the exclusions applied. The real estate company tried to argue that because its real estate agents were trained in identifying mold-related hazards, the claim did not fit the exclusion clause. The court did not agree, and the real estate company was held liable. The court held that the exclusion clauses in the policy prevented insurance coverage for the injuries.

In light of this case and other court decisions on this topic, real estate companies and professionals find it difficult to know what to do when mold is suspected or found on a property. There are no federal requirements to disclose mold contamination at this time, and only a few states require disclosure. Real estate professionals should remind buyers that sellers cannot disclose what they do not know. Also, real estate professionals should advise buyers that they have not only the right but also the burden to discover the presence of mold.

IN PRACTICE

Real estate professionals may need to take extra steps to protect themselves from liability. Those who suspect that mold is present in a home should ask many questions about leaks, floods, and prior damage and remind the sellers to honestly and truthfully disclose any insurance claims regarding mold and other water issues. Any conversation with a seller should be followed up with a summary of the conversation in writing, even if just an email, particularly if the seller says that there has never been any instance of water damage to the property and the real estate professional suspects that this is not the truth. Copies of all emails and other communications with the seller should be kept in the office's records of the transaction, in case they are ever needed.

GROUNDWATER PROTECTION

Groundwater, water that exists under the earth's surface within the tiny spaces or crevices in geological formations, forms the **water table**, the natural level at which the ground is saturated. The water table may be several hundred feet underground or near the surface. When the earth's natural filtering systems are inadequate to ensure the availability of pure water, any contamination of underground water threatens the supply of pure, clean water for private wells or public water systems. Numerous state and federal laws have been enacted to preserve and protect the water supply.

Groundwater can be contaminated from a number of sources, including runoff from waste disposal sites, leaking underground storage tanks, septic systems, dry wells, and storm drains, as well as the illegal disposal of hazardous materials and regular use of insecticides and herbicides. Because water flows from one place to another, contamination can spread far from its source. Once the contamination has been identified, its source can be eliminated. Although the water may eventually become clean, the process can be time consuming and extremely expensive.

The Safe Drinking Water Act

The Safe Drinking Water Act (SDWA) was passed in 1974 (and amended in 1986 and 1996) to protect public health by regulating the nation's public drinking water supply. The SDWA authorizes the EPA to set national health-based standards for drinking water. The amendments strengthened the law by increasing source water protection, operator training, funding for water system improvements, and public information. For example, the EPA now requires that water suppliers report any health risk situation within 24 hours, instead of the 72 hours mandated originally. One of the EPA's recent concerns is the effect on groundwater of the byproducts produced by hydraulic fracturing (fracking), the process used to extract natural gas from the deep layers of rock in which it is embedded. A regularly updated report by the EPA can be found at www.epa.gov/hfstudy. In December 2016, the EPA issued the final Executive Summary of its ongoing investigation.

www.epa.gov/hfstudy

Most property disclosure forms require sellers to identify the property's water source, such as well water, municipal water supply, or some other source. Anything other than a municipal water supply should be tested. Also, sellers are generally required to identify the type and location of any septic system used on the property because an incorrectly placed or poorly functioning system can contaminate the water source.

IN PRACTICE

Real estate professionals should educate their sellers about full and honest disclosure concerning the property's water supply and septic systems. Buyers should be educated about potential groundwater contamination sources both on and off a property. Real estate professionals should always recommend testing the water supply when it is not part of a municipal source.

Wetlands protection

The Federal Water Pollution Control Act of 1948 was amended in 1972 and is now known as the Clean Water Act. Under the authority of the Clean Water Act, the EPA is concerned with protecting and improving the quality of wetlands, areas where water covers the soil all or part of the time. Wetlands include swamps, marshes, bogs, and even wet meadows, river overflows, and mud flats, as well as natural ponds. They can be habitats for fish and wildlife and also serve as water storage as well as drainage areas. More information is available at www.epa.gov/wetlands.

www.epa.gov/wetlands

UNDERGROUND STORAGE TANKS

Underground storage tanks (USTs) are commonly found on sites where petroleum products are used or where gas stations and auto repair shops are or were located. They also may be found in a number of other commercial and industrial establishments, including printing and chemical plants, wood treatment plants, paper mills, paint manufacturers, dry cleaners, food processing plants, and chemical storage or process waste plants. Military bases and airports are also common sites for underground tanks. In residential areas, tanks can be used to store heating oil.

Legal requirements

The Resource Conservation and Recovery Act (RCRA) is the federal law that gives the EPA authority to develop a program for proper management of underground storage tanks, as well as hazardous and nonhazardous solid waste. Information on program requirements can be found at www.epa.gov/rcra.

www.epa.gov/rcra

Federal and state laws impose strict requirements on a landowner whose property contains an underground storage tank. The regulations apply to tanks that contain hazardous substances or liquid petroleum products and that store at least 10% of their volume underground. Some states also have adopted laws regulating underground storage tanks that are more stringent than the federal laws. UST owners are required to register all tanks and adhere to strict technical and administrative requirements that govern

- installation,
- maintenance,
- corrosion prevention,
- overspill prevention,
- monitoring, and
- recordkeeping.

Owners are also required to provide evidence of sufficient financial resources to cover any damage that might result from a leak.

The following types of tanks are among those that are exempt from the federal regulations:

- Tanks that hold less than 110 gallons
- Farm and residential tanks that hold 1,100 gallons or less of motor fuel used for noncommercial purposes
- Tanks that store heating oil burned on the premises
- Tanks on or above the floor of underground areas, such as basements or tunnels
- Septic tanks and systems for collecting storm water and wastewater

Most seller property disclosures are required only for residential properties. Most of the problematic USTs are found in commercial and industrial properties, placing the duty of discovery squarely on the buyer. Because many of the older tanks have never been registered and exempt tanks are not required to be registered, real estate professionals and their buyers should be particularly alert to the presence of fill pipes, vent lines, stained soil, and fumes or odors, any of which may indicate the presence of a UST. Detection, removal, and cleanup of surrounding contaminated soil can be expensive, so it is important to deal with these issues before, not after, closing.

IN PRACTICE

Whenever a real estate professional is in doubt about whether or not a property contains USTs, a contingency should be added to the property buyer's offer allowing the buyer to have the property inspected for USTs.

WASTE DISPOSAL SITES AND BROWNFIELDS

The RCRA, as well as state and local regulations, governs the location, construction, content, and maintenance of landfill sites built to accommodate the vast quantities of garbage produced every day in America. Commercial or industrial sites that are no longer is use but which may contain toxic waste are also regulated.

Waste disposal sites

A landfill begins as enormous hole in the ground, either excavated for the purpose of waste disposal or left over from surface mining operations. The hole is lined with clay or a synthetic liner to prevent leakage of waste material into the water supply. A system of underground drainage pipes permits the monitoring of leaks and leaching. Waste is laid on the liner at the bottom of the excavation, and a layer of topsoil is then compacted onto the waste. The layering procedure is repeated until the landfill is full, with the layers mounded up sometimes as high as several hundred feet.

Capping is the process of laying two to four feet of soil over the top of the site and then planting grass on it to enhance the landfill's aesthetic value and prevent erosion. A ventilation pipe runs from the landfill's base through the cap to vent off accumulated natural gases created by the decomposing waste. Test wells around landfill operations are installed to constantly monitor the groundwater in the surrounding area, and soil analyses test for contamination.

Capped landfills have been used as parks and golf courses. Rapid suburban growth has resulted in housing developments and office campuses being built on landfill sites. Most newer landfill sites are well documented, but the locations of many older landfill sites are no longer known.

Special hazardous waste disposal sites contain radioactive waste from nuclear power plants, toxic chemicals, and waste materials produced by medical, scientific, and industrial processes. Additional waste disposal sites used as on-site garbage dumps are located on rural property, such as farms, ranches, and residences. Some materials, such as radioactive waste, are sealed in containers buried deep underground and placed in *tombs* designed to last thousands of years. These disposal sites are usually limited to extremely remote locations, well away from populated areas or farmland.

Hazardous and radioactive waste disposal sites are subject to strict state and federal regulation to prevent the escape of toxic substances.

Brownfields

Brownfields are defunct, derelict, or abandoned commercial or industrial sites, many of which may contain toxic waste. According to the U.S. General Accounting Office, several hundred thousand brownfields plague communities as eyesores and potentially dangerous and hazardous properties, often contributing to the decline of property values.

The Brownfields Law

The **Small Business Liability Relief and Brownfields Revitalization Act** (or Brownfields Law) was signed into law in 2002. The Brownfields Law provides funds to assess and clean up brownfields, clarifies liability protections, and provides tax incentives toward enhancing state and tribal response programs. The law is also important for property owners and developers because it shields innocent developers from liability for toxic wastes that existed at a site prior

www.epa.gov
/brownfields

to the purchase of property. In effect, a property owner who neither caused nor contributed to the contamination is not liable for the cleanup. Significantly, the law encourages the development of abandoned properties, some of which are located in prime urban real estate areas. Information on the Brownfields Law can be found at www.epa.gov/brownfields.

ENVIRONMENTAL LIABILITY

While the EPA oversees laws intended to preserve and enhance the environment, most federal laws encourage state and local governments to enact their own legislation.

Comprehensive Environmental Response, Compensation, and Liability Act

The **Comprehensive Environmental Response, Compensation, and Liability Act (CERCLA)** was created in 1980. It established a fund, initially $1.6 billion, called the Superfund, to clean up uncontrolled hazardous waste sites and to respond to spills. The act created a process for identifying potential responsible parties (PRPs) and for ordering them to take responsibility for the cleanup action. CERCLA is administered and enforced by the EPA. Superfund information can be found at www.epa.gov/superfund.

www.epa.gov
/superfund

Liability

A landowner is liable under CERCLA when a release or a threat of release of a hazardous substance has occurred on the landowner's property. Regardless of whether the contamination is the result of the landowner's actions or those of others, the owner can be held responsible for the cleanup. This liability includes the cleanup not only of the landowner's property but also of any neighboring property that has been contaminated. A landowner who is not responsible for the contamination can seek reimbursement for the cleanup costs from previous landowners, any other responsible party, or the Superfund. If other parties are not available, however, even a landowner who did not cause the problem could be solely responsible for the cleanup costs. This *strict liability* was modified somewhat by an amendment to the Superfund law that is described in the next part of this section.

Once the EPA determines that hazardous material has been released into the environment, the agency is authorized to begin remedial action. First, it attempts to identify the potentially responsible parties (PRPs). If the PRPs agree to cooperate in the cleanup, they must also agree about how to divide the cost. If the PRPs do not voluntarily undertake the cleanup, EPA may hire its own contractors to do the necessary work. The EPA then bills the PRPs for the cost. If the PRPs refuse to pay, the EPA can seek damages in court for up to three times the actual cost of the cleanup.

Liability under the Superfund is considered strict, joint and several, and retroactive. Strict liability means that the owner is responsible to the injured party without excuse. Joint and several liability means that each individual owner is personally responsible for the total damages. If only one of the owners is financially able to handle the total damages, that owner must pay the total and collect the proportionate shares from the other owners whenever possible. Retroactive liability means that the liability is not limited to the current owner but includes prior owners during the time the site was contaminated.

Superfund Amendments and Reauthorization Act

The **Superfund Amendments and Reauthorization Act (SARA)** created an "innocent landowner" immunity status. It recognized that, in certain cases, a landowner in the chain of ownership was completely innocent of all wrongdoing and therefore should not be held liable. The innocent landowner immunity clause established the criteria by which to judge whether a person or business could be exempted from liability. The criteria included the following:

■ The pollution was caused by a third party.

■ The property was acquired after the fact.

■ The landowner had no actual or constructive knowledge of the damage.

■ Due care was exercised when the property was purchased (the landowner made a reasonable search, called an environmental or Phase I site assessment) to determine that no damage to the property existed.

■ Reasonable precautions were taken in the exercise of ownership rights.

The most serious effects on property value associated with environmental problems involve the presence of undisclosed landfills and hazardous waste sites. Real estate professionals can encourage buyers to consult www.epa.gov/superfund to determine whether a property of interest is located near a Superfund site. Buyers should also speak with neighbors about activities that have taken place on or near a property.

IN PRACTICE

The buyer of commercial, industrial, and even some residential and agricultural properties should include a contingency in an offer to purchase that allows the buyer to hire an environmental engineer to conduct an environmental site assessment (discussed in the next section). A residential property located next to a dry cleaner or gas station, or a farm which uses overhead tanks to pump fuel into farm machinery, with the possibility of spills, can have hidden issues that may result in liability for the buyer. In other words, the parties should do everything possible to avoid surprises.

DEALING WITH ENVIRONMENTAL ISSUES

A real estate professional can avoid liability for environmental issues by
■ becoming familiar with common environmental problems in the licensee's area,
■ looking for signs of environmental contamination,
■ suggesting (and including as a contingency) an environmental audit if the licensee suspects contamination, and
■ giving no advice on environmental issues.

Although federal and state laws have defined many of the liabilities involved in environmental issues, common law (case law based on judicial precedent) is often used for further interpretation. The real estate professional and all others involved in a real estate transaction must be aware of both actual and potential liability.

Sellers often carry the most exposure to liability. Purchasers may be held liable even if they didn't cause the contamination. Lenders may end up owning worthless assets if owners default on loans rather than undertake expensive cleanup efforts. Real estate professionals could be held liable for improper disclosure; therefore, it is necessary to be aware of the potential environmental risks from neighboring properties, such as gas stations, manufacturing plants, or even funeral homes.

Additional exposure is created for individuals involved in other aspects of real estate transactions. For example, real estate appraisers must identify and adjust for environmental problems. Adjustments to market value typically reflect the cleanup cost plus a factor of the degree of panic and suspicion that exists in the current market. Although the sales price can be affected dramatically, the underlying market value might possibly remain relatively equal to others in the neighborhood. The real estate appraiser's greatest responsibility is to the lender, which depends on the appraiser to identify values affected by environmental hazards. Although the lender may be protected under certain conditions by virtue of the 1986 amendments to the Superfund act, the lender must be aware of any potential problems and may require additional environmental reports.

Insurance carriers also might be affected. Mortgage insurance companies protect lenders' mortgage investments and might be required to carry part of the ultimate responsibility in cases of loss. More important, a hazard insurance carrier might be directly responsible for damages if such coverage was included in the initial policy.

Discovery of environmental hazards

Real estate professionals are not expected to have the technical expertise necessary to discover the presence of environmental hazards. Nevertheless, they are presumed by the public to have special knowledge about real estate, so real estate professionals must be aware of possible hazards and where to seek professional help.

The most appropriate people on whom a real estate professional can rely for sound environmental information are scientific or technical experts. Environmental auditors (or *environmental assessors*) are scientific or technical experts who can provide the most comprehensive studies. Developers and purchasers of commercial and industrial properties (and even purchasers of some agricultural and residential properties) often rely on an environmental assessment that includes the property's history of use, a current-use review, and an investigation into the existence of reported or known contamination sources in the subject area that may affect the property. Testing of soil, water, air, and structures can be conducted, if warranted.

Not only do environmental experts detect environmental problems, they can usually offer guidance about how best to resolve the conditions. Although an environmental audit or assessment may occur at any stage in a transaction, they are most frequently a contingency that must be satisfied before closing.

IN PRACTICE

An environmental assessment and accompanying tests conducted by an environmental consultants can take time. The real estate professional should be aware of the time required and encourage the prospective property buyer to contact the environmental consultants as soon as it is known that such tests are needed, either before an offer to purchase is made or as a contingency in the offer. In some cases, the need for such an assessment may be enough to convince a prospective buyer to avoid the property entirely.

Environmental site assessments

An **environmental site assessment** (ESA) is often performed on a property to show that due care was exercised in determining whether any environmental impairments exist. The assessment can help prevent parties from becoming involved in contaminated property and work as a defense to liability. It is often requested by a lending institution, developer, or a potential buyer. The assessment is commonly performed in phases, such as Phase 1 or Phase 2. A Phase 1 ESA is requested first to determine whether any potential environmental problems exist at or near the subject property that may cause impairment. A Phase 2 ESA includes soil, water, and other testing, and is performed if warranted. There are no federal regulations that define what an environmental assessment must include, but the American Society for Testing and Materials (ASTM), an international organization, has established standards that have been adopted by many states. Go to www.astm.org for more information.

www.astm.org

Environmental impact statements

A federally funded project requires that an **environmental impact statement (EIS)** be performed. The statement details the impact the project will have on the environment. It can include information about air quality, noise, public health and safety, energy consumption, population density, wildlife, vegetation, and the need for sewer and water facilities. Increasingly, these statements are also being required for private development.

Disclosure of environmental hazards

Most state laws address the issue of disclosure of known material facts regarding a residential property of one to four units. In some states, real estate professionals may be liable if they should have known of a condition, even if the seller neglected to make the disclosure. Very few states require disclosure of environmental issues with commercial and industrial property. Real estate professionals specializing in these properties should emphasize to prospective buyers the importance of professional environmental audits in the absence of required disclosures.

KEY POINT REVIEW

Asbestos is a mineral composed of fibers that have fireproofing and insulating qualities, but it is a health hazard when fibers break down (become **friable**) and are inhaled. Asbestos has been banned for use in insulation since **1978**. **Encapsulation** can prevent asbestos fibers from becoming airborne.

Lead can be found in pipes, pipe solder, paints, air, and soil. **Lead-based paint** is found in many of the housing units built before 1978. Lead accumulates in the body and can damage the brain, nervous system, kidneys, and blood.

The **Lead-Based Paint Hazard Reduction Act of 1992 (LBPHRA)** requires disclosure of known lead-based paint hazards to potential buyers or renters.

Real estate professionals must provide buyers and lessees with *Protect Your Family from Lead in Your Home*, a pamphlet created by EPA, HUD, and the Consumer Product Safety Commission. Contractors and remodelers who disturb painted surfaces in homes, schools, and child care facilities built before 1978 must be trained and certified in the EPA's lead-based work practices. The pamphlet *Renovate Right* must be given to the property owner before work begins.

Radon is an odorless, tasteless, **radioactive gas** produced by the natural decay of radioactive substances in the ground and is found throughout the United States. Radon gas may cause lung cancer. Testing for radon in buildings is not a federal requirement.

Formaldehyde, described as a hazardous air pollutant in the Clean Air Act Amendments of 1990, is used for building and household products, such as **urea-formaldehyde foam insulation (UFFI)**, and may cause respiratory problems, eye and skin irritations, and possibly cancer. Since 1985, it has been regulated by HUD for use in wood products.

Real estate professionals should check state formaldehyde disclosure requirements, and appraisers should note the presence of formaldehyde.

Carbon monoxide (CO) is a colorless, odorless gas that is by-product of fuel burning. Inhaling CO may cause carbon monoxide poisoning, which can result in death unless the gas is properly vented. CO is detectable with available carbon monoxide detectors, which may be required by state law.

Polychlorinated biphenyls (PCBs), which are suspected of causing health problems, may be found in electrical equipment. The manufacture and commercial distribution of PCBs has been banned since **1979**.

Chlorofluorocarbons (CFCs), used in refrigerators, aerosol sprays, paints, solvents, and foam applications, are no longer manufactured worldwide, for the most part since 1996.

The **EPA** has guidelines for remediation and/or cleanup of mold and moisture problems in schools and commercial buildings. Real estate professionals should recommend a **mold inspection** if mold is evident or suspected because of water problems.

Groundwater is found under the earth's surface and forms the water table. The **Safe Drinking Water Act (SDWA)** of 1974 regulates the public drinking water supply. On transfer of property, any water source other than a municipal supply should be tested, as should any septic system. The EPA protects and improves the quality of wetlands under the Clean Water Act.

Underground storage tanks (USTs), which contain petroleum products, industrial chemicals, and other substances are subject to federal law (regulated by EPA) and state law When a purchase is being considered, a careful inspection of any property on which USTs are suspected should be conducted.

Waste disposal sites can be owned by municipalities, be part of commercial enterprises, or be found on farms and other rural properties. A landfill disposal site, whether excavated or created in previously mined property, is **lined** to prevent seepage, **capped** with soil for aesthetic reasons, and **vented** to release gases created by decomposing waste.

Brownfields legislation encourages development of abandoned properties by shielding innocent developers from liability for toxic wastes that existed at a site prior to purchase.

The **Comprehensive Environmental Response, Compensation, and Liability Act (CERCLA)** is administered and enforced by EPA. CERCLA established a **Superfund** to clean up uncontrolled hazardous waste sites and identifies **potential responsible parties (PRPs)**.

Strict liability means that the landowner has no defense to the responsibility for cleanup; **joint and several liability** means that each of several landowners is responsible for the entire cleanup; and **retroactive liability** occurs when the present owner and previous owners are considered responsible for cleanup. CERCLA also defines when **innocent landowner immunity** applies.

Environmental liability issues for **real estate professionals** include discovery of environmental hazards by questioning the owner and recommending an **environmental site assessment (ESA)**. A **Phase 1 ESA** is a physical examination of the property and investigation of its history; a **Phase 2 ESA** includes sampling of soil and other materials, and is performed if it appears a problem may exist. An **environmental impact statement (EIS)** is required for federally funded projects and may be required by the state or locality.

State laws cover **disclosure of known material facts regarding property condition**, which may include environmental hazards.

UNIT 21 QUIZ

1. Regarding the federal Lead-Based Paint Hazard Reduction Act, which statement is *TRUE*?
   A. All residential housing built before 1978 must be tested for the presence of lead-based paint before being listed for sale or rent.
   B. A disclosure statement must be attached to all sales contracts and leases involving residential properties built before 1978.
   C. A lead-hazard pamphlet must be distributed to all prospective buyers but not to tenants.
   D. Purchasers of housing built before 1978 must be given five days to test the property for the presence of lead-based paint.

2. The term *encapsulation* refers to
   A. the process of sealing a landfill with three to four feet of topsoil.
   B. the way in which insulation is applied to pipes and wiring systems.
   C. the method of sealing disintegrating asbestos.
   D. the way in which lead-based paint particles become airborne.

3. A real estate professional showed a pre–World War I house to a prospective buyer. The buyer has two toddlers and is worried about potential health hazards. Which of the following is *TRUE*?
   A. There is a risk that urea-formaldehyde foam insulation was used in the original construction.
   B. The real estate professional can offer to personally inspect for lead and remove any lead risks.
   C. Because of the age of the house, there is a good likelihood of the presence of lead-based paint.
   D. Removal of lead-based paint and asbestos hazards is covered by standard title insurance policies.

4. Which of the following is *TRUE* regarding asbestos?
   A. Improper removal of asbestos can cause further contamination of a building.
   B. Asbestos causes health problems only when it is eaten.
   C. The level of asbestos in a building is affected by weather conditions.
   D. HUD requires that all asbestos-containing materials be removed from all residential buildings.

5. All of the following may contribute to the growth of mold *EXCEPT*
   A. low humidity.
   B. presence of EIFS.
   C. roof leaks.
   D. improperly installed gutters.

6. Federal underground storage tank (UST) regulations require that
   A. home fuel oil tanks in basements be registered with the EPA.
   B. septic tanks be pumped every five years.
   C. liquid petroleum tanks that store at least 10% of their volume underground be in compliance.
   D. states not develop regulations more stringent than the federal requirements.

7. Which of the following describes the process of creating a landfill site?
   A. Waste is liquefied, treated, and pumped through pipes to tombs under the water table.
   B. Waste and topsoil are layered in a pit, mounded up, and then covered with dirt and plants.
   C. Waste is compacted and sealed in a container, then placed in a tomb designed to last several thousand years.
   D. Waste is buried in an underground concrete vault.

8. With the exception of the innocent landowner, liability under the Superfund is
   A. limited to the owner of record.
   B. joint and several and retroactive, but not strict.
   C. voluntary.
   D. strict, joint and several, and retroactive.

9. Radon poses the greatest potential health risk to people when it is
   A. contained in insulation material used in residential properties during the 1970s.
   B. found in high concentrations in unimproved land.
   C. trapped and concentrated in inadequately ventilated areas.
   D. emitted by malfunctioning or inadequately ventilated appliances.

10. What do urea-formaldehyde foam insulation (UFFI), lead-based paint, and asbestos have in common?
    A. They all pose a risk to humans because they may emit harmful gases.
    B. They all were banned in 1978.
    C. All three were used in insulating materials.
    D. They were all used at one time in residential construction.

11. A method of sealing off disintegrating asbestos is called
    A. capping.
    B. encapsulation.
    C. containment.
    D. contamination closure.

12. All of the following are true about lead-based paint *EXCEPT*
    A. it was commonly used in residences before 1978.
    B. renovation by a contractor of a residence that has lead-based paint requires education and certification.
    C. all residential buildings must be tested for lead-based paint.
    D. it is most dangerous when ingested.

13. The *MOST* common source of harmful lead in older residential properties is
    A. asbestos.
    B. basements.
    C. appliances.
    D. alkyd oil-based paint.

14. Urea-formaldehyde is found in residential properties in
    A. lead-based paints.
    B. insulating foam.
    C. home appliances.
    D. USTs.

15. In regulations regarding lead-based paints, HUD requires that
    A. homeowners test for its presence.
    B. paint be removed from surfaces before selling.
    C. known lead-based paint hazards be disclosed.
    D. only homeowners deal with its removal.

16. Radon is
    A. only found in the eastern United States.
    B. easy to detect because of its odor.
    C. a known human carcinogen.
    D. not found in older homes.

17. Contamination from underground storage tanks is
    A. found only in petroleum stations.
    B. addressed by EPA regulations.
    C. only caused by tanks currently in use.
    D. easily detected and eliminated.

18. All of the following are true about underground water contamination *EXCEPT*
    A. it is a minor problem in the United States.
    B. any contamination of underground water can threaten the supply of pure, clean water from private wells and public water systems.
    C. protective state and federal laws concerning water supply have been enacted.
    D. real estate professionals need to be aware of potential contamination sources.

19. CERCLA regulations for administration of the Superfund, which helps pay for cleanup of uncontrolled hazardous waste sites,
    A. exempt from responsibility those sites that contaminate neighboring properties.
    B. release from liability those owners of contaminated property who did not actually cause known contamination.
    C. make no provision for recovering Superfund expenses incurred in cleanup operations.
    D. impose strict, joint and several, and retroactive liability on potentially responsible parties.

20. Asbestos dust can cause
    A. lung disease.
    B. radiation sickness.
    C. skin cancer.
    D. AIDS.

APPENDIX

STATE LICENSING AGENCIES

Alabama
https://arec.alabama.gov/arec/

Alaska
www.commerce.alaska.gov/web/cbpl/professionallicensing/realestatecommission.aspx

Arizona
www.re.state.az.us

Arkansas
http://arec.arkansas.gov

California
www.dre.ca.gov

Colorado
www.colorado.gov/pacific/dora/division-real-estate

Connecticut
www.ct.gov/dcp/cwp/view.asp?a=1624&q=276076

Delaware
dpr.delaware.gov/boards/realestate/

District of Columbia
www.pearsonvue.com/dc/realestate/

Florida
www.myfloridalicense.com/dbpr/

Georgia
www.grec.state.ga.us

Hawaii
cca.hawaii.gov/reb/

Idaho
https://irec.idaho.gov/

Illinois
www.idfpr.com

Indiana
www.in.gov/pla/real.htm

Iowa
https://plb.iowa.gov/board/real-estate-sales-brokers

Kansas
www.krec.ks.govw

Kentucky
https://krec.ky.gov

Louisiana
www.lrec.state.la.us

Maine
www.maine.gov/pfr/professionallicensing/professions/real_estate/

Maryland
www.dllr.state.md.us/license/mrec/

Massachusetts
www.mass.gov/orgs/board-of-registration-of-real-estate-brokers-and-salespersons

Michigan
http://www.michigan.gov/lara/0,4601,7-154-72600_72602_72731_72871---,00%20.html

Minnesota
www.mn.gov/commerce/licensees/real-estate/

Mississippi
www.mrec.state.ms.us

Missouri
www.pr.mo.gov/realestate.asp

Montana
http://boards.bsd.dli.mt.gov/rre

Nebraska
www.nrec.ne.gov

Nevada
http://red.nv.gov

New Hampshire
www.oplc.nh.gov/real-estate-commission.htm

New Jersey
www.state.nj.us/dobi/division_rec/

New Mexico
www.rld.state.nm.us/Default.aspx?aspxerrorpath=/boards/Real%C2%AC_Estate_Commission
.aspx

New York
www.dos.ny.gov/licensing/re_broker/re_broker.html

North Carolina
www.ncrec.gov

North Dakota
www.realestatend.org

Ohio
www.com.state.oh.us/real/

Oklahoma
www.ok.gov/OREC/

Oregon
www.oregon.gov/REA/pages/index.aspx

Pennsylvania
www.dos.pa.gov/ProfessionalLicensing/BoardsCommissions/RealEstateCommission/Pages
/default.aspx

Rhode Island
www.dbr.state.ri.us/divisions/commlicensing/realestate.php

South Carolina
www.llr.state.sc.us/pol/rec/

South Dakota
http://dlr.sd.gov/

Tennessee
www.tn.gov/regboards/trec/

Texas
www.trec.texas.gov

Utah
https://realestate.utah.gov/realestate/index.html

Vermont
www.sec.state.vt.us/professional-regulation/list-of-professions/real-estate-commission.aspx

Virginia
www.dpor.virginia.gov/boards/real-estate/

Washington
www.dol.wa.gov/business/realestate/realestatecommission.html

West Virginia
http://rec.wv.gov/Pages/default.aspx

Wisconsin
https://dsps.wi.gov/Pages/Professions/REBroker/Default.aspx

Wyoming
http://realestate.wyo.gov

MATH FAQs

INTRODUCTION

Math is an integral part of the real estate profession. The amount and complexity of the math a real estate professional or consumer encounters will vary, depending on the area of real estate involved. Calculators and computers are great time-savers, but a solid, basic knowledge of math is still important. It is a matter of taking the math concepts and adapting them to the real estate profession.

This review covers the basics of real estate math in the real-world situations that will be encountered, as well as the math problems a prospective licensee will most likely find on the real estate licensing examination. Even those who are uncomfortable working with numbers will find that this clear and simple review will reinforce concepts that haven't been encountered for many years—and maybe alert you to a few tricks and shortcuts, too.

Study, review, and practice help overcome stress and anxiety so that everyone can become comfortable with math. With practice and review, your confidence and ability in real estate math will grow.

Using this math review

This math review is organized in a way that makes it easy to look up just the information needed. The subject matter is presented in a straightforward manner with a minimum of wordy explanations and a maximum of quick tips, examples, formulas, memory aids, and shortcuts to help you become confident in real estate math.

Divided into sections, the review is divided into the following five general subject areas:

1. Calculators

2. Measurement

3. Fractions

4. Percentages

5. Proration

Within each general subject heading are a series of frequently asked questions (FAQs) and brief, clear explanations. The Math FAQs provide a good, general review of real estate math principles, but can also be used for a last-minute review of difficult issues or even as a reference in daily real estate practice.

Special features

Some math concepts have been explained earlier in the text in pertinent units. In this review you will find general explanations of additional concepts, as well as **Take Note** tips that offer insight into both real estate math in general and the real estate exam's math content in particular. The **Example** feature applies formulas and concepts to practical situations to show how the concept works in the real world. Practice problems at the end of the review provide the opportunity to apply one's understanding in an exam-style context.

INTRODUCTION TO CALCULATORS

Basic calculators are permitted when taking most state licensing examinations. The rules usually require that the calculator be silent, handheld, battery-operated, and nonprinting. Many states will not allow test takers to use a real estate or financial calculator while taking the real estate exam. Check with your state regarding the appropriate calculator for your exam.

What kind of calculator do I need?

A basic calculator with functions for addition (+), subtraction (–), multiplication (×), and division (÷) is sufficient for licensing examinations. A calculator with a battery only or solar power with a battery backup is recommended over solar-powered only. Choose a calculator that is most comfortable for you; allow yourself time to learn to use it correctly and to become comfortable with it before you take the licensing examination.

Calculators with specific real estate functions

Many business or financial calculators have additional functions that are very beneficial to the real estate professional. Some of the relevant information that can be provided or found is indicated by keys for "N" (number of interest compounding periods/number of payments), "I" (interest rate per period), "PV" (present value of money/loan), "PMT" (amount of payment), and "FV" (future value of money). Business or financial calculators vary according to brand and/or model; therefore, the user's manual should always be followed to use the calculator properly. For example, some calculators indicate "TERM" instead of "N"; therefore, the number of years of the term is entered instead of the number of payments or compounding periods. Some have "LOAN" instead of "PV." Some instruct the user to enter the interest rate as an annual rate instead of a monthly rate. A business or financial calculator that contains these extra functions may prove useful, but anyone taking a licensing examination should always check with the state real estate commission to find out if the calculator can be used during the exam. No matter which calculator is chosen, the user should always read the user's manual.

FIGURE M.1:   Calculator Functions to Look For

TAKE NOTE

Be careful! Business or financial calculators often have been preset to round to two decimal places. The user's manual will indicate how to change any presettings to float or to display to a minimum of five decimal places. That change will provide an answer with enough decimal places to match multiple-choice answers on an exam. The calculations in this FAQ section are rounded to three decimal places except for those dealing with money. Those are rounded to the nearest cent. Proration problems are computed by carrying the division to three decimal places, and then rounding to the nearest cent only after the final proration figure is determined.

How do I use the percent key?

If you use the "%" key on calculators to solve percentage problems, read the user's manual for the key's proper use. Some calculators require the use of the "%" key or the "=" key *but never both in the same calculation*. Other calculators require the use of *both* the "%" key and the "=" key to get a correct answer. No matter which calculator you choose, read the user's manual.

EXAMPLE

If a property sold for $100,000 and a 7% commission was paid to the real estate professional, how much was the real estate professional paid?

The answer to this question can be determined two ways, as illustrated below.

Convert 7% to the decimal 0.07. (How to convert percentages to decimals is shown in Section 3.) Touch $100,000 into your calculator, then the × or multiplication key, then 0.07, then the = key to read $7,000.

Or, touch in $100,000, then the × or multiplication key, then 7, then the % key. If your calculator now reads $7,000, you've finished the question. If, when you touch the % key, it reads 0.07, then you must touch the = key to complete the calculation.

The use of the % key allows the calculator to convert to the proper decimal place, and there is no question about the placement of the decimal. The choice is yours: you can convert the percentage to a decimal or use the % key for the conversion.

MEASUREMENT PROBLEMS

What are linear measurements?

Linear measurement is line measurement. Linear measures are used for length or distance (e.g., length of a wall). Linear measures include feet, yards, inches, and miles. When the terms

- *foot,*
- *linear foot,*
- *running foot,* or
- *front foot*

are used, you are being asked to determine the *total length* of the dimension, whether measured in a straight line, crooked line, or curved line. The abbreviation for feet is '. Thus, 12 feet can be written as 12'. The abbreviation for inches is ". Thus, 12 inches can be written as 12".

What does the term *front foot* refer to?

When the term *front foot* is used, you are dealing with the number of units on the **frontage** of a lot. The frontage is usually the street frontage, but it might be the water frontage if the lot is on a river, lake, or ocean. If two dimensions are given for a tract of land and they are not labeled, the first dimension is the frontage. The word *width* also refers to frontage; the length is the *depth* of the property.

How do I convert one kind of linear measurement to another?

12 inches = 1 foot

     inches ÷ 12 = feet (144 inches ÷ 12 = 12 feet)

     feet × 12 = inches (12 feet × 12 = 144 inches)

36 inches = 1 yard

     inches ÷ 36 = yards (144 inches ÷ 36 = 4 yards)

     yards × 36 = inches (4 yards × 36 = 144 inches)

3 feet = 1 yard

     feet ÷ 3 = yards (12 feet ÷ 3 = 4 yards)

     yards × 3 = feet (4 yards × 3 = 12 feet)

5,280 feet = 1 mile

     feet ÷ 5,280 = miles (10,560 feet ÷ 5,280 = 2 miles)

     miles × 5,280 = feet (2 miles × 5,280 = 10,560 feet)

16½ feet = 1 rod

     feet ÷ 16.5 = rods (82.5 feet ÷ 16.5 = 5 rods)

     rods × 16.5 = feet (5 rods × 16.5 = 82.5 feet)

320 rods = 1 mile

     rods ÷ 320 = miles (640 rods ÷ 320 = 2 miles)

     miles × 320 = rods (2 miles × 320 = 640 rods)

EXAMPLE

A rectangular lot is 50 feet by 150 feet. The cost to fence this lot is priced per linear/running foot. How many linear/running feet will be used to calculate the price of the fence?

```
                           150'
  50'                                              50'

                           150'
```

50 feet + 150 feet + 50 feet + 150 feet = 400 linear/running feet

400 linear/running feet is the answer.

EXAMPLE

A parcel of land that fronts on Interstate 45 in Houston, Texas, is for sale at $5,000 per front foot. What will it cost to purchase this parcel of land if the dimensions are 150 feet by 100 feet?

150 is the frontage because it is the first dimension given.

150 front feet × $5,000 = $750,000 cost

$750,000 is the answer.

How do I solve for area measurement?

Area is the two-dimensional surface of an object. Area is quoted in *square units* or in *acres*. A linear measure multiplied by another linear measure always equals a square measure: feet times feet equals square feet; miles times miles equals square miles, yards times yards equals square yards, and so on. We will look at calculating the area of squares, rectangles, and triangles. Squares and rectangles are four-sided objects. All four sides of a square are the same length. Opposite sides of a rectangle are the same length. A triangle is a three-sided object. The three sides of a triangle can be the same length or two or three different lengths.

TAKE NOTE

When two dimensions are given, assume they refer to a figure that is a rectangle unless told otherwise.

How do I convert one kind of area measurement to another?

144 square inches = 1 square foot

square inches ÷ 144 = square feet (14,400 square inches ÷ 144 = 100 square feet)

square feet × 144 = square inches (100 square feet × 144 = 14,400 square inches)

1,296 square inches = 1 square yard

square inches ÷ 1,296 = square yards (12,960 ÷ 1,296 = 10 square yards)

square yards × 1,296 = square inches (10 square yards × 1,296 = 12,960 square yards)

9 square feet = 1 square yard

    square feet ÷ 9 = square yards (90 square feet ÷ 9 = 10 square yards)

    square yards × 9 = square feet (10 square yards × 9 = 90 square feet)

43,560 square feet = 1 acre

    square feet ÷ 43,560 = acres (87,120 ÷ 43,560 = 2 acres)

    acres × 43,560 = square feet (2 acres × 43,560 = 87,120 square feet)

640 acres = 1 section = 1 square mile

    acres ÷ 640 = sections (square miles) (1,280 acres ÷ 640 = 2 sections)

    sections (square miles) × 640 = acres (2 sections × 640 = 1,280 acres)

How do I determine the area of a square or rectangle?

length × width = area of a square or rectangle

E X A M P L E

How many square feet are in a room 15'6" × 30'9"? Remember, we must use like dimensions, so the inches must be converted to feet.

    6" ÷ 12 = 0.5' + 15' = 15.5' wide

    9" ÷ 12 = 0.75' + 30' = 30.75' long

    30.75' × 15.5' = 476.625 square feet

476.625 square feet is the answer.

E X A M P L E

If carpet costs $63 per square yard to install, what would it cost to carpet the room in the previous example?

    476.625 square feet ÷ 9 = 52.958333 square yards × $63 per square yard = $3,336.375, or $3,336.38 rounded

$3,336.38 is the answer.

E X A M P L E

How many acres are there in a parcel of land that measures 450' × 484'?

    484' × 450' = 217,800 square feet ÷ 43,560 = 5 acres of land

5 acres is the answer.

How do I determine the area of a triangle?

½ (base × height) = area of a triangle

or

(base × height) ÷ 2 = area of a triangle

EXAMPLE

How many square feet are contained in a triangular parcel of land that is 400 feet on the base and 200 feet high?

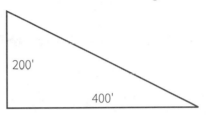

(400' × 200') ÷ 2 = 40,000 square feet

40,000 square feet is the answer.

EXAMPLE

How many acres are in a three-sided tract of land that is 300' on the base and 400' high?

(300' × 400') ÷ 2 = 60,000 square feet ÷ 43,560 = 1.377 acres

1.377 acres is the answer (rounded to three decimal places).

How do I solve for volume?

Volume is the space inside a three-dimensional object. Volume is measured in *cubic units*. We will look at calculating the volume of boxes that have rectangular sides and triangular prisms. There are always three measures: length, width, and height. Multiplying the three measures expressed in the same kind of units results in cubic units—for example, feet times feet times feet equals cubic feet.

How do I convert from one kind of volume measurement to another?

1,728 cubic inches = 1 cubic foot

cubic inches ÷ 1,728 = cubic feet
(17,280 cubic inches ÷ 1,728 = 10 cubic feet)

cubic feet × 1,728 = cubic inches
(10 cubic feet × 1,728 = 17,280 cubic inches)

46,656 cubic inches = 1 cubic yard

> cubic inches ÷ 46,656 = cubic yards
> (93,312 cubic inches ÷ 46,656 = 2 cubic yards)
>
> cubic yards × 46,656 = cubic inches
> (2 cubic yards × 46,656 = 93,312 cubic inches)

27 cubic feet = 1 cubic yard

> cubic feet ÷ 27 = cubic yards (270 cubic feet ÷ 27 = 10 cubic yards)
> cubic yards × 27 = cubic feet (10 cubic yards × 27 = 270 cubic feet)

How do I determine the volume of a room?

For purposes of determining volume, think of a room as though it were a box.

> length × width × height = volume of a box

EXAMPLE

A building is 500 feet long, 400 feet wide, and 25 feet high. How many cubic feet of space are in this building?

> 500' × 400' × 25' = 5,000,000 cubic feet

5,000,000 cubic feet is the answer.

EXAMPLE

How many cubic yards of concrete would it take to build a sidewalk measuring 120 feet long; 2 feet, 6 inches wide; and 3 inches thick?

> 6" ÷ 12' = 0.5' + 2' = 2.5' wide
>
> 3" ÷ 12' = 0.25' thick
>
> 120' × 2.5' × 0.25' = 75 cubic feet ÷ 27 = 2.778 cubic yards
> (rounded to three decimal places)

2.778 cubic yards is the answer.

How do I determine the volume of a triangular prism?

The terms *A-frame*, *A-shaped*, or *gable roof* on an exam describe a triangular prism.

> ½ (base × height × width) = volume of a triangular prism

or

> (base × height × width) ÷ 2 = volume of a triangular prism

E X A M P L E

An A-frame cabin in the mountains is 50 feet long and 30 feet wide. The cabin is 25 feet high from the base to the highest point. How many cubic feet of space does this A-frame cabin contain?

50' × 30' × 25' ÷ 2 = 18,750 cubic feet

18,750 cubic feet is the answer.

E X A M P L E

A building is 40 feet by 25 feet with a 10-foot-high ceiling. The building has a gable roof that is 8 feet high at the tallest point. How many cubic feet are in this structure, including the roof?

40' × 25' × 10' = 10,000 cubic feet in the building

40' × 25' × 8' ÷ 2 = 4,000 cubic feet in the gable roof

10,000 cubic feet + 4,000 cubic feet = 14,000 cubic feet

14,000 cubic feet is the answer.

FRACTIONS, DECIMALS, AND PERCENTAGES

What are the parts of a fraction?

A fraction shows one number over another number. The **denominator** on the bottom of the fraction shows the number of equal parts in the whole or total. The **numerator** on the top of the fraction shows the number of those parts with which you are working. In the example below, the whole or total has been divided into eight equal parts, and you have seven of those equal parts.

$$\frac{\text{numerator}}{\text{denominator}} \qquad \frac{\text{(top number)}}{\text{(bottom number)}}$$

What is meant by a *proper* and an *improper* fraction?

The value of a proper fraction is always less than one whole. ⅞ is an example of a proper fraction. ⅞ represents 7 parts out of 8 parts needed to make one whole. All proper fractions have a numerator smaller than the denominator—for example, ⅝ or ¾.

The fraction ¹¹⁄₈ is an example of an **improper fraction**. The value of an improper fraction is always equal to or greater than one whole. The improper fraction ¹¹⁄₈ states that you have 11 parts but only need 8 parts to make one whole. All improper fractions have a numerator larger than the denominator.

What is a mixed number?

11½ is a **mixed number**. It consists of a whole number and a fraction.

How do I multiply fractions?

When multiplying fractions, numerator is multiplied by numerator, and denominator by denominator. Let's start with an easy question. What is ½ × ¾?

First multiply the numerators (top numbers), 1 × 3 = 3. Then, multiply the denominators (bottom numbers), 2 × 4 = 8. Thus, ½ × ¾ = ⅜.

What is 4⅔ × 10⅝? The first step is to convert the whole number 4 into thirds. This is done by multiplying the whole number 4 by the denominator of the fraction, which is 3, so that 4 × 3 = 12. Thus, the whole number 4 is equal to ¹²⁄₃ and 4⅔ is equal to ¹²⁄₃ + ⅔ or ¹⁴⁄₃.

The next step is to convert the whole number 10 into eighths. This is done by multiplying the whole number 10 by the denominator of the fraction, 8. Thus, the whole number 10 is equal to ⁸⁰⁄₈ and ⁸⁰⁄₈ + ⅝ = ⁸⁵⁄₈.

So, what is ¹⁴⁄₃ × ⁸⁵⁄₈? First, 14 × 85 = 1,190. Then, 3 × 8 = 24. Finally, ¹,¹⁹⁰⁄₂₄ = 49.583.

An easier way to solve the problem is to convert the fractions to decimals.

⅔ is equal to 2 ÷ 3, or 0.667 (rounded to three decimal places)

⅝ is equal to 5 ÷ 8, or 0.625

4.667 × 10.625 = 49.587 (rounded to three decimal places)

When working with fractions or decimal equivalents, you will find that the answers will be close but not exact, depending on how many places the answer is computed before rounding.

How do I divide fractions?

Dividing fractions is a two-step process. What is ¾ ÷ ¼?

First, invert the second fraction by exchanging the numerator and denominator, then multiply the fractions and simplify the result. In this example, invert the ¼ to ⁴⁄₁. Then, ¾ × ⁴⁄₁ = ¹²⁄₄. Finally, 12 ÷ 4 = 3.

You may also convert ¾ to the decimal 0.75 and ¼ to the decimal 0.25.

0.75 ÷ 0.25 = 3 (There are three decimal parts of 0.25 in the figure 0.75.)

What is 100⅞ ÷ ¾?

100 × 8 = 800

800 + 7 = ⁸⁰⁷⁄₈

¾ is inverted to ⁴⁄₃.

⁸⁰⁷⁄₈ × ⁴⁄₃ = 807 × 4 = 3,228; 8 × 3 = 24

³,²²⁸⁄₂₄ = 3,228 ÷ 24 = 134.5

Or:

7 ÷ 8 = 0.875 and 3 ÷ 4 = 0.75

100.875 ÷ 0.75 = 134.5

How do I convert fractions to decimals?

Fractions will sometimes be used in real estate math problems. Because calculators may be used on most licensing examinations, it is best to convert fractions to decimals.

T A K E   N O T E

To convert a fraction to a decimal, divide the numerator (top number) by the denominator (bottom number).

For example:

⅞ = 7 ÷ 8 = 0.875

11⅛ = 11 ÷ 8 = 1.375

11½ = 1 ÷ 2 = 0.5 + 11 = 11.5

Once fractions have been converted to decimals, other calculations can be easily completed using the calculator. Note that many calculators automatically display the zero before the decimal point.

How do I add or subtract decimals?

Line up the decimals, add or subtract, and bring the decimal down in the answer. You may add zeros if necessary as placeholders. For example, 0.5 is the same as 0.50, or .5.

```
  0.50        8.20
+ 3.25      − 0.75
= 3.75      = 7.45
```

T A K E   N O T E

When you use a calculator, the decimal will be in the correct place in the answer (0.5 + 3.25 = 3.75, and 8.2 − 0.75 = 7.45).

How do I multiply decimals?

Multiply the numbers, then count the number of decimal places in each number. Next, start with the last number on the right and move the decimal the total number of decimal places to the left in the answer.

Multiply as you normally would to get the 1,500, then count the four decimal places in the numbers (0.20 and 0.75). In the 1,500, start at the last zero on the right and count four decimal places to the left. The decimal is placed to the left of the 1.

```
  0.20
× 0.75
  100
  140
0.1500 or 0.15
```

T A K E   N O T E

When you use a calculator, the decimal will be in the correct place in the answer (0.2 × 0.75 = 0.15).

How do I divide decimals?

Divide the **dividend** (the number being divided) by the **divisor** (the number you are dividing by) and bring the decimal in the dividend straight up in the **quotient** (answer). If the divisor has a decimal, move the decimal to the right of the divisor and move the decimal the same number of places to the right in the dividend. Now divide as stated above.

$$
\begin{array}{r}
0.75 \\
2\overline{)1.50} \\
1.4 \\
10 \\
10 \\
0
\end{array}
\qquad
0.5\overline{)15.5} =
\begin{array}{r}
31. \\
5\overline{)155.} \\
15 \\
05 \\
5 \\
0
\end{array}
$$

T A K E   N O T E

When you use a calculator, you can have a decimal in the divisor and the decimal will be in the correct place in the answer (1.5 ÷ 2 = 0.75, and 15.5 ÷ 0.5 = 31).

What is a percentage?

Percent (%) means *per hundred* or *per hundred parts*. The whole or total always represents 100%.

5% = 5 parts of 100 parts, or 5 ÷ 100 = 0.05 or ½₀

75% = 75 parts of 100 parts, or 75 ÷ 100 = 0.75 or ¾

120% = 120 parts of 100 parts, or 120 ÷ 100 = 1.2 or 1⅕

How can I convert a percentage to a decimal?

Move the decimal *two places* to the *left* and *drop* the % sign.

20% = 20 ÷ 100 = 0.20 or 0.2

1% = 1 ÷ 100 = 0.01

12¼% = 12.25%, 12.25 ÷ 100 = 0.1225

See Figure M.2.

How can I convert a decimal to a percentage?

Move the decimal *two places* to the *right* and *add* the % sign.

0.25 = 25%

0.9 = 90%

0.0875 = 8.75% or 8¾%

See Figure M.2.

FIGURE M.2:   Converting Decimal to Percentage and Percentage to Decimal

Decimal to Percentage

.10 ⟹ 10%

Move decimal two places right
to find the percentage

Percentage to Decimal

.10 ⟸ 10%

Move percentage two places left
to find the decimal

How do I multiply by percentages?

$500 \times 25\% = 500 \times {}^{25}\!/_{100} = {}^{12,500}\!/_{100} =$ **125**

or

$500 \times 25\% = 125$, or $500 \times 0.25 =$ **125**

How do I divide by percentages?

$100 \div 5\% = 100 \div {}^{5}\!/_{100} = 100 \times {}^{100}\!/_{5} = {}^{10,000}\!/_{5} =$ **2,000**

or

$100 \div 5\% =$ **2,000**

or

$100 \div 0.05 =$ **2,000**

Is there any easy way to remember how to solve percentage problems?

The following three formulas are important for solving all percentage problems:

total × rate = part

part ÷ rate = total

part ÷ total = rate

What is the x-bar method?

The x-bar is another tool to use to solve percentage problems. For some people, the "three-formula method" is more difficult to remember than the visual image of an x-bar in which the horizontal line stands for a division and the x-brace supporting the horizontal line stands for a multiplication.

$$\frac{part}{total \quad \times \quad rate}$$

How do I use the x-bar?

The procedure for using the x-bar is as follows:

1. Enter the two *known* items in the correct places.

2. If there is a multiplication sign between the two items, you *multiply* to equal the missing item.

3. If the line between the two items is *horizontal*, you *divide* to equal the missing item. When you divide, the top (part) always goes into the calculator first and is divided by the bottom (total or rate).

The following examples show how the x-bar can be used to solve percentage problems. These examples deal with discounts because everyone can relate to buying an item that is on sale. Later, we will see how the x-bar can be used for many types of real estate problems.

EXAMPLE

John purchased a new suit that was marked $500. How much did John save if the suit was on sale for 20% off?

$$\frac{part}{\$500 \quad \times \quad 20\%}$$

$500 × 20% = $100

$100 is the answer.

How much did John pay for the suit?

$500 total price – $100 discount = **$400 paid**

or

100% total price – 20% discount = 80% paid

$$\frac{part}{\$500 \quad \times \quad 80\%}$$

$500 × 80% = **$400**

EXAMPLE

Richard paid $112.50 for a dress that was reduced 25%. How much was it originally marked?

100% original price – 25% discount = 75% paid

$$\frac{\$112.50}{\text{total}} \quad \times \quad 75\%$$

$112.50 ÷ 75% = **$150**

EXAMPLE

Sols paid $127.50 for a coat that was marked down from the original price of $150. What percentage of discount did Sol receive?

$150 original price – $127.50 discount price = $22.50 discount

$$\frac{\$22.50}{\$150} \quad \times \quad \text{rate}$$

$22.50 ÷ $150 = 0.15, or **15%**

Or

$127.50 ÷ $150 = 0.85, or 85%

85% was the percentage paid; therefore

100% original price – 85% paid = **15% discount**

How should I approach tricky word problems?

Five important steps must be taken to solve word problems.

1. *Read* the problem carefully and completely. Never touch the calculator until you have read the entire problem.

2. *Analyze* the problem to determine what is being asked, what facts are given that *will* be needed to solve for the answer, and what facts are given that *will not* be needed to solve for the answer. Eliminate any information and/or numbers given that are not needed to solve the problem. Take the remaining information and/or numbers and determine which will be needed first, second, and so on, depending on the number of steps it will take to solve the problem.

3. *Choose* the proper formula(s) and steps it will take to solve the problem.

4. *Insert* the known elements and calculate the answer.

5. *Check* your answer to be sure you keyed in the numbers and functions properly on your calculator. Be sure you finished the problem. For example, when the problem asks for the salesperson's or sales associate's share of a commission, do not stop at the broker's share of the commission and mark that answer just because it is one of the choices.

PERCENTAGE PROBLEMS

How do I solve commission problems?

As it is used in a problem involving a real estate transaction, a full **commission** will be a percentage of the sales price, unless it is stated differently in the problem. Remember that full commission rates, commission splits between brokers, and commission shares between the broker and the sales associates are always negotiable. Always read a problem carefully to determine the correct rate(s).

$$\underline{\text{sales price} \quad \times \quad \text{full commission rate}}$$
$$\text{full commission}$$

sales price × full commission rate = full commission

full commission ÷ full commission rate = sales price

full commission ÷ sales price = full commission rate

$$\underline{\text{full brokerage commission} \quad \times \quad \% \text{ of full brokerage commission to the broker}}$$
$$\text{broker's share of the commission}$$

| full brokerage commission | × | % of full commission to the broker | = | broker's share of the commission |

| broker's share of the commission | ÷ | % of full commission to the broker | = | full commission |

| broker's share of the commission | ÷ | full brokerage commission | = | % of full brokerage commission to the broker |

$$\underline{\text{broker's share of the commission} \quad \times \quad \text{sales associate's } \% \text{ of the broker's share}}$$
$$\text{sales associate's share of the commission}$$

| broker's share of the commission | ÷ | sales associate's % of the broker's share | = | sales associate's share of the commission |

| sales associate's share of the commission | ÷ | sales associate's % of the broker's share | = | broker's share of the commission |

| sales associate's share of the commission | ÷ | broker's share of the commission | = | sales associate's % of the broker's share |

EXAMPLE

A seller listed a home for $200,000 and agreed to pay a commission of 5%. The home sold four weeks later for 90% of the list price. The listing broker agreed to give the selling broker 50% of the commission. The listing broker paid the listing sales associate 50% of her share of the commission, and the selling broker paid the selling sales associate 60% of his share of the commission. How much compensation did the selling sales associate receive?

$$\frac{\text{sales price}}{\$200,000 \text{ list price}} \times 90\%$$

$200,000 × 90% = $180,000 sales price.

$$\frac{\text{full commission}}{\$180,000 \text{ list price}} \times 5\%$$

$180,000 × 5% = $9,000 full commission.

$$\frac{\text{listing broker's commission split}}{\$9,000 \text{ full commission}} \times 50\%$$

$9,000 × 50% = $4,500 listing broker's commission split

$$\frac{\text{selling sales associate's commission}}{\$4,500 \text{ listing broker's commission split}} \times 60\%$$

$4,500 × 60% = $2,700 selling sales associate's commission

$2,700 selling salesperson's commission is the answer.

What is meant by seller's dollars after commission?

The first deduction from the sales price in a real estate transaction typically is the real estate commission. For example, if a house sold for $100,000 and a 5% commission was paid to the listing broker, that means the broker's compensation was $5,000. The seller still has 95% of the sales price, or $95,000. The seller's dollars after commission will be used to pay the seller's other expenses, including any outstanding mortgages secured by the property, and hopefully will leave some money for the seller. The sales price is 100%. Thus, 100% − commission % = percent after commission. The x-bar can be applied to the sales price, seller's dollars after commission, and percentage after commission to provide the formulas shown below.

$$\frac{\text{seller's dollars after commission}}{\text{sales price} \times \text{percentage after commission}}$$

sales price × percentage after commission = seller's dollars after commission

seller's dollars after commission ÷ percentage after commission = sales price

seller's dollars after commission ÷ sales price = percentage after commission

EXAMPLE

After deducting $5,850 in closing costs and a 5% broker's commission, the sellers received their original cost of $175,000 plus a $4,400 profit. What was the sales price of the property?

$5,850 closing costs + $175,000 original cost + $4,400 profit = $185,250 seller's dollars after commission

100% sales price – 5% commission = 95% after commission

$$\frac{\$185,250 \text{ seller's dollars after commission}}{\text{sales price}} \quad \times \quad 95\% \text{ after commission}$$

$185,250 ÷ 95% = $195,000

$195,000 sales price is the answer.

How do I determine interest?

Interest is the cost of using money. The amount of interest paid is determined by the agreed annual interest rate, the amount of money borrowed (loan amount) or the amount of money still owed (loan balance), and the period of time the money is held. When a lender grants a loan for real estate, the loan-to-value ratio (LTV) is the percentage of the sales price or appraised value, whichever is less, that the lender is willing to lend.

$$\frac{\text{loan amount}}{\text{sales price or appraised value (whichever is less)}} \quad \times \quad \text{loan-to-value ratio (LTV)}$$

loan amount ÷ sales price or appraised value (whichever is less) = loan-to-value ratio (LTV)

sales price or appraised value (whichever is less) × loan-to-value ratio (LTV) = loan amount

loan amount ÷ loan-to-value ratio (LTV) = sales price or appraised value (whichever is less)

$$\frac{\text{annual interest}}{\text{loan amount (principal)}} \quad \times \quad \text{annual interest rate}$$

loan amount (principal) × annual interest rate = annual interest

annual interest ÷ annual interest rate = loan amount (principal)

annual interest ÷ loan amount (principal) = annual interest rate

EXAMPLE

A parcel of rural land sold for $335,200. The lender approved a 90% loan at 4.5% for 30 years. The appraised value on this parcel was $335,500. How much interest is paid to the lender in the first monthly payment?

$$\frac{\text{loan amount}}{\$335{,}200 \text{ sales price}} \quad \times \quad 90\%$$

$335,200 × 90% = $301,680 loan amount

$$\frac{\text{annual interest}}{\$301{,}680 \text{ loan amount}} \quad \times \quad 4.5\%$$

$301,680 × 4.5% = $13,575.60 annual interest

$13,575.60 annual interest ÷ 12 months = $1,131.30 monthly interest

$1,131.30 interest in the first monthly payment is the answer.

How do I determine monthly principal and interest payments?

A **loan payment factor** can be used to calculate the monthly principal and interest payment on a loan. The factor represents the monthly principal and interest payment to amortize a $1,000 loan and is based on the annual interest rate and the term of the loan.

(loan amount ÷ $1,000) × loan payment factor = monthly PI payment

monthly PI payment ÷ loan payment factor = loan amount

EXAMPLE

If a lender uses a loan payment factor of $6.99 per $1,000 of loan amount, what will be the monthly PI (principal and interest) payment?

($301,680 loan amount ÷ $1,000) × $6.99 = $2,108.74 monthly PI payment (rounded to the nearest cent)

$2,108.74 monthly PI payment is the answer.

How do I solve problems about points?

The word *point* means percent. One **point** equals 1% of the loan amount.

Two points mean 2%, or ½ point means ½%. A loan point is a percentage of the loan amount.

$$\frac{\text{amount paid for points}}{\text{loan amount}} \quad \times \quad \text{points as percentage of loan}$$

loan amount × points as percentage of loan = amount paid for points

amount paid for points ÷ points as percentage of loan = loan amount

amount paid for points ÷ loan amount = points as percentage of loan

E X A M P L E

The lender will charge 3½ discount points on an $800,000 loan. What will be the total amount paid as discount points at closing?

$$\frac{\text{amount paid for points}}{\$800{,}000 \text{ loan amount} \quad \times \quad 3.5\%}$$

$800,000 × 3.5% = $28,000

$28,000 paid for points is the answer.

How do I determine profit?

A **profit** is made when we sell something for more than we paid for it. If we sell something for less than we paid for it, we have suffered a **loss**.

sales price – seller's cost = profit

When setting the x-bar, the whole is the original investment or cost (i.e., the total amount paid by the seller, including the original purchase price and the cost of any improvements made after the purchase). The seller's cost must be the whole thing (the 100%) because percentages of profit or loss are percentages of the money invested. A 20% loss is 20% of the amount invested.

$$\frac{\text{profit}}{\text{seller's cost} \quad \times \quad \text{percentage of profit}}$$

seller's cost × percentage of profit = profit

profit ÷ percentage of profit = seller's cost

profit ÷ seller's cost = percentage of profit

The seller's cost plus the amount of the profit equals the sales price. Unfortunately, not every sale results in a profit to the seller. The seller's cost minus the amount of any loss equals the sales price. (100% cost ± % profit = % sales price)

$$\frac{\text{sales price}}{\text{seller's cost} \quad \times \quad \text{percentage sold of cost}}$$

seller's cost × percentage sold of cost = sales price

sales price ÷ percentage sold of cost = seller's cost

sales price ÷ seller's cost = percentage sold of cost

EXAMPLE

A home listed for $285,000 and sold for $275,000, which gave the seller a 10% profit over the seller's cost. What was the seller's cost?

100% seller's cost + 10% profit = 110% sales price

$$\frac{\$275{,}000 \text{ sales price}}{\text{seller's cost} \quad \times \quad 110\%}$$

$275,000 ÷ 110% = $250,000 seller's cost

$250,000 seller's cost is the answer.

EXAMPLE

Marco invested in a mountain cabin a few years ago and made no improvements to the property. He just sold the cabin for $80,640, losing 16% of his investment. What did the cabin cost Marco?

100% seller's cost – 16% loss = 84% today's value

$$\frac{\$80{,}640 \text{ sales price}}{\text{seller's cost} \quad \times \quad 84\%}$$

$80,640 ÷ 0.84 = $96,000 seller's cost

$96,000 seller's cost is the answer.

How do I estimate value for income-producing properties?

When appraising income-producing property, an opinion of value can be formed by using the property's annual net operating income (NOI) and the current market rate of return or capitalization ("cap") rate. Annual scheduled gross income is adjusted for vacancies and credit losses to arrive at the annual effective gross income. The annual operating expenses are deducted from the annual effective gross income to arrive at the annual NOI.

Vacancy/credit loss is usually expressed as a percentage of the scheduled gross.

scheduled gross income – vacancies and credit losses = effective gross income

effective gross income – annual operating expenses = NOI

$$\frac{\text{NOI}}{\text{value} \quad \times \quad \text{capitalization rate}}$$

value × capitalization rate = NOI

NOI ÷ capitalization rate = value

NOI ÷ value = capitalization rate

EXAMPLE

An office building produces $132,600 annual gross income. If the annual expenses are $30,600 and the appraiser uses an 8.5% cap rate, what is the estimated value?

$132,600 annual gross income – $30,600 annual expenses = $102,000 NOI

$$\frac{\$102,000 \text{ NOI}}{\text{value} \quad \times \quad 8.5\% \text{ cap rate}}$$

$102,000 ÷ 8.5% = $1,200,000 value

$1,200,000 value is the answer.

The above formulas also can be used to calculate either the return on the real estate investment (ROI) or the monthly NOI. The total becomes *original cost* or *investment* instead of value.

EXAMPLE

An investor spends $335,000 for a property that should produce a 9% rate of return. What monthly NOI will the investor receive?

$$\frac{\text{NOI}}{\$335,000 \text{ investment} \quad \times \quad 9\%}$$

$335,000 × 9% = $30,150

$30,150 NOI ÷ 12 months = $2,512.50 monthly NOI

$2,512.50 monthly NOI is the answer.

How do I solve problems involving percentage leases?

When establishing the rent to be charged for retail space, a percentage lease may be used instead of a lease based simply on dollars per square foot. In a **percentage lease**, a base or minimum monthly rent is paid plus a percentage of the gross sales in excess of an amount set in the lease. The percentage lease also can be set up as a percentage of the total gross sales or of the base/minimum rent, whichever is larger. The discussion that follows considers the minimum plus percentage lease only.

$$\text{gross sales} \quad - \quad \begin{array}{c}\text{gross sales not subject} \\ \text{to the percentage}\end{array} \quad = \quad \begin{array}{c}\text{gross sales subject} \\ \text{to the percentage}\end{array}$$

$$\frac{\text{percentage rent}}{\text{gross sales subject to the percentage} \quad \times \quad \% \text{ in the lease}}$$

gross sales subject to the percentage × % in the lease = percentage rent

percentage rent ÷ % in the lease = gross sales subject to the percentage

percentage rent ÷ gross sales subject to the percentage = % in the lease

Add the percentage rent and the base/minimum rent to find the total rent.

EXAMPLE

A lease calls for monthly minimum rent of $900 plus 3% of annual gross sales in excess of $270,000. What was the annual rent in a year when the annual gross sales were $350,600?

$900 monthly minimum rent × 12 months = $10,800 annual minimum rent

$350,600 annual gross sales – $270,000 annual gross sales not subject to the percentage = $80,600 annual gross sales subject to the percentage

$$\frac{\text{percentage rent}}{\begin{matrix}\$80,600 \text{ annual gross} \\ \text{subject to the percentage}\end{matrix} \quad X \quad 3\%}$$

$80,600 × 3% = $2,418 percentage rent

$10,800 annual minimum rent + $2,418 percentage rent = $13,218 total annual rent

$13,218 total annual rent is the answer.

PRORATION PROBLEMS

To **prorate** means to divide proportionately. Some expenses and income may be prorated for the closing of a real estate transaction. We will look at prorating interest on a loan, ad valorem taxes on a property, homeowners insurance on a property, and rent on income-producing property. All the calculations in this section are carried to three decimal places and then rounded to the nearest cent in the final step.

What are the different calendars used for prorating?

When we prorate, we calculate the number of days owed for the expense or the rental income. The days may be calculated using a *banker's year, statutory year*, or *calendar year*. The **banker's year** and **statutory year** are the same because they both contain 12 months with 30 days in each month. The total number of days in both a banker's year and a statutory year is 360 days. The **calendar year** contains 12 months with 28 to 31 days in each month. The total number of days in a calendar year is 365. The total number of days in a calendar *leap* year (every fourth year) is 366. The following chart shows the days in each month.

	Banker's or Statutory Year	Calendar	Calendar Leap Year
January	30	31	31
February	30	28	29
March	30	31	31
April	30	30	30
May	30	31	31
June	30	30	30
July	30	31	31
August	30	31	31
September	30	30	30
October	30	31	31
November	30	30	30
December	30	31	31
Total days in a year	360	365	366

What is the difference between prorating *through* and prorating *to* the day of closing?

In a proration problem, an examinee will be told whether to prorate *through* the day of closing or *to* the day of closing. **This is very important when calculating the days owed.** When prorating *through* the day of closing, the *seller* is responsible for the day of closing. When prorating *to* the day of closing, the *buyer* is responsible for the day of closing.

How do I calculate proration problems?

Once the number of days owed is known, the amount of the expense or income per day must be found. Either the annual amount is divided by the total days in the year to get the daily amount, or the monthly amount is divided by the total days in the month to get the daily amount.

TAKE NOTE

The correct type of year (banker's or statutory year of 360 days, calendar year of 365 days, or calendar leap year of 366 days) must be used when computing the daily amount.

The final step is to multiply the amount per day by the number of days owed to get the prorated amount.

What is the difference between debit and credit in a proration problem?

To calculate a proration problem, it is necessary to know how expenses and income are posted on the closing statement. **Debit** takes money from a person. **Credit** gives money to a person. (See Figure M.3.) When the prorated amount involves both the buyer and the seller, there will always be a double entry (i.e., the item appears twice, once as a debit to one party and once as a credit to the other party). If the seller owes the buyer, the prorated amount will be debited to the seller and credited to the buyer. If the buyer owes the seller, the prorated amount will be debited to the buyer and credited to the seller. When the prorated amount involves the buyer and someone other than the seller, there will be only a single entry. When the prorated amount involves the seller and someone other than the buyer, there will be only a single entry.

The five questions to ask when prorating are:

1. What calendar is to be used?

2. Is the expense paid in arrears or in advance?

3. Who has or will pay the expense?

4. Who has earned or received income?

5. When will the expense be paid?

FIGURE M.3:   The Debit/Credit Flow

	Buyer	Seller
Sales Price	DEBIT	CREDIT
Tenants' Security Deposits	CREDIT	DEBIT
Fuel Oil (in tank)	DEBIT	CREDIT
Prorated Accrued Water Bill	CREDIT	DEBIT
Unearned Rents	CREDIT	DEBIT
Tax Reserve Account	DEBIT	CREDIT

Different items are treated differently as credits or debits to the buyer or the seller on a closing statement. Utility payments may not appear on the statement if the utility provider sends a final bill to the seller based on the date provided.

How do I calculate interest in a proration problem?

When a loan is assumed or paid off, the accrued interest for the month of closing must be prorated. Interest is paid in arrears; therefore, the monthly payment made on the first day of the month pays interest for the entire previous month. The payment includes interest *up to but not including* the day of the payment unless specified otherwise. Not all payments are due on the first day of the month; therefore, attention must be paid to the stated day the interest has been paid through. The sellers owe unpaid interest (also called accrued, earned, or current interest) from the date of the last payment to or through the closing date.

If the prorations are to be calculated *through* the day of closing, the seller will owe payments *including* the day of closing. If the prorations are to be calculated *to* the day of closing, the seller will *owe up to but not including* the day of closing. Remember to use the correct type of year: the banker's or statutory year of 360 days, the calendar year of 365 days, or the calendar leap year of 366 days. When a loan is paid off, unpaid interest is calculated and added to the outstanding loan balance and is a debit *to the seller only*. Loan payoff is the sum of the principal balance and the accrued interest. On an assumption of the loan, the interest proration is a debit to the *seller* and a credit to the *buyer*.

EXAMPLE

A home was purchased on April 4 for $110,000, and the closing was set for the following May 8. The buyer assumed the seller's $93,600 loan balance on an original loan amount of $96,000 with 6.5% interest and monthly payments of $612.62 due on the first day of each month. How much will the interest proration be, using a banker's year and prorating through the day of closing? Who will be debited and who will be credited?

Banker's Year/Statutory Year

Step 1: Find the exact number of days of earned or accrued interest.

Seller owes 8 days (May 1 *through* May 8).

Note: It would be 7 days (8 days minus 1 day) if the problem had said prorate *to* the day of closing.

Step 2: Find the daily interest charge.

Outstanding loan balance × annual interest rate = annual interest

Annual interest ÷ 360 days per year = daily interest

$93,600 × 6.5% = $6,084 annual interest

$6,084 ÷ 360 days = $16.90 daily interest

Step 3: Compute the total amount of accrued interest.

Daily interest × days owed = interest proration

$16.90 daily interest × 8 days = $135.20

$135.20 debit seller, credit buyer is the answer.

Calendar Year (if the problem had said to use a calendar year)

Step 1: Find the exact number of days of earned or accrued interest.

Seller owes 8 days (May 1 *through* May 8).

Note: It would be 7 days (8 days minus 1 day) if the problem had said prorate *to* the day of closing.

Step 2: Find the daily interest charge.

Outstanding loan balance × annual interest rate = annual interest

Annual interest ÷ 365 days per year = daily interest

$93,600 × 6.5% = $6,084 annual interest

$6,084 ÷ 365 days = $16.668 daily interest

Step 3: Compute the total amount of accrued interest.

Daily interest × days owed = interest proration

$16.668 daily interest × 8 days = $133.344

$133.34 debit seller, credit buyer is the answer (rounded to the nearest cent).

How do I prorate taxes?

Real estate taxes are normally assessed from January 1 through December 31. The tax rate is *always* applied *to the assessed value of the property* instead of the market value, although some jurisdictions treat market value as the assessed value. Taxes are usually paid in arrears; therefore, the seller will owe the buyer for accrued taxes from January 1 *through* the day of closing or *to* the day of closing. The most recent tax bill is used to compute the proration, and this is usually the past year's tax bill. Remember to use the correct type of year: a banker's or statutory year has 360 days, a calendar year has 365 days, and a calendar leap year has 366 days.

If the taxes are paid in arrears, the tax proration will be a debit to the *seller* and a credit to the *buyer*. If the taxes are paid in advance, the tax proration will be a debit to the *buyer* and a credit to the *seller*.

EXAMPLE

The market value of a condominium is $115,000. For tax purposes, the property is assessed at 90% of the market value. The annual tax rate is $2.50 per $100 of assessed value. If the closing is on March 13, what is the prorated amount for the current tax year? Prorations are calculated through the day of closing and using a statutory year.

Banker's Year/Statutory Year

Step 1: Find the exact number of days of accrued taxes from the beginning of the tax period (January 1) up to and including the day of closing (March 13).

2 months (January and February) × 30 days per month = 60 days

60 + 13 days in March = 73 days

Note: It would be 72 days (73 days minus 1 day) if the problem had said prorate *to* the day of closing.

Step 2: Calculate the annual taxes.

Market value × assessment ratio = assessed value

(Assessed value ÷ $100) × tax rate per hundred = annual tax

$115,000 × 90% = $103,500

($103,500 ÷ $100) × $2.50 = $2,587.50 annual tax

Step 3: Find the tax amount per day.

Annual tax ÷ 360 days per year = daily tax

$2,587.50 ÷ 360 days = $7.188 daily tax

Step 4: Compute the prorated tax amount.

Daily tax × days owed = tax proration

$7.188 per day × 73 days = $524.724

$524.72 debit seller, credit buyer is the answer (rounded to the nearest cent).

Calendar Year (if the problem had said to use a calendar year)

Step 1: Find the exact number of days of accrued tax from the beginning of the tax period (January 1) up to and including the day of closing (March 13).

31 days in January + 28 days in February + 13 days in March = 72 days

Note: It would be 71 days (72 days minus 1 day) if the problem had said prorate *to* the day of closing.

Step 2: Calculate the annual tax.

Market value × assessment ratio = assessed value

(Assessed value ÷ $100) × tax rate per hundred = annual tax

$115,000 × 90% = $103,500

($103,500 ÷ $100) × $2.50 = $2,587.50 annual tax

Step 3: Find the tax amount per day.

Annual tax ÷ 365 days per year = daily tax

$2,587.50 ÷ 365 days = $7.089

Step 4: Compute the prorated tax amount.

Daily tax × days owed = tax proration

$7.089 per day × 72 days = $510.408

$510.41 debit seller, credit buyer is the answer (rounded to the nearest cent).

How do I prorate rent?

When prorating rents, the amount of rent collected for the month of closing is the only amount prorated. The seller owes the buyer for the unearned rent starting with the day after closing through the end of the month if prorating *through* the day of closing. The seller owes the buyer for the unearned rent starting with the day of closing through the end of the month if prorating *to* the day of closing. If security deposits are being held by the seller, they are not prorated; therefore, the entire amount of the security deposits are transferred to the buyer. The actual number of days in the month of closing is always used for rent prorations, unless the problem provides differently. Both the rent proration and the security deposit amount will be a debit to the *seller* and a credit to the *buyer*.

EXAMPLE

A buyer is purchasing an apartment complex that contains 15 units that rent for $450 per month each. A $450 security deposit is being held on each unit. The sale is to close on March 14, and the March rent has been received for all 15 units. Compute the rent proration by prorating through the day of closing. Compute the security deposit.

Calendar Days (remember to use actual days in the month unless specified differently)

Step 1: Compute the unearned days of rent for the month of closing.

> 31   days in March
> – 14   day of closing
> 17   days of unearned rent

> Note: It would be 18 days (17 days plus 1 day) if the problem had said prorate *to* the day of closing.

Step 2: Compute the daily rent. Monthly rent × number of units paid = total rent collected ÷ number of actual days in the month of closing = daily rent.

> $450 × 15 units = $6,750 monthly rent collected

> $6,750 ÷ 31 days in March = $217.742 daily rent

Step 3: Compute the prorated rent amount.

> Daily rent × days of unearned rent. $217.742 daily rent × 17 days = $3,701.614

Step 4: Compute the security deposit.

> $450 per unit × 15 units = $6,750

> **$3,701.61 rent proration (rounded to the nearest cent)** and **$6,750 security deposit** are the answers. They are both *debit seller* and *credit buyer*.

REAL ESTATE MATH PRACTICE PROBLEMS

1. The value of a property is $91,000 today. What was the original cost if the property has lost 35% of its value over the past seven years?
   A. $67,407.41
   B. $95,789.47
   C. $122,850.00
   D. $140,000.00

2. What was the price per front foot for a 100' × 125' lot that sold for $125,000?
   A. $10
   B. $556
   C. $1,000
   D. $1,250

3. If the bank makes a 90% loan on a house valued at $88,500, how much additional cash is required as a down payment if the buyer has already paid $4,500 in earnest money?
   A. $3,500
   B. $4,000
   C. $4,350
   D. $8,850

4. What did the sellers pay for their home if they sold it for $298,672, which gave them a 12% profit over their original cost? Round your answer to the nearest cent.
   A. $243,671.43
   B. $266,671.43
   C. $312,512.64
   D. $334,512.64

5. What would be an estimate of value for a building producing $11,250 annual net income and showing a rate of return of 9%?
   A. $101,250
   B. $122,625
   C. $123,626
   D. $125,000

6. The sale of a home is to close on September 28. Included in the sale is a garage apartment that is rented for $350 per month. The tenant has paid the September rent. What is the rent proration, using actual days and prorating through the day of closing? Round your answer to the nearest cent.
   A. $325.67
   B. $23.33
   C. $350.00
   D. $175.00

7. What is the total cost of paving a driveway 15' wide, 40' long, and 4" thick if the concrete to be used costs $60.00 per cubic yard and labor costs $1.25 per square foot?
   A. $527.25
   B. $693.75
   C. $1,194.00
   D. $1,581.75

8. An owner agrees to list property on the condition that the sale proceeds be at least $47,300 after the owner pays a 5% broker's commission and $1,150 in closing costs. At what price must the property sell?
   A. $48,450
   B. $50,815
   C. $50,875
   D. $51,000

9. A gift shop pays rent of $600 per month plus 2.5% of gross annual sales in excess of $50,000. What was the average monthly rent last year if gross annual sales were $75,000? Round your answer to the nearest cent.
   A. $1,125.00
   B. $756.25
   C. $600.00
   D. $652.08

10. A tenant's monthly rent is $825. What is the rent as a percentage of an annual income of $41,000? Round your answer to the nearest percent.
    A. 18%
    B. 24%
    C. 33%
    D. 40%

11. Two brokers split the 6% commission on the sale of a $324,000 home. The selling broker's sales associate was paid 70% of the selling broker's share. The listing broker's sales associate was paid 30% of the listing broker's share. How much did the listing broker's sales associate receive?
    A. $2,916
    B. $6,804
    C. $19,440
    D. $20,275

12. Find the number of square feet in a lot with a frontage of 75 feet, 6 inches, and a depth of 140 feet, 9 inches.
    A. 216.25
    B. 10,626.625
    C. 10,652.04
    D. 25,510.875

13. A 28-unit apartment house is being valued using the income approach. Each unit rents for $775 a month, an amount that is consistent with like rental units in the vicinity. For the past five years, the annual expenses of operation for the property have averaged $82,460 and the building has maintained a consistent vacancy rate of 5%. A potential investor is only interested if the cap rate is at least 9.5%. What is the property's likely value using these variables?
    A. $2,741,100
    B. $868,000
    C. $1,736,000
    D. $1,873,100

14. How much interest will the seller owe the buyer for a closing date of August 10 if the outstanding loan balance is $43,580? The interest rate on this assumable loan is 6%, and the last payment was paid on August 1. Prorations are to be done through the day of closing, using a statutory year.
    A. $72.63
    B. $145.20
    C. $290.47
    D. $508.20

15. The buyer has agreed to a $175,000 sales price, 2.5 loan discount points, and a 1% loan origination fee. If the buyer receives a 90% loan to value, how much will the buyer owe at closing for points and the origination fee?
    A. $1,575.00
    B. $3,937.50
    C. $5,512.50
    D. $6,125.00

16. Calculate eight months' interest on a $5,000 interest-only loan at 9.5%.
    A. $39.58
    B. $237.50
    C. $316.66
    D. $475.00

17. A 100-acre farm is subdivided into lots for homes. The streets require one-eighth of the entire property, and the remaining acreage is divided into 140 lots of approximately the same size. About how many square feet are in each lot?
    A. 27,225
    B. 31,114
    C. 35,004
    D. 43,560

18. The annual tax bill on a home was $1,282 and was paid in December. The home sold the following March and will close on April 23. How much will the tax proration be, using a calendar year and prorating to the day of closing?
    A. $393.34
    B. $396.89
    C. $402.41
    D. $427.33

19. What is the monthly net operating income on an investment of $115,000 if the rate of return is 12.5%? Round your answer to the nearest cent.
    A. $1,150.00
    B. $1,197.92
    C. $7,666.67
    D. $14,375.00

20. A sales associate sells a property for $258,500. The sales associate's employment agreement provides for a 60% share of the employing broker's commission. The commission due the selling broker is 2½%. What is the selling sales associate's share of the commission?
    A. $2,106.00
    B. $3,877.50
    C. $6,462.50
    D. $10,340.00

21. A developer buys 348,480 square feet of land at $0.75 per square foot and divides the land into half-acre lots. If the developer keeps three lots and sells the others for $24,125 each, what percentage of profit does the developer realize?
    A. 16.7%
    B. 20%
    C. 32.2%
    D. 47.4%

22. A landscaping contract for services for May 1 through October 31 totaling $2,500 has been paid in full for the current year. The house is sold and scheduled to close on July 16 and the buyers are assuming the sellers' landscaping agreement. What is the amount of the proration for this expense if a banker's year is used and all prorations are made through the day of closing? Round your answer to the nearest cent.
    A. $1,444.46
    B. $1,642.42
    C. $1,785.50
    D. $1,790.25

23. What is the interest rate on a $10,000 loan that requires a semiannual interest payment of $450?
    A. 7%
    B. 9%
    C. 11%
    D. 13.5%

24. A warehouse is 80 feet wide and 120 feet long with ceilings 14 feet high. If 1,200 square feet of floor surface has been partitioned off, floor to ceiling, for an office, how many cubic feet of space will be left in the warehouse?
    A. 117,600
    B. 133,200
    C. 134,400
    D. 151,200

25. An office building produces $68,580 annual net operating income. What price would an investor pay for this property to show a minimum return of 12% on the investment?
    A. $489,857
    B. $571,500
    C. $685,800
    D. $768,096

26. A buyer is assuming the balance of a seller's second mortgage loan. The interest rate is 8%, and the last monthly payment of $578.16 was paid on April 1, leaving an outstanding balance of $18,450. Using a banker's year, compute the interest to be paid by the seller if the sale is to close on April 19. Prorate through the day of closing.
    A. $77.90
    B. $82.00
    C. $110.83
    D. $123.00

27. A lot purchased five years ago for $15,000 has appreciated a total of 17.5% since its purchase. What is it worth today?
    A. $12,375
    B. $15,525
    C. $17,250
    D. $17,625

28. A lot has a frontage of 100 feet and a depth of 150 feet. If the building line regulations call for a setback of 25 feet at the front, 10 feet at the back, and 6 feet on each side, how many square feet of usable space are left for the building?
    A. 9,350
    B. 10,120
    C. 11,750
    D. 15,000

29. A lease calls for rent of $1,000 per month plus 2% of annual sales in excess of $100,000. What is the annual rent if the annual sales are $150,000?
    A. $12,000
    B. $13,000
    C. $14,000
    D. $15,000

30. Taxes on a home for the current tax year amount to $6,468. The home was sold in July, and the sale closed on August 29. The seller had not paid any of the tax owed for the current year prior to the closing. What was the prorated tax amount using a calendar year if the proration was calculated to the day of closing?
    A. $4,252.93
    B. $4,607.34
    C. $5,280.50
    D. $6,468.00

31. A tract of land measures 1.25 acres. The lot is 150 feet deep. How much will the lot sell for at $65 per front foot?
    A. $8,125
    B. $9,750
    C. $23,595
    D. $25,420

32. If a 6.5% full brokerage commission was $5,200, what was the sales price of the house?
    A. $77,200
    B. $80,000
    C. $80,400
    D. $86,600

33. A buyer earns $60,000 per year and can qualify for a monthly PITI payment equal to 25% of monthly salary. If the annual tax and insurance on a prospective purchase is $678.24, what loan amount will the buyer qualify for if the monthly PI payment factor is $10.29 per $1,000 of loan amount?
    A. $99,987
    B. $108,965
    C. $112,784
    D. $115,980

34. Find the cost of building a house 29' × 34' × 17' with a gable roof 8' high at the highest point. The cost of construction is $2.25 per cubic foot.
    A. $27,731.25
    B. $37,714.50
    C. $46,588.50
    D. $55,462.50

35. An amount of $50,000 is invested at a rate of return of 12%. What is the net operating income?
    A. $4,167
    B. $5,000
    C. $5,600
    D. $6,000

36. Monthly interest on a loan with a 9.25% annual interest rate is $65.53. What is the loan amount rounded to the nearest hundred dollars?
    A. $1,400
    B. $2,800
    C. $6,300
    D. $8,500

37. What percentage of profit will there be if a property buyer pays $20,500 for a lot, builds a home on the lot that costs $133,000, and then sells the lot and house together for $194,550? Round your answer to the nearest percent.
    A. 13%
    B. 23%
    C. 27%
    D. 45%

38. The buyer is purchasing a fourplex and closing on November 4. Each apartment rents for $875 per month. As of November 1, one apartment is vacant and the other tenants have paid their November rent. Compute the rent proration through the day of closing.
    A. $345.00
    B. $1,993.33
    C. $2,275.00
    D. $3,935.72

39. An income-producing property has $62,500 annual gross income and monthly expenses of $1,530. What is an estimate of the property's value using a 10% capitalization rate?
    A. $183,600
    B. $441,400
    C. $609,700
    D. $625,000

40. A new house and lot cost the buyer $565,000. Of this total price, the lot was estimated to be worth $130,000. The buyer held the property for eight years. If average market prices of comparable properties in the area increased by 32% over that period, what would be the total value of the property at the end of eight years?
    A. $695,300
    B. $745,800
    C. $810,900
    D. $925,800

41. The seller received a $121,600 check at closing after paying a 7% brokerage commission, $31,000 in other closing costs, and a $135,700 loan payoff. What was the total sales price?
    A. $288,300
    B. $306,300
    C. $308,500
    D. $310,000

42. A fence is being built to enclose a lot 125 feet by 350 feet. If there will be one 10-foot gate, how many running feet of fence will be needed?
    A. 465
    B. 600
    C. 940
    D. 960

43. A buyer pays $9,500 each for four parcels of land, subdivides them into six parcels, and sells each of the six parcels for $7,500. What is the buyer's percentage of profit? Round your answer to the nearest percent.
    A. 16%
    B. 18%
    C. 22%
    D. 38%

44. A property sells for $295,200. If it has appreciated for a total of 20% over the past five years, what did the owner pay for the property five years ago?
    A. $175,000
    B. $246,000
    C. $286,000
    D. $320,000

45. A teacher earns an annual income of $60,000, and the teacher's spouse earns $2,400 per month. How much can the couple pay monthly for their mortgage payment if the lender uses a 28% qualifying ratio?
    A. $672
    B. $1,400
    C. $2,072
    D. $2,352

46. If a buyer borrows $4,400, agreeing to pay back principal and interest in 18 months, what annual interest rate is the buyer paying if the total payback is $5,588?
    A. 15%
    B. 18%
    C. 21.3%
    D. 27%

47. If you purchase a lot that is 125' × 150' for $6,468.75, what price did you pay per front foot?
    A. $23.52
    B. $43.13
    C. $51.75
    D. $64.69

48. A buyer is granted a 90% loan for $340,500. How much will the monthly principal and interest payment be, using a loan payment factor of $7.16 per $1,000 of loan?
    A. $2,194.18
    B. $2,437.98
    C. $3,064.50
    D. $4,755.59

49. Calculate the amount of the total commission earned by a broker on a rural property selling for $61,000 if 6% is paid on the first $50,000 of the sales price and 3% is paid on the amount over $50,000.
    A. $3,330
    B. $3,600
    C. $3,830
    D. $3,930

50. A 50' × 100' lot has a 2,400-square-foot house on it that contains four bedrooms and three bathrooms. What percentage of the lot is not taken up by the house?
    A. 21%
    B. 48%
    C. 50%
    D. 52%

ANSWER KEY FOR REAL ESTATE MATH PRACTICE PROBLEMS

1. **D $140,000.00 original cost**

    100% original cost – 35% total depreciation = 65% today's value

    $$\frac{\$91,000 \text{ today's value}}{\text{original cost} \quad \times \quad 65\%}$$

    $91,000 ÷ 65% = $140,000 original cost

2. **D $1,250 per front foot**

    $125,000 sales price ÷ 100 front feet = $1,250 per front foot

3. **C $4,350 due at closing**

    100% value – 90% LTV = 10% down payment

    $$\frac{\$8,850 \text{ down payment}}{\$88,500 \text{ value} \quad \times \quad 10\%}$$

    $88,500 × 10% = $8,850

    $8,850 down payment – $4,500 earnest money = $4,350 due at closing

4. **B $266,671.43 original cost**

    100% original cost + 12% profit = 112% sales price

    $$\frac{\$298,672 \text{ sales price}}{\text{original cost} \quad \times \quad 112\%}$$

    $298,672 ÷ 112% = $266,671.43 original cost

5. **D $125,000 value**

    $$\frac{\$11,250 \text{ annual net income}}{\text{value} \quad \times \quad 9\%}$$

    $11,250 ÷ 9% = $125,000 value

6. **B $23.33 rent proration**

    30 days in September – 28 day of closing = 2 days due

    $350 monthly rent ÷ 30 days = $11.666667 per day × 2 days = $23.33 rent proration

7. **C $1,194.00 total cost**

    4" ÷ 12 = 0.333'

    Concrete: 40' × 15' × 0.333' = 199.8 cubic feet

    199.8 ÷ 27 = 7.4 cubic yards

    7.4 × $60 per cubic yard = $444

    Labor: 40' × 15' = 600 square feet

    600 × $1.25 per square foot = $750

    $444 concrete + $750 labor = $1,194.00 total cost

8. **D $51,000 sales price**

    $47,300 net to seller + $1,150 closing costs = $48,450 seller's dollars after commission

    100% sales price – 5% commission = 95% seller's percentage after commission

    $$\frac{\$48,450 \text{ seller's dollars after commission}}{\text{sales price} \quad \times \quad 95\%}$$

    $48,450 ÷ 95% = $51,000 sales price

9. **D $652.08 average monthly rent**

    $75,000 gross annual sales – $50,000 = $25,000 gross annual sales subject to 2.5%

    $$\frac{\text{annual percentage rent}}{\substack{\$25,000 \text{ gross sales} \\ \text{subject to the percentage}} \quad \times \quad 2.5\%}$$

    $25,000 × 2.5% = $625 annual percentage rent

    $625 annual percentage rent ÷ 12 months = $52.08 monthly percentage rent

    $600 monthly minimum rent + $52.08 monthly percentage rent = $652.08 average monthly rent

10. **B 24%**

    $825 monthly rent × 12 months = $9,900 annual rent

    $$\frac{\$9,900 \text{ annual rent}}{\substack{\$41,000 \\ \text{annual income}} \quad \times \quad \substack{\text{percent of} \\ \text{annual income}}}$$

    $9,900 ÷ $41,000 = 0.241 or 24% (rounded to the nearest percent)

11. **A**   **$2,916 commission to listing broker's sales associate**

$$\frac{\text{full commission}}{\$324,000 \text{ sales price} \quad \times \quad 6\%}$$

$324,000 × 6% = $19,440 full commission

$19,440 ÷ 2 brokers = $9,720 each broker's commission split

$$\frac{\text{listing broker's sales associate's commission}}{\$9,720 \text{ broker's commission split} \quad \times \quad 30\%}$$

$9,720 × 30% = $2,916 sales associate's commission

12. **B**   **10,626.625 square feet**

6" ÷ 12 = 0.5'

0.5' + 75' = 75.5' frontage

9" ÷ 12 = 0.75'

0.75' + 140' = 140.75' depth

140.75' × 75.5' = 10,626.625 square feet

13. **C**   **$1,736,000 value**

$775 monthly rent × 28 units × 12 months = $260,400 annual scheduled gross income

$260,400 − 5% vacancy rate = $247,380 annual effective gross income

$247,380 − $82,460 annual expenses = $164,920 annual net operating income

$$\frac{\$164,920 \text{ annual net operating income}}{\text{property value} \quad \times \quad 9.5\%}$$

$164,920 ÷ 9.5% = $1,736,000 property value

14. **A**   **$72.60 interest due**

Seller owes buyer 10 days (August 1 through August 10)

$$\frac{\text{annual interest}}{\$43,580 \text{ loan balance} \quad \times \quad 6\%}$$

$43,580 × 6% = $2,614.80 annual interest

$2,614.80 annual interest ÷ 360 days = $7.263 per day

$7.263 × 10 days = $72.63 interest due

15. **C**   **$5,512.50 points and origination fee**

2.5 loan discount points + 1 point origination fee = 3.5 points

$$\frac{\text{loan}}{\$175,000 \text{ sales price} \quad \times \quad 90\%}$$

$175,000 × 90% = $157,500 loan

$$\frac{\text{discount points and origination fee}}{\$157,500 \text{ loan} \quad \times \quad 3.5\%}$$

$157,500 loan × 3.5% = $5,512.50 points and origination fee

16. **C**   **$316.66 interest**

$$\frac{\text{annual interest}}{\$5,000 \text{ loan} \quad \times \quad 9.5\%}$$

$5,000 loan × 9.5% = $475 annual interest

$475 ÷ 12 months = $39.583 monthly interest

$39.583 × 8 months = $316.664 interest or $316.66 (rounded to the nearest cent)

17. **A**   **27,225 square feet per lot**

⅛ = 1 ÷ 8 = 0.125 for streets

100 acres × 0.125 = 12.5 acres for streets

100 acres − 12.5 acres for streets = 87.5 acres for lots

87.5 × 43,560 square feet per acre = 3,811,500 square feet buildable land

3,811,500 ÷ 140 lots = 27,225 square feet per lot

18. **A**   **$393.34 tax proration**

Seller owes the buyer January 1 to April 23

31	January
+ 28	February
+ 31	March
+ 22	April
112	days due

$1,282 annual tax ÷ 365 days = $3.512 per day

$3.512 × 112 days = $393.344 tax proration or $393.34 (rounded to the nearest cent)

19. **B** **$1,197.92 monthly NOI**

$$\frac{\text{annual NOI}}{\$115,000 \text{ investment}} \quad \times \quad 12.5\%$$

$115,000 × 12.5% = $14,375 annual NOI

$14,375 ÷ 12 months = $1,197.92 monthly NOI

20. **B** **$3,877.50 sales associate's commission**

$$\frac{\text{broker's commission}}{\$258,500 \text{ sales price}} \quad \times \quad 2\frac{1}{2}\%$$

$258,500 × 2½ % = $6,462.50 broker's commission

$$\frac{\text{sales associate's commission}}{\$6,462.50 \text{ broker's commission}} \quad \times \quad 60\%$$

$6,462.50 × 60% = $3,877.50 salesperson's commission

21. **B** **20% profit**

348,480 square feet × $0.75 per square foot = $261,360 cost

348,480 square feet ÷ 43,560 = 8 acres

8 acres × 2 lots per acre = 16 lots

16 lots − 3 lots = 13 lots sold

13 lots × $24,125 each = $313,625 total sales price

$313,625 sales price − $261,360 cost = $52,265 profit

$$\frac{\$52,265 \text{ profit}}{\$261,360 \text{ cost}} \quad \times \quad \text{percentage profit}$$

$52,265 ÷ $261,360 = 0.199973 or 20% profit

22. **A** **$1,444.46 landscaping proration**

May 1 through October 31 = 6 months or 180 days

30	July
− 16	closing date
14	days left in July
+ 30	August
+ 30	September
+ 30	October
104	days due

$2,500 landscaping expense ÷ 180 days = $13.889 per day

$13.889 × 104 days due = $1,444.456 or $1444.46 landscaping proration (rounded to the nearest cent)

23. **B** **9% interest rate**

$450 semiannual interest × 2 = $900 annual interest

$$\frac{\$900 \text{ annual interest}}{\$10,000 \text{ loan}} \quad \times \quad \text{interest rate}$$

$900 annual interest ÷ $10,000 loan = 0.09 or 9% interest rate

24. **A** **117,600 cubic feet**

120' × 80' = 9,600 square feet in building

9,600 − 1,200 square feet for office = 8,400 square feet left in warehouse

8,400 × 14-foot ceiling = 117,600 cubic feet left in warehouse

25. **B** **$571,500 price**

$$\frac{\$68,580 \text{ annual NOI}}{\text{price}} \quad \times \quad 12\% \text{ cap rate}$$

$68,580 ÷ 12% = $571,500 price

26. **A** **$77.90 interest proration**

Seller owes buyer 19 days (April 1 *through* April 19)

$$\frac{\text{annual interest}}{\$18,450 \text{ loan balance}} \quad \times \quad 8\%$$

$18,450 × 8% = $1,476

$1,476 annual interest ÷ 360 days = $4.10 per day

$4.10 × 19 days = $77.90 interest proration

27. **D** **$17,625 today's value**

100% cost + 17.5% total appreciation = 117.5% today's value

$$\frac{\text{today's value}}{\$15,000 \text{ original cost}} \quad \times \quad 117.5\%$$

$15,000 × 117.5% = $17,625 today's value

28. **B** **10,120 buildable square feet left**

Front and back setbacks are 25' + 10' = 35'

150' depth − 35' setback = 115' left

Side setbacks are 6' + 6" = 12"

100' frontage − 12' = 88' left

115' × 88' = 10,120 buildable square feet left

29. **B** **$13,000 annual rent**

$1,000 monthly minimum rent × 12 months = $12,000 annual minimum rent

$150,000 annual sales − $100,000 = $50,000 annual sales subject to 2%

$$\frac{\text{annual percentage rent}}{\$50,000 \text{ annual sales}} \times 2\%$$

$50,000 × 2% = $1,000

$12,000 annual minimum rent + $1,000 annual percentage rent = $13,000 annual rent

30. **A** **$4,252.93 tax proration**

Seller owes buyer January 1 to August 29

	31	January
+	28	February
+	31	March
+	30	April
+	31	May
+	30	June
+	31	July
+	28	August
	240	days due

$6,468 annual tax ÷ 365 days = $17.72055 per day

$17.72055 × 240 days = $4,252.93 tax proration

31. **C** **$23,595 sales price**

1.25 acres × 43,560 = 54,450 square feet

54,450 ÷ 150' deep = 363' frontage

363' × $65 per front foot = $23,595 sales price

32. **B** **$80,000 sales price**

$$\frac{\$5,200 \text{ full commission}}{\text{sales price}} \times 6.5\%$$

$5,200 full commission ÷ 6.5% = $80,000 sales price

33. **D** **$115,980 loan**

$60,000 annual salary ÷ 12 months = $5,000 monthly salary

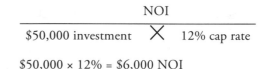

$$\frac{\text{monthly PITI}}{\$5,000 \text{ monthly salary}} \times 25\%$$

$5,000 × 25% = $1,250 monthly PITI

$678.24 annual taxes and insurance ÷ 12 months = $56.52 monthly TI

$1,250 monthly PITI − $56.52 monthly TI = $1,193.48 monthly PI

$1,193.48 monthly PI payment ÷ $10.29 = 115.9845 or 115.98 (rounded to the nearest cent)

115.98 × $1,000 = $115,980 loan

34. **C** **$46,588.50 construction cost**

29' × 34' × 17' = 16,762 cubic feet in house

29' × 34' × 8' ÷ 2 = 3,944 cubic feet in attic

16,762 cubic feet + 3,944 cubic feet = 20,706 cubic feet total

20,706 × $2.25 per cubic foot = $46,588.50 construction cost

35. **D** **$6,000 NOI**

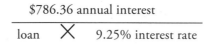

$$\frac{\text{NOI}}{\$50,000 \text{ investment}} \times 12\% \text{ cap rate}$$

$50,000 × 12% = $6,000 NOI

36. **D** **$8,500 loan**

$65.53 monthly interest × 12 months = $786.36 annual interest

$$\frac{\$786.36 \text{ annual interest}}{\text{loan}} \times 9.25\% \text{ interest rate}$$

$786.36 ÷ 9.25% = $8,501.19 (rounded to the nearest cent) = $8,500 loan rounded to the nearest hundred dollars.

37. **C** **27%**

$20,500 cost of lot + $133,000 cost of home = $153,500 total cost

$194,550 sales price – $153,500 total cost = $41,050 profit

$$\frac{\$41,050 \text{ profit}}{\$153,500 \text{ total cost}} \quad \times \quad \% \text{ profit}$$

$41,050 ÷ $153,500 = 0.267 or 27% profit (rounded to the nearest percent)

38. **C** **$2,275 rent proration**

30	November
– 4	day of closing
26	days due

$875 monthly rent × 3 units = $2,625 monthly rent

$2,625 ÷ 30 days = $87.50 per day

$87.50 × 26 days = $2,275 rent proration

39. **B** **$441,400 estimated value**

$1,530 monthly expenses × 12 months = $18,360 annual expenses

$62,500 annual gross income – $18,360 annual expenses = $44,140 NOI

$$\frac{\$44,140 \text{ NOI}}{\text{estimated value}} \quad \times \quad 10\% \text{ cap rate}$$

$44,140 ÷ 10% = $441,400 estimated value

40. **B** **$745,800 appreciated property value**

100% cost + 32% appreciation = 132% appreciated property value

$$\frac{\text{appreciated property value}}{\$565,000 \text{ cost of property}} \quad \times \quad 132\% \text{ appreciation}$$

$565,000 cost × 132% = $745,800 appreciated property value

41. **D** **$310,000 sales price**

$121,600 seller's net + $31,000 closing costs + $135,700 loan payoff = $288,300 seller's dollars after commission

100% sales price – 7% commission = 93% seller's dollars after commission

$$\frac{\$288,300 \text{ seller's dollars after commission}}{\text{sales price}} \quad \times \quad 93\%$$

$288,300 ÷ 93% = $310,000 sales price

42. **C** **940 running feet**

125' + 350' + 125' + 350' – 10' gate = 940 running feet

43. **B** **18% profit**

$9,500 cost × 4 parcels = $38,000 total cost

$7,500 sales price × 6 parcels = $45,000 sales price

$45,000 sales price – $38,000 cost = $7,000 profit

$$\frac{\$7,000 \text{ profit}}{\$38,000 \text{ cost}} \quad \times \quad \text{percentage profit}$$

$7,000 ÷ $38,000 cost = 0.18421 or 18% profit (rounded to the nearest percent)

44. **B** **$246,000 original cost**

100% cost + 20% total appreciation = 120% appreciated property value

$$\frac{\$295,200 \text{ appreciated property value}}{\text{original cost}} \quad \times \quad 120\%$$

$295,200 ÷ 120% = $246,000 original cost

45. **C** **$2,072 monthly payment**

$60,000 annual salary ÷ 12 months = $5,000 monthly salary

$5,000 + $2,400 monthly salary = $7,400 total monthly salary

$$\frac{\text{monthly payment}}{\$7,400 \text{ monthly salary}} \quad \times \quad 28\%$$

$7,400 × 28% = $2,072 monthly payment

46. **B**   **18% annual interest rate**

$5,588 payback (principal + interest) − $4,400 loan (principal) = $1,188 interest for 18 months

$1,188 ÷ 18 months = $66 monthly interest

$66 × 12 months = $792 annual interest

$$\frac{\$792 \text{ annual interest}}{\$4,400 \text{ loan}} \quad X \quad \text{annual interest rate}$$

$792 ÷ $4,400 = 0.18 or 18% annual interest rate

47. **C**   **$51.75 per front foot**

$6,468.75 price ÷ 125 front feet = $51.75 per front foot

48. **B**   **$2,437.98 monthly principal and interest payment**

$340,500 loan ÷ $1,000 = 340.5

340.5 × $7.16 = $2,437.98 monthly principal and interest payment

49. **A**   **$3,330 total commission**

$$\frac{\text{commission}}{\text{first } \$50,000 \text{ of sales price}} \quad X \quad 6\%$$

$50,000 × 6% = $3,000 commission

$61,000 sales price − $50,000 sales price at 6% = $11,000 sales price at 3%

$$\frac{\text{commission}}{\$11,000 \text{ of sales price above } \$50,000} \quad X \quad 3\%$$

$11,000 × 3% = $330 commission

$3,000 commission + $330 commission = $3,330 total commission

50. **D**   **52% not taken up by house**

50' × 100' = 5,000 square feet of lot − 2,400 square feet of house = 2,600 square feet not taken up by house

$$\frac{2,600 \text{ square feet not taken up by house}}{5,000 \text{ square feet of lot}} \quad X \quad \text{percentage not taken up by house}$$

2,600 ÷ 5,000 = 0.52 or 52% not taken up by house

SAMPLE EXAMINATIONS

PREVIEW: TESTING SERVICES

In some states, the real estate commission writes and administers the real estate licensing examinations. In others, a commercial testing service prepares two-part examinations that include both state-specific license law questions and questions on broader national issues and general principles. Most states use the examinations produced by one of the commercial testing services, which include Applied Measurement Professionals (AMP), www.goamp.com; Pearson VUE, https://home.pearsonvue.com; Prometric, www.prometric.com; and PSI Examination Services (PSI), https://candidate.psiexams.com; and others.

The sample examinations included here are not intended to be a review of *Modern Real Estate Practice* or your real estate course. Rather, they are designed to imitate real estate licensing exams, any one of which may emphasize some concepts and ignore others. The answer key for these sample examinations includes the relevant unit from which each question was drawn. Questions that involve mathematical calculations in addition to one or more real estate concepts will refer you to the math skills review in "Math FAQs." If your answer is not correct, it is advisable to restudy the suggested material. *Note that proration calculations here are based on a 30-day month unless otherwise stated. Additionally, decimals are rounded to two places, or the nearest cent.*

SAMPLE EXAM 1

1. Which of the following is a lien on real estate?
   A. Recorded easement
   B. Recorded mortgage
   C. Encroachment
   D. Deed restriction

2. A sales contract was signed by a minor. Which term describes this contract?
   A. Voidable
   B. Breached
   C. Discharged
   D. Void

3. A real estate professional receives a check for earnest money from a buyer and deposits the money in the real estate professional's personal interest-bearing checking account over the weekend. This action exposes the real estate professional to a charge of
   A. commingling.
   B. novation.
   C. subrogation.
   D. accretion.

4. A borrower takes out a mortgage loan that requires monthly payments of $875.70 for 20 years and a final payment of $24,095. This is what type of loan?
   A. Wraparound
   B. Accelerated
   C. Balloon
   D. Variable

5. If a borrower computed the interest charged for the previous month on a $260,000 loan balance as $1,300, what is the borrower's interest rate to the nearest half percent?
   A. 6%
   B. 6½%
   C. 5%
   D. 5½%

6. A real estate professional signs a contract with a buyer. Under the contract, the real estate professional agrees to help the buyer find a suitable property and to represent the buyer in negotiations with the seller. The buyer may not sign an agreement with any other real estate professional. What kind of agreement has this real estate professional signed?
   A. Exclusive buyer listing agreement
   B. Exclusive buyer representation agreement
   C. Open buyer agency agreement
   D. Option contract

7. A grantor conveys property by delivering a deed. The deed contains five covenants. This is *MOST* likely
   A. a general warranty deed.
   B. a quitclaim deed.
   C. a bargain and sale deed.
   D. a deed in trust.

8. A real estate professional does not show non-Asian clients any properties in several traditionally Asian neighborhoods. The real estate professional bases this practice on the need to preserve the valuable cultural integrity of Asian immigrant communities. Which statement is *TRUE* regarding the real estate professional's policy?
   A. The real estate professional's policy is steering and violates federal and state fair housing laws regardless of motivation.
   B. Because the real estate professional is not attempting to restrict the rights of any single minority group, the practice does not constitute steering.
   C. The real estate professional's policy is steering, but it does not violate the fair housing laws because cultural preservation is the motive, not exclusion or discrimination.
   D. The real estate professional's policy has the effect, but not the intent, of steering.

9. A woman grants a life estate to her son-in-law and stipulates that, upon his death, the title to the property will pass to her grandson. The grandson's interest is known as
   A. a remainder.
   B. a reversion.
   C. an estate at sufferance.
   D. an estate for years.

10. A primary benefit of property held in joint tenancy is
    A. ownership by a maximum of two people.
    B. the fractional interests of the owners, which can be different.
    C. the fact that additional owners may be added later.
    D. the right of survivorship.

11. A licensed real estate sales associate has a written contract with the employing broker that specifies that the sales associate will not be treated as an employee for federal tax purposes. The sales associate's entire income is from sales commissions rather than an hourly wage. Based on these facts, the sales associate will be treated by the IRS as
    A. a real estate assistant.
    B. an employee.
    C. a subagent.
    D. a qualified real estate agent.

12. The states in which the owner gives up legal title of mortgaged real estate are known as
    A. title theory states.
    B. lien theory states.
    C. statutory title states.
    D. strict title forfeiture states.

13. The form of tenancy that will expire on a specific date is
    A. a joint tenancy.
    B. a tenancy for years.
    C. a tenancy at sufferance.
    D. a tenancy by the entirety.

14. A large home that lacks sufficient indoor plumbing suffers from which condition?
    A. Functional obsolescence
    B. Curable physical deterioration
    C. Incurable physical deterioration
    D. External obsolescence

15. A developer built a structure that has six stories. Several years later, an ordinance was passed in that area banning any building six stories or higher. This building is
    A. a nonconforming use.
    B. a situation in which the structure would have to be demolished.
    C. a conditional use.
    D. a violation of the zoning laws.

16. Assuming that the listing agent and the selling agent in a transaction split their commission equally, what was the sales price of the property if the commission rate was 5.5% and the listing agent received $12,584?
    A. $228,800
    B. $242,871
    C. $457,600
    D. $692,120

17. A real estate broker specializes in helping both buyers and sellers with the necessary paperwork involved in transferring property. Although not an agent of either party, the broker may not disclose either party's confidential information to the other. The broker is *BEST* described as
    A. a buyer's broker.
    B. an independent contractor.
    C. a dual agent.
    D. a transaction broker.

18. Three women owned a house as joint tenants. In the year 2009, one died. Last month, another died. Based on these facts, which of the following correctly describes the remaining woman's ownership interest in the house?
    A. Joint tenancy with the deceased owners' heirs
    B. Tenancy in common with the deceased owners' heirs
    C. Severalty
    D. Partitioned tenancy by the entirety

19. The listing and selling brokers agree to split a 7% commission 50-50 on a $295,900 land sale. The listing broker gives the listing sales associate 50% of the listing broker's share, and the selling broker gives the selling sales associate 65% of that share. How much does the selling sales associate earn from the sale after deducting expenses of $1,300? Round your answer to the nearest cent.
    A. $5,178.00
    B. $5,431.73
    C. $6,731.73
    D. $10,356.50

20. Police powers include all of the following *EXCEPT*
    A. zoning.
    B. deed restrictions.
    C. building codes.
    D. density requirements.

21. A seller wants to net $165,000 from the sale of a house after paying the broker's fee of 6% and other closing costs of $2,635. The seller's gross sales price will be
    A. $152,465.
    B. $152,623.
    C. $174,900.
    D. $178,335.

22. Three acres equals how many square feet?
    A. 43,560
    B. 130,680
    C. 156,840
    D. 27,878,400

23. A buyer is purchasing a condominium unit in a subdivision and obtains financing from a local bank. In this situation, which term *BEST* describes this buyer?
    A. Vendor
    B. Mortgagor
    C. Grantor
    D. Lessor

24. The current value of a property is $140,000. The property is assessed at 40% of its current value for real estate tax purposes, with an equalization factor of 1.5 applied to the assessed value. If the tax rate is $4 per $100 of assessed valuation, what is the amount of tax due on the property?
    A. $840
    B. $2,100
    C. $2,240
    D. $3,360

25. A building was sold for $260,000, with the purchaser putting 10% down and obtaining a loan for the balance. The lending institution charged a 1% loan origination fee. What was the total cash used for the purchase?
    A. $2,340
    B. $23,400
    C. $26,000
    D. $28,340

26. A parcel of vacant land has an assessed valuation of $274,550. If the assessment is 85% of market value, what is the market value?
    A. $315,732
    B. $320,000
    C. $323,000
    D. $1,830,333

27. Which of the following *BEST* describes a capitalization rate?
    A. Amount determined by the gross rent multiplier
    B. Rate of return an income property will produce
    C. Mathematical value determined by a sales price
    D. Rate at which the amount of depreciation in a property is measured

28. A parcel of land described as "the NW¼ and the SW¼ of Section 6, T4N, R8W of the Third Principal Meridian" was sold for $875 per acre. The listing agent will receive a 5% commission on the total sales price. How much will the agent receive?
    A. $1,750
    B. $5,040
    C. $14,000
    D. $15,040

29. If a house was sold for $360,000 and the buyer obtained a mortgage loan for $288,000, how much money would the buyer pay in discount points if the lender charged two points?
    A. $5,760
    B. $6,000
    C. $6,600
    D. $7,200

30. The commission rate is 7% on a sale of $250,000. What is the dollar amount of the commission?
    A. $1,750
    B. $3,571
    C. $17,500
    D. $35,000

31. A prospective buyer signs an offer to purchase a residential property. All the following circumstances would automatically terminate the offer *EXCEPT*
    A. the buyer signed a written offer to buy a house and then died.
    B. the buyer revoked the offer between the presentation and a possible acceptance.
    C. the seller made a counteroffer.
    D. the seller received a better offer from another buyer.

32. A buyer purchased a home under a land contract. Until the contract is paid in full, or the buyer meets statutory requirements, the buyer
    A. holds legal title to the premises.
    B. has no legal interest in the property.
    C. possesses a legal life estate in the premises.
    D. has equitable title in the property.

33. A buyer and a seller sign a contract for the sale of real property. A few days later, they decide to change many of the terms of the contract, while retaining the basic intent to buy and sell. The process by which the new contract replaces the old one is called
    A. assignment.
    B. novation.
    C. assemblage.
    D. rescission.

34. Using the services of a mortgage broker, a buyer borrowed $25,000 from a private lender. After the loan costs were deducted, the buyer received $24,255. What is the face amount of the note?
    A. $645
    B. $4,255
    C. $24,255
    D. $25,000

35. Whose signature is necessary for a signed offer to purchase real estate to become a contract?
    A. Buyer's only
    B. Buyer's and seller's
    C. Seller's only
    D. Seller's and seller's agent's

36. A borrower has just made the final payment on a mortgage loan. Regardless of this fact, the records will still show a lien on the mortgaged property until which event occurs?
    A. A mortgage satisfaction document is recorded.
    B. A reconveyance of the mortgage document is delivered to the mortgage holder.
    C. A novation of the mortgage document takes place.
    D. An estoppel of the mortgage document is filed with the clerk of the county in which the mortgagee is located.

37. If the annual net income from a commercial property is $75,000 and the capitalization rate is 8%, what is the property worth if the income approach is used?
    A. $600,000
    B. $694,000
    C. $810,000
    D. $937,500

38. A real estate professional enters into a listing agreement with a seller in which the seller will receive $120,000 from the sale of a vacant lot and the real estate professional will receive any sale proceeds exceeding that amount. This is what type of listing?
    A. Exclusive agency
    B. Net
    C. Exclusive right to sell
    D. Multiple

39. Under a cooperative form of ownership, an owner
    A. is a shareholder in the corporation.
    B. owns the unit outright and a share of the common areas.
    C. will have to take out a new mortgage loan on a newly acquired unit.
    D. receives a fixed-term lease for the unit.

40. A known defect or a cloud on the title to property may be cured by
    A. obtaining quitclaim deeds from all appropriate parties.
    B. recording the title after closing.
    C. paying cash for the property at the settlement.
    D. purchasing a title insurance policy at closing.

41. A seller signed an exclusive right-to-sell agreement with a real estate professional. If the seller finds a suitable buyer with no assistance, the real estate professional is entitled to
    A. full compensation from the buyer.
    B. no compensation from the seller.
    C. partial compensation.
    D. full compensation from the seller.

42. Under the terms of a net lease, a commercial tenant would usually be directly responsible for paying all the following property expenses *EXCEPT*
    A. maintenance expenses.
    B. mortgage debt service.
    C. fire and extended-coverage insurance.
    D. real estate taxes.

43. The Civil Rights Act of 1866 prohibits discrimination based on
    A. sex.
    B. religion.
    C. race.
    D. familial status.

44. What would it cost to put new carpeting in a room measuring 45 feet by 20 feet if the carpet costs $16.95 per square yard, plus a $250 installation charge?
    A. $1,250
    B. $1,695
    C. $1,945
    D. $15,255

45. What is the difference between a general lien and a specific lien?
    A. A general lien cannot be enforced in court, while a specific lien can.
    B. A specific lien is held by only one person, while a general lien must be held by two or more people.
    C. A general lien is a lien against personal property, while a specific lien is a lien against real estate.
    D. A specific lien is a lien against a certain parcel of real estate or other property, while a general lien covers all of a debtor's property.

46. In an option to purchase real estate, which statement is *TRUE* of the optionee?
    A. The optionee must purchase the property but may do so at any time within the option period.
    B. The optionee is limited to a refund of the option consideration if the option is exercised.
    C. The optionee cannot obtain third-party financing on the property until after the option has expired.
    D. The optionee has no obligation to purchase the property during the option period.

47. A village board has decided that a parking lot near the central business district would enhance the beauty, safety, and vitality of the community by keeping cars from parking on the busiest streets. Unfortunately, a house is located on part of the land best suited for the new parking lot. Based on these facts, which statement is *TRUE*?
    A. The homeowner's constitutional right to own property cannot be infringed by the village under any circumstances.
    B. The village may tear down the house and build the parking lot without paying the homeowner any compensation, through the village's constitutional authority under the takings clause.
    C. The village may tear down the house if it first pays the homeowner fair value after meeting legal requirements.
    D. The village may not seize the house because it has insufficient reason to do so.

48. How many acres are there in the N½ of the SW¼ and the NE¼ of the SE¼ of a section?
    A. 20
    B. 40
    C. 80
    D. 120

49. A home is the smallest in a neighborhood of large, expensive houses. The effect of the other houses on the value of the small home is known as
    A. regression.
    B. progression.
    C. substitution.
    D. contribution.

50. A lien that arises as a result of a judgment, estate or inheritance taxes, a decedent's debts, or federal taxes is what type of lien?
    A. Specific
    B. General
    C. Voluntary
    D. Equitable

51. All of the following will terminate an offer to purchase real estate *EXCEPT*
    A. failure to accept the offer within a prescribed period.
    B. revocation by the offeror communicated to the offeree after acceptance.
    C. a conditional acceptance of the offer by the offeree.
    D. the death of the offeror or offeree.

52. Two homeowners are joint tenants. One of the owners sells that interest to another person. What is the remaining owner's relationship to the new tenant regarding the property?
    A. Joint tenants
    B. Tenants in common
    C. Tenants by the entirety
    D. No relationship, because he cannot sell his joint tenancy interest

53. Two friends enter into a six-month oral lease. If one friend defaults, the other may
    A. not bring a court action because leases must be in writing for a court to review them.
    B. not bring a court action because the statute of frauds governs six-month leases.
    C. bring a court action because six-month leases need not be in writing to be enforceable.
    D. bring a court action because the statute of limitations does not apply to oral leases, regardless of their term.

54. On Monday, a prospective buyer offers to purchase a vacant lot for $25,000. On Tuesday, the owner counteroffers to sell the lot for $29,000. On Friday, the owner withdraws the counteroffer and accepts the buyer's original offer of $25,000. Under these circumstances, which statement is *TRUE*?
    A. A valid agreement exists because the seller accepted the buyer's offer exactly as it was made, regardless of the fact that it was not accepted immediately.
    B. A valid agreement exists because the seller accepted before the buyer provided notice that the offer was withdrawn.
    C. No valid agreement exists because the buyer's offer was not accepted within 72 hours of its having been made.
    D. No valid agreement exists because the seller's counteroffer was a rejection of the buyer's offer, and once rejected, it cannot be accepted later.

55. A doctor's neighbors use the doctor's driveway to reach their garage, which is on their property. The doctor's attorney explains that the neighbors have the right to use the driveway. The doctor's property is
    A. the dominant tenement.
    B. the servient tenement.
    C. the fee simple defeasible estate.
    D. the fee simple determinable estate.

56. If the quarterly interest at 7.5% is $562.50, what is the principal amount of the loan?
    A. $7,500
    B. $15,000
    C. $30,000
    D. $75,000

57. A deed conveys ownership to the grantee "so long as the existing building is not torn down." What type of estate does this deed create?
    A. Fee simple determinable estate
    B. Homestead estate
    C. Fee simple absolute estate
    D. Life estate pur autre vie, with the measuring life being the building's expected structural lifetime

58. If the mortgage loan is 80% of the appraised value of a house and the interest rate of 6% amounts to $460 for the first month, what is the appraised value of the house?
    A. $55,200
    B. $73,600
    C. $92,000
    D. $115,000

59. Local zoning ordinances may regulate all of the following *EXCEPT*
    A. height of buildings in an area.
    B. density of population.
    C. appropriate use of buildings in an area.
    D. market value of a property.

60. A real estate professional took a listing and later discovered that the client had been declared incompetent by a court. What is the current status of the listing?
    A. The listing is unaffected because the real estate professional acted in good faith as the owner's agent.
    B. The listing is of no value to the real estate professional because the contract is void.
    C. The listing entitles the real estate professional to collect a commission from the client's guardian or trustee if the real estate professional produces a buyer.
    D. The listing must be renegotiated between the real estate professional and the client, based on the new information.

61. After a borrower's default on home mortgage loan payments, the lender obtained a court order to foreclose on the property. At the foreclosure sale, the property sold for $164,000; the unpaid balance on the loan at the time of foreclosure was $178,000. If state law permits, what must the lender do to recover the $14,000 that the borrower still owes?
    A. Sue for specific performance
    B. Sue for damages
    C. Seek a deficiency judgment
    D. Seek a judgment by default

62. Which activity is forbidden by the federal Fair Housing Act?
    A. Limitation by religion and nationality in the sale of a single-family home where the property is listed by a licensed real estate professional
    B. Limitation to members only in noncommercial lodgings of a private club
    C. Limitations against familial status and disability in the rental of a unit in an owner-occupied three-family dwelling when no discriminatory advertising is used
    D. Limitation by religion and sex in noncommercial housing in a convent or monastery

63. A buyer purchases a $137,000 property, depositing $3,000 as earnest money. The buyer obtains a 75% loan-to-value (LTV) loan with no additional items to be prorated and no closing costs to the buyer. How much more cash will the buyer need at the settlement?
    A. $31,250
    B. $33,500
    C. $34,250
    D. $37,250

64. A real estate professional arrives to present a purchase offer to a seller who is seriously ill and finds the seller's two adult children also present. The children angrily urge the seller to accept the offer, even though it is much less than the asking price for the property. If the seller accepts the offer, the seller may not be bound by it because
    A. the real estate professional improperly presented an offer that was less than the asking price.
    B. the real estate professional's failure to protect the seller from the children constituted a violation of the real estate professional's fiduciary duties.
    C. the seller's rights under the ADA have been violated by the seller's children.
    D. the seller was under undue influence from the seller's children, so the contract is voidable.

65. A property is sold. The deed of conveyance contained only the following guarantee: "This property was not encumbered during the time the seller owned it except as noted in this deed." What type of deed makes such a covenant?
    A. General warranty
    B. Special warranty
    C. Bargain and sale
    D. Quitclaim

66. An unmarried couple own a parcel of real estate. Each owns an undivided interest, with one owning one-third and the other owning two-thirds. The form of ownership under which the couple own their property is
    A. severalty.
    B. joint tenancy.
    C. tenancy at will.
    D. tenancy in common.

67. A buyer agrees to purchase a house for $184,500. The buyer pays $2,000 as earnest money and obtains a new mortgage loan for $167,600. The purchase contract provides for a March 15 settlement. The buyer and the sellers prorate the current year's real estate taxes of $1,880.96, which have been prepaid. The buyer has additional closing costs of $1,250, and the sellers have other closing costs of $850. How much cash must the buyer bring to the settlement?
    A. $16,389.09
    B. $17,639.10
    C. $17,839.09
    D. $19,639.10.

68. A real estate professional listed a house for $247,900. A member of a racial minority group saw the house and was interested in it. When the prospective buyer asked the real estate professional the price of the house, the real estate professional said that it was listed for $253,000 and that the seller was very firm on the price. Under the federal Fair Housing Act of 1968, such a statement is
    A. legal because the law requires only that the buyer be given the opportunity to buy the house.
    B. legal because the representation was made by the real estate professional and not directly by the owner.
    C. illegal because the difference in the offering price and the quoted price was greater than 10%.
    D. illegal because the terms of the potential sale were changed for the prospective buyer.

69. Property was placed in a trust. When the owner died, the owner's will directed the trustee to sell the property and distribute the proceeds of the sale to the named heirs. The trustee sold the property in accordance with the will. What type of deed was delivered at settlement?
    A. Trustee's deed
    B. Trustor's deed
    C. Deed of trust
    D. Reconveyance deed

70. An appraiser has been hired to prepare an appraisal report of a property for loan purposes. The property is an elegant old mansion that is now used as a restaurant. Which approach to value should the appraiser probably give the greatest weight when making this appraisal?
    A. Income
    B. Sales comparison
    C. Depreciated cost
    D. Functional obsolescence

71. A borrower applies for a mortgage, and the loan officer suggests that the borrower consider a term mortgage loan. Which statement *BEST* explains what the loan officer means?
    A. All the interest is paid at the end of the term.
    B. The debt is partially amortized over the life of the loan.
    C. The length of the term is limited by state law.
    D. The entire principal amount is due at the end of the term.

72. A condominium community has a swimming pool, sauna, and tennis courts. These facilities are *MOST* likely owned by
    A. the condominium board.
    B. the corporation in which the unit owners hold stock.
    C. the unit owners in the form of proportional divided interests.
    D. the unit owners in the form of percentage undivided interests.

73. At closing for a typical real estate transaction, the buyer's earnest money deposit is
    A. a credit to the buyer only.
    B. a credit to the seller, debit to the buyer.
    C. a credit to the buyer and the seller.
    D. a debit to the buyer only.

74. At closing for a typical real estate transaction, property tax not yet due is
    A. a credit to the buyer, debit to the seller.
    B. a credit to the seller only.
    C. a debit to the seller only.
    D. a debit to the buyer, credit to the seller.

75. Real property can become personal property by the process known as
    A. annexation.
    B. severance.
    C. hypothecation.
    D. accretion.

76. A property owners gives a friend permission to park a camper in the yard for a few weeks. The friend is not charged rent for the use of the yard. The property owner has given the friend
    A. a revocable trust.
    B. an estate for years.
    C. a license.
    D. a permissive encroachment.

77. What is the cost of constructing a fence 6 feet, 6 inches, high around a lot measuring 90 feet by 175 feet, if the cost of erecting the fence is $1.25 per linear foot and the cost of materials is $0.825 per square foot of fence? Round your answer to the nearest cent.
    A. $1,752.62
    B. $2,054.63
    C. $2,084.62
    D. $3,504.63

78. A seller signs a listing agreement with a real estate professional. A second real estate professional from a different firm obtains a buyer for the property, and the first real estate professional does not receive a commission. The first real estate professional does not sue the seller, even though the seller compensated the second real estate professional. The listing agreement between the seller and the first real estate professional was probably which type?
    A. Exclusive right to sell
    B. Open
    C. Exclusive agency
    D. Dual agency

79. Antitrust laws do *NOT* prohibit real estate
    A. companies agreeing on fees charged to sellers.
    B. professionals allocating markets based on the value of homes.
    C. companies from allocating markets based on the location of commercial buildings.
    D. brokers from imposing a standard commission rate on all transactions handled by the sales associates employed by the office.

80. A tenant leased an apartment from a property owner. Because the owner failed to perform routine maintenance, the apartment building's central heating plant broke down in the fall. The owner neglected to have the heating system repaired, and the tenant had no heat for the first six weeks of winter. The tenant reported this problem repeatedly to the owner. Although eight months remained on his lease, the tenant moved out of the apartment and refused to pay any rent. If the owner sues to recover the outstanding rent, what would be the tenant's *BEST* defense?
    A. Because the tenant lived in the apartment for more than 25% of the lease term, he was entitled to move out at any time without penalty.
    B. The tenant was entitled to vacate the premises because the landlord's failure to repair the heating system constituted abandonment.
    C. Because the apartment was made uninhabitable, the landlord's actions resulted in actual eviction.
    D. The landlord's actions resulted in constructive eviction.

SAMPLE EXAM 2

1. A tenant's landlord plans to sell the building in which the tenant lives to the state so that a freeway can be built. The tenant's lease has expired, but the landlord permits the tenant to stay in the apartment until the building is torn down. The tenant continues to pay the rent as prescribed in the lease. What kind of tenancy does this tenant have?
   A. Holdover tenancy
   B. Month-to-month tenancy
   C. Tenancy at sufferance
   D. Tenancy at will

2. The owner of a house wants to fence the yard for the family pet. When the fence is erected, the fencing materials become real estate through
   A. severance.
   B. subrogation.
   C. annexation.
   D. attachment.

3. A seller is interested in selling a house as quickly as possible and believes that the best way to do this is to have several real estate professionals compete against each other for the commission. The listing agreements with four different real estate professionals specifically promise that if one of them finds a buyer for the property, the seller will be obligated to pay a commission to that real estate professional only. What type of agreement has the seller entered into?
   A. Executed
   B. Discharged
   C. Unilateral
   D. Bilateral

4. In some states, by paying the debt after a foreclosure sale, the delinquent borrower has the right to regain the property under which of the following?
   A. Novation
   B. Redemption
   C. Reversion
   D. Recovery

5. A country music singer who owns a cattle ranch enters into a sale-and-leaseback agreement with a local dentist. Which statement is *TRUE* of this arrangement?
   A. The singer retains title to the ranch.
   B. The dentist receives possession of the property.
   C. The dentist is the lessor.
   D. The singer is the lessor.

6. A real estate professional is employed by a buyer. When the real estate professional finds a property that the buyer might be interested in buying, she is careful to find out as much as possible about the property's owners and why their property is on the market. The real estate professional's efforts to keep the buyer informed of all facts that could affect a transaction is the duty of
   A. accounting.
   B. loyalty.
   C. confidentiality.
   D. disclosure.

7. A parcel of vacant land 80 feet wide and 200 feet deep was sold for $500 per front foot. How much money would a real estate professional receive as a 60% share of a 10% commission on the sale?
   A. $1,600
   B. $2,400
   C. $6,000
   D. $4,000

8. Which situation does *NOT* violate the federal Fair Housing Act?
   A. The refusal of a property manager to rent an apartment to a Muslim couple who are otherwise qualified
   B. The general policy of a loan company to avoid granting home improvement loans to individuals living in transitional neighborhoods
   C. The intentional neglect of a real estate professional to show an Asian family any property listings in neighborhoods other than those with a majority of Asian residents.
   D. A widow's insistence on renting her spare bedroom only to another widowed woman

9. If a storage tank that measures 12 feet by 9 feet by 8 feet is designed to store gas that costs $1.82 per cubic foot, what does it cost to fill the tank to one-half of its capacity? Round your answer to the nearest dollar.
   A. $685
   B. $786
   C. $864
   D. $1,572

10. A buyer bought a house for $225,000. The house, which had originally sold for $148,250, appraised for $210,500. Based on these facts, if the buyer applies for an 80% mortgage, what will be the amount of the loan?
    A. $118,600
    B. $168,400
    C. $180,000
    D. $196,750

11. A purchaser offers to buy a seller's property by signing a purchase contract. The seller accepts the offer. What kind of title interest does the buyer have in the property at this point?
    A. Legal
    B. Equitable
    C. Defeasible
    D. No title interest

12. Which federal law requires that finance charges be stated as an annual percentage rate?
    A. Truth in Lending Act
    B. Real Estate Settlement Procedures Act (RESPA)
    C. Equal Credit Opportunity Act (ECOA)
    D. Fair Housing Act

13. A seller signed a 90-day listing agreement with a real estate professional. Two weeks later, the seller was killed in an accident. What is the present status of the listing?
    A. The listing agreement is binding on the seller's estate for the remainder of the 90 days.
    B. Because the seller's intention to sell was clearly defined, the listing agreement is still in effect and the real estate professional may proceed to market the property on behalf of the seller's estate.
    C. The listing agreement is binding on the seller's estate only if the real estate professional can produce an offer to purchase the property within the remainder of the listing period.
    D. The listing agreement was terminated automatically when the seller died.

14. A resident of Metro City conveys the ownership of an office building to a nursing home. The nursing home agrees that the rental income produced by the building will pay for the expenses of caring for the grantor's parents. When both parents have died, ownership of the office building will revert to the grantor. The estate held by the nursing home is
    A. a remainder life estate.
    B. a legal life estate.
    C. a life estate pur autre vie.
    D. a temporary leasehold estate.

15. A buyer signs a buyer representation agreement under which the real estate professional will help this client find a three-bedroom house in the $185,000 to $200,000 price range. A seller comes into the real estate professional's office and signs a listing agreement to sell a two-bedroom condominium for $170,000. Based on these facts, which statement is *TRUE*?
    A. The buyer is the real estate professional's client; the seller is the real estate professional's customer.
    B. The buyer is the real estate professional's customer; the seller is the real estate professional's client.
    C. While both the buyer and the seller are clients, the real estate professional owes the fiduciary duties of an agent only to the seller.
    D. Because both the buyer and the seller are the real estate professional's clients, the real estate professional owes the fiduciary duties of an agent to both.

16. In a township, which statement is *TRUE*?
    A. Section 31 lies to the east of Section 32.
    B. Section 18 is by law set aside for school purposes.
    C. Section 6 lies in the northeast corner of the township.
    D. Section 16 lies to the north of Section 21.

17. A real estate professional representing a seller is asked by the client to make sure that the deed to the buyer does not reveal the actual sales price. In this case, the real estate professional
    A. must inform the client that only the actual price of the real estate may appear on the deed.
    B. may ask that a deed be prepared that shows only nominal consideration of $10.
    C. should inform the seller that either the full price should be stated in the deed or all references to consideration should be removed from it.
    D. may show a price on the deed other than the actual price, provided that the variance is not greater than 10% of the purchase price.

18. A real estate professional obtained a listing agreement to act as the agent in the sale of a house. An unrepresented buyer has been found for the property, and all agreements have been signed. As agent of the seller, the real estate professional is responsible for which activity?
    A. Completing the buyer's loan application
    B. Making sure that the buyer receives copies of all documents the seller is required to deliver to the buyer
    C. Ensuring that the buyer is qualified for the new mortgage loan
    D. Scheduling the buyer's inspection of the property

19. A broker's employment agreement with a sales associate provides a commission share of 65% to the sales associate. What is the sales associate's compensation if the sales price of a property is $895,000, the broker is entitled to a 6½% commission, and there is no cooperating broker?
    A. $16,621.43
    B. $34,905.00
    C. $37,813.75
    D. $58,175.00

20. Which step is among those an appraiser would use in preparing a real property appraisal using the cost approach?
    A. Estimate the replacement cost of the improvements
    B. Deduct for the depreciation of the land and buildings
    C. Determine the original cost and adjust for depreciation
    D. Review the sales prices of comparable properties

21. When a mortgage lender provides the buyer with statements of all fees and charges the seller will incur, the lender is complying with requirements that originated under which federal law?
    A. Equal Credit Opportunity Act (ECOA)
    B. Truth in Lending Act (Regulation Z)
    C. Real Estate Settlement Procedures Act (RESPA)
    D. Fair Housing Act

22. The landlord of an apartment building neglected to repair the building's plumbing system. As a result, the apartments did not receive water. If a tenant's unit becomes uninhabitable, what is the *MOST* likely result?
    A. Suit for possession
    B. Claim of constructive eviction
    C. Tenancy at sufferance
    D. Suit for negligence

23. A property owner conveys a life estate to a cousin. Under the terms of the owner's conveyance, the property will pass to the cousin's children on the cousin's death. Which interest in the property *BEST* describes that of the children during the cousin's lifetime?
    A. Remainder
    B. Reversion
    C. Life estate pur autre vie
    D. Redemption

24. At closing, prorations for unpaid real estate taxes are shown as
    A. a credit to the seller and a debit to the buyer.
    B. a debit to the seller and a credit to the buyer.
    C. a credit to both the seller and the buyer.
    D. a debit to both the seller and the buyer.

25. What type of lease establishes a rental payment and requires the lessor to pay for the taxes, insurance, and maintenance on the property?
    A. Percentage
    B. Net
    C. Expense only
    D. Gross

26. A conventional mortgage loan closed on July 1 for $165,000 at 3.75% interest amortized over 25 years at $857.06 per month. Using a 360-day year and interest paid in arrears, what would the principal amount be after the monthly payment was made August 1?
    A. $164,936.30
    B. $164,484.38
    C. $164,142.94
    D. $164,658.57

27. In the preceding question, what would the interest portion of the payment be?
    A. $17.19
    B. $257.81
    C. $515.63
    D. $618.75

28. A seller lists her home with a real estate professional for $220,000 but tells the real estate professional, who is acting as the seller's agent, "I've got to sell quickly because of a job transfer. If necessary, I can accept a price as low as $175,000." The real estate professional tells a prospective buyer to offer $180,000 "because the seller is desperate to sell." The seller accepts the buyer's offer. In this situation, which statement is *TRUE*?
    A. The real estate professional violated an established agency relationship with the seller.
    B. The real estate professional's action did not violate any agency relationship with the seller because the real estate professional did not actually reveal the seller's lowest acceptable price.
    C. The real estate professional acted properly to obtain a quick offer on the seller's property, in accordance with the seller's instructions.
    D. The real estate professional violated established fiduciary duties toward the buyer by failing to disclose that the seller would accept a lower price than the buyer offered.

29. Which of the following *BEST* describes the capitalization rate under the income approach to appraising real estate?
    A. Rate at which a property increases in value
    B. Rate of return a property earns as an investment
    C. Rate of capital required to keep a property operating most efficiently
    D. Maximum rate of return allowed by law on an investment

30. At closing, the cost of the lender's title insurance policy required for a new loan is usually shown as which of the following?
    A. Credit to the seller
    B. Credit to the buyer
    C. Debit to the seller
    D. Debit to the buyer

31. An FHA-insured loan in the amount of $157,500 at 4½% for 30 years closed on July 17. The first monthly payment is due on September 1. Using a 360-day year and assuming that interest is being paid for the day of closing, what was the amount of the interest payment the buyer had to make at the settlement?
    A. $19.69
    B. $275.63
    C. $295.35
    D. $315.04

32. If a home that cost $342,500 three years ago is now valued at 127% of its original cost, what is its current market value?
    A. $364,750
    B. $395,000
    C. $424,500
    D. $434,975

33. A buyer makes an offer on a property and the seller accepts. Three weeks later, the buyer announces that "the deal's off" and refuses to go through with the sale. If the seller is entitled to keep the buyer's earnest money deposit, there *MOST* likely is what kind of clause in the sales contract?
    A. Liquidated damages clause
    B. Contingent damages clause
    C. Actual damages clause
    D. Revocation clause

34. A search of the public record regarding title to a property is *MOST* likely to provide information about which item?
    A. Encroachments
    B. Rights of parties in possession
    C. Inaccurate survey
    D. Mechanics' liens

35. A rectangular lot is worth $193,600. This value is the equivalent of $4.40 per square foot. If one lot dimension is 200 feet, what is the other dimension?
    A. 110 feet
    B. 220 feet
    C. 400 feet
    D. 880 feet

36. A real estate professional listed an agricultural property at an 8% commission rate. After the sale of the property and the settlement had taken place, the seller discovered that the real estate professional had been listing other properties at a 6% commission rate. Based on this information, which statement is *TRUE*?
    A. The real estate professional has done nothing wrong because a commission rate is always negotiable between the parties.
    B. If the real estate professional inflated the usual commission rate for the area, the real estate professional may be subject to discipline by the state real estate commission.
    C. The seller is entitled to rescind the transaction based on the principle of lack of reality of consent.
    D. The seller is entitled to a refund from the real estate professional of 2% of the commission.

37. A renter has six months remaining on her apartment lease. The monthly rent is $875. The renter moves out of the apartment for four months, and a friend moves in. The friend pays the renter a monthly rental of $700, and the renter continues paying the full rental amount under her lease to the landlord. This is an example of
    A. subletting.
    B. assignment.
    C. rescission and renewal.
    D. surrender.

38. One real estate professional asked another, "Will I have to prove that I was the procuring cause in order to collect a commission if my seller sells the property without my help?" The other real estate professional answered, "No, not if you have
    A. an option listing."
    B. an open listing."
    C. an exclusive agency listing."
    D. an exclusive right-to-sell listing."

39. The capitalization rate on a property reflects (among other things) which factor?
    A. Risk of the investment
    B. Replacement cost of the improvements
    C. Real estate taxes
    D. Debt service

40. An investor wants to buy a nearby apartment building and wants to sell a factory to finance the purchase. The investor also wants to incur as little tax liability as possible. What is the best way to accomplish the investor's goals?
    A. Buy the apartment building before selling the factory
    B. Pay more for the apartment building than the investor receives for the factory
    C. Exchange the factory for the apartment building
    D. Give the factory to a charity and use the tax write-off to purchase the apartment building

41. After a buyer purchased a property from a seller, they both decided to rescind the recorded transfer. To do this, what must happen?
    A. The buyer must return the deed to the seller.
    B. The parties must record a notice of rescission.
    C. The parties must simply destroy the original deed in the presence of witnesses.
    D. The buyer must make a new deed to the seller.

42. A farmer owns the W½ of the NW¼ of the NW¼ of a section. The adjoining property can be purchased for $300 per acre. Owning all of the NW¼ of the section would cost the farmer
    A. $6,000.
    B. $12,000.
    C. $42,000.
    D. $48,000.

43. A real estate professional received a deposit, along with a written offer from a buyer. The offer stated: "The offeror will leave this offer open for the seller's acceptance for a period of 10 days." On the fifth day, and before acceptance by the seller, the offeror notified the real estate professional that the offer was withdrawn and demanded the return of the deposit. Which statement is *TRUE* in this situation?
    A. The offeror cannot withdraw the offer; it must be held open for the full 10-day period, as promised.
    B. The offeror has the right to withdraw the offer and secure the return of the deposit any time before being notified of the seller's acceptance.
    C. The offeror can withdraw the offer, and the seller and the real estate professional will each retain one-half of the forfeited deposit.
    D. While the offeror can withdraw the offer, the real estate professional is legally entitled to declare the deposit forfeited and retain all of it in lieu of the lost commission.

44. A building's owner pays a property manager an 8½% commission based on the unit's annualized rent for each new tenant. Last year, the manager signed five new tenants—three at $795 per month, one at $1,200 per month, and one at $900 per month. What was the total amount of the property manager's new-tenant commissions for that year?
    A. $381.23
    B. $2,952.90
    C. $3,685.47
    D. $4,574.70

45. The monthly rent on a warehouse is $1 per cubic yard. Assuming the warehouse is 36 feet by 200 feet by 12 feet high, what is the annual rent?
    A. $3,200
    B. $9,600
    C. $38,400
    D. $115,200

46. If a veteran wishes to refinance a home by changing to a VA-guaranteed loan and the lender insists on 3½ discount points, which option is available to the veteran?
    A. Refinance with a VA loan, provided the lender charges no discount points
    B. Refinance with a VA loan, provided the lender charges no more than two discount points
    C. Be required to pay a maximum of 1% of the loan as an origination fee
    D. Proceed with the refinance loan and pay the discount points

47. A woman owned property that she conveyed to a man "so long as no real estate broker or salesperson ever sets foot on the property." If a broker or a salesperson visits the property, ownership will revert to the woman. Based on these two conveyances, which statement is *TRUE*?
    A. The man holds the property in fee simple determinable.
    B. The man holds the property in fee simple defeasible, subject to a condition subsequent.
    C. The man may not transfer ownership of the property without the woman's permission.
    D. The woman has retained a right of re-entry with regard to the property.

48. A real estate transaction has a closing date of November 15. The seller, who is responsible for costs up to and including the date of settlement, has already paid the property taxes of $11,160 for the calendar year. On the closing statement, the buyer will be
    A. debited $1,395.
    B. debited $9,765.
    C. credited $1,395.
    D. credited $9,765.

49. After a storeowner's spouse died, he could no longer maintain the store. A woman who wished to open a store agreed to move into the entire space and pay for the remaining seven years on the lease. The landlord agreed to the arrangement. This is known as a lease
    A. assumption.
    B. assignment.
    C. surrender.
    D. breach.

50. A purchaser buys a house for $234,500 by making a $25,000 cash down payment and taking out a $209,500 mortgage for 30 years. The lot value is $80,000. If the purchaser wants to depreciate the property over a period of 27½ years, what will be the annual depreciation amount using the straight-line method? Round your answer to the nearest cent.
    A. $3,818.18
    B. $4,709.09
    C. $5,618.18
    D. $7,444.44

51. A property manager leased a store for three years. The first year, the store's rent was $1,000 per month, and the rent was to increase 10% per year thereafter. The manager received a 7% commission for the first year, 5% for the second year, and 3% for the balance of the lease. What was the total commission earned by the property manager?
    A. $840.40
    B. $1,613.10
    C. $1,935.60
    D. $2,785.40

52. Against a recorded deed from the owner of record, the party with the weakest position is
    A. a person with a prior unrecorded deed and who is not in possession.
    B. a person in possession with a prior unrecorded deed.
    C. a tenant in possession with nine months remaining on the lease.
    D. a painter who is half-finished painting the house at the time of the sale and who has not yet been paid.

53. A married couple files their income taxes jointly. Last year they sold their home for $340,000. Seven years ago, when they were first married, they bought the house for $250,000 and have lived in it ever since. Based on these facts, which statement is *TRUE*?
    A. Under current tax law, the couple will owe a capital gains tax this year on their $90,000 gain.
    B. Current tax law permits the couple to exclude up to $250,000 in capital gain from their income tax.
    C. Because their gain is less than $500,000, the couple will owe no capital gains tax this year.
    D. Under current tax law, the couple will be entitled to a penalty-free withdrawal of up to $10,000 from a 401(k) retirement account to use as a down payment.

54. A squatter moved into an abandoned home and lived there for some years. Ultimately, the squatter was granted title to the property by a court. Which element is *NOT* basic to acquiring title in this manner?
    A. Permission of the true owner
    B. Open and notorious use
    C. Occupancy for a period of time prescribed by state law
    D. Occupancy hostile to the best interests of the true owner

55. Maria, Frank, and Judy are joint tenants. Judy sells her interest to Laura, and then Frank dies. As a result, which statement is *TRUE*?
    A. Frank's heirs are joint tenants with Laura and Maria.
    B. Frank's heirs and Maria are joint tenants, but Laura is a tenant in common.
    C. Maria is a tenant in common with Laura and Frank's heirs.
    D. Maria and Laura are tenants in common.

56. At closing, the selling price is
    A. a debit to the buyer.
    B. a debit to the seller.
    C. a credit to the buyer.
    D. greater than the loan amount.

57. The state wants to acquire a strip of farmland to build a highway. Does the state have the right to acquire this land for public use?
    A. Yes, the state's right is called condemnation.
    B. Yes, the state's right is called eminent domain.
    C. Yes, the state's right is called escheat.
    D. No, under the U.S. Constitution, private property may never be taken by state governments or by the federal government.

58. A decedent's estate was distributed by will as follows: 54% to the surviving spouse, 18% to the children, 16% to the grandchildren, and the remainder to the decedent's college. The college received $79,000. How much did the children receive? Round your answer to the nearest dollar.
    A. $105,333
    B. $118,500
    C. $355,500
    D. $658,333

59. Which of the following is an example of external obsolescence?
    A. Numerous pillars supporting the ceiling in a store
    B. Leaks in the roof of a warehouse, making the premises unusable and, therefore, unrentable
    C. Coal cellar in a house with central heating
    D. Vacant, abandoned, and run-down buildings in an area

60. Which phrase, when placed in a print advertisement, would *MOST* nearly comply with the requirements of the Truth in Lending Act (Regulation Z)?
    A. "5½% interest"
    B. "5½% rate"
    C. "5½% annual interest"
    D. "5½% annual percentage rate"

61. Which statement is *FALSE* regarding a capitalization rate?
    A. The rate increases when the risk increases.
    B. An increase in rate, while other elements remain the same, means a decrease in value.
    C. The net income is divided by the rate to estimate value.
    D. A decrease in rate, while other elements remain the same, results in a decrease in value.

62. The Equal Credit Opportunity Act (ECOA) makes it illegal for lenders to refuse credit to or otherwise discriminate against which applicant?
    A. Parent of twins who receives public assistance and cannot afford the monthly mortgage payments
    B. New homebuyer who does not have a credit history
    C. Single person who receives public assistance
    D. Unemployed person with no job prospects and no identifiable source of income

63. When a man died, a deed was found in his desk drawer. Although the deed had never been recorded, it was signed, dated, and acknowledged. The deed gave the man's house to a local charity. The will, however, provided as follows: "I leave all of the real and personal property that I own to my beloved niece." In this situation, the house *MOST* likely will go to
    A. the charity, because acknowledgment creates a presumption of delivery.
    B. the charity, because the man's intent was clear from the deed.
    C. the niece, because the deed was never delivered to or accepted by the charity.
    D. the niece, because the deed had not been recorded.

64. If a borrower takes out a $90,000 loan at 7½% interest to be repaid at the end of 15 years with interest paid annually, what is the total interest that the borrower will pay over the life of the loan?
    A. $10,125
    B. $80,000
    C. $101,250
    D. $180,000

65. After an offer is accepted, the seller finds that the real estate professional was the undisclosed agent for the buyer, as well as the agent for the seller. The seller may
    A. withdraw without obligation to the real estate professional or the buyer.
    B. withdraw but be subject to liquidated damages.
    C. withdraw but only with the concurrence of the buyer.
    D. refuse to sell but be subject to a suit for specific performance.

66. To net the owner $90,000 after a 6% commission is paid, what would the list price would have to be? Round your answer to the nearest dollar.
    A. $95,400
    B. $95,745
    C. $95,906
    D. $96,000

67. Which circumstance would *MOST* likely be legal under the provisions of the federal Fair Housing Act?
    A. A lender refuses to make loans in areas where more than 25% of the population is Hispanic.
    B. A private social club that discriminates against no protected group in granting membership refuses to rent a suite in its members-only vacation facility to a Nigerian family who are not members of the club.
    C. A church excludes Middle Easterners from membership and rents its nonprofit housing to church members only.
    D. A real estate professional directs prospective buyers away from areas where they are likely to feel uncomfortable because of their race.

68. It is discovered after a sale of a parcel of land that the land parcel is 10% smaller than the seller represented it to be. The real estate professional who passed this information on to the buyer is
    A. not liable as long as the real estate professional only repeated the seller's data.
    B. not liable if the misrepresentation was unintentional.
    C. not liable if the buyer actually inspected the parcel.
    D. liable if the real estate professional knew or should have known of the discrepancy.

69. An easement terminates
    A. automatically.
    B. when the owner of the servient tenement wishes to do so.
    C. if the owners of the dominant and servient tenements become one and the same.
    D. when a property owner dies.

70. Which activity is *NOT* a violation of the Real Estate Settlement Procedures Act (RESPA)?
    A. Providing a Closing Disclosure to a borrower four days before the closing
    B. Accepting a kickback on a loan subject to RESPA requirements
    C. Requiring the buyer to use a particular title insurance company
    D. Accepting a fee or charging for services that were not performed

71. The rescission provisions of the Truth in Lending Act (Regulation Z) apply to which transaction?
    A. Home purchase loans
    B. Construction lending
    C. Business financing
    D. Consumer credit

72. A property has a net income of $30,000. An appraiser decides to use a 12% capitalization rate rather than a 10% rate on this property. The use of the higher rate results in
    A. a 2% increase in the appraised value.
    B. a $50,000 increase in the appraised value.
    C. a $50,000 decrease in the appraised value.
    D. no change in the appraised value.

73. The section in a purchase contract that would provide for the buyer to forfeit any earnest money if the buyer fails to complete the purchase is known as a provision for
    A. liquidated damages.
    B. punitive damages.
    C. hypothecation.
    D. subordination.

74. In one commercial building, a tenant intends to start a small health food shop. An identical, adjacent building houses a showroom leased to a major national retailing chain. Both tenants have long-term leases with identical rents. If the appraiser uses a capitalization rate for the store leased to the national retailing chain that is lower than the rate for the other building, which statement is *TRUE*?
    A. The indicated value of the chain's property will be lower than the indicated value of the food-shop property.
    B. The indicated value of the chain's property will be higher than the indicated value of the food-shop property.
    C. The appraiser would then be compelled to make use of the sales comparison approach to value.
    D. It would indicate the appraiser believes a building occupied by a chain-store tenant is more valuable than an identical one occupied by a health food shop.

75. An insurance company agreed to provide a developer with financing for a shopping center at 7% interest plus an equity position. What type of loan is this?
    A. Package
    B. Participation
    C. Open-end
    D. Blanket

76. A $100,000 loan at 6% could be amortized with monthly payments of $644 on a 15-year basis or payments of $600 on a 30-year basis. The 30-year loan results in total payments of what percentage of the 15-year total payments? Round your answer to the nearest whole percentage.
    A. 106%
    B. 158%
    C. 186%
    D. 154%

77. According to an appraisal prepared for a loan approval, a property is worth $425,000. The previous homeowner bought the property for $290,000 and added $50,000 in improvements, for a total of $340,000. The property sold in foreclosure for $325,000. Which amount represents the property's market price?
    A. $290,000
    B. $325,000
    C. $425,000
    D. $340,000

78. What is the amount of tax payable if a property's assessed value is $185,000 and the tax rate is 40 mills in a community in which an equalization factor of 110% is used?
    A. $4,625.00
    B. $5,087.50
    C. $7,400.40
    D. $8,140.00

79. At closing, how will a proration of prepaid water, gas, and electric charges be reflected?
    A. Debit to the seller, credit to the buyer
    B. Debit to the buyer, credit to the seller
    C. Debit to the buyer only
    D. Credit to the seller only

80. An apartment manager decides not to purchase flood insurance. Instead, the manager installs raised platforms in the basement storage areas and has the furnace placed on eight-inch legs. This form of risk management is known as
    A. avoiding the risk.
    B. controlling the risk.
    C. retaining the risk.
    D. transfering the risk.

GLOSSARY

Note: Most of the entries in this glossary reference specific pages in *Modern Real Estate Practice, 20th Edition*. Page references are for where a term is defined or explained. Page references are not provided for terms that are included here because they are used in everyday professional practice or are of historical interest.

abstract of title   The condensed history of the recorded ownership of a particular parcel of real estate, consisting of a summary of the original grant and all subsequent conveyances and encumbrances affecting the property and a certification by the abstractor that the history is complete and accurate. (106)

accelerated cost recovery system (ACRS)   Method for claiming tax deductions for certain property purchased before 1987 in which it was possible to claim greater deductions in the early years of ownership, gradually reducing the amount deducted in each year of useful life.

acceleration clause   The clause in a mortgage or deed of trust that can be enforced to make the entire debt due immediately if the borrower defaults on an installment payment or other obligation. (215)

accession   Acquiring title to additions or improvements to real property as a result of the annexation of fixtures or the accretion of alluvial deposits along the banks of streams. (27)

accretion   The increase or addition of land by the deposit of sand or soil washed up naturally from a river, lake, or sea.

accrued depreciation   Loss in a property's value resulting from physical deterioration, external depreciation, and functional obsolescence. (23)

accrued items   On a closing statement, items of expense that are incurred but not yet payable, such as interest on a mortgage loan or taxes on real property. (317)

acknowledgment   A formal declaration made before a duly authorized officer, usually a notary public, by a person who has signed a document. (87)

acre   A measure of land equal to 43,560 square feet, 4,840 square yards, 4,047 square meters, 160 square rods, or 0.4047 hectares. (77)

action to quiet title   A court action that establishes ownership when ownership cannot be traced through an unbroken chain of title. (106)

actual eviction   The legal process that results in a tenant's being physically removed from leased premises. (337)

actual notice   Express information or fact; that which is known; direct knowledge. (104)

ad valorem tax   A tax levied according to value, generally used to refer to real estate tax. Also called the *general tax*. (290)

addendum   Any provision added to an existing contract without altering the content of the original. Must be signed by all parties. (200)

adjustable-rate mortgage (ARM)   A loan characterized by a fluctuating interest rate, usually one tied to a bank or savings and loan association cost-of-funds index. (219)

adjusted basis   *See* basis. (12)

administrative law judge (ALJ)   The official who presides over a hearing involving a government agency and someone affected by a decision of that agency. The ALJ hears evidence, including the testimony of witnesses, and renders a decision. (356)

administrator   A court-selected person who assists with the settlement of an estate of a person who died without leaving a will. A woman might be called an *administratrix*, although *administrator* is the term used most often to refer to either a man or a woman. (96)

adverse possession   The actual, open, notorious, hostile, and continuous possession of another's land under a claim of title. Possession for a statutory period may be a means of acquiring title. (93)

affidavit of title   A written statement, made under oath by a seller or grantor of real property and acknowledged by a notary public, in which grantors (1) identify themselves and indicate marital status, (2) certify that since the examination of the title, on the date of the contract no defects have occurred in the title, and (3) certify that they are in possession of the property (if applicable). (258)

affiliated business arrangement (ABA)   Practice of one company offering a package of services to consumers. (264)

agency   The relationship between a principal and an agent wherein the agent is authorized to represent the principal in certain transactions. (137)

agency by ratification   An agency relationship created after the fact.

agent   One who acts or has the power to act for another. A fiduciary relationship is created under the *law of agency* when a property owner, as the principal, executes a listing agreement or management contract authorizing a licensed real estate broker to be his or her agent. A prospective property buyer may authorize a real estate broker to act as the buyer's agent to find a suitable property. (137)

air lots   Designated airspace over a piece of land. An air lot, like surface property, may be transferred. (76)

air rights   The right to use the open space above a property, usually allowing the surface to be used for another purpose. (21)

alienation   The act of transferring property to another. Alienation may be voluntary, such as by gift or sale, or involuntary, as through eminent domain or adverse possession. (84, 92)

alienation clause   The clause in a mortgage or deed of trust stating that the balance of the secured debt becomes immediately due and payable at the lender's option if the property is sold by the borrower. In effect, this clause prevents the borrower from assigning the debt without the lender's approval. (217)

allodial system   A system of land ownership in which land is held free and clear of any rent or service due to the government; commonly contrasted to the feudal system. Land is held under the allodial system in the United States.

amendment   A change to the existing content of a contract (i.e., if words or provisions are added to or deleted from the body of the contract). Must be initialed by all parties. (199)

American Land Title Association (ALTA) policy
A title insurance policy that protects the interest in a collateral property of a mortgage lender who originates a new real estate loan. (109)

Americans with Disabilities Act (ADA)   Act addresses rights of individuals with disabilities in employment and public accommodations. (352, 377)

amortized loan   A loan in which the principal, as well as the interest, is payable in monthly or other periodic installments over the term of the loan. (218)

annexation   Process of converting personal property into real property. (25)

annual percentage rate (APR)   The relationship of the total finance charges associated with a loan. This must be disclosed to borrowers by lenders under the Truth in Lending Act (TILA). (246)

anticipation   The appraisal principle holding that value can increase or decrease based on the expectation of some future benefit or detriment produced by the property. (313)

antitrust laws   Laws designed to preserve the free enterprise of the open marketplace by making illegal certain private conspiracies and combinations formed to minimize competition. Most violations of antitrust laws in the real estate business involve either *price-fixing* (real estate professionals conspiring to set fixed compensation rates) or *allocation of customers or markets* (real estate professionals agreeing to limit their areas of trade or dealing to certain areas or properties). (124)

appointed agency   *See* designated agency. (149)

appraisal   An estimate of the quantity, quality, or value of something. The process through which conclusions of property value are obtained; also refers to the report that sets forth the process of estimation and conclusion of value. (302)

appraisal report   An opinion of a property's market value given to a lender or client with detailed market information. (302)

appraiser   An independent person trained to provide an unbiased estimate of value. (2)

Appraiser Independence Requirements (AIR)
Regulations issued by Fannie Mae that must be followed by appraisers to ensure accurate and objective appraisals. (302)

appreciation   An increase in the worth or value of a property due to economic or related causes, which may prove to be either temporary or permanent; opposite of depreciation. (11)

appurtenance   A right, privilege, or improvement belonging to, and passing with, the land; "runs with the land." (20)

area   A level surface or piece of ground; the size of a surface; the amount of a two-dimensional object.

area preference People's desire for one area over another, based on a number of factors such as history, reputation, convenience, scenic beauty, and location. (24)

asbestos A mineral once used in insulation and other materials that can cause respiratory diseases. (403)

assemblage The combining of two or more adjoining lots into one larger tract to increase their total value. (314)

assessed value The value set on property for taxation purposes. (291)

assessment The imposition of a tax, charge, or levy, usually according to established rates. (291)

assessment equalization factor A factor (number) by which the assessed value of a property is multiplied to arrive at a value for the property that is in line with statewide tax assessments. The *ad valorem tax* would be based on this adjusted value. An equalization factor may be applied to raise or lower assessments in a particular district or county. (291)

assigned agency *See* designated agency. (149)

assignment The transfer in writing of interest in a bond, mortgage, lease, or other instrument. (190)

associate licensee A licensed real estate salesperson who is employed by or associated with the broker to perform brokerage activities on behalf of or for the broker. (2)

assumption of mortgage Acquiring title to property on which there is an existing mortgage and agreeing to be personally liable for the terms and conditions of the mortgage, including payments. (217)

attachment The act of taking a person's property into legal custody by writ or other judicial order to hold it available for application to that person's debt to a creditor. (295)

attorney's opinion of title An abstract of title that an attorney has examined and has certified to be, in the attorney's opinion, an accurate statement of the facts concerning the property's ownership. (108)

automatic extension clause A listing agreement clause stating that the agreement will continue automatically for a certain period of time after its expiration date. In many states, use of this clause is discouraged or prohibited. (163)

avulsion The sudden tearing away of land, as by earthquake, flood, volcanic action, or the sudden change in the course of a stream. (23)

balance The appraisal principle stating that the greatest value in a property will occur when the type and size of the improvements are proportional to each other as well as the land.

balloon payment A final payment of a mortgage loan that is considerably larger than the required periodic payments because the loan amount was not fully amortized. (221)

bargain and sale deed A deed that carries with it no warranties against liens or other encumbrances but that does imply that the grantor has the right to convey title. The grantor may add warranties to the deed. (89)

base line The main imaginary line running east and west and crossing a principal meridian at a definite point; used by surveyors for reference in locating and describing land under the rectangular (government) survey system of legal description. (70)

basis The financial interest that the Internal Revenue Service attributes to an owner of an investment property for the purpose of determining annual depreciation and gain or loss on the sale of the asset. If a property was acquired by purchase, the owner's basis is the cost of the property plus the value of any capital expenditures for improvements to the property, minus any depreciation allowable or actually taken. This new basis is called the *adjusted basis*. (12)

benchmarks Permanent reference marks or points established for use by surveyors in measuring differences in elevation. (77)

beneficiary (1) The person for whom a trust operates or in whose behalf the income from a trust estate is drawn. (55) (2) A lender in a deed of trust loan transaction. (214)

bilateral contract *See* contract. (188)

binder An agreement that may accompany an earnest money deposit for the purchase of real property as evidence of the purchaser's good faith and intent to complete the transaction. (196)

blanket loan A mortgage covering more than one parcel of real estate, providing for each parcel's partial release from the mortgage lien upon repayment of a definite portion of the debt. (244)

blockbusting The illegal practice of inducing homeowners to sell their properties by making representations regarding the entry or prospective entry of persons of a particular race or national origin into the neighborhood. (353)

blue-sky laws Common name for those state and federal laws that regulate the registration and sale of investment securities.

boot   Money or property given to make up any difference in value or equity between two properties in an *exchange*.

boycott   When individuals or businesses withhold their patronage to a business as a protest or to reduce competition. (125)

branch office   A secondary place of business apart from the principal or main office from which real estate business is conducted. A branch office usually must be run by a licensed real estate professional. (118)

breach of contract   Violation of any terms or conditions in a contract without legal excuse; for example, failure to make a payment when it is due. (193)

bring down   A second title search that is made after the closing and before any new documents are filed. (258)

broker   One who acts as an intermediary on behalf of others for a fee or commission. (2)

broker protection clause   Clause in a contract that protects a broker from losing a commission in the event a transaction is not completed or is intentionally delayed until after the listing expires. (163)

brokerage   The bringing together of parties interested in making a real estate transaction. (117)

broker's price opinion (BPO)   An opinion of real estate value commissioned by a bank or an attorney and provided by a broker. (304)

brownfields   Defunct, derelict, or abandoned commercial or industrial sites; many have toxic wastes. (413)

budget comparison statement   Compares actual results with the original budget, often giving either percentages or a numerical variance of actual versus projected income and expenses. (372)

buffer zone   A strip of land, usually used as a park or designated for a similar use, separating land dedicated to one use from land dedicated to another use (e.g., residential from commercial). (390)

building code   An ordinance that specifies minimum standards of construction for buildings to protect public safety and health. (392)

building permit   Written governmental permission for the construction, alteration, or demolition of an improvement, showing compliance with building codes and zoning ordinances. (391)

building-related illness (BRI)   An illness due to air quality problems, typically toxic substances or pathogens; a clinically diagnosed condition. Symptoms include asthma, allergies, and hypersensitivity. (377)

bundle of legal rights   The concept of land ownership that includes ownership of all legal rights to the land—possession, control within the law, enjoyment, exclusion, and disposition. (19)

buydown   A financing technique used to reduce the monthly payments for the first few years of a loan. Funds in the form of discount points are given to the lender by the builder or the seller to buy down or lower the effective interest rate paid by the buyer, thus reducing the monthly payments for a set time. (245)

buyer representation agreement   A principal-agent relationship in which the real estate professional acts on behalf of the buyer, usually as an agent, with fiduciary responsibilities to the buyer. (140)

buyer's agent   A real estate professional who is under contract to locate property for a buyer and represent the buyer's interests in a transaction. (141)

buyer's broker   A residential real estate professional who represents prospective buyers exclusively.

buyer's representative   A residential real estate professional who represents the prospective purchaser in a transaction, often through a sales associate of the broker. The buyer's representative who acts as a buyer's agent owes the buyer-principal the common-law or statutory agency duties. (162)

capital gain   Profit earned from the sale of an asset. (12)

capitalization   A mathematical process for estimating the value of a property using a proper rate of return on the investment and the annual net operating income expected to be produced by the property. The formula is expressed as follows: income ÷ rate = value.

capitalization rate   The rate of return a property will produce on the owner's investment. (319)

capping   The process of laying two to four feet of soil over the top of a landfill site and then planting grass on it to enhance the aesthetic value and prevent erosion. (413)

carbon monoxide (CO)   A colorless, odorless gas that occurs as a by-product of fuel combustion that may result in death in poorly ventilated areas. (408)

cash flow   The net spendable income from an investment, determined by deducting all operating and fixed expenses from the gross income. When expenses exceed income, a *negative cash flow* results. (372)

cash flow report A monthly statement that details the financial status of the property. (371)

caveat emptor A Latin phrase meaning "let the buyer beware." (3, 138)

CC&Rs *See* covenants, conditions, and restrictions. (395)

certificate of occupancy Permission by the municipal inspector to occupy a completed building structure after being inspected and having complied with building codes. (393)

certificate of reasonable value (CRV) A form indicating the appraised value of a property being financed with a VA loan. (242)

certificate of sale The document generally given to the purchaser at a tax foreclosure sale. A certificate of sale does not convey title; normally, it is an instrument certifying that the holder received title to the property after the redemption period passed and that the holder paid the property taxes for that interim period. (293)

certificate of title A statement of opinion on the status of the title to a parcel of real property based on an examination of specified public records. (107)

chain of title The succession of conveyances, from some accepted starting point, whereby the present holder of real property derives title. (105)

change The appraisal principle that holds that no physical or economic condition remains constant. (313)

chattel *See* personal property. (24)

chlorofluorocarbons (CFCs) Nontoxic, nonflammable chemicals containing atoms of carbon, chlorine, and fluorine, such as air conditioners and refrigerators. CFCs are safe in application but cause ozone depletion. (409)

Civil Rights Act of 1866 An act that prohibits racial discrimination in the sale and rental of housing. (346)

client The principal in an agency relationship or other form of representation. (139)

closing An event where promises made in a sales contract are fulfilled and mortgage loan funds (if any) are distributed to the buyer. (255)

Closing Disclosure The CFPB form that itemizes all charges that are normally paid by a borrower and a seller in connection with settlement, whether required by the lender or another party, or paid by the lender or any other person. (265)

closing escrow Process of settlement in which the buyer and the seller never meet; the paperwork is handled by an escrow agent. (260)

closing statement A detailed cash accounting of a real estate transaction showing all cash received, all charges and credits made, and all cash paid out in the transaction. (275)

cloud on the title Any document, claim, unreleased lien, or encumbrance that may impair the title to real property or make the title doubtful; usually revealed by a title search and removed by either a quitclaim deed or suit to quiet title. (42, 90)

code of ethics A written system of standards for ethical conduct. (126)

codicil A supplement or an addition to a will, executed with the same formalities as a will, which normally does not revoke the entire will. (95)

coinsurance clause A clause in insurance policies covering real property that requires the policyholder to maintain fire insurance coverage generally equal to at least 80% of the property's actual replacement cost. (227)

collateral Something having value that is given to secure repayment of a debt. (288)

commingling The illegal act by a real estate professional of placing client or customer funds with personal funds. By law, real estate professionals are required to maintain a separate *trust* or *escrow account* for other parties' funds held temporarily by the real estate professional. (144)

commission Payment to a real estate professional for services rendered, such as in the sale or purchase of real property; usually a percentage of the selling price of the property. (120)

common elements Parts of a property that are necessary or convenient to the existence, maintenance, and safety of a condominium or are normally in common use by all the condominium residents. Each condominium owner has an undivided ownership interest in the common elements. (58)

common law The body of law based on custom, usage, and court decisions. (138)

community association management Provides a team of property managers, accounting staff, office staff, and property consultants to manage property. (367)

community property   A system of property ownership based on the theory that each spouse has an equal interest in the property acquired by the efforts of either spouse during marriage. A holdover of Spanish law found predominantly in the western U.S. states; the system was unknown under English common law. (54)

Community Reinvestment Act of 1977 (CRA)   Under the act, which was revised most recently in 2008, financial institutions are expected to meet the deposit and credit needs of their communities; participate and invest in local community development and rehabilitation projects; and participate in loan programs for housing, small businesses, and small farms. (248)

comparables   Properties used in an appraisal report that are substantially equivalent to the subject property.

comparative market analysis (CMA)   A comparison of the prices of recently sold homes that are similar to a listing seller's home in terms of location, style, and amenities. (163)

competent party   A person who has the capacity to be engaged in a legal contract; being of sound mind and body.

competition   The appraisal principle stating that excess profits generate competition. (313)

Comprehensive Environmental Response, Compensation, and Liability Act (CERCLA)   A federal law administered by the Environmental Protection Agency that establishes a process for identifying parties responsible for creating hazardous waste sites, forcing liable parties to clean up toxic sites, bringing legal action against responsible parties, and funding the abatement of toxic sites. *See also* Superfund. (414)

Comprehensive Loss Underwriting Exchange (CLUE)   A database of consumer claims history that allows insurance companies to access prior claims information in the underwriting and rating process. (227)

comprehensive plan   *See* master plan. (388)

computerized loan origination (CLO)   An electronic network for handling loan applications through remote computer terminals linked to various lenders' computers.

conciliation   A form of alternative dispute resolution in which a conciliator meets with each of the parties separately to help them settle their differences voluntarily, without the formality of a hearing or trial. (356)

condemnation   A judicial or administrative proceeding to exercise the power of eminent domain, through which a government agency takes private property for public use and compensates the owner. (42–43)

conditional-use permit   Written governmental permission allowing a use inconsistent with zoning but necessary for the common good, such as locating an emergency medical facility in a predominantly residential area. (392)

condominium   The absolute ownership of a unit in a multiunit building based on a legal description of the airspace the unit actually occupies, or a separate dwelling unit in a multiunit development, plus an undivided interest in the ownership of the common elements in the building or development, which are owned jointly with the other condominium unit owners. (58)

confession of judgment clause   Permits judgment to be entered against a debtor without the creditor's having to institute legal proceedings.

conformity   The appraisal principle holding that the greater the similarity among properties in an area, the better they will hold their value. (313)

consent   Expressing or implying permission, approval, or agreement of an action or decision. (140)

consideration   (1) That received by the grantor in exchange for the deed. (86) (2) Something of value that induces a person to enter into a contract. (190)

construction loan   *See* interim financing. (245)

constructive annexation   The combination of items into real property that are not fixed or fastened to the property. (27)

constructive eviction   Actions of a landlord that so materially disturb or impair a tenant's enjoyment of the leased premises that the tenant is effectively forced to move out and terminate the lease without liability for any further rent. (338)

constructive notice   Notice given to the world by recorded documents. All persons are charged with knowledge of such documents and their contents, whether or not they have actually examined them. Possession of property is also considered constructive notice that the person in possession has an interest in the property. (104)

consumer   An individual who purchases goods or services that are not for resale.

contingencies   Provisions in a contract that require a certain act to be done or a certain event to occur before the contract becomes binding. (199)

contract   A legally enforceable promise or set of promises that must be performed and for which, if a breach of the promise occurs, the law provides a remedy. A contract may be either *unilateral*, by which only one party is bound to act, or *bilateral*, by which all parties to the instrument are legally bound to act as prescribed. (188)

contract broker   *See* nonagent. (149)

contribution   The appraisal principle stating that the value of any component of a property is what it gives to the value of the whole or what its absence detracts from that value. (313)

controlled business arrangement   An arrangement that offers consumers a package of services (e.g., a real estate firm, title insurance company, mortgage broker, and home inspection company).

conventional loan   A loan that requires no federally sponsored insurance or guarantee. (239)

conversion   The illegal use of money received on behalf of the principal. (144)

conveyance   A term used to refer to any document that transfers title to real property. The term is also used in describing the act of transferring.

cooperating broker   *See* listing broker. (161)

cooperative   A residential multiunit building whose title is held by a trust or corporation that is owned by and operated for the benefit of people living within the building who are the beneficial owners of the trust or shareholders of the corporation, each possessing a proprietary lease to a property unit. (60)

co-ownership   Title ownership held by two or more persons. (50)

corporation   An entity or organization, created by operation of law, whose rights of doing business are essentially the same as those of an individual. The entity has continuous existence until it is dissolved according to legal procedures. (57)

corrective maintenance   Correction of problems after they have occurred. (376)

cost   The total amount of money incurred for products or services.

cost approach   The process of estimating the value of a property by adding to the estimated land value the appraiser's estimate of the reproduction or replacement cost of the building, less depreciation. (317)

cost recovery   An Internal Revenue Service term for *depreciation*. (12)

counteroffer   A new offer made in response to an offer received. It has the effect of rejecting the original offer, which cannot be accepted thereafter unless revived by the offeror. (196)

covenant   A written agreement between two or more parties in which a party or parties pledge to perform or not perform specified acts with regard to property; usually found in such real estate documents as deeds, mortgages, leases, and contracts for deed. (88)

covenant of quiet enjoyment   The covenant implied by law by which a landlord guarantees that a tenant may take possession of leased premises and that the landlord will not interfere in the tenant's possession or use of the property. (89)

covenants, conditions, and restrictions (CC&Rs)   Private agreements that affect land use. They may be enforced by an owner of real estate that benefits from them and can be included in the seller's deed to the buyer. (395)

credit   On a closing statement, an amount entered in a person's favor—either an amount the party has paid or an amount for which the party must be reimbursed. (275)

curtesy   A life estate, usually a fractional interest, given by some states to the surviving husband in real estate owned by his deceased wife. Most states have recognized other marital property rights and abolished curtesy. (37)

customer   The third party or nonrepresented consumer for whom some level of service is provided. (139)

datum   A horizontal plane from which heights and depths are measured. (76)

debit   On a closing statement, an amount charged; that is, an amount that the debited party must pay. (275)

debt to income (DTI)   Information about an applicant's gross income and total debt that lenders generally look at as a percentage to determine qualification for a loan. (210)

decedent   A person who has died.

deed   A written instrument that, when executed and delivered, conveys title to or an interest in real estate. (84)

deed in lieu of foreclosure   A deed given by the mortgagor to the mortgagee when the mortgagor is in default under the terms of the mortgage. If accepted by the mortgagee, this is a way for the mortgagor to avoid foreclosure. (223)

deed in trust   An instrument that grants a trustee under a land trust full power to sell, mortgage, and subdivide a parcel of real estate. The beneficiary controls the trustee's use of these powers under the provisions of the trust agreement. (90)

deed of reconveyance   A document that a trustee uses to transfer the title back to the trustor (borrower) when the note is repaid. (229)

deed of trust   *See* trust deed. (214)

deed of trust lien   *See* trust deed lien.

deed restrictions   Clauses in a deed limiting the future uses of the property. Deed restrictions may impose a vast variety of limitations and conditions—for example, they may limit the density of buildings, dictate the types of structures that can be erected, or prevent buildings from being used for specific purposes or even from being used at all. (395)

default   The nonperformance of a duty, whether arising under a contract or otherwise; failure to meet an obligation when due.

defeasance clause   A clause used in leases and mortgages that cancels a specified right upon the occurrence of a certain condition, such as cancellation of a mortgage upon repayment of the mortgage loan. (216)

defeasible fee estate   An estate in which the holder has a fee simple title that may be divested upon the occurrence or nonoccurrence of a specified event. There are two categories of defeasible fee estates: fee simple on condition precedent (fee simple determinable) and fee simple on condition subsequent. (35)

deficiency judgment   A personal judgment levied against the borrower when a foreclosure sale does not produce sufficient funds to pay the mortgage debt in full. In some states, a deficiency judgment cannot be sought when the mortgage debt was used to purchase, and is secured by, the borrower's principal residence. (224)

delinquent taxes   Taxes that are unpaid and past due.

delivery and acceptance   When the title to property is delivered by the grantor and accepted by the grantee. (88)

demand   The amount of goods people are willing and able to buy at a given price; often coupled with *supply*. (8)

demographics   The study and description of a population. (9)

denominator   The number written below the line in a fraction. (435)

density zoning   Zoning ordinances that restrict the maximum average number of housing units per acre that may be built within a particular area, generally a subdivision. (395)

Department of Housing and Urban Development (HUD)   Federal agency that has established rules and regulations that further interpret the practices affected by federal law; for example, HUD distributes an equal housing opportunity poster. (348)

depreciation   (1) In appraisal, a loss of value in property due to any cause, including *physical deterioration, functional obsolescence,* and *external obsolescence.* (318) (2) In real estate investment, a deduction for tax purposes taken over the period of ownership of income property, based on the property's acquisition cost. (12)

descent   Acquisition of an estate by inheritance in which an heir succeeds to the property by operation of law. (94)

designated agency   A process that accommodates an *in-house* sale in which two different agents are involved. The broker designates one agent to represent the seller and one agent to represent the buyer. (149)

designated agent   A real estate professional authorized by a broker to act as the agent for a specific principal in a particular transaction; also may be called *assigned agent* or *appointed agent.* (149)

determinable fee estate   A fee simple estate providing that the property returns to the original grantor or heirs when a specified condition occurs, indicating that the property is no longer being used for the purpose prescribed. (35)

developer   One who attempts to put land to its most profitable use through the construction of improvements. (394)

development   The construction of improvements that benefit land. (3)

devise   A transfer of real property by will. The decedent is the devisor, and the recipient is the devisee. (95)

discharge   The act of terminating a contract or agreement; this may be done when it has been completely performed for by another party's breach or default. (192)

disclaimer   A statement indicating no legal responsibility for information; no warranties or representations have been made. (127)

disclosure   Relevant information or facts that are known or should have been known. (143)

discount point   A unit of measurement used for various loan charges; one point equals 1% of the amount of the loan. (212)

discount rate   The interest rate set by the Federal Reserve that member institutions are charged when they borrow money through the Fed. (234)

divisor   A number or quantity divided into another. (438)

Do Not Call Registry   A national registry, managed by the Federal Trade Commission, that lists the phone numbers of consumers who have indicated their preference to limit the telemarketing calls they receive. (130)

dominant tenement   A property that includes in its ownership the appurtenant right to use an easement over another person's property for a specific purpose. (39)

dower   The legal right or interest, recognized in some states, that a wife acquires in the property her husband held or acquired during their marriage. During the husband's lifetime, the right is only a possibility of an interest; upon his death, it can become an interest in land. (37)

dual agency   Representing both parties to a transaction. This is unethical unless both parties agree to it, and it is illegal in some states. (147)

due-on-sale clause   A provision in the mortgage stating that the entire balance of the note is immediately due and payable if the mortgagor transfers (sells) the property. (217)

duress   Unlawful constraint or action exercised upon a person whereby the person is forced to perform an act against her will. A contract entered into under duress is voidable.

dwelling   Any building or part of a building designed for occupancy as a residence by one or more families. (348)

earnest money   Money deposited by a buyer under the terms of a contract, to be forfeited if the buyer defaults but to be applied to the purchase price if the sale is closed. (196)

easement   A right to use the land of another for a specific purpose, such as for a right-of-way or utilities; an incorporeal interest in land because it does not include a right of possession. (38)

easement appurtenant   An easement that is annexed to the ownership of one parcel and allows the owner the use of the neighbor's land. (39)

easement by implication   An easement that occurs when a party's actions reflect the intention to create an easement.

easement by necessity   An easement allowed by law as necessary for the full enjoyment of a parcel of real estate (e.g., a right of ingress and egress over a grantor's land). (40)

easement by prescription   An easement acquired by open, notorious, continuous, hostile and adverse use of the property for the period of time prescribed by state law. (40)

easement in gross   An easement that is not created for the benefit of any land owned by the owner of the easement but that attaches *personally to the easement owner*. For example, a right granted by a property owner to a friend to use a portion of the property for the rest of the friend's life would be an easement in gross. (39)

economic life   The number of years during which an improvement will add value to land. (318)

electronic contracting   A process of integrating information electronically in a real estate transaction between clients, lender, and title and closing agents. (129)

Electronic Signatures in Global and National Commerce Act (E-Sign)   An act that makes contracts (including signatures) and records legally enforceable regardless of the medium in which they are created. (129)

emblements   Growing crops, such as corn, that are produced annually through labor and industry; also called *fructus industriales*. (25)

eminent domain   The right of a government or municipal quasi-public body to acquire property for public use through a court action called *condemnation*, in which the court decides that the use is a public use and determines the compensation to be paid to the owner. (42)

employee   For tax purposes, someone who works as a direct employee of an employer and has employee status. The employer is obligated to withhold income taxes and Social Security taxes from the compensation of employees. *See also* independent contractor. (118)

employment agreement   *See* employment contract. (117)

employment contract   A document evidencing formal employment between employer and employee or between principal and agent or representative. In the real estate business, this generally takes the form of the agreement between broker and sales associate, client representation agreement (including a listing agreement or buyer representation agreement), or property management agreement. (2, 140, 160)

enabling acts   State legislation that confers zoning and other powers on municipal governments. (388)

encapsulation A method of controlling environmental contamination by sealing off a dangerous substance, such as asbestos. (403)

encroachment A building or some portion of it—a wall or fence, for instance—that extends beyond the land of the owner and illegally intrudes on the land of an adjoining owner or a public street or alley. (41)

encumbrance Anything—such as a mortgage, tax, or judgment lien; an easement; a restriction on the use of the land; or an outstanding dower right—that may diminish the value or use and enjoyment of a property. (38)

enforceable contract A contract that meets all the elements of a valid contract, including compliance with any applicable statute of frauds or other law that requires it to be in writing and signed by the parties. (192)

environmental impact statement (EIS) A statement that details the impact a project will have on the environment. (417)

environmental site assessment (ESA) An evaluation of property to show that due care was exercised in the determination of environmental impairments. (416)

Equal Credit Opportunity Act (ECOA) The federal law that prohibits discrimination in the extension of credit because of race, color, religion, national origin, sex, age, marital status, or receipt of public assistance. (248)

equalization The raising or lowering of assessed values for tax purposes in a particular county or taxing district to make them equal to assessments in other counties or districts. (291)

equalization factor A factor (number) by which the assessed value of a property is multiplied to arrive at a value for the property that is in line with statewide tax assessments. The *ad valorem tax* would be based on this adjusted value. (291)

equitable lien *See* statutory lien. (288)

equitable right of redemption The right of a defaulted property owner to recover the property before its sale by paying the appropriate fees and charges. (293)

equitable title The interest held by a vendee (buyer) under a contract for deed or an installment contract in which title is not immediately transferred; the equitable right to obtain absolute ownership to property when legal title is held in another's name. (197, 214)

equity The interest or value that an owner has in property over and above any indebtedness. (9)

equity buildup That portion of the loan payment directed toward the principal rather than the interest, plus any gain in property value due to appreciation. (11)

erosion The gradual and sometimes imperceptible wearing away of the land by natural forces, such as wind, rain, and flowing water. (23)

escheat The reversion of property to the state or county, as provided by state law, in cases in which a decedent dies intestate without heirs capable of inheriting, or when the property is abandoned. (44)

escrow The closing of a transaction through a third party called an *escrow agent*, or *escrowee*, who receives certain funds and documents to be delivered upon the performance of conditions outlined in the escrow instructions. (262)

escrow account The trust account established by a real estate professional under the provisions of the license law for the purpose of holding funds on behalf of the real estate professional's principal or some other person until the consummation or termination of a transaction; trust account established by an escrow agent to hold funds pending distribution at the closing of a transaction. (277)

escrow closing Occurs when a disinterested third party is authorized to act as escrow agent (escrow holder) and to coordinate the closing activities on behalf of the buyer and the seller. (262)

escrow contract An agreement between a buyer, a seller, and an escrow holder setting forth rights and responsibilities of each.

escrow instructions A document that sets forth the duties of the escrow agent, as well as the requirements and obligations of the parties, when a transaction is closed through an escrow. (262)

estate (tenancy) at sufferance The tenancy of a lessee who lawfully comes into possession of a landlord's real estate but who continues to occupy the premises improperly after the lease rights have expired. (330)

estate (tenancy) at will An estate that gives the lessee the right to possession until the estate is terminated by either party; the term of this estate is indefinite. (330)

estate for term *See* estate for years. (329)

estate (tenancy) for years An interest for a certain, exact period of time in property leased for a specified consideration. (329)

estate (tenancy) from period to period An interest in leased property that continues from period to period—week to week, month to month, or year to year. (329)

estate in land   The degree, quantity, nature, and extent of interest a person has in real property. (34)

estate tax   Federal tax on a decedent's real and personal property. (296)

estoppel   Method of creating an agency relationship in which someone states incorrectly that another person is his agent and a third person relies on that representation.

estoppel certificate   A document in which a borrower certifies the amount owed on a mortgage loan and the rate of interest.

ethics   The system of moral principles and rules that becomes the standard for professional conduct. (126)

eviction   A legal process to oust a person from possession of real estate. (337)

evidence of title   Proof of ownership of property; commonly a certificate of title, an abstract of title with lawyer's opinion, title insurance, or a Torrens registration certificate. (108)

exception   The exclusion of a part of the property conveyed. (87)

exchange   A transaction in which all or part of the consideration is the transfer of *like-kind* property (e.g., real estate for real estate).

exclusive agency listing   A listing contract under which the owner appoints a real estate professional as her exclusive agent for a designated period of time to sell the specified property, on the owner's stated terms, for a commission. The owner reserves the right to sell the property without paying anyone a commission if the sale is to a prospect who has not been introduced or claimed by the real estate professional. (160)

exclusive buyer representation agreement Agreement in which the buyer works with only one broker, although the broker is free to represent other buyer clients. (175)

exclusive right-to-sell listing   A listing contract under which the owner appoints a real estate professional as his exclusive agent for a designated period of time to sell the specified property on the owner's stated terms and agrees to pay the real estate professional a commission when the property is sold, whether by the real estate professional, the owner, or another real estate professional. (160)

executed contract   A contract in which all parties have fulfilled their promises and thus performed the contract. (189)

execution   The signing and delivery of an instrument. Also, a legal order directing an official to enforce a judgment against the property of a debtor.

executor   An appointed person who carries out the directions of a will. A woman might be referred to as *executrix*, although executor is the term most commonly used to refer to either a man or a woman. (96)

executory contract   A contract under which something remains to be done by one or more of the parties. (189)

express agency   An agency relationship based on a formal agreement between the parties. (140)

express agreement   An oral or written contract in which the parties state the contract's terms and express their intentions in words. (140)

express contract   *See* express agreement. (140)

external depreciation   Reduction in a property's value caused by outside factors (i.e., those that are off the property). (317)

external obsolescence   Incurable depreciation caused by factors not on the subject property, such as environmental or economic factors. (318)

facilitator   *See* nonagent. (139)

Fair Housing Act   The federal law that prohibits discrimination in housing based on race, color, religion, sex, disability, familial status, and national origin. (347)

Fair Housing Amendments Act of 1988   Expansion of the Fair Housing Act to include families with children and those with physical or mental disabilities. (347)

familial status   One or more individuals under age 18 living with a parent or guardian; also includes a woman who is pregnant and anyone who is in the process of assuming custody of a child under age 18. (348)

Fannie Mae   A government-supervised enterprise established to purchase any kind of mortgage loans in the secondary mortgage market from the primary lenders. (237)

Farmer Mac   The Federal Agricultural Mortgage Corporation—a privately owned and publicly traded company established by Congress to create a secondary market for agricultural mortgage and rural utilities loans and the portions of agricultural and rural development loans guaranteed by the U.S. Department of Agriculture (USDA). (238)

Federal Deposit Insurance Corporation (FDIC) An independent federal agency established by Congress to examine and supervise financial institutions, manage receiverships, and insure deposits (currently up to $250,000 per depositor per financial institution). (235)

Federal Emergency Management Agency (FEMA) A federal agency that is responsible for assisting the nation in preparing for, protecting against, responding to, and recovering from hazards. (227)

federal funds rate The rate recommended by the Federal Reserve for the member banks to charge each other on short-term loans. These rates form the basis on which the banks determine the percentage rate of interest they will charge their loan customers.

Federal Home Loan Mortgage Corporation *See* Freddie Mac. (237)

Federal National Mortgage Association *See* Fannie Mae. (238)

Federal Reserve System (Fed) The country's central banking system, which establishes the nation's monetary policy by regulating the supply of money and interest rates. (234)

fee-for-service Arrangement by which a consumer asks a real estate professional to perform specific real estate services for an agreed-upon fee. (123)

fee simple The highest interest in real estate recognized by the law; the holder is entitled to all rights to the property. (35)

fee simple absolute The maximum possible estate or right of ownership of real property, continuing forever. (35)

fee simple defeasible *See* defeasible fee estate. (35)

fee simple determinable A fee simple estate qualified by a special limitation. Language used to describe the limitation includes the words *so long as, while,* or *during.* (35)

fee simple subject to a condition subsequent An estate carrying the limitation that, if it is no longer used for the purpose conveyed, it reverts to the original grantor by the right of reentry. (35)

feudal system A system of ownership usually associated with precolonial England, in which the king or other sovereign is the source of all rights. The right to possess real property was granted by the sovereign to an individual as a life estate only. Upon the death of the individual, title passed back to the sovereign, not to the decedent's heirs.

FHA-insured loan A loan insured by the Federal Housing Administration and made by an approved lender in accordance with FHA regulations. (240)

fiduciary One in whom trust and confidence is placed; a reference to a real estate professional employed under the terms of a listing contract or buyer representation agreement. (55,137)

fiduciary relationship A relationship of trust and confidence, as between trustee and beneficiary, attorney and client, or principal and agent. (142)

Financial Institutions Reform, Recovery, and Enforcement Act (FIRREA) This act restructured the savings and loan association regulatory system; enacted in response to the savings and loan crisis of the 1980s. (302)

financing The business of providing the funds that make real estate transactions possible. (3)

first mortgage A mortgage that has priority over all other mortgages. (218)

fiscal policy The government's policy in regard to taxation and spending programs. The balance between these two areas determines the amount of money the government will withdraw from or feed into the economy, which can counter economic peaks and slumps.

fixture An item of personal property that has been converted to real property by being permanently affixed to the realty. (26)

forcible detainer Removal of a tenant from a rental property by the landlord if the tenant has breached one of the terms of the lease agreement, in compliance with statutory law.

foreclosure A legal procedure whereby property used as security for a debt is sold to satisfy the debt in the event of default in payment of the mortgage note or default of other terms in the mortgage document. The foreclosure procedure brings the rights of the parties to a conclusion and passes the title in the mortgaged property to either the holder of the mortgage or a third party who may purchase the realty at the foreclosure sale. Depending on the priority of the foreclosed mortgage, the property may be sold free of all other encumbrances incurred prior to the sale. (222)

formal will/witnessed will A document having written instructions of property disbursements upon the death of the owner. The document must be signed and witnessed.

formaldehyde An air pollutant that is a colorless chemical used to manufacture building materials and many household products, such as particleboard, hardwood plywood paneling, and urea-formaldehyde foam insulation. (407)

fraud Deception intended to cause a person to give up property or a lawful right. (150)

Freddie Mac A government-supervised enterprise established to purchase primarily conventional mortgage loans in the secondary mortgage market. (237)

freehold estate An estate in land in which ownership is for an indeterminate length of time, in contrast to a *leasehold estate*. (34)

front footage The measurement of a parcel of land by the number of feet of street or road frontage. (429–430)

frontage The length of property along the street or waterfront. (430)

fully amortized loan A loan consisting of equal, regular payments satisfying the total payment of principal and interest by the due date. (218)

functional obsolescence A loss of value to an improvement to real estate arising from problems of design or utility. (318)

future interest A person's present right to an interest in real property that will not result in possession or enjoyment until sometime in the future, such as a reversion or right of reentry. (36)

gap A defect in the chain of title of a particular parcel of real estate; a missing document or conveyance that raises doubt as to the present ownership of the land. (106)

general agent One who is authorized by a principal to represent the principal in a specific range of matters. (145)

general lien The right of a creditor to have all of a debtor's property—both real and personal—sold to satisfy a debt. (288)

general partnership *See* partnership. (57)

general real estate tax A tax that is made up of the taxes levied on the real estate by government agencies and municipalities. (290)

general warranty deed A deed in which the grantor fully warrants good, clear title to the premises. Used in most real estate deed transfers, a general warranty deed offers the greatest protection of any deed. (88)

Ginnie Mae A government agency that plays an important role in the secondary mortgage market. It guarantees mortgage-backed securities using FHA-insured and VA-guaranteed loans as collateral. (238)

good and indefeasible title A title that cannot be annulled or rendered void.

Good Faith Estimate (GFE) An estimate of all closing fees that was formerly provided to a borrower within three days of the loan application as was required by the Real Estate Settlement Procedures Act (RESPA).

Government National Mortgage Association *See* Ginnie Mae. (238)

government-sponsored enterprises (GSEs) Organizations created by the federal government (Fannie Mae, Freddie Mac, Farmer Mac, Ginnie Mae) to help increase loan opportunities for homebuyers. (237)

government survey system *See* rectangular (government) survey system. (70)

graduated-payment mortgage (GPM) A loan in which the monthly principal and interest payments increase by a certain percentage each year for a certain number of years and then level off for the remaining loan term.

grantee A person who receives a transfer of real property from a grantor. (84)

granting clause Words in a deed of conveyance that state the grantor's intention to convey the property at the present time. This clause is generally worded as "convey and warrant"; "grant"; "grant, bargain, and sell"; or the like. (86)

grantor The owner transferring title to or an interest in real property to a grantee. (84)

gross income multiplier (GIM) A figure used as a multiplier of the gross annual income of a property to produce an estimate of the property's value; usually used for commercial property. (321)

gross lease A lease of property according to which a landlord pays all property charges regularly incurred through ownership, such as repairs, taxes, insurance, and operating expenses. Most residential leases are gross leases. (335)

gross rent multiplier (GRM) The figure used as a multiplier of the gross monthly income of a property to produce an estimate of the property's value; usually used for single-family residential property. (321)

ground lease A lease of land only, on which the tenant usually owns a building or is required to build as specified in the lease. Such leases are usually long-term net leases; the tenant's rights and obligations continue until the lease expires or is terminated through default. (336)

groundwater Water that exists under the earth's surface within the tiny spaces or crevices in geological formations. (410)

growing-equity mortgage   A loan in which the monthly payments increase annually, with the increased amount being used to directly reduce the principal balance outstanding and thus shorten the overall term of the loan. (219)

habendum clause   That part of a deed beginning with the words "to have and to hold," following the granting clause and defining the extent of ownership the grantor is conveying. (86)

habitability   A property that is suitable for living in or on.

heir   One who might inherit or succeed to an interest in land under the state law of descent when the owner dies without leaving a valid will. (95)

highest and best use   The legally permitted and physically possible use of a property that would produce the greatest net income and, thereby, develop the highest value. (313)

holdover tenancy   A tenancy in which a lessee retains possession of leased property after the lease has expired and the landlord, by continuing to accept rent, agrees to the tenant's continued occupancy as defined by state law. (329)

holographic will   A will that is written, dated, and signed in the testator's handwriting. (95)

home equity loan   A loan under which a property owner uses the property as collateral and can then draw funds up to a prearranged amount against the property. Also called a *home equity line of credit*, or *HELOC*. (246)

home inspection   A thorough visual survey of a property's structure, systems, and site conditions conducted by a professional. (3)

Home Mortgage Disclosure Act   A federal law, implemented at its creation by Regulation C of the Federal Reserve, that requires lenders to annually disclose the number of loan applications and loans made in certain areas to avoid the practice of redlining. On July 21, 2011, the rule-making authority of the law was transferred to the Consumer Financial Protection Bureau.

homeowners insurance   Insurance that covers a residential real estate owner against financial loss from fire, theft, public liability, and other common risks. (226)

homestead   Land that is owned and occupied as the family home. In many states, a portion of the area or value of this land is protected or exempt from judgments for debts other than those secured by the property. (37)

Housing for Older Persons Act of 1995 (HOPA)   Amended the Fair Housing Act to provide that housing intended for persons aged 55 or older no longer needs to have significant facilities and services designed for the elderly. (348)

HUD-1   A form that was formerly used to itemize fees and services charged to a borrower and seller during a real estate transaction.

hydraulic fracturing (fracking)   The process used to extract natural gas from the deep layers of rock in which it is embedded. (21, 411)

hypothecation   To pledge property as security for an obligation or loan without giving up possession of it. (213)

immobility   The fact that property cannot be relocated to satisfy demand where supply is low, nor can buyers always relocate to areas with greater supply. (7, 18)

implied agency   If the actions of the parties imply that they have mutually consented to an agency relationship, an implied agency relationship is formed. (140)

implied agreement   A contract under which the agreement of the parties is demonstrated by their acts and conduct. (141)

implied contract   *See* implied agreement. (141)

implied warranty of habitability   A theory in landlord/tenant law in which the landlord renting residential property implies that the property is habitable and fit for its intended use.

impound accounts   An account that the mortgage lender may require a borrower to have to accumulate funds to pay future real estate taxes and insurance premiums. (277)

improvement   (1) Any structure, usually privately owned, erected on a site to enhance the value of the property (e.g., a building, fence, or driveway). (2) A publicly owned structure added to or benefiting land (e.g., a curb, sidewalk, street, or sewer). (24)

income approach   The process of estimating the value of an income-producing property through capitalization of the annual net income expected to be produced by the property during its remaining useful life. (319)

income property   Property held for current income as well as a potential profit upon its sale.

incorporeal right   A nonpossessory right in real estate (e.g., an easement or a right-of-way).

independent contractor   Someone who is retained to perform a certain act but who is subject to the control and direction of another only as to the end result and not as to the way in which the act is performed. Unlike an employee, an independent contractor pays for all expenses and Social Security and income taxes and receives no employee benefits. Most real estate sales associates are independent contractors, meeting the Internal Revenue Service definition for a qualified real estate agent. (119)

index   An objective economic indicator to which the interest rate for an adjustable-rate mortgage is tied. (219)

inflation   The gradual reduction of the purchasing power of the dollar, usually related directly to increases in the money supply by the federal government. (7)

inheritance taxes   State-imposed taxes on a decedent's real and personal property. (296)

installment sale   A transaction in which the sales price is paid in two or more installments over two or more years. If the sale meets certain requirements, a taxpayer can postpone reporting such income until future years by paying tax each year only on the proceeds received that year. (200)

interest   A charge made by a lender for the use of money. (211)

interest-only loan   A loan that only requires the payment of interest for a stated period of time with the principal due at the end of the term. (218)

interim financing   A short-term loan usually made during the construction phase of a building project (often referred to as a *construction loan*). (245)

intermediary   *See* nonagent. (139)

Internal Revenue Service tax lien   A lien charged by the Internal Revenue Service for nonpayment of income taxes. (296)

Internet Data Exchange (IDX) policy   Policy that allows all multiple listing service (MLS) members to restrict internet access to MLS property listings. (127)

Interstate Land Sales Full Disclosure Act (ILSA)   A federal law that regulates the sale of certain real estate in interstate commerce. (396)

intestate   The condition of a property owner who dies without leaving a valid will. Title to the property will pass to the decedent's heirs, as provided in the state law of descent. (93)

intrinsic value   An appraisal term referring to the value of a property unaffected by a person's personal preferences. (11)

inverse condemnation   An action brought by a property owner seeking just compensation for diminished use and value of land because of an adjacent property's public use. (43)

investment   Money directed toward the purchase, improvement, and development of an asset in expectation of income or profits. (10)

involuntary alienation   *See* alienation. (92)

involuntary lien   A lien placed on property without the consent of the property owner. (288)

joint tenancy   Ownership of real estate between two or more parties who have been named in one conveyance as joint tenants. Upon the death of a joint tenant, the decedent's interest usually passes to the surviving joint tenant or tenants by the *right of survivorship*. (51)

judgment   The formal decision of a court upon the respective rights and claims of the parties to an action or suit. After a judgment has been entered and recorded with the county recorder, it usually becomes a general lien on the property of the defendant. (295)

judicial precedent   In law, the requirements established by prior court decisions within the jurisdiction of the dispute. (415)

jumbo loan   *See* nonconforming loan. (239)

junior lien   An obligation, such as a second mortgage, that is subordinate in right or lien priority to an existing lien on the same property. (289)

laches   An equitable doctrine used by courts to bar a legal claim or to prevent the assertion of a right because of undue delay or failure to assert the claim or right. (396)

land   The earth's surface, extending downward to the center of the earth and upward infinitely into space, including things permanently attached by nature, such as trees. (18)

land contract   *See* installment sale. (200)

land trust   A trust in which property is conveyed, and in which real estate is the only asset. (56)

latent defect   A hidden structural defect that could not be discovered by ordinary inspection and that threatens a property's soundness or the safety of its inhabitants. Some states impose on property sellers and real estate professionals a duty to inspect for and disclose latent defects. (151)

law of agency   *See* agency. (139)

law of diminishing returns   Point at which additional property improvements do not increase the property's income or value. (314)

law of increasing returns   Applies as long as money being spent on property improvements produces an increase in the property's income or value. (314)

lead   Used as a pigment and drying agent in alkyd oil-based paint in about 75% of housing built before 1978. An elevated level of lead in the body can cause serious damage to the brain, kidneys, nervous system, and red blood cells. Children younger than six are most vulnerable. (404)

Lead-Based Paint Hazard Reduction Act (LBPHRA)   Federal legislation requiring disclosure of the presence of any known lead-based paint hazards to potential buyers or renters. The law does not require that anyone test for the presence of lead-based paint, however. (404)

lease   A written or oral contract between a landlord (the lessor) and a tenant (the lessee) that transfers the right to exclusive possession and use of the landlord's real property to the lessee for a specified period of time and for a stated consideration (rent). By state law, leases for longer than a certain period of time (generally one year) must be in writing to be enforceable. (328)

lease option   A lease under which the tenant has the right to purchase the property at an agreed-upon price either during the lease term or at its end. (337)

lease purchase   The purchase of real property, the consummation of which is preceded by a lease, usually long term, that is typically done for tax or financing purposes. (336)

leasehold estate   A tenant's right to occupy real estate during the term of a lease, generally considered a personal property interest, although a long-term lease may be eligible for treatment as real property for financing purposes. (35, 328)

legacy   A disposition of money or personal property by will. (95)

legal description   A description of a specific parcel of real estate complete enough for an independent surveyor to locate and identify it. (67)

legal life estate   A form of life estate established by state law, rather than created voluntarily by an owner. It becomes effective when certain events occur. *See* dower, curtesy, and homestead for legal life estates used in some states. (37)

legally competent parties   People who are recognized by law as being able to contract with others; those of legal age and sound mind. (188)

lessee   *See* lease. (328)

lessor   *See* lease. (328)

leverage   The use of borrowed money to finance an investment. (11)

levy   To assess; to seize or collect. To levy a tax is to assess a property and set the rate of taxation. To levy an execution is to officially seize the property of a person in order to satisfy an obligation. (292)

liability coverage   Feature of homeowners insurance that covers injuries or losses sustained within the home. (226)

license   (1) In real estate practice, the privilege or right granted to a person by a state to operate as a real estate broker or salesperson. (2) The revocable permission for a temporary use of land—a personal right that cannot be sold. (41)

lien   A right given by law to certain creditors to have their debts paid out of the property of a defaulting debtor, usually by means of a court sale. (288)

lien theory   Principle in which the mortgagor retains both legal and equitable title to property that serves as security for a debt. The mortgagee has a lien on the property, but the mortgage is nothing more than collateral for the loan. (213)

life cycle costing   In property management, comparing one type of equipment with another based on both purchase cost and operating cost over its expected useful lifetime.

life estate   An interest in real or personal property that is limited in duration to the lifetime of its owner or some other designated person or persons. (36)

life tenant   A person in possession of a life estate. (36)

limited agent   *See* special agent. (145)

limited liability company (LLC)   A form of business organization that combines the most attractive features of limited partnerships and corporations. (57)

limited partnership   *See* partnership. (57)

linear measurement   Measurement in a straight line. (429)

liquidated damages   An amount predetermined by the parties to a contract as the total compensation to an injured party should the other party breach the contract. (197)

liquidity   The ability to sell an asset and convert it into cash, at a price close to its true value, in a short period of time. (12)

lis pendens   A recorded legal document giving constructive notice that an action affecting a particular property has been filed in either a state or a federal court. (42, 295)

listing agreement   A contract between an owner (as principal) and a real estate professional (as representative of the owner) by which the real estate professional is employed to find a buyer for the owner's real estate on the owner's terms, for which service the owner agrees to pay a commission or other form of compensation. (140)

listing broker   The broker from whose office a listing agreement is initiated. (138)

littoral rights   (1) A landowner's claim to use water in large navigable lakes and oceans adjacent to her property. (2) The ownership rights to land bordering these bodies of water up to the high-water mark. (22)

living trust   A trust that is created during the trustor's lifetime. (56)

Loan Estimate   A CFPB form that highlights the information that historically has been the most important to consumers. Interest rate, monthly payment, and total closing costs are clearly presented on the first page. (265)

loan origination fee   A fee charged to the borrower by the lender for making a mortgage loan. The fee is usually computed as a percentage of the loan amount. (211)

loan-to-value ratio (LTV)   The relationship between the amount of the mortgage loan and the value of the real estate being pledged as collateral. (210)

lot-and-block (recorded plat) method   A method of describing real property that identifies a parcel of land by reference to lot and block numbers within a subdivision, as specified on a recorded subdivision plat. (74)

management agreement   A contract between the owner of income property and a management firm or individual property manager that outlines the scope of the manager's authority. (369)

management plan   A highly detailed plan that lays out the owner's objectives for a property, as well as what the property manager wants to accomplish and how, including all budgetary information. (370)

managing broker   The real estate professional who is responsible for supervision of the real estate professionals who act on behalf of the brokerage; may also be called a supervising broker. (118)

manufactured home   A permanent installation built to federal specifications, providing a principal residence or a vacation home. (6)

manufactured housing   Dwellings that are built off site and trucked to a building lot where they are installed or assembled. (25)

margin   A premium added to the index rate representing the lender's cost of doing business. (219)

market   A place where goods can be bought and sold and a price established. (6)

market data approach   Also known as the *sales comparison approach*. An estimate of value obtained by comparing property being appraised with recently sold comparable properties. (315)

market value   The most probable price that a property would bring in an arm's-length transaction under normal conditions on the open market. (312)

marketable title   Good or clear title, reasonably free from the risk of litigation over possible defects. (107)

master plan   A comprehensive government plan to guide the long-term physical development of a particular area. (388)

master-planned community   A planned combination of diverse land uses, such as housing, recreation, and shopping, in one contained development or subdivision; also called a planned unit development (PUD). (6)

mechanic's lien   A statutory lien created in favor of contractors, laborers, material suppliers, and others who have performed work or furnished materials in the erection or repair of a building. (294)

Megan's Law   Federal legislation that promotes the establishment of state registration systems to maintain residential information on every person who kidnaps children, commits sexual crimes against children, or commits sexually violent crimes. (152)

meridian   One of a set of imaginary lines running north and south and crossing a base line at a definite point, used in the rectangular (government) survey system of property description. (70)

metes-and-bounds method   A method used to describe a parcel of land that begins at a well-marked point and follows the property's boundaries, using directions and distances around the tract, back to the place of beginning. (68)

mill   One-tenth of one cent. Some states use a mill rate to compute real estate taxes; for example, a rate of 52 mills would indicate a tax of $0.052 for each dollar of assessed valuation of a property. (292)

minimum level of services   The services that real estate professionals must provide to clients, as prescribed differently by certain states; for example, assisting clients in negotiation and answering questions from clients about offers, counteroffers, and contingencies. (123)

ministerial acts   The necessary paperwork and formalities involved in transferring ownership of real property. (149)

minor   A person who has not reached the age of majority and, therefore, does not have legal capacity to transfer title to real property. (85)

mixed use   Property that accommodates more than one use, such as commercial use and residential use. (4)

Model Real Estate Time-Share Act   An act that governs the management, use, and termination of time-share units. (62)

modular home   A type of factory-built housing with components that are assembled at a building site on a prepared foundation. (6)

mold   A form of fungus that can be found almost anywhere and can grow on almost any organic substance, so long as moisture and oxygen are present. Mold growth can gradually destroy what it is growing on, as well as cause serious health problems. (409)

monetary policy   Governmental regulation of the amount of money in circulation through such institutions as the Federal Reserve Board. (8, 234)

month-to-month tenancy   A periodic tenancy under which the tenant rents for one month at a time. In the absence of a rental agreement (oral or written), a tenancy is generally considered to be month to month. (329)

monument   A fixed natural or artificial object used to establish real estate boundaries for a metes-and-bounds description. (68)

mortgage   A conditional transfer or pledge of real estate as security for the payment of a debt. Also, the document creating a mortgage lien. (213)

mortgage banker   A mortgage loan company that originates, services, and sell loans to investors.

mortgage broker   An agent of a lender who brings the lender and the borrower together. The broker receives a fee for this service.

Mortgage Disclosure Improvement Act (MDIA)   Enacted in July 2008 as an amendment to the Truth in Lending Act (TILA) to require mortgage loan cost disclosures to consumers. Early disclosure (a good-faith estimate) of mortgage loan cost must be provided within three business days of receiving a consumer's application for a mortgage loan; a creditor must wait seven business days after providing the early disclosures before closing the loan; and a creditor must provide new disclosures and wait an additional three business days before closing the loan, if a change occurs that makes the annual percentage rate quoted in the early disclosure inaccurate beyond a specified tolerance.

mortgage insurance premium (MIP)   The FHA insurance that is a percentage of the loan amount that the borrower is charged as a premium. (240)

mortgage lien   A lien or charge on the property of a mortgagor that secures the underlying debt obligation. (294)

mortgage servicing transfer statement   Disclosure required by the lender if the lender intends to sell or assign the right to service the loan to another loan servicer. The loan servicer must notify the borrower 15 days before the effective date of the loan transfer, including in the notice the name and address of the new servicer, toll-free telephone numbers, and the date the new servicer will begin accepting payments. (264)

mortgagee   A lender in a mortgage loan transaction. (213)

mortgagor   A borrower in a mortgage loan transaction. (213)

multiperil policies   Insurance policies that offer protection from a range of potential perils, such as fire, hazard, public liability, and casualty. (381)

multiple listing clause   A provision in an exclusive listing for the authority and obligation on the part of the listing agent to distribute the listing to other real estate professionals in a multiple listing organization. (161)

multiple listing service (MLS) A marketing organization composed of member real estate professionals who agree to share their listing agreements with one another in the hope of procuring ready, willing, and able buyers for their properties more quickly than they could on their own. Most multiple listing services accept exclusive right-to-sell or exclusive agency listings from their member real estate professionals. (120)

mutual assent Requirement that there must be complete agreement between the parties about the purpose and terms of a contract. (189)

National Association of REALTORS® (NAR) The largest real estate organization in the world; NAR members subscribe to a strict code of ethics. Active members are allowed to use the trademarked designation, REALTORS®. (125)

National Do Not Call Registry *See* Do Not Call Registry. (130)

negative amortization Process by which the amount of the loan increases. The mortgagor sets a payment cap, or maximum amount for payments, but the difference between the payment made and the full payment amount is added to the remaining mortgage balance. (219)

negligent misrepresentation Occurs when the real estate professional should have known that a statement about a material fact was false. (150)

negotiable instrument A written promise or order to pay a specific sum of money that may be transferred by endorsement or delivery. The transferee then has the original payee's right to payment. (210)

net lease A lease requiring the tenant to pay not only rent but also costs incurred in maintaining the property, including taxes, insurance, utilities, and repairs. (335)

net listing A listing based on the net price the seller will receive if the property is sold. Under a net listing, the real estate professional can offer the property for sale at the highest price obtainable to increase the commission. This type of listing is illegal in many states. (161)

net operating income (NOI) The income projected for an income-producing property after deducting anticipated vacancy and collection losses and operating expenses. (319)

niche marketing The target marketing of specific demographic populations, within the bounds of fair housing laws. (9)

nonagent An intermediary between a buyer and a seller, or a landlord and a tenant, who assists one or both parties with a transaction without representing either. Also known as a *facilitator, transaction broker, transaction coordinator,* and *contract broker.* (139)

nonconforming loan A loan that exceeds the Federal Housing Finance Agency (FHFA) loan limits; also called a *jumbo loan.* (239)

nonconforming use A use of property that is permitted to continue after a zoning ordinance prohibiting it has been established for the area. (391)

nondisturbance clause A mortgage clause stating that the mortgagee agrees not to terminate the tenancies of the lessees in the event the mortgagee forecloses on the mortgagor-lessor's building. (334)

nonhomogeneity A lack of uniformity; dissimilarity. Because no two parcels of land are exactly alike, real estate is said to be nonhomogeneous. (19)

notarization Certification by a notary or other authorized official of the validity of a signature on a document. (85)

note *See* promissory note. (210)

novation Substituting a new obligation for an old one or substituting new parties to an existing obligation. (193)

numerator The number written above the line of a fraction representing the number to be divided by the denominator. (435)

nuncupative will An oral will declared by the testator in his final illness, made before witnesses and afterward reduced to writing; not permitted by all states. (95)

obsolescence The loss of value due to property features that are outmoded or less useful. Obsolescence may be functional or external. (318)

occupancy permit A permit issued by the appropriate local governing body to establish that the property is suitable for habitation by meeting certain safety and health standards. (393)

offer and acceptance Two essential components of a valid contract; a "meeting of the minds." An offer is a promise made by the offeror, requesting something in exchange for that promise. Acceptance is a promise by the offeree to be bound by the exact terms proposed by the offeror. (189)

offeror/offeree The person who makes the offer is the offeror. The person to whom the offer is made is the offeree. (189)

Office of the Comptroller of the Currency (OCC) Government agency which sets standards and regulations for fiduciary lenders. (235)

open-end loan A mortgage loan that is expandable by increments up to a maximum dollar amount, with the full loan being secured by the same original mortgage. (244)

open listing A listing contract under which the real estate professional's compensation is contingent on the real estate professional producing a ready, willing, and able buyer before the property is sold by the seller or another real estate professional. (161)

operating budget A property's anticipated financial performance in the present and future. It gives the owner a sense of expected profit. (371)

option An agreement to keep open for a set period an offer to sell or purchase property. (200)

ostensible agency A form of implied agency relationship created by the actions of the parties involved rather than by written agreement or document.

owelty lien A lien created by the order of the court to make an equitable partition of property when otherwise an agreeable partition is impossible or impractical (i.e., in a divorce). The owelty lien allows the party acquiring the interest of a co-owner to place a lien on the entire property.

owner financing The seller is the primary lender, securing the property by means of a deed, note and mortgage, deed of trust, or contract for deed. In its traditional form, the buyer takes possession of the property and the seller retains legal title until paid in full, but some states have softened this outcome to provide that the buyer is entitled to legal title after a specified period of successful loan payments. (200)

P&I Principal and interest.

package loan A real estate loan used to finance the purchase of both real property and personal property, such as in the purchase of a new home that includes carpeting, window coverings, and major appliances. (244)

panic selling The illegal practice of soliciting people in a neighborhood to sell their homes because of fear or alarm; also referred to as blockbusting. (353)

participation mortgage A mortgage loan wherein the lender has a partial equity interest in the property or receives a portion of the income from the property.

partition The division of cotenants' interests in real property when the parties do not all voluntarily agree to terminate the co-ownership; takes place through a court procedure. (53)

partnership An association of two or more individuals who carry on a continuing business for profit as co-owners. Under the law, a partnership is regarded as a group of individuals rather than as a single entity separate from the individual owners. A *general partnership* is a typical form of joint venture in which each general partner shares in the administration, profits, and losses of the operation. A *limited partnership* is a business arrangement whereby the operation is administered by one or more general partners and funded, by and large, by limited or silent partners, who are by law responsible for losses only to the extent of their investments. (57)

party wall An exterior wall of a building that straddles the boundary line between two lots, or a commonly shared partition wall between two connected properties. (39)

passing papers When parties to a transaction sit around a table and exchange copies of documents as the documents are executed. (260)

patent A grant or franchise of land from the U.S. government.

payment cap The limit on the amount the monthly payment can be increased on an adjustable-rate mortgage when the interest rate is adjusted. (219)

payoff statement *See* reduction certificate. (258)

percent One part in a hundred. (438)

percentage lease A lease, commonly used for commercial property, whose rental is based on the tenant's gross sales at the premises; it usually stipulates a base monthly rental plus a percentage of any gross sales above a certain amount. (335)

percolation test A test of the soil to determine whether it will absorb and drain water adequately to use a septic system for sewage disposal.

periodic tenancy *See* estate from period to period. (329)

personal property Items, called *chattels*, that do not fit into the definition of real property; movable objects. (24)

personalty Personal property. (24)

physical deterioration A reduction in a property's value resulting from a decline in physical condition; can be caused by action of the elements or by ordinary wear and tear. (318)

PITI The basic costs of owning a home—mortgage principal and interest, real estate taxes, and hazard insurance. (209)

PITT The four unities of tenants in a joint tenancy: possession, interest, time, and title. (52)

planned unit development (PUD) A planned combination of diverse land uses, such as housing, recreation, and shopping, in one contained development or subdivision. (390)

plat map A map of a town, section, or subdivision indicating the location and boundaries of individual properties. (394)

plottage The increase in value or utility resulting from the consolidation *(assemblage)* of two or more adjacent lots into one larger lot. (314)

point A term used for a percentage of the principal loan amount charged by the lender. Each point is equal to 1% of the loan amount. (212)

point of beginning (POB) In a metes-and-bounds legal description, the starting point of the survey, situated in one corner of the parcel; all metes-and-bounds descriptions must follow the boundaries of the parcel back to the point of beginning. (68)

police power The government's right to impose laws, statutes, and ordinances, including zoning ordinances and building codes, to protect the public health, safety, and welfare. (42)

polychlorinated biphenyls (PCBs) Used as an insulating material in dielectric oil. It can linger in the environment for long periods of time and can cause health problems. (408)

possession Owning or occupying a property. (52)

power of attorney A written instrument authorizing a person, the *attorney-in-fact*, to act as agent for another person to the extent indicated in the instrument. (87)

prepaid items On a closing statement, items that have been paid in advance by the seller, such as fuel costs and some real estate taxes, for which the seller must be reimbursed by the buyer. (279)

prepayment penalty A charge imposed on a borrower who pays off the loan principal early. This penalty compensates the lender for interest and other charges that would otherwise be lost. (212)

preventive maintenance Small repairs that help prevent bigger problems and expenses. (376)

price The amount of money paid for an item or service. (7, 312)

price-fixing *See* antitrust laws. (124)

primary mortgage market The mortgage market in which loans are originated, consisting of lenders such as commercial banks, savings associations, and mutual savings banks. (235)

principal (1) A sum loaned or employed as a fund or an investment, as distinguished from its income or profits. (444) (2) The original amount (as in a loan) of the total due and payable at a certain date. (209) (3) A main party to a transaction—the person for whom an agent works. (139)

principal meridian The main imaginary line running north and south and crossing a base line at a definite point; used by surveyors for reference in locating and describing land under the rectangular (government) survey system of legal description. (70)

prior appropriation A concept of water ownership in which the landowner's right to use available water is based on a government-administered permit system. (23)

priority The order of position or time. The priority of liens is generally determined by the chronological order in which the lien documents are recorded; tax liens, however, have priority even over previously recorded liens. (289)

private mortgage insurance (PMI) Insurance provided by a private carrier that protects a lender against a loss in the event of a foreclosure and deficiency. (239)

probate A legal process by which a court determines who will inherit a decedent's property and what the estate's assets are. (94)

procuring cause The effort that brings about the desired result. Under an open listing, the real estate professional who is the procuring cause of the sale receives the commission. (121)

profit Making a gain from an investment after subtracting expenses. (10)

profit and loss statement A general financial picture based on the monthly cash flow reports; does not include itemized information. (375)

progression An appraisal principle that the value of a lesser-quality property is favorably affected by the presence of a better-quality property. (314)

promissory note A financing instrument that states the terms of the underlying obligation, is signed by its maker, and is negotiable (transferable to a third party). (210)

property manager Someone who manages real estate for another person for compensation. Duties include collecting rents, maintaining the property, and keeping up all accounting. (366)

property reports The mandatory federal and state documents compiled by subdividers and developers to provide potential purchasers with facts about a property prior to a purchase.

proprietary lease A lease given by the corporation that owns a cooperative apartment building to a shareholder who has the right as a tenant to an individual unit. (5)

prorations Expenses, either prepaid or paid in arrears, that are divided or distributed between the buyer and the seller at the closing. (278)

protected class Any group of people designated as such by the Department of Housing and Urban Development (HUD) in consideration of federal civil rights legislation. Individual states and local jurisdictions provide such designation to additional groups as well. (347)

public ownership Government-owned property.

puffing Exaggerated or superlative comments or opinions. (150)

pur autre vie "For the life of another." A life estate pur autre vie is a life estate that is measured by the life of a person or persons other than the grantee. (36)

purchase money mortgage A note secured by a mortgage or deed of trust given by a buyer, as borrower, to a seller, as lender, as part of the purchase price of the real estate. (201)

purchase option The right given by a lease to the tenant to purchase the property at a predetermined price within a certain period, possibly the lease term. (334)

pyramiding The process of acquiring additional property by refinancing property already owned and investing the loan proceeds in additional properties.

quiet title A court action to remove a cloud on the title. (106)

quitclaim deed A conveyance that transfers whatever interest the grantor has in the specified real estate, without warranties or obligations. (90)

quotient The number resulting from dividing one number by another. (438)

radon A naturally occurring gas that is suspected of causing lung cancer. (407)

range A strip of land six miles wide, extending north and south and numbered east and west according to its distance from the principal meridian in the rectangular (government) survey system of legal description. (71)

rate cap The limit on the amount the interest rate can be increased at each adjustment period in an adjustable rate loan. The cap may also set the maximum interest rate that can be charged during the life of the loan. (219)

ratification Method of creating an agency relationship in which the principal accepts the conduct of someone who acted without prior authorization as the principal's agent.

ready, willing, and able buyer Person who is prepared to buy property on the seller's terms and is ready to take positive steps to consummate the transaction. (121)

real estate Land; a portion of the earth's surface extending downward to the center of the earth and upward infinitely into space, including all things permanently attached to it, whether naturally or artificially. (19)

real estate broker A person licensed to arrange the buying, selling, leasing, or exchange of real property for a fee. (2)

real estate investment syndicate *See* syndicate. (236)

real estate investment trust (REIT) Trust ownership of real estate by a group of individuals who purchase certificates of ownership in the trust, which in turn invests the money in real property and distributes the profits back to the investors free of corporate income tax.

real estate license law State law enacted to protect the public from fraud, dishonesty, and incompetence on the part of those they hire to represent them in the purchase and sale of real estate. (116)

real estate licensee In real estate practice, a person who has the skills and knowledge to be licensed as a real estate broker or salesperson. (2)

real estate mortgage investment conduit (REMIC) A tax entity that issues multiple classes of investor interests (securities) backed by a pool of mortgages.

real estate recovery fund A fund established in some states from real estate license revenues to cover claims of aggrieved parties who have suffered monetary damage through the actions of a real estate professional.

Real Estate Settlement Procedures Act (RESPA) The federal law that requires certain disclosures to consumers about mortgage loan settlements. The law also prohibits the payment or receipt of kickbacks and certain kinds of referral fees. (249, 263)

real property The interests, benefits, and rights inherent in real estate ownership; often used as a synonym for real estate. (19)

REALTOR®   A registered trademarked term reserved for the sole use of active members of state and local REALTOR® associations affiliated with the National Association of REALTORS®. (125)

reconciliation   The final step in the appraisal process, in which the appraiser considers the estimates of value received from the sales comparison, cost, and income approaches to arrive at a final opinion of market value for the subject property. (321)

reconveyance deed   A deed used by a trustee under a deed of trust to return title to the trustor. (91)

recorded plat   A map of a subdivision filed as a public record showing the location and boundaries of the individual parcels. (74)

recording   The act of entering or recording documents affecting or conveying interests in real estate in the recorder's office established in each county. Until it is recorded, a deed or a mortgage ordinarily is not effective against subsequent purchasers or mortgagees. (104)

rectangular (government) survey system   A system established in 1785 by the federal government, providing for surveying and describing land by reference to principal meridians and base lines. (70)

redemption   The right of a defaulted property owner to recover property by curing the default. (224)

redemption period   A period of time established by state law during which property owners have the right to redeem their real estate from a foreclosure or tax sale by paying the sales price, interest, and costs. Many states do not have mortgage redemption laws. (224)

redlining   The illegal practice by a lending institution of denying loans or restricting their number for certain areas of a community. (355)

reduction certificate (payoff statement)   The document signed by a lender indicating the amount required to pay a loan balance in full and satisfy the debt; used in the settlement process to protect both the seller's and the buyer's interests. (258)

regression   An appraisal principle that the value of a better-quality property is affected adversely by the presence of a lesser-quality property. (314)

Regulation Z   Implements the Truth in Lending Act (TILA), requiring credit institutions to inform borrowers of the true cost of obtaining credit. (246)

release deed   A document, also known as a *deed of reconveyance*, that transfers all rights given a trustee under a deed of trust loan back to the grantor after the loan has been fully repaid. (258)

release of lien   A lien on a property that is now free from a mortgage. (289)

remainder interest   The remnant of an estate that has been conveyed to take effect and be enjoyed after the termination of a prior estate, such as when an owner conveys a life estate to one party and the remainder to another. (36)

renewal option   A clause in a lease that grants the lessee the privilege of renewing the lease. (334)

rent   A fixed, periodic payment made by a tenant of a property to the owner for possession and use, usually by prior agreement of the parties. (328)

rent schedule   A statement of proposed rental rates, determined by the owner or the property manager or both, based on a building's estimated expenses, market supply and demand, and the owner's long-range goals for the property.

replacement cost   The construction cost at current prices of a property that is not necessarily an exact duplicate of the subject property but serves the same purpose or function as the original. (227)

representation   The role of a real estate professional acting on behalf of a client in a real estate transaction.

reproduction cost   The construction cost at current prices of an exact duplicate of the subject property.

rescission   The practice of one party canceling or terminating a contract, which has the effect of returning the parties to their original positions before the contract was made. (194)

reservation   Something that is retained by the seller (i.e., a life estate or an access easement). (86)

Resolution Trust Corporation (RTC)   Created in 1989 by the Financial Institutions Reform, Recovery, and Enforcement Act (FIRREA) to liquidate the assets of failed savings and loan associations. In 1995, the responsibilities of RTC were transferred to the Savings Association Insurance Fund of the Federal Deposit Insurance Corporation.

restrictive covenant   A clause in a deed that limits the way the real estate ownership may be used. (395)

reverse mortgage   A loan by which a homeowner receives a lump sum, monthly payments, or a line of credit based on the homeowner's equity in the property secured by the mortgage. The loan must be repaid at a prearranged date, upon the death of the owner, or upon the sale of the property. (222)

reversionary interest   The remnant of an estate that the grantor holds after granting a life estate to another person. (36)

reversionary right   The return of the rights of possession and quiet enjoyment to the lessor at the expiration of a lease. (328)

revocation   Canceling or annulling licensed privileges or rights. (190)

right of first refusal   A clause allowing the tenant the opportunity to buy the property before the owner accepts an offer from another party. (334)

right of survivorship   *See* joint tenancy. (51)

right-of-way   The right given by one landowner to another to pass over the land, construct a roadway, or use as a pathway, without actually transferring ownership. (38)

riparian rights   An owner's rights in land that borders on or includes a stream, river, or lake. These rights include access to and use of the water. (22)

risk management   Evaluation and selection of appropriate property and other insurance. (380)

routine maintenance   Day-to-day duties such as cleaning common areas, performing minor carpentry and plumbing adjustments, and providing regularly scheduled upkeep of heating, air-conditioning, and landscaping. (376)

rules and regulations   Real estate licensing authority orders that govern real estate professionals' activities, having the same force and effect as statutory law.

Safe Drinking Water Act   An act to protect public health by authorizing the EPA to set national health-based standards for drinking water. (411)

sale-and-leaseback   A transaction in which the owner sells improved property and, as part of the same transaction, signs a long-term lease to remain in possession of the premises. (245)

sales associate   A person who performs real estate activities while employed by a licensed real estate broker. (2)

sales comparison approach   The process of estimating the value of a property by examining and comparing sales and listings of comparable properties. (315)

sales price   The amount of money paid to a seller for the product sold. (315)

salesperson   *See* sales associate. (2)

satisfaction   Release or discharge when a note has been fully paid, returning to the borrower all interest in the real estate originally conveyed to the lender. Entering this release in the public record shows that the debt has been removed from the property. (91, 213)

satisfaction of mortgage   A document acknowledging the payment of a mortgage debt. (213)

secondary mortgage market   A market for the purchase and sale of existing mortgages, designed to provide greater liquidity for mortgages. Mortgages are first originated in the *primary mortgage market*. (236)

section   A portion of a township under the rectangular (government) survey system. A township is divided into 36 sections, numbered 1 through 36. A section is a square with mile-long sides and an area of one square mile, or 640 acres. (72)

security   *See* collateral. (212)

security deposit   A payment by a tenant, held by the landlord during the lease term, and kept (wholly or partially) on default or on destruction of the premises by the tenant. (332)

seller's broker   The real estate broker who represents only the seller in transactions.

seller's disclosure notice   Documents completed by the seller of a home listing any known issues of the property, including home improvements made.

separate property   Under community property law, property owned solely by either spouse before the marriage, acquired by gift or inheritance during the marriage, or purchased with separate funds after the marriage. (54)

servient tenement   Land on which an easement exists in favor of an adjacent property, called the *dominant tenement*. (39)

setback   The amount of space local zoning regulations require between a lot line and a building. (389)

settlement and transfer   *See* closing. (260)

Settlement Statement (HUD-1)   The special HUD form, recently replaced by a new form created by the Consumer Financial Protection Bureau, that itemized all charges to be paid by a borrower and a seller in connection with the settlement of a real estate transaction. Also called the HUD-1 form.

severalty   Ownership of real property by one person only; also called *sole ownership*. (50)

severance   Changing an item of real estate to personal property by detaching it from the land (e.g., cutting down a tree). (25)

shared appreciation mortgage (SAM)   A mortgage loan in which the lender, in exchange for a loan with a favorable interest rate, participates in the profits (if any) the borrower receives when the property is eventually sold.

short sale   Sale of property in which the sales price is less than the remaining indebtedness. (225)

sick building syndrome (SBS)   An illness caused by poor air quality, typically in large commercial buildings. Symptoms include fatigue, nausea, headache, and sensitivity to odors. (377, 407)

single agency   Agency relationship in which the agent represents only one party to a transaction. (145)

situs   The location of land for legal purposes; the jurisdiction in which land is located. (24)

Small Business Liability Relief and Brownfields Revitalization Act   Law that provides funds to assess and clean up brownfields, clarifies liability protections, and provides tax incentives toward enhancing state and tribal response programs (also known as Brownfields Law). (413)

special agent   One who is authorized by a principal to perform a single act or transaction; a real estate professional is usually a special agent authorized to find a ready, willing, and able buyer for a particular property, when representing a seller, or a special agent authorized to find a suitable property, when representing a buyer. (145)

special assessment   A tax or levy customarily imposed against only those specific parcels of real estate that will benefit from a proposed public improvement like a street or sewer. (293)

special warranty deed   A deed in which the grantor warrants, or guarantees, the title only against defects arising during the period of the grantor's tenure and ownership of the property and not against defects existing before that time, generally using the language, "by, through, or under the grantor but not otherwise." (89)

specific lien   A lien affecting or attaching only to a certain, identified parcel of land or piece of property. (288)

specific performance   A legal action to compel a party to carry out the terms of a contract. (193)

spot survey   A survey that shows the location, size, and shape of buildings on the lot, in addition to the lot's legal description. (75)

spot zoning   Granting a particular parcel a classification that differs from the classification of other land in the immediate area; may be considered illegal.

statute of frauds   That part of a state law that requires certain instruments, such as deeds, real estate sales contracts, and certain leases, to be in writing to be legally enforceable. (188)

statute of limitations   That law pertaining to the period of time within which certain actions must be brought to court. (193)

statutory lien   A lien imposed on property by statute—a tax lien, for example—in contrast to an *equitable lien*, which arises out of common law. (288)

statutory right of redemption   The right of a defaulted property owner to recover the property after its sale by paying the appropriate fees and charges. (293)

statutory year   A year composed of 12 months, with each month consisting of 30 days, for a total of 360 days in the year. Also called a *banker's year*. (279, 449)

steering   The illegal practice of channeling home seekers to particular areas based on their race, national origin, religion, or other protected classification. (354)

stigmatized property   A property that has acquired an undesirable reputation due to an event that occurred on or near it, such as violent crime, gang-related activity, illness, or personal tragedy. Some states restrict the disclosure of information about stigmatized properties. (152)

straight-line depreciation   Depreciation taken periodically in equal amounts over an asset's useful life. (319)

straight loan   A loan in which only interest is paid during the term of the loan, with the entire principal amount due with the final interest payment. (218)

subagent   A cooperating agent working with the broker on behalf of the broker's client. (146)

subdivider   One who buys undeveloped land, divides it into smaller, usable lots and sells the lots to potential users. (394)

subdivision   A tract of land divided by the owner, known as the *subdivider*, into blocks, building lots, and streets according to a recorded subdivision plat, which must comply with local ordinances and regulations. (2)

subdivision and development ordinances Municipal ordinances that establish requirements for subdivisions and development.

subdivision plat *See* plat map. (74)

subject to Buyer takes title of property and makes payments on the existing loan but is not personally obligated to pay the debt in full. Original seller might continue to be liable for debt.

"subject to" A clause in a contract specifying exceptions or contingencies of a purchase. (217)

subjective value The perceived value of an item based on the benefits given to the owner.

sublease *See* subletting. (333)

subletting The leasing of premises by a lessee to a third party for part of the lessee's remaining term. *See* also assignment. (333)

subordination Relegation to a lesser position, usually in respect to a right or security. (218, 289)

subordination agreement A written agreement between holders of liens on a property that changes the priority of mortgage, judgment, and other liens under certain circumstances. (218, 289)

subrogation The right acquired by the title company to any remedy or damages available to the insured when a title company makes a payment to settle a claim covered by a policy. (108)

substitution An appraisal principle that the maximum value of a property tends to be set by the cost of purchasing an equally desirable and valuable substitute property, assuming that no costly delay is encountered in making the substitution. (315)

subsurface rights Ownership rights in a parcel of real estate to the water, minerals, gas, oil, and so forth that lie beneath the surface of the property. (20)

suit for possession A court suit initiated by a landlord to evict a tenant from leased premises after the tenant has breached one of the terms of the lease or has held possession of the property after the lease's expiration. (337)

suit for specific performance *See* specific performance. (193)

suit to quiet title A court action intended to establish or settle the title to a particular property, especially when there is a cloud on the title. (106)

Superfund Popular name of the hazardous-waste cleanup fund established by the Comprehensive Environmental Response, Compensation, and Liability Act (CERCLA). (414)

Superfund Amendments and Reauthorization Act (SARA) An amendatory statute that contains stronger cleanup standards for contaminated sites, increased funding for Superfund, and clarifications of lender liability and innocent landowner immunity. *See* Comprehensive Environmental Response, Compensation, and Liability Act (CERCLA). (415)

supply The amount of goods available for sale in the market. The term is often coupled with *demand*. (7)

supply and demand The appraisal principle that follows the interrelationship of the supply of and demand for real estate. Because appraising is based on economic concepts, this principle recognizes that real property is subject to the influences of the marketplace as with any other commodity. (7)

surety bonds An agreement by an insurance or bonding company to be responsible for certain possible defaults, debts, or obligations incurred by an insured party; in essence, a policy insuring one's personal and/or financial integrity. In the real estate business, a surety bond is generally used to ensure that a particular project will be completed at a certain date or that a contract will be performed as stated. (381)

surface rights Ownership rights in a parcel of real estate that are limited to the surface of the property and do not include the space above it *(air rights)* or the substances below the surface *(subsurface rights)*. (20)

survey The process by which boundaries are measured and land areas are determined; the on-site measurement of lot lines, dimensions, and position of a house on a lot, including the determination of any existing encroachments or easements. (67)

syndicate A combination of people or firms formed to accomplish a business venture of mutual interest by pooling resources. In a *real estate investment syndicate*, the parties own and/or develop property, with the main profit generally arising from the sale of the property. (236)

tacking Concept providing that successive periods of continuous occupation by different parties may be combined to reach the required total number of years needed to establish a claim for a prescriptive easement. (40)

taking Process of land being taken from a property owner for public use through eminent domain with the requirement that the owner be compensated fairly. (43)

tax basis   The point from which gains and losses are figured for tax purposes. (12)

tax credit   An amount by which tax owed is reduced directly. (10)

tax deed   An instrument, similar to a certificate of sale, given to a purchaser at a tax sale. *See also* certificate of sale. (293)

tax levy   The formal action taken to impose a tax, usually by vote of a taxing district's governing body. (292)

tax lien   A charge against property, created by operation of law. Tax liens and assessments take priority over all other liens. (290)

tax sale   A court-ordered sale of real property to raise money to cover delinquent taxes. (293)

taxation   The process by which a government body raises monies to fund its operation. (44)

tenancy by the entirety   The joint ownership, recognized in some states, of property acquired by husband and wife during marriage. Upon the death of one spouse, the survivor becomes the owner of the property. (54)

tenancy in common (TIC)   A form of co-ownership by which each owner holds an undivided interest in real property as if each were sole owner. Each individual owner has the right to partition. Unlike joint tenants, tenants in common have the right of inheritance. (50)

tenant   One who holds or possesses lands or tenements by any kind of right or title.

tenant improvements   Alterations to the interior of a building to meet the functional demands of the tenant. Also known as *build-outs*. (376)

tenant's insurance   Insurance on the personal belongings of tenants. (381)

testamentary trust   A trust that is established by will after one's death. (56)

testate   Having made and left a valid will. (94)

testator   A person who has made a valid will. A woman might be referred to as a *testatrix*, although *testator* can be used for either a man or a woman. (95)

tie-in agreement   Agreement to sell one product only if the buyer purchases another product as well; also called a *tying agreement*. (125)

tiers   Strips of land that are six miles wide, extending east and west and numbered north and south according to their distance from the base line in the rectangular (government) survey system of legal description. (71)

"time is of the essence"   A phrase in a contract that requires the performance of a certain act within a stated period of time. (192)

time-share   A form of ownership interest that may include an estate interest in property and that allows use of the property for a fixed or variable time period. (61)

title   (1) The right to ownership or the ownership of land. (2) The evidence of ownership of land. (84)

title insurance   A policy insuring a property owner or mortgagee against loss by reason of defects in the title to a parcel of real estate, other than encumbrances, defects, and matters specifically excluded by the policy. (108)

title search   The examination of public records relating to real estate to determine the current state of the ownership. (106)

title theory   Principle in which the mortgagor conveys *legal title* to the mortgagee (or some other designated individual) and retains *equitable title* and the *right of possession*. In effect, because the lender holds legal title, the lender has the right to immediate possession of the real estate and rents from the mortgaged property if the mortgagor defaults. (214)

Title VIII of Civil Rights Act of 1968 (Fair Housing Act)   As since amended, the Fair Housing Act prohibits discrimination in housing based on race, color, religion, national origin, sex, familial status, or disability. (347)

Torrens system   A method of evidencing title by registration with the proper public authority, generally called the *registrar*; named for its founder, Sir Robert Torrens. (110)

town house   A type of residential dwelling with two floors that is connected to one or more dwellings by a common wall or walls. Title to the unit and lot vest in the owner who shares a fractional interest with other owners in any common areas. (59)

township   The principal unit of the rectangular (government) survey system. A township is a 6-mile square of 36 square miles. (71)

township lines   All the lines in a rectangular survey system that run east and west, parallel to the base line and six miles apart. (71)

township strips   *See* tier. (71)

trade fixture   An article installed by a tenant under the terms of a lease that is removable by the tenant before the lease expires. (27)

transaction broker   Helps both the buyer and the seller with paperwork and formalities in transferring ownership of real property, but who is not an agent of either party. (149)

transaction coordinator   *See* nonagent. (139, 149)

transfer tax   Tax stamps required to be affixed to a deed by state and/or local law. (91)

triggering terms   Specific credit terms, such as down payment, monthly payment, and amount of finance charge or term of loan. (247)

trust   A fiduciary arrangement whereby property is conveyed to a person or an institution, called a *trustee*, to be held and administered on behalf of another person, called a *beneficiary*. The one who conveys the trust is called the *trustor*. (55)

trust deed   An instrument used to create a mortgage lien by which the borrower conveys title to a trustee, who holds it as security for the benefit of the note holder (the lender); also called a *deed of trust*. (214)

trustee   One to whom something is entrusted and who holds legal title to property and administers the property for the benefit of a beneficiary. Can also be a member of a board entrusted with the administration of an institution or organization, such as a cooperative. (55)

trustee's deed   A deed executed by a trustee conveying land held in a trust. (91)

trustor   A borrower in a deed of trust loan transaction; one who places property in a trust. Also called a grantor or settler. (55)

Truth in Lending Act (TILA)   Federal government regulates the lending practices of mortgage lenders through this act. (246)

unbundling services   Offering only the real estate services that a client requires. (124)

underground storage tanks (USTs)   Commonly found on sites where petroleum products are used or where gas stations and auto repair shops are located, and subject to federal and state regulations. In residential areas, tanks are used to store heating oil. Over time, neglected tanks may leak hazardous substances into the environment. (411)

undivided interest   *See* tenancy in common. (50)

unenforceable contract   A contract that has all the elements of a valid contract, yet neither party can sue the other to force performance of it. For example, an unsigned contract is generally unenforceable. (192)

Uniform Electronic Transactions Act (UETA)   Sets forth rules for entering into an enforceable contract using electronic means. (129)

Uniform Partnership Act   Law that provides for the continuation of an existing business if a partner in a general partnership dies, withdraws, or goes bankrupt. (57)

Uniform Residential Appraisal Report (URAR)   The appraisal form created by Fannie Mae and Freddie Mac that is required for most residential real estate transactions. (305)

Uniform Standards of Professional Appraisal Practice (USPAP)   A set of standards developed by the Appraisal Foundation that details information required for a property appraisal. (303)

unilateral contract   A one-sided contract wherein one party makes a promise so as to induce a second party to do something. The second party is not legally bound to perform; however, if the second party does comply, the first party is obligated to keep the promise. (189)

uniqueness   The idea that no matter how identical they may appear, no two parcels of real estate are ever exactly alike. (7)

unity of ownership   The four unities that are traditionally needed to create a joint tenancy—unity of title, time, interest, and possession. (52)

unity of possession   Co-owners of a tenancy in common are each entitled to possession and use of the entire property, even though each hold only a fractional ownership interest. (52)

universal agent   A person empowered to do anything the principal could do personally. (144)

urea-formaldehyde foam insulation (UFFI)   Insulating foam that can release harmful formaldehyde gases. Formaldehyde causes some individuals to suffer respiratory problems, as well as eye and skin irritations. (408)

usury   Charging interest at a higher rate than the maximum rate established by state law. (211)

VA-guaranteed loan   A mortgage loan on approved property made to a qualified veteran by an authorized lender and guaranteed by the U.S. Department of Veterans Affairs in order to limit the lender's possible loss. (242)

valid contract   A contract that complies with all the essentials of a contract and is binding and enforceable on all parties to it. (191)

value   The power of a good or service to command other goods in exchange for the present worth of future rights to its income or amenities. (312)

variable rate mortgage   A mortgage loan in which the interest rate varies depending on market conditions. (247)

variance   Permission obtained from zoning authorities to build a structure or conduct a use that is expressly prohibited by the current zoning laws; an exception from the zoning ordinances. (392)

vendee   A buyer, usually under the terms of a land contract. (200)

vendor   A seller, usually under the terms of a land contract. (200)

vendor's lien   A lien that belongs to a vendor for the unpaid purchase price of land, where the vendor has not taken any other lien or security beyond the personal obligation of the purchaser. (288)

void contract   A contract that has no legal force or effect because it does not meet the essential elements of a contract. (191)

voidable contract   A contract that seems to be valid on the surface but may be rejected or disaffirmed by one or both of the parties. (191)

volume   The amount of space of a three-dimensional object. (433)

voluntary alienation   *See* alienation. (84)

voluntary lien   A lien placed on property with the knowledge and consent of the property owner. (288)

warranty clause   A part of the deed in which the seller warrants the title conveyed to the buyer.

waste   An improper use or an abuse of a property by a possessor who holds less than fee ownership, such as a tenant, life tenant, or vendee. Such waste ordinarily impairs the value of the land or the interest of the person holding the title or the reversionary rights.

water rights   Common law rights held by owners of land adjacent to rivers, lakes, or oceans; includes restrictions on those rights and land ownership. (22)

water table   The natural level at which the ground is saturated. The water table may be several hundred feet underground or near the surface. (410)

will   A written document, properly witnessed, providing for the transfer of title to property owned by the deceased, called the *testator*. (94)

workers' compensation acts   State laws that require an employer to obtain insurance coverage to protect employees who are injured in the course of their employment. (381)

wraparound loan   A method of refinancing in which the new mortgage is placed in a secondary, or subordinate, position; the new mortgage includes both the unpaid principal balance of the first mortgage and whatever additional sums are advanced by the lender. In essence, it is an additional mortgage in which another lender refinances a borrower by lending an amount over the existing first mortgage amount without disturbing the existence of the first mortgage.

writ of attachment   A document ordered by the court to have a sheriff enter a leased property to give possession back to the owner. (295)

x-bar method   A math tool used to solve percentage problems, indicating what values to multiply or divide to arrive at the unknown value. (440)

zoning   A regulatory tool that helps communities regulate and control how land is used. (389)

zoning board of appeals   A board that must be formed when the local legislature adopts a new zoning law, to provide for property owners to object to the application of the law to their property.

zoning ordinance   An exercise of police power by a municipality to regulate and control the character and use of property.

ANSWER KEY

Unit 1 Quiz

1. **B** The answer is a real estate appraiser. Although real estate professionals, counselors, and inspectors also look closely at a specific property, only an appraiser is qualified to produce a formal opinion of value—an appraisal. (2)

2. **B** The answer is price tends to drop. If demand is constant and supply increases, sellers compete with each other by lowering prices. (7)

3. **D** The answer is governmental monetary policy. Population, demographics, and employment impact demand for a commodity, but governmental monetary policy strongly influences the supply and value of property in a local market. (8)

4. **C** The answer is wage levels and employment opportunities. When wage levels and job expansion are increasing, workers are more likely to buy real estate; when job opportunities are scarce or wage levels low, demand for real estate usually drops. (9)

5. **B** The answer is specializations within the real estate industry. All are specializations in the field of real estate, and every real estate professional must have a basic knowledge of these specialties. (2–3)

6. **D** The answer is fair housing. Fair housing laws prohibit discriminatory practices against protected classes of individuals. (6)

7. **B** The answer is houses will likely become more expensive. The expected arrival of 2,000 employees and their families in a small town will cause sellers to raise their prices in expectation of the greatly increased demand and the long time it takes to build new housing. It becomes a *sellers' market*, and the many buyers will have to compete for the few houses available. (7–8)

8. **A** The answer is real estate counselor. Advising and guiding investors and other buyers is counseling them. Many states require a person to have a real estate license to serve as a real estate advisor/counselor for a fee because it involves skills and duties closely related to real estate brokerage. (4)

9. **D** The answer is mortgage loan originators. Federal law requires mortgage loan originators to qualify for the Nationwide Multistate Licensing System and Registry. (3)

10. **A** The answer is special purpose. Special-purpose properties include schools, churches, cemeteries, and municipal service buildings. (4)

11. **B** The answer is price tends to fall. Under the concept of supply and demand, if demand decreases and supply remains the same, producers need to attract more customers, and so prices fall. (7–8)

12. **B** The answer is capital gain. This is essentially the profit earned from the sale of an asset. (12)

13. **B** The answer is leverage. As a rule, an investor can receive a maximum return from the initial investment by making a small down payment, paying a low interest rate, and spreading mortgage payments over as long a period as possible. (11)

14. **B** The answer is developmental. Residential, agricultural, and industrial are all classifications of real estate. Development can occur with any of these types. (3)

15. **D** The answer is monetary policy. Government monetary policies affect the supply of land available for development. Population, demographics, and wage levels affect demand for real estate. (8)

16. **C** The answer is degree of standardization of the property's price. Uniqueness and immobility of product and parties to the transaction, not the standardization of the product price, govern the way the market reacts to the pressures of supply and demand. (8–9)

17. **B** The answer is a home inspector. The home inspector, who prepares an analytical report of a visual inspection of the property's structure and systems, is becoming more important in the real estate transaction as more consumers rely on these reports when buying property. (3)

18. **A** The answer is cost recovery. Depreciation, or cost recovery, allows an investor to recover the cost of an income-producing asset through tax deductions over the asset's useful life. (12)

19. **C**   The answer is a property manager. The basic responsibility of the property manager is to protect the owner's investment and maximize the return on investment. (2–3)

20. **B**   The answer is demographics. Information about members of a population group is called demographics. These factors are important because they contribute to the amount and type of housing needed. (9)

Unit 2 Quiz

1. **C**   The answer is annual crops. Common law treats annual crops, those that must be planted each year, as the personal property of the person who planted and tended them. When a farm is sold, trees, air rights, and mineral rights may all convey, but the annual crops (*fructus industriales* or emblements)—lacking effective contractual agreement to the contrary—are still the personal property of the tenant farmer or other person who planted them. The farmer may return and harvest them in season. (25)

2. **B**   The answer is the shelves and tables are trade fixtures and may be properly removed by the tenant before the lease expires, and the tenant would be responsible to the landlord for any damage that the removal causes to the premises. Common law protects business tenants who install fixtures for their business by treating these trade fixtures as tenants' personal property and giving tenants the right to remove the fixtures before the end of the lease. Any damage to the building due to removal of the fixtures must be repaired by the departing tenant. A real estate professional who participates in the sale of business properties should make known to purchasers what, if any, trade fixtures will not convey with the building. (27)

3. **C**   The answer is uniqueness. The characteristics of each property differ from one another; this is also called heterogeneity. (19)

4. **C**   The answer is chattels. Fixtures, fructus naturales, and realty are all real property. (24)

5. **C**   The answer is doctrine of prior appropriation. Many states whose water is in relatively short supply have passed statutes authorizing a system of prior appropriation in which owners downstream do not necessarily have to wait for "what's left" after those upstream have drawn their fill. Priority—who is allowed to appropriate water first—is established, instead, by the date of approved filing and continued conformity with any rules and limitations on use imposed by the jurisdiction. (23)

6. **B**   The answer is the heir of the deceased inherits the property as is. The daughter inherits exactly what the man owned just before his death: a location on the earth's surface, everything below it to the center of the earth, and the space above it toward infinity. (18)

7. **A**   The answer is the cost of the item when it was purchased. The overall test in determining whether an item is a fixture or real property is the intention of the person installing it, how uniquely adapted the item is to the property in which it is installed, how the item was installed and the damage its removal would cause, and what the parties have agreed to. The original cost of the installation, although important to one or the other of the parties, is not considered in this decision. (26)

8. **A**   The answer is indestructibility. The ability to make improvements, preference for the area, and relative scarcity of similar property are all economic matters. The land's indestructibility is a physical matter, even though it is subject to both natural and human forces. (19)

9. **A**   The answer is severance. When we sever something, we cut it loose. Severing (felling) a tree from its roots converts it from realty—real(proper)ty—to personalty—personal(proper)ty. The process is called severance. (25)

10. **A**   The answer is ceiling fans are usually considered real estate. Whatever fixtures are present in the structure at the time of contract, and not mentioned in the contract, convey with the property (pass to the purchaser). Replacement fixtures are not personal property of the resident; they became real estate when annexed (attached) to the building. (25)

11. **C**   The answer is subsurface rights. *Sub* means under or beneath. *Subsurface* then, is below the surface—the place where most minerals are found. (20)

12. **B**   The answer is personal property. The lumber will become realty if and when it is later affixed in the course of construction. Until then, it is personal property—a chattel—of the landowner. (24)

13. **C**   The answer is a fixture or personal property. The overall test in determining whether an item is a fixture (real property) is the intention of the person installing it, how uniquely adapted the item is to the property in which it is installed, how item was installed and the damage its removal would cause, the relationship of the parties, and what the parties have agreed to. (25–26)

14. **D** The answer is appurtenances. *Appurtenances* are rights or privileges associated with the property, although not necessarily part of the property. (20)

15. **A** The answer is the company's action constitutes improvement of the property. The technical term *improvement* refers to any permanent structure—building, fence, shed, or prefabricated structure—erected on a property, despite the inherent value of the structure or what is stored in it. (24)

16. **C** The answer is riparian rights. Riparian rights are common law rights granted owners of land along the course of a river. (22)

17. **B** The answer is exclude utility meter readers. The right of exclusion generally allows an owner to exclude someone else from entering the property, but this does not include the right to exclude the utility meter reader. (19)

18. **C** The answer is personalty. An item used in conducting business is considered a trade fixture and can be removed by the tenant. It is considered personal property (personalty) even though it may be attached to a building. (22)

19. **B** The answer is area preference. Area preference, or location, is also known as situs and is the single most important economic characteristic of land. (24)

20. **D** The answer is patio furniture. Personal property, such as patio furniture, is movable. A fireplace, bathtubs, and awnings are all attached to the property and considered real property. (24–25)

Unit 3 Quiz

1. **B** The answer is eminent domain. The right is eminent domain; the process by which the right is exercised is condemnation. Escheat and police power are other examples of government limitations on rights of private ownership. (42–43)

2. **A** The answer is fee simple absolute. Fee simple is an absolute ownership—an inheritable interest "with no strings attached." A life estate is noninheritable; fee on condition subsequent and determinable fees are both estates involving another person with an interest called "possibility of (either reverter or) re-entry." (35)

3. **C** The answer is a fee simple determinable. A determinable fee estate has a special limitation and may end automatically if there is noncompliance with that stipulation. Language such as *so long as* or *while* characterize this estate. The hospital's

ownership of the lot would come to an end if the property were to be no longer used for hospital purposes, and the lot would immediately become the property of the former owner or that owner's heirs. (35)

4. **C** The answer is the servient tenement. Your driveway is on the property over which the easement runs and is the servient tenement. The adjacent property owned by the neighbors is known as the dominant tenement. (39)

5. **C** The answer is a personal privilege. A *license* is a personal, revocable right of use. It is temporary in that it can be withdrawn at will by the one who issued it. (41)

6. **D** The answer is runs with the land. An easement appurtenant can only be created if the adjacent properties involved have different owners. This easement runs with the land and transfers with the deed. (39)

7. **C** The answer is eminent domain. Eminent domain is the right of the government to acquire privately owned real estate for public use. (42–43)

8. **A** The answer is remainder. The four governmental powers that limit private rights to ownership of land are represented by the acronym PETE (police power, eminent domain, taxation, and escheat). (42)

9. **B** The answer is an easement. An *easement* is a right of use or passage, not of ownership—nor is it is an example of encroachment or the exercise of a government's police power. (38–39)

10. **C** The answer is homestead. Homestead rights are granted by statute in some states to provide some protection to debtors and their families against the execution of judgment liens on their homes by the action of unsecured creditors. (37)

11. **B** The answer is a remainder. Until the owner dies, the church will have a remainder interest. The owner reserved a life estate. The church may legally sell its future (remainder) interest, even during the lifetime of the life tenant. (36)

12. **B** The answer is an encroachment. To build over a property line is to encroach on the property of another. (41)

13. **C** The answer is homestead rights. Homestead rights are granted by statute in some states to provide some protection to debtors and their families against the execution of judgment liens on their homes by the action of unsecured creditors. (37)

14. **D**   The answer is a license. Such permission given to an individual is personal, nontransferable, and can be withdrawn. (41)

15. **B**   The answer is occupied as the family home. In many states, a portion of the area or value of this land is protected or exempt from judgments for debts other than those secured by the property. (37)

16. **B**   The answer is a lien. Unpaid real estate taxes are a lien on the property because they are a charge against the property that provides security for a debt or an obligation of the property owner. (38)

17. **A**   The answer is an easement in gross. *Easements in gross* are individual rights to use someone's land, as in the case of the utility company. A commercial (but not a personal) easement in gross can be assigned, conveyed, and inherited. (39)

18. **A**   The answer is escheat. Escheat is a process by which the state may acquire privately owned real or personal property. State laws provide for ownership to transfer, or escheat, to the state when an owner dies and leaves no heirs (as defined by the law) and there is no will or living trust instrument that directs how the real estate is to be distributed. (44)

19. **A**   The answer is easement by necessity. An easement by necessity arises when there is no ingress or egress (entry or exit) from one piece of property without crossing over a parcel of land owned by another. An easement of necessity is not merely for convenience or imposed to validate a shortcut. (40)

20. **D**   The answer is release of the right of easement to the dominant tenement. An easement is terminated when the owner of the dominant tenement releases that right to the owner of the servient tenement. (39)

Unit 4 Quiz

1. **D**   The answer is joint tenancy. A joint tenancy can only be created by an intentional act and requires the four unities—PITT—to be present. (52)

2. **B**   The answer is tenants in common. When joint tenancy is not clearly prescribed by the deed, grantees take title as tenants in common—to avoid accidental joint tenancy. Unmarried persons are unable to hold community property or be tenants by the entirety because both are reserved for married couples. (50–51)

3. **A**   The answer is the other two owners remain joint tenants. When one of three joint tenants sells to a new person, the other two remain joint tenants with respect to each other. The new person is a tenant in common, and not owner in severalty of the entire property because severalty is sole ownership. (53)

4. **B**   The answer is condominium. When a person owns part of a development in fee and a percentage of the rest in common with the other unit owners, this is condominium ownership. (58)

5. **C**   The answer is a trustee. The trustor creates a trust that is held for the benefit of the beneficiary who will ultimately benefit from the trust. A third party, the trustee, holds legal title to the property and carries out the trustor's instructions. (55)

6. **D**   The answer is community property. This arrangement falls under community property law, which is found—with some variations in details—in Arizona, California, Idaho, Louisiana, Nevada, New Mexico, Texas, Washington, Wisconsin, and as an option in Alaska. (54)

7. **B**   The answer is a tenant in common. If the deceased had been a joint tenant, the property would not have passed to an heir as prescribed in her will because joint tenancy supersedes a will. The deceased also was not a tenant by the entirety, a category reserved for spouses. Nor was the deceased an owner in severalty because that requires property to be held by only one person. (50)

8. **A**   The answer is a trust. Trusts protect beneficiaries. Partnerships can protect limited partners; corporations can protect stockholder-owners. (55)

9. **D**   The answer is cooperative. In a cooperative, a corporation holds title to the property and offers stock shares to the residents, who then receive a proprietary lease to the apartment. (60–61)

10. **C**   The answer is time-share. When a person holds an interest in property for a stated time each year, that person is sharing the property according to a time plan. It is a time-share. (61)

11. **C**   The answer is severalty. The term *person* does not always refer to a natural individual—a human; the law regards a corporation as an artificial person. Because this is so, a corporation can own real estate in severalty (alone). (50)

12. **D**   The answer is severalty. *Severalty ownership* is ownership by one person severed—cut off—from all others. (50)

13. **D** The answer is an estate by the entirety. Married persons may own property together as tenants in common, joint tenants, or as community property. Being more than one person, a couple cannot own in severalty. The right of survivorship is a distinguishing feature of tenancy by the entirety, which some states recognize as a form of joint tenancy reserved for a married couple. (54-55)

14. **B** The answer is cooperative unit ownership. Because it involves receiving shares of stock and a leasehold—both of which are considered by common law to be personal property—cooperative ownership is personal, not real, property. (60–61)

15. **B** The answer is joint tenancy. Upon the death of one party in a joint tenancy arrangement, all remaining interests do not pass to the heirs or according to the will but to the surviving joint tenant. (53)

16. **C** The answer is shareholder stock. The documents that show ownership in a cooperative are shares of stock in the cooperative corporation and a proprietary lease. (60)

17. **B** The answer is a time-share. A real property interest and the right to use the facilities for a certain period of time is called a time-share. (61)

18. **B** The answer is the last survivor becomes a severalty owner. Tenancy by the entirety is a type of joint tenancy recognized by some states that is reserved for married couples. In both, there is a right of survivorship. The last survivor becomes sole (severalty) owner. (54)

19. **B** The answer is ownership in severalty. When just one individual owns property, the form of ownership is known as ownership in severalty. (50)

20. **A** The answer is the surviving owner or owners. *Survivorship* means that the interest of a deceased cotenant will pass to, and be divided equally among, the still-living (surviving) cotenants. (54)

Unit 5 Quiz

1. **B** The answer is the N½ of the NE¼ of the SW¼ and the SE¼ of the NW¼. The location and size of a property can be determined using the rectangular survey system. (73)

2. **D** The answer is within the rectangular survey system area in which the land being surveyed is located. No matter how many ranges or tiers it takes, the description must always refer to the principal

meridian and the base line of the survey system area in which the land being described is located. (70)

3. **D** The answer is 80. A section contains 640 acres. A ½ of ¼ of 640 equals 80 acres. Using decimals, the equation is $0.5 \times 0.25 \times 640 = 80$. (77)

4. **B** The answer is metes and bounds. Monuments are the turning points in the metes-and-bounds method of describing property. In this method, natural, tangible features, such as a distinctive rock or a great tree, were sometimes used as monuments. The path of a stream might serve as all or part of a boundary line. *Metes* means distance; *bounds* refers to direction (not boundaries). The description gives distance in a compass direction from the point of beginning (POB) and then from each succeeding monument, until it returns to the POB. (76–77)

5. **C** The answer is Section 36. Starting with the upper left corner as number 1, sections of a township are numbered right to left, left to right, right to left, and so on until reaching number 36. (72)

6. **C** The answer is C. Starting with the upper left corner as number 1, sections of a township are numbered right to left, left to right, right to left, and so on until reaching number 36. (72)

7. **A** The answer is Section 7. Starting with the upper left corner as number 1, sections of a township are numbered right to left, left to right, right to left, and so on until reaching number 36. (72)

8. **A** The answer is Section 1. Starting with the upper left corner as number 1, sections of a township are numbered right to left, left to right, right to left, and so on until reaching number 36. (72)

9. **A** The answer is Area 1. The location and size of a property can be determined using the rectangular survey system. (73)

10. **C** The answer is $46,827. An acre consists of 43,560 square feet; therefore, a half-acre has 21,780 square feet. If each square foot sells for $2.15, 21,780 sq. ft. × $2.15 per sq. ft. = $46,827. (77)

11. **A** The answer is 80 acres. The area described is a triangle formed when a quarter of a section is cut from one corner to the opposite corner. A section has 640 acres, a quarter-section has 160 acres, and half of that quarter has 80 acres. (77)

12. **D** The answer is $180,000. Disregard all elements of the description except those showing area. It is a quarter of a quarter of a section, or ¹⁄₁₆ of 640, or 40

acres. When sold, each acre brought $4,500, so the gross selling price is calculated as follows: 40 acres × $4,500 = $180,000. (77)

13. **C** The answer is a principal meridian. A property description based on the rectangular survey system must always make reference to the principal meridian and the base line of the survey system area in which the property lies. This description makes no reference to a principal meridian. (70)

14. **B** The answer is $6,000. Price divided by area (in square feet) gives cost per square foot. The area is 4.5 times the size of one acre, or 4.5 × 43,560 sq. ft. = 196,020 sq. ft. Then, $78,400 divided by 196,020 sq. ft. = $0.3996 (essentially, $0.40) per square foot. Determining the purchase price of a 100-by-150-foot lot at the same cost per square foot requires finding the area of the lot: 100 × 150 = 15,000 sq. ft. Multiply this area by $0.40: 15,000 sq. ft. × $0.40 = $6,000. (77)

15. **B** The answer is base lines, principal meridians, and townships. Base lines, meridians, and townships are elements of the rectangular survey system, not the metes-and-bounds system. (70–71)

16. **B** The answer is 81. The area of ten acres in square feet is figured as follows: 10 acres × 43,560 sq. ft. = 435,600 sq. ft. Reserving 26,000 square feet for roads leaves 409,600 square feet. The area of each lot is to be not less than 5,000 square feet: 50' ×100' = 5,000 sq. ft. Divide the available square footage by the square footage needed for each lot: 409,600 sq. ft. ÷ 5,000 square feet = 81.92. Because each lot must be "not less than 50 feet × 100 feet," the property can be subdivided into 81 such lots (77)

17. **B** The answer is 2.94. The parcel is 256,000 square feet: 400' × 640' = 256,000 sq. ft. Half of it is 128,000 square feet. Each acre requires 43,560 square feet. Therefore: 128,000 sq. ft. ÷ 43,560 sq. ft. per acre = 2.938 acres (rounded to three decimal places). The nearest answer is 2.94. (77)

18. **B** The answer is four miles. The shortest distance from Section 1 to Section 36 is from the bottom of Section 1 to the top of Section 36, or four miles. (72)

19. **B** The answer is 16. Section 16 is one of the centrally located sections in the standard township and is designated as the school section. (72)

20. **C** The answer is street address. A legal description is a precise method of identifying a parcel of land and includes metes-and-bounds, rectangular survey, and lot-and-block as methods that can be used for identification. A street address is not a legal description and, therefore, not as precise. (67–68)

Unit 6 Quiz

1. **A** The answer is state law. Although all the listed items influence it somewhat, state law has the greatest influence on requirements for a valid real property conveyance. (95)

2. **A** The answer is the grantor. Either the grantor, or someone acting under the grantor's authority, must execute (sign) every deed, and the grantor must have legal capacity to do so. (84)

3. **D** The answer is voidable. Real estate contracts entered into by minors are generally voidable by the minor until the minor reaches the age of majority—18 in most states—or shortly thereafter. (85)

4. **A** The answer is a power of attorney. That document is a power of attorney; the person named in it is an attorney-in-fact. Deeds do not authorize one person to act for another. (87)

5. **B** The answer is general warranty. In the general warranty—often just called warranty—deed, the grantor makes more promises and gives the grantee more covenants than in any other deed. (88)

6. **A** The answer is special warranty. The quoted granting clause does not use the word *quitclaim* but does use the word *convey*, so it is not a quitclaim deed. It does not use the words *warrant generally*, so it is not a general warranty deed, and it does not use the phrase *bargain and sell*. A special warranty deed uses such words as *remise*, *alienate*, and *convey*. (89)

7. **D** The answer is ensures that the title will be good against the title claims of third parties. *Quiet enjoyment* means freedom from claims of third parties—persons other than grantor and grantee. (89)

8. **B** The answer is bargain and sale. By giving a bargain and sale deed, the grantor implies ownership and possession of the property, but there are no express warranties against encumbrances. (89)

9. **C** The answer is Step 3. Title in this case was transferred upon delivery and acceptance of the deed. At that moment, the deed was binding between the parties. The purchaser, when later recording the deed, was then also protected against third parties. (88)

10. **B**   The answer is an acknowledgment. P gave this acknowledgment as to the validity and voluntary nature of P's signature to a notary. The notary took P's acknowledgment and attached a seal. (87)

11. **C**   The answer is involuntary alienation. Transfer of title by devise (will), descent (death intestate), or escheat (for lack of a will and lack of heirs) all occur after death. Involuntary alienation, such as condemnation, foreclosure sale, or tax sale, can occur during a person's lifetime. (92)

12. **B**   The answer is adverse possession. Adverse possession is (hostile) possession of real estate without the permission of the owner and contrary to the owner's best interests. If it continues in an open, conspicuous (notorious) way for the time set by statute (the statutory period), the adverse possessor may take legal action to be declared the owner on the basis of all these facts. (93)

13. **D**   The answer is involuntary alienation. The right of eminent domain allows a government entity to compel the transfer of a property to that entity for a price set by court process—condemnation. This transfer of title (alienation) is forced and so is involuntary. When a person dies without a will (intestate) and without heirs, the property passes (escheats) to the state. This process was neither planned nor initiated by the owner before death and so is classified as involuntary. (92)

14. **A**   The answer is further assurances. Any promise to obtain documents to make the title good is the covenant of further assurance. The covenants of quiet enjoyment, seisin, and warranty forever are not addressed. (89)

15. **A**   The answer is warranty forever. The grantor promises to compensate the grantee for the loss sustained if the title fails at any time in the future in the covenant of warranty forever. (89)

16. **C**   The answer is intestate. A person who dies testate leaves a valid will; one who dies intestate does not. A person who makes a last will and testament is a testator. A devisee is one who receives a gift of real estate (a devise) through a will. A legatee is one who receives a gift of personal property (legacy) through a will. (93)

17. **D**   The answer is will. A will transfers title to real estate upon the death of the testator. Deeds must be delivered and accepted during the lifetime of the grantor to transfer title. (94–95)

18. **C**   The answer is according to the state laws of descent. A requirement for a valid will is mental competency of the testator at the time of writing the will. Because of mental incompetence, the owner in question died without a valid will. Consequently,

the property will pass to people chosen by state law (statute) to receive property when a decedent has no will (dies intestate). (94)

19. **C**   The answer is in both the county where the decedent resided and the county in which the property is located. There will be two probates conducted: one in the county where the decedent resided and another in the county where the real estate is located. (96–97)

20. **D**   The answer is the habendum clause. The habendum clause defines or explains the ownership to be enjoyed by the grantee, and its provisions must agree with those stated in the granting clause. The habendum clause begins with the words *to have and to hold*. (86)

Unit 7 Quiz

1. **A**   The answer is anyone. Real estate records are public records, open to all members of the public. (104)

2. **A**   The answer is recording gives constructive notice to the world of the rights and interests claimed by a party in a particular parcel of real estate. The recording of an instrument affecting real estate puts the transaction into the public record so that anyone interested in the title of a parcel will know where to look. *Constructive notice* means that everyone is charged with knowledge of such documents. (104)

3. **C**   The answer is the seller did not mortgage the property. The fact that no mortgage is on record against the property indicates, with a reasonable degree of certainty, that the seller did not mortgage the property. (106–107)

4. **A**   The answer is priority. Time of recordation is an important consideration in establishing the priority of claims in the event of a sale. (105)

5. **A**   The answer is the buyer. Constructive notice can be given in either or both of two ways: taking possession and/or recording one's deed. The buyer took possession. The relative who purchased the property from the seller's heirs was responsible for both checking the public records (which still showed the seller as owner because the buyer had not yet recorded the purchase) and visiting the property to inquire into the rights of any parties in possession. The relative-purchaser's investigation would have revealed that the seller's heirs did not have the right to sell the property in question. (104)

6. **D**   The answer is can be sold if a buyer agrees to take it subject to the encumbrances. A buyer can agree to purchase property with existing encumbrances, such as a lien that the purchaser will assume. (106–107)

7. **D**   The answer is deed to the current owner signed by the last seller. The existence of a deed to the current owner is not evidence that the owner actually received title. The absence of any deed, however, would indicate that the owner probably does not have title. A favorable attorney's opinion based on examination of an abstract (the report of a title search) and a policy of title insurance are strong evidence of title held by the owner. (108)

8. **A**   The answer is the record of a property's ownership. *Chain of title* is the entire history, or record, of transactions affecting a property, while an *abstract* is a summary of relevant facts found when examining the history. Title insurance is used to protect against defects in the record of a property's ownership and is issued only after a title examination, which evaluates the public records of the property. (105–106)

9. **C**   The answer is a marketable title. Title that is good enough that a reasonably well-informed person would accept it is called marketable title. (107)

10. **A**   The answer is searches the public records and then summarizes the events and proceedings that affect title. Abstractors search public records concerning property and prepare a relatively brief, written summary of their findings. This report is the abstract of title. Title insurance companies and attorneys who are asked to give an opinion of title rely on these abstracts. (106)

11. **C**   The answer is they do not need the original deed if it has been recorded. If the homeowners' deed was copied into the public record after they received it, that copy is all that is needed to start a title search. The original is not needed. (104–105)

12. **C**   The answer is lenders. A mortgagee title policy protects the mortgagee—the lender. An owner's policy protects the owner, heirs, and devisees. (108–109)

13. **A**   The answer is improperly delivered deeds. The rights of persons in possession (prior to purchase) are not covered by the basic title insurance policy, but they are covered by extended coverage policies. Changes in land use related to zoning are not covered in any type of title insurance. Standard coverage will protect against improperly delivered deeds. (109–110)

14. **C**   The answer is an abstract of title. An abstract of title summarizes the various events and proceedings that affected the title throughout its history. (106)

15. **C**   The answer is unrecorded rights of parties in possession. All are covered except unrecorded rights of parties in possession. These are covered by an extended coverage policy. (109)

16. **A**   The answer is policies of title insurance. Deeds are never considered title evidence. Policies of title insurance provide the best title evidence. (108)

17. **C**   The answer is they guarantee marketable title. Proof of ownership is evidence that title is marketable. Such proof, while it cannot be found in public records, can be assured through a certificate of title, title insurance, or a Torrens certificate. (107)

18. **A**   The answer is C has been given constructive notice of the prior sale because B promptly recorded the deed. C is presumed to know all these facts, even if C doesn't examine the public record and therefore never gets actual notice of the sale to B. Actual notice to a buyer is not necessary if a deed has been recorded. The courts construe recording of a deed as notice to the world. C is construed (i.e., considered) to have notice. C has no claim to the property that B owns, even if C later "buys" it from B. Recording the deed to real estate gives constructive notice to the world (which includes C) of the grantee's (B's) claim of ownership. (105)

19. **B**   The answer is to ensure that the seller can deliver marketable title. Title insurance is considered the best defense of title and is assurance that the grantee is actually acquiring ownership and that the title is marketable. (108)

20. **C**   The answer is the amount of coverage is commensurate with the loan amount. A lender's policy is used for the benefit of the mortgagee. The amount of coverage depends on the amount of the mortgage loan and is decreased as the loan balance is reduced. (109)

Unit 8 Quiz

1. **B**   The answer is the client must make an express or implied agreement to pay a commission to the broker. A broker's contract of employment by a client is the listing or buyer representation agreement signed by them both. A valid employment agreement is one of the usual requirements in a suit for a brokerage commission; it is proof of employment. (117–118)

2. **C**   The answer is independent contractors. Most real estate sales associates (whether licensed as brokers or salespersons) are said to be independent contractors. They receive gross earnings—paid as though they were self-employed—with no withholding of

income taxes or employer contributions to Social Security or Medicare, workers' compensation, and unemployment insurance. (119)

3. **B** The answer is an employee. Because her earnings were more than half in hourly wages, the IRS would not consider her to be an independent contractor within the definition of a qualified real estate agent, but would treat her as an employee of the broker. (118)

4. **B** The answer is work set hours. An employee not only accepts the actual duties assigned by the employer but also agrees to the manner in which the employer wants them performed. (118)

5. **A** The answer is Terry has a real estate license. Most states have very specific rules about what a licensed assistant and an unlicensed assistant may do and how they can be compensated. Usually, an unlicensed personal assistant working for a sales associate can be paid by the sales associate, but a licensed personal assistant working for a sales associate must be paid by the employing broker. (120)

6. **D** The answer is conduct in compliance with statutory law and regulations. Brokers may dictate behavior as it complies to laws and regulations, but they may not dictate working schedules or attendance at sales meetings. (118–119)

7. **D** The answer is $270,000 plus attorney's fees and costs. Under federal law, victims of such activities in restraint of trade (antitrust activities) are entitled to treble (triple) damages plus attorney's fees and costs if the alleged perpetrators are found guilty. (125)

8. **A** The answer is the agreement does not violate antitrust laws. Because both sales associates are in the same firm, their agreement is not an intercompany agreement to allocate markets; it is merely fixing responsibility within one company and is quite proper and not subject to antitrust law. (125)

9. **C** The answer is the rules and regulations have the same force and effect as the license law itself. Each state has a licensing authority with power to issue licenses and create regulations that enforce the statutes of the real estate law. (116)

10. **D** The answer is a member of the National Association of REALTORS® (NAR). People are licensed by their respective states to be real estate brokers or salespersons (also called sales associates or associate licensees). A licensee who then joins the National Association of REALTORS® is called a REALTOR®. (125)

11. **D** The answer is the broker may, as a matter of office policy, legally set the minimum commission rate acceptable for the firm. Brokers have the right to set commissions within their own firm. This is not an antitrust violation. Sales associates who wish to continue with that broker can be required to comply. (124)

12. **A** The answer is $14,575. The associate's income statement for the month: $11,370 + $6,875 = $18,245 total earnings. $1,500 desk fee + $2,170 other = $3,670 total expenses. $18,245 total earnings – $3,670 total expenses = $14,575 net earnings. (122)

13. **C** The answer is $6,929.68. Amount the listing sales associate's broker received: $329,985 × 5% × 60% = $9,899.55 Amount the listing broker kept: $9,899.55 × 30% = $2969.87 (rounded to the nearest cent). The sales associate's earnings: $9,899.55 – $2,969.87 = $6,929.68. (122)

14. **B** The answer is $6,621.25. Total commission to the firm: $234,500 × 6.5% = $15,242.50. The sales associate's commission is computed in three parts: (1) Use $2,500 of the $15,242.50 for a commission at 30% = $750. (2) Use another $5,000 of the $15,242.50 for commission at 40% = $2,000. So far, the sales associate has received commissions on $7,500: $2,500 + $5,000. The licensee now gets 50 percent commission on the $7,742.50 that is left: $15,242.50 – $7,500 = $7,742.50. (3) The commission on $7,742.50 at 50% = $3,871.25. Total of three parts of the sales associate's commission: $750 + $2,000 + $3,871.25 = $6,621.25. (122)

15. **D** The answer is UETA. The law sets forth basic rules for entering an enforceable contract using electronic means. The primary purpose of UETA is to remove barriers in electronic commerce that would otherwise prevent enforceability of contracts. (129)

16. **C** The answer is mutual agreement with the broker. All commissions must be paid through the broker, and the amount the sales associate receives is set by mutual agreement between these two parties. (121)

17. **C** The answer is price-fixing. Antitrust laws prohibit group boycotting, allocation of customers and markets, tie-in agreements, and price-fixing. Price-fixing occurs when competing brokers set a standard commission rate. (124)

18. **B** The answer is procuring cause. A broker who starts a chain of events that results in a sale and does so without abandoning the transaction, may be considered the procuring cause of sale. (121)

19. **B**   The answer is perform all work unsupervised by the managing broker. The IRS's three requirements to be treated as a qualified real estate agent, and thus self-employed, are that the real estate professional (1) is a real estate licensee, (2) has a written agreement with the broker indicating the licensee will not be treated as an employee by broker contributions to Social Security or the withholding of income taxes, and (3) earns a substantial portion of income from the firm in commissions, not wages. An independent contractor is not free from supervision by the managing broker. (118–119)

20. **D**   The answer is a negotiated share of commissions on transactions. An independent contractor may not receive any employee benefits and must not be treated as an employee for federal tax purposes. An independent contractor may negotiate with the broker for commissions on transactions. (118–119)

Unit 9 Quiz

1. **D**   The answer is the agent's relationship to the principal. The relationship of the agent to the principal involves care, obedience, loyalty, disclosure, accounting, and confidentiality (COLD AC)—a fiduciary relationship. A person with legal power to act for another is an *attorney-in-fact* most real estate agents do not have such power. (142)

2. **A**   The answer is special. A broker serves a client—either a buyer or a seller—usually by performing the specific brokerage act spelled out in the employment contract (representation agreement). A specific assignment creates a special agency. (145)

3. **A**   The answer is the broker is obligated to render loyalty to the seller. Loyalty to the client-seller requires confidentiality—not revealing confidential information; it involves obedience—not publishing a price different from the one set by the client; and it requires disclosure of any fact or action which might affect the principal or the relationship between the agent and principal. (143)

4. **B**   The answer is the seller is the broker's client; the buyer is a customer. One who lists property with a broker is the broker's client. A prospective purchaser who refuses buyer representation is a customer. Customers are not owed fiduciary duties but may later contract with the broker for buyer representation. (150)

5. **C**   The answer is both parties consent in writing to the dual agency. Dual agency requires nothing less than written, informed consent from both parties.

Any family relationship of the parties or whether they have legal representation does not change this rule. (147)

6. **B**   The answer is the owner declares personal bankruptcy. Common law holds that the bankruptcy of either the broker or the seller ends the agency relationship created by the listing. (149)

7. **D**   The answer is the buyer and the seller are represented by the same company. Designated agency is a process that accommodates an in-house sale in which two different sales associates of the same broker are involved. The broker designates one sales associate to represent the seller and one sales associate to represent the buyer. (149)

8. **D**   The answer is all lawful instructions of the owner. Lawful instructions from one's broker require obedience. An agency statute may modify aspects of the common law of agency. Caveat emptor is a warning to purchasers, not brokers. (142–143)

9. **C**   The answer is the buyer wanted to work with a new agent, but the terms of agency had not yet expired and the current agent did not agree to terminate. Termination of agency requires mutual agreement by all parties to cancel the contract. (149)

10. **C**   The answer is disclosure was improper and possibly illegal, regardless of the agent's motive. Such action is an example of the agent's failure to maintain confidentiality—a breach of the agent's fiduciary duty. (144)

11. **C**   The answer is the seller and the buyer must be informed of the situation and agree in writing to the broker's representing both of them. Both buyer and seller must give informed, generally written, consent for dual representation. (147–148)

12. **C**   The answer is it is part of a body of law established by tradition and court decisions. The basic framework of the agency law that governs the legal responsibilities of real estate brokers to the people they represent is known as *common law*. (138)

13. **C**   The answer is a transactional brokerage. A nonagent (transactional broker, facilitator, coordinator, or contract broker) is not an agent of either party. A nonagent's job is simply to help both the buyer and the seller with the necessary paperwork and formalities involved in transferring ownership of real property. (149)

14. **A**   The answer is care. The broker was careless in failing to check zoning for a proposed business. To be careless is to fail to use proper care. (142)

15. **D** The answer is the broker is merely puffing. The broker was puffing—stating something that anyone with common sense and open eyes would know to be an exaggeration. (150)

16. **B** The answer is disclosure. The agent's duty of disclosure requires that the principal be informed of all facts or information that might affect a transaction. (143)

17. **A** The answer is a broker acting for both parties in the same transaction. In dual agency, the agent represents two principals in the same transaction. Because the agency originates with the broker, dual agency arises when the broker is the agent of both parties to a transaction, such as the buyer *and* the seller. (147)

18. **C** The answer is a fiduciary. The client in an agency relationship is the principal to whom the agent gives advice and counsel. The agency agreement usually authorizes the broker to act for the principal. The agent's fiduciary relationship of trust and confidence with the principal means that the broker owes the principal certain specific duties. (142)

19. **A** The answer is must promote and safeguard the seller's best interests. A broker acting as the agent of the seller is responsible to the seller and must promote and safeguard the seller's best interest. (139)

20. **D** The answer is both parties have been informed and agree in writing to the dual representation. Real estate licensing laws that permit dual agency typically require that the buyer and the seller must be *informed* of the nature of the proposed relationship and give *written consent* to the broker's representation of both parties in the same transaction. (147–148)

Unit 10 Quiz

1. **A** The answer is the broker. Only a licensed broker may enter into brokerage agreements. The broker's sales associates have authority only to assist in negotiating the agreements. The sales associate is the agent of the broker, but only the broker is the agent of the client and a party to the representation agreement. The sales associate is not a party to it. (160)

2. **C** The answer is both types of listings give the responsibility of representing the seller to one broker only. Each listing is exclusive, meaning it is granted to one broker exclusively. While the exclusive agency listing would allow the seller to find a buyer without paying a commission, the exclusive right-to-sell listing would require a commission to be paid even if the seller alone procured the buyer. Open listings impose no limit on the number of additional brokers that might be hired by the seller. (160–161)

3. **C** The answer is on April 15, the owner and agent cancel the agreement. Mutual agreement by the owner and the agent would terminate a listing agreement before its expiration date. The death of the owner or the destruction of the property also would end the listing agreement before the expiration date. (162)

4. **A** The answer is no commission. Only the exclusive right-to-sell listing earns the listing broker a commission if someone else sells the property during the term of the agreement. (160)

5. **B** The answer is 5.5%. Commission rate × selling price = commission, so commission ÷ selling price = commission rate; therefore, $26,675 commission ÷ $485,000 selling price = 0.055, or 5.5% commission rate. (172–173)

6. **D** The answer is a net listing. Whether an open, an exclusive agency, or an exclusive right-to-sell, any listing that allows the broker to keep all of the selling price over the net amount that the seller requires is a net listing. Net listings are illegal in many states. (161)

7. **A** The answer is under each, the seller avoids paying the broker a commission if the seller sells the property to someone the broker did not procure. Both open and exclusive agency listings allow owners to sell without broker aid and thus avoid paying a commission. (160–161)

8. **C** The answer is the seller. Although a listing agent, an appraiser, and an attorney voice their opinions, the seller finally sets the listing (offering) price for a property. (172)

9. **A** The answer is it is an employment contract for the professional services of the broker. The listing is the broker's contract of employment by the seller. It is not a contract between the seller and any buyer and so cannot be enforced on the seller by a buyer, even though the buyer might make an offer that is the "mirror image" of the terms of the listing. In such an event, however, the seller may owe the broker a full commission for having produced the result the listing called for: an able buyer who is ready and willing to buy according to the terms of the listing. (163)

10. **D** The answer is $183,333. Two steps are involved: (1) Find the firm's full commission. (2) Find the selling price using the full commission and the rate. (1) $3,575 amount to salesperson = 30% × full commission; $3,575 amount to salesperson ÷ 30% = $11,916.67 full commission (rounded to the nearest cent). (2) $11,916.67 full commission ÷ 6.5% brokerage rate = $183,333.38 sales price (rounded to the nearest cent). The closest answer is $183,333. (172–173)

11. **C** The answer is both brokers. The broker with the open listing who procures the buyer is due a full commission. The broker with an exclusive right-to-sell listing is due a full commission if the listed property is sold by anyone during the term of the listing. Both these events occurred. Two full commissions are due. (160–161)

12. **B** The answer is owes a commission to the broker. The broker has fulfilled all the requirements. Even though no contract is signed with the willing buyer, the broker is due a full commission. The seller does not have to sell, just pay the commission. (161)

13. **C** The answer is an exclusive buyer representation agreement. An exclusive buyer representation agreement binds the buyer to compensate the agent whenever the buyer purchases a property of the type described in the contract, even if the buyer finds the property independently. (175)

14. **B** The answer is the broker can represent other buyers. The broker is free to represent other buyers; the buyer cannot sign an agreement or work with another broker while the first agreement is still in effect. (175)

15. **C** The answer is an exclusive right-to-sell listing. In an exclusive right to sell listing, a commission will be owed to a broker regardless of which party sells the house. In exclusive agency and open listings, the seller retains the right to sell without obligation to the broker. (160)

16. **B** The answer is a definite contract termination date. Failing to specify a definite termination date in a real estate listing can be grounds for suspension or revocation of a license in most states. Automatic extensions have been discouraged by courts. Broker protection clauses and MLS clauses are not required. (162)

17. **B** The answer is net listing. A net listing may be prohibited by state law. (161)

18. **C** The answer is the agent of the seller. As agent, the broker represents the seller with whom the broker executed the listing agreement. (160)

19. **B** The answer is a multiple listing clause. A multiple listing service (MLS) is a marketing organization whose broker members make their own exclusive listings available through other brokers. (161)

20. **B** The answer is death of the sales associate who worked with the buyer. A listing agreement is a personal service agreement between a broker and a seller, not between a sales associate and a seller. (162)

Unit 11 Quiz

1. **C** The answer is a bilateral contract. A bilateral contract is a legally enforceable agreement under which two parties exchange promises to do something for each other. (188)

2. **B** The answer is unenforceable. The parties may like to do business this way and proceed to carry out their oral agreement. There is no law against it; however, under the Statute of Frauds, an oral agreement for the sale of real property is unenforceable. (192)

3. **D** The answer is both parties to the contract exchange binding promises. When both parties to a contract are bound by it, the contract is said to be bilateral. A contract yet to be performed is executory. A contract that binds only one party to act is unilateral. A contract made with a minor is usually voidable by the minor. (188)

4. **B** The answer is executory. A contract is executory when its terms have not yet been carried out. When the contract's terms have been fulfilled, it is said to be executed. (189)

5. **C** The answer is void. A contract is void when a consideration is not stated because consideration is an essential element of a contract. (191)

6. **D** The answer is transfer of the property. The buyer wants the seller to do what was promised in the sales agreement: convey the property. The buyer wants the seller to perform the specific actions as agreed. (193)

7. **A** The answer is have both parties initial or sign in the margin near each change. All parties must initial or sign the changes. To draw a new contract would be to invite a new round of negotiation. Letters approving all changes might then be treated as part of the contract, but such a cumbersome procedure is seldom used. (199)

8. **A** The answer is equitable. Upon formation of the agreement of sale between the seller and the buyer, the buyer received equitable title. Upon later delivery and acceptance of the deed, the buyer will also receive legal title—sometimes called actual title. (200)

9. **A** The answer is a contingency. The contract is said to be contingent upon the attorney's approval. If the contingency is not satisfied—if the attorney doesn't approve—the contract is null and void. (199)

10. **D** The answer is illegal. Earnest money does not belong to the brokerage and must be placed in an escrow (trust) account. To convert that money for personal use is illegal, regardless of any plan to later reimburse the account. It doesn't make any difference if there remains enough money in the trust account to cover immediate client needs. (196–197)

11. **B** The answer is seller only. The potential buyer (optionee) who purchases an option to purchase is not bound to purchase the property. Should the optionee decide to exercise the option, the optionor (seller) is bound to proceed with the sale in keeping with all the details contained in the option. (200)

12. **D** The answer is land sales contract. This arrangement has a variety of names: contract for a deed, land contract, installment contract, land sales contract, and more. Its most important characteristic is that no deed is given to the buyer (vendee) until all the payments in the contract have been made, although some states give the buyer an equitable interest in the property after a specified period of successful payments. (200)

13. **D** The answer is has only an equitable interest in the property's title. The purchaser (vendee) holds equitable title during the executory period, while the seller (vendor) retains legal title. (200)

14. **C** The answer is in writing to be enforceable. A statute of frauds calls for real estate sales contracts to be in writing. Such statutes do not address who writes the agreements or on what forms they are written. Earnest money is not an essential feature of a contract of sale, although it is often mistakenly said to be. (188)

15. **D** The answer is relieved of the original offer. When the original offer is rejected by the seller, it ceases to exist. The buyer may accept or reject the seller's counteroffer, or make a counter to the counteroffer. (196)

16. **B** The answer is put the deposit in an account, as provided by state law. Most states require real estate professionals to place earnest money and other funds held in trust in a specified account used only for such money. Real estate professionals who mix the company's money with deposits and trust funds are guilty of commingling funds. (196–197)

17. **A** The answer is the contract is voidable. A person suffering from a mental illness may either declare the contract void or hold the seller of the real estate to the contract. That is to say, the contract is voidable, but only by the person who is mentally ill. (191)

18. **B** The answer is an offer. A written offer to buy property—an offer that has not been seen or acted upon by the property owner—is simply an offer. Even if the offer had been for full price, no contract would yet exist and the offeror would have no claim on the offeree. (190)

19. **D** The answer is if the closing date passes and no closing takes place, the contract may be rescinded by the party who was ready to settle on the scheduled date. "Time is of the essence" refers to the settlement date. If one party fails to go to settlement by that date, the other party may rescind (cancel) the contract. (192)

20. **B** The answer is option. The buyer has purchased an option. The $500 is the option price. If the option isn't exercised within the three-month option period, the option will lapse. (200)

Unit 12 Quiz

1. **B** The answer is $3,600. A point is 1 percent of the amount borrowed (the loan amount). Three points would be three times as much: 3% × $120,000 = $3,600. (212)

2. **A** The answer is the mortgagor. A buyer who signs a mortgage—the document to be given to the lender—is a mortgagor. The buyer is also the maker (obligor) on the note. (213)

3. **C** The answer is the mortgagee. Because it receives the mortgage document, the mortgage company is the mortgagee. (213)

4. **A** The answer is the trustor. A borrower gives a deed of trust to a trustee and a note to the lender, thus becoming a trustor on the deed of trust and a maker—or obligor—on the note. The deed is held by the trustee, and the lender is the beneficiary of the trust. (214)

5. **C** The answer is a straight loan. A straight loan (also known as a term loan or interest-only loan) essentially divides the loan into two amounts to be paid off separately. The borrower makes periodic payments of interest only, followed by the payment of the principal in full at the end of the term. (218)

6. **B** The answer is a usury law. A law that set limits on rates of interest that may be charged is a usury law. Usury is charging a higher interest rate than the law allows for a specific kind of loan. Federal law currently exempts federally related residential first mortgage loans from state usury laws. (211)

7. **D** The answer is statutory redemption. The redemption of property by paying off the mortgage debt plus interest and other charges after foreclosure is the right of statutory redemption. It is only possible in states that have statutes permitting it. All states, however, permit redemption before the foreclosure sale; this right is the right of equitable redemption. (224)

8. **D** The answer is acceleration. The *acceleration* (speed-up) clause allows the lender to declare the entire loan balance due upon borrower default. The *alienation* clause allows the lender to accelerate the balance due if borrowers alienate (transfer) their mortgaged property. The *defeasance* clause requires the lender to release its lien claim against the property when the entire debt has been paid. (215)

9. **A** The answer is satisfaction of mortgage. A document that indicates the mortgage has been fully paid off is a satisfaction of mortgage, sometime called a satisfaction piece. (216)

10. **A** The answer is a homeowner age 62 or older. Reverse mortgages are available to homeowners age 62 or older. (222)

11. **C** The answer is an amortized loan. An amortized loan is paid off in regular periodic payments that include both principal and interest over a term of years. (218)

12. **B** The answer is a defeasance clause. A defeasance clause requires a lender to execute a satisfaction when the note has been fully paid. (216)

13. **B** The answer is power of sale. A power-of-sale provision in a mortgage permits the lender to foreclose and sell a mortgaged property that is in default without petitioning to get the court to conduct the sale. Nevertheless, the procedure is often supervised—although not conducted—by the court. (223)

14. **D** The answer is seek a deficiency judgment. A deficiency judgment entitles the mortgagee to a personal judgment against the borrower for the unpaid balance when a foreclosure sale does not produce enough cash to pay the loan balance in full after deducting expenses and accrued unpaid interest. It may also be obtained against any endorsers or guarantors of the note and against any owners of the mortgaged property who assumed the debt by written agreement. (224)

15. **B** The answer is the loan amount. Discount points are based on a percentage of the loan amount, not the purchase price. (212)

16. **A** The answer is lien theory. This state is a lien theory state. The court is enlisted to order and oversee the mortgage foreclosure procedure. (213)

17. **D** The answer is title theory. In title theory states, the mortgagor actually gives legal title to the mortgagee (or some other designated individual) and retains equitable title. Legal title is returned to the mortgagor only when the debt is paid in full (or some other obligation is performed). (214)

18. **B** The answer is a growing-equity mortgage. The growing-equity mortgage uses a fixed interest rate, but payments of principal are increased according to an index or schedule. The total payment thus increases, and the loan is paid off more quickly. (219)

19. **B** The answer is a subordination agreement. If the original (first mortgage) lender signs a subordination agreement, another loan made more recently (later) may be allowed to take first place; the original loan then drops to second place in priority. (218)

20. **B** The answer is assumed the seller's mortgage. Purchasers who buy a property and formally assume an existing mortgage debt become liable for any deficiency arising from a foreclosure sale. Purchasers who buy a property subject to an existing mortgage are not liable for such a deficiency; the original borrower is still liable for the debt. (217)

Unit 13 Quiz

1. **D** The answer is a purchase money mortgage. The term purchase money mortgage can mean either owner financing or any mortgage used as acquisition debt in the purchase of a property. Here the owner-seller took back a mortgage for $47,000. An owner takeback is a purchase-money mortgage. (244)

2. **D** The answer is buydown. The builder brought down the purchaser's interest rate for two years by paying the lender advance interest. This is a buydown arrangement. (245)

3. **C** The answer is credit union. The credit union is a participant in the primary market; the other three are major, active participants in buying and reselling existing mortgages—secondary market activity. (236–237)

4. **C** The answer is the Fair Credit Reporting Act. If a loan application is rejected after consideration of a credit report, the federal Fair Credit Reporting Act (FCRA) specifies the information that the lender must provide to the loan applicant. The loan applicant has the right to a free copy of any credit report that was considered in the loan application process. Additional state protections may also apply. (248)

5. **B** The answer is a life insurance company. Life insurance companies make mortgage loans on large projects but rarely, if ever, on individual home purchases. (236–237)

6. **A** The answer is the Federal Housing Finance Agency. Fannie Mae has shareholders but is under the conservatorship of the Federal Housing Finance Agency (FHFA). It creates mortgage-backed securities using pool of mortgages as collateral and deals in conventional, FHA, and VA loans. (237)

7. **D** The answer is Regulation Z of the Truth in Lending Act. The Truth in Lending Act is enforced by Regulation Z, which was enacted by the Federal Reserve Board. Regulation Z provides strict rules for real estate advertisements in all media that refer to mortgage financing terms. (246)

8. **B** The answer is the blanket loan. This is a blanket loan with a provision for partial release as properties are sold. In a blanket loan, a borrower puts up several parcels of real estate to be used as security for the debt. (244)

9. **C** The answer is approved lenders. An FHA-insured loan is insured by the agency, and funds must be made available by FHA-approved lenders. (240)

10. **B** The answer is brokerage commissions. Regulation Z has to do with disclosing details of the proposed loan. It does not deal with brokerage commissions. (246)

11. **B** The answer is junior. A HELOC is junior to the original lien. The original lien takes priority over the HELOC. (246)

12. **A** The answer is a package loan. A package loan is a real estate loan used to finance the purchase of both real property and personal property, such as in the purchase of a new home that includes window coverings and major appliances. (244)

13. **B** The answer is buy and pool blocks of conventional mortgages. Freddie Mac—the Federal Home Loan Mortgage Corporation (FHLMC)—buys and gathers into bundles (pools) existing conventional mortgages. Freddie Mac raises money to do this by selling bonds backed by these pools of mortgages. (237)

14. **D** The answer is amount of income. Lenders may reject applicants who have insufficient income for the loans they are requesting, but lenders may not discriminate based on any of the other criteria listed. (248)

15. **B** The answer is an open-end loan. An open-end loan provides a security interest when a note is executed by the borrower to the lender, but also secures any future advances of funds made by the lender to the borrower. (244)

16. **B** The answer is the Farm Service Agency. The Farm Service Agency (FSA) is a federal agency of the Department of Agriculture. The FSA offers programs to help families purchase or operate family farms and has taken over the functions of the former Farmers Home Administration (FmHA). (243)

17. **C** The answer is $91,600. The loan-to-value ratio will be based on the relationship of the loan to either the appraisal or the purchase price, whichever is less. In this case, the appraisal is less. Therefore, the loan will be 80 percent of $114,500, which equals $91,600. (238)

18. **B** The answer is the certificate of eligibility. The veteran must apply for a certificate of eligibility. This certificate sets forth the maximum guarantee to which the veteran is entitled, but the veteran must still qualify for the loan with the lender. (242)

19. **C** The answer is the Community Reinvestment Act. Under the Community Reinvestment Act of 1977 (CRA), financial institutions are expected to meet the deposit and credit needs of their communities, participate and invest in local community development and rehabilitation projects, and participate in loan programs for housing, small businesses, and small farms. (248–249)

20. **D** The answer is Truth in Lending Act (Regulation Z). Regulation Z of the Truth in Lending Act requires that trigger terms about mortgage financing in any

kind of advertising must also include additional disclosures in the advertisement. (246–247)

Unit 14 Quiz

1. **D**   The answer is the seller usually pays the expenses for the day of closing. Presumably, the sellers woke up in the house on the day of settlement; that day is theirs to enjoy and to pay for. Closings are rarely, if ever, conducted by real estate sales associates. Either the buyer or the seller—whichever orders title evidence—pays for the closing. In the sale of an income property, the seller typically receives the rents for the day of closing. (278)

2. **B**   The answer is the seller. Removal of encumbrance is the (financial) responsibility of the seller. (259)

3. **D**   The answer is when the deed is delivered and accepted. Although the buyer received equitable title upon contract, legal title does not pass until delivery and acceptance of the deed. If the buyer, or someone acting on the buyer's behalf, records the deed, acceptance is presumed. (258)

4. **A**   The answer is title insurance commitment. Credit report, application for the mortgage loan, and appraisal of the subject property are all required by a lender well before closing. The title insurance binder is due at closing. (258)

5. **D**   The answer is cash needed to complete the purchase. The buyer is normally responsible for depositing the cash needed to complete the transaction. (276)

6. **C**   The answer is residential transactions financed by federally related mortgage loans. Except for owner financing, very few loans for the purchase of residential properties are not—or will not sometime be— federally related, either directly or indirectly. For example, if they are not insured or guaranteed by FHA or VA, they may still be later traded on the secondary mortgage market by Fannie Mae, Freddie Mac, or other government-sponsored enterprises. (263)

7. **C**   The answer is a lending institution. A mortgage reduction certificate, issued by the seller's lender, confirms the balance remaining on a loan to be assumed as well as the interest rate and the date through which interest has been paid. (258)

8. **B**   The answer is a credit to the buyer. The purchasers see to it that money is available in the form of a mortgage loan for the purchase of the property. They are given credit for getting this money to the table. (276)

9. **B**   The answer is a credit to the buyer. The purchaser's earnest (deposit) money is usually shown in a contract of sale as credited toward closing expenses and, if there is enough, toward any down payment. (276)

10. **D**   The answer is credit the seller $9,750; debit the buyer $9,750. The sellers should get credit for the unused portion of their prepaid real estate taxes. When taxes are paid on a calendar-year basis, the sellers get credit for that portion of the year between closing and December 31. A property with an annual real estate tax of $18,000 is taxed $1,500 per month ($18,000 ÷ 12 months = $1,500). Between June 15 and December 31 there are 6½ months. So 6½ times the monthly taxes of $1,500 yields a proration of $9,750 to be credited to the seller and the same amount debited (charged) to the buyer at closing. (280)

11. **C**   The answer is the seller owes the buyer $450. The sellers have housed the tenant for half a month and so have earned one-half of the $900 month's rent they received. But they owe the rent for the second half of the month, $450, to the purchaser. (280)

12. **A**   The answer is the buyer. When investors buy an income property, rental security deposits held by the former owner are transferred to them. Buyers are credited for all existing security deposits at closing. (276)

13. **C**   The answer is $100,300. A purchase for $850,000 with 10% down requires a mortgage loan of $765,000 ($850,000 − $85,000 = $765,000). A point is 1% of the loan amount, or $7,650 (1% × $765,000 = $7,650). The buyer must bring 2 points (2 × $7,650 = $15,300) plus the down payment ($85,000) to the closing ($15,300 + $ 85,000 = $100,300). (280)

14. **B**   The answer is lender charges for taking and underwriting the loan. Lender charges for taking and underwriting the loan stated on the Closing Disclosure must be the same or less than the charge noted on the Loan Estimate form. (265)

15. **C**   The answer is a debit to the seller. When the sellers have engaged the agent, they will be debited (charged) for the agent's commission at closing. (276)

16. **B**   The answer is bills relating to the property that the buyer must pay. *Accrued items* are those property-related expenses (bills) that remain on the property as it is sold and that the purchasers will have to pay later. (279)

17. **D** The answer is credited to the seller. *Prepaid items* are expenses that have been paid by seller but are not fully used up, such as fuel oil. These items are prorated and appear as a credit to the seller. (279)

18. **D** The answer is ensure that buyers know all settlement costs that will be charged to them. RESPA seeks to ensure that borrowers know the financial repercussions of the transaction, including all settlement costs that will be charged to them. (263)

19. **B** The answer is *Your Home Loan Toolkit*. It provides numerous resources for further information as well as a line-by-line description of the Loan Disclosure form. (274)

20. **B** The answer is three business days. If the APR has changed more than 0.125% before closing, the TILA-RESPA Integrated Disclosure Act (TRID) provides that a lender must provide a new Closing Disclosure and extend the closing three business days. (265)

Unit 15 Quiz

1. **D** The answer is general. A general lien attaches to all of a debtor's property as opposed to a specific lien, which affects only a specific property. (288)

2. **B** The answer is order in which liens will be paid if property is sold to satisfy a debt. Priority of liens refers to the order in which claims against a property will be paid off. In general, the rule for priority of liens is "first come, first served," but there are some exceptions, such as taxes and assessments. (289)

3. **B** The answer is special assessment lien. Specific improvements are paid for by special assessments. (293)

4. **C** The answer is judgment. A judgment lien is not just on some specific assets but on the assets of the debtor in general. (295)

5. **B** The answer is real estate taxes due. Unpaid real estate taxes take priority when property is liquidated at a foreclosure sale. They are a statutory lien with priority over liens created by contract, such as mortgages. (289)

6. **D** The answer is $4,800. A mill is $\frac{1}{1000}$ of a dollar: $0.001. The mill rate is the tax on every dollar of the assessed value of property. A rate of 40 mills ($0.040) is applied to 75% of the $160,000 market value of the property: $160,000 × 75% = $120,000, and $120,000 × $0.040 = $4,800. (292)

7. **C** The answer is real property tax. The real property (ad valorem) tax falls on those who own real property, such as homeowners. (290)

8. **C** The answer is record a notice of the lien and file a court suit within the time required by state law. In this situation, the contractor has specific, statutory rights that are limited to the real property for which the contractor performed work or supplied materials. (294)

9. **D** The answer is $1,477. Tax = assessed value × equalization factor × tax rate. The millage rate is the tax on each dollar of assessed value: 1 mill = $0.001; 25 mills = $0.025. Therefore: $47,250 × 125% = $59,062.50, and $59,062.50 × $0.025 = $1,476.56. The best answer is $1,477. (291–292)

10. **C** The answer is mortgage lien. A mortgage lien is created voluntarily by the borrower. The borrower names specific property in the mortgage agreement that serves as security for the lender. (294)

11. **D** The answer is judgment. The seller could seek a monetary judgment based on a vendor's (seller's) lien for unpaid portions of the purchase price not secured by a mortgage. (295)

12. **D** The answer is lis pendens. A recorded lis pendens—a notice of action pending—warns any potential purchaser that a property is subject to a pending legal action. Such a notice might prompt a buyer to consider very. (295)

13. **C** The answer is they take priority over mechanic's liens. Real estate taxes and special assessments take priority over all other liens. (289)

14. **B** The answer is unpaid mortgage loan. Encumbrances such as easements and encroachments do not involve liens. A license is a personal, revocable privilege. A mortgage agreement creates a voluntary, specific lien. (294)

15. **B** The answer is it involves a debtor-creditor relationship. Both involve a debtor-creditor relationship. A mortgage lien is specific, not general, and is voluntary and entered by the lender. The lien is executed by legal action upon default of the borrower. (294)

16. **D** The answer is real estate professionals. Contractors, subcontractors, and surveyors all have standing to seek a mechanic's lien. Real estate professionals typically do not have the right to place liens on property they have sold and for which they have not been paid the commission owed to them. (294)

17. **D** The answer is the equitable right of redemption. An equitable right of redemption exists because it is only fair (equitable) that a property owner be permitted to save the property before a tax sale—or even a foreclosure sale—by paying the amount owed in full. (293)

18. **A** The answer is real estate tax lien. A real estate tax lien is always on a specific piece of realty; it happens without permission of the property owner and so is involuntary; it is created by statute. Therefore, it is specific, involuntary, and statutory. (290)

19. **B** The answer is ad valorem taxes. Confusingly, the general real estate tax—the ad valorem tax—creates a specific lien. The word *general*, in this context, distinguishes this tax from a special assessment for a specific project or neighborhood. (290)

20. **D** The answer is apartment buildings. Properties such as public hospitals and public parks, as well as religious institutions such as synagogues and churches, are usually exempt from real estate taxes. Apartment buildings, typically operated as investment properties, are taxed. (290–291)

Unit 16 Quiz

1. **C** The answer is income approach. The income approach uses the rate of investment return, which is the relationship between the appraised value and the net annual income. (319)

2. **B** The answer is scarcity. The characteristics of value are remembered by the acronym DUST: demand, utility, scarcity, and transferability. (312)

3. **B** The answer is plottage. The principal of plottage is that additional market value can be obtained in some instances by combining, and selling as a single parcel, two or more contiguous (i.e., adjacent) properties. This value exceeds the combined total that the individual properties would bring if sold separately. (314)

4. **B** The answer is market price. Market price is a property's asking, offer, or sales price. (312)

5. **D** The answer is regression. The value of larger lavish homes in a modest neighborhood will be drawn down by the presence of modest less lavish homes; regression is the opposite of progression. (314)

6. **A** The answer is progression. The value of modest homes in an area may increase with the presence of luxurious homes. This is an example of the principle of progression. (314)

7. **D** The answer is accelerated depreciation. Functional obsolescence, physical deterioration, and external (economic) obsolescence are all sources of depreciation as a loss in value. Depreciation also refers to a deduction for income tax purposes. Accelerated depreciation falls within this definition and is not used for appraisal purposes. (318)

8. **C** The answer is analyzing the results obtained by the different approaches to value to form an opinion of value. The three approaches to value typically produce three different values. An in-depth analysis of these values is required to determine the most valid, logical, and reliable approach that will provide the final opinion of value. (321)

9. **A** The answer is 8%. Net annual income ÷ market value = capitalization rate ($24,000 ÷ $300,000 = 0.08, or 8%). Given any two elements, the third can be calculated. (320)

10. **C** The answer is accrued depreciation. Depreciation is one of the calculations used in the replacement (cost) approach and not in the income approach. (317)

11. **C** The answer is income approach. The income approach is likely to be given the most weight in an analysis of income-producing property. Circumstances may dictate a different approach when, for instance, the property's current use is no longer its highest and best use. (319)

12. **C** The answer is an estimate of the most probable price it should bring. An appraisal is the appraiser's opinion of a property's market value—the price a property would most probably bring. (302)

13. **B** The answer is estimate value. Capitalization (the income approach) requires the use of the net operating income, and capitalization rate to find value. (319)

14. **C** The answer is loss of value due to any reason. Depreciation is loss of value from any reason. Some examples of such causes are physical deterioration (wearing out and/or deferred maintenance), external (economic) obsolescence, and functional obsolescence (lack of modernity or good design). (318)

15. **D** The answer is differences in original cost. None of the approaches to appraisal considers the original (historical) cost of a property. The other three factors would be relevant to the sales comparison—sometimes called the market data—approach. Original cost, however, is used in computations of book-value depreciation for tax purposes. (315–321)

16. **D**   The answer is none of these. A comparative market analysis is based on recently closed properties, those currently on the market, and expired listings. It is prepared by a real estate professional and is not as detailed as an appraisal performed by a licensed or certified appraiser. (303)

17. **A**   The answer is methodical collection and analysis of data. The appraisal process is an orderly set of procedures used to collect and analyze data to arrive at a justifiable conclusion of value. (304)

18. **B**   The answer is functional obsolescence. Depending on the other homes in the marketplace, a home with four bedrooms and only one bathroom may be undesirable. (318)

19. **B**   The answer is competition. A successful project invites imitators (competitors) to do the same thing nearby. This drives profits down for a developer and costs down for a consumer-buyer. (313)

20. **C**   The answer is value. They all affect value—the most probable price a property will bring. (312)

Unit 17 Quiz

1. **C**   The answer is a landlord charges a commercial tenant separate amounts for the rented land and for the leased building. When a tenant has separate leases and pays separate rents on the building and the ground under it, the second agreement is a ground lease. The consideration paid for it is ground rent. (336)

2. **C**   The answer is a percentage lease. When a business tenant pays rent that varies according to the tenant's gross business receipts, the arrangement is called a percentage lease. In such a situation, the landlord shares in the tenant's business risk because of the possibility of receiving no more in rent than the minimum fixed amount. (335)

3. **D**   The answer is the tenant may be entitled to recover damages from the landlord. The tenant suffering financial losses (damages) because of the landlord's negligence could enter an action against (sue) the landlord for those damages. (337–338)

4. **C**   The answer is actual eviction. A tenant's breach of a lease can result in actual eviction, whereas landlord negligence can result in a tenant's being forced to move, and this is known as constructive eviction. (337)

5. **B**   The answer is a sublessor. The tenant is the tenant of the landlord (lessor) and, in turn, is the landlord of the friend. In this *sandwich* position, the tenant is a sublessor. (333)

6. **D**   The answer is an estate at sufferance. An estate at sufferance is created when a tenant who lawfully occupied the property continues to stay on after the expiration date of the lease without the permission of the landlord. If the lease does not have a "holdover" clause that governs the rights of both landlord and tenant, state law will govern. (330)

7. **C**   The answer is do nothing because the agreement will terminate automatically at the end of the current term. In common law, a tenant for a specified period (one who holds a lease for years) does not have to give notice because the lease ends by contractual agreement. Nor does the landlord have to give the tenant notice in such a case, unless required to do so by state law. (329)

8. **B**   The answer is the landlord can file suit for possession. The tenant is a tenant at sufferance. The landlord may regain possession through a legal process known as an actual eviction. (337)

9. **B**   The answer is order a new water heater and deduct the payment from the rent. The landlord's behavior provides a basis for any of the actions except ordering a new water heater and having the bill sent to the landlord. A lease typically does not provide for the tenant to replace a water heater or other appliance. State law may require that a residence meet identified minimum standards of habitability, which may or may not include the provision of hot water. (332)

10. **B**   The answer is from period to period. When a lease renews itself periodically, the arrangement is known as a leasehold from period to period, or a periodic tenancy. (329)

11. **B**   The answer is consideration for the use of real property. Consideration is the exchange of something of value by the tenant in return for possession of property owned by another person. (331)

12. **A**   The answer is mortgage debt service. Under a net lease, the tenant pays all property expenses, including taxes and insurance, utilities, maintenance, and so on, but not debt service (the landlord's mortgage payment). (335)

13. **B**   The answer is a lease in which the tenant pays rent, plus all—or most—of the operating expenses related to the property. (335)

14. **D** The answer is a tenancy at sufferance. A tenant who stays after the end of the lease without the landlord's permission holds a tenancy at sufferance. (330)

15. **A** The answer is an estate for years. When this leasehold interest expires, the lessee is required to vacate the premises and surrender possession to the lessor. No notice is necessary as the lease agreement states a specific expiration date; state law may require notice of intent to terminate a residential lease. (329)

16. **A** The answer is an agreement in which the tenant pays a fixed rent and some or all of the utilities and the landlord pays all taxes, insurance, and other expenses related to the property. In a gross lease, the tenant pays no part of the property's operating expenses other than utilities. (335)

17. **C** The answer is graduated. An agreement in which tenant agrees to pay predicted, regular increases during its term is called a graduated lease. (336)

18. **D** The answer is index. When the rental varies with an outside index, such as the consumer price index, the agreement is called an index lease. (336)

19. **C** The answer is tenancy at will. The only lease that is terminated by death, of either the landlord or the tenant, is a tenancy at will. A relationship at will continues only so long as both parties continue to mutually agree. If one party dies, a mutual agreement no longer exists. (330)

20. **C** The answer is constructive eviction. Constructive eviction terminates the lease when the landlord breaches any clause of the lease agreement. The tenant must prove that the premises have become unusable because of the conscious neglect of the landlord. (338)

Unit 18 Quiz

1. **C** The answer is refusing to make a mortgage loan to a member of a protected class because of a poor credit history. Bad credit can cause anyone to be rejected, even those who are members of protected classes. (347)

2. **A** The answer is must be taken directly to federal courts. Complaints under the Civil Rights Act of 1866 are heard in federal courts. (357)

3. **D** The answer is it provides no exceptions that would permit racial discrimination. Unlike other exemptions permitted under the federal Fair Housing Act of 1968, the Civil Rights Act of 1866 allows no exceptions that would permit discrimination on the basis of race. (346)

4. **B** The answer is blockbusting. Such statements, made by a person in real estate brokerage, constitute blockbusting—usually an attempt to get listings by frightening owners into selling by encouraging the belief that a member of a protected class is moving into the neighborhood. To do this for financial gain is a violation of the federal Fair Housing Act. (353)

5. **C** The answer is steering. A person who guides prospects either toward or away from certain neighborhoods based on racial, ethnic, religious, or similar concerns is guilty of steering. This practice is outlawed by the federal Fair Housing Act. Whether it is done to promote housing segregation or integration or whether it was intentional or unintentional is immaterial. (354)

6. **A** The answer is redlining. Failure to lend or to insure in areas largely populated by a protected group is a violation of the federal Fair Housing Act of 1968. It is redlining. (355)

7. **B** The answer is the owner of a 20-unit residential apartment building renting to men only. Sex is a protected category under the federal Fair Housing Act but the owner of the building doesn't qualify for any exception to the law. Even if the owner lives in one of the units, doesn't use a broker, and does not advertise discriminatorily, the property is not an exception to the law because it has more than four units. (347)

8. **A** The answer is the ethnicity of the residents of the area. Redlining refers to literally drawing a line around a particular area and refusing to make loans in that area because of the ethnicity of the residents, rather than looking at the economic qualifications of the applicant. (355)

9. **A** The answer is HUD. The federal Fair Housing Act is administered by the Office of Fair Housing and Equal Opportunity under the direction of the secretary of HUD. Upon receiving a complaint, HUD initiates an investigation. (348)

10. **B** The answer is includes a restriction that 80% of the units be occupied by persons aged 55 or older. The Fair Housing Act allows for two exemptions to familial status protection in housing for older persons. One permissible exemption is for housing in which 80% of the units are occupied by persons 55 years of age or older. (348)

11. **A** The answer is racial discrimination is prohibited by any party in the sale or rental of real estate. The *Jones v. Mayer* decision held that the Civil Rights Act of 1866, banning all limitation on property rights on the basis of race, is the law of the land. Racial discrimination by anyone in the sale or rental of any kind of property violates this law. (346)

12. **B** The answer is explain to the owners that the instruction violates federal law and that the real estate professional cannot comply with it. The fiduciary duty of obedience requires that the broker obey all LAWFUL instructions. This is not a lawful instruction as it requires a violation of the Fair Housing Act. If the owners are adamant, to avoid breaking the law, the real estate professional must terminate the representation. (347)

13. **A** The answer is $19,987. A fine of not more than $19,987 is possible for a first violation. (356)

14. **C** The answer is the man may file a complaint alleging discrimination on the basis of familial status. The salesperson and, by implication, the broker and the property owners/principals have violated the prohibition against familial-status discrimination. Anyone in charge of one or more children under age 18 who is denied access because of the children is the victim of discrimination based on familial status. (348)

15. **D** The answer is the ad should not mention St. John's Church. Reference to a nearby church implies religious preference. This violates HUD advertising regulations designed to enforce the Federal Fair Housing Act. (354)

16. **A** The answer is within two years of the discriminatory act. A civil suit alleging an act of discrimination under the Fair Housing Act may be filed in federal court within two years of the discriminatory act. A complaint may be filed with HUD within one year of the alleged discriminatory act. (357)

17. **D** The answer is discriminating on the basis of marital status. Marital status is not one of the seven protected classes under the federal Fair Housing Act. (347)

18. **B** The answer is requiring a person with a disability to establish an escrow account for the costs to restore a property after it has been modified. A landlord may negotiate, as part of a restoration agreement, a provision requiring the tenant to pay an amount not exceeding the cost of restoration into an interest-bearing escrow account. The interest in the account accrues to the benefit of the tenant. (350)

19. **D** The answer is the tenant is entitled to make the necessary alterations. People with disabilities must be permitted to make reasonable modifications to the premises at their own expense. (352)

20. **A** The answer is in all states. The federal Fair Housing Act applies to all states, and many states and municipalities have their own fair housing laws. (347)

Unit 19 Quiz

1. **B** The answer is workers' compensation. Workers' compensation insurance protects employers against claims for on-the-job injuries to their employees. (381)

2. **C** The answer is risk management. Ways to manage risk are to avoid it (removing source of risk), to control it (take safety measures), to shift or transfer it (insure), or to retain it (increase deductible). (380)

3. **B** The answer is tenant improvements. Tenant improvements are alterations to the interior of the building to meet a tenant's particular space needs. (376)

4. **C** The answer is liability. Liability insurance protects an insured who becomes obliged to pay (liable) for damage or injury to others. (381)

5. **C** The answer is restrictions regarding ages of children. A management agreement should include an adequate description of the property, compensation arrangements, and what the manager's authority is to be. Restricting occupancy based on ages of children violates the federal Fair Housing Act and may also violate state and local laws. (370)

6. **B** The answer is retaining risk. The deductible is the part of risk that the insured retains. (380)

7. **D** The answer is environmental concerns that a property manager may have to address. These are all environmental issues that might impact any managed property. (377)

8. **A** The answer is the building's owner. The management contract establishes the agency relationship between the property manager and the owner. (369)

9. **C** The answer is building repairs. Cash reserves are needed to deal with unscheduled or variable expenses such as unexpected building repairs. (371)

10. **A** The answer is supply and demand factors. Rents (unless subject to governmental intervention) are controlled by market forces—supply and demand. (372)

11. **C** The answer is consequential loss, use, and occupancy. Consequential loss policies—also called business interruption insurance—offset loss of rental income due to disasters that keep a property from being used. (381)

12. **C** The answer is a surety bond. The manager can protect the owner by urging the purchase of a surety bond on the building employee at the time the employee is hired. Property managers usually formulate and recommend insurance plans for an owner's consideration and decision. (381)

13. **C** The answer is a monthly rate per unit. A rental rate for residential space is usually stated as the monthly rate per unit (the entire living space). (372)

14. **B** The answer is corrective. Fixing something that is not working properly (malfunctioning) is making a corrective repair. (376)

15. **B** The answer is a general agent. While residential real estate brokers are special agents in each transaction, property managers are typically general agents; their work usually continues and involves multiple representations of the same principal (owner/investor/landlord) because they are involved in ongoing dealings with many tenants. (369)

16. **B** The answer is a profit and loss statement. The profit and loss statement provides a general financial picture based on monthly cash flow reports. Only the interest portion of the debt service is reflected as an expense. (372)

17. **B** The answer is multiperil. Because such insurance addresses several sources of financial loss, it is called a multiperil policy. (381)

18. **C** The answer is Americans with Disabilities Act. The Americans with Disabilities Act (ADA) requires that places of public accommodation remove existing barriers when readily achievable to provide access to facilities and services. (377–378)

19. **C** The answer is commercial and public accommodations. The ADA impacts commercial properties and public accommodations. Type of ownership has no bearing on compliance. (377–378)

20. **D** The answer is the Equal Credit Opportunity Act. A lease is an extension of credit, so the property manager must comply with the provisions of the Equal Credit Opportunity Act (ECOA) and be consistent when evaluating the financial information provided on rental applications. (379)

Unit 20 Quiz

1. **A** The answer is a restrictive covenant. It is a restrictive covenant—in this case, a limitation placed on the entire subdivision by its developer and recorded with the plat of subdivision. It is an example of private land-use control. (395)

2. **A** The answer is conditional-use permit. Conditional use is based on benefit to the community despite a deviation from zoning. (392)

3. **B** The answer is covenants, conditions, and restrictions. Restrictive covenants are private—not public—land-use controls. (295)

4. **C** The answer is ethnicity of owners. Police powers may control the use, size, details of construction, and density of occupancy—but not who may own buildings. (388)

5. **C** The answer is provide evidence of compliance with municipal regulations. A building permit is issued only after municipal regulations have been complied with. It is, therefore, evidence of such compliance. (393)

6. **A** The answer is by state enabling acts. Zoning powers lie with state governments. Local zoning power is conferred on local jurisdictions by the state through enabling acts. (388)

7. **A** The answer is nonconforming use. Allowing a nonconforming use is a way to grandfather in a use that was present before the enactment of certain zoning restrictions forbade it. Once allowed, the use may continue for a stipulated length of time and with limited right of transfer to a later buyer. (391)

8. **D** The answer is the zoning ordinance. Zoning ordinances deal with the uses to which properties in various parts of the jurisdiction can be put. (390)

9. **B** The answer is allowable race of purchasers. No deed restrictions may limit ownership or occupancy based on an individual's race or national origin. (395)

10. **A** The answer is court injunction. Deed restrictions are private land-use controls and can only be enforced by a suit for injunctive relief. The courts can prevent someone from violating a recorded restriction by issuing an injunction—forcing the violator to remove the violation or stop the activity. (395)

11. **A** The answer is a subdivider. Dividing land for later construction or sale is subdividing. (394)

12. **C** The answer is a subdivision plat map. A *plat* is a map. A *subdivision plat* is a map of a subdivision showing at least those details required by local subdivision regulations. (394)

13. **B** The answer is gross density. Public land-use controls commonly seek to control density—such as how many living units will be allowed per acre. (395)

14. **A** The answer is an exception to a zoning ordinance. A variance permits a use that does not meet current zoning requirements. (392)

15. **B** The answer is comprehensive plan. A community's comprehensive plan seeks to address all these issues for the foreseeable future. (388)

16. **D** The answer is prices of residential and commercial lots. Prices are not a matter of public record and are subject to constant change. They do not belong on the recorded plat of subdivision. (394)

17. **A** The answer is the municipality. The plat for a proposed subdivision usually must be approved by the municipality before it can be recorded; when property does not fall within city limits, the county may have this responsibility. (394)

18. **D** The answer is apply to and bind successive owners of the property. The deed conveying a particular lot in a subdivision will refer to the plat or declaration of restrictions, thus limiting the title conveyed and binding all grantees. (395)

19. **A** The answer is provide each purchaser with a printed report disclosing details of the property. The printed report summarizes the developer's detailed filing with HUD and reveals to the purchaser any legal and financial or physical difficulties the project is facing. Buyers who are not given this report can rescind the contract up to seven days after a copy is delivered or until settlement occurs. (396–397)

20. **C** The answer is after building construction work has been inspected and found satisfactory by the municipal inspector. The certificate of occupancy is necessary before a building can be occupied. (393)

Unit 21 Quiz

1. **B** The answer is a disclosure statement must be attached to all sales contracts and leases involving residential properties built before 1978. Although no remediation of the property is required, a lead-based paint warning disclosure statement must be completed and signed by the parties and a copy attached to any sales contract or lease for a residential property built before 1978. In the disclosure statement, buyers and renters acknowledge receiving a HUD booklet about protecting one's family from lead-based paint hazards. (404)

2. **C** The answer is the method of sealing disintegrating asbestos. Wrapping or enclosing with an airtight covering is encapsulating. This is the safest way of dealing with much of the friable (flaking) asbestos that already exists in housing and office buildings. (403)

3. **C** The answer is because of the age of the house, there is a good likelihood of the presence of lead-based paint. Pre–World War I means before 1914. Lead-based paint and varnishes were commonly used in housing interiors until it was outlawed in 1978. There is great likelihood that lead-based products are present in such an old building, even if many layers of non-lead products have been applied over them. (404)

4. **A** The answer is improper removal of asbestos can cause further contamination of a building. Removal must only be done by skilled, licensed contractors. Once disturbed, asbestos can remain suspended in air for long periods of time before settling and then being disturbed once again. (403)

5. **A** The answer is low humidity. Mold grows where there is moisture, such as where a roof leaks, or where water is not routed away properly by the gutters. EIFS is a building material that can trap moisture in a house. (409)

6. **C** The answer is liquid petroleum tanks that store at least 10% of their volume underground be in compliance. Federal regulations impose strict requirements on landowners about USTs. States may impose even more stringent controls. Exceptions to federal regulations include septic tanks and home heating oil tanks. (411–412)

7. **B** The answer is waste and topsoil are layered in a pit, mounded up, and then covered with dirt and plants. Putting down alternate layers of waste and topsoil in a pit, and then capping it with soil and vegetation, creates a landfill. (413)

8. **D** The answer is strict, joint and several, and retroactive. Strict means that the victim's fault does not reduce the violation; joint and several means that if everyone associated with the problem is judged

responsible, any one of the parties might have to pay the entire fine and all damages, not just a party's proportionate share; retroactive means that present violations can be charged as well as violations that occurred before the laws were passed. The Superfund Amendments and Reauthorization Act (SARA) created an exception for the innocent landowner who is completely innocent of all wrongdoing and thus should not be subject to liability. (414)

9. **C** The answer is trapped and concentrated in inadequately ventilated areas. When radon gas accumulates in a poorly ventilated area in a structure or in a mine, its harmful effects increase. (407)

10. **D** The answer is they were all used at one time in residential construction. Only UFFI and asbestos are insulating materials. Only UFFI emits harmful gas. Only lead-based paint was banned in 1978. But all three of these materials were once used in residential construction. (404–408)

11. **B** The answer is encapsulation. Encapsulation, or the sealing off of disintegrating asbestos, is an alternate method of asbestos control that may be preferable to removal in certain circumstances. (403)

12. **C** The answer is all residential buildings must be tested for lead-based paint. The EPA requires that sellers or landlords must disclose known information on lead-based paint and hazards for residential buildings built before 1978. (404)

13. **D** The answer is alkyd oil-based paint. Lead was used as a pigment and drying agent in alkyd oil-based paint that is common on doors, windows, and other woodwork. The federal government estimates that lead is present in about 75% of all private housing built before 1978. (404)

14. **B** The answer is insulating foam. In the 1970s, many homeowners had urea-formaldehyde foam insulation installed in their homes to conserve energy. (408)

15. **C** The answer is known lead-based paint hazards be disclosed. HUD issued the Lead-Based Paint Hazard Reduction Act of 1992, which requires disclosure of any known lead-based paint hazards to potential buyers or renters. (404)

16. **C** The answer is a known human carcinogen. Radon can cause health problems and has been classified as a Class A known human carcinogen. It can be found anywhere in the United States. (407)

17. **B** The answer is addressed by EPA regulations. The federal underground storage tank program is regulated by the EPA. The regulations apply to tanks that contain hazardous substances or liquid petroleum products and that store at least 10% of their volume underground. (412)

18. **A** The answer is it is a minor problem in the United States. According to the EPA, approximately 40% of the 3 million to 5 million underground storage tanks that exist in the United States are leaking. (412)

19. **D** The answer is impose strict, join and several, and retroactive liability on potentially responsible parties. Strict liability means that the owner is responsible to the injured party without excuse. Joint and several liability means that each of the individual owners is personally responsible for the total damages. If only one of the owners is financially able to handle the total damages, that owner must pay the total and collect the proportionate shares from the other owners whenever possible. Retroactive liability means that the liability is not limited to the current owner but includes people who have owned the site in the past. (414)

20. **A** The answer is lung disease. Lung disease can be caused by asbestos dust. (403)

Sample Exam 1

1. **B** (294)	21. **D** (442)	41. **D** (160)	61. **C** (230)
2. **A** (191)	22. **B** (77)	42. **B** (335)	62. **A** (347)
3. **A** (144)	23. **B** (213)	43. **C** (346)	63. **A** (280–281)
4. **C** (221)	24. **D** (293)	44. **C** (431)	64. **D** (191)
5. **A** (444)	25. **D** (212)	45. **D** (288)	65. **B** (89)
6. **B** (175)	26. **C** (292)	46. **D** (200)	66. **D** (50)
7. **A** (88–89)	27. **B** (319)	47. **C** (42–43)	67. **B** (280–281)
8. **A** (354)	28. **C** (77, 442)	48. **D** (73)	68. **D** (347)
9. **A** (36)	29. **A** (212)	49. **B** (314)	69. **A** (91)
10. **D** (51)	30. **C** (442)	50. **B** (288)	70. **A** (319)
11. **D** (119)	31. **D** (195–196)	51. **B** (193–194)	71. **D** (218)
12. **A** (214)	32. **D** (200)	52. **B** (52–54)	72. **D** (58–59)
13. **B** (329)	33. **B** (193)	53. **C** (328)	73. **A** (276)
14. **A** (318)	34. **D** (211)	54. **D** (196)	74. **A** (276)
15. **A** (391)	35. **B** (196)	55. **B** (39)	75. **B** (25)
16. **C** (392)	36. **A** (213)	56. **C** (441)	76. **C** (41)
17. **D** (149)	37. **D** (319–320)	57. **A** (35)	77. **D** (429–430)
18. **C** (52–53)	38. **B** (161)	58. **D** (441)	78. **B** (161)
19. **B** (122)	39. **A** (60)	59. **D** (389–390)	79. **D** (124–125)
20. **B** (388)	40. **A** (90)	60. **B** (191)	80. **D** (338)

Sample Exam 2

1. **D** (330)	21. **C** (249)	41. **D** (194, 247)	61. **D** (319)
2. **C** (25)	22. **B** (338)	42. **C** (77)	62. **C** (248)
3. **C** (189)	23. **A** (36)	43. **B** (189–190)	63. **C** (105)
4. **B** (224)	24. **B** (276)	44. **D** (442)	64. **C** (441)
5. **C** (245)	25. **D** (335)	45. **C** (431)	65. **A** (189–190)
6. **D** (142)	26. **D** (449–455)	46. **D** (242–243)	66. **B** (441)
7. **B** (430)	27. **C** (449–455)	47. **A** (35)	67. **B** (347)
8. **D** (347)	28. **A** (138)	48. **A** (449–455)	68. **D** (150)
9. **B** (433)	29. **B** (319)	49. **B** (192)	69. **C** (41)
10. **B** (441)	30. **D** (276)	50. **C** (319)	70. **A** (263–264)
11. **B** (197)	31. **B** (449–455)	51. **C** (442)	71. **D** (246)
12. **A** (246)	32. **D** (441)	52. **A** (105)	72. **C** (441)
13. **D** (162)	33. **A** (193)	53. **C** (10)	73. **A** (193)
14. **C** (36)	34. **D** (294)	54. **A** (93)	74. **A** (319–320)
15. **D** (142)	35. **B** (431)	55. **D** (51–53)	75. **B** (510)
16. **D** (72)	36. **A** (175)	56. **A** (276)	76. **C** (220)
17. **B** (86)	37. **A** (333)	57. **B** (42–43)	77. **B** (312)
18. **B** (138)	38. **D** (160)	58. **B** (442)	78. **D** (292)
19. **C** (442)	39. **A** (319)	59. **D** (318)	79. **B** (276)
20. **A** (317)	40. **C** (12)	60. **D** (247)	80. **B** (380)

LIST OF FIGURES

INDEX

Notes

Notes

Notes

Notes